SpringBoard®

English Language Arts

California Edition

Teacher Edition

Grade 8

CollegeBoard

ABOUT THE COLLEGE BOARD

The College Board is a mission-driven not-for-profit organization that connects students to college success and opportunity. Founded in 1900, the College Board was created to expand access to higher education. Today, the membership association is made up of more than 6,000 of the world's leading educational institutions and is dedicated to promoting excellence and equity in education. Each year, the College Board helps more than seven million students prepare for a successful transition to college through programs and services in college readiness and college success—including the SAT® and the Advanced Placement Program®. The organization also serves the education community through research and advocacy on behalf of students, educators, and schools. For further information, visit www.collegeboard.com.

ISBN: 1-4573-0471-6
ISBN: 978-1-4573-0471-2

1 2 3 4 5 6 7 8 16 17 18 19 20 21 22
Printed in the United States of America

ACKNOWLEDGMENTS

The College Board gratefully acknowledges the outstanding work of the classroom teachers and writers who have been integral to the development of this revised program. The end product is testimony to their expertise, understanding of student learning needs, and dedication to rigorous and accessible English Language Arts instruction.

Pat Bishop
Writing Coach (Retired)
Hillsborough Schools
Tampa, Florida

Amanda Breuer
English Teacher
Tetzlaff Accelerated Learning Academy
Cerritos, California

Susie Challancin
English Teacher
Bellevue School District 405
Bellevue, Washington

Bryant Crisp
English Teacher
Charlotte Mecklenburg Schools
Charlotte, North Carolina

Paul DeMaret
English Teacher
Poudre School District
Fort Collins, Colorado

Kathy Galford
English Teacher
Chesapeake Public Schools
Chesapeake, Virginia

Michelle Lewis
Curriculum Coordinator
Spokane Public Schools
Spokane, Washington

Julie Manley
English Teacher
Bellevue School District 405
Bellevue, Washington

Le'Andra Myers
English Teacher
Pasco School District
Pasco, Washington

Stephanie Sharpe
English Teacher
Hillsborough Schools
Tampa, Florida

Susan Van Doren
English Teacher
Douglas County School District Minden, Nevada

SPRINGBOARD ENGLISH LANGUAGE ARTS DEVELOPMENT

Lori O'Dea
Executive Director
Content Development

Doug Waugh
Executive Director
Product Management

Joely Negedly
Senior Director
Grades 6–12 English and Social Studies Curriculum and Instruction

JoEllen Victoreen
English Language Arts Instructional Manager

Sarah Balistreri
English Language Arts Editor

Jennifer Duva
English Language Arts Editor

Rebecca Grudzina
English Language Arts Editor

Spencer Gonçalves
Assistant ELA Editor

Jessica Pippin
Assistant ELA Editor

RESEARCH AND PLANNING ADVISORS

We also wish to thank the members of our SpringBoard Advisory Council and the many educators who gave generously of their time and their ideas as we conducted research for both the print and online programs. Your suggestions and reactions to ideas helped immeasurably as we planned the revisions. We gratefully acknowledge the teachers and administrators in the following districts.

ABC Unified School District
Cerritos, California

Bellevue School District 405
Bellevue, Washington

Charleston County School District
Charleston, South Carolina

Clark County School District
Las Vegas, Nevada

Denver Public Schools
Denver, Colorado

Hillsborough County Public Schools
Tampa, Florida

Kenton County School District
Fort Wright, Kentucky

Los Angeles Unified School District
Los Angeles, California

Milwaukee Public Schools
Milwaukee, Wisconsin

Newton County Schools
Covington, Georgia

Noblesville Schools
Noblesville, Indiana

Oakland Unified School District
Oakland, California

Orange County Public Schools
Orlando, Florida

Peninsula School District
Gig Harbor, Washington

Quakertown Community School District
Quakertown, Pennsylvania

St. Vrain School District
Longmont, Colorado

Scottsdale Public Schools
Phoenix, Arizona

Seminole County Public Schools
Sanford, Florida

Spokane Public Schools
Spokane, Washington

GRADE 8

Contents

*Texts not included in these materials.

Unit 2 The Challenge of Utopia

Activities

*Texts not included in these materials.

Unit 3 The Challenge to Make a Difference

Activities

*Texts not included in these materials.

Unit 4 The Challenge of Comedy

Activities

*Texts not included in these materials.

To the Teacher

Welcome to SpringBoard English Language Arts, a college- and career-readiness program for ALL students. Beginning in middle school, SpringBoard helps students develop the knowledge and skills needed for Advanced Placement as well as for success in college and beyond without remediation. This flexible framework is created by teachers for teachers and may be used as a core curriculum that will make rigor and the California Common Core State Standards (CA CCSS) accessible for students.

This new edition of SpringBoard was designed from the start to meet the needs of California students and teachers and was built on current research on best instructional practices and pedagogy. SpringBoard helps accelerate the full implementation of the CA CCSS for ELA/Literacy so all students can achieve the outcomes defined in the new standards:

- Higher-order critical thinking skills
- Precision in reading and writing
- Accurate analysis and evaluation
- Problem-solving skills
- Deeper conceptual understanding
- Expanded academic vocabulary
- Media literacy

SpringBoard asks teachers to slow down, clear away the clutter, and focus on work worth doing. With SpringBoard, students read deeply, write using evidence, and develop the critical-thinking skills needed to be successful in high school, college, and beyond. The CA CCSS for ELA/Literacy identify what students should know; the English Language Arts/English Language Development Framework focuses on teaching and learning, providing direction for how to implement the Standards. Designed in response to both the Standards and the Framework, SpringBoard is a carefully scaffolded curriculum that gives teachers the tools to address the rigor outlined by the Common Core, ensuring that all students can achieve their highest potential.

KEY THEMES OF ENGLISH LANGUAGE ARTS/LITERACY AND ENGLISH LANGUAGE DEVELOPMENT INSTRUCTION

Reading, Making Meaning, and Analyzing Complex Texts

SpringBoard is designed to help students make meaning of complex texts and prepare them for the rigorous textual analysis expected of them in Advanced Placement (AP) English and college courses. The skills students acquire in SpringBoard allow them to think critically about and respond thoughtfully to important topics in all disciplines, and in society.

- Literary and informational texts were selected to be both challenging and engaging for students, with film for comparison and analysis.
- Explicit instruction in close reading and the opportunity to annotate within the student text develop analysis skills.
- Guided discussion questions lead to high-level, academic analysis, rather than simple, literal meaning.
- A wide range of research-based reading strategies empowers students and helps them develop fluency.
- Scaffolded instruction and practice with complex text move students toward learning independence.

Understanding Text Complexity

Understanding text complexity is a central concern of curriculum developers and teachers alike. Students should be reading texts that are appropriately challenging—not so challenging that students get frustrated and give up, and not so easy that students get bored and stagnate. Discerning the complexity of a text involves quantitative measures, as well as some subjective knowledge of the individual student. In this Teacher Edition, an analysis based on the three-part model for determining text complexity is included for each prose text.

Text Complexity
The Diary of a Young Girl
Wednesday, 13 January, 1943
by Anne Frank
Overall: Complex
Lexile: 970
Qualitative: Moderate Difficulty
Task: Moderate (Analyze)

- **Quantitative** measures are indicated with Lexile scores obtained by computer software.
- **Qualitative** measures are indicated as High, Moderate, or Low Difficulty. These ratings were determined by experienced teachers who carefully considered the meaning, purpose, structure, language, and knowledge demands of each text.
- **Task** requirements are indicated as High, Moderate, or Low based on the cognitive demands of the task associated with the text. Anderson and Krathwohl's taxonomy was used for this analysis, and verbs such as *evaluate, analyze,* and *understand* are included as descriptors. (Reader variables such as motivation and background must be determined at the classroom level.)

For each prose text, an overall complexity is given. This overall indicator is a combination of the Lexile, qualitative, and task indicators.

After analyzing each text based on the three-part model, teachers assigned an overall rating of Accessible, Complex, or Very Complex, with Complex representing on-grade-level texts. The overall ratings began with Lexile scores, and adjustments were made based on qualitative and task measures.

Complete, descriptive text complexity analysis documents for each prose passage can be found in the Teacher Resources section of SpringBoard Digital.

The Practice of Reading Closely

SpringBoard has always presented high-quality literary and informational texts for students to analyze and enjoy or appreciate. The program explicitly guides students through the steps of close reading, giving them the skills they will need for lifelong learning. During the first read, students are encouraged to engage with the text and annotate it with questions and thoughts. When they return to the text for a second read, students search for answers and evidence in response to thoughtful text-dependent questions found after each passage. The questions have been written to tap into the complexity of the text: thematic complexity, structural or linguistic complexity, or content knowledge demands. By attending to the questions, students dig into the heart of the text and practice their literary analysis skills.

The Common Core State Standards require all students to engage with authentic, complex texts. Not all students, however, are able to access such texts independently. SpringBoard's teacher guidance offers a variety of supports to bridge this gap. Before reading any text, teachers are encouraged to select an appropriate reading mode for the class based on the complexity of the passage. These possible modes include independent reading, partner reading, choral reading, or reading aloud in groups or as a whole class. Teachers are also given guidance on how to support students while working on the Text Dependent Questions. All of these supports strive to bring readers up to the level of the text, not the level of the text down to the reader.

Reading Independently

SpringBoard understands the critical need for students to read widely and independently, and provides a structure that teachers can use as an independent reading plan. Twice a unit, at the beginning and after the first Embedded Assessment, students are given the opportunity select a title from a wide array of informational and literary texts based on complexity, content, or interest. SpringBoard's list of suggested titles relates thematically to each unit, but it is not an exhaustive list. Students are free to do their own research and select a title that intrigues them. Once they have selected a title, they set a plan for their reading and begin filling out an Independent Reading Log graphic organizer.

While students work their way through each unit, it is expected that they will be given time regularly and frequently, in class and outside of class, to accomplish their independent reading. Periodic Independent Reading Links prompt students to respond to questions, conduct further research, connect texts and themes, discuss ideas in book talks, and recommend their titles to their peers. Finally, an Independent Reading Checkpoint before each Embedded Assessment asks students to reflect on their reading and log it in their Reader/Writer Notebook.

Language Development

Grammar and Vocabulary

The ability to know and understand how language functions is a crucial skill in being able to use language effectively and purposefully in a variety of contexts. Students must not only master the conventions of standard English, they must be able to choose vocabulary, syntax, and punctuation to express themselves effectively according to task, purpose, and audience.

Language skills and knowledge are incorporated as part of an integrated approach to reading, writing, speaking, and listening and focuses on language as a flexible tool that can be adapted for specific contexts.

SpringBoard includes specific **Language and Writer's Craft** activities and supporting **Grammar and Usage** sidebar definitions to provide language instruction and grammar support in the context of the reading and writing of the units of instruction.

Within the *Writing Workshop with Grammar Activities* component, grammar mini-lessons and exercises provide practice with the essential rules for conventional usage, while also encouraging students to consider how making conscious choices about diction, grammar, conventions, vocabulary, and style enhances meaning.

Reading tasks emphasize an analysis of style and application that transfers to students' own effective use of language in writing.

Vocabulary development is critically important to learning. SpringBoard has a multifaceted and integrated approach to vocabulary study that includes:

- **Academic Vocabulary** features that discuss Tier Two terms and concepts the students will use in academic discourse
- **Literary Term** features that equip students with the Tier Three language from the domains of literature, literary analysis, writing, and rhetoric
- **Word Connections** features that introduce roots and affixes as tools for decoding meaning, etymology, cognates, word relationships like antonyms and synonyms, and multiple-meaning words
- **Academic Vocabulary in Context** features that gloss Tier Two terms for students at the point of use when the text lacks context clues to aid in comprehension

Effective Expression

Speaking and Listening

A focus on Speaking and Listening as a significant element of an integrated ELA classroom has long been a hallmark of the SpringBoard program. SpringBoard provides ample opportunities for students to practice the art of collaborative thinking and planning built around structured academic conversations and collaborative tasks.

- Focused discussions, such as Socratic Seminars, Debates, and Literature Circles develop a student-centered classroom in which listening attentively and contributing orally is fostered.
- Direct instruction in establishing norms and behaviors for effective collaborative work is provided and practiced.
- Multiple opportunities for student presentations, including speeches, oral discussions, and interpretive performances allow students to practice speaking and listening in a variety of oral contexts to better prepare them for the wide variety of oral communication tasks they will encounter in college and career.
- Students are expected to support their oral communication with the appropriate and persuasive use of media and visual displays.
- Specific strategies for collaboration and oral communication are taught and practiced leading to the development of independent, skillful conduct of academic discussions.

Writing

SpringBoard provides multiple opportunities for authentic, task-based writing and writing to sources. As students are learning to write, they learn to consider task, audience, and purpose in structuring and organizing their writing. Direct instruction in writing in different modes—narrative, argumentative, and expository—is a primary focus of unit instruction.

- Guided instruction focuses on the major modes of writing arguments, expository/explanatory texts, and narratives, while also allowing students opportunities to develop creative writing skills.
- Instruction emphasizes writing process while modeling the incorporation of details, reasons, and textual evidence to support ideas.
- Structured opportunities are provided that require short and extended student research in order to practice evaluating sources, gathering relevant evidence, and citing and reporting findings accurately.
- A wide range of research-based strategies that take students through the writing process are embedded within the instructional activities to encourage best practices and sustain independent student learning.

- Mode-specific writing workshops, formative writing prompts, and performance-based Embedded Assessments with Scoring Guides provide regular practice.

Content Knowledge

SpringBoard helps students build content knowledge primarily through engagement with a wide range of high-quality literary and informational texts. These include novels, short stories, personal narratives, myths, poetry, drama, speeches, and news articles, as well as historical and science texts. Extending this core reading program with a rich independent reading program ensures that SpringBoard students are reading widely and becoming broadly literate.

SpringBoard units are designed thematically so that students can delve deeply into an exploration of themes such as heroism, utopia, comedy, perspectives, and consequences. Through close reading and analysis of texts, critical viewing of select films, wide-ranging independent reading, and lively, engaging classroom discussion, students have the opportunity to acquire and build upon extensive content knowledge.

AP Connections

A powerful feature of SpringBoard is the robust alignment to Advanced Placement (AP) Language and Literature. While not every student will take an AP class, we believe strongly that ALL students should be equipped with the higher-order thinking skills, knowledge, and behaviors necessary to be successful in AP classes and post-secondary education. SpringBoard focuses on content connections, pre-AP strategies, and writing tasks anchored in the skills and knowledge necessary to be successful on the AP exams. Explicit AP Connections as noted in the Planning the Unit section serve as a pathway across the grades. Examples of these connections include:

- close reading and analysis of both literary and nonfiction texts
- analyzing relationships among author's purpose, literary/stylistic devices, rhetorical appeals, and desired effects for intended audiences
- writing with an attention to selecting textual evidence and organizational patterns according to purpose and audience
- writing to interpret and evaluate multiple perspective in literature
- developing the control of language and command of conventions required for academic writing

Foundational Skills

SpringBoard supports the development of foundational skills for students who have not received instruction in these important skills at the primary level and/or have not developed sufficient skills in these foundations to become successful at the secondary level. The *Routines for Teaching Foundational Skills* component offers lessons and techniques for SpringBoard English Language Arts and English Language Development teachers to provide additional instruction to secondary students who are still developing foundational skills.

RESEARCH-BASED PEDAGOGY

As classroom practitioners, SpringBoard writers understand the role that research plays in curricular design and in creating effective English Language Arts instruction. They also have the hands-on experience to know what works in the classroom. Incorporating both research from experts in the field and practical experience, SpringBoard starts with the desired skills and knowledge and scaffolds the instruction students need to achieve learning goals.

SpringBoard uses the widely respected Wiggins and McTighe "Understanding by Design" instructional model. The program "back maps" the essential skills and knowledge students need to prepare for the courses, including Advanced Placement, that are the "on ramps" to college and career. Each unit begins by unpacking the Embedded Assessment, and there are multiple formative assessments throughout each unit to measure progress toward that goal. This instructional design assures teachers and students that everyday activities are building a foundation of skills and knowledge that will help students perform on the assessments, which ultimately align with the standards.

Standards → **Embedded Assessments** → **Instruction**

Standards: The CCSS define what students should know and be able to do.

Embedded Assessments: These performance-based assessments are built around CCSS and measure evidence of student learning in connection to the standards.

Instruction: Scaffolded activities help students develop the skills and knowledge to be successful on the assessments.

SpringBoard's lesson design also takes into account the work of the American Institutes for Research in its focus on students moving through multiple levels of cognitive engagement: progressing fluidly from understanding and comprehension, to analysis, and ultimately to synthesis and the creation of new content through the Embedded Assessment. Each lesson is designed to allow for the type of facilitation and flexibility referenced by Charlotte Danielson in her work on teacher instruction. We have also integrated the research of Marzano and Pickering by building students' background knowledge in the area of Academic Vocabulary development. Finally, SpringBoard is directly informed by Robyn Jackson's work on rigorous instruction. As Jackson suggests, our content requires students to be "active, not passive," and our units feature activities that stress "implicit meaning, ambiguity, layers, and complexity."

FEATURES OF THE TEACHER EDITION

In support of the work that teachers do to provide their students' with the tools and strategies they need to be successful, SpringBoard has integrated into the Teacher Edition various features that aid teachers' in their navigation of the program.

Planning the Unit

At the start of every unit, teachers will encounter the Planning the Unit section. This is a resource for teachers to use as a planning tool for the upcoming unit. These pages provide information about

- the **context** of the unit by locating the unit within the grade and scope of California Common Core State Standards
- the **instructional sequence** of the unit by explaining the purpose, progression, and connections among the activities and how each activity scaffolds toward the Embedded Assessment
- the **pacing** of the unit by providing an overview of the activities in the unit and showing teachers their natural groupings in order to support them in identifying appropriate assessment opportunities,
- the **Embedded Assessments** by unpacking the skills and knowledge necessary for students to be successful on the two major assessments in the unit,

- the **supports for writing** by offering teachers additional support for the instruction of writing in the classroom
- the **independent reading** by suggesting a wealth of texts for students to read independently based on difficulty, content, and interest
- the **instructional components** by providing a concise list of all the resources available to teachers and students to achieve the learning of the unit

Prepared with this information, teachers can feel confident before they begin the unit.

Instructional Roadmap

Throughout the activities in the SpringBoard program, teachers are supported through the inclusion of an instructional roadmap alongside the student pages. This roadmap follows the PLAN-TEACH-ASSESS-ADAPT structure. In the PLAN section, teachers are provided with a list of materials they will need for the activity as well as suggested pacing. During the TEACH portion of the roadmap, teachers are furnished with instructional steps to guide them through the activity. Along the way, teachers are offered tips and strategies from expert SpringBoard teacher-writers to enhance their instruction in the Teacher to Teacher call-out boxes. In ASSESS, opportunities are called out for teachers to assess student progress. Finally, teachers are presented with suggestions to ADAPT the activity.

LEVELED DIFFERENTIATED INSTRUCTION

Throughout the activities in the SpringBoard program, teachers will find Leveled Differentiated Instruction features designed to help them support students with the challenging tasks embedded in the program. The differentiation scaffolds learning for students at four levels: **Emerging, Expanding, Bridging**, and **Support**. The first three indicate English language proficiency levels. The level indicated as Support scaffolds learning for students who struggle with understanding the text or completing the task. A fifth level, **Stretch**, offers extensions for students ready to be challenged beyond the scope of the activity. Throughout the Teacher Edition, this leveled differentiated instruction is labeled with the following icons:

Em Ex Br Support Stretch

The three English language proficiency levels represent a continuum across which students will move during the school year, with students at the Emerging level receiving significant support, and with the support gradually decreasing for students at the Expanding and Bridging levels. A set of 26 graphic organizers designed to support student achievement of the California English Language Development Standards is included in the Resources section of this Teacher Edition, as well as in the Student Edition. These are frequently referenced in the Leveled Differentiated Instruction and are intended as learning tools that teachers and students can use in many activities.

SpringBoard strives to give students at all levels the opportunity to succeed within the framework of a rigorous and standards aligned curriculum. Teachers will discover that the scaffolds provided are designed for each level of learners' particular needs, and provide them with learning tools they will revisit throughout the program. The ultimate goal is to support teachers in building student capacity so they can successfully participate in or complete a task in order to build the knowledge and skills to be able to perform the task independently at some future point.

ASSESSMENT

Multiple and varied forms of assessment are a hallmark of SpringBoard ELA instruction. The program offers short-, medium-, and long-cycle opportunities to monitor student progress throughout the year. *Assessment for learning* is the philosophical basis of assessment opportunities in SpringBoard, and we make assessment and evaluation transparent and explicit so students and teachers can focus more deliberately on the key skills and knowledge to be learned.

- **Text-Dependent Comprehension Questions, Writing Prompts**, and **Check Your Understanding** assignments ask students to demonstrate evidence of understanding and analysis of texts and the independent ability to draw conclusions and apply new learning.
- **Short-Cycle Assessments** offer formative checks of understanding several times across a unit and are grouped according to skills and knowledge that span several activities. These multiple-choice assessments are available online through SpringBoard Digital.
- **End-of-Unit Assessments** are aligned to the Learning Targets and standards of each unit and include 20 multiple-choice and five open-response questions per unit. Teachers may choose to use these as a precursor or complement to the final Embedded Assessment for the unit. These assessments are available online through SpringBoard Digital.
- **Embedded Assessments** give students performance-based opportunities to demonstrate mastery of skills and knowledge visually, orally, and in writing. Assessment-specific **Scoring Guides** set clear expectations for students, while **English Language Development Rubrics** accompanying the Embedded Assessments help teachers gauge their English Learners' progress on the ELD continuum.
- **Reflection** questions follow each Embedded Assessment and provide opportunities for students to self-assess and identify strategies that worked for them as they take real ownership of their learning.

WRITING WORKSHOP WITH GRAMMAR ACTIVITIES

SpringBoard instruction in writing is addressed in two integrated ways:

- through project-based, scaffolded writing assessments in the student texts
- through SpringBoard *Writing Workshop with Grammar Activities*

To support students in becoming effective writers, these writing workshops offer guided experiences in specific rhetorical and grammar and usage skills, emphasizing practice and mastery of specific writing modes. The SpringBoard writing workshops offer direct instruction to support and extend mastery of the writing process and commonly assessed writing products. Each workshop guides students through writing in a specific mode by creating opportunities for students to write three separate texts in the mode under study; one that is constructed as a class with direct guidance from the teacher, one that is peer constructed with teacher support, and one that is written independently.

The SpringBoard writing workshops provide extensive practice in writing in the essential modes of narrative, argumentative, and expository/explanatory, as well as in creative modes. Each writing workshop follows a clear sequence of writing development of prewriting, drafting, and revision, taking students through instruction in organizational structure, presentation of ideas, use of stylistic techniques, use of sentence structure for effect, and the incorporation of grammar and language conventions. All writing workshops are accompanied by a Scoring Guide that outlines the performance expectations for each writing mode and provides an evaluation tool for the Learning Targets identified at each grade level.

Ten different writing workshops are available for each grade level. In addition to direct instruction in the writing process, and in the essential major areas of narrative, argumentative, and expository writing, other workshops support writing responses to literature, short stories, poetry, dramatic scripts, procedural texts and research based texts. These workshops include a **Grammar Handbook** to be used as a reference, and **Grammar Activities** to support grammar and usage skill acquisition aligned to every unit of the SpringBoard ELA.

ENGAGING AND INTERACTIVE DIGITAL EDITION

SpringBoard has introduced a bold new generation of digital teaching and learning resources. Both the Teacher and Student Editions have been developed using state-of-the-art responsive web design, so they work seamlessly on any device from laptop and smart phone to tablet and interactive whiteboards. In addition to providing all content online, the new SpringBoard Digital program includes the following:

- A full digital toolbox for teachers to **plan and personalize lessons**, track student progress, and communicate with students
- A one-click **Correlations Viewer** with links between grade-level standards and exact standards-related content locations
- Digital "sticky" notes that can be inserted on-screen and offer on-demand **planning and notation** for teacher suggestions or student work
- The ability to edit teaching commentary, personalizing it by adding notes and comments to lessons
- A full digital toolbox that enables students to annotate, underline, circle, highlight, and interact with the text
- A digital notebook for students to record notes and view their interactive work, including writing and portfolio work
- The full ability to edit, save, and send

A Letter from SpringBoard

We at SpringBoard have learned a lot as we have taken the ideas, suggestions, and best practices from teachers like you and placed them in a program that puts students at the center of instruction. The California Common Core State Standards tell us "what" students should know, and we believe teachers can use SpringBoard as a tool to address "how" to meet the rigor of the Standards and ensure that all students achieve their highest potential.

SpringBoard is truly a unique program, and the materials reflect the experiences and expertise of teachers in every state. At first glance, many users see the teacher suggestions as a "script" that can take away some of their autonomy and creativity. This is not the intent. We know that the dedicated teachers who use this instructional framework already have a variety of experiences that they can, and should, bring to the table. We at SpringBoard celebrate and embrace the amazing work that is already being done in the field and hope that all teachers who use our program can truly make it their own. Our talented group of writers, teachers, trainers, and coaches has learned a great deal in working with instructors and leaders across the country, and we feel it is important to share a few thoughts with you.

We believe in starting each unit by showing students the Embedded Assessment assignment. By asking students to identify the skills and knowledge they will need to know and be able to apply, we are inviting our students to take ownership of their education. No longer will we hear comments like "This is busy work" or "Why are we doing this today?" Instead, at the end of every class period we can ask our students what they learned and how it connects to the assessment. Their answers will validate instruction and help them understand why every day is important.

Process is as important as content, so the focus should be on both. Learning content is important, but learning how to learn is equally important to ensure students gain the skills to read and make meaning of any text or to write in multiple modes. Choose the reading and writing strategies that work well with your students (sometimes this changes from class to class), and differentiate your instruction based on your students' needs. Having common assessments and lesson pathways allows you to focus on instruction and adjust that instruction according to what you see in your students' work. This model also fosters rich discussions about your choices in your professional learning communities and district meetings.

Finally, we hope you will take time to become a part of the larger SpringBoard **community** of teachers who are focused on preparing ALL students for college and career success. Let yourself be inspired and challenged during professional development, find support through our online community, and share your opinions with us. The SpringBoard family welcomes you. We hope the high-quality tasks, models of instruction, and professional support that SpringBoard offers will help you in your work with the CA CCSS and Framework, and in your own instructional growth and success.

Sincerely,

The SpringBoard Team

California Common Core State Standards

Reading Standards for Literature

Key Ideas and Details	RL.8.1	Cite the textual evidence that most strongly supports an analysis of what the text says explicitly as well as inferences drawn from the text.
	RL.8.2	Determine a theme or central idea of a text and analyze its development over the course of the text, including its relationship to the characters, setting, and plot; provide an objective summary of the text.
	RL.8.3	Analyze how particular lines of dialogue or incidents in a story or drama propel the action, reveal aspects of a character, or provoke a decision.
Craft and Structure	RL.8.4	Determine the meaning of words and phrases as they are used in a text, including figurative and connotative meanings; analyze the impact of specific word choices on meaning and tone, including analogies or allusions to other texts. **(See grade 8 Language standards 4–6 for additional expectations.) CA**
	RL.8.5	Compare and contrast the structure of two or more texts and analyze how the differing structure of each text contributes to its meaning and style.
	RL.8.6	Analyze how differences in the points of view of the characters and the audience or reader (e.g., created through the use of dramatic irony) create such effects as suspense or humor.
Integration of Knowledge and Ideas	RL.8.7	Analyze the extent to which a filmed or live production of a story or drama stays faithful to or departs from the text or script, evaluating the choices made by the director or actors.
	RL.8.8	(Not applicable to literature)
	RL.8.9	Analyze how a modern work of fiction draws on themes, patterns of events, or character types from myths, traditional stories, or religious works such as the Bible, including describing how the material is rendered new.
Range of Reading and Text Complexity	RL.8.10	By the end of the year, read and comprehend literature, including stories, dramas, and poems, at the high end of grades 6–8 text complexity band independently and proficiently.

Reading Standards for Informational Text

Key Ideas and Details	RI.8.1	Cite the textual evidence that most strongly supports an analysis of what the text says explicitly as well as inferences drawn from the text.
	RI.8.2	Determine a central idea of a text and analyze its development over the course of the text, including its relationship to supporting ideas; provide an objective summary of the text.
	RI.8.3	Analyze how a text makes connections among and distinctions between individuals, ideas, or events (e.g., through comparisons, analogies, or categories).
Craft and Structure	RI.8.4	Determine the meaning of words and phrases as they are used in a text, including figurative, connotative, and technical meanings; analyze the impact of specific word choices on meaning and tone, including analogies or allusions to other texts. **(See grade 8 Language standards 4–6 for additional expectations.) CA**
	RI.8.5	Analyze in detail the structure of a specific paragraph in a text, including the role of particular sentences in developing and refining a key concept.
	RI.8.5a	**Analyze the use of text features (e.g., graphics, headers, captions) in consumer materials. CA**
	RI.8.6	Determine an author's point of view or purpose in a text and analyze how the author acknowledges and responds to conflicting evidence or viewpoints.
Integration of Knowledge and Ideas	RI.8.7	Evaluate the advantages and disadvantages of using different mediums (e.g., print or digital text, video, multimedia) to present a particular topic or idea.
	RI.8.8	Delineate and evaluate the argument and specific claims in a text, assessing whether the reasoning is sound and the evidence is relevant and sufficient; recognize when irrelevant evidence is introduced.
	RI.8.9	Analyze a case in which two or more texts provide conflicting information on the same topic and identify where the texts disagree on matters of fact or interpretation.
Range of Reading and Text Complexity	RI.8.10	By the end of the year, read and comprehend literary nonfiction at the high end of the grades 6–8 text complexity band independently and proficiently.

Writing Standards

Text Types and Purposes	W.8.1	Write arguments to support claims with clear reasons and relevant evidence.
	W.8.1a	Introduce claim(s), acknowledge and distinguish the claim(s) from alternate or opposing claims, and organize the reasons and evidence logically.
	W.8.1b	Support claim(s) with logical reasoning and relevant evidence, using accurate, credible sources and demonstrating an understanding of the topic or text.
	W.8.1c	Use words, phrases, and clauses to create cohesion and clarify the relationships among claim(s), counterclaims, reasons, and evidence.
	W.8.1d	Establish and maintain a formal style.
	W.8.1e	Provide a concluding statement or section that follows from and supports the argument presented.
	W.8.2	Write informative/explanatory texts, **including career development documents (e.g., simple business letters and job applications),** to examine a topic and convey ideas, concepts, and information through the selection, organization, and analysis of relevant content. **CA**
	W.8.2a	Introduce a topic **or thesis statement** clearly, previewing what is to follow; organize ideas, concepts, and information into broader categories; include formatting (e.g., headings), graphics (e.g., charts, tables), and multimedia when useful to aiding comprehension. **CA**
	W.8.2b	Develop the topic with relevant, well-chosen facts, definitions, concrete details, quotations, or other information and examples.
	W.8.2c	Use appropriate and varied transitions to create cohesion and clarify the relationships among ideas and concepts.
	W.8.2d	Use precise language and domain-specific vocabulary to inform about or explain the topic.
	W.8.2e	Establish and maintain a formal style.
	W.8.2f	Provide a concluding statement or section that follows from and supports the information or explanation presented.
	W.8.3	Write narratives to develop real or imagined experiences or events using effective technique, relevant descriptive details, and well-structured event sequences.
	W.8.3a	Engage and orient the reader by establishing a context and point of view and introducing a narrator and/or characters; organize an event sequence that unfolds naturally and logically.

Writing Standards

Text Types and Purposes	W.8.3b	Use narrative techniques, such as dialogue, pacing, description, and reflection, to develop experiences, events, and/or characters.
	W.8.3c	Use a variety of transition words, phrases, and clauses to convey sequence, signal shifts from one time frame or setting to another, and show the relationships among experiences and events.
	W.8.3d	Use precise words and phrases, relevant descriptive details, and sensory language to capture the action and convey experiences and events.
	W.8.3e	Provide a conclusion that follows from and reflects on the narrated experiences or events.
Production and Distribution of Writing	W.8.4	Produce clear and coherent writing in which the development, organization, and style are appropriate to task, purpose, and audience. (Grade-specific expectations for writing types are defined in standards 1–3 above.)
	W.8.5	With some guidance and support from peers and adults, develop and strengthen writing as needed by planning, revising, editing, rewriting, or trying a new approach, focusing on how well purpose and audience have been addressed. (Editing for conventions should demonstrate command of Language standards 1–3 up to and including grade 8.)
	W.8.6	Use technology, including the Internet, to produce and publish writing and present the relationships between information and ideas efficiently as well as to interact and collaborate with others.
Research to Build and Present Knowledge	W.8.7	Conduct short research projects to answer a question (including a self-generated question), drawing on several sources and generating additional related, focused questions that allow for multiple avenues of exploration.
	W.8.8	Gather relevant information from multiple print and digital sources, using search terms effectively; assess the credibility and accuracy of each source; and quote or paraphrase the data and conclusions of others while avoiding plagiarism and following a standard format for citation.
	W.8.9	Draw evidence from literary or informational texts to support analysis, reflection, and research.
	W.8.9a	Apply grade 8 Reading standards to literature (e.g., "Analyze how a modern work of fiction draws on themes, patterns of events, or character types from myths, traditional stories, or religious works such as the Bible, including describing how the material is rendered new").
	W.8.9b	Apply grade 8 Reading standards to literary nonfiction (e.g., "Delineate and evaluate the argument and specific claims in a text, assessing whether the reasoning is sound and the evidence is relevant and sufficient; recognize when irrelevant evidence is introduced").
Range of Writing	W.8.10	Write routinely over extended time frames (time for research, reflection, and revision) and shorter time frames (a single sitting or a day or two) for a range of discipline-specific tasks, purposes, and audiences.

Speaking and Listening Standards

Comprehension and Collaboration	SL.8.1	Engage effectively in a range of collaborative discussions (one-on-one, in groups, and teacher-led) with diverse partners on grade 8 topics, texts, and issues, building on others' ideas and expressing their own clearly.
	SL.8.1a	Come to discussions prepared, having read or researched material under study; explicitly draw on that preparation by referring to evidence on the topic, text, or issue to probe and reflect on ideas under discussion.
	SL.8.1b	Follow rules for collegial discussions and decision-making, track progress toward specific goals and deadlines, and define individual roles as needed.
	SL.8.1c	Pose questions that connect the ideas of several speakers and respond to others' questions and comments with relevant evidence, observations, and ideas.
	SL.8.1d	Acknowledge new information expressed by others, and, when warranted, qualify or justify their own views in light of the evidence presented.
	SL.8.2	Analyze the purpose of information presented in diverse media and formats (e.g., visually, quantitatively, orally) and evaluate the motives (e.g., social, commercial, political) behind its presentation.
	SL.8.3	Delineate a speaker's argument and specific claims, evaluating the soundness of the reasoning and relevance and sufficiency of the evidence and identifying when irrelevant evidence is introduced.
Presentation of Knowledge and Ideas	SL.8.4	Present claims and findings **(e.g., argument, narrative, response to literature presentations),** emphasizing salient points in a focused, coherent manner with relevant evidence, sound valid reasoning, and well-chosen details; use appropriate eye contact, adequate volume, and clear pronunciation. **CA**
	SL.8.4a	**Plan and present a narrative that: establishes a context and point of view, presents a logical sequence, uses narrative techniques (e.g., dialogue, pacing, description, sensory language), uses a variety of transitions, and provides a conclusion that reflects the experience. CA**
	SL.8.5	Integrate multimedia and visual displays into presentations to clarify information, strengthen claims and evidence, and add interest.
	SL.8.6	Adapt speech to a variety of contexts and tasks, demonstrating command of formal English when indicated or appropriate. (See grade 8 Language standards 1 and 3 for specific expectations.)

Language Standards

Conventions of Standard English	L.8.1	Demonstrate command of the conventions of standard English grammar and usage when writing or speaking.
	L.8.1a	Explain the function of verbals (gerunds, participles, infinitives) in general and their function in particular sentences.
	L.8.1b	Form and use verbs in the active and passive voice.
	L.8.1c	Form and use verbs in the indicative, imperative, interrogative, conditional, and subjunctive mood.
	L.8.1d	Recognize and correct inappropriate shifts in verb voice and mood.
	L.8.2	Demonstrate command of the conventions of standard English capitalization, punctuation, and spelling when writing.
	L.8.2a	Use punctuation (comma, ellipsis, dash) to indicate a pause or break.
	L.8.2b	Use an ellipsis to indicate an omission.
	L.8.2c	Spell correctly.
Knowledge of Language	L.8.3	Use knowledge of language and its conventions when writing, speaking, reading, or listening.
	L.8.3a	Use verbs in the active and passive voice and in the conditional and subjunctive mood to achieve particular effects (e.g., emphasizing the actor or the action; expressing uncertainty or describing a state contrary to fact).
Vocabulary Acquisition and Use	L.8.4	Determine or clarify the meaning of unknown and multiple-meaning words or phrases based on grade 8 reading and content, choosing flexibly from a range of strategies.
	L.8.4a	Use context (e.g., the overall meaning of a sentence or paragraph; a word's position or function in a sentence) as a clue to the meaning of a word or phrase.
	L.8.4b	Use common, grade-appropriate Greek or Latin affixes and roots as clues to the meaning of a word (e.g., precede, recede, secede).
	L.8.4c	Consult general and specialized reference materials (e.g., dictionaries, glossaries, thesauruses), both print and digital, to find the pronunciation of a word or determine or clarify its precise meaning or its part of speech **or trace the etymology of words. CA**
	L.8.4d	Verify the preliminary determination of the meaning of a word or phrase (e.g., by checking the inferred meaning in context or in a dictionary).

Language Standards

Vocabulary Acquisition and Use	L.8.5	Demonstrate understanding of figurative language, word relationships, and nuances in word meanings.
	L.8.5a	Interpret figures of speech (e.g. verbal irony, puns) in context.
	L.8.5b	Use the relationship between particular words to better understand each of the words.
	L.8.5c	Distinguish among the connotations (associations) of words with similar denotations (definitions) (e.g., bullheaded, willful, firm, persistent, resolute).
	L.8.6	Acquire and use accurately grade-appropriate general academic and domain-specific words and phrases; gather vocabulary knowledge when considering a word or phrase important to comprehension or expression.

California English Language Development Standards

Part I: Interacting in Meaningful Ways

Communicative Modes	Standard Code	Emerging	Expanding	Bridging
Collaborative	PI.8.1	**Exchanging information/ideas** Engage in conversational exchanges and express ideas on familiar topics by asking and answering *yes–no* and *wh-* questions and responding using simple phrases.	**Exchanging information/ideas** Contribute to class, group, and partner discussions by following turn-taking rules, asking relevant questions, affirming others, adding relevant information, and paraphrasing key ideas.	**Exchanging information/ideas** Contribute to class, group, and partner discussions by following turn-taking rules, asking relevant questions, affirming others, adding relevant information and evidence, paraphrasing key ideas, building on responses, and providing useful feedback.
	PI.8.2	**Interacting via written English** Engage in short written exchanges with peers and collaborate on simple written texts on familiar topics, using technology when appropriate.	**Interacting via written English** Engage in longer written exchanges with peers and collaborate on more detailed written texts on a variety of topics, using technology when appropriate.	**Interacting via written English** Engage in extended written exchanges with peers and collaborate on complex written texts on a variety of topics, using technology when appropriate.
	PI.8.3	**Supporting opinions and persuading others** Negotiate with or persuade others in conversations (e.g., to gain and hold the floor or to ask for clarification) using learned phrases (e.g., *I think . . . Would you please repeat that?*) and open responses.	**Supporting opinions and persuading others** Negotiate with or persuade others in conversations (e.g., to provide counter-arguments) using learned phrases (*I agree with X, but . . .*) and open responses.	**Supporting opinions and persuading others** Negotiate with or persuade others in conversations using an appropriate register (e.g., to acknowledge new information and justify views) using a variety of learned phrases, indirect reported speech (e.g., *I heard you say X, and that's a good point. I still think Y, though, because . . .*) and open responses.
	PI.8.4	**Adapting language choices** Adjust language choices according to social setting (e.g., classroom, break time) and audience (e.g., peers, teacher).	**Adapting language choices** Adjust language choices according to purpose (e.g., explaining, persuading, entertaining), task, and audience.	**Adapting language choices** Adjust language choices according to task (e.g., facilitating a science experiment, providing peer feedback on a writing assignment), purpose, and audience.

Communicative Modes	Standard Code	Emerging	Expanding	Bridging
Interpretive	PI.8.5	**Listening actively** Demonstrate active listening in oral presentation activities by asking and answering basic questions with prompting and substantial support.	**Listening actively** Demonstrate active listening in oral presentation activities by asking and answering detailed questions with occasional prompting and moderate support.	**Listening actively** Demonstrate active listening in oral presentation activities by asking and answering detailed questions with minimal prompting and support.
	PI.8.6a	**Reading/viewing closely** Explain ideas, phenomena, processes, and text relationships (e.g., compare/contrast, cause/effect, problem/solution) based on close reading of a variety of grade-appropriate texts and viewing of multimedia with substantial support.	**Reading/viewing closely** Explain ideas, phenomena, processes, and text relationships (e.g., compare/contrast, cause/effect, problem/solution) based on close reading of a variety of grade-appropriate texts and viewing of multimedia with moderate support.	**Reading/viewing closely** Explain ideas, phenomena, processes, and text relationships (e.g., compare/contrast, cause/effect, problem/solution) based on close reading of a variety of grade-level texts and viewing of multimedia with light support.
	PI.8.6b	**Reading/viewing closely** Express inferences and conclusions drawn based on close reading of grade-appropriate texts and viewing of multimedia using some frequently used verbs (e.g., *shows that, based on*).	**Reading/viewing closely** Express inferences and conclusions drawn based on close reading of grade-appropriate texts and viewing of multimedia using a variety of verbs (e.g., *suggests that, leads to*).	**Reading/viewing closely** Express inferences and conclusions drawn based on close reading of grade-level texts and viewing of multimedia using a variety of precise academic verbs (e.g., *indicates that, influences*).
	PI.8.6c	**Reading/viewing closely** Use knowledge of morphology (e.g., affixes, roots, and base words), context, reference materials, and visual cues to determine the meanings of unknown and multiple-meaning words on familiar topics.	**Reading/viewing closely** Use knowledge of morphology (e.g., affixes, roots, and base words), context, reference materials, and visual cues to determine the meanings of unknown and multiple-meaning words on familiar and new topics.	**Reading/viewing closely** Use knowledge of morphology (e.g., affixes, roots, and base words), context, reference materials, and visual cues to determine the meanings, including figurative and connotative meanings, of unknown and multiple-meaning words on a variety of new topics.

Communicative Modes	Standard Code	Emerging	Expanding	Bridging
Interpretive	PI.8.7	**Evaluating language choices** Explain how well writers and speakers use language to support ideas and arguments with detailed evidence (e.g., identifying the precise vocabulary used to present evidence, or the phrasing used to signal a shift in meaning) when provided with substantial support.	**Evaluating language choices** Explain how well writers and speakers use specific language to present ideas or support arguments and provide detailed evidence (e.g., showing the clarity of the phrasing used to present an argument) when provided with moderate support.	**Evaluating language choices** Explain how well writers and speakers use specific language resources to present ideas or support arguments and provide detailed evidence (e.g., identifying the specific language used to present ideas and claims that are well supported and distinguishing them from those that are not) when provided with light support.
	PI.8.8	**Analyzing language choices** Explain how phrasing or different common words with similar meanings (e.g., choosing to use the word persistent versus the term *hard worker*) produce different effects on the audience.	**Analyzing language choices** Explain how phrasing or different words with similar meanings (e.g., describing a character as *stubborn* versus *persistent*) or figurative language (e.g., *Let me throw some light onto the topic.*) produce shades of meaning and different effects on the audience.	**Analyzing language choices** Explain how phrasing or different words with similar meanings (e.g., *cunning* versus *smart*, *stammer* versus *say*) or figurative language (e.g., *Let me throw some light onto the topic.*) produce shades of meaning, nuances, and different effects on the audience.
Productive	PI.8.9	**Presenting** Plan and deliver brief informative oral presentations on concrete topics.	**Presenting** Plan and deliver longer oral presentations on a variety of topics using details and evidence to support ideas.	**Presenting** Plan and deliver longer oral presentations on a variety of concrete and abstract topics using reasoning and evidence to support ideas and using a growing understanding of register.
	PI.8.10a	**Writing** Write short literary and informational texts (e.g., an argument about whether the government should fund research using stem cells) collaboratively (e.g., with peers) and independently.	**Writing** Write longer literary and informational texts (e.g., an argument about whether the government should fund research using stem cells) collaboratively (e.g., with peers) and independently using appropriate text organization.	**Writing** Write longer and more detailed literary and informational texts (e.g., an argument about whether the government should fund research using stem cells) collaboratively (e.g., with peers) and independently using appropriate text organization and growing understanding of register.

Communicative Modes	Standard Code	Emerging	Expanding	Bridging
Productive	PI.8.10b	**Writing** Write brief summaries of texts and experiences using complete sentences and key words (e.g., from notes or graphic organizers).	**Writing** Write increasingly concise summaries of texts and experiences using complete sentences and key words (e.g., from notes or graphic organizers).	**Writing** Write clear and coherent summaries of texts and experiences using complete and concise sentences and key words (e.g., from notes or graphic organizers).
	PI.8.11a	**Justifying/arguing** Justify opinions by providing some textual evidence or relevant background knowledge with substantial support.	**Justifying/arguing** Justify opinions or persuade others by providing relevant textual evidence or relevant background knowledge with moderate support.	**Justifying/arguing** Justify opinions or persuade others by providing detailed and relevant textual evidence or relevant background knowledge with light support.
	PI.8.11b	**Justifying/arguing** Express attitude and opinions or temper statements with familiar modal expressions (e.g., *can, may*).	**Justifying/arguing** Express attitude and opinions or temper statements with a variety of familiar modal expressions (e.g., *possibly/likely, could/would*).	**Justifying/arguing** Express attitude and opinions or temper statements with nuanced modal expressions (e.g., *potentially/certainly/absolutely, should/might*).
	PI.8.12a	**Selecting language resources** Use a select number of general academic words (e.g., *specific, contrast*) and domain-specific words (e.g., *scene, cell, fraction*) to create some precision while speaking and writing.	**Selecting language resources** Use a growing set of academic words (e.g., *specific, contrast, significant, function*), domain-specific words (e.g., *scene, irony, suspense, analogy, cell membrane, fraction*), synonyms, and antonyms to create precision and shades of meaning while speaking and writing.	**Selecting language resources** Use an expanded set of general academic words (e.g., *specific, contrast, significant, function, adequate, analysis*), domain-specific words (e.g., *scene, irony, suspense, analogy, cell membrane, fraction*), synonyms, antonyms, and figurative language to create precision and shades of meaning while speaking and writing.
	PI.8.12b	**Selecting language resources** Use knowledge of morphology to appropriately select affixes in basic ways (e.g., *She likes X. He walked to school.*).	**Selecting language resources** Use knowledge of morphology to appropriately select affixes in a growing number of ways to manipulate language (e.g., *She likes walking to school. That's impossible.*).	**Selecting language resources** Use knowledge of morphology to appropriately select affixes in a variety of ways to manipulate language (e.g., *changing destroy* → *destruction, probably* → *probability, reluctant* → *reluctantly*).

Part II: Learning About How English Works

Language Processes	Standard Code	Emerging	Expanding	Bridging
Structuring Cohesive Texts	PII.8.1	**Understanding text structure** Apply understanding of how different text types are organized to express ideas (e.g., how narratives are organized sequentially) to comprehending texts and to writing brief arguments, informative/explanatory texts and narratives.	**Understanding text structure** Apply understanding of the organizational features of different text types (e.g., how narratives are organized by an event sequence that unfolds naturally versus how arguments are organized around reasons and evidence) to comprehending texts and to writing increasingly clear and coherent arguments, informative/explanatory texts and narratives.	**Understanding text structure** Apply understanding of the organizational structure of different text types (e.g., how narratives are organized by an event sequence that unfolds naturally versus how arguments are organized around reasons and evidence) to comprehending texts and to writing clear and cohesive arguments, informative/explanatory texts and narratives.
	PII.8.2a	**Understanding cohesion** Apply knowledge of familiar language resources for referring to make texts more cohesive (e.g., how pronouns refer back to nouns in text) to comprehending and writing brief texts.	**Understanding cohesion** Apply knowledge of familiar language resources for referring to make texts more cohesive (e.g., how pronouns refer back to nouns in text, how using synonyms helps avoid repetition) to comprehending and writing texts with increasing cohesion.	**Understanding cohesion** Apply knowledge of familiar language resources for referring to make texts more cohesive (e.g., how pronouns, synonyms, or nominalizations are used to refer backward in a text) to comprehending texts and writing cohesive texts.
	PII.8.2b	**Understanding cohesion** Apply basic understanding of how ideas, events, or reasons are linked throughout a text using everyday connecting words or phrases (e.g., *at the end, next*) to comprehending and writing brief texts.	**Understanding cohesion** Apply growing understanding of how ideas, events, or reasons are linked throughout a text using a variety of connecting words or phrases (e.g., *for example, as a result, on the other hand*) to comprehending and writing texts with increasing cohesion.	**Understanding cohesion** Apply increasing understanding of how ideas, events, or reasons are linked throughout a text using an increasing variety of academic connecting and transitional words or phrases (e.g., *for instance, in addition, consequently*) to comprehending and writing texts with increasing cohesion.

Language Processes	Standard Code	Emerging	Expanding	Bridging
Expanding and Enriching Ideas	PII.8.3	**Using verbs and verb phrases** Use a variety of verbs in different tenses (e.g., present, past, future) and aspects (e.g., simple, progressive) appropriate for the text type and discipline (e.g., simple past and past progressive for recounting an experience) on familiar topics.	**Using verbs and verb phrases** Use a variety of verbs in different tenses (e.g., present, past, future) and aspects (e.g., simple, progressive, perfect) appropriate for the task, text type, and discipline (e.g., the present perfect to describe previously made claims or conclusions) on an increasing variety of topics.	**Using verbs and verb phrases** Use a variety of verbs in different tenses (e.g., present, past, future), aspects (e.g., simple, progressive, perfect), voices (active and passive), and moods (e.g., declarative, interrogative, subjunctive) appropriate for the task, text type, and discipline (e.g., the passive voice in simple past to describe the methods of a scientific experiment) on a variety of topics.
	PII.8.4	**Using nouns and noun phrases** Expand noun phrases in basic ways (e.g., adding a sensory adjective to a noun) in order to enrich the meaning of sentences and add details about ideas, people, things, etc.	**Using nouns and noun phrases** Expand noun phrases in a growing number of ways (e.g., adding prepositional or adjective phrases) in order to enrich the meaning of sentences and add details about ideas, people, things, etc.	**Using nouns and noun phrases** Expand noun phrases in an increasing variety of ways (e.g., embedding relative or complement clauses) in order to enrich the meaning of sentences and add details about ideas, people, things, etc.
	PII.8.5	**Modifying to add details** Expand sentences with simple adverbials (e.g., adverbs, adverb phrases, prepositional phrases) to provide details (e.g., time, manner, place, cause) about a familiar activity or process.	**Modifying to add details** Expand sentences with adverbials (e.g., adverbs, adverb phrases, prepositional phrases) to provide details (e.g., time, manner, place, cause) about a familiar or new activity or process.	**Modifying to add details** Expand sentences with increasingly complex adverbials (e.g., adverbs, adverb phrases and clauses, prepositional phrases) to provide details (e.g., time, manner, place, cause) about a variety of familiar and new activities and processes.

Language Processes	Standard Code	Emerging	Expanding	Bridging
Connecting and Condensing Ideas	PII.8.6	**Connecting ideas** Combine clauses in a few basic ways to make connections between and join ideas (e.g., creating compound sentences using *and, but, so;* creating complex sentences using *because*).	**Connecting ideas** Combine clauses in an increasing variety of ways (e.g., creating compound and complex sentences) to make connections between and join ideas, for example, to express a reason (e.g., *He stayed at home on Sunday to study for Monday' s exam.*) or to make a concession (e.g., *She studied all night even though she wasn' t feeling well.*).	**Connecting ideas** Combine clauses in a wide variety of ways (e.g., creating compound and complex sentences, and compound- complex sentences) to make connections between and join ideas, for example, to show the relationship between multiple events or ideas (e.g., *After eating lunch, the students worked in groups while their teacher walked around the room.*) or to evaluate an argument (e.g., *The author claims X, although there is a lack of evidence to support this claim.*).
	PII.8.7	**Condensing ideas** Condense ideas in simple ways (e.g., by compounding verbs, adding prepositional phrases, or through simple embedded clauses or other ways of condensing as in, This is a story about a girl. The girl changed the world. ⟶ This is a story about a girl *who changed the world.*) to create precise and detailed sentences.	**Condensing ideas** Condense ideas in an increasing variety of ways (e.g., through various types of embedded clauses and other ways of condensing, as in, Organic vegetables are food. They're made without chemical fertilizers. They're made without chemical insecticides. ⟶ Organic vegetables are foods *that are made without chemical fertilizers or insecticides.*) to create precise and detailed sentences.	**Condensing ideas** Condense ideas in a variety of ways (e.g., through various types of embedded clauses, ways of condensing, and nominalization as in, They *destroyed* the rainforest. Lots of animals *died*. ⟶ The *destruction* of the rainforest led to the *death* of many animals.) to create precise and detailed sentences.
Foundational Literacy Skills: **Literacy in an Alphabetic Writing System** • Print concepts • Phonological awareness • Phonics and word recognition • Fluency	PIII.8	**See Appendix A for information on teaching reading foundational skills to English learners of various profiles based on age, native language, native language writing system, schooling experience, and literacy experience and proficiency. Some considerations are:** • Native language and literacy (e.g., phoneme awareness or print concept skills in native language) should be assessed for potential transference to English language and literacy. • Similarities between native language and English should be highlighted (e.g., phonemes or letters that are the same in both languages). • Differences between native language and English should be highlighted (e.g., some phonemes in English may not exist in the student's native language; native language syntax may be different from English syntax).		

Planning the Unit

UNIT 1

Context

The word *heroism* is often used, yet rarely defined. We hear it on the news, read it in newspapers, see it in movies. We are bombarded with the media's version of heroism, and we accept it as truth. This unit shows students how to take an everyday concept such as *heroism* and think about it analytically and creatively from diverse perspectives. Students study heroes from across time and cultures to discover similarities and differences between mythological, literary and real-life heroes, and to distinguish the media's heroes from their own.

Instructional Sequence

The first half of the unit explores and connects the Hero's Journey archetype, narrative writing, and visual techniques. Students apply their understanding of these skills and concepts by conceptualizing, drafting, visualizing, and revising an original Hero's Journey narrative. This work directly prepares students for Embedded Assessment 1.

The second half of the unit shifts from narrative to expository writing as students go deeper into the concept of *heroism*. Students analyze a variety of literary and informational texts to form an original definition of *heroism*, and they learn how to structure their ideas to write a definition essay.

CollegeBoard

AP/College Readiness

In this unit, students will focus on refining these important skills and knowledge areas for AP/College Readiness:

- Analyzing writer's craft (Activities 1.3, 1.6, 1.14, 1.16)
- Using textual evidence to support a literary interpretation (Activities 1.3, 1.4, 1.7, 1.12)
- Making meaning of a wide variety of texts of literary merit (Activities 1.6, 1.7, 1.9, 1.13, 1.14)
- Applying a literary archetype to literary text (Activities 1.5, 1.6, 1.7, 1.9)
- Writing for a variety of purposes (Activities 1.2, 1.3, 1.6, 1.13, 1.16)
- Analyzing an image as text (Activities 1.3, 1.4, 1.5)

Unpacked Embedded Assessments

Embedded Assessment 1: Writing a Hero's Journey Narrative	Embedded Assessment 2: Writing a Definition Essay
Skills and Knowledge: • Create a believable, original protagonist. • Establish context through point of view, setting, and conflict. • Use details, dialogue, and description for effect. • Sequence plot based on the Hero's Journey archetype. • Use transitions to link events and signal shifts. • Use connotative diction, vivid verbs, sensory language, and figurative language for effect. • Demonstrate command of conventions. • Use visual techniques to enhance illustrations.	**Skills and Knowledge:** • Establish a clear thesis in a focused introduction. • Use strategies of definition to define *heroism*. • Support thesis with relevant detail, evidence, and explanations. • Embed and cite direct quotations. • Sequence ideas logically. • Use transitions and topic sentences to create coherence. • Provide a relevant conclusion. • Use diction to create tone. • Demonstrate command of conventions.

Instructional Activities and Pacing

Total: 34 class periods	Description
1.1–1.2 2 class periods	Students are introduced to the unit's Essential Questions and vocabulary before unpacking Embedded Assessment 1 and selecting a text for independent reading. This process clarifies expectations for learning and sets a purpose for activities that lead up to the Hero's Journey narrative. Next, students analyze quotes to explore the unit's thematic topics of *challenge* and *heroism*.
1.3–1.4 4 class periods	Students learn how to write an effective narrative beginning by studying an excerpt a classic novel. They learn how a writer sets the context for the story by describing the setting, establishing a point of view, and introducing a conflict. Next, they learn how to use visual techniques for effect (e.g. , to set the context and create mood), and they practice transforming written imagery and detail into illustrations.
1.5–1.9 10 class periods	This series of activities uses print and nonprint texts to examine the Hero's Journey archetype plot structure, which is divided into three distinct stages: Departure, Initiation, and Return. As students study each stage, they strengthen their understanding of narrative elements (e.g., plot, characterization, theme), and narrative and visual techniques. They apply what they learn by creating heroes, sending them on a journey, and illustrating key events. After drafting the beginning and middle of a narrative, students work in writing groups to create a writer's checklist and to provide specific feedback for revision and editing. They continue to revise after drafting the end of their narrative. Students will use the knowledge gained in these activities to successfully develop content and structure, use language for effect, and illustrate events in Embedded Assessment 1.
Embedded Assessment 1 3 class periods	By the time students encounter the Embedded Assessment, they will have already drafted, revised, and illustrated an original Hero's Journey narrative. After collaborating in writing groups to strengthen their writing through revision and editing, students will publish and present their story and reflect on their learning.
1.10–1.11 2 class periods	The first activity serves as a transition from the first to the second half of the unit. Students begin by reflecting on their learning in the first half, unpacking Embedded Assessment 2, and selecting a new independent reading text. Next, students compare and contrast narrative and expository writing to see that their work in the first half of the unit supports learning in the second half. After students are introduced to the concept of *definition*, they study connotative diction to understand nuance in tone. This sets a foundation for upcoming reading and writing activities.
1.12–1.14 6 class periods	In preparation for writing a heroism definition essay, students read a wide variety of literary and informational texts featuring diverse heroes and learn three key strategies of definition. Students use these texts to spark research and ideas for their definition essay, and they use the strategies to guide close reading and structure their writing.

1.15 1 class periods	A definition essay is a synthesis essay: students must effectively combine a variety of sources to support an original definition of *heroism*. In this activity, students learn how to use transitions to create coherence and how to embed quotations to support ideas.
1.16–1.17 3 class periods	The negation strategy is often the most challenging strategy for students because it requires a writer to acknowledge and counter someone else's definition of a term or concept. It is simple when defining an object, but complex when defining a concept. Students practice using the negation strategy to strengthen and balance their original definition of *heroism*. Next, students focus on the structure of an essay: the introduction, the body, and the conclusion. After learning important elements of each type of paragraph, students analyze sample paragraphs and evaluate effectiveness of each. Once students have a clear understanding of the required structure, they draft a thesis and outline ideas for their essay.
Embedded Assessment 2 3 class periods	Students will prepare an outline for the hero definition essay before the Embedded Assessment. Using the writing process and collaborating in writing groups, students prepare their essay for publication and then reflect on learning.

Unit Resources at a Glance

Readings	Writing Tasks	Language Skills
Excerpt from *A Wrinkle in Time*, by Madeleine L'Engle "Saturday at the Canal" by Gary Soto "The Drummer Boy of Shiloh," by Ray Bradbury Excerpt from the *Odyssey* by Homer "A Man" by Nina Cassian "Soldier home after losing his leg in Afghanistan" by Gale Flege "Sonnet 116" by William Shakespeare "Where I Find My Heroes," by Oliver Stone Excerpt from White House Funeral Sermon for Abraham Lincoln, by Dr. Phineas D. Gurley "O Captain! My Captain!" by Walt Whitman "Frederick Douglass," by Robert Hayden Excerpt from *The Narrative of the Life of Frederick Douglass, an American Slave*, by Frederick Douglass "A Definition of a Gentleman," by John Henry Newman	Quickwrite: Connect heroism to challenge Expository Writing Prompts • Relate disability to heroism. • How does a hero function? • Explain examples of heroes. • Define a hero. Narrative Writing Prompts • Change the point of view • What might happen in Departure stage? • What might happen in Initiation stage? • What might happen in Return Stage?	**Language and Writers Craft** Revising and Editing Verbs and Mood Transitions and Quotations **Grammar and Usage** Mood in Verbs Prepositional Phrases Appositives
Strategy Introduction	**Speaking and Listening**	**Family Connections**
Self-Editing/Peer Editing TP-CASTT Free Writing	Think Pair Share Collaborative Discussion Writing Groups	Suggestions for Independent Reading Family Letters (English and Spanish) Student Reports

English Language Development	Independent Reading	Assessments
Leveled Differentiated Instruction ELD Graphic Organizers *SpringBoard English Language Development,* Student Edition, Grade 8, Unit 1 *SpringBoard English Language Development,* Teacher Edition Grade 8, Unit 1	Independent Reading Links Independent Reading Checkpoints Independent Reading Log Reader/Writer Notebook Suggestions for Independent Reading	Check Your Understanding Writing Prompts Embedded Assessment One: Writing a Hero's Journey Narrative Embedded Assessment Two: Writing a Definition Essay Short-Cycle Assessments Unit Assessments

SpringBoard Writing Workshop with Grammar Activities, Grade 8	SpringBoard Close Reading Workshop, Grade 8	Routines for Teaching Foundational Skills
Writing Workshop 3: Expository Writing: Compare and Contrast Writing Workshop 4: Narrative Writing: Short Story Writing Workshop 8: Poetry Grammar Activities: Unit 1 Grammar Handbook	Close Reading Workshop 1: Close Reading of Informational/Literary Nonfiction Texts Close Reading Workshop 3: Close Reading of Poetry	Phonics and Word Recognition Mini-lessons Fluency Mini-lessons

Suggestions for Independent Reading

This list, divided into the categories of **Literature** and **Nonfiction/Informational Text**, comprises titles related to the themes and content of the unit. For their independent reading, students can select from this wide array of titles, which have been chosen based on complexity and interest. You can also encourage students to do their own research and select titles that intrigue them.

Unit 1: The Challenge of Heroism		
Literature		
Author	**Title**	**Lexile**
Alexie, Sherman	*Reservation Blues*	670L
Alvarez, Julia	*Before We Were Free*	890L
Anderson, Laurie Halse	*Fever 1793*	580L
Avi	*Crispin: The Cross of Lead*	780L
Butler, Octavia	*The Parable of the Sower*	710L
Coelho, Paul	*The Alchemist*	910L
Crew, Linda	*Children of the River*	700L
Crutcher, Chris	*Whale Talk*	1000L
Dashner, James	*The Maze Runner*	770L
Ellis, Deborah	*The Breadwinner*	630L
Hinton, S.E.	*The Outsiders*	750L
Jeffrey, Gary	*African Myths*	N/A
Johnston, E.K.	*The Story of Owen: Dragon Slayer of Trondheim*	1020L
Jones, Diana Wynne	*Howl's Moving Castle*	800L
L'Engle, Madeline	*A Wrinkle in Time*	740L
Lewis, C.S.	*The Chronicles of Narnia* series	N/A
Lewis, Richard	*The Killing Sea*	760L
Lupica, Mike	*Hero*	730L
O'Connor, George	*Athena: Grey-Eyed Goddess*	720L
Paolini, Christopher	*Eragon*	710L
Park, Linda Sue	*When My Name Was Keoko*	610L
Paulsen, Gary	*Soldier's Heart*	1000L
Pierce, Tamora	*Alanna of Trebond*	690L
Riordan, Rick	*Heroes of Olympus series*	N/A
Robbins, Trina	*Freedom Songs: A Tale of the Underground Railroad*	580L
Robbins, Trina	*Lily Renee, Escape Artist: From Holocaust Survivor to Comic Book Pioneer*	510L
Selznick, Brian	*The Invention of Hugo Cabret* (Graphic Novel)	820L
Sepetys, Ruta	*Between Shades of Gray*	490L
Storrie, Paul	*Hercules: The 12 Labors*	N/A
White, T.E.	*The Once and Future King*	1080L

Nonfiction/Informational Text		
Author	**Title**	**Lexile**
Bardhan-Quallen, Sudipta	*Up-Close: Jane Goodall*	N/A
Beales, Melba Pattilo	*Warriors Don't Cry*	N/A
Bradley, James	*Flags of Our Fathers*	950L
Chin-Lee, Cynthia	*Akira to Zoltan: 26 Men Who Changed the World*	N/A
Chin-Lee, Cynthia	*Amelia to Zora: 26 Women Who Changed the World*	N/A
Freedman, Russell	*Eleanor Roosevelt: A Life of Discovery*	1100L
Freedman, Russell	*Kids at Work: Lewis Hine and the Crusade Against Child Labor*	1140L
Hillenbrand, Laura	*Unbroken: An Olympian's Journey from Airman to Castaway to Captive* (Young Adult Adaptation)	850L
Hurley, Michael	*World's Greatest Olympians*	960L
Krull, Kathleen	*Lives of Extraordinary Women: Rulers, Rebels (and What the Neighbors Thought)*	1150L
Myers, Walter Dean	*The Greatest: Muhammad Ali*	N/A
Peet, Mal	*The Keeper*	780L
Wells, Susan	*Amelia Earhart: The Thrill of it All*	N/A
Yousafzai, Malala	*I Am Malala*	830L

The Challenge of Heroism

Visual Prompt: What do you picture when you hear the word *hero*? What words and images immediately come to mind?

Unit Overview

This unit focuses on the challenges of *heroism*. Because this word is used every day—in television shows, movies, video games, books, the news, school, and conversations—we rarely take time to actually think about what it means. In this unit, you will research, read, and write to develop a more complex understanding of this important societal and cultural concept.

UNIT 1

Read aloud the Unit Overview, asking students to **mark the text** by highlighting words and phrases that help them **predict** what the unit will be about. Share responses in partner, small-group, or whole-class discussion.

Have students look at the photograph and respond to the visual prompt. You may want to have students **think-pair-share** to write a short response or discuss their responses as a class.

TEACHER TO TEACHER

Have students begin to think about the concept of heroism and about what it means to be a hero. Do they have the same ideas about what a hero is now as they did when they were younger?

ELL Support

ELD Modes and Processes

Collaborative: Students work with partners to analyze quotations.

Interpretive: Students use active listening, knowledge of morphology, and context to understand the meaning of words and concepts. Students also analyze visual techniques in a film and visualize a scene based on close reading.

Productive: Students write about an imagined hero in order to practice narrative writing. Students also write to analyze a newspaper article.

Structuring Cohesive Texts: Students use connecting words to organize a paragraph about the sequence of a text and to strengthen the organization of their narrative writing.

Expanding and Enriching Ideas: Students use a variety of verbs and verb phrases to enhance their writing.

UNIT 1

Have students read the goals for the unit and mark any words that are unfamiliar to them. Have students add these words to the classroom Word Wall, along with definitions.

You may also want to post these goals in a visible place in the classroom for the duration of this unit, allowing you and your students to revisit the goals easily and gauge progress toward achieving goals throughout the unit.

VOCABULARY DEVELOPMENT

Important terms in this unit are divided into Academic Vocabulary (those words that are used in multiple curriculum areas) and Literary Terms, which are specific to the student of literature and language arts.

Adding to vocabulary knowledge is essential for reading fluency. Students will encounter new vocabulary in this course in multiple ways:

- Academic Vocabulary
- Literary Terms
- Academic Vocabulary in Context (unfamiliar terms glossed in text selections)
- Word Connections
- Oral discussions

Encourage students to keep a **Reader/Writer Notebook** in which they record new words and their meanings (and pronunciations if needed). Having students use word-study graphic organizers to study key vocabulary terms in depth will greatly enhance their understanding of new word, as well as their connection to unit concepts and to the broader use of academic terms.

See the Resources section at the back of this book for examples of graphic organizers suitable for word study. As students become more familiar with using graphic organizers to explore the meaning of a word, you may want them to create their own graphic organizers.

UNIT 1

The Challenge of Heroism

GOALS:

- To create and present an original illustrated narrative based on the Hero's Journey archetype
- To analyze and synthesize a variety of texts to develop an original definition of *hero*
- To analyze and evaluate expository texts for ideas, structure, and language
- To develop expository texts using strategies of definition

ACADEMIC VOCABULARY
context
technique
concise
nuance
function
negation
coherence

Literary Terms
archetype
imagery
setting
point of view
conflict
mood
protagonist
plot
pacing
epic
tone
diction
denotation
connotation
allegory

Contents

Activities

ELL Support (continued)

English Language Development Standards

ELD.PI.8.1 Bridging* Contribute to class, group, and partner discussions by following turn-taking rules, asking relevant questions, affirming others, adding relevant information and evidence, paraphrasing key ideas, building on responses, and providing useful feedback. **ELD.PI.8.5 Bridging*** Demonstrate active listening in oral presentation activities by asking and answering detailed questions with minimal prompting and support. **ELD.PI.8.6a Expanding*** Explain ideas, phenomena, processes, and text relationships based on close reading of a variety of grade-appropriate texts and viewing of multimedia with moderate support. **ELD.PI.8.6c Expanding*** Use knowledge of morphology, context, reference materials, and visual cues to determine the meanings of unknown and multiple-meaning words on familiar and new topics. **ELD.PI.8.7 Expanding*** Explain how well writers and speakers use specific language to

© 2017 College Board. All rights reserved.

*Texts not included in these materials.

Language and Writer's Craft
- Revising and Editing (1.8)
- Verbs and Mood (1.8)
- Transitions and Quotations (1.15)

MY INDEPENDENT READING LIST

LANGUAGE AND WRITER'S CRAFT

Each unit includes Language and Writer's Craft features as well as Grammar & Usage content. You may want students to devote a section of their Reader/Writer Notebooks to their study of language and grammar. Encourage students to make notes about their understanding of specific grammar rules and how to use language in their writing to create specific effects.

CONTENTS

Have the students **skim/scan** the activities and texts to find a Wow (an activity that looks interesting) and a Whoa (an activity that looks challenging). Share responses in partner, small-group, or whole-class discussion.

INDEPENDENT READING

In the first half of the unit, while preparing to write a Hero's Journey narrative, students will have the opportunity to read another text. Stories about fictional heroic figures, such as from mythical tales, are recommended, but student choice is paramount. The Planning the Unit section of the Teacher's Edition and the Resources section of the Student Edition contain information, Reading Logs, and Reading Lists to help you and your students find the right book.

TEACHER TO TEACHER

The SpringBoard program has been designed to allow students to interact with the text by making notes in their books and marking text to facilitate **close reading.** In addition to making notes in the text, students are expected to use their Reader/Writer Notebooks often: for vocabulary study, answering text-dependent reading comprehension questions, reflections, some writing assignments, notes in response to the Independent Reading Links, capturing thoughts about learning strategies and how to use them, and so on. The Reader/Writer Notebooks are not listed as part of the materials for each activity, but the expectation is that students will have access to them.

ELL Support (continued)

present ideas or support arguments and provide detailed evidence when provided with moderate support. **ELD.PI.8.10a Bridging*** Write longer and more detailed literary and informational texts collaboratively and independently using appropriate text organization and growing understanding of register. **ELD.PII.8.2b Bridging*** Apply increasing understanding of how ideas, events, or reasons are linked throughout a text using an increasing variety of academic connecting and transitional words or phrases to comprehending and writing texts with increasing cohesion. **ELD.PII.8.3 Expanding*** Use a variety of verbs in different tenses and aspects appropriate for the task, text type, and discipline on an increasing variety of topics.

*The citation reflects the highest level supported. Support is also offered for the lower levels

ACTIVITY 1.1

▶PLAN

Materials: unpacking graphic organizer models (optional)
Suggested Pacing: 1 50-minute class period (with the Unit Overview and Contents pages)

▶TEACH

1 Read aloud the learning targets. **Activate prior knowledge** by asking students to share prior learning that could help them meet these goals.

2 Have students read the Making Connections paragraph and highlight any unknown words. Discuss the meanings.

3 Have students briefly answer and discuss each Essential Question.

4 Guide students in using the **QHT** strategy if they are unfamiliar with it.

Q: I have questions/never heard of it.

H: I have heard of it/it is familiar.

T: I could teach this concept.

TEACHER TO TEACHER

Create a class **QHT** chart to use with Academic Vocabulary and Literary Terms throughout the year. Move the terms from the "Q" column into the "H" and "T" columns as students become more comfortable with the Academic Vocabulary.

5 Read aloud the assignment for the first Embedded Assessment. Have students **mark the text** and **think-pair-share** the skills and knowledge they will need for success.

6 Unpack the assignment with students. Post the unpacking graphic during the unit so students can make connections between each activity and requirements for the assessment. Consider using one of these approaches:

- Create a web on poster paper, and list the skills and knowledge.
- Use the Embedded Assessment Scoring Guide, and list the skills and knowledge under the matching criteria.

ACTIVITY 1.1

Previewing the Unit

LEARNING STRATEGIES: Think-Pair-Share, QHT, Close Reading, Marking the Text, Paraphrasing, Graphic Organizer

Literary Terms
An **archetype** is a character, symbol, story pattern, or other element that is common to human experience across cultures and that occurs frequently in literature, myth, and folklore.

INDEPENDENT READING LINK
In this unit you will be reading excerpts from many hero stories. Select a full-length work about a mythological or real hero to extend your learning. Book lists are available in the back of this textbook, and you can use book discussions and recommendations from classmates to help you choose. Use your Reader/Writer Notebook and your Independent Reading Log to keep notes on what you are reading and answer questions that come up.

My Notes

Learning Targets

- Discuss the big ideas and vocabulary for the unit.
- Demonstrate an understanding of the skills and knowledge needed to complete Embedded Assessment 1 successfully.

Making Connections

This unit introduces the challenge theme by examining how we define heroes. You will be introduced to the **archetype** of the hero's journey and will study various examples of heroes and how their journeys fit the archetype. You will also have the opportunity to expand your writing skills into new forms of expository writing, focusing on writing an essay of definition about heroism.

Essential Questions

Based on your current thinking, how would you answer these questions?

1. What defines a hero?

2. How does the Hero's Journey archetype appear in stories throughout time?

Developing Vocabulary

Create a chart to use the **QHT** strategy to sort the Academic Vocabulary and the Literary Terms from the Contents page.

Unpacking Embedded Assessment 1

Closely read the assignment for Embedded Assessment 1: Writing a Hero's Journey Narrative.

> Think about all the heroes you have encountered in fiction and in real life. What type of hero appeals to you? Write and create an illustrated narrative about an original hero. Use the Hero's Journey archetype to develop and structure your ideas. Orally present your narrative to your classmates.

Find the Scoring Guide and work with your class to paraphrase the expectations for the assignment. Create a graphic organizer to use as a visual reminder of the required skills and concepts. Copy the graphic organizer into your Reader/Writer Notebook.

After each activity in the first half of this unit, use this graphic organizer to guide reflection about what you have learned and what you still need to learn in order to be successful in the Embedded Assessment.

COMMON CORE STATE STANDARDS

Focus Standard:

L.8.6: Acquire and use accurately grade-appropriate general academic and domain-specific words and phrases; gather vocabulary knowledge when considering a word or phrase important to comprehension or expression.

Additional Standards Addressed:

RL.8.10

© 2017 College Board. All rights reserved.

Understanding Challenges

ACTIVITY 1.2

Learning Target

- Analyze quotes and identify connections between the concepts of *challenges* and *heroism*.
- Collaborate to discuss and orally present an explanation of the meaning of text.

LEARNING STRATEGIES: Diffusing, Paraphrasing, Graphic Organizer, Brainstorming, Note-taking, Sketching

Independent Reading Plan

1. Create an INDEPENDENT READING PLAN for the text you have chosen.
   - I have chosen to read title
     by author
     because reason from previewing or connected with student's prior experience
   - I will create time to read by student strategies for creating reading time
   - I should finish this text by date

The Concept of Challenge

2. When you hear the word *challenges,* what comes to mind? Is the word positive or negative? How can challenges be helpful to an individual? How can they be harmful?

3. Your teacher will assign quotes from the graphic organizer on the next page. Read your assigned quote and diffuse the text by identifying and defining unfamiliar words. In the graphic organizer, paraphrase the quote and brainstorm examples from life or literature that support the speaker's idea about challenges.

4. Categorize the quote based on how the speaker defines *challenge*: as an obstacle, a difficult task, or an opportunity. Circle or highlight the appropriate category in the third column.

5. Be able to discuss how the speaker's definition of *challenge* connects to the concept of *heroism*.

My Notes

ACTIVITY 1.2

PLAN

Materials: access to an online or print dictionary and thesaurus
Suggested Pacing: 1 50-minute class period

TEACH

1 Ask students to create a section in their Reader/Writer Notebooks for independent reading. **Activate prior knowledge** by asking them to reflect on their successful experiences with choosing a text to read independently. Students should consider the content and manageability of their independent reading selections.

2 Help students prepare for independent reading, including selecting appropriate materials to read. Guide students in **previewing** texts, analyzing the visuals and text on both the front and back covers.

TEACHER TO TEACHER

If your library has a digital catalogue, teach students to use the search function to find texts on topics of interest.

3 Students should independently read the start of the text, considering content and manageability. Guide students in choosing an appropriate text and creating an Independent Reading Plan that they will revisit throughout the unit.

4 Ask students to **quickwrite** a response to question 2. Briefly discuss as a class.

5 Form groups of four and assign one quote from the graphic organizer on the following page to each group. Assign a role to each group member (leader, recorder, illustrator, or presenter). The leader will read the quote aloud and facilitate the discussion; the recorder will take accurate notes; the illustrator will capture ideas for a visual display; and the presenter will organize and assign speaking parts.

COMMON CORE STATE STANDARDS

Focus Standards:

RL.8.4: Determine the meaning of words and phrases as they are used in a text, including figurative and connotative meanings; analyze the impact of specific word choices on meaning and tone, including analogies or allusions to other texts.

SL.8.1: Engage effectively in a range of collaborative discussions (one-on-one, in groups, and teacher-led) with diverse partners on Grade 8 topics, texts, and issues, building on others' ideas and expressing their own clearly.

Additional Standards Addressed:

RL.8.3; RL.8.10; W.8.10; SL.8.1a; SL.8.4; SL.8.5; SL.8.6

TEACHER TO TEACHER

Explain that even though each student is responsible for one main role, all students should be actively engaged in all steps of the process the entire time. For example, all students should participate in creating the poster even though the illustrator is in charge.

6 Circulate to check for understanding as groups work to comprehend, analyze, and **visualize** the quote.

Leveled Differentiated Instruction

In this activity, students may benefit from discussing the meaning of the quotations with a partner and recording ideas from the discussion.

Em Help students express their ideas by asking and answering simple questions about the quotes. Have students record ideas from the discussion using a **Collaborative Dialogue** graphic organizer.

Ex Have students respond to their discussion partners by adding relevant information and paraphrasing key ideas. Encourage students to take notes based on the discussion.

Br Have students respond to their discussion partners by adding relevant information, paraphrasing key ideas, and providing useful feedback. Encourage students to take notes based on the discussion.

Stretch Ask students to work with their discussion partners to analyze the rest of the quotes and take notes based on the discussion. Then partners should choose a favorite quote and plan a brief oral presentation about one of the quotes to share with the class. Remind students to speak clearly and with expression during their presentation.

Understanding Challenges

Quote		A Challenge Is . . .
A. "The true measure of a man is not how he behaves in moments of comfort and convenience, but how he stands at times of controversy and challenges." —Rev. Dr. Martin Luther King, Jr. (clergyman, activist)	**Paraphrase:** People should be judged by how well they behave in difficult situations rather than how they behave in easy situations. **Examples:**	**an obstacle** **a difficult task** **an opportunity**
B. "Accept the challenges so that you can feel the exhilaration of victory." —George S. Patton (U.S. Army officer)	**Paraphrase:** Taking on difficult challenges allows a person to have a greater sense of victory. **Examples:**	**an obstacle** **a difficult task** **an opportunity**
C. "The block of granite which was an obstacle in the pathway of the weak became a stepping-stone in the pathway of the strong." —Thomas Carlyle (writer, essayist, historian)	**Paraphrase:** Strong people make opportunities of obstacles. **Examples:**	**an obstacle** **a difficult task** **an opportunity**
D. "Life's challenges are not supposed to paralyze you; they're supposed to help you discover who you are." —Bernice Johnson Reagon (singer, composer, scholar, activist)	**Paraphrase:** Challenges are opportunities to discover yourself and your strengths. **Examples:**	**an obstacle** **a difficult task** **an opportunity**

© 2017 College Board. All rights reserved.

6. Create a poster that represents the meaning of your quote. You will use this visual display to clarify and add interest during your presentation.

7. Assign speaking parts for the presentation.

Element of Presentation	Speaker
(a) Fluently read the quote and explain the meaning.	
(b) Provide specific examples from life.	
(c) Explain the group's categorization of the quote.	
(d) Explain how the quote connects to the concept of heroism.	

8. Present using appropriate eye contact, adequate volume, and clear pronunciation. Use your visual effectively.

9. As other groups present, listen to them, try to comprehend their main points, and take notes in the graphic organizer.

Check Your Understanding

Quickwrite: Think about the content of all four quotes. How does the concept of *challenge* connect to the concept of *heroism*?

My Notes

ACTIVITY 1.2 continued

7 Once groups have completed the analysis of their quote using the **graphic organizer** and the questions in the text, remind each group's presenter to assign speaking parts for the presentation.

8 As each group presents, remind students to listen actively and take notes.

9 Students should respond to the **Quickwrite** prompt as a way to synthesize the ideas in the group presentations.

ASSESS

Listen to presentations and review posters to determine the accuracy of the students' analyses. Use a class discussion of the **Quickwrite** to determine students' ability to synthesize sources and make a connection between concepts.

ADAPT

This activity requires speaking and listening skills. Depending on the class, you might want to spend time at the beginning of the activity to set specific norms and expectations. You might also ask students to work with a partner instead of a group, and instead of presentations, you could ask students to participate in a **gallery walk** (students display their work and then circulate around the room, studying others' work).

© 2017 College Board. All rights reserved.

ACTIVITY 1.3

▶PLAN

Suggested Pacing: 2 50-minute class periods

▶TEACH

1 Read the Preview and the Setting a Purpose for Reading sections with your students. Help them understand the literary terms they encounter.

2 **FIRST READ:** Based on the complexity of the passage and your knowledge of your students, you may choose to conduct the first reading in a variety of ways:

- independent reading
- paired reading
- small group reading
- choral reading
- read aloud

ACTIVITY 1.3

Opening with Imagery

LEARNING STRATEGIES: Marking the Text, Discussion Groups, Rereading, Summarizing, Predicting, Substituting, Adding

Learning Targets

- Analyze the imagery in a novel excerpt to understand how it reveals the context of the story.
- Revise writing by substituting a different point of view and adding imagery for effect.

Preview

In this activity, you will read an excerpt from a novel and think about how the author uses **imagery** to set up a scene and **conflict**.

Setting a Purpose for Reading

- Imagery and detail are the tools authors use to help readers visualize important elements of the story. As you read, underline words and phrases that you can easily picture in your mind.
- Circle unknown words and phrases. Try to determine the meaning of the words by using context clues, word parts, or a dictionary.

Literary Terms
Imagery is descriptive or figurative language used to create word pictures in a reader's mind.
Conflict is a struggle between opposing forces, either internal or external. Common conflicts are man vs. self, man vs. man, man vs. society, and man vs. nature.

ABOUT THE AUTHOR
Madeleine L'Engle (1918–2007) authored numerous books for children and adults. Her best-known work, *A Wrinkle in Time,* won the 1963 Newbery Medal for best children's book of the year. Oddly enough, L'Engle submitted her manuscript for this book to 26 different publishers—all of whom rejected it. The 27th agreed to its publication. L'Engle's work also included plays and poetry, as well as her autobiography. *A Wrinkle in Time* is part of a series. Other books in the series are *A Wind in the Door, A Swiftly Tilting Planet, Many Waters,* and *An Acceptable Time.*

INDEPENDENT READING LINK
Read and Connect
Examine the opening chapter of your independent reading book and write about how it sets the context for the hero's challenges. What mood does the author set in the opening of your book? How is it similar or different from the mood that is set in the opening of the passage you will read on the next two pages?

Novel

from A Wrinkle in Time

by Madeleine L'Engle
Excerpt from Chapter 6, "The Happy Medium"

1 Below them the town was laid out in harsh **angular** patterns. The houses in the outskirts were all exactly alike, small square boxes painted gray. Each had a small, rectangular plot of lawn in front, with a straight line of dull-looking flowers edging the path to the door. Meg had a feeling that if she could count the flowers there would be exactly the same number for each house. In front of all the houses children were playing. Some were skipping rope, some were bouncing balls. Meg felt vaguely that something was wrong with their play. It seemed exactly like children playing around any housing development at home, and yet there was something different about it. She looked at Calvin, and saw that he, too, was puzzled.

2 "Look!" Charles Wallace said suddenly. "They're skipping and bouncing in rhythm! Everyone's doing it at exactly the same moment."

angular: at sharp angles; not curved

COMMON CORE STATE STANDARDS

Focus Standards:

RL.8.4: Determine the meaning of words and phrases as they are used in a text, including figurative and connotative meanings; analyze the impact of specific word choices on meaning and tone, including analogies or allusions to other texts.

W.8.3d: Use precise words and phrases, relevant descriptive details, and sensory language to capture the action and convey experiences and events.

Additional Standards Addressed:

RL.8.1; RL.8.2; RL.8.10; W.8.5; W.8.10; L.8.6

© 2017 College Board. All rights reserved.

3 This was so. As the skipping rope hit the pavement, so did the ball. As the rope curved over the head of the jumping child, the child with the ball caught the ball. Down came the ropes. Down came the balls. Over and over again. Up. Down. All in rhythm. All identical. Like the houses. Like the path. Like the flowers.

4 Then the doors of all the houses opened simultaneously, and out came women like a row of paper dolls. The print of their dresses was different, but they all gave the appearance of being the same. Each woman stood on the steps of her house. Each clapped. Each child with the ball caught the ball. Each child with the skipping rope folded the rope. Each child turned and walked into the house. The doors clicked shut behind them.

5 "How can they do it?" Meg asked wonderingly. "We couldn't do it that way if we tried. What does it mean?"

6 "Let's go back." Calvin's voice was urgent.

7 "Back?" Charles Wallace asked. "Where?"

8 "I don't know. Anywhere. Back to the hill. Back to Mrs Whatsit and Mrs Who and Mrs Which. I don't like this."

9 "But they aren't there. Do you think they'd come to us if we turned back now?"

10 "I don't like it." Calvin said again.

11 "Come *on*." Impatience made Meg squeak. "You *know* we can't go back. Mrs Whatsit *said* to go into the town." She started on down the street and the two boys followed her. The houses, all identical, continued, as far as the eye could reach.

12 Then, all at once, they saw the same thing, and stopped to watch. In front of one of the houses stood a little boy with a ball, and he was bouncing it. But he bounced it rather badly and with no particular rhythm, sometimes dropping it and running after it with awkward, **furtive** leaps, sometimes throwing it up into the air and trying to catch it. The door of his house opened and out ran one of the mother figures. She looked wildly up and down the street, saw the children and put her hand to her mouth as though to stifle a scream, grabbed the little boy and rushed indoors with him. The ball dropped from his fingers and rolled out into the street.

My Notes

furtive: sneaky or shifty

Second Read

- Reread the excerpt to answer these text-dependent questions.
- Write any additional questions you have about the text in your Reader/Writer Notebook.

1. **Craft and Structure:** Look at paragraph 4. What are some synonyms of the word *simultaneously*? Why did L'Engle choose "simultaneously"?

   Simultaneously means "at the same time," "together," "at once," or "concurrently." L'Engle chose the word "simultaneously" because it is the most precise word to express both "at the same time" and "together." RL.8.4

2. **Key Ideas and Details:** Make an inference about Calvin's reaction in paragraph 6. Why does he react that way?

   Calvin is both disturbed by and suspicious of the vision of conformity he sees. RL.8.3

SCAFFOLDING THE TEXT-DEPENDENT QUESTIONS

1. Craft and Structure (RL.8.4) **Look at paragraph 4. What are some synonyms of the word *simultaneously*? Why did L'Engle choose "simultaneously"?** Read paragraphs 2 and 3, and look for words and phrases that are describing the action taking place. Is the action in paragraph 4 the same as in these other paragraphs? What then does the word *simultaneously* mean? How is the sentence different if we say "at the same time"?

2. Key Ideas and Details (RL.8.3) **Make an inference about Calvin's reaction in paragraph 6. Why does he react that way?** Reread the sentences that follow paragraph 6. What is Calvin referring to when he says, "I don't like this"? Find evidence to support your answer.

3. Key Ideas and Details (RL.8.1) **How does paragraph 12 clarify what the conflict is?** Reread the Literary Terms box that defines the word *conflict*. What happens in this paragraph? How is the action in this paragraph different from the action in the beginning of the excerpt? What is the conflict that paragraph 12 introduces?

ACTIVITY 1.3 continued

Text Complexity
Overall: Complex
Lexile: 740L
Qualitative: Moderate Difficulty
Task: Challenging (Create)

3 As students are reading, monitor their progress. Be sure they are engaged with the text and annotating words and phrases that show imagery. Evaluate whether the selected reading mode is effective.

4 Based on the observations you made during the first reading, you may want to adjust your reading mode. For example, you may decide for the second reading to read aloud certain complex passages, or you may group students differently.

5 **SECOND READ:** During the second reading, students will be returning to the text to answer the text-dependent comprehension questions. You may choose to have students reread and work on the questions in a variety of ways:

- independently
- in pairs
- in small groups
- together as a class

6 Have students answer the text-dependent questions. If they have difficulty, scaffold the questions by rephrasing them or breaking them down into smaller parts. See the Scaffolding the Text-Dependent Questions boxes for suggestions.

Leveled Differentiated Instruction

In this activity, ask students to visualize a scene from the text based on their close reading. Then ask students to draw a sketch of the scene they visualized.

Em Guide students to write words from the text that relate to their sketch. Then discuss how the words contributed to the scene.

Ex Have students write sentences about how well certain words in the text led them to visualize the scene using the sentence frame. *The word ___ helped me picture ___.*

ACTIVITY 1.3 continued

7 Form **discussion groups**, and ask students to work through the Working from the Text activities. After students have responded, have them discuss why the passage is an effective opening to a scene.

8 Have students respond to the writing prompt independently. Then have students return to **discussion groups** and **share and respond**, using the requirements as a guide.

ASSESS

When groups finish the Working from the Text activities, discuss responses as a class. Students should revise their responses throughout the discussion to indicate new learning.

Review student responses to the writing prompt to determine how well students understand *point of view* and *imagery.*

ADAPT

To support student writing, model how to change point of view, add imagery, and use diction for effect. Then, work as a class to revise a small section of the text. For students who are ready, extend learning by asking them to write another paragraph emulating the author's style.

You might choose to have students use the opening of their independent reading novel with this writing prompt.

ACTIVITY 1.3 continued

Opening with Imagery

Literary Terms
Setting is the time and place in which a narrative occurs. **Point of view** is the perspective from which a story is told.
In **first-person point of view** a character tells the story from his or her own perspective.
In **third-person point of view** a narrator (not a character) tells the story.

ACADEMIC VOCABULARY
You know the word **context** from context clues to define words. **Context** also refers to the circumstances or facts that surround a particular event or situation. In a story or novel, **contextual** information can help you understand the time and place as well as the situation in the story.

My Notes

3. **Key Ideas and Details:** How does paragraph 12 clarify what the conflict is?

Before paragraph 12, it seems as though the main conflict is between the people in this strange place and Meg and her companions. This is expressed by how suspicious and unnerved Meg and her companions are. Paragraph 12, however, introduces a conflict between the "synchronized" members of this community and those who are not in sync. The woman is nervous, which indicates she knows there is a conflict between her and everyone else. RL.8.1

Working from the Text

4. Context can help you make meaning of unknown words in a text. Context also has a broader form: the context of a whole story or situation. What is the context created in the passage and how do the imagery and details create it?

5. The author establishes a setting and point of view in the opening of the narrative. Using evidence from the text, summarize the setting and point of view.

6. Make a prediction about the story based on the conflict created in this opening passage.

Check Your Understanding

WRITING to SOURCES **Narrative Writing Prompt:** Think about the opening of Chapter 6 from Madeleine L'Engle's novel *A Wrinkle in Time*. What would be the effect if it were written from a different point of view? Revise a selected section of the excerpt. Be sure to:

- **Substitute** third-person point of view with first-person point of view.
- **Add** imagery to strengthen the description of the setting.
- **Add** details to communicate the character's perspective.

© 2017 College Board. All rights reserved.

Visual Techniques

ACTIVITY 1.4

Learning Targets

- Apply knowledge of new vocabulary to analyze visual text collaboratively.
- Create a visual for *A Wrinkle in Time* using a variety of visual techniques for effect.

LEARNING STRATEGIES: Close Reading, Rereading, Drafting, Discussion Groups, Sharing and Responding

As part of the requirements for Embedded Assessment 1, you will be creating an illustrated narrative. Understanding how filmmakers create visuals for films can help you transform written imagery and detail into illustrations or film images.

1. The following information will increase your understanding of **visual techniques.**

ACADEMIC VOCABULARY
A **technique** is a way of carrying out a particular task, so **visual techniques** are ways images can be used to convey narration.

VISUAL TECHNIQUES
Framing: Borders of the image. A single shot can be thought of as a frame for the picture. **Shot:** A single piece of film, uninterrupted by cuts. **Long shot (LS):** A shot from some distance (also called a *full shot*). A long shot of a person shows the full body. It may suggest the isolation or vulnerability of the character. **Medium shot (MS):** The most common shot. The camera seems to be a medium distance from the object being filmed. A medium shot shows a person from the waist up. **Close-up shot (CU):** The image takes up at least 80 percent of the frame. **Extreme close-up shot (ECU):** The image being shot is a part of a whole, such as an eye or a hand.
Camera Angles **Eye level:** A shot taken from a normal height (character's eye level). Most shots are eye level because it is the most natural angle. **High angle:** The camera is above the subject. This angle usually has the effect of making the subject look smaller than normal, giving him or her the appearance of being weak, powerless, or trapped. **Low angle:** The camera shoots the subject from below. This angle usually has the effect of making the subject look larger than normal, and therefore strong, powerful, or threatening.
Camera Point of View **Subjective:** A shot taken from a character's point of view, as though the camera lens is the character's eyes. **Objective:** A shot from a neutral point of view, as though the camera lens is an outside, objective witness to the events as they unfold.
Lighting **High key:** A scene flooded with light, creating a bright and open **mood**. **Low key:** A scene flooded with shadows and darkness, creating suspense or suspicion. **Neutral:** Neither high key nor low key—even lighting in the shot.

My Notes

Literary Terms
Mood is the overall emotion, which is created by the author's language and tone and the subject matter.

COMMON CORE STATE STANDARDS

Focus Standards:

L.8.6: Acquire and use accurately grade-appropriate general academic and domain-specific words and phrases; gather vocabulary knowledge when considering a word or phrase important to comprehension or expression.

W.8.2: Write informative/explanatory texts, including career development documents, to examine a topic and convey ideas, concepts, and information through the selection, organization, and analysis of relevant content.

Additional Standards Addressed:

RL.8.1; W.8.2a; W.8.2b; W.8.10; SL.8.2

ACTIVITY 1.4

PLAN

Materials: DVD to show opening scene of a film, pictures (advertisements, artwork, etc.) that demonstrate the visual techniques
Suggested Pacing: 2 50-minute class periods

TEACH

1 To **activate prior knowledge**, ask students to share their knowledge of visual techniques. Encourage artists and filmmakers in the room to share what they know throughout the lesson.

2 Use still photos or scenes from a film to illustrate the terms as you briefly explain each of the visual techniques, and continue to check for understanding along the way. Explain that in Embedded Assessment 1, students will need to be able to show their understanding of lighting by using colors for effect.

3 You may want to move students into small groups at this point. Display a series of pictures or a sequence of shots from a film, and ask students to identify each combination of visual techniques. Guide groups as they work to distinguish between types of shots, camera angles, and lighting.

ACTIVITY 1.4 continued

TEACHER TO TEACHER

Consider using commercials, art, and/or graphic novels throughout the unit to prompt analysis of visual techniques.

4 Once students seem comfortable with the techniques, ask students to respond to Student Step 2, which will prepare them for viewing the film.

5 Divide the class into three groups, and assign each group a focus for a **close reading** of the film. Ask the first third to focus on Section 1 (Framing), the second third to focus on Section 2 (Angles), and the final third to focus on Section 3 (POV and Lighting). Point out that sound is another important technique, but it is not our focus at this time.

Leveled Differentiated Instruction

In this activity, you may want to have some students complete an alternative **Active Listening Notes** graphic organizer to record visual techniques in the film clips.

Em Help students use an **Active Listening Notes** graphic organizer to record words and phrases about what they see and hear in the film clip.

Ex Have students use an **Active Listening Notes** graphic organizer to record complete sentences about what they see and hear in the film clip.

TEACHER TO TEACHER

The opening scene from almost any film would be appropriate for teaching visual techniques. The opening of *ET: The Extra-Terrestrial* is especially good. Scenes from *The Lion King* or *Up* also work well for this activity since many students are already quite familiar with the story line. Each of these stories contains elements of the Hero's Journey archetype that can be used for the next activity.

ACTIVITY 1.4 continued

Visual Techniques

Literary Terms
A **protagonist** is the leading character or a major character in a drama, movie, novel, or other fictional text.

2. Pretend you are directing an action movie. What mood would you want to create? Which combination of techniques would you use to create that mood? Explain your choices.

Possible responses include moods of danger, adventure, humor, or suspicion. Possible techniques include lighting, camera framing and angles, and subjective point of view.

3. While viewing the opening sequence of a film, identify the director's use of visual techniques. Record your observations in the chart below.

Section 1: Framing	
What **framing** is used to film the protagonist? (LS, MS, CU, ECU)	Why do you think the director chose this framing?

Section 2: Angles	
What **angles** are used to film the opening scene? (eye level, high angle, low angle)	Why do you think the director chose these angles?

Section 3: Lighting and Point of View	
What kind of **lighting** is used? (high key, low key, neutral)	Why do you think the director used this lighting?
From which camera point of view is this shot?	Why did the director choose this point of view?

4. Analyze the techniques you observed. What **mood** is created by the techniques used by the director?

My Notes

Check Your Understanding

5. Explain how the director uses a combination of visual techniques to create a specific mood. Provide supporting detail and commentary for the first technique, using the frame below to guide your response. Then write supporting details for the other two techniques.

Topic Sentence:

The director of [*film title*] uses [technique 1], [technique 2], and [technique 3] to create a ________________ mood in the opening sequence of his/her film.

Supporting Detail:

For example, he/she uses [technique 1] to ________________________.

Commentary: [connect the supporting detail to the mood]

6. Revisit the excerpt from the novel *A Wrinkle in Time*. Analyze the mood and provide textual evidence to support your interpretation.

Mood:
Possible moods include suspense, puzzlement, worry, and forboding.

Textual Evidence:
Possible textual evidence includes the following:
"Meg felt vaguely that something was wrong with their play."
"The houses, all identical, continued, as far as the eye could reach."

Textual Evidence:
Calvin said, "I don't like this."
"The mother...put her hand to her mouth as though to stifle a scream."

7. Imagine that you are codirecting a film version of *A Wrinkle in Time*. Work with your partner to plan and draft a visual of one frame (or no more than 3 frames) that represents imagery from the text. Use a variety of film techniques for effect.

ACTIVITY 1.4 continued

6 Show the opening scene (after the credits) of a film at least twice. To take effective notes on shots and angles, students need only list what they see after each type of technique (e.g., High Angle: a little boy).

7 As a class, discuss the techniques and analyze the intended effect of each. Each group should be responsible for leading the discussion that relates to their assigned section. During the discussion, students should listen and take notes to complete the **graphic organizer.**

8 Define *mood*, and ask pairs of students to identify at least two words that describe the mood of this opening sequence.

9 Check Your Understanding asks students to explain the use of visual techniques to create mood. Briefly review elements of an effective expository paragraph.

10 Form pairs and ask students to write a response to Student Step 6. Call on students to read their work aloud; provide feedback relating to their ideas and use of language.

11 Form new pairs and ask students to complete Student Step 7. Explain that the level of thinking and use of technique in the visual are more important than artistic ability.

12 Briefly discuss qualities of an effective title, and then ask students to create an original title for their frame(s).

13 Form **discussion groups** by combining pairs. Ask students to **share and respond** by evaluating titles and identifying and evaluating the use of visual techniques for effect.

▶ASSESS

Review students' drafts to identify challenges with applying visual techniques for effect. Select a few models to share with the class, and ask these students to explain their thinking and use of technique.

▶ADAPT

To support learning, create a model frame or two prior to asking students to create their own. That way you will be able to share the process you went through, including your challenges and successes. You may want to discuss with students how they might divide up the text scenes. To extend learning, ask "artists" to draft multiple frames that represent the entire opening. Frames should contain different combinations of techniques for effect. Ask students to present their work to the class.

Visual Techniques

Plan:

Technique	Explanation	Intended Effect
Shot:		
Angle:		
Lighting:		

Draft:

Title: ______________________________

© 2017 College Board. All rights reserved.

Understanding the Hero's Journey Archetype

ACTIVITY 1.5

Learning Targets

- Analyze how a film uses the Hero's Journey to structure its plot.
- Apply the Hero's Journey archetype to a new text.

LEARNING STRATEGIES: Metacognitive Markers, Rereading, Close Reading, Graphic Organizer, Note-taking, Collaborative Discussion

The Archetype of the Hero's Journey

In literature, an **archetype** is a character, symbol, story pattern, or other element that is common to human experience across cultures. It refers to a common plot pattern or to a character type such as the Innocent, the Mother Figure, or the Hero, or to images that occur in the literature of all cultures.

The archetype of the **Hero's Journey** describes a plot pattern that shows the development of a hero. The information below describes the structure of a Hero's Journey.

Joseph Campbell, an American anthropologist, writer, and lecturer, studied the myths and stories of multiple cultures and began to notice common plot patterns. In *The Hero With a Thousand Faces,* Campbell defines common elements of the Hero's Journey. Campbell found that most journey myths had three parts:

- Departure: The hero leaves home to venture into the unknown on some sort of quest.
- Initiation: The hero faces a series of problems.
- Return: With the help of a friend, the hero returns home successfully.

While these elements may be referred to as the stages of the Hero's Journey, these stages may not always be presented in the exact same order, and some stories do not contain every element of the journey.

WORD CONNECTIONS

Etymology

Etymology is the study of the origin of words. Many English words come from other languages, including Latin, German, and Greek. Knowing a word's etymology can help you determine the meaning of unfamiliar words. The Greek prefix *arch-* in **archetype** means "first," and the root *-type-* means "model." When first used in the 14th century, it meant "original pattern from which copies are made." Today it is used to denote a story element common to many people or a perfect example of something.

Preview

In this activity, you will read a poem and think about how it fits into the archetype of the Hero's Journey.

Setting a Purpose for Reading

- Read the poem sentence by sentence. Remember that the lines of poems are often only parts of a sentence. Read until you come to punctuation that notates the end of a sentence.
- Underline any phrases you do not understand.
- Circle unknown words and phrases. Try to determine the meaning of the words by using context clues, word parts, or a dictionary.

My Notes

ABOUT THE AUTHOR

Gary Soto was born in 1952 and raised in Fresno, California. Being of Mexican-American heritage, many of his works present life growing up in the barrio, a Spanish-speaking neighborhood. He has also worked extensively with groups that help improve the lives of others with Hispanic heritage. Soto's perspective has been shared with the world through award-winning poems, novels, short stories, and film. Fresno is now home to the Gary Soto Literary Museum.

ACTIVITY 1.5

PLAN

Materials: film clips that represent Stage 2 and Stage 3 of the Hero's Journey

Suggested Pacing: 1 50-minute class period

TEACH

1 Read aloud the information about archetypes, the Hero's Journey.

2 Read the Preview and the Setting a Purpose for Reading sections with your students.

3 **FIRST READ:** Based on the complexity of the passage and your knowledge of your students, you may choose to conduct the first reading in a variety of ways:

- independent reading
- paired reading
- small group reading
- choral reading
- read aloud

COMMON CORE STATE STANDARDS

Focus Standards:

RL.8.1: Cite the textual evidence that most strongly supports an analysis of what the text says explicitly as well as inferences drawn from the text.

RL.8.7: Analyze the extent to which a filmed or live production of a story or drama stays faithful to or departs from the text or script, evaluating the choices made by the director or actors.

Additional Standards Addressed:

RL.8.2; RL.8.3; RL.8.9; L.8.6

ACTIVITY 1.5 continued

4 As students are reading, monitor their progress. Be sure they are engaged with the text, reading fluently and annotating words and phrases they don't understand. Evaluate whether the selected reading mode is effective.

5 Based on the observations you made during the first reading, you may want to adjust your reading mode. For example, you may decide for the second reading to read aloud certain complex phrases, or you may group students differently.

6 **SECOND READ:** During the second reading, students will be returning to the text to answer the text-dependent comprehension questions. You may choose to have students reread and work on the questions in a variety of ways:

- independently
- in pairs
- in small groups
- together as a class

7 Have students answer the text-dependent questions. If they have difficulty, scaffold the questions by rephrasing them or breaking them down into smaller parts. See the Scaffolding the Text-Dependent Questions boxes for suggestions.

Understanding the Hero's Journey Archetype

Literary Terms
Plot is the sequence of related events that make up a story. There are five main elements of plot: exposition, rising action, climax, falling action, and resolution.

My Notes

Poetry

Saturday at the Canal

by Gary Soto

I was hoping to be happy by seventeen.
School was a sharp check mark in the roll book,
An obnoxious tuba playing at noon because our team
Was going to win at night. The teachers were
Too close to dying to understand. The hallways
Stank of poor grades and unwashed hair. Thus,
A friend and I sat watching the water on Saturday,
Neither of us talking much, just warming ourselves
By hurling large rocks at the dusty ground
And feeling awful because San Francisco was a postcard
On a bedroom wall. We wanted to go there,
Hitchhike under the last migrating birds
And be with people who knew more than three chords
On a guitar. We didn't drink or smoke,
But our hair was shoulder length, wild when
The wind picked up and the shadows of
This loneliness gripped loose dirt. By bus or car,
By the sway of train over a long bridge,
We wanted to get out. The years froze
As we sat on the bank. Our eyes followed the water,
White-tipped but dark underneath, racing out of town.

Second Read

- Reread the poem to answer these text-dependent questions.
- Write any additional questions you have about the text in your Reader/Writer Notebook.

1. **Key Ideas and Details:** What is the speaker's opinion of school? What details in the poem show this?

The speaker in the poem sees school as a lifeless, boring place, "a check mark in the roll book" where the hallways "stank of poor grades" and the teachers were "too old to understand." RL.8.3

SCAFFOLDING THE TEXT-DEPENDENT QUESTIONS

1. Key Ideas and Details (RL.8.3) **What is the speaker's opinion of school? What details in the poem show this?** How does the first line set up the mood of boredom and alienation the speaker feels? How does his attitude toward school show this alienation?

2. Key Ideas and Details (RL.8.3) **What does the phrase "San Francisco was a postcard on a bedroom wall" imply?** Why did the boys feel "awful" about the postcard on the wall? Where did the boys want to go? Why?

3. Key Ideas and Details (RL.8.2) **What part of the Hero's Journey is this poem leading to? How do you know?** During the entire poem, what are the boys doing? What do they want to be doing? What attitude about their life is evoked by the phrases, "the loneliness gripped..." and "the years froze?"

© 2017 College Board. All rights reserved.

2. **Key Ideas and Details:** What does the phrase "San Francisco was a postcard on a bedroom wall" imply?

San Francisco is a destination or journey that holds some promise of adventure, but that the boys feel hopeless to embark upon. RL.8.3

3. **Key Ideas and Details:** What part of the Hero's Journey is this poem leading to? How do you know?

This poem sets the scene for Departure, "The Call to Adventure." The boys are lonely, alienated, bored. They are ready for adventure, for their ordinary life to be disrupted, but they have not yet been called. Their adventure is a "postcard." RL.8.2

My Notes

Working from the Text

Embedded Assessment 2 requires you to use the Hero's Journey to sequence and structure events in your narrative. You already know the basic elements of **plot** development. All plot development includes:

Exposition: Events that set the context for the story: the **setting** (time and place), **characters,** and central **conflict** are introduced.

Rising Action: Events that develop the plot and lead to the climax.

Climax: The main event; the turning point, or highest point of tension in the story.

Falling Action: The events that lead to the resolution.

Resolution: Conflict is completely resolved and the lesson has been learned.

As you study the the stages of the **Hero's Journey archetype,** think how the stages of the journey fit with the development of plot. As you read, use metacognitive markers to indicate your level of understanding and to guide future discussion: ? = questions, ! = connections, and * = comments.

Hero's Journey Archetype

Stage 1: Departure

Steps	Explanation	Example
1. **The Call to Adventure** The future hero is first given notice that his or her life is going to change.	The story's **exposition** introduces the hero, and soon the hero's normal life is disrupted. Something changes; the hero faces a problem, obstacle, or challenge.	Bruce Wayne's parents are murdered when he is a young boy. Soon after, he falls into a well that is home to thousands of bats, and he is filled with fear.

ACTIVITY 1.5 continued

8 Ask students to read and **mark** the Hero's Journey Archetype chart to deepen their understanding of various concepts. Use the first step—The Call to Adventure—to model the process of using **metacognitive markers** while reading.

9 As you discuss the stages and steps of the journey archetype, ask students to make connections to the elements of plot: exposition, rising action, climax, falling action.

TEACHER TO TEACHER

Scenes from *Batman Begins* are provided as examples of each of the steps within the stages of the journey archetype. Students may also be familiar with a hero's journey story such as that presented in *The Lion King*, *The Hobbit*, or *Star Wars: A New Hope*.

© 2017 College Board. All rights reserved.

Leveled Differentiated Instruction

In this activity, students may need extra support to understand the meaning of the word *archetype*.

Em Help students complete an **Unknown Word Solver** graphic organizer. Model completing the word parts section of the organizer based on the Word Connections information in the student edition. Then guide students to complete the rest of the organizer.

Ex Ask students to complete an **Unknown Word Solver** graphic organizer independently. Then have partners share their completed organizers in order to confirm their understanding of the word *archetype*.

Understanding the Hero's Journey Archetype

Hero's Journey Archetype		
Steps	**Explanation**	**Example**
Stage 1: Departure (Continued)		
2. **Refusal of the Call** The future hero often refuses to accept the call to adventure. The refusal may stem from a sense of duty, an obligation, a fear, or insecurity.	At first the hero is reluctant to accept the change. Usually this reluctance presents itself as second thoughts or personal doubt. Hesitation, whether brief or lengthy, humanizes the hero for the reader.	Instead of following in his parents' footsteps and seeking positive solutions to the problems of Gotham City, Bruce Wayne disappears and ends up in a foreign prison.
3. **The Beginning of the Adventure** The hero begins the adventure, leaving the known limits of his or her world to venture into an unknown and dangerous realm where the rules and limits are unknown.	The hero finally accepts the call and begins a physical, spiritual, and/or emotional journey to achieve a boon, something that is helpful or beneficial.	After leaving prison, Bruce Wayne is invited to the top of the mountain to find what he is looking for.
Stage 2: Initiation		
4. **The Road of Trials** The hero experiences and is transformed by a series of tests, tasks, or challenges. The hero usually fails one or more of these tests, which often occur in threes.	The story develops **rising action** as the hero faces a series of challenges that become increasingly difficult as the story unfolds.	After being trained as a ninja, Bruce Wayne must face his fear of bats as well as his fear of death.
5. **The Experience with Unconditional Love** During the Road of Trials, the hero experiences support (physical and/or mental) from a friend, family member, mentor, etc.	This love often drives the hero to continue on the journey, even when the hero doubts him/herself.	Bruce Wayne remembers and is inspired by the love of his parents as well as the values they stood for.
6. **The Ultimate Boon** The goal of the quest is achieved. The boon can be a physical object or an intangible item such as knowledge, courage, or love. The Road of Trials makes the hero strong enough to achieve this goal.	The story reaches the **climax** as the hero gains what he or she set out to achieve. The Call to Adventure (what the hero is asked to do), the Beginning of the Adventure (what the hero sets out to do), and the Ultimate Boon (what the hero achieves) must connect.	Batman defeats the League of Shadows and saves Gotham City.

Hero's Journey Archetype

Stage 3: Return		
7. **Refusal of the Return** When the goal of the adventure is accomplished, the hero may refuse to return with the boon or gift, either because the hero doubts the return will bring change, or because the hero prefers to stay in a better place rather than return to a normal life of pain and trouble.	The **falling action** begins as the hero begins to think about the Return. Sometimes the hero does not want to look back after achieving the boon. Sometimes the hero likes the "new world" better. This step is similar to the Refusal of the Call (in both cases, the hero does not take action right away).	Bruce Wayne must decide if he should rebuild his burned home and his life in Gotham City, living as Bruce Wayne and Batman.
8. **The Magic Flight** The hero experiences adventure and perhaps danger as he or she **returns** to life as it was before the Call to Adventure.	For some heroes, the journey "home" (psychological or physical) can be just as dangerous as the journey out. Forces (sometimes magical or supernatural) may keep the hero from returning. This step is similar to The Road of Trials.	After defeating the League of Shadows, Batman decides he must dedicate his life to Gotham City, fighting crime and returning order.
9. **Rescue from Without** Just as the hero may need guides and assistance on the quest, oftentimes he or she must have powerful guides and rescuers to bring him or her back to everyday life. Sometimes the hero does not realize that it is time to return, that he or she can return, or that others are relying on him or her to return.	Just as it looks as if the hero will not make it home with the boon, the hero is "rescued." The rescuer is sometimes the same person who provided love or support throughout the journey.	Alfred serves as Bruce Wayne's mentor and guide as Wayne struggles to do what is right.
10. **The Crossing or Return Threshold** At this final point in the adventure, the hero must retain the wisdom gained on the quest, integrate that wisdom into his or her previous life, and perhaps decide how to share the wisdom with the rest of the world.	The final step is the story's **resolution,** when the hero returns with the boon. The theme is typically revealed at this point. To determine theme, think about the hero's struggles, transformation, and achievement. The reader is expected to learn a lesson about life though the hero's experience.	Bruce Wayne learns that he must always face his fears. Even though the situation in Gotham City is bleak, it is not without hope. He must make personal sacrifices to give hope to the people.

© 2017 College Board. All rights reserved.

10 After reading the information in the chart, use the metacognitive markers to guide discussion and check for understanding. Begin with questions and then discuss connections and comments.

TEACHER TO TEACHER

Since the Road of Trials is part of the rising action, it is the longest part of the story. When students write their narrative, they may want to develop three major complications that transform the hero. The hero should fail at least one of these conflicts but grow stronger because of the failure.

11 You might use the responses in the Example column of the Hero's Journey Archetype chart to help students make connections to the plot diagram. Create sets of 10 cards by writing each response on a card. Then give each group of students a set of the cards, and ask them to arrange the cards on a plot diagram. Or ask students to plot the sequence of events of *The Lion King* according to the Hero's Journey.

Understanding the Hero's Journey Archetype

My Notes

Literary Terms

Pacing is a narrative technique that refers to the amount of time a writer gives to describing each event and the amount of time a writer takes to develop each stage in the plot. Some events and stages are shorter or longer than others.

4. How do the elements of plot structure connect to the Hero's Journey? Use the diagram below to show your understanding.

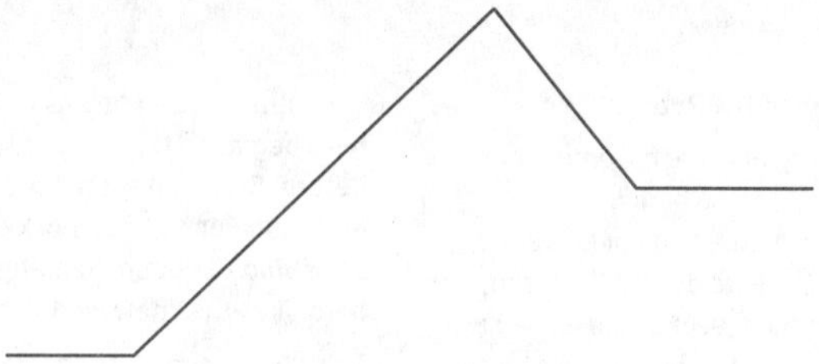

5. In addition to using description for effect, another narrative technique is **pacing**. Notice how the plot diagram gives an idea of how rising action is paced in contrast to falling action. How does a writer effectively **pace** plot events?

© 2017 College Board. All rights reserved.

Check Your Understanding

In your discussion group, choose a familiar story that contains a hero's journey and work to connect the story's plot to each step in the Hero's Journey archetype. If the story does not contain one of the steps, indicate it with an X in the space provided.

Text: ______________________________

Stage 1: Departure
1. **The Call to Adventure:**
2. **Refusal of the Call:**
3. **The Beginning of the Adventure:**
Stage 2: Initiation
4. **The Road of Trials:** (a) (b) (c)
5. **The Experience with Unconditional Love:**
6. **The Ultimate Boon:**
Stage 3: Return
7. **Refusal of the Return:**
8. **The Magic Flight:**
9. **Rescue from Without:**
10. **The Crossing or Return Threshold:** (Theme Statement)

ASSESS

Form **discussion groups**, and ask students to apply the archetype to a new text (from memory). Review student work to determine if students are able to accurately connect elements of the Hero's Journey to a text.

ADAPT

To **support** learning, work through another example as a class before asking students to work without direct guidance. To **extend** learning, ask students to illustrate a part or all of the Hero's Journey and present their analysis to the class. Students will have the opportunity to analyze a variety of texts with a specific emphasis on each of the three stages in upcoming activities.

© 2017 College Board. All rights reserved.

ACTIVITY 1.6

▶PLAN

Suggested Pacing: 2 50-minute class periods

▶TEACH

1 Guide students through the "The Departure" section. Explain that as students work through the activity, they should begin thinking about ideas for their own Hero's Journey narrative. Remind students that their hero can be real or imagined.

2 Read the Preview and the Setting a Purpose for Reading sections with your students. Help them understand the literary terms they encounter.

3 **FIRST READ:** Based on the complexity of the passage and your knowledge of your students, you may choose to conduct the first reading in a variety of ways:

- independent reading
- paired reading
- small group reading
- choral reading
- read aloud

ACTIVITY 1.6

The Departure

LEARNING STRATEGIES: Marking the Text, Close Reading, Diffusing, Rereading, Summarizing, Sketching, Visualizing

Learning Targets

- Analyze a story for archetypal structure and narrative techniques.
- Draft the opening of an original Hero's Journey narrative.
- Demonstrate understanding of visual techniques used for effect by illustrating an event.

The Departure

Joseph Campbell describes the first stage of the Hero's Journey as the hero's departure or separation. The Departure Stage consists of three steps: the Call to Adventure, Refusal of the Call, and the Beginning of the Adventure.

Preview

In this activity, you will read a story about a hero's departure and begin creating a hero of your own.

Setting a Purpose for Reading

- As you read, think about the stages of a hero's journey. Put a star next to parts of this story that show the stages of Joby's journey.
- Circle unknown words and phrases. Try to determine the meaning of the words by using context clues, word parts, or a dictionary.

My Notes

ABOUT THE AUTHOR

Ray Bradbury (1920–2012) authored the novel *Fahrenheit 451*, which was first published in 1953. Bradbury called his books fantasy rather than science fiction because he wrote stories that could not happen in real life. Other well-known works by Bradbury include *The Martian Chronicles* and *Something Wicked This Way Comes*. Bradbury also authored hundreds of short stories and even wrote and published his own fan magazine.

INDEPENDENT READING LINK

Read and Respond

What kinds of challenges has the hero of your independent reading text encountered? What do these challenges or obstacles reveal about the character? Write your response in your Reader/Writer Notebook.

Short Story

"The Drummer Boy of Shiloh"

by Ray Bradbury

1 In the April night, more than once, blossoms fell from the orchard trees and lit with rustling taps on the drumskin. At midnight a peach stone left miraculously on a branch through winter flicked by a bird fell swift and unseen struck once like panic, which jerked the boy upright. In silence he listened to his own heart **ruffle** away away—at last gone from his ears and back in his chest again.

ruffle: to flutter or move in a slow, wavy pattern

2 After that, he turned the drum on its side, where its great lunar face peered at him whenever he opened his eyes.

COMMON CORE STATE STANDARDS

Focus Standards:

RL.8.3: Analyze how particular lines of dialogue or incidents in a story or drama propel the action, reveal aspects of a character, or provoke a decision.

W.8.3: Write narratives to develop real or imagined experiences or events using effective technique, relevant descriptive details, and well-structured event sequences.

W.8.3a: Engage and orient the reader by establishing a context and point of view and introducing a narrator and/or characters; organize an event sequence that unfolds naturally and logically.

W.8.3d: Use precise words and phrases, relevant descriptive details, and sensory language to capture the action and convey experiences and events.

Additional Standards Addressed:

RL.8.1; RL.8.2; RL.8.4; RL.8.10; W.8.3b; W.8.4; W.8.10: L.8.4a; L.8.4c

3 His face, alert or at rest, was solemn. It was indeed a solemn night for a boy just turned fourteen in the peach field near the Owl Creek not far from the church at Shiloh.[1]

4 "...thirty-one, thirty-two, thirty-three..."

5 Unable to see, he stopped counting.

6 Beyond the thirty-three familiar shadows, forty thousand men, exhausted by nervous expectation, unable to sleep for **romantic** dreams of battles yet unfought, lay crazily askew in their uniforms. A mile yet farther on, another army was strewn **helter-skelter**, turning slow, basting themselves with the thought of what they would do when the time came: a leap, a yell, a blind plunge their strategy, raw youth their protection and **benediction**.

romantic: fondly imaginary
helter-skelter: in a confused or disorderly way
benediction: a prayer or blessing

7 Now and again the boy heard a vast wind come up, that gently stirred the air. But he knew what it was—the army here, the army there, whispering to itself in the dark. Some men talking to others, others murmuring to themselves, and all so quiet it was like a natural element arisen from South or North with the motion of the earth toward dawn.

8 What the men whispered the boy could only guess, and he guessed that it was: "Me, I'm the one, I'm the one of all the rest who won't die. I'll live through it. I'll go home. The band will play. And I'll be there to hear it."

9 Yes, thought the boy, that's all very well for them, they can give as good as they get!

10 For with the careless bones of the young men harvested by the night and **bindled** around campfires were the similarly strewn steel bones of their rifles, with bayonets fixed like eternal lightning lost in the orchard grass.

bindled: held together in a sack

11 Me, thought the boy, I got only a drum, two sticks to beat it and no shield.

12 There wasn't a man-boy on the ground tonight who did not have a shield he cast, riveted or carved himself on his way to his first attack, compounded of remote but nonetheless firm and fiery family devotion, flag-blown patriotism and cocksure **immortality** strengthened by the touchstone of very real gunpowder; ramrod, Minié ball and flint. But without these last the boy felt his family move yet farther off away in the dark, as if one of those great prairie-burning trains ha d chanted them away never to return—leaving him with this drum which was worse than a toy in the game to be played tomorrow or some day much too soon.[2]

immortality: the ability to live forever

13 The boy turned on his side. A moth brushed his face, but it was peach blossom. A peach blossom flicked him, but it was a moth. Nothing stayed put. Nothing had a name. Nothing was as it once was.

14 If he lay very still when the dawn came up and the soldiers put on their bravery with their caps, perhaps they might go away, the war with them, and not notice him lying small here, no more than a toy himself.

15 "Well ... now," said a voice.

16 The boy shut up his eyes to hide inside himself, but it was too late. Someone, walking by in the night, stood over him.

WORD CONNECTIONS

Etymology

In the past, people would test the quality of gold or silver by rubbing a stone across it and analyzing the color of the streak it left. The 15th-century Middle English word *touch* meant "to test," so this stone became known as a *touchstone*. This term is now a metaphor for any method used to test the quality or effectiveness of something else.

[1] **Shiloh** (n.): site of a Civil War battle in 1862; now a national military park in southwest Tennessee
[2] **Minié ball:** a type of rifle bullet that became prominent during the Civil War

ACTIVITY 1.6 continued

Text Complexity
Overall: Very Complex
Lexile: 960L
Qualitative: Moderate Difficulty
Task: Challenging (Evaluate)

4 As students are reading, monitor their progress. Be sure they are engaged with the text and annotating the stages of Joby's journey. Evaluate whether the selected reading mode is effective.

5 Based on the observations you made during the first reading, you may want to adjust your reading mode. For example, you may decide for the second reading to read aloud certain complex passages, or you may group students differently.

6 **SECOND READ:** During the second reading, students will be returning to the text to answer the text-dependent comprehension questions. You may choose to have students reread and work on the questions in a variety of ways:

- independently
- in pairs
- in small groups
- together as a class

SCAFFOLDING THE TEXT-DEPENDENT QUESTIONS

1. Key Ideas and Details (RL.8.3) **What textual evidence in the first paragraph shows that the boy is afraid?** Try to hear the sound of a peach stone hitting the skin of your drum as it lay beside you in the darkness. How could that cause a panicky feeling?

2. Craft and Structure (RL.8.4) **The word "harvested" is used figuratively in paragraph 10. How do you know it is used figuratively, and why did the author choose this word?** What is the boy counting? What is beyond the forms of the soldiers the boy can barely see in the night time? Visually, what would this vast army of soldiers look like?

3. Craft and Structure (RL.8.4) **Consult reference materials to find the meanings of "ramrod" and "flint." Relate these words to the meaning of the last sentence in paragraph 12. How does the sentence convey the boy's mood?** From the opening scene, what is the boy's

The Departure

My Notes

17 "Well," said the voice quietly, "here's a soldier crying before the fight. Good. Get it over. Won't be time once it all starts."

18 And the voice was about to move on when the boy, startled, touched the drum at his elbow. The man above, hearing this, stopped. The boy could feel his eyes, sense him slowly bending near. A hand must have come down out of the night, for there was a little rat-tat as the fingernails brushed and the man's breath fanned his face.

19 "Why, it's the drummer boy, isn't it?"

20 The boy nodded not knowing if his nod was seen. "Sir, is that you?" he said.

21 "I assume it is." The man's knees cracked as he bent still closer.

22 He smelled as all fathers should smell, of salt sweat, ginger, tobacco, horse, and boot leather, and the earth he walked upon. He had many eyes. No, not eyes—brass buttons that watched the boy.

23 He could only be, and was, the general.

24 "What's your name, boy?" he asked.

25 "Joby," whispered the boy, starting to sit up.

26 "All right Joby, don't stir." A hand pressed his chest gently and the boy relaxed. "How long you been with us, Joby?"

27 "Three weeks, sir."

28 "Run off from home or joined legitimately, boy?"

29 Silence.

30 ". . . Fool question," said the general. "Do you shave yet, boy? Even more of a … fool. There's your cheek, fell right off the tree overhead. And the others here not much older. Raw, raw, the lot of you. You ready for tomorrow or the next day, Joby?"

31 "I think so, sir."

32 "You want to cry some more, go on ahead. I did the same last night."

33 "You, sir?"

34 "It's the truth. Thinking of everything ahead. Both sides figuring the other side will just give up, and soon, and the war done in weeks, and us all home. Well, that's not how it's going to be. And maybe that's why I cried."

35 "Yes, sir," said Joby.

36 The general must have taken out a cigar now, for the dark was suddenly filled with the smell of tobacco unlit as yet, but chewed as the man thought what next to say.

37 "It's going to be a crazy time," said the general. "Counting both sides, there's a hundred thousand men, give or take a few thousand out there tonight, not one as can spit a sparrow off a tree, or knows a horse clod from a Minié ball. Stand up, bare the breast, ask to be a target, thank them and sit down, that's us, that's them. We should turn tail and train four months, they should do the same. But here we are, taken with spring fever and thinking it blood lust, taking our sulfur with cannons instead of with molasses, as it should be, going to be a hero, going to live forever. And I can see all of

mood this night before the battle? How does describing his drums as "worse than a toy" help convey his mood about the battle to come?

4. Key Ideas and Details (RL.8.3) **How did Joby join the army? What is significant about that?** How old is Joby? Is he old enough to fight in the Army? Does he have a gun to fight with? What does the general mean when he calls Joby "raw"?

5. Craft and Structure (RL.8.4) **Consult reference materials to find the meaning of "drowse." How does that word choice create a contrast in paragraph 44?** What does the phrase "sleep forever" mean? What does the beat of a drum have to do with movement?

6. Key Ideas and Details (RL.8.3) **What shift happens in paragraphs 44, 45, and 46? Use textual evidence in your answer.** Before the general talks to him, how does Joby feel about his drums? How important does the general think the drummer boy is to the success of the army in battle? Why does the general talk to Joby about the importance of the drum beat?

ACTIVITY 1.6 continued

them over there nodding agreement, save the other way around. It's wrong, boy, it's wrong as a head put on hindside front and a man marching backward through life... More innocents will get shot out of pure ... enthusiasm than ever got shot before. Owl Creek was full of boys splashing around in the noonday sun just a few hours ago. I fear it will be full of boys again, just floating, at sundown tomorrow, not caring where the tide takes them."

38 The general stopped and made a little pile of winter leaves and twigs in the darkness, as if he might at any moment strike fire to them to see his way through the coming days when the sun might not show its face because of what was happening here and just beyond.

39 The boy watched the hand stirring the leaves and opened his lips to say something, but did not say it. The general heard the boy's breath and spoke himself.

40 "Why am I telling you this? That's what you wanted to ask, eh? Well, when you got a bunch of wild horses on a loose rein somewhere somehow you got to bring order, rein them in. These lads, fresh out of the milkshed, don't know what I know, and I can't tell them: men actually die in war. So each is his own army. I got to make one army of them. And for that, boy, I need you.

41 "Me!" The boy's lips barely twitched.

42 "Now, boy," said the general quietly, "you are the heart of the army. Think of that. You're the heart of the army. Listen, now."

43 And, lying there, Joby listened. And the general spoke on.

44 If he, Joby, beat slow tomorrow, the heart would beat slow in the men. They would lag by the wayside. They would drowse in the fields on their muskets. They would sleep for ever, after that, in those same fields—their hearts slowed by a drummer boy and stopped by enemy lead.

45 But if he beat a sure, steady, ever faster rhythm, then, then their knees would come up in a long line down over that hill, one knee after the other, like a wave on the ocean shore! Had he seen the ocean ever? Seen the waves rolling in like a well-ordered cavalry charge to the sand? Well, that was it that's what he wanted, that's what was needed! Joby was his right hand and his left. He gave the orders, but Joby set the pace!

46 So bring the right knee up and the right foot out and the left knee up and the left foot out. One following the other in good time, in brisk time. Move the blood up the body and made the head proud and the spine stiff and the jaw **resolute**. Focus the eye and set the teeth, flare the nostrils and tighten the hands, put steel armor all over the men, for blood moving fast in them does indeed make men feel as if they'd put on steel. He must keep at it, at it! Long and steady, steady and long! The men, even though shot or torn, those wounds got in hot blood—in blood he'd helped stir—would feel less pain. If their blood was cold, it would be more than slaughter, it would be murderous nightmare and pain best not told and no one to guess.

47 The general spoke and stopped, letting his breath **slack** off. Then after a moment, he said, "So there you are, that's it. Will you do that, boy? Do you know now you're general of the army when the general's left behind?"

48 The boy nodded mutely.

49 "You'll run them through for me then boy?"

My Notes

resolute: determined

slack: to diminish or fade away

© 2017 College Board. All rights reserved.

7. Key Ideas and Details (RL.8.3) **How does the general's comment, "Do you know now you're general of the army when the general's left behind?" prove to be a decisive moment in the conversation between him and Joby?** Up to this point the boy has thought of his drums as a toy, and wishes he had a gun instead. After the general's speech to him, what is Joby ready to do? How does Joby's role as the drummer make him "the general of the army"?

7 Define *dialogue*, and explain that students will be expected to use dialogue in their original narrative (Embedded Assessment 1). Point out that the dialogue in this drama moves the plot forward and develops the characters.

The Departure

My Notes

50 "Yes, sir."

51 "Good. And maybe, many nights from tonight, many years from now, when you're as old or far much older than me, when they ask you what you did in this awful time, you will tell them—one part humble and one part proud—'I was the drummer boy at the battle of Owl Creek,' or the Tennessee River, or maybe they'll just name it after the church there. 'I was the drummer boy at Shiloh.' Who will ever hear those words and not know you, boy, or what you thought this night, or what you'll think tomorrow or the next day when we must get up on our legs and move!"

52 The general stood up. "Well then … Bless you, boy. Good night."

53 "Good night, sir." And tobacco, brass, boot polish, salt sweat and leather, the man moved away through the grass.

54 Joby lay for a moment, staring but unable to see where the man had gone. He swallowed. He wiped his eyes. He cleared his throat. He settled himself. Then, at last, very slowly and firmly, he turned the drum so that it faced up toward the sky.

55 He lay next to it, his arm around it, feeling the tremor, the touch, the muted thunder as, all the rest of the April night in the year 1862, near the Tennessee River, not far from the Owl Creek, very close to the church named Shiloh, the peach blossoms fell on the drum.

Second Read

- Reread the excerpt to answer these text-dependent questions.
- Write any additional questions you have about the text in your Reader/Writer Notebook.

1. **Key Ideas and Details:** What textual evidence in the beginning of the story shows that the boy is afraid?

   At the beginning the boy is "jerked upright" by the sound of an unseen peach stone hitting his drumskin, and in that instant his heart is beating so loud he can hear it in response to unexpected panic. RL.8.3

2. **Craft and Structure:** The word "harvested" is used figuratively in paragraph 10. How do you know it is used figuratively, and why did the author choose this word?

   Harvested is usually used in reference to crops bundled on a field. In this case, "harvested" is used as a visual image of the men of the army gathered together in bunches as they sleep in a vast field and await daybreak. RL.8.4

3. **Craft and Structure:** Consult reference materials to find the meanings of "ramrod" and "flint." Relate these words to the meaning of the sentence in paragraph 12. How does the sentence convey the boy's mood?

A ramrod is the stick used to cram ammunition down the muzzle of a gun, and a flint is a piece of stone used to create a spark to ignite gunpowder. Joby realizes that the soldiers can be comforted and confident in battle because they have such equipment to help them fight. Joby, howerver, lacks such comfort because he only has a drum and sticks. RL.8.4

4. **Key Ideas and Details:** How did Joby join the army? What is significant about that?

Joby did not join legitimately because at 14, he is too young to join. He ran off and joined up as a drummer boy. He is very young, and as the general says, "raw." He has only been in the army for 3 weeks. He is not ready for battle. RL.8.3

5. **Craft and Structure:** Consult reference material to find the meaning of the word "drowse." How does that word create a contrast in paragraph 44?

"Drowse," meaning "a light sleep" or "half sleep," is used to set up a contrast to the image that the soldiers would "sleep forever" if the drummer boy were to beat the drum slowly. Slow drumming would guarantee the soldiers would die. RL.8.4

6. **Key Ideas and Details:** What shift happens in paragraphs 44, 45, and 46? Use textual evidence in your answer.

The shift occurs as the general impresses the boy with the importance of keeping the men moving quickly in an "ever faster rhythm," "like a wave on the ocean," their hearts beating steadily and quickly to keep "the blood moving fast in them." The general convinces the boy of the importance of his role in the battle. RL.8.3

7. **Key Ideas and Details:** How does the general's comment, "Do you know now you're general of the army when the general's left behind?" prove to be a decisive moment in the conversation between him and Joby?

In this comment the general makes Joby understand his importance to the army. Joby leads the army by keeping the drum beat steady and strong to inspire the men and keep them resolute and focused. RL.8.3

My Notes

8 Form pairs, and ask students to work collaboratively to complete the Working from the Text section. When students are finished, discuss student responses to check for understanding.

The Departure

My Notes

Working from the Text

8. Summarize the Departure Stage of the Hero's Journey as it relates to Joby in "The Drummer Boy." Which stage is Joby in? Embed at least one direct quotation in your summary to strengthen your response.

   The Call to Adventure has already occurred when the story begins. The boy, Joby, is now experiencing an internal conflict that characterizes the Refusal of the Call—he wants to be part of the army, but he is afraid because he "has no shield." He has only a drum, "worse than a toy." This fear threatens to overcome his courage and commitment to accompany the army in the coming battle. It is at this time that the general comes by and convinces Joby of his crucial role in encouraging the troops and maintaining their courage. Joby is now ready to begin his adventure.

9. Write a main idea statement to express how Joby is now ready to start his journey. How did the author communicate this idea? Provide textual evidence to support your interpretation.

   Theme:

   Joby gains a sense of the importance of his purpose and his role, which helps set the stage for heroism.

   Evidence:

   "He wiped his eyes. He cleared his throat. He settled himself. Then, at last, very slowly and firmly, he turned the drum so that it faced up toward the sky.

10. Reread a chunk of the text to identify and evaluate the narrative elements listed in the graphic organizer on the next page.

Structure: Exposition	What descriptive detail does the author provide?	How effective is the description?
Setting 1862; night before the Battle of Shiloh	Anonymous soldiers; darkness; under a peach tree with blossoms falling	The author effectively portrays the quiet before battle when fears are most likely to reveal themselves.
Character Fourteen-year-old volunteer drummer boy	Alone; has a drum; crying and afraid	The reader can clearly imagine the youth and vulnerability of the drummer boy.
Conflict Internal: fear vs. duty	Crying; contrasts his two sticks to soldiers with guns as being better prepared to go into battle	The reader sympathizes with the boy's sense of his vulnerability; he has only a drum; he has no gun.
Techniques	**How does the author use each element to develop the story?**	**How effective is the author's technique?**
Description	Shadowy; nighttime; the lack of clear visibility is like the boy's need for more clarity of purpose, so he is not overcome by fear	The scene is obscure as is the boy's fear; he hides his fear in the darkness.
Dialogue	General's dialogue gives the boy a sense of his importance and purpose	The general's words are inspiring; this is the turning point for the boy.
Pacing	The pace is fairly slow, measured, and thoughtful. It is a conversation between wisdom and innocence the night before a battle.	The pacing is effective for a story about a boy experiencing fear and how he is pulled out of his fear.

Check Your Understanding

Use your imagination to create an original hero. In the left column (or on notebook paper or in your Reader/Writer Notebook), sketch your image of a hero. Label unique characteristics and give him or her a meaningful name. In the right column, use the prompting questions to brainstorm ideas for a story.

My Notes

9 Have students continue to work in pairs or small groups as they complete the **graphic organizer**.

10 Ask students to independently complete the Check Your Understanding. Explain that although this is practice, they can use any or all of these ideas for Embedded Assessment 1. Remind students that the excerpt from *A Wrinkle in Time* is a great example of a narrative opening; it may help to revisit it.

Leveled Differentiated Instruction

In this activity, some students may draw a picture of the hero they envisioned. Writing about their picture will prepare students for the narrative writing prompt.

Em Help students write a narrative sentence about their picture using the sentence frame, *[name the hero] is [tell something about the hero].*

Ex Guide students to write several narrative sentences about their picture. Ask students to write about what the hero looks like and what makes him or her special. Encourage students to use appropriate text organization in their writing.

Br Have students write several more detailed narrative sentences about their picture. Encourage students to use appropriate text organization and register in their writing.

© 2017 College Board. All rights reserved.

11 You may choose to review visual techniques by displaying unfamiliar visuals and asking students to identify the different shots, angles, and colors (related to lighting). Then, ask students to explain how visual techniques are used for effect. Display these visuals (and others) for future reference.

12 As students prepare to illustrate an event from their draft, encourage them to add as many frames as they need to capture the event.

▶ASSESS

Review student work to determine the quality of the narrative and the visual. Identify skills that are still at the emerging level (to focus on in future activities), and select student exemplars to share with the class.

▶ADAPT

To support learning, provide additional examples of the Departure Stage in narratives. Provide copies of a different example for each stage, at different stations in the room. Form discussion groups, and ask students to rotate through each station, reading, analyzing, evaluating, and taking notes to record ideas for their own narrative. To save time, you could ask each group to become experts on one example and then have groups present their analysis and evaluation to the class.

The Departure

My Notes

The Hero: ____________ (name)	The Story Exposition
Use these questions to spark ideas. Is the hero male or female? Young or old? Beautiful or unattractive? Well liked or misunderstood? Conspicuous (obvious) or nondescript (ordinary)?	**Setting:** (In what kind of place does your hero live? Does he or she live in the past, present, or future?) **Character:** (What are the hero's strengths and weaknesses? Who are the hero's family and friends? What does the hero do every day? What does the hero want in life? What do others want from the hero?) **Conflicts:** (What challenges might the hero experience? How might the hero transform into someone stronger?)

Narrative Writing Prompt

Think about the hero you just envisioned. What might the hero experience in the Departure Stage of his or her journey? Draft the beginning of a narrative using the three steps in this stage (The Call, The Refusal, and The Beginning) to guide your structure and development. Be sure to:

- Establish a context (exposition) and point of view (first person or third person).
- Use narrative techniques such as dialogue, pacing, and description to develop experiences, events, and/or characters.
- Use details and imagery to create mood.

Visualize an event in your draft. Use visual techniques to capture imagery, emphasize an important idea, and/or add interest.

The Initiation

ACTIVITY 1.7

Learning Targets

- Analyze an excerpt of an epic poem for archetype and narrative techniques.
- Demonstrate understanding of these concepts by drafting and illustrating an event in a hero's Road of Trials stage.

Preview

In this activity, you will read and analyze an excerpt from an epic poem.

Setting a Purpose for Reading

- Read the excerpt and make observations and inferences about Odysseus's character. Make note of words that describe his appearance, as well as his own words, actions, thoughts, and feelings. Also note how others react to him.
- Circle unknown words and phrases. Try to determine the meaning of the words by using context clues, word parts, or a dictionary.

ABOUT THE AUTHOR
Homer is the traditionally accepted author of two famous epic poems, the *Iliad* and the *Odyssey*. No biography of Homer exists, and scholars disagree about whether he was the sole author or whether *Homer* was a name chosen by several writers who contributed to the works. Some scholars believe that the poems evolved through oral tradition over a period of centuries and are the collective work of many poets.

LEARNING STRATEGIES:
Marking the Text, Note-taking, Shared Reading, Close Reading, Rereading, Diffusing, Skimming/Scanning, Visualizing

WORD CONNECTIONS

Cognates

The English word *initiation* has at its root *-init-*, which comes from the Latin word *initialis*, meaning "beginning." Its Spanish cognate is *iniciación*, which derives from *iniciar*, meaning "to begin."

Literary Terms

An **epic** is a long narrative about the deeds of heroes or gods.

INDEPENDENT READING LINK

Read and Discuss

Think about the hero of the book you are reading outside of class. Meet with a partner and describe the mental and physical strengths your book's hero possesses that will be important when facing challenges and obstacles. Talk to classmates who chose a different independent reading book than you. Discuss how the strengths of your book's hero are similar to those of the heroes in their books.

Epic

From the ODYSSEY

by Homer
Translation by Tony Kline

Book IX: 152–192
ODYSSEUS TELLS HIS TALE: THE CYCLOPS'S CAVE

1 Looking across to the land of the neighboring Cyclops,[1] we could see smoke and hear their voices, and the sound of their sheep and goats. Sun set and darkness fell, and we settled to our rest on the shore.

2 As soon as rosy-fingered Dawn appeared, I gathered my men together, saying: "The rest of you loyal friends stay here, while I and my crew take ship and try and find out who these men are, whether they are cruel, savage and lawless, or good to strangers, and in their hearts fear the gods."

[1] **Cyclops:** one-eyed giants

ACTIVITY 1.7

PLAN

Suggested Pacing: 3 50-minute class periods

TEACH

1 Read the Preview and the Setting a Purpose for Reading sections with your students. Help them understand the literary terms they encounter.

2 **FIRST READ:** Based on the complexity of the passage and your knowledge of your students, you may choose to conduct the first reading in a variety of ways:

- independent reading
- paired reading
- small group reading
- choral reading
- read aloud

COMMON CORE STATE STANDARDS

Focus Standards:

RL.8.3: Analyze how particular lines of dialogue or incidents in a story or drama propel the action, reveal aspects of a character, or provoke a decision.

W.8.3: Write narratives to develop real or imagined experiences or events using effective technique, relevant descriptive details, and well-structured event sequences.

W.8.3a: Engage and orient the reader by establishing a context and point of view and introducing a narrator and/or characters; organize an event sequence that unfolds naturally and logically.

W.8.3d: Use precise words and phrases, relevant descriptive details, and sensory language to capture the action and convey experiences and events.

ACTIVITY 1.7 continued

Text Complexity
Overall: Complex
Lexile: 1130L
Qualitative: Moderate Difficulty
Task: Moderate (Analyze)

TEACHER TO TEACHER

To **support** or **extend** learning, use alternate translations of the text. Note that though *The Odyssey* is considered an epic poem, it is often (as here) translated into prose. Audio support could also be provided.

3 As students are reading, monitor their progress. Be sure they are engaged with the text and annotating details about Odysseus. Evaluate whether the selected reading mode is effective.

4 Based on the observations you made during the first reading, you may want to adjust your reading mode. For example, you may decide for the second reading to read aloud certain complex passages, or you may group students differently.

The Initiation

My Notes

3 With this I went aboard and ordered my crew to follow and loose the cables. They boarded swiftly and took their place on the benches then sitting in their rows struck the grey water with their oars. When we had reached the nearby shore, we saw a deep cave overhung with laurels at the cliff's edge close to the sea. Large herds of sheep and goats were penned there at night and round it was a raised yard walled by deep-set stones, tall pines and high-crowned oaks. There a giant spent the night, one that grazed his herds far off, alone, and keeping clear of others, lived in lawless solitude. He was born a monster and a wonder, not like any ordinary human, but like some wooded peak of the high mountains, that stands there isolated to our gaze.

Book IX: 193–255

ODYSSEUS TELLS HIS TALE: POLYPHEMUS RETURNS

talent: an ancient coin
draught: a liquid that one drinks

4 Then I ordered the rest of my loyal friends to stay there and guard the ship, while I selected the twelve best men and went forward. I took with me a goatskin filled with dark sweet wine that Maron, son of Euanthes, priest of Apollo, guardian god of Ismarus, had given me, because out of respect we protected him, his wife and child. He offered me splendid gifts, seven **talents** of well-wrought gold, and a silver mixing-bowl: and wine, twelve jars in all, sweet unmixed wine, a divine **draught**. None of his serving-men and maids knew of this store, only he and his loyal wife, and one housekeeper. When they drank that honeyed red wine, he would pour a full cup into twenty of water, and the bouquet that rose from the mixing bowl was wonderfully sweet: in truth no one could hold back. I filled a large goatskin with the wine, and took it along, with some food in a bag, since my instincts told me the giant would come at us quickly, a savage being with huge strength, knowing nothing of right or law.

WORD CONNECTIONS

Etymology

The English word *bouquet* comes from a French word of the same spelling meaning "little wood." The term derives from the Medieval Latin word *boscus*, which means "grove."

whey: the watery part of milk

5 Soon we came to the cave, and found him absent; he was grazing his well-fed flocks in the fields. So we went inside and marveled at its contents. There were baskets full of cheeses, and pens crowded with lambs and kids, each flock with its firstlings, later ones, and newborn separated. The pails and bowls for milking, all solidly made, were swimming with **whey**. At first my men begged me to take some cheeses and go, then to drive the lambs and kids from the pens down to the swift ship and set sail. But I would not listen, though it would have been best, wishing to see the giant himself, and test his hospitality. When he did appear he proved no joy to my men.

curdled: separated the solid parts out of milk

6 So we lit a fire and made an offering, and helped ourselves to the cheese, and sat in the cave eating, waiting for him to return, shepherding his flocks. He arrived bearing a huge weight of dry wood to burn at suppertime, and he flung it down inside the cave with a crash. Gripped by terror we shrank back into a deep corner. He drove his well-fed flocks into the wide cave, the ones he milked, leaving the rams and he-goats outside in the broad courtyard. Then he lifted his door, a huge stone, and set it in place. Twenty-two four-wheeled wagons could not have carried it, yet such was the great rocky mass he used for a door. Then he sat and milked the ewes, and bleating goats in order, putting her young to each. Next he **curdled** half of the white milk, and stored the whey in wicker baskets, leaving the rest in pails for him to drink for his supper. When he had busied himself at his tasks, and kindled a fire, he suddenly saw us, and said: "Strangers, who are you? Where do you sail from over the sea-roads? Are you on business, or do you roam at random, like pirates who chance their lives to bring evil to others?"

COMMON CORE STATE STANDARDS

Additional Standards Addressed:

RL.8.1; RL.8.2; RL.8.4; RL.8.10; W.8.3b; W.8.3c; W.8.4; L.8.4b; L.8.6

ACTIVITY 1.7
continued

Book IX: 256–306
ODYSSEUS TELLS HIS TALE: TRAPPED

7 Our spirits fell at his words, in terror at his loud voice and monstrous size. Nevertheless I answered him, saying: "We are Achaeans, returning from Troy, driven over the ocean depths by every wind that blows. Heading for home we were forced to take another route, a different course, as Zeus,[1] I suppose, intended. We are followers of Agamemnon, Atreus' son, whose fame spreads widest on earth, so great was that city he **sacked** and host he **slew**. But we, for our part, come as suppliants to your knees, hoping for hospitality, and the kindness that is due to strangers. Good sir, do not refuse us: respect the gods. We are **suppliants** and Zeus protects visitors and suppliants, Zeus the god of guests, who follows the steps of sacred travelers."

8 His answer was **devoid** of pity. "Stranger, you are a foreigner or a fool, telling me to fear and **revere** the gods, since the Cyclopes care nothing for **aegis**-bearing Zeus: we are greater than they. I would spare neither you nor your friends, to evade Zeus' anger, but only as my own heart prompted. But tell me, now, where you moored your fine ship, when you landed. Was it somewhere nearby, or further off? I'd like to know."

sacked: attacked a city and stole from it
slew: killed
suppliants: people who beg
devoid: absent
revere: to regard with devotion and awe
aegis: protection

9 His words were designed to fool me, but failed. I was too wise for that, and answered him with cunning words: "Poseidon,[2] Earth-Shaker, smashed my ship to pieces, wrecking her on the rocks that edge your island, driving her close to the headland so the wind threw her onshore. But I and my men here escaped destruction."

10 Devoid of pity, he was silent in response, but leaping up laid hands on my crew. Two he seized and dashed to the ground like **whelps**, and their brains ran out and stained the earth. He tore them limb from limb for his supper, eating the flesh and entrails, bone and marrow, like a mountain lion, leaving nothing. Helplessly we watched these cruel acts, raising our hands to heaven and weeping. When the Cyclops had filled his huge stomach with human flesh, and had drunk pure milk, he lay down in the cave, stretched out among his flocks. Then I formed a courageous plan to steal up to him, draw my sharp sword, and feeling for the place where the midriff supports the liver, stab him there. But the next thought checked me. Trapped in the cave we would certainly die, since we'd have no way to move the great stone from the wide entrance. So, sighing, we waited for bright day.

whelp: a young child or animal

My Notes

Book IX: 307–359
ODYSSEUS TELLS HIS TALE: OFFERING THE CYCLOPS WINE

11 As soon as rosy-fingered Dawn appeared, Cyclops relit the fire. Then he milked the ewes, and bleating goats in order, putting her young to each. When he had busied himself at his tasks, he again seized two of my men and began to eat them. When he had finished he drove his well-fed flocks from the cave, effortlessly lifting the huge door stone, and replacing it again like the cap on a quiver. Then whistling loudly he turned his flocks out on to the mountain slopes, leaving me with murder in my heart searching for a way to take vengeance on him, if Athene[3] would grant me inspiration. The best plan seemed to be this:

[1] **Zeus:** the king of the gods
[2] **Poseidon:** god of the sea and of earthquakes
[3] **Athene:** goddess of wisdom, the arts, and war

SCAFFOLDING THE TEXT-DEPENDENT QUESTIONS

1. Key Ideas and Details (RL.8.1) **Why does Odysseus go to the land of the Cyclops? What evidence in the first paragraph tells you this?** Is Odysseus simply curious about the giants or did he mean to do them harm?

2. Key Ideas and Details (RL.8.3) **What does the following quote from paragraph 5 reveal about Odysseus's character? "But I would not listen, though it would have been best, wishing to see the giant himself, and test his hospitality. When he did appear he proved no joy to my men."** How does this comment from Odysseus set up for later action in the story? How does this statement make Odysseus seem more sympathetic as a leader?

3. Key Ideas and Details (RL.8.3) **Based on the words and actions of the Cyclops, how would you describe his character and his perspective?** Reread paragraphs 7–10. Odysseus greets the giant politely, but almost immediately the Cyclops shows his true intentions. List all the actions the Cyclops has taken against Odysseus and his men.

The Initiation

cast lots: to throw a set of objects in order to impartially decide something

premonition: a vision of the future

ambrosia and nectar: the food and drink that the gods ate

fuddled: made confusing

subtle: not obvious

12 The Cyclops' huge club, a trunk of green olive wood he had cut to take with him as soon as it was seasoned, lay next to a sheep pen. It was so large and thick that it looked to us like the mast of a twenty-oared black ship, a broad-beamed merchant vessel that sails the deep ocean. Approaching it, I cut off a six-foot length, gave it to my men and told them to smooth the wood. Then standing by it I sharpened the end to a point, and hardened the point in the blazing fire, after which I hid it carefully in a one of the heaps of dung that lay around the cave. I ordered the men to **cast lots** as to which of them should dare to help me raise the stake and twist it into the Cyclops' eye when sweet sleep took him. The lot fell on the very ones I would have chosen, four of them, with myself making a fifth.

13 He returned at evening, shepherding his well-fed flocks. He herded them swiftly, every one, into the deep cave, leaving none in the broad yard, commanded to do so by a god, or because of some **premonition**. Then he lifted the huge door stone and set it in place, and sat down to milk the ewes and bleating goats in order, putting her young to each. But when he had busied himself at his tasks, he again seized two of my men and began to eat them. That was when I went up to him, holding an ivy-wood bowl full of dark wine, and said: "Here, Cyclops, have some wine to follow your meal of human flesh, so you can taste the sort of drink we carried in our ship. I was bringing the drink to you as a gift, hoping you might pity me and help me on my homeward path: but your savagery is past bearing. Cruel man, why would anyone on earth ever visit you again, when you behave so badly?"

14 At this, he took the cup and drained it, and found the sweet drink so delightful he asked for another draught: "Give me more, freely, then quickly tell me your name so I may give you a guest gift, one that will please you. Among us Cyclopes the fertile earth produces rich grape clusters, and Zeus' rain swells them: but this is a taste from a stream of **ambrosia and nectar**."

Book IX: 360–412

ODYSSEUS TELLS HIS TALE: BLINDING THE CYCLOPS

15 As he finished speaking I handed him the bright wine. Three times I poured and gave it to him, and three times, foolishly, he drained it. When the wine had **fuddled** his wits I tried him with **subtle** words: "Cyclops, you asked my name, and I will tell it: give me afterwards a guest gift as you promised. My name is Nobody. Nobody, my father, mother, and friends call me."

16 Those were my words, and this his cruel answer: "Then, my gift is this. I will eat Nobody last of all his company, and all the others before him."

17 As he spoke, he reeled and toppled over on his back, his thick neck twisted to one side, and all-conquering sleep overpowered him. In his drunken slumber he vomited wine and pieces of human flesh. Then I thrust the stake into the depth of the ashes to heat it, and inspired my men with encouraging words, so none would hang back from fear. When the olivewood stake was glowing hot, and ready to catch fire despite its greenness, I drew it from the coals, then my men stood round me, and a god breathed courage into us. They held the sharpened olivewood stake, and thrust it into his eye, while I threw my weight on the end, and twisted it round and round, as a man bores the timbers of a ship with a drill that others twirl lower down with a strap held at both ends, and so keep the drill continuously moving. We took the red-hot stake and twisted it round and round like that in his eye, and the blood poured out despite the heat. His lids and brows were scorched by flame from the burning eyeball, and its

My Notes

SCAFFOLDING THE TEXT-DEPENDENT QUESTIONS

4. Key Ideas and Details (RL.8.3) **What does the following reflection reveal about Odysseus's character? "His words were designed to fool me, but failed. I was too wise for that, and answered him with cunning words."** Did the Cyclops ever intend to treat Odysseus and his men with hospitality and concern? Once the Cyclops finds out that Odysseus and his men are stranded on the island, what does he do? Why does Odysseus lie to the Cyclops?

5. Craft and Structure (RL.8.4) **List the verbs used in the blinding of the Cyclops. What effect do these verbs have on the pacing of this event?** Review with students the importance of verbs to pacing and creating a vivid picture. Choose one or two of the verbs for closer analysis—"thrust," "twisted," "hissed"—to show how they move the scene forward.

6. Key Ideas and Details (RL.8.3) **Why does Odysseus give the Cyclops a false name? How**

roots crackled with fire. As a great axe or adze causes a vast hissing when the smith dips it in cool water to temper it, strengthening the iron, so his eye hissed against the olivewood stake. Then he screamed, terribly, and the rock echoed. Seized by terror we shrank back, as he wrenched the stake, wet with blood, from his eye. He flung it away in frenzy, and called to the Cyclops, his neighbors who lived in caves on the windy heights. They heard his cry, and crowding in from every side they stood by the cave mouth and asked what was wrong: "Polyphemus, what terrible pain is this that makes you call through deathless night, and wake us? Is a mortal stealing your flocks, or trying to kill you by violence or **treachery**?"

treachery: a betrayal of trust

18 Out of the cave came mighty Polyphemus' voice: "Nobody, my friends, is trying to kill me by violence or treachery."

19 To this they replied with winged words: "If you are alone, and nobody does you violence, it's an inescapable sickness that comes from Zeus: pray to the Lord Poseidon, our father."

My Notes

Book IX: 413–479
ODYSSEUS TELLS HIS TALE: ESCAPE

20 Off they went, while I laughed to myself at how the name and the clever scheme had deceived him. Meanwhile the Cyclops, groaning and in pain, groped around and labored to lift the stone from the door. Then he sat in the entrance, arms outstretched, to catch anyone stealing past among his sheep. That was how foolish he must have thought I was. I considered the best way of escaping, and saving myself, and my men from death. I dreamed up all sorts of tricks and schemes, as a man will in a life or death matter: it was an evil situation. This was the plan that seemed best. The rams were fat with thick **fleeces**, fine large beasts with deep black wool. These I silently tied together in threes, with twists of willow on which that lawless monster, Polyphemus, slept. The middle one was to carry one of my men, with the other two on either side to protect him. So there was a man to every three sheep. As for me I took the pick of the flock, and curled below his shaggy belly, gripped his back and lay there face upwards, patiently gripping his fine fleece tight in my hands. Then, sighing, we waited for the light.

fleece: the coat of wool on a ram

21 As soon as rosy-fingered Dawn appeared, the males rushed out to graze, while the un-milked females udders bursting bleated in the pens. Their master, tormented by agonies of pain, felt the backs of the sheep as they passed him, but foolishly failed to see my men tied under the rams' bellies. My ram went last, burdened by the weight of his fleece, and me and my teeming thoughts. And as he felt its back, mighty Polyphemus spoke to him:

22 "My fine ram, why leave the cave like this last of the flock? You have never lagged behind before, always the first to step out proudly and graze on the tender grass shoots, always first to reach the flowing river, and first to show your wish to return at evening to the fold. Today you are last of all. You must surely be grieving over your master's eye, blinded by an evil man and his wicked friends, when my wits were fuddled with wine: Nobody, I say, has not yet escaped death. If you only had senses like me, and the power of speech to tell me where he hides himself from my anger, then I'd strike him down, his brains would be sprinkled all over the floor of the cave, and my heart would be eased of the pain that nothing, Nobody, has brought me."

SCAFFOLDING THE TEXT-DEPENDENT QUESTIONS

does it help him? Ask students if this trick was necessary. Has the Cyclops proven himself to be an honest hospitable giant?

7. Key Ideas and Details (RL.8.2) **Summarize paragraphs 21 and 22. How do Odysseus and his men escape? What makes paragraph 22 dramatic?** Why does the Cyclops feel sorry for himself? How is he to blame for his own misfortune?

8. Key Ideas and Details (RL.8.3) **The adventure on the Road of Trials concludes with Odysseus having the last word of dialogue. Is this an effective way to end? Why or why not?** In his last words what message or moral does Odysseus want to impress upon his enemy and all his potential enemies?

ACTIVITY 1.7 continued

5 SECOND READ: During the second reading, students will be returning to the text to answer the text-dependent comprehension questions. You may choose to have students reread and work on the questions in a variety of ways:

- independently
- in pairs
- in small groups
- together as a class

6 Have students answer the text-dependent questions. If they have difficulty, scaffold the questions by rephrasing them or breaking them down into smaller parts. See the Scaffolding the Text-Dependent Questions boxes for suggestions.

ACTIVITY 1.7 continued

The Initiation

My Notes

23 With this he drove the ram away from him out of doors, and I loosed myself when the ram was a little way from the cave, then untied my men. Swiftly, keeping an eye behind us, we shepherded those long-limbed sheep, rich and fat, down to the ship. And a welcome sight, indeed, to our dear friends were we, escapees from death, though they wept and sighed for the others we lost. I would not let them weep though, but stopped them all with a nod and a frown. I told them to haul the host of fine-fleeced sheep on board and put to sea. They boarded swiftly and took their place on the benches then sitting in their rows struck the grey water with their oars. When we were almost out of earshot, I shouted to the Cyclops, mocking him: "It seems he was not such a weakling, then, Cyclops, that man whose friends you meant to tear apart and eat in your echoing cave. Stubborn brute not shrinking from murdering your guests in your own house, your evil deeds were bound for sure to fall on your own head. Zeus and the other gods have had their revenge on you."

Second Read

- Reread the excerpt to answer these text-dependent questions.
- Write any additional questions you have about the text in your Reader/Writer Notebook.

1. **Key Ideas and Details:** Why does Odysseus go to the land of the Cyclops? What evidence in the first two paragraphs tells you this?

   Odysseus goes to the land of the Cyclops to "find out who these men are, whether they are cruel, savage and lawless, or good to strangers, and in their hearts fear the gods." RL.8.1

2. **Key Ideas and Details:** What does the following quote from paragraph 5 reveal about Odysseus's character? "But I would not listen, though it would have been best, wishing to see the giant himself, and test his hospitality. When he did appear he proved no joy to my men."

   Odysseus admits that his judgment was poor; he takes responsibility for the harm done to his men. RL.8.3

3. **Key Ideas and Details:** Based on the words and actions of the Cyclops, how would you describe his character and his perspective?

   The Cyclops sees himself as superior to the gods and is monstrous in his eagerness to eat the strangers. RL.8.3

4. **Key Ideas and Details:** What does the following reflection reveal about Odysseus's character? "His words were designed to fool me, but failed. I was too wise for that, and answered him with cunning words."

   Odysseus is smart and self-confident. He understands that the Cyclops may attack his ship and so answers him with a lie. Odysseus uses the giant's answer to gauge his character. RL.8.3

5. **Craft and Structure:** List the verbs used in the blinding of the Cyclops. What effect do these verbs have on the pacing of this event?

The following verbs and verbals are used in the blinding of the Cyclops: thrust, glowing, twisted, poured out, scorched, burning, crackled, hissing. The effect of these words is to speed up the action. RL.8.4

6. **Key Ideas and Details:** Why does Odysseus give the Cyclops a false name? How does it help him?

Odysseus tells the Cyclops his name is "Nobody." In paragraph 18, Polyphemus yells to his friends for help, saying, "Nobody...is trying to kill me..." and so his friends think he is imagining the violence. RL.8.3

7. **Key Ideas and Details:** Summarize paragraphs 21 and 22. How do Odysseus and his men escape? What makes paragraph 22 dramatic?

Odysseus had each of his men hide underneath the bellies of three rams tied together. When the rams ran outside the cave, the Cyclops felt only the back of the rams and could not see or feel the men underneath. This scene is dramatic because it is the final display of the superiority of Odysseus and his men over the cruel and self-pitying monster who was determined to eat them all. RL.8.2

8. **Key Ideas and Details:** The adventure on the "Road of Trials" concludes with Odysseus having the last word of dialogue. Is this an effective way to end? Why or why not?

The hero is able to show the superiority of himself and his men who are supported by the gods against monsters such as the Cyclops. RL.8.3

Working from the Text

9. Use this chart to organize your notes about Odysseus. Fill in the description column with your notes and then analyze what this information means about Odysseus. Fill in the analysis column with descriptive words.

My Notes

Leveled Differentiated Instruction

In this activity, it may be helpful for students to write a paragraph to be sure they understand the sequence of the story. Have students complete a **Paragraph Frame for Sequencing** graphic organizer for these chapters in the *Odyssey*.

Em Help students add connecting words to their paragraphs such as *at the end, next*.

Ex Guide students to add a variety of connecting words to their paragraphs such as *as a result, on the other hand*.

Br Have students add an increasing variety of connecting words to their paragraphs such as *in addition, consequently*.

7 Complete the Working from the Text section. The questions focus on the author's technique, so it is important that all students have a chance to contribute to each response.

The Initiation

Element of Character Development	Description	Analysis
Appearance (Adjectives)	There is no mention of Odysseus's appearance. It is implied that he is very strong and commanding.	
Actions (Verbs)	makes most of his men wait on the ship, takes only his twelve best men with him puts himself between his men and the Cyclops and confronts the Cyclops himself creates a stake from a large piece of wood and drives it into the Cyclops's eye figures out that he can escape from the cave without the Cyclops seeing him by riding underneath a sheep	honorable/selfless/strong leader physically and mentally strong resourceful
Words (Verbs)	speaks with and tries to rationalize with the Cyclops first, instead of harming him right away tells the Cyclops his name is "Nobody," so when the Cyclops is injured, he tells his friends "Nobody" has caused him harm	reasonable witty/clever
Thoughts/Feelings	Odysseus is outraged that the giant would deny him and his men hospitality and actually harm them. He plans and carries out revenge.	
Others' Reactions	Little evidence of others' reactions except that his men follow him without question	

The Road of Trials (physical and mental challenges) and Outcome (success or failure)

1.

2.

3.

4. Which step in the Intitiation Stage would best describe these chapters from the *Odyssey*?

These chapters represent one incident in The Road of Trials.

5. Analyze the ***structure*** of the narrative: Map out the sequence of events. What is the turning point for Odysseus and his men?

Sequence of events:

(1) Odysseus prepares to meet the Cyclops; Odysseus and his men are trapped in the cave.

(2) Rather than offering hospitality, the monster eats two of Odysseus's men.

(3) After the monster eats two more men the next morning, Odysseus devises a plan to poke out the eye of the Cyclops.

(4) Odysseus gets the Cyclops drunk, and then the men poke a burning stick in the monster's one eye, blinding him.

(5) The turning point comes when Polyphemus tries to get help from his fellow Cyclops, but, because he is tricked into using the word "Nobody," his fellow monsters do not believe he has been attacked.

(6) The next day, the remaining men and Odysseus escape by riding under and in between sheep as they leave the case for their pasture.

6. Analyze the transitions used in the storytelling. How does the author use transitions to convey sequence and signal shifts?

The story includes transitions of time, such as "As soon as rosy-fingered Dawn appeared..."; "At this..."; and "He returned at evening..."

7. What is the ***mood*** of this adventure? How does the author create the mood?

The mood represents outrage, disgust, terror, trepidation, and fear. The author creates these moods by describing events and the characters' reactions.

My Notes

TEACHER TO TEACHER

You may want to answer the first question as a whole group to set the context. You could ask separate groups or segments of the class to work on the next two questions, since they will need to skim the text again before forming a response, and then discuss as a whole group, culminating in a whole-class discussion of the last question.

ACTIVITY 1.7 continued

▶ASSESS

Have students respond to the writing prompt independently. Remind students that they can use any or all of this work in Embedded Assessment 1. Review student work to determine the quality of the narrative and the visual. Identify skills that are still at the emerging level (to focus on in future activities), and select student models to share with the class.

▶ADAPT

If multiple students are struggling with the same thing, stop the class and offer a **brainstorming** session to generate ideas. You could also support learning by using **visual prompts** to spark ideas or by allowing students to work with a partner.

The Initiation

My Notes

Check Your Understanding

Narrative Writing Prompt

Think about the hero you created in the previous activity. What might the hero experience in the Initiation Stage of his or her journey? Draft an event using your understanding of the Road of Trials to guide your structure and development. Be sure to:

- Use narrative techniques such as dialogue, pacing, and description, and to develop experiences, events, and/or characters.
- Use diction, detail, and imagery to create tone and mood.
- Sequence the event logically and naturally, and use transitions to connect ideas.

Visualize a key moment in the event. Use visual techniques to capture imagery, emphasize an important idea, and/or add interest. Challenge yourself to use a different combination of visual techniques for effect in each frame.

Language and Writer's Craft: Revising and Editing

ACTIVITY 1.8

Learning Targets

- Identify and apply effective techniques and strategies for writing groups.
- Revise and edit a narrative draft through a collaborative writing group.

LEARNING STRATEGIES: Collaborative Discussion, Sharing and Responding, Summarizing, Self-Editing/Peer-Editing

Writing Group Roles

For groups to be effective, each member must participate to help achieve the goals of the group. The purpose of writing groups is to:

- Provide an open-minded place to read, respond to, and revise writing.
- Provide meaningful feedback to improve writing based on specific criteria.
- Create specific roles to solicit and manage sharing and responding.
- Focus on posing open-ended questions for the writer to consider.

Writing group members have roles and responsibilities.

My Notes

Role	Guidelines	Discussion / Response Starters
The Reader: Reads the text silently, then aloud. Begins the conversation after reading.	The Reader's purpose is to share an understanding of the writer's words. The Reader sees the physical structure of the draft and may comment on that as well. The Reader follows all listeners' guidelines as well.	Reader's and Listeners' **compliments:** • I liked the words you used, such as . . . • I like the way you described . . . • This piece made me feel . . . • This piece reminded me of . . . • I noticed your use of ______ from the Hero's Journey when you . . .
The Listeners: Take notes and prepare open-ended questions for the writer or make constructive statements.	The Listeners begin with positive statements, using "I" statements to talk about the writing, not the writer. The Listeners use the **writer's checklist** to produce thoughtful questions that will help strengthen the writing.	Reader's and Listeners' **comments and suggestions:** • I really enjoyed the part where . . . • What parts are you having trouble with? • What do you plan to do next? • I was confused when . . .
The Writer: Listens to the draft, takes notes, responds to questions, and asks questions for clarification.	As his or her work is being read aloud by another, the Writer can get an overall impression of the piece. The Writer takes notes on needed changes. The Writer asks questions to get feedback that will lead to effective revision.	Writer's **questions:** • What do you want to know more about? • Which part does not make sense? • Which section of the text does not work? • How can I improve this part?

ACTIVITY 1.8

PLAN

Suggested Pacing: 2 50-minute class periods

TEACH

1 Preview the four parts of the activity: Writing Groups, Revision, Editing, and Reflection.

2 Lead a discussion on effective writing groups. As students read the information about writing groups, have them circle important words and concepts.

3 After students independently read the description of the writing group roles, ask them to summarize the assignment and guidelines for each "job." Students must know exactly what is expected of them prior to beginning the group discussion.

COMMON CORE STATE STANDARDS

Focus Standard:

W.8.5: With some guidance and support from peers and adults, develop and strengthen writing as needed by planning, revising, editing, rewriting, or trying a new approach, focusing on how well purpose and audience have been addressed. (Editing for conventions should demonstrate command of Language standards 1–3 up to and including Grade 8 here.)

Additional Standards Addressed:

RL.8.3; W.8.10; SL.8.1a; SL.8.1b; SL.8.1c; SL.8.1d; L.8.1c; L.8.1d; L.8.2c

4 Have students read about the revision process; then, in Student Step 3, have them consider questions they can ask members of their writing group to aid in revision.

Language and Writer's Craft: Revising and Editing

My Notes

1. Summarize the purpose and process of working in a successful writing group.

The Revision Process

Very few people are able to write a perfect first draft, so revising is a typical part of the writing process—even for famous writers. In an interview done for *The Paris Review* in 1956, the interviewer asked Ernest Hemingway about his writing.

Interviewer: How much rewriting do you do?
Hemingway: It depends. I rewrote the ending of *Farewell to Arms*, the last page of it, 39 times before I was satisfied.
Interviewer: Was there some technical problem there? What was it that had stumped you?
Hemingway: Getting the words right.
(From Ernest Hemingway, "The Art of Fiction," *The Paris Review* Interview, 1956)

2. Writing groups can help you revise and get your words right. In the last two activities, you started a narrative about a hero. As you think about revising your draft, what are some guiding questions you might ask? You might use the Embedded Assessment 1 Scoring Guide to prompt your questions to focus on ideas, organization, and your use of language.
   - Who is your hero, and how is he or she original?
   - What is your hero's *calling*? What will your hero experience on his or her *Road of Trials*? What will be your hero's *boon*? What *wisdom* will be *gained* by the end of the story?
   - How did you use [specific technique or element of language] for effect?
   - How did you sequence events? How did you transition between ideas?

Introducing the Strategy: Self-Editing, Peer-Editing

Editing your writing is a part of the writing process (self-editing). This strategy can be used with a partner (peer-editing) to examine a text closely to identify areas that may need to be corrected for language, grammar, punctuation, capitalization, or spelling.

3. In addition to asking questions, having a writer's checklist can help you revise. Next you will work with members of your writing group to create, on separate paper, a ***writer's checklist*** for your Hero's Journey narrative. This checklist should reflect your group's ideas about the following:
   - **Ideas:** Think of the purpose of the writing, the topic, and the details.
   - **Structure:** Think of the writing mode and purpose, as well as organization of the writing.
   - **Use of language:** Think about figurative language, descriptive details, transitions, diction, etc.

You may want to check the Scoring Guide for Embedded Assessment 1 for further ideas.

4. After completing your writer's checklist, your writing group will read and discuss each member's draft of the Hero's Journey narrative. Group members should trade roles of Reader, Listener, and Writer as they proceed through each draft, following the information in the chart on the previous pages.

Using Resources and References to Revise

How does a writer improve a text through revision? Deep revision takes time and effort. Skilled writers do the following:

- **Add** ideas and language to enhance effect.
- **Delete** irrelevant, unclear, and repetitive ideas and language to improve pacing and effect.
- **Rearrange** ideas to improve sequence.
- **Substitute** ideas and language for effect.

5. Use the writer's checklist you created, the feedback from your peers, and the revision strategies above to guide your revision. Share one of your revisions with the class by explaining specifically what you revised and how it improved your writing.

Editing a Draft

6. New writers sometimes confuse revision with editing or proofreading. Both are extremely important in creating a polished piece of writing, but they are different and separate processes.
   - Revision focuses on ideas, organization, and language and involves adding, deleting, rearranging, and substituting words, sentences, and entire paragraphs.

My Notes

5 Form **writing groups.** Each group will begin by creating a **writer's checklist** of ways to improve ideas, organization, and language. Students should consult the Embedded Assessment 1 Scoring Guide as they develop their lists.

6 Next, writing groups will discuss each member's Hero's Journey draft. Students should rotate through the roles as each has his or her draft read and discussed.

7 Read the information under Using Resources and References to Revise, and have students share their own revisions in small groups.

8 Make sure students understand that revision and editing are two distinct steps in the writing process. Ask a variety of students to state the differences in their own words.

ACTIVITY 1.8 continued

9 At the beginning of the Language and Writer's Craft, distinguish between mood in a story and mood in a sentence.

10 As a class, read the definitions and examples of grammatical moods. Give or ask students for additional examples of each mood. Have students **think-pair-share** their analysis of the excerpt before discussing the mood as a class.

ACTIVITY 1.8 continued

Language and Writer's Craft: Revising and Editing

GRAMMAR & USAGE
Mood
Mood is the form of the verb that shows the mode or manner in which a thought is expressed.

My Notes

- Editing focuses on conventions of standard English. It involves close proofreading and consulting reference sources to correct errors in grammar and usage, capitalization, punctuation, and spelling.
- After drafting a text, students often either revise *or* edit rather than doing both. Skipping either step in the writing process greatly affects the quality of your final draft.

Language and Writer's Craft: Verbs and Mood

Strong writers form and use verbs in the correct **mood**. The list below shows the moods of English verbs. Most of these should be familiar to you because you use them all the time in your writing. Rank the moods 1–5 for your familiarity with each one, with 1 as the most familiar and 5 the least familiar.

Indicative Mood: Verbs that indicate a fact or opinion.

I am too ill to go to school today.

Imperative Mood: Verbs that express a command or request.

Go to school. Please get up and get dressed.

Interrogative Mood: Verbs that ask a question.

Are you going to school? Do you feel ill?

Conditional Mood: Verbs that express something that hasn't happened or something that can happen if a certain condition is met.

I would have gone to school yesterday if I had felt well.

You should ask your teacher about the assignments you missed.

Subjunctive Mood: Verbs that describe a state that is uncertain or contrary to fact. When using the verb "to be" in the subjunctive, always use *were* rather than *was.*

I wish my cold were better today.

If you were to go to school, what would you learn?

7. Look at this excerpt from *A Wrinkle in Time* and identify how the author uses mood in each sentence.

(1) Below them the town was laid out in harsh angular patterns. (2) The houses in the outskirts were all exactly alike, small square boxes painted gray. (3) Each had a small, rectangular plot of lawn in front, with a straight line of dull-looking flowers edging the path to the door. (4) Meg had a feeling that if she could count the flowers there would be exactly the same number for each house. (5) In front of all the houses children were playing.

Sentences 1–3 and 5 are in the indicative mood. Sentence 4 is in the conditional mood.

8. Now look at the verbs in italics in the draft paragraph below. Edit the forms of the verbs that do not match the mood of the sentence in which they appear. Write the correct verb above the incorrect one.

(1) Jera *could look* at the great troll that now blocked her path. (2) It *should have swung* its enormous club through the air almost lazily, though it wasn't yet moving toward her. (3) "What if it *was* to attack?" Jera thought. (4) "I *can make* a plan." (5) She scanned the area immediately around her and looked for a means of escape. (6) "If I *was* to jump across the brook," she thought, "I *can reach* that small cave." (7) She jumped to her left as the club descended toward her.

(1) looked (indicative), (2) swung (indicative), (3) were (subjunctive), (4) should make (conditional), (6) were (subjunctive) and could reach (conditional)

9. Work with the class to create examples for each type of mood:
- **Indicative Mood:**
- **Imperative Mood:**
- **Interrogative Mood:**
- **Conditional Mood:**
- **Subjunctive Mood:**

10. Analyze the author's use of mood in the following excerpt:

"Now, boy," said the general quietly, "*you* are the heart of the army. Think of that. You're the heart of the army. Listen, now."

And, lying there, Joby listened. And the general spoke on.

If he, Joby, beat slow tomorrow, the heart would beat slow in the men. They would lag by the wayside. They would drowse in the fields on their muskets. They would sleep for ever, after that, in those same fields—their hearts slowed by a drummer boy and stopped by enemy lead.

But if he beat a sure, steady, ever faster rhythm, then, then their knees would come up in a long line down over that hill, one knee after the other, like a wave on the ocean shore! Had he seen the ocean ever? Seen the waves rolling in like a well-ordered cavalry charge to the sand? Well, that's what he wanted, that's what was needed! Joby was his right hand and his left. He gave the orders, but Joby set the pace!

Indicative, Imperative: "Listen, now."

Conditional: "If ..." (beginning of third paragraph); "But if..." (beginning of fourth paragraph); sentence ending "... stopped by enemy lead."

Conditional, Interrogative, Indicative: Last sentence of last paragraph

My Notes

ACTIVITY 1.8 continued

11 Have students work individually or in small groups to complete Student Steps 9–11.

Leveled Differentiated Instruction

In this activity, students may need extra support with editing their writing for a variety of verbs in different tenses. Have students answer questions to practice using verbs in different tenses.

Em Help students use the sentence frames to write responses to the following questions. *What did you eat yesterday?* Yesterday I ate ___. *Where were you born?* I was born in ___. *How old were you when you started school?* I was ___ when I started school.

Ex Guide students to write several sentences in the present perfect tense in response to the following questions: *How many times have you exercised so far this week? What is the latest you have ever slept in? What places has your family visited?*

ACTIVITY 1.8 continued

12 Form pairs, and then allow time for students to work collaboratively to edit their hero narrative drafts. They should pay particular attention to the use of correct mood. Remind them to create a new **writer's checklist** specific to conventions before they begin.

13 Ask students to respond to the reflection questions and to briefly share their responses with the class.

▶ASSESS

Circulate to check for understanding of an effective writing group process. As students revise, review their work to determine the quality and effectiveness of their revisions and to provide ideas for deeper revision if necessary. As students edit, review their work to determine the quality and effectiveness of their editing and to provide further ideas for editing if necessary.

▶ADAPT

To support learning, use the **fishbowl** strategy (see page 118) to model the group process before you ask students to work in their own groups. In addition, provide a bank of questions for students to use during the discussion.

If students need more practice with collaborating in writing groups, revising, or editing in order to be successful on the upcoming Embedded Assessment, continue to model effective strategies and build mini-lessons into the final activity.

Language and Writer's Craft: Revising and Editing

My Notes

11. Respond to the following questions:
    - Which verb moods would you use to show something that *might* happen?
      Conditional; subjunctive
    - Which verb mood would you use to state a fact?
      Indicative
    - Which would you use in commands or demands?
      Imperative
    - How does changing the verb mood affect the meaning of your sentence?
      From fact to possibility or uncertainty; from questioning to commanding

Check Your Understanding

It is essential that writers take the time to edit drafts to correct errors in grammar and usage, capitalization, punctuation, and spelling. Return to your draft and self-edit and peer-edit to strengthen the grammar and language conventions in your draft. Be sure to create a new writer's checklist that contains specific areas of concern.

Reflection: Reflect on your experience.

1. How did working with peers help you to revise and edit?
2. How did your revisions and editing strengthen your draft?
3. Did you meet your speaking and listening goals? Why or why not?

The Return

ACTIVITY 1.9

Learning Targets

- Analyze a narrative for archetype and narrative techniques.
- Draft and illustrate the final event in a narrative.

LEARNING STRATEGIES: Marking the Text, Shared Reading, Close Reading, Rereading, Diffusing, Skimming/Scanning, Drafting, Visualizing

The Return

While some stories end once the hero has achieved the Ultimate Boon (the goal he or she set out to achieve), most stories continue into the final stage: The Return.

Preview

In this activity, you wil read another excerpt from *A Wrinkle in Time* and think about the archetype of the Hero's Return.

Setting a Purpose for Reading

- As you read, identify steps in the Hero's Return. Mark the text to indicate evidence of each step. Highlight transitions that indicate sequencing through time.
- Circle unknown words and phrases. Try to determine the meaning of the words by using context clues, word parts, or a dictionary.
- Meg is posed with a riddle in paragraph 3 which she must try and solve. When you read the riddle, make a prediction about the answer and write it in the My Notes section. Revise it as you get more information. You will eventually confirm your prediction later in the passage.

WORD CONNECTIONS

Roots and Affixes

The prefix *re-*, as in *return*, is a very common and useful Latin prefix that means "again" or "back." You can see it in many English words, such as *replay*, *rewrite*, *replace*, *regenerate*, *reproduce*, *recall*, *recreate*, and so on.

My Notes

ACTIVITY 1.9

PLAN

Suggested Pacing: 2 50-minute class periods

TEACH

1 Review the four steps within the last stage, The Return, in order to **activate prior knowledge** and to prepare students for the text.

2 Read the Preview and the Setting a Purpose for Reading sections with your students. Help them understand the literary terms they encounter.

3 **FIRST READ:** Based on the complexity of the passage and your knowledge of your students, you may choose to conduct the first reading in a variety of ways:

- independent reading
- paired reading
- small group reading
- choral reading
- read aloud

TEACHER TO TEACHER

Chunk the text in advance, based on steps and/or stages in the Hero's Journey archetype.

COMMON CORE STATE STANDARDS

Focus Standards:

RL.8.3: Analyze how particular lines of dialogue or incidents in a story or drama propel the action, reveal aspects of a character, or provoke a decision.

W.8.3e: Provide a conclusion that follows from and reflects on the narrated experiences or events.

Additional Standards Addressed:

RL.8.1: RL.8.2; RL.8.4; RL.8.10; W.8.3a; W.8.3b; W.8.3c; W.8.3d; W.8.4; W.8.5; L.8.4b; L.8.6

Text Complexity
Overall: Complex
Lexile: 770L
Qualitative: Moderate Difficulty
Task: Moderate (Analyze)

4 As students are reading, monitor their progress. Be sure they are engaged with the text and annotating words and phrases that show imagery. Evaluate whether the selected reading mode is effective.

5 Based on the observations you made during the first reading, you may want to adjust your reading mode. For example, you may decide for the second reading to read aloud certain complex passages, or you may group students differently.

The Return

My Notes

eerie: spooky; inspiring fear

GRAMMAR & USAGE
Prepositional Phrases

Prepositional phrases add detail in sentences by showing relationships of time, direction, or location. Prepositional phrases function as adjectives or adverbs. Note the examples in Madeleine L'Engle's writing. In paragraph 2, she uses several prepositional phrases to add detail:

"... she was standing breathlessly on her feet on the same hill on which they had first landed on Camazotz."

The first two prepositional phrases are adverbial phrases because they modify the verb *was standing*. The phrase "on which they had first landed on Camazotz" is an adjective phrase modifying the noun *hill*.

In your writing, look for opportunities to add detail with prepositional phrases.

Novel

from A Wrinkle in Time

by Madeleine L'Engle
Excerpt from Chapter 12, "The Foolish and the Weak"

This excerpt comes near the end of Meg Murry's journey. She has found her father and they have escaped Camazotz, but they were forced to leave behind her younger brother Charles Wallace in the grip of the "Black Thing." Now Meg must return to Camazotz to get her brother.

1 Immediately Meg was swept into darkness, into nothingness, and then into the icy devouring cold of the Black Thing. Mrs Which won't let it get me, she thought over and over while the cold of the Black Thing seemed to crunch at her bones.

2 Then they were through it, and she was standing breathlessly on her feet on the same hill on which they had first landed on Camazotz. She was cold and a little numb, but no worse than she had often been in the winter in the country when she had spent an afternoon skating on the pond. She looked around. She was completely alone. Her heart began to pound.

3 Then, seeming to echo from all around her, came Mrs Which's unforgettable voice, "I hhave nnott ggivenn yyou mmyy ggifftt. *Yyou hhave ssomethinngg thatt ITT hhass nnott.* Thiss ssomethinngg iss yyourr onlly wweapponn. Bbutt yyou mmusstt ffinndd itt fforr yyourrssellff." Then the voice ceased, and Meg knew that she was alone.

4 She walked slowly down the hill, her heart thumping painfully against her ribs. There below her was the same row of identical houses they had seen before, and beyond these the linear buildings of the city. She walked along the quiet street. It was dark and the street was deserted. No children playing ball or skipping rope. No mother figures at the doors. No father figures returning from work. In the same window of each house was a light, and as Meg walked down the street all the lights were extinguished simultaneously. Was it because of her presence, or was it simply that it was time for lights out?

5 She felt numb, beyond rage or disappointment or even fear. She put one foot ahead of the other with precise regularity, not allowing her pace to lag. She was not thinking; she was not planning; she was simply walking slowly but steadily toward the city and the domed building where IT lay.

6 Now she approached the outlying buildings of the city. In each of them was a vertical line of light, but it was a **dim**, eerie light, not the warm light of stairways in cities at home. And there were no isolated brightly lit windows where someone was working late, or an office was being cleaned. Out of each building came one man, perhaps a watchman, and each man started walking the width of the building. They appeared not to see her, At any rate they paid no attention to her whatsoever, and she went on past them.

SCAFFOLDING THE TEXT-DEPENDENT QUESTIONS

1. Craft and Structure (RL.8.4) **The word "devouring" is used in paragraph 1. What is the effect of this word choice on the mood of the opening?** "Devour" means to eat hungrily, but how does the addition of contextual diction such as "icy," "cold of the Black thing," and "crunch at her bones" create a mood that doesn't have anything to do with eating?

2. Knowledge and Ideas (RL.8.3) **Why does the author use mathematical terms like "linear" and "vertical" to describe the scene?** How does describing the houses as identical and the streets as deserted contribute to the mood of barrenness and harshness? How is the light of the city described?

3. Key Ideas and Details (RL.8.3) **What can you infer about IT as a character in the novel? Provide textual evidence to support your inferences.** Examine paragraphs 29 to 39 to find what Meg realizes about the pulsing,

7 What have I got that IT hasn't got? she thought suddenly. What have I possibly got?

8 Now she was walking by the tallest of the business buildings. More dim vertical lines of light. The walls glowed slightly to give a faint illumination to the streets. CENTRAL Central Intelligence was ahead of her. Was the man with red eyes still sitting there? Or was he allowed to go to bed? But this was not where she must go, though the man with red eyes seemed the kind old gentleman he claimed to be when compared with IT. But he was no longer of any **consequence** in the search for Charles Wallace. She must go directly to IT.

9 IT isn't used to being resisted. Father said that's how he managed, and how Calvin and I managed as long as we did. Father saved me then. There's nobody here to save me now. I have to do it myself. I have to resist IT by myself. Is that what I have that IT hasn't got? No, I'm sure IT can resist. IT just isn't used to having *other* people resist.

10 CENTRAL Central Intelligence blocked with its huge rectangle the end of the square. She turned to walk around it, and almost **imperceptibly** her steps slowed.

11 It was not far to the great dome which housed IT.

12 I'm going to Charles Wallace. That's what's important. That's what I have to think of. I wish I could feel numb again the way I did at first. Suppose IT has him somewhere else? Suppose he isn't there?

13 I have to go there first, anyhow. That's the only way I can find out.

14 Her steps got slower and slower as she passed the great bronzed doors, the huge slabs of the CENTRAL Central Intelligence building, as she finally saw ahead of her the strange, light, pulsing dome of IT.

15 Father said it was all right for me to be afraid. He said to go ahead and be afraid. And Mrs Who said—I don't understand what she said but I think it was meant to make me not hate being only me, and me being the way I am. And Mrs Whatsit said to remember that she loves me. That's what I have to think about. Not about being afraid. Or not as smart as IT. Mrs Whatsit loves me. That's quite something, to be loved by someone like Mrs Whatsit.

16 She was there.

17 No matter how slowly her feet had taken her at the end, they had taken her there.

18 Directly ahead of her was the circular building, its walls glowing with **violet** flame, its silvery roof pulsing with a light that seemed to Meg to be insane. Again she could feel the light, neither warm nor cold, but reaching out to touch her, pulling her toward IT.

19 There was a sudden sucking, and she was within.

20 It was as though the wind had been knocked out of her. She gasped for breath, for breath in her own rhythm, not the **permeating** pulsing of IT. She could feel the inexorable beat within her body, controlling her heart, her lungs.

consequence: importance

My Notes

imperceptibly: in a manner that is hardly noticeable

violet: a purplish-blue color

permeating: spreading everywhere

WORD CONNECTIONS

Roots and Affixes

In the word *inexorable*, the prefix *in-* means "not." It has the same meaning in *ineffective* and *inexperienced*. The suffix *-able* means "worthy of," as in *debatable* and *laughable*. The root *-exor-* comes from Latin and means "to plead for." Put together, inexorable can be seen to mean "not worthy of pleading for," or in this usage, "unable to be stopped."

"nauseating" power of IT that has her brother trapped in its grip.

4. Key Ideas and Details (RL.8.2) **Throughout the story, how do others assist Meg in her quest to rescue her brother?** Examine paragraph 15 to find the people whose advice is helping her.

5. Craft and Structure (RL.8.4) **What word in paragraph 32 tells you the meaning of the word "loathing"?** Note the entire context: "it was not anger," "it was hatred."

6. Key Ideas and Details (RL.8.1) **What is the power of "The Black Thing," of IT, that Meg must battle against? Choose a line that best expresses IT's power and explain your choice.** Examine paragraph 32 to find a line that shows Meg is being taken in by IT.

7. Knowledge and Ideas (RL.8.2) **How does Meg use the Ultimate Boon to conquer the power of IT?** Examine paragraphs 50 to 53. What does Meg say that brings Charles Wallace back to her?

ACTIVITY 1.9
continued

The Return

nauseating: making feel ill
reiterating: repeating

My Notes

21 But not herself. Not Meg. It did not quite have her.

22 She blinked her eyes rapidly and against the rhythm until the redness before them cleared and she could see. There was the brain, there was IT, lying pulsing and quivering on the dais, soft and exposed and **nauseating**. Charles Wallace was crouched beside IT, his eyes still slowly twirling, his jaw still slack, as she had seen him before, with a **tic** in his forehead **reiterating** the revolting rhythm of IT.

23 As she saw him it was again as though she had been punched in the stomach, for she had to realize afresh that she was seeing Charles, and yet it was not Charles at all. Where was Charles Wallace, her own beloved Charles Wallace?

24 What is it I have got that IT hasn't got?

25 "You have nothing that IT hasn't got," Charles Wallace said coldly. "How nice to have you back, dear sister. We have been waiting for you. We knew that Mrs Whatsit would send you. She is our friend, you know."

26 For an appalling moment Meg believed, and in that moment she felt her brain being gathered up into IT.

27 "No!" she screamed at the top of her lungs. "No! You lie!"

28 For a moment she was free from ITs clutches again.

29 As long as I can stay angry enough IT can't get me.

30 Is that what I have that IT doesn't have?

31 "Nonsense," Charles Wallace said. "You have nothing that IT doesn't have."

32 "You're lying," she replied, and she felt only anger toward this boy who was not Charles Wallace at all. No, it was not anger, it was loathing; it was hatred, sheer and unadulterated, and as she became lost in hatred she also began to be lost in IT. The red miasma swam before her eyes; her stomach churned in ITs rhythm. Her body trembled with the strength of her hatred and the strength of IT.

vestige: a bit or trace of something

33 With the last **vestige** of consciousness she jerked her mind and body. Hate was nothing that IT didn't have. IT knew all about hate.

34 "You are lying about that, and you were lying about Mrs Whatsit!" she screamed.

35 "Mrs Whatsit hates you," Charles Wallace said.

36 And that was where IT made ITs fatal mistake, for as Meg said, automatically, "Mrs Whatsit loves me; that's what she told me, that she loves me," suddenly she knew.

37 She knew!

38 Love.

39 That was what she had that IT did not have.

40 She had Mrs Whatsit's love, and her father's, and her mother's, and the real Charles Wallace's love, and the twins', and Aunt Beast's.

41 And she had her love for them.

WORD CONNECTIONS

Etymology

The word *miasma* appeared in the 1660s as a Modern Latin word meaning "noxious vapors." It derives from the same Greek word that means "stain" or "pollution." Now it is used to mean a poisonous atmosphere.

8. Craft and Structure (RL.8.4) **What is the meaning of the word "animated" in paragraph 50? Cite textual evidence in your response.** Find the importance of the word "thing" in the sentence. Why is this "thing" not Charles Wallace but just an animated version of him?

9. Key Ideas and Details (RL.8.2) **Identify and explain how this section of the story is an example of a stage of The Return in the archetype of the Hero's Journey.** Look back to the Stages of the Hero's Journey on page 15 and apply The Return stage to the action of the excerpt.

© 2017 College Board. All rights reserved.

ACTIVITY 1.9 continued

42 But how could she use it? What was she meant to do?

43 If she could give love to IT perhaps it would shrivel up and die, for she was sure that IT could not withstand love. But she, in all her weakness and foolishness and baseness and nothingness, was incapable of loving IT. Perhaps it was not too much to ask of her, but she could not do it.

44 But she could love Charles Wallace.

45 She could stand there and she could love Charles Wallace.

46 Her own Charles Wallace, the real Charles Wallace, the child for whom she had come back to Camazotz, to IT, the baby who was so much more than she was, and who was yet so utterly **vulnerable**.

47 She could love Charles Wallace.

48 Charles. Charles, I love you. My baby brother who always takes care of me. Come back to me, Charles Wallace, come away from IT, come back, come home. I love you, Charles. Oh, Charles Wallace, I love you.

49 Tears were streaming down her cheeks, but she was unaware of them.

50 Now she was even able to look at him, at this animated thing that was not her own Charles Wallace at all. She was able to look and love.

51 I love you. Charles Wallace, you are my darling and my dear and the light of my life and the treasure of my heart, I love you. I love you. I love you.

52 Slowly his mouth closed. Slowly his eyes stopped their twirling. The tic in the forehead ceased its revolting twitch. Slowly he advanced toward her.

53 "I love you!" she cried. "I love you, Charles! I love you!"

54 Then suddenly he was running, pelting, he was in her arms, he was shrieking with sobs. "Meg! Meg! Meg!"

55 "I love you, Charles!" she cried again, her sobs almost as loud as his, her tears mingling with his. "I love you! I love you! I love you!"

56 A whirl of darkness. An icy cold blast. An angry, resentful howl that seemed to tear through her. Darkness again. Through the darkness to save her came a sense of Mrs Whatsit's presence, so that she knew it could not be IT who now had her in its clutches.

57 And then the feel of earth beneath her, of something in her arms, and she was rolling over on the sweet-smelling **autumnal** earth, and Charles Wallace was crying out, "Meg! Oh, Meg!"

58 Now she was hugging him close to her, and his little arms were clasped tightly about her neck. "Meg, you saved me! You saved me!" he said over and over.

59 "Meg!" came a call, and there were her father and Calvin hurrying through the darkness toward them.

60 Still holding Charles she struggled to stand up and look around. "Father! Cal! Where are we?"

My Notes

vulnerable: susceptible to danger

autumnal: related to autumn

The Return

contagious: passed from one person to another
gravely: seriously

My Notes

61 Charles Wallace, holding her hand tightly, was looking around, too, and suddenly he laughed, his own, sweet, **contagious** laugh. "In the twins' vegetable garden! And we landed in the broccoli!"

62 Meg began to laugh, too, at the same time that she was trying to hug her father, to hug Calvin, and not to let go of Charles Wallace for one second.

63 "Meg, you did it!" Calvin shouted. "You saved Charles!"

64 "I'm very proud of you, my daughter." Mr. Murry kissed her **gravely**, then turned toward the house. "Now I must go in to Mother." Meg could tell that he was trying to control his anxiety and eagerness.

65 "Look!" she pointed to the house, and there were the twins and Mrs. Murry walking toward them through the long, wet grass.

66 "First thing tomorrow I must get some new glasses," Mr. Murry said, squinting in the moonlight, and then starting to run toward his wife.

67 Dennys's voice came crossly over the lawn. "Hey, Meg, it's bedtime."

68 Sandy suddenly yelled, "Father!"

69 Mr. Murry was running across the lawn, Mrs. Murry running toward him, and they were in each other's arms, and then there was a tremendous happy jumble of arms and legs and hugging, the older Murrys and Meg and Charles Wallace and the twins, and Calvin grinning by them until Meg reached out and pulled him in and Mrs. Murry gave him a special hug all of his own. They were talking and laughing all at once, when they were startled by a crash, and Fortinbras, who could bear being left out of the happiness not one second longer, catapulted his sleek black body right through the screened door to the kitchen. He dashed across the lawn to join in the joy, and almost knocked them all over with the exuberance of his greeting.

70 Meg knew all at once that Mrs Whatsit, Mrs Who, and Mrs Which must be near, because all through her she felt a flooding of joy and of love that was even greater and deeper than the joy and love which were already there.

71 She stopped laughing and listened, and Charles listened, too. "Hush."

72 Then there was a whirring, and Mrs Whatsit, Mrs Who, and Mrs Which were standing in front of them, and the joy and love were so tangible that Meg felt that if she only knew where to reach she could touch it with her bare hands.

73 Mrs Whatsit said breathlessly, "Oh, my darlings, I'm sorry we don't have time to say good-by to you properly. You see, we have to—"

74 But they never learned what it was that Mrs Whatsit, Mrs Who, and Mrs Which had to do, for there was a gust of wind, and they were gone.

WORD CONNECTIONS

Cognates

The English word *tangible* is spelled the same as, but pronounced differently than, its Spanish cognate with the same meaning. The Spanish word *catapultar* is a cognate of the English verb *catapult*.

Second Read

- Reread the excerpt to answer these text-dependent questions.
- Write any additional questions you have about the text in your Reader/Writer Notebook.

1. **Craft and Structure:** The word "devouring" is used in paragraph 1. What is the effect of this word choice on the mood of the opening?

   The effect of using "devouring" is to create a violent, destructive mood of eerie danger. RL.8.4

2. **Knowledge and Ideas:** Why does the author use mathematical terms like "linear" and "vertical" to describe the scene?

   Mathematical terms indicate precision and angularity and create harsh outlines. This diction vividly describes how uniform, barren, and organized the city is. RL.8.3

3. **Key Ideas and Details:** What can you infer about IT as a character in the novel? Provide textual evidence to support your inferences.

   IT as a character is a powerful force that feeds on anger and hatred and is conquered by love. IT has trapped someone Meg loves with the force of hatred: "Charles Wallace was crouched beside IT, his eyes still slowly twirling, his jaw still slack..." RL.8.3

4. **Key Ideas and Details:** Throughout the story, how do others assist Meg in her quest to rescue her brother?

   Meg's father helps by telling her it is okay to be afraid. Mrs Whatsit reminds Meg that she is loved. This help gives her confidence to attempt the rescue of her brother. RL.8.2

5. **Craft and Structure:** What word in paragraph 32 tells you the meaning of the word "loathing"?

   hatred RL.8.4

6. **Key Ideas and Details:** What is the power of "the Black Thing," of IT, that Meg must battle against? Choose a line that best expresses IT's power and explain your choice.

   The power of IT is hate, fear, and loathing. "As she became lost in hatred she also began to be lost in IT." RL.8.1

My Notes

ACTIVITY 1.9 continued

6 **SECOND READ:** During the second reading, students will be returning to the text to answer the text-dependent comprehension questions. You may choose to have students reread and work on the questions in a variety of ways:

- independently
- in pairs
- in small groups
- together as a class

7 Have students answer the text-dependent questions. If they have difficulty, scaffold the questions by rephrasing them or breaking them down into smaller parts. See the Scaffolding the Text-Dependent Questions boxes for suggestions.

TEACHER TO TEACHER

You may want to revisit the graphic organizer in Activity 1.5 to reread the steps and explanation for each step of the Return. Ask students to provide specific textual evidence of how this excerpt illustrates these steps.

8 Form pairs and ask students to complete the Working from the Text questions about the author's technique (Student Steps 10–12). Tell students that because of the difficulty of the questions, they will need to **skim/scan** parts of the text before forming a response.

9 As a class, ask students to share their responses in order to determine their level of understanding. Provide additional clarification and instruction when necessary.

The Return

My Notes

7. **Knowledge and Ideas:** How does Meg use "the Ultimate Boon" to conquer the power of IT?

   Meg realizes that "the Ultimate Boon is love. She uses this gift from Mrs Whatsit to challenge the power of IT and pull Charles Wallace out of ITs grip by telling him, "I love you! I love you! I love you!" RL.8.2

8. **Craft and Structure:** What is the meaning of the word "animated" in paragraph 50? Cite textual evidence in your response.

   Animated here means to have the appearance of being alive. Charles Wallace is described as having twirling eyes and a slack jaw, and in paragraph 23 as "not being Charles at all." RL.8.4

9. **Knowledge and Ideas:** Identify and explain how this section of the story is an example of a stage of The Return in the archetype of the Hero's Journey.

   The story has elements of The Return stage because it includes the Magic Flight when Meg must return to rescue her brother. It also embodies the Rescue from Without when she is reminded by Mrs Whatsit's comment of the power of love, and finally The Crossing is represented when Meg returns to her family with her brother and rediscovers the power of love in her family. RL.8.2

Working from the Text

10. What steps in The Return stage are illustrated in this section of the novel *A Wrinkle in Time*?

    Magic Flight: Meg must return for Charles Wallace.
    Rescue from Without: When Meg is reminded of the power of love, she uses it to rescue Charles Wallace.
    The Crossing: Meg rediscovers love for and within her family.

11. Quote examples of Meg's dialogue and internal thoughts (reflections) that show her anxiety and fear about the task she has to do.

    "What have I got that IT hasn't got?"
    "Mrs Whatsit loves me."

12. What does Meg learn during her attempt to conquer the challenge?

    Meg learns that hatred and loathing are not sources of strength; love is a source of strength.

ACTIVITY 1.9
continued

Narrative Writing Prompt

Revisit your hero narrative. What might your hero learn by the end of the Return Stage in his or her journey? Draft an ending to your narrative using your understanding of the Crossing/Return Threshold to guide your development. Add at least two frames of visuals to support your narrative. Be sure to:

- Use narrative techniques such as dialogue, pacing, and description to communicate ideas.
- Use connotative diction and imagery for effect.
- Sequence the event logically and naturally (with the beginning and middle).
- Visualize the theme or major idea of your journey story. Use visual techniques for effect. Challenge yourself to use two frames to communicate one theme.

Check Your Understanding

Revise your draft by adding transitions to strengthen organization and convey sequence, signal shifts, and show the relationships among experiences and events. How does the use of transitions strengthen your writing?

Independent Reading Checkpoint

What accomplishments did the protagonist in your independent reading text achieve? What vivid language did the author use to describe these accomplishments? Explain why you think these accomplishments do or do not make this character a hero.

My Notes

ACTIVITY 1.9 continued

10 Have students independently complete the writing prompt draft and the illustration. Remind students that they can use any or all of this work in Embedded Assessment 1. Check for understanding by having students revise their drafts.

ASSESS

Review student work to determine the quality of the narrative and the visual, and to select student models to share with the class.

ADAPT

At this point, students should feel confident in their ability to create an illustrated narrative about a hero. If students demonstrate emerging skills or express confusion, take the time to provide additional models and/or mini-lessons.

Leveled Differentiated Instruction

In this activity, have students create a bank of additional transitions to add to their writing.

Em Help students review their bank of transitions to be sure it includes everyday words and phrases such as *at the end, next.*

Ex Guide students to review their bank of transitions to be sure it includes a variety of words and phrases such as *for example, as a result, on the other hand.*

Br Have students review their bank of transitions to be sure it includes an increasing variety of words and phrases such as *for instance, in addition, consequently.*

INDEPENDENT READING CHECKPOINT

Have students complete the Independent Reading Checkpoint.

EMBEDDED ASSESSMENT 1

Suggested Pacing: 3 50-minute class periods (depending on homework)

TEACHER TO TEACHER

If students have access to computers, small groups of students might try using a wiki or a tool such as Google Docs to create a collaborative story. With these programs you can keep track of students' contributions, which creates accountability and encourages group collaboration.

The oral presentation of this assignment can be accomplished by presenting to small groups rather than the whole class. You can also have students display their narratives and deliver an oral summary in a carousel fashion.

1 Planning and Prewriting: Consider suggesting the outline of the Hero's Journey or a Freytag model as the basis of an outline. Also, discuss with students the idea of reordering the sequence of events in a story so that they might start at the end and then use a flashback to recount the events.

2 Drafting: Try to determine what narrative elements students will have the hardest time with and offer more support in those areas. Be sure students understand the importance of a well-crafted resolution or conclusion to the story.

3 Evaluating and Revising the Draft: You might allow members of writing groups to support each other during the process of drafting and/or revising their stories. If so, the meeting should be short and focused on discussing one element, such as the main conflict or an effective resolution or conclusion to their story.

4 Checking and Editing: Proofreading and editing are especially appropriate for a writing group activity. Not only can students use writing processing tools, they can remind each other about spelling, grammatical mood, and transitions.

Reflection: After students have completed this task, remind them to respond to the reflection questions.

EMBEDDED ASSESSMENT 1

Writing a Hero's Journey Narrative

My Notes

Technology TIP:

Avoid using images in a way that would violate copyright law. You may download or copy an image for personal use and provide the source, but you may not broadcast the image without the owner's permission.

Assignment

Think about all the heroes you have encountered in fiction and real life. What type of hero appeals to you? Write and create an illustrated narrative about an original hero. Use the Hero's Journey archetype to develop and structure your ideas. Orally present your narrative to your classmates.

Planning and Prewriting: Take time to make a plan for your narrative.

- What characteristics will your hero possess and what setting will you choose?
- What are the essential elements of a narrative that you will need to include?
- What prewriting strategies will you use to plan the organization?

Drafting: Create a draft that includes the elements of an effective narrative.

- How will you introduce characters, context, and setting and establish a point of view?
- How will you use dialogue, details, and description to create an original, believable hero?
- How will you sequence events logically and naturally using steps of the Hero's Journey archetype?
- How will you provide a conclusion or resolution that follows from and reflects on the events of the narrative?
- How will you find or create illustrations to capture key imagery, emphasize ideas, or add interest?

Evaluating and Revising: Create opportunities to review and revise your work.

- When will you share your work with your writing group?
- What is your plan to incorporate suggestions and ideas for revisions into your draft?
- How can you improve connotative diction and imagery to create tone and mood?
- How can the Scoring Guide help you evaluate how well your draft meets the requirements of the assignment?

Checking and Editing: Confirm that your final draft is ready for publication.

- How will you proofread and edit your draft to demonstrate command of the conventions of standard English capitalization, punctuation, spelling, grammar, and usage?
- How will you create a title and assemble your illustrations in an appealing manner?
- How will you prepare a final draft for publication and presentation?

Reflection

After completing this Embedded Assessment, think about how you went about accomplishing this task, and respond to the following:

- How did your understanding of the Hero's Journey archetype help you create an original narrative?

COMMON CORE STATE STANDARDS

Focus Standards:

W.8.3a: Engage and orient the reader by establishing a context and point of view and introducing a narrator and/or characters; organize an event sequence that unfolds naturally and logically.

W.8.3b: Use narrative techniques, such as dialogue, pacing, and description, and reflection, to develop experiences, events, and/or characters.

W.8.3c: Use a variety of transition words, phrases, and clauses to convey sequence, signal shifts from one time frame or setting to another, and show the relationships among experiences and events.

W.8.3d: Use precise words and phrases, relevant descriptive details, and sensory language to capture the action and convey experiences and events.

W.8.3e: Provide a conclusion that follows from and reflects on the narrated experiences or events.

Writing a Hero's Journey Narrative

EMBEDDED ASSESSMENT 1

SCORING GUIDE

Scoring Criteria	Exemplary	Proficient	Emerging	Incomplete
Ideas	The narrative • creates a complex, original protagonist • establishes a clear point of view, setting, and conflict • uses precise and engaging details, dialogue, imagery and description • includes a variety of enhancing visuals.	The narrative • creates a believable, original protagonist • establishes point of view, setting, and conflict • uses adequate details, dialogue, imagery, and description • includes sufficient visuals.	The narrative • creates an unoriginal or undeveloped protagonist • establishes a weak point of view, setting, or conflict • uses inadequate narrative techniques • includes insufficient, unrelated, or inappropriate visuals.	The narrative • lacks a protagonist • does not establish point of view, setting, or conflict • uses minimal narrative techniques • includes few or no visuals.
Structure	The narrative • engages and orients the reader with detailed exposition • sequences events in the plot effectively, including a variety of steps from the Hero's Journey archetype • uses a variety of transitional strategies effectively and purposefully • provides a thoughtful resolution.	The narrative • orients the reader with adequate exposition • sequences events in the plot logically, including some steps of the Hero's Journey archetype • uses transitional words, phrases, and clauses to link events and signal shifts • provides a logical resolution.	The narrative • provides weak or vague exposition • sequences events unevenly, including minimal or unclear steps of the Hero's Journey archetype • uses inconsistent, repetitive, or basic transitional words, phrases, and clauses • provides a weak or disconnected resolution.	The narrative • lacks exposition • has minimal plot with no apparent connection to the Hero's Journey archetype • uses few or no transitional strategies • lacks a resolution.
Use of Language	The narrative • is presented using effective volume, clarity and eye contact. • demonstrates command of the conventions of standard English capitalization, punctuation, spelling, grammar, and usage (including appropriate use of a variety of moods).	The narrative • is presented using appropriate volume, pronunciation, and eye contact. • demonstrates adequate command of the conventions of standard English capitalization, punctuation, spelling, grammar, and usage (including appropriate use of moods).	The narrative • is presented with some attention to eye contact, volume, and pace of delivery. • demonstrates partial or inconsistent command of the conventions of standard English capitalization, punctuation, spelling, grammar, and usage.	The narrative • is presented with little attention to eye contact, volume and pacing. • lacks command of the conventions of standard English capitalization, punctuation, spelling, grammar, and usage; frequent errors obscure meaning.

COMMON CORE STATE STANDARDS

SL.8.4a: Plan and present a narrative that establishes a context and point of view, presents a logical sequence, uses narrative techniques (e.g., dialogue, pacing, description, sensory language), uses a variety of transitions, and provides a conclusion that reflects the experience.

Additional Standards Addressed:
W.8.4; W.8.5; W.8.6; W.8.10; L.8.1c; L.8.2c

EMBEDDED ASSESSMENT 1 continued

This is an opportunity to ask students to be reflective about their learning and academic growth.

Portfolio During the course of this first unit of Grade 8, you have had your students create and keep their work. Creating and keeping the Embedded Assessments is part of a process that helps you and your students measure their academic growth over time. By looking back on previous work and forward to setting learning goals for the future, students can take more control over their learning and determine what works best for them to meet learning expectations.

This is an opportunity for students to reflect on their cognitive skills. You'll notice that the questions ask them to think about their work on the Embedded Assessment, what worked for them, and what they would change for future work.

If you have been asking students to keep work in a folder, now is the time to create a more permanent place for students to keep their work. A three-ring binder can work, as can hanging folders in milk crates. However you decide to do this, you will want to divide student work by unit and Embedded Assessment. Since this is the first Embedded Assessment of the year, you might ask students to collect and organize all their work by creating a table of contents for each activity that scaffolded the Embedded Assessment.

You can require students to keep all work for now, and then after the second Embedded Assessment, you might ask them to cull their work and choose the work they think best represents growth in skills and knowledge.

SCORING GUIDE

When you score this Embedded Assessment, you may wish to download and print copies of the Scoring Guide from SpringBoard Digital. In this way you can have a copy to mark for each student's work.

To identify additional areas where your English learners could use additional support, see the English Language Development Rubric for Embedded Assessment 1 on page 98a.

ACTIVITY 1.10

▶PLAN

Suggested Pacing: 1 50-minute class period

▶TEACH

1 Read Making Connections as an introduction to the major goals of the unit. Help students see how their understanding will progress during the unit from the traditional depiction of a hero in myths and tales to a more fully realized conception of a hero.

2 The answer to Essential Question 1, "What defines a hero?" should begin the discussion of the definition. You might ask students to list preliminary ideas, such as adjectives or phrases that come to mind.

3 Have students re-sort the Academic Vocabulary and Literary Terms from the first half of the unit and then answer the reflection questions based on their sort.

4 Facilitate a close reading of the Embedded Assessment 2 assignment. Unpacking this Embedded Assessment will bring up some new vocabulary that will need to be discussed, such as *negation* and *function*. These terms will be explained in detail later, but it would be helpful to acknowledge them now.

5 For unpacking, use a **graphic organizer** similar to the one used for Embedded Assessment 1 to help students understand the process of identifying the skills and knowledge they will need for Embedded Assessment 2.

6 You may consider doing a close reading of the Scoring Guide criteria, focusing on the "Proficient" column. Instruct students to mark the text by underlining or highlighting key skills (verbs) and knowledge (nouns).

ACTIVITY 1.10

Previewing Embedded Assessment 2 and the Definition Essay

LEARNING STRATEGIES: QHT, Close Reading, Paraphrasing, Graphic Organizer

My Notes

ACADEMIC VOCABULARY
It is important to be precise and **concise** in writing and speaking. To be **concise** is to be brief and to the point. **Conciseness** is expressing a great deal in just a few words.

Learning Targets

- Reflect on previous learning and make connections to new learning.
- Identify and analyze the skills and knowledge necessary to be successful in completing Embedded Assessment 2.

Making Connections

In the first part of this unit you learned about the archetype of the Hero's Journey, and you wrote your own illustrated narrative depicting a protagonist who makes a heroic journey. In this half of the unit you will continue thinking about heroism and what makes a hero; your work will culminate in an essay in which you create your definition of a hero.

Essential Questions

Reflect on your understanding of Essential Question 1: How has your understanding of the Hero's Journey changed over the course of this unit? Then, respond to Essential Question 2, which will be the focus of the rest of the unit: How does the Hero's Journey archetype appear in stories throughout time?

Developing Vocabulary

Re-sort the vocabulary from the first half of the unit, using the QHT strategy. Compare the new sort with your original sort. How has your understanding changed? Select one word and write a **concise** statement about how your understanding of the word has changed over the course of this unit.

Unpacking Embedded Assessment 2

Read the assignment for Embedded Assessment 2 closely to identify and analyze the components of the assignment.

> Think about people who deserve status as a hero from the past, from the present, from life, and from literature. What defines a hero? Write a multi-paragraph essay that develops your definition of heroism. Be sure to use strategies of definition (function, example, and negation) to guide your writing.

Using the assignment and the Scoring Guide, work with your class to analyze the prompt and create a graphic organizer to use as a visual reminder of the required concepts (what you need to know) and skills (what you need to do). Copy the graphic organizer in your Reader/Writer Notebook.

After each activity, use this graphic to guide reflection about what you have learned and what you still need to learn in order to be successful on the Embedded Assessment.

COMMON CORE STATE STANDARDS

Focus Standard:

L.8.6: Acquire and use accurately grade-appropriate general academic and domain-specific words and phrases; gather vocabulary knowledge when considering a word or phrase important to comprehension or expression.

Additional Standards Addressed:

RI.8.10

Preparing for Expository Writing

1. How are expository and narrative writing similar? How are they different? List ideas below, and then create a graphic organizer on separate paper to show your thinking.

Similarities	Differences

My Notes

Preparing for Expository Writing

2. You are often asked to define vocabulary terms and to explain your understanding of what something means. Abstract concepts, such as heroism, can also be defined. Practice thinking about how to define an abstract concept by working in a small group or with a partner to develop a list of words that describe each of the concepts below.
   - freedom
   - responsibility
   - sacrifice
   - friendship

3. Next, working with the same partner or group, choose one of the concepts above and write a short paragraph that defines and explains the concept.

INDEPENDENT READING LINK

Read and Research

Continue your exploration of the *heroes* theme by choosing a fiction or nonfiction text about a historical or modern hero for your independent reading.

Research the author of the text to find out why they might have chosen to write about this particular hero.

ACTIVITY 1.10 continued

7 Use the Scoring Guides for Embedded Assessment 1 and Embedded Assessment 2 to compare and contrast the two writing modes. It is important that students understand that their learning in the first half of the unit applies to the second half.

8 Help students become more familiar with defining concepts by having them work individually, in pairs, or in small groups to brainstorm words that describe the concepts listed. Other concepts that you might give students are *achievement*, *success*, and *justice*.

9 Next, have the same partners or groups choose one of the concepts and draft a short paragraph that defines and explains their thinking about it.

10 Guide students in the selection of a new independent reading text.

ACTIVITY 1.11

▶PLAN

Materials: index cards for Word Wall, dictionaries
Suggested Pacing: 1 50-minute class period

▶TEACH

1 As students read the opening sections, have them highlight or underline key terms. After the class reads the definition of each term in the Literary Terms box, ask a student volunteer to make and display a Word Wall card. Each word should be placed in a way that shows the relationship between words. For example, diction is used to create tone, so the *diction* card should be placed on top of or to the left of *tone*. *Denotation* and *connotation* define *diction*, so those words should be stacked and placed on top of or to the left of *diction*. Be sure students understand how connotation can evoke certain feelings that determine tone.

2 Check for understanding by asking students to respond to and discuss the questions that follow. Use the **Think-Write-Pair-Share** strategy to ensure that all students are thinking through the questions. This strategy is an extension of Think-Pair-Share that asks students to write before they pair and share ideas.

3 For Student Step 4, explain that in the past, students have probably used a word like *angry* to describe tone. While it is true that a speaker may be angry, there are many levels of *angry*, so this word does not precisely describe how the speaker feels. The synonyms in the list on the following page give much more precise and accurate descriptions.

ACTIVITY 1.11

The Nuance of Tone

LEARNING STRATEGIES: Note-taking, Graphic Organizer, Discussion Groups

Literary Terms

Tone is a writer's or speaker's attitude toward a subject.
Diction is a writer's or speaker's choice of words.
Denotation is the direct meaning of a word or expression, as distinguished from the ideas or meanings associated with it or suggested by it.
Connotation is the implied associations, meanings, or emotions associated with a word.

ACADEMIC VOCABULARY
Nuance refers to a subtle difference or distinction in meaning.

My Notes

Learning Target

- Explain how nuances in tone words arise from connotation.

Understanding Tone

In literature, being able to recognize the **tone** of a story or poem or essay is an important skill in understanding the author's purpose. An author who is trying to create a comedy skit needs to choose content and language that communicates humor rather than sadness. Writers purposefully select diction to create an appropriate tone.

1. What is the connection between **tone** and **diction**? Many words have a similar **denotation**, but one must learn to distinguish among the **connotations** of these words in order to accurately identify meaning and tone. Careful readers and writers understand **nuances** (subtle differences) in word meanings. This means that they recognize that words have varying levels of meaning.

   Examples: *house*, *home*, *abode*, *estate*, *shack*, *mansion*, and *hut* all describe or **denotate** a place to live, but each has a different **connotation** that determines meaning and tone.

2. Create examples like the one above illustrating ranges of words that have the same denotation but different connotations. Independently, write your examples below, and then pair with another student to share your words.

   Examples:
   walk, saunter, skulk, slither, march, prance, stomp
   talk, argue, converse, interrogate, gossip, whisper

3. Use one of the examples you just created to discuss how connotation connects to tone.

   Readers have certain associations with the word *gossip* as opposed to *argue*, or *walk* as opposed to *stomp*. Choosing one word over another implies a certain feeling or attitude by a writer.

Identifying Nuances in Diction

4. On the following page are some common tone words and their **synonyms**. Use a dictionary to determine or clarify each synonym's precise meaning. After taking notes on the denotation of each word, number the words to indicate the various levels of meaning, from least intense to most intense (1 = least intense). If your group feels that two words have the same connotation and level of meaning, give them the same ranking.

COMMON CORE STATE STANDARDS

Focus Standards:

L.8.5b: Use the relationship between particular words to better understand each of the words.

L.8.5c: Distinguish among the connotations (associations) of words with similar denotations (definitions) (e.g., bullheaded, willful, firm, persistent, resolute).

Additional Standards Addressed:

SL.8.4; SL.8.6; L.8.4c; L.8.4d; L.8.6

© 2017 College Board. All rights reserved.

Angry: upset, enraged, irritated, sharp, vexed, livid, infuriated, incensed
Happy: mirthful, joyful, jovial, ecstatic, light-hearted, exultant, jubilant, giddy
Sad: poignant, despondent, sentimental, lugubrious, morose, woeful, mournful, desolate
Honest: sincere, candid, outspoken, forthright, frank, unbiased, blunt
Calm: placid, still, bored, composed, peaceful, tranquil, serene, soothing
Nervous: anxious, apprehensive, hesitant, fretful, agitated, jittery, afraid
Smart: wise, perceptive, quick-witted, clever, sagacious, intellectual, brainy, bright, sharp

My Notes

5. Prepare to present your findings to the class. Use the outline below to prepare for your presentation.

Our group studied words that have the same denotation as ____________.
The most intense word is ____________, which means ____________.
One would feel ____________ if / when ____________ [specific situation].
The least intense word is ____________, which means ____________.
One would feel ____________ if / when ____________ [specific situation].
Our favorite word is ____________, which means ____________.
One would feel ____________ if / when ____________ [specific situation].

6. While other groups present, listen to comprehend, and take notes. You will be responsible for applying this vocabulary in future activities.

Check Your Understanding

Which words would you use to describe the protagonist of the story you wrote? Which words would be appropriate to define a hero?

ACTIVITY 1.11 continued

4 Model the process of working with nuances by using a **Think Aloud** to show students how to distinguish between the nuances of meaning surrounding the synonyms for *angry*.

5 Form small groups, and assign one of the six remaining tone words to each group. As students work, circulate to check for understanding and to clarify confusion.

6 Have groups use the template to prepare a brief presentation on their word and synonyms, and then have each group present to the class. Use the list of tone words to guide the order of presentations.

7 After the presentations, ask students to identify a pair of antonyms that share the same level of intensity. For example, *despondent* and *ecstatic* are both fairly intense opposites for *serene* and *agitated*. You might also have students use the words they have learned to describe a hero or the protagonist of the story they wrote.

ASSESS

During the presentations, listen for accuracy and ask questions to check for understanding. Make sure that students are recording information during others' presentations.

ADAPT

To support struggling students, reduce the list of synonyms to three for each tone word (least intense, most intense, and one in the middle). You could also turn the activity into a manipulative exercise by asking groups to create a Word Wall card for each synonym before they begin sorting the words.

To extend learning, ask students to find their own tone word and synonyms.

As an alternative to presentations, students can also work through all the words in pairs or small groups and use the template as an exit slip.

ACTIVITY 1.12

▶PLAN

Materials: sentence strips, dictionaries

Suggested Pacing: 2 50-minute class periods

▶TEACH

1 With students, read the Preview and the introduction to the **TP-CASTT** strategy.

2 Use the "Strategy" column of the graphic organizer that begins on page 64 to review the elements of **TP-CASTT**. Check for understanding, and clarify if there is any confusion.

3 Read the title of the poem "A Man" aloud. Ask students to **predict** what the poem will be about and record it on the **TP-CASTT** chart.

4 **FIRST READ:** Based on the complexity of the passage and your knowledge of your students, you may choose to conduct the first reading in a variety of ways:

- independent reading
- paired reading
- small group reading
- choral reading
- read aloud

ACTIVITY 1.12

Physical and Emotional Challenges

LEARNING STRATEGIES: TP-CASTT, Diffusing, Rereading, Paraphrasing, Summarizing, Close Reading, Marking the Text, Free Writing

My Notes

Learning Targets

- Analyze and compare the structure of a literary and an informational text on similar subjects.
- Make thematic connections relating to heroism in a written response.

Preview

In this activity, you will read a poem and an informational text on similar subjects and compare them.

Introducing the Strategy: TP-CASTT

This reading strategy is used to analyze a poetic text by identifying and discussing each topic in the acronym: *Title*, *Paraphrase*, *Connotation*, *Attitude*, *Shift*, *Theme*, and *Title* again. The strategy is a guide designed to lead you in an analysis of a literary text. It is most effective if you begin at the top and work your way down the elements. However, you will find that as you study one element, you will naturally begin to explore others. For example, a study of *connotation* often leads to a discussion of ***tone*** and *shifts*. Revisiting the *title* often leads to a discussion of the *theme*.

Setting a Purpose for Reading

- As you read, connect this poem to the ideas of challenge, the Hero's Journey, and heroism. Put an exclamation mark next to phrases, stanzas, or paragraphs that remind you of these ideas.
- Circle unknown words and phrases. Try to determine the meaning of the words by using context clues, word parts, or a dictionary.

ABOUT THE AUTHOR

Nina Cassian was born in Romania in 1924 and now lives in New York City. She has written more than 50 volumes of work, including poetry, fiction, and books for children. Cassian is also a journalist, film critic, and composer of classical music.

Poetry

A Man

by Nina Cassian

While fighting for his country, he lost an arm
And was suddenly afraid:
"From now on, I shall only be able to do things by halves.
I shall reap half a harvest.

COMMON CORE STATE STANDARDS

Focus Standards:

RL.8.2: Determine a theme or central idea of a text and analyze its development over the course of the text, including its relationship to the characters, setting, and plot; provide an objective summary of the text.

RL.8.5: Compare and contrast the structure of two or more texts and analyze how the differing structure of each text contributes to its meaning and style.

Additional Standards Addressed:

RL.8.3; RL.8.4; RL.8.10; RI.8.1; RI.8.3; RI.8.4; RI.8.5; RI.8.6; RI.8.10; W.8.10; L.8.4a; L.8.5a; L.8.6

I shall be able to play either the tune
or the accompaniment on the piano,
but never both parts together.
I shall be able to bang with only one fist
on doors, and worst of all
I shall only be able to half hold
my love close to me.
There will be things I cannot do at all,
applaud for example,
at shows where everyone applauds."
From that moment on, he set himself to do
everything with twice as much enthusiasm.
And where the arm had been torn away
a wing grew.

Second Read

- Reread the poem to answer these text-dependent questions.
- Write any additional questions you have about the text in your Reader/Writer Notebook.

1. **Key Ideas and Details:** What kinds of things is the man afraid of not being able to do? What do these worries tell you about his character?

The man is afraid that without an arm he can only do things by halves: half a harvest, half a tune on the piano, only half hold his love. Moreover he is afraid because there are things he cannot do at all: applaud. The man wants to be able to embrace the world entirely despite his loss of an arm. RL.8.2

2. **Craft and Structure:** Is the last sentence of this poem meant to be understood literally or figuratively? How does the connotation of "wing" help create the mood of the poem?

The "wing" in the last stanza is not literal; it is metaphorical. Wings have the connotation of flight and of rising above one's circumstances and challenges. RL.8.4

Working from the Text

3. Use the TP-CASTT strategy to analyze the poem. Record your responses in the graphic organizer that follows. Read the poem several times, each time discussing aspects of the TP-CASTT strategy and recording your responses.

My Notes

ACTIVITY 1.12 continued

5 As students are reading, monitor their progress. Be sure they are engaged with the text and connecting it to the bigger ideas of the unit. Evaluate whether the selected reading mode is effective.

6 Based on the observations you made during the first reading, you may want to adjust your reading mode. For example, you may decide for the second reading to read aloud certain complex passages, or you may group students differently.

7 **SECOND READ:** During the second reading, students will be returning to the text to answer the text-dependent comprehension questions. You may choose to have students reread and work on the questions in a variety of ways:

- independently
- in pairs
- in small groups
- together as a class

8 Have students answer the text-dependent questions. If they have difficulty, scaffold the questions by rephrasing them or breaking them down into smaller parts. See the Scaffolding the Text-Dependent Questions boxes for suggestions.

SCAFFOLDING THE TEXT-DEPENDENT QUESTIONS

1. Key Ideas and Details (RL.8.2) **What kinds of things is the man afraid of not being able to do? What do these worries tell you about his character?** Examine the lines in quotation marks. What are his worries?

2. Craft and Structure (RL.8.4) **Is the last sentence of this poem meant to be understood literally or figuratively? How does the connotation of "wing" help create the mood of the poem?** Are wings usually a hopeful thing or a despairing thing? When does the man grow a wing? Does the man grow a wing before or after he decides to be positive?

9 Continue to lead students through the elements of the **TP-CASTT** strategy. Discuss each element and have students contribute ideas to the analysis. Students should **mark/annotate** the text and **take notes** throughout the discussion. As you discuss the author's attitude, challenge students to apply their knowledge of nuances of tone words. Remember that the responses in the graphic organizer are suggested possible responses. Students may think of alternate, and equally valid, responses. It is more important to students to struggle and discuss than to think that there is one correct answer.

Physical and Emotional Challenges

Strategy	Response / Analysis
Title: Think about the title before reading the text to predict what it will be about.	**Prediction:** This poem will be about a man who might represent Everyman, all men, ordinary people. Note the difference between "A" and "the."
Paraphrase: After diffusing the text, translate the most challenging lines of the poem into your own words (you may need to reread the text several times). Then briefly summarize the poem.	**Poem Summary:** A man has lost an arm during a war. He is afraid the quality of his life will be cut in half from now on, but he resolves to work twice as hard to make up for it.
Connotation: Mark the text by highlighting the diction (words and phrases) used for positive effect (color 1) and/or negative effect (color 2). Then, study the diction to determine a pattern (e.g., mostly negative begins negatively but ends positively) and record your analysis.	**Pattern: (+/–)** Positive: fighting for his country; do everything with twice as much enthusiasm; wing grew Negative: lost; afraid; only be able to do things by halves; worst of all; things I cannot do at all; arm torn Pattern: mostly negative; ends positively
Attitude (Tone): Determine how the writer or speaker feels about the subject of the poem. (There might be more than one tone.) Highlight words that convey tone. Be sure to use precise tone words (e.g. mournful, not sad). Finally, summarize the tone.	**Tone Summary:** At first the speaker is fearful and woeful, but by the end he is inspired, determined, and hopeful.
Shift: Identify shifts, such as in the speaker, setting, subject, tone, or images. After **marking the text** with a star and numbering each, study and explain the shifts.	**Shifts:** There is a shift from third-person narrator to first-person speaker, which is the voice of the injured soldier, and back to third person. A shift in tone also occurs at the end of line 15. The voice of fear and the sense of loss shift to an attitude of resolve and a sense of enthusiasm and rebirth.
Title: Examine the title to determine the deeper meaning. Look beyond the literal, even if the title is simple (e.g. "Choices"). Record ideas.	**Deeper Meaning:** The title maintains its sense that this man is Everyman; that this man's experience is intended to be inspirational to all people who live with a tragic loss. It is this man's positive response to a life-altering challenge that makes the difference.
Theme: Determine the message about life implied in the poem. After you identify a subject (e.g. friendship), write a statement about the subject that sounds like a piece of advice (e.g, For a friendship to survive, one must be selfless, not selfish). Record your theme statement(s).	**Theme Statement(s):** • People conquer their greatest fears by resolving to have a positive outlook. • Out of great tragedy can come a new spirit of determination and hope. • One can overcome one's greatest fears by changing one's attitude to enthusiastic self-acceptance. • Physical challenges can be overcome through a change in attitude.

4. After reading the poem several times, return to the TP-CASTT graphic organizer and write a brief paragraph to summarize the poem and state its meaning.

My Notes

Setting a Purpose for Reading

- As you read this newspaper article, think about its audience and purpose. Write ideas you have in the My Notes section.
- Circle unknown words and phrases. Try to determine the meaning of the words by using context clues, word parts, or a dictionary.

Article

Soldier home after losing his leg in AFGHANISTAN

by Gale Fiege

1 LAKE STEVENS – It started out as just another day in the Zabul Province of southern Afghanistan.

2 On Sept. 18, 2010, Army Pfc. Tristan Eugene Segers, a 2002 graduate of Lake Stevens High School, was driving his armored patrol vehicle when a homemade bomb exploded in the road underneath Segers' floorboard.

3 One of the vehicle's 800-pound tires was found a half-mile away.

4 Just below his knee, Segers' right leg was gone. He had **shrapnel** sticking out of his eyeballs, face and arms.

shrapnel: small fragments of a bomb after it explodes

5 After nearly two years of surgeries and rehabilitation in Texas, Segers, a handsome 28-year-old, moved back to Snohomish County last week in time to celebrate Independence Day with his folks in the home where he grew up.

GRAMMAR & USAGE
Appositives

An **appositive** is a noun or noun phrase that gives further detail or explanation of the noun next to it. An appositive is not necessary to the meaning of the sentence and is usually set off by commas. For example, the writer of this article uses an appositive in the second paragraph to describe Eugene Segers: "... Eugene Segers, a 2002 graduate of Lake Stevens High School, was driving..."

ACTIVITY 1.12 continued

10 Explain that students will now use a similar process with an informational text. Emphasize that although the **TP-CASTT** strategy is usually used with poetry, readers can also use it to guide analysis of other types of texts. Review the Setting a Purpose for Reading section with students.

Text Complexity
Overall: Complex
Lexile: 1050L
Qualitative: Moderate Difficulty
Task: Accessible (Understand)

11 FIRST READ: Based on the complexity of the passage and your knowledge of your students, you may choose to conduct the first reading in a variety of ways:

- independent reading
- paired reading
- small group reading
- choral reading
- read aloud

Leveled Differentiated Instruction

While students read this article, have them fill out a **Key Idea and Details Chart** graphic organizer.

Em Have students write short phrases to complete the **Key Idea and Details Chart** graphic organizer.

Ex Have students write complete sentences to complete the **Key Idea and Details Chart** graphic organizer.

SCAFFOLDING THE TEXT-DEPENDENT QUESTIONS

5. Key Ideas and Details (RI.8.2) **What is the purpose of the first four paragraphs of this article?** What happened to Army Pfc. Segers? How are the facts of the wounding important to setting the context of the article?

6. Craft and Structure (RI.8.4) **The author uses the word "folks" in paragraph 5 to mean family. What effect does this word choice have?** How is "my folks" different from saying "my parents"? If I refer to strangers as just folks, how does that make them less alien or strange?

7. Key Ideas and Details (RI.8.2) **Choose a statement made by Segers that expresses the central idea driving Segers's life now. What facts in the story support this idea?** Examine paragraph 10 to find a statement that expresses Segers's ideas about his injury.

8. Knowledge and Ideas (RI.8.4) **Notice how the language changes as it describes his army assignment. What is an "elite" infantry unit? What are "personnel recovery missions?"** How does paragraph 12 give a sense of Segers's status in the Army?

12 As students are reading, monitor their progress. Be sure they are engaged with the text and noting its audience and purpose. Evaluate whether the selected reading mode is effective.

13 Based on the observations you made during the first reading, you may want to adjust your reading mode. For example, you may decide for the second reading to read aloud certain complex passages, or you may group students differently.

14 **SECOND READ:** During the second reading, students will be returning to the text to answer the text-dependent comprehension questions. You may choose to have students reread and work on the questions in a variety of ways:

- independently
- in pairs
- in small groups
- together as a class

Physical and Emotional Challenges

WORD CONNECTIONS

Etymology

The English word *culinary* appeared in the 1630s having derived from the Latin word *culinarius* which means "of the kitchen." About 20 years later it took on the meaning "of cooking." The English word *kiln*, which is an oven, also comes from the same Latin root.

6 Segers is married now to his high school girlfriend, Lindsay Blanchard. They are expecting a baby boy in October. He plans to return to culinary arts school this fall and they are about to move into an apartment in the Bothell area.

7 Until his official Army retirement date on Aug. 21, he is Cpl. Segers, the owner of a Purple Heart.[1]

8 Segers wears shorts in the warm summer weather, not even pretending to hide his prosthetic leg. He has run a marathon. A specially designed gas pedal is on the left side of his slate-gray Toyota Tacoma truck.

9 Nothing is stopping him.

10 "Everybody's injury is different and everybody handles it in their own way. There is no way to measure it, whether it's physical or mental," Segers said. "I just kept telling the doctors that I didn't want my life to be different than it was before. Of course, the loss of a leg changed me. But it doesn't define me or the rest of my life."

11 Segers was enjoying a promising start to a career as a chef when the economic recession forced him to consider joining the Army. He figured he would serve in the family tradition set by his father and grandfather.

grueling: physically demanding
elite: made of the best and most able

12 After **grueling** training in the hot Georgia sun, he landed a spot in the Army's 101st Airborne Pathfinder Division, an **elite** infantry unit, and was sent to Afghanistan in February 2010 to work on personnel recovery missions.

13 After the explosion, Segers was stabilized and flown to the Army hospital in Landstuhl, Germany.

My Notes

14 "My eyes were completely bandaged and I was in a lot of pain. The stretchers were on bunks in the airplane, so when I woke up it felt like I was in a coffin," Segers said. "I was so glad to hear the voice of my buddy, Andrew Leonard, a guy from Boston who had been injured earlier."

15 Tristan Segers can't say enough good things about the surgeons, psychiatrists, physical therapists and other staff at the Army hospital, as well as the numerous charitable organizations such as the Fisher House Foundation that help wounded veterans

rigorous: full of difficulty

16 "I was truly cared for," he said. "The rehabilitation was **rigorous** and I pushed it, building back my muscles and learning to use the prosthetic leg.

17 "But they never told me I was doing a good job for fear that I might get complacent. There were many guys there who had given up on life."

18 "Most of the time when people see my leg, they think I've been in a car accident or something. But sometimes an old veteran will stop me and thank me for my service," Segers said. "I didn't do anything special, but if the progress I have made motivates another wounded veteran to keep going, then that's great."

Second Read

- Reread the article to answer these text-dependent questions.
- Write any additional questions you have about the text in your Reader/Writer Notebook.

[1] **Purple Heart:** a medal given to U.S. Army personnel who are injured in the line of duty

© 2017 College Board. All rights reserved.

5. **Key Ideas and Details:** What is the purpose of the first four paragraphs of this article?

   The first four paragraphs state the facts of Segers's injury. RL.8.2

6. **Craft and Structure:** The author uses the word "folks" in paragraph 5 to mean family. What effect does this word choice have?

   "Folks" is a casual, informal word for parents or family, so it makes the tone simple and relatable. It creates a level of hominess or comfort. RL.8.4

7. **Key Ideas and Details:** Choose a statement made by Segers that expresses the central idea driving Segers's life now. What facts in the story support this idea?

   "Of course, the loss of a leg changed me. But it doesn't define me or the rest of my life." Facts that support that statement include that he is married, has a career and a child, and runs a marathon. RL.8.2

8. **Knowledge and Ideas:** Notice how the language changes as it describes his Army assignment. What is an "elite" infantry unit? What are "personnel recovery missions"?

   The language becomes technical: "elite" means a superior or especially talented group, and his work was to bring soldiers back from the front lines. RL.8.4

Working from the Text

9. Think about the audience and purpose of the poem "A Man" and the newspaper article you just read. Compare the purpose and audience for the two texts.
10. In both texts, the subject faces physical and mental challenges. How are these challenges similar and different?
11. An informational article and a poem would seem to have different purposes. How does the language of the texts differ?

    The impact of the poem comes from the use of imagery and the figurative language at the end, whereas the article uses very straightforward and clear language with no imagery or figures of speech.

12. Which piece had a greater impact on you? How did it affect you?

Check Your Understanding

Write a thematic statement about heroism that connects the texts.

A hero faces the challenge of a serious wartime injury with courage and optimism.

A life-changing wound can make an ordinary man become extraordinary.

Heroes may need courage both on the battlefield and at home.

My Notes

15 Have students answer the text-dependent questions. If they have difficulty, scaffold the questions by rephrasing them or breaking them down into smaller parts. See the Scaffolding the Text-Dependent Questions boxes for suggestions.

16 Ask students to independently complete Working from the Text questions 9–12. Briefly discuss Student Steps 9 and 10. Then, share, select, and display model theme statements.

17 Remind students that the theme should connect the concepts of *challenges* and *heroism*. Ask students individually to write an interpretive statement that captures the theme. Then have students **pair-share**. As a class, share theme statements, record the theme statements on sentence strips, select the strongest, and display for future reference.

18 After explaining the purpose of the **Freewriting** strategy, give students time to form a response to the writing prompt. Remind them that the ultimate goal is to develop an original definition of *heroism*, and this writing is part of the process.

19 Ask student volunteers to share ideas from their **freewrite**. Encourage students to add to their work if they hear a good idea.

ASSESS

As students read the news article in small groups, circulate to check for understanding of the process and for accurate analysis.

ADAPT

For students struggling to write a personal connection or struggling to connect the text to the concept of *challenge*, consider bringing in a film clip to allow students to visualize physical challenges. Possible video topics include Luca "Bboy LazyLegz" Patuelli (a breakdancer with spinal muscle atrophy), Wounded Warriors (wounded veterans), and Serena (an agility dog with three legs).

Physical and Emotional Challenges

My Notes

Introducing the Strategy: Free Writing

The **free writing** strategy allows writers to write freely without pressure to be correct or complete. A free write gives a writer the freedom to write in an informal style and get ideas on paper in preparation for a more complete and formal writing assignment. This strategy helps writers refine and clarify thoughts, spark new ideas, and/or generate content during drafting or revision.

Expository Writing Prompt

Free write about the topic of physical and mental challenges and their connection to heroism. Be sure to:

- Capture as many ideas as you can.
- Explore your ideas about the ways people react to challenges, not only physically or mentally but also changes in what they do with their lives.

Definition Strategies

ACTIVITY 1.13

Learning Targets

- Identify and apply definition strategies of function, example, and negation.
- Form an initial definition of heroism.

LEARNING STRATEGIES: Brainstorming, Manipulatives, Graphic Organizer, Prewriting

Writing to Define

For Embedded Assessment 2, you will be writing a definition essay to share your personal understanding of the concept of heroism. To write this definition of heroism, you will need various strategies and knowledge to create an expanded definition of the concept. First, you can expand your collection of words that describe heroes and heroism.

1. **Defining heroes:** Generate a list of
   - **Adjectives** that could describe what a hero is:
     A hero is (adjective) brave, courageous, self-sacrificing, fearless, etc.
   - **Nouns** that could define what a hero shows:
     A hero shows (noun) courage, selflessness, bravery, fearlessness, temerity, determination, etc.
   - **Verbs** that could define what a hero does:
     A hero (verb) fights, perseveres, moves forward, sacrifices, thinks of others, etc.
2. After sharing and consulting additional resources such as a thesaurus, group and then sort synonyms to represent the nuances of the words (subtle differences in meanings). Record these terms in your Reader/Writer Notebook for future reference.

Defining a Concept

Part of defining any concept is finding ways to describe the concept to make it clear to others. Writers of a **definition essay** use **strategies of definition** to clarify, develop, and organize ideas. The three **definition** strategies you will learn in this unit are **function, example,** and **negation.**

- **Definition by function:** Paragraphs using the **function** strategy explain how the concept functions or operates in the real world.
- **Definition by example:** Paragraphs using the **example** strategy use specific examples of the concept from texts or life.
- **Definition by negation:** Paragraphs using the **negation** strategy explain what something is by showing what it is not. A nonexample should be based on what someone else would say is an example. If no one would disagree with the negation, it is ineffective.

My Notes

ACTIVITY 1.13

▶PLAN

Materials: dictionaries, thesauruses, index cards, children's book about friendship or family (optional)
Suggested Pacing: 1 50-minute class period

▶TEACH

1 After students independently **brainstorm** as many words as they can to define a heroic person, ask them to share and compare their words in small groups. All students should add words to their lists as they share. Then, direct groups to expand their lists further by searching through a thesaurus or a dictionary for additional synonyms or other appropriate words.

2 Distribute eight index cards to each group. Ask the group to select eight words from their lists created in Step 1 and write them on index cards to use as **manipulatives.** After students have discussed and sorted their words into parts of speech, allow groups to share their ideas. As a class, use the categories to create a Word Wall.

3 Remind students that Embedded Assessment 2 requires them to write an essay based on an original definition of *heroism*. Read and briefly discuss the purpose of each definition strategy. You might use this opportunity to discuss whether students used the negation strategy in the opening activity—that is, did they define a hero by saying what it is *not*?

COMMON CORE STATE STANDARDS

Focus Standards:

L.8.6: Acquire and use accurately grade-appropriate general academic and domain-specific words and phrases; gather vocabulary knowledge when considering a word or phrase important to comprehension or expression.

RI.8.2: Determine a central idea of a text and analyze its development over the course of the text, including its relationship to supporting ideas; provide an objective summary of the text.

RI.8.3: Analyze how a text makes connections among and distinctions between individuals, ideas, or events (e.g., through comparisons, analogies, or categories).

Additional Standards Addressed:

RL.8.10; RI.8.1; RI.8.4; RI.8.5; RI.8.10; W.8.2a; W.8.2b; W.8.2c; W.8.2d; W.8.4; W.8.5; W.8.7; W.8.10; L.8.5c

4 The exercise in Student Step 3 lists examples of the three types of definition strategies and asks students to identify the types. Each of the passages is dominated by one type of strategy, but contains others also. In small groups, have students examine each passage closely, first determining the topic being defined and then the definition strategy or strategies being used.

Leveled Differentiated Instruction

In this activity, you may want to introduce the definition strategies by using a children's book about family or friendship. As you read the story aloud, have students demonstrate active listening to discuss content relating to function, example, or negation.

Em Help students ask and answer basic questions about the definition strategies as you read the story aloud.

Ex Guide students to ask and answer detailed questions about the definition strategies as you read the story aloud. Prompt and support students' questions and answers as necessary.

Br Instruct students to ask and answer detailed questions about the definition strategies as you read the story aloud.

Definition Strategies

ACADEMIC VOCABULARY

Describing the **function** of something is telling how something is used. The verb *to function* means "to act as or to operate as."

Just as a **negative** answer would be a no, to **negate** is to deny or make ineffective. The noun *negation* means "showing what something is not in order to prove what it is."

My Notes

3. Read the following passages of definition and decide whether they contain definition by **function**, example, and/or **negation**. Be able to explain why you categorized ideas as you did. First, highlight the topic being defined. Then, decide the type of definition being used.
   - "But just for the purposes of this discussion, let us say: one's family are those toward whom one feels loyalty and obligation, and/or from whom one derives identity, and/or to whom one gives identity, and/or with whom one shares habits, tastes, stories, customs, memories." (Marilynn Robinson, "Family." *The Death of Adam: Essays on Modern Thought*. Houghton Mifflin, 1998) (family as it functions in the real world)
   - "It's always seemed odd to me that *nonfiction* is defined, not by what it *is*, but by what it is *not*. It is *not* fiction. But then again, it is also *not* poetry, or technical writing or libretto. It's like defining classical music as *nonjazz*." (Philip Gerard, *Creative Nonfiction*. Story Press, 1996) (negation; it starts with what nonfiction is not)
   - "Love is patient and kind; love does not envy or boast; it is not arrogant or rude. It does not insist on its own way; it is not irritable or resentful; it does not rejoice at wrongdoing, but rejoices with the truth. Love bears all things, believes all things, hopes all things, endures all things. Love never ends." (*The Bible*, I Corinthians 13:4–8a) (negation and function of love)
   - "Let me not to the marriage of true minds
     admit impediments. Love is not love
     which alters when it alteration finds,
     or bends with the remover to remove:

     O no! It is an ever-fixed mark
     that looks on tempests and is never shaken;
     it is the star to every wandering bark,
     whose worth's unknown, although his height be taken.

     Love's not time's fool, though rosy lips and cheeks
     within his bending sickle's compass come:
     love alters not with his brief hours and weeks,
     but bears it out even to the edge of doom.

     If this be error and upon me proved,
     I never writ, nor no man ever loved."

     ("Sonnet 116," by William Shakespeare) (negation and function of love)

- From *To Kill a Mockingbird* – Atticus speaks to Jem about Mrs. Dubose:

  "You know, she was a great lady."

  "A lady?" Jem raised his head. His face was scarlet. "After all those things she said about you, a lady?"

  "She was. She had her own views about things, a lot different from mine, maybe ... son, I told you that if you hadn't lost your head I'd have made you go read to her. I wanted you to see something about her—I wanted you to see what real courage is, instead of getting the idea that courage is a man with a gun in his hand. It's when you know you're licked before you begin but you begin anyway and you see it through no matter what. You rarely win, but sometimes you do. Mrs. Dubose won, all ninety-eight pounds of her. According to her views, she died beholden to nothing and nobody. She was the bravest person I ever knew." (Mrs. Dubose is an example of courage.)

My Notes

Setting a Purpose for Reading

- As you read, put exclamation marks next to the author's definition of heroism.
- Highlight details the author gives to support his definition.
- Circle unknown words and phrases. Try to determine the meaning of the words by using context clues, word parts, or a dictionary.

ABOUT THE AUTHOR
Oliver Stone became a movie director after serving in the Vietnam War. Stone's films have explored historical subjects, such as the Vietnam War and President Kennedy's assassination. Three of Stone's films—*Midnight Express* (for which he wrote the screenplay), *Platoon*, and *Born on the Fourth of July*—have earned Academy Awards.

Article

Where I Find My Heroes

by Oliver Stone
from McCall's Magazine, November 1992

1 It's not true that there are no heroes anymore—but it is true that my own concept of heroism has changed radically over time. When I was young and I read the Random House biographies, my heroes were always people like George Washington and General Custer and Abraham Lincoln and Teddy Roosevelt. Men, generally, and doers. Women—with the exception of Clara Barton, Florence Nightingale, and Joan of Arc — got **short shrift**. Most history was oriented toward male heroes.

short shrift: little attention

2 But as I've gotten older, and since I've been to war, I've been forced to reexamine the nature of life and of heroism. What is true? Where are the myths?

ACTIVITY 1.13 continued

Text Complexity
Overall: Complex
Lexile: 960L
Qualitative: Low Difficulty
Task: Moderate (Analyze)

5 Read the Setting a Purpose for Reading sections with your students.

6 **FIRST READ:** Based on the complexity of the passage and your knowledge of your students, you may choose to conduct the first reading in a variety of ways:

- independent reading
- paired reading
- small group reading
- choral reading
- read aloud

SCAFFOLDING THE TEXT-DEPENDENT QUESTIONS

4. Key Ideas and Details (RI.8.2) **What is the connection among the examples of heroes Stone lists in paragraph 5?** Reread paragraph 4 to see how Stone defines a hero. How does this set up the listing of heros in paragraph 5?

ACTIVITY 1.13 continued

7 As students are reading, monitor their progress. Be sure they are engaged with the text and taking notes. Evaluate whether the selected reading mode is effective.

8 Based on the observations you made during the first reading, you may want to adjust your reading mode. For example, you may decide for the second reading to read aloud certain complex passages, or you may group students differently.

9 **SECOND READ:** During the second reading, students will be returning to the text to answer the text-dependent comprehension question. You may choose to have students reread and work on the question in a variety of ways:

- independently
- in pairs
- in small groups
- together as a class

10 Have students answer the text-dependent question. If they have difficulty, scaffold the question by rephrasing it or breaking it down into smaller parts. See the Scaffolding the Text-Dependent Questions boxes for suggestions.

11 Form small groups, and have students develop answers to the Working from the Text questions together. Note that Stone also defines a hero by function when he says that heroes try "to be greater than oneself," "to grow," and to be "a higher human being."

Definition Strategies

WORD CONNECTIONS

Etymology

The English word *advocate* was first used in the mid-1300s to refer to someone who argues a case in court. It was derived from the French word *avocar*, meaning "spokesman," which was itself derived from the Latin *advocatus*, meaning "one called to aid." The word *voice* also derives from the Latin root *vocare*, which means "call." The word *advocate* was first used as a verb in the 1640s.

3 The simple acts of heroism are often overlooked—that's very clear to me not only in war but in peace. I'm not **debunking** all of history: Crossing the Delaware was a magnificent action. But I am saying that I think the meaning of heroism has a lot to do with evolving into a higher human being. I came into contact with it when I worked with Ron Kovic, the **paraplegic** Vietnam vet, on *Born on the Fourth of July*. I was impressed by his life change, from a patriotic and strong-willed athlete to someone who had to deal with the total surrender of his body, who grew into a nonviolent and peaceful advocate of change in the Martin Luther King, Jr., and Gandhi tradition. So heroism is tied to an evolution of consciousness. . . .

4 Since the war, I've had children, and I'm wrestling now with the everyday problems of trying to share my knowledge with them without overwhelming them. It's difficult to be a father, to be a mother, and I think that to be a kind and loving parent is an act of heroism. So there you go—heroes are everyday, common people. Most of what they do goes unheralded, unappreciated. And that, ironically, is heroism: not to be recognized.

5 Who is heroic? Scientists who spend years of their lives trying to find cures for diseases. The teenager who says no to crack. The inner-city kid who works at McDonald's instead of selling drugs. The kid who stands alone instead of joining a gang, which would give him an instant identity. The celebrity who remains modest and treats others with respect, or who uses his position to help society. The student who defers the immediate pleasure of making money and finishes college or high school. People who take risks despite fears. People in wheelchairs who don't give up. . . .

6 We have a lot of **corruption** in our society. But we mustn't assume that everything is always basely motivated. We should allow for the heroic impulse—which is to be greater than oneself, to try to find another version of oneself, to grow. That's where virtue comes from. And we must allow our young generation to **strive** for virtue, instead of **ridiculing** it.

debunking: proving false
paraplegic: not having movement in the legs
corruption: fraud
strive: to work hard for
ridiculing: making fun of

My Notes

Second Read

- Reread the article to answer these text-dependent questions.
- Write any additional questions you have about the text in your Reader/Writer Notebook.

4. **Key Ideas and Details:** What is the connection among the examples of heroes Stone lists in paragraph 5?

   They are all ordinary people making choices and taking risks to realize a larger, better sense of self. RI.8.2

Working from the Text

5. How is Stone's definition of a hero different from the traditional idea of a hero as represented by the examples in paragraph 1?

   Stone's definition of a hero includes "everyday, common people" who perform "simple acts of heroism."

6. State Stone's definition of heroism in one concise statement.

   Stone defines heroes as common, ordinary people who daily act in virtuous, self-sacrificing ways to help others or themselves.

INDEPENDENT READING LINK

Read and Respond

Think about how you could use the protagonist of the book you are reading as part of a definition of a hero. How is he/she an example of a heroic type? Write your response in your Reader/Writer Notebook.

© 2017 College Board. All rights reserved.

7. How does Stone use the example strategy to support his definition? Cite textual evidence to support your analysis.

Stone gives several examples of heroic actions that ordinary people perform every day, such as scientists searching for cures to disease or kids who refuse to join gangs.

8. How do the final sentences provide a call to action and a final clarification of heroism?

Stone ends with the idea of the "heroic impulse" toward growth and being greater than oneself. Stone calls for adults to allow the younger generation to continue to admire and strive for heroism.

9. The heroes mentioned by Oliver Stone are listed below. Choose one or think of one of your own. Do a quick search to determine what made the person a hero.

- George Washington
- General Custer
- Abraham Lincoln
- Teddy Roosevelt
- Martin Luther King, Jr.
- Clara Barton
- Florence Nightingale
- Joan of Arc
- Ron Kovic
- Mohandas Gandhi

Beginning a Definition of Hero

10. After reading and thinking about definition strategies and heroes, use the graphic organizer that follows to begin organizing your definition of a hero according to the three different strategies for definition: function, example, and negation.

My Notes

12 Have individuals or groups do some quick research on one of the heroes mentioned in Stone's article. Students should report their findings to the class.

13 The **graphic organizer** is intended to create a visual representation of the Embedded Assessment 2 writing task by asking students to draft ideas to fit the three strategies. Have students use the organizer to consider how the ideas they have generated so far might fit into the overall essay structure.

14 The writing prompt is designed to give students practice writing using one definition strategy. You can modify this by changing the strategy or by asking students to try using all the strategies.

▶ASSESS

In responding to the writing prompt, students should be able to provide ideas for the required definition strategy that demonstrates a thoughtful definition of their chosen concept. In using the graphic organizer, students should be able to accurately classify their current ideas as relating to function, example, or negation.

▶ADAPT

To support learning, you might want to use additional visual prompts and/or models to explain the differences between the definition strategies. You might also allow students to work on the Heroism graphic organizer in pairs. To extend learning, you could ask students to begin researching heroism independently.

Definition Strategies

My Notes

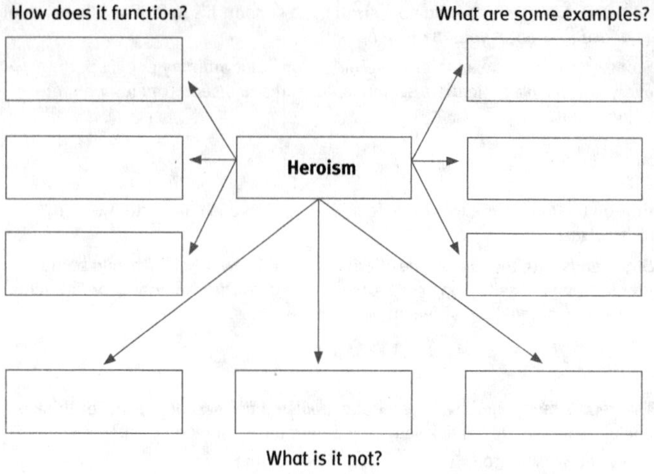

Check Your Understanding

Expository Writing Prompt

Think about how to define a hero by how he or she functions or acts. Draft a paragraph that establishes the function of a hero. Cite examples from texts you have read throughout this unit. Remember that the function strategy explains how an idea or concept operates in the world. Be sure to:

- Begin with a topic sentence that states how a hero functions in the world.
- Provide supporting detail (paraphrased and directly quoted) from life and from the texts you have read and provide commentary to develop ideas.
- Use transitions to create coherence.

Revise the language in your draft by creating figurative imagery (a metaphor) to express an idea.

A gentleman's behavior is like the polish on furniture, making daily use more pleasurable and careful.

A family, like a pillow, muffles and cushions us from the harshness of strangers.

© 2017 College Board. All rights reserved.

Historical Heroes: Examples

ACTIVITY 1.14

Learning Targets

- Compare a poem of tribute to an autobiographical excerpt and analyze how the structure contributes to meaning.
- Draft a written response using the example definition strategy.

Preview

In this activity, you will read several texts about Abraham Lincoln and Frederick Douglass. Think about how they each present their subjects in different ways.

Setting a Purpose for Reading

- The next two texts were written to remember and praise Abraham Lincoln after his assassination. As you read, underline words and phrases that the authors use to portray Lincoln as a heroic figure.
- You may use the TP-CASTT strategy to aid your analysis of the poem.
- Circle unknown words and phrases. Try to determine the meaning of the words by using context clues, word parts, or a dictionary.

LEARNING STRATEGIES: TP-CASTT, Diffusing, Close Reading, Marking the Text, Paraphrasing, Summarizing, Rereading

My Notes

ACTIVITY 1.14

PLAN

Suggested Pacing: 3 50-minute class periods

TEACH

1 Read the Preview and the Setting a Purpose for Reading sections with your students. Help them understand the literary terms they encounter.

2 **FIRST READ:** Based on the complexity of the passage and your knowledge of your students, you may choose to conduct the first reading in a variety of ways:

- independent reading
- paired reading
- small group reading
- choral reading
- read aloud

COMMON CORE STATE STANDARDS

Focus Standards:

RI.8.3: Analyze how a text makes connections among and distinctions between individuals, ideas, or events (e.g., through comparisons, analogies, or categories).

W.8.9: Draw evidence from literary or informational texts to support analysis, reflection, and research.

W.8.9a: Apply *Grade 8 Reading standards* to literature (e.g., "Analyze how a modern work of fiction draws on themes, patterns of events, or character types from myths, traditional stories, or religious works such as the Bible, including describing how the material is rendered new").

W.8.9b: Apply *Grade 8 Reading standards* to literary nonfiction (e.g., "Delineate and evaluate the argument and specific claims in a text, assessing whether the reasoning is sound and

Text Complexity
Overall: Complex
Lexile: 1130L
Qualitative: Moderate Difficulty
Task: Moderate (Analyze)

3 As students are reading, monitor their progress. Be sure they are engaged with the text and annotating it. Evaluate whether the selected reading mode is effective.

4 Based on the observations you made during the first reading, you may want to adjust your reading mode. For example, you may decide for the second reading to read aloud certain complex passages, or you may group students differently.

5 **SECOND READ:** During the second reading, students will be returning to the text to answer the text-dependent comprehension questions. You may choose to have students reread and work on the questions in a variety of ways:

- independently
- in pairs
- in small groups
- together as a class

Historical Heroes: Examples

My Notes

ABOUT THE AUTHOR
Dr. Phineas D. Gurley (1816–1868) was the pastor of the New York Avenue Presbyterian Church (in Washington, D.C.), which Abraham Lincoln attended during his presidency. Gurley was also Chaplain of the United States Senate. Gurley preached this funeral sermon in the White House East Room on April 19, 1865, four days after Lincoln's assassination.

Article

White House Funeral Sermon for Abraham Lincoln

by Dr. Phineas D. Gurley

He is dead; but the God in whom he trusted lives, and He can guide and strengthen his successor, as He guided and strengthened him. He is dead; but the memory of his virtues, of his wise and patriotic counsels and labors, of his calm and steady faith in God lives, is precious, and will be a power for good in the country quite down to the end of time. He is dead; but the cause he so **ardently** loved, so ably, patiently, faithfully represented and defended—not for himself only, not for us only, but for all people in all their coming generations, till time shall be no more—that cause survives his fall, and will survive it. The light of its brightening prospects flashes cheeringly to-day athwart[1] the gloom occasioned by his death, and the language of God's united **providences** is telling us that, though the friends of Liberty die, Liberty itself is **immortal**. There is no assassin strong enough and no weapon deadly enough to **quench** its inextinguishable life, or arrest its onward march to the conquest and empire of the world. This is our confidence, and this is our consolation, as we weep and mourn to-day. Though our beloved President is slain, our beloved country is saved. And so we sing of mercy as well as of judgment. Tears of gratitude mingle with those of sorrow. While there is darkness, there is also the dawning of a brighter, happier day upon our stricken and weary land. God be praised that our fallen Chief lived long enough to see the day dawn and the daystar of joy and peace arise upon the nation. He saw it, and he was glad. Alas! alas! He only saw the *dawn*. When the *sun* has risen, full-orbed and glorious, and a happy reunited people are rejoicing in its light—alas! alas! it will shine upon his grave. But that grave will be a precious and a **consecrated** spot. The friends of Liberty and of the Union will **repair** to it in years and ages to come, to pronounce the memory of its occupant blessed, and, gathering from his very ashes, and from the rehearsal of his deeds and virtues, fresh **incentives** to patriotism, they will there renew their vows of fidelity[2] to their country and their God.

ardently: passionately
providences: guardianship exercised by a deity
immortal: living forever
quench: to put an end to
consecrated: blessed
repair: to go often
incentives: reasons to do something

[1] **athwart:** across or against
[2] **fidelity:** loyalty, faithfulness to a person, cause, or belief

COMMON CORE STATE STANDARDS

the evidence is relevant and sufficient; recognize when irrelevant evidence is introduced").

Additional Standards Addressed:

RL.8.1; RL.8.4; RL.8.10; RI.8.1; RI.8.2; RI.8.3; RI.8.5; RI.8.10; W.8.2a; W.8.2b; W.8.2d; W.8.2e; W.8.4; W.8.10; L.8.5a; L.8.5b; L.8.5c; L.8.6

SCAFFOLDING THE TEXT-DEPENDENT QUESTIONS

1. Key Ideas and Details (RI.8.1) **Choose a sentence that shows that Dr. Gurley sees hope within the sorrow of Lincoln's death. Explain how your answer shows this.** Begin by reading the sentence "He is dead; but the cause he so ardently loved...survives his fall." Discuss how hope exists within the grief of loss.

Second Read

- Reread the sermon to answer these text-dependent questions.
- Write any additional questions you have about the text in your Reader/Writer Notebook.

1. **Key Ideas and Details:** Choose a sentence that shows that Dr. Gurley sees hope within the sorrow of Lincoln's death. Explain how your choice shows this.

   Answers will vary, but students may choose "though the friends of Liberty die, Liberty itself is immortal." it expresses that the cause for which Lincoln gave his life will survive him and prosper. RI.8.1

2. **Craft and Structure:** What does the word "arrest" mean in this sermon? How do you know?

   Arrest means to stop or slow down. The context helps the reader to understand. Liberty is said to be "immortal" and nothing can kill it or stop its "onward march." RL.8.4

3. **Knowledge and Ideas:** How do Dr. Gurley's contrasting statements echo the feeling of that moment in history?

   The contrast between grief and hope echoes the feelings of the nation in that the country grieves for the assassination of a beloved President even as it rejoices that the war is over, the Union is preserved, and Liberty has been protected. RL.8.2

ABOUT THE AUTHOR
Walt Whitman (1819–1892) is now considered one of America's greatest poets, but his untraditional poetry was not well received during his lifetime. As a young man, he worked as a printer and a journalist while writing free-verse poetry. His collection of poems, *Leaves of Grass*, first came out in 1855, and he revised and added to it several times over the years. During the Civil War, he worked in Washington, first caring for injured soldiers in hospitals and later as a government clerk.

My Notes

ACTIVITY 1.14 continued

6 Have students answer the text-dependent questions. If they have difficulty, scaffold the questions by rephrasing them or breaking them down into smaller parts. See the Scaffolding the Text-Dependent Questions boxes for suggestions.

TEACHER TO TEACHER

This passage is paired with Walt Whitman's poetic tribute to Lincoln. Whitman seems more focused on Lincoln's determination to save the American nation, whereas Dr. Gurley is more focused on Lincoln's dedication to liberty for all.

2. Craft and Structure (RI.8.4) **What does the word "arrest" mean in this sermon? How do you know?** How is this meaning of "arrest" like the common meaning of arresting someone for a crime? What would it mean to "arrest" the spread of a disease?
3. Knowledge and Ideas (RI.8.2) **How do Dr. Gurley's contrasting statements echo the feeling of that moment in history?** Despite the grief at the death of President Lincoln, what is the event that gives hope to the country?

7 **FIRST READ:** Based on the complexity of the passage and your knowledge of your students, you may choose to conduct the first reading in a variety of ways:

- independent reading
- paired reading
- small group reading
- choral reading
- read aloud

8 As students are reading, monitor their progress. Be sure they are engaged with the text and annotating it. Evaluate whether the selected reading mode is effective.

9 Based on the observations you made during the first reading, you may want to adjust your reading mode. For example, you may decide for the second reading to read aloud certain complex passages, or you may group students differently.

Historical Heroes: Examples

Literary Terms
An **allegory** is a literary technique of extending a metaphor through an entire poem or story so that objects, persons, and actions in the text are equated with meanings that lie outside the text.

Poetry

O Captain! My Captain!

by Walt Whitman

O Captain! my Captain! our fearful trip is done;
The ship has weather'd every **rack**, the prize we sought is won;
The port is near, the bells I hear, the people all exulting,
While follow eyes the steady keel, the **vessel** grim and daring:
But O heart! heart! heart!
O the bleeding drops of red,
Where on the deck my Captain lies,
Fallen cold and dead.

O Captain! my Captain! rise up and hear the bells;
Rise up—for you the flag is flung—for you the bugle trills;
For you bouquets and ribbon'd wreaths—for you the shores a-crowding,
For you they call, the swaying mass, their eager faces turning;
Here Captain! dear father!
This arm beneath your head;
It is some dream that on the deck,
You've fallen cold and dead.

My Captain does not answer, his lips are pale and still;
My father does not feel my arm, he has no pulse nor will;
The ship is anchored safe and sound, its voyage closed and done;
From fearful trip the victor ship comes in with object won:
Exult O shores, and ring O bells!
But I with **mournful** tread,
Walk the deck my Captain lies,
Fallen cold and dead.

rack: a windy storm
vessel: a ship

mournful: sad

My Notes

4. Key Ideas and Details (RL.8.4) **As an allegory representing the death of Abraham Lincoln, what does the Captain represent? What does the ship represent? What does the trip or voyage represent?** You might need to reexamine the definition of an allegory. What is the direct connection between the captain of a ship and the president of a country?

5. Craft and Structure (RL.8.4) **How does Whitman establish the same mood of sorrow and hope in his poem as Dr. Gurley does in his sermon?** What are some words that sound sad in the sermon? What are some words that sound hopeful? How are these ideas connected?

Second Read

- Reread the poem to answer these text-dependent questions.
- Write any additional questions you have about the text in your Reader/Writer Notebook.

4. **Key Ideas and Details:** As an allegory representing the death of Abraham Lincoln, who does the Captain represent? What does the ship represent? What does the trip or voyage represent?

   The captain represents Lincoln; the ship represents the country; the voyage represents the Civil War. RL.8.4

5. **Craft and Structure:** How does Whitman establish the same mood of sorrow and hope in his poem as Dr. Gurley does in his sermon? Explain by choosing a line that represents the mood.

   "From fearful trip the victor ship comes in with object won." This line expresses the feeling of sadness and fear even as it expresses that the trip was a success. RL.8.4

Setting a Purpose for Reading

- The next two texts are about Frederick Douglass. One is a poem written as a tribute. The other is an excerpt from Douglass's autobiography. Underline words and phrases that link Douglass to the concept of a hero.
- Circle unknown words and phrases. Try to determine the meaning of the words by using context clues, word parts, or a dictionary.

ABOUT THE AUTHOR
Robert Hayden (1913–1980) was born in Detroit, Michigan. He had a life-long love of literature and became a teacher and writer. Through his work for the Federal Writers' Project in the 1930s, he studied African-American history and folk life, both of which became inspirations for his works of poetry. Slavery and emancipation were recurring themes in his work.

My Notes

10 SECOND READ: During the second reading, students will be returning to the text to answer the text-dependent comprehension questions. You may choose to have students reread and work on the questions in a variety of ways:

- independently
- in pairs
- in small groups
- together as a class

11 Have students answer the text-dependent questions. If they have difficulty, scaffold the questions by rephrasing them or breaking them down into smaller parts. See the Scaffolding the Text-Dependent Questions boxes for suggestions.

ACTIVITY 1.14 continued

12 **FIRST READ:** Based on the complexity of the passage and your knowledge of your students, you may choose to conduct the first reading in a variety of ways:

- independent reading
- paired reading
- small group reading
- choral reading
- read aloud

13 As students are reading, monitor their progress. Be sure they are engaged with the text and annotating it. Evaluate whether the selected reading mode is effective.

14 Based on the observations you made during the first reading, you may want to adjust your reading mode. For example, you may decide for the second reading to read aloud certain complex passages, or you may group students differently.

15 **SECOND READ:** During the second reading, students will be returning to the text to answer the text-dependent comprehension questions. You may choose to have students reread and work on the questions in a variety of ways:

- independently
- in pairs
- in small groups
- together as a class

16 Have students answer the text-dependent questions. If they have difficulty, scaffold the questions by rephrasing them or breaking them down into smaller parts. See the Scaffolding the Text-Dependent Questions boxes for suggestions.

Historical Heroes: Examples

My Notes

diastole: the act of the heart filling with blood
systole: the act of the heart pumping blood
gaudy: showy in a tasteless way
exiled: forced to leave one's native land
rhetoric: language or speech

Poetry

Frederick Douglass

by Robert Hayden

When it is finally ours, this freedom, this liberty, this beautiful
and terrible thing, needful to man as air,
usable as earth; when it belongs at last to all,
when it is truly instinct, brain matter, **diastole, systole,**
reflex action; when it is finally won; when it is more
than the **gaudy** mumbo jumbo of politicians:
this man, this Douglass, this former slave, this Negro
beaten to his knees, **exiled**, visioning a world
where none is lonely, none hunted, alien,
this man, superb in love and logic, this man
shall be remembered. Oh, not with statues' **rhetoric**,
not with legends and poems and wreaths of bronze alone,
but with the lives grown out of his life, the lives
fleshing his dream of the beautiful, needful thing.

Second Read

- Reread the excerpt to answer these text-dependent questions.
- Write any additional questions you have about the text in your Reader/Writer Notebook.

6. **Craft and Structure:** In the first six lines, circle all the uses of the word "it" and "thing." What is "it"? How is it described?

   "It" is freedom and liberty. Descriptive words are "beautiful, terrible, needful, and usable." RL.8.4

7. **Knowledge and Ideas:** How is the cause of both Lincoln and Douglass the same according to these tributes?

   Both dedicated themselves to helping others gain freedom and liberty. RL.8.1

6. Craft and Structure (RL.8.4) **In the first six lines, circle all of the uses of the word "it" and "thing." What is "it"? How is it described?** Note that "it" is defined in the first line as both liberty and freedom. Note what adjectives are associated with it: "beautiful," "terrible," "needful," usable.

7. Knowledge and Ideas (RL.8.1) **How is the cause of both Lincoln and Douglass the same according to these tributes?** Reexamine your notes about the cause that Dr. Gurley says that Lincoln lived and died for. Then look at the first line of Hayden's poem about Douglass to find what Douglass stood for.

© 2017 College Board. All rights reserved.

ABOUT THE AUTHOR
Frederick Douglass (1818?–1895) was born into slavery in Maryland. He learned to read as a house servant in Baltimore. In 1838, Douglass escaped from his plantation and settled in Massachusetts. After spending two years abroad, he published an antislavery newspaper and was an advisor to President Lincoln during the Civil War. He was later appointed to positions in the U.S. government never before achieved by an African American.

My Notes

Autobiography

from The Narrative of the Life of Frederick Douglass, an American Slave

by Frederick Douglass

1 I felt assured that if I failed in this attempt, my case would be a hopeless one—it would seal my fate as a slave forever. I could not hope to get off with anything less than the severest punishment and being placed beyond the means of escape. It required no very vivid imagination to depict the most frightful scenes through which I should have to pass in case I failed. The wretchedness of slavery, and the blessedness of freedom, were perpetually before me. It was life and death with me. But I remained firm, and, according to my resolution, on the third day of September, 1838, I left my chains, and succeeded in reaching New York without the slightest interruption of any kind. How I did so—what means I adopted—what direction I travelled, and by what mode of conveyance—I must leave unexplained, for the reasons before mentioned.

2 I have been frequently asked how I felt when I found myself in a free State. I have never been able to answer the question with any satisfaction to myself. It was a moment of the highest excitement I ever experienced. I suppose I felt as one may imagine the unarmed **mariner** to feel when he is rescued by a friendly man-of-war from the pursuit of a pirate. In writing to a dear friend, immediately after my arrival at New York, I said I felt like one who had escaped a den of hungry lions. This state of mind, however very soon subsided; and I was again seized with a feeling of great insecurity and loneliness. I was yet liable to be taken and subjected to all the tortures of slavery. This in itself was enough to **damp** the **ardor** of my enthusiasm. But the loneliness overcame me. There I was in the midst of thousands, and yet a perfect stranger; without home and without friends, in the midst of thousands of my own brethren—children of a common Father, and yet I dared not to unfold to any one of them my sad condition. I was afraid to speak to any one for fear of speaking to the wrong one, and thereby falling into the hands of money-loving kidnappers, whose business it was to lie in wait for the panting fugitive, as the ferocious beasts of the forest lie in wait for their prey. [I]n the midst of plenty, yet suffering the terrible gnawing of hunger—in the midst of houses, yet having no home—among fellow-men, yet feeling as if in the midst of wild beasts, whose greediness to swallow up the trembling and half-famished **fugitive** is only equalled by that with which the monsters of the deep swallow up the trembling and half-famished fish upon which they subsist—I say let him be placed in this most trying situation—the situation in which I was placed—then, and not till then, will he fully appreciate the hardships of, and know how to sympathize with, the toil-worn and whip-scarred fugitive slave.

WORD CONNECTIONS

Prefixes and Suffixes

In the word *subjected*, the Latin prefix *sub-* means "below" or "less than." It has the same meaning in *submarine* and *subset*. The Latin root *-ject-* means "to throw." It appears in words like *trajectory* and *reject*.

mariner: one who works on a ship

damp: lessen

ardor: strong devotion

fugitive: one who flees

Text Complexity
Overall: Complex
Lexile: 1230L
Qualitative: Moderate Difficulty
Task: Moderate (Analyze)

17 **FIRST READ:** Based on the complexity of the passage and your knowledge of your students, you may choose to conduct the first reading in a variety of ways:

- independent reading
- paired reading
- small group reading
- choral reading
- read aloud

18 As students are reading, monitor their progress. Be sure they are engaged with the text and annotating it. Evaluate whether the selected reading mode is effective.

19 Based on the observations you made during the first reading, you may want to adjust your reading mode. For example, you may decide for the second reading to read aloud certain complex passages, or you may group students differently.

8. Key Idea and Details (RI.8.1) **What images in paragraph 2 does Douglass use to describe his first feelings of freedom and his fear of capture?** You might choose one of the images and then have students find another. Start with "unarmed mariner...rescued...from the pursuit of a pirate."

9. Key Ideas and Details (RI.8.2) **What did the "Liberator" write about? Why did it send a "thrill of joy" through Douglass's soul?** Reread paragraph 3 to determine what subjects set Douglass's "soul on fire."

10. Key Ideas and Details (RI.8.2) **What kind of mental, emotional, and physical courage did Douglass convey in this excerpt from his autobiography?** How did a slave have to be physically courageous to escape slavery? Think about the emotional fears that would plague a former slave.

© 2017 College Board. All rights reserved.

20 **SECOND READ:** During the second reading, students will be returning to the text to answer the text-dependent comprehension questions. You may choose to have students reread and work on the questions in a variety of ways:

- independently
- in pairs
- in small groups
- together as a class

21 Have students answer the text-dependent questions. If they have difficulty, scaffold the questions by rephrasing them or breaking them down into smaller parts. See the Scaffolding the Text-Dependent Questions boxes for suggestions.

Historical Heroes: Examples

brethren: people sharing in a similar situation
bonds: ties used to keep one in place
scathing: harshly critical
denunciations: formal accusations of wrongful activities

My Notes

3 In about four months after I went to New Bedford, there came a young man to me, and inquired if I did not wish to take the "Liberator." I told him I did; but just having made my escape from slavery, I remarked that I was unable to pay for it then. I, however, finally became a subscriber to it. The paper came, and I read it from week to week with such feelings as it would be quite idle for me to attempt to describe. The paper became my meat and my drink. My soul was set all on fire. Its sympathy for my **brethren** in **bonds**—its **scathing denunciations** of slaveholders—its faithful exposures of slavery—and its powerful attacks upon the upholders of the institution—sent a thrill of joy through my soul, such as I had never felt before!

4 I had not long been a reader of the "Liberator," before I got a pretty correct idea of the principles, measures and spirit of the anti-slavery reform. I did with a joyful heart, and never felt happier than when in an anti-slavery meeting. I seldom had much to say at the meetings, because what I wanted to say was said so much better by others. But, while attending an anti-slavery convention at Nantucket, on the 11th of August, 1841, I felt strongly moved to speak, and was at the same time much urged to do so by Mr. William C. Collin, a gentleman who had heard me speak in the colored people's meeting at New Bedford. It was a severe cross, and I took it up reluctantly. The truth was, I felt myself a slave, and the idea of speaking to white people weighed me down. I spoke but a few moments, when I felt a degree of freedom, and said what I desired with considerable ease. From that time until now, I have been engaged in pleading the cause of my brethren—with what success, and with what devotion, I leave those acquainted with my labors to decide.

Second Read

- Reread the excerpt to answer these text-dependent questions.
- Write any additional questions you have about the text in your Reader/Writer Notebook.

8. **Key Ideas and Details:** What images in paragraph 2 does Douglass use to describe his first feelings of freedom and his fear of capture?

Images include "A mariner ... rescued ... from the pursuit of pirates," "One who had escaped a den of hungry lions," and "Kidnappers ... ferocious beasts ... lie in wait." RI.8.1

9. **Key Ideas and Details:** What did the "Liberator" write about? Why did it send "a thrill of joy" through Douglass's soul?

The Liberator wrote with sympathy about slaves, denounced slaveholders, and attacked the upholders of slavery, which is what gave Douglass a thrill of joy to see these issues being exposed publicly. RI.8.2

10. **Key Ideas and Details:** What kind of mental, emotional, and physical courage did Douglass convey in this excerpt from his autobiography?

the physical courage to escape slavery; the emotional courage to face freedom alone, without others; the mental courage to speak out at antislavery meeting RI.8.2

© 2017 College Board. All rights reserved.

Working from the Text

11. Compare Hayden's poem to Douglass's autobiographic narrative. What topic of the autobiographic narrative do you see reflected in Robert Hayden's tribute to Douglass?
Robert Hayden emphasizes the liberty that Douglass sought as "beautiful and terrible." Douglass's autobiographical selection gives first-hand evidence of how he sees his liberty as full of fears and yet beautiful enough to pursue with devotion.

12. Review the elements of a well-developed expository body paragraph before responding to the Writing Prompt.
    - **Topic Sentence:** Paragraphs begin with a sentence that includes a subject and an interpretation. The two main functions of a topic sentence are to make a point that supports the thesis of the essay and to indicate the main idea of a paragraph.
    - **Supporting Detail:** Specific and relevant facts, details, examples, and quotations are used to support the topic sentence and thesis and to develop ideas.
    - **Commentary:** Commentary explains the significance of the supporting detail in relation to the thesis, which further develops ideas. It also brings a sense of closure to the paragraph.

Check Your Understanding

WRITING to SOURCES **Expository Writing Prompt**

Think about the four texts you just read. How were Abraham Lincoln and Frederick Douglass heroic? Draft a definition paragraph using the example strategy. Be sure to:

- Begin with a topic sentence that answers the prompt.
- Provide supporting detail and commentary to develop ideas.
- Use **formal style** and appropriate diction for the purpose and audience.

Reflect on your writing: Discuss how the use of the example strategy strengthens a definition.

Sample topic sentences:

1. Lincoln and Douglass are important examples of heroes because they championed the right to freedom and liberty.
2. Both Lincoln and Douglass struggled for freedom for others.
3. Douglass and Lincoln dedicated their public lives to the fight for liberty.

My Notes

TEACHER TO TEACHER

You may want students to return to the Heroism graphic so they can add elements and evidence gleaned from the tributes to and the autobiography of Lincoln and Douglass as examples of heroic figures. If so, be sure they can explain why these men are examples of heroism.

22 Review elements of a well-developed body paragraph. Explain that commentary is usually the most challenging part for students since it requires in-depth analysis and clear explanations.

23 Ask students to independently respond to the writing prompt.

24 As a class, discuss the final reflection question.

ASSESS

Review students' work to check that students were able to do the following:

- Accurately analyze the second poem for each element of **TP-CASTT.**
- Draft a response that uses the example strategy and meets the stated criteria.

ADAPT

To support learning, write a model of an example paragraph in response to the prompt, and/or allow students to co-construct the draft (as a class, in groups, or with a partner). If students struggle with any aspect of the analysis or writing, display and discuss a successful student model.

ACTIVITY 1.15

▶PLAN

Suggested Pacing: 1 50-minute class period

▶TEACH

1 Explain that transitions and embedded quotations contribute to a successful expository paragraph.

2 Discuss the purpose of transitions, and then ask students to read the list of transitions, noting especially the different purposes and identifying unfamiliar transitions.

ACTIVITY 1.15

Language and Writer's Craft: Transitions and Quotations

LEARNING STRATEGIES: Marking the Draft, Adding, Substituting

ACADEMIC VOCABULARY
Coherence is the clear and orderly presentation of ideas in a paragraph or essay.

Learning Target

- Examine and appropriately apply transitions and embedded quotations to create coherence in writing.

Reviewing and Extending Transitions

You have learned that transitions connect ideas. Writers use transitional words and phrases to create **coherence** and to help readers move smoothly through the essay. In formal writing, transitions establish relationships between one thought and the next, both within and between body paragraphs.

Transitions are used for different purposes:

To offer evidence:	To introduce an interpretation:	To compare and contrast:
Most important, For example, For instance, According to ___________, To illustrate, In this case,	Therefore, For these reasons, Consequently, Furthermore, In addition, Moreover, Thus,	Although ___________, Even though ________, Instead, On the other hand, On the contrary, Rather, Yet, / But, / However, Still, Nevertheless, In contrast, Similarly, Likewise, In the same way,
To add information:	**To clarify:**	**To conclude:**
Additionally, In addition, For example, For instance, Likewise, Finally, Equally important, Again,	In other words, For instance, That is, Put another way,	As a result, Therefore, Thus, Finally,

COMMON CORE STATE STANDARDS

Focus Standards:

W.8.2b: Develop the topic with relevant, well-chosen facts, definitions, concrete details, quotations, or other information and examples.

W.8.2c: Use appropriate and varied transitions to create cohesion and clarify the relationships among ideas and concepts.

Additional Standards Addressed:

W.8.4; W.8.5; W.8.8; L.8.4b; L.8.6

1. The following sample paragraph is based on a folklore story from China about a girl, Mulan, who chooses to go to war in place of her ill father. Mark the draft to indicate where transitions could be added.

Using the chart on the previous page, determine what kinds of transitions are appropriate to this expository paragraph. Then, revise the writer's organization by adding or substituting transitional words and phrases to create coherence.

Mulan is courageous because she has the ability to disregard fear for a greater good. Mulan takes her father's place in the Chinese army because she knows that he is hurt. It is a crime punishable by death to impersonate a man and a soldier. Mulan has the strength and the nerve to stand up for her father and protect him. She gathers all of her courage and leaves before anyone can stop her, which is what courage is all about. Her pluck allows her to face the impossible and not think about the outcome, the fear or the danger, until she is far enough to be ready for it. The heroes that we look up to are everyday heroes, ordinary, average people who have conquered huge challenges by finding the strength and the courage within themselves to continue on. "A hero is an ordinary individual who finds the strength to persevere and endure in spite of overwhelming obstacles" (Christopher Reeve). Mulan is an ordinary girl who finds courage and strength to continue training and fighting in battles, even though she may be frightened. It is impossible to endure and overcome fearful obstacles when you have fear of them. Courage is what gives heroes the drive to move forward. The heroes that have the courage and the will to move on are the heroes that we all know and admire, the ones that we strive to be like.

Transitions that could be added include "First" (beginning of sentence 2); "Although" (beginning of sentence 3 to introduce the clause "It is a crime punishable by death to impersonal a man and a soldier"); "In spite of her fears" (phrase at beginning of sentence 4); "In most cases" (phrase at beginning of sentence 6); "In just this way" (phrase at beginning of sentence 8).

WORD CONNECTIONS

Roots and Affixes

Coherence contains the Latin root *-her-*, meaning "to stick" and the prefix *co-* meaning "together." The root also appears in *cohere*, *coherent*, *adhere*, and *inherent*.

My Notes

ACTIVITY 1.15 continued

3 After clarifying the meaning and purpose of each transition, introduce the sample text about *Mulan*. It may be necessary to prime students' prior knowledge of *Mulan* with a brief review of the plot and a brief discussion of heroic characters from folklore. Either guide students through the revisions using direct instruction, or ask students to work independently or in pairs to revise. Students can write their transitions in the text or in the My Notes section.

ACTIVITY 1.15 continued

4 Paraphrasing and embedding quotations are two ways to add important support to explanations and arguments. A brief discussion of the value of paraphrasing and quoting can be part of this activity.

5 After discussing the **TLQC** strategy, ask the class to think of a mnemonic to remember TLQC (e.g., *The little queen cries*).

ACTIVITY 1.15 continued

Language and Writer's Craft: Transitions and Quotations

My Notes

Providing Support for a Claim

Supporting details can be paraphrased or directly quoted, depending on the writer's purpose and intended effect. Examine the difference between a paraphrase and an embedded quotation.

Paraphrase: Early in the story, Mulan reveals that she knows she will hurt her family if she is true to herself (*Mulan*).

Embedded Quotation: Early in the story, Mulan reveals her fears when she sings, "Now I see, that if I were truly to be myself, I would break my family's heart" (*Mulan* 5).

Note that an embedded quotation shows a more detailed and precise knowledge of the text.

A direct quotation *should not*:	A direct quotation *should*:
contain a simple idea that a writer could easily paraphrase	contain a complex idea that is thought-provoking
repeat an idea that has already been said	add another layer of depth to the writing
stand alone	be smoothly embedded into the writing; begin with a transition and lead-in
be lengthy	be no more than three lines

Use the acronym TLQC to help you remember how to embed a quotation smoothly. The letters stand for Transition, Lead-in, Quote, Citation.

Element	Definition/Purpose	Example
Transition	Use as a bridge to link ideas and strengthen cohesion and fluency.	**Early in the story,** Mulan reveals her fears when she sings, "Now I see, that if I were truly to be myself, I would break my family's heart."
Lead-in	Use to set the context for the information in the quote (complex sentences work well).	Early in the story, **Mulan reveals her fears when she sings,** "Now I see, that if I were truly to be myself, I would break my family's heart."
Quote	Use ideas from a credible source to strengthen your ideas, illustrate a point, and/or support your controlling idea.	Early in the story, Mulan reveals her fears when she sings, **"Now I see, that if I were truly to be myself, I would break my family's heart."**
Citation	Include author's last name and page number to give credit to the author and to make your writing credible to the reader.	Early in the story, Mulan reveals her fears when she sings, "Now I see, that if I were truly to be myself, I would break my family's heart" (***Mulan* 5**).

Note: If you are citing a different type of source, such as a website, provide the first piece of information listed in a source citation.

2. Return to the sample paragraph and revise the writer's ideas about *Mulan* by smoothly embedding Christopher Reeve's quote (already there, but not carefully embedded) and by adding the following quotation from the film:

   Mulan: "It's going to take a miracle to get me into the army."
   Possible revisions:
   Mulan is a good example of Christopher Reeve's statement that "a hero ... finds the strength to persevere and endure in spite of overwhelming obstacles." Her pluck allows her to face the impossible because she knows "it's going to take a miracle to get [me] into the army."

My Notes

Check Your Understanding

Return to the paragraph you wrote about Lincoln and Douglass as historical heroes. Mark your draft to indicate missing or ineffective transitions. Then, revise the organization by adding or substituting transitional words and phrases to create coherence. Next, find a significant quote in two of the texts you have read and add those ideas into your paragraph by smoothly embedding the quotes.

Reflection: What types of transitions did you add during your revision? Why? How do the direct quotations strengthen your ideas?

6 Guide students through the revisions of the sample text.

7 Ask students to revise their own writing from the previous activity by adding transitions and embedded quotations. Call on a few students to share their work with the class, and provide feedback about the effectiveness of the revisions.

ASSESS

Review students' revised paragraphs to assess students' ability to apply these skills to their own writing.

ADAPT

These skills are important, and students should know that they are essential to success on the Embedded Assessment. To support learning, provide students with only a few key transitions (instead of the entire chart). You might also allow students to work in **discussion groups** during the revision work. Encourage students to go beyond one-word transitions into transitional phrases and clauses as seen in the sample revisions.

ACTIVITY 1.16

▶PLAN

Suggested Pacing: 1 50-minute class period

▶TEACH

1 Guide students through the review of the negation strategy.

2 Read the Preview and the Setting a Purpose for Reading sections with your students. Help them understand the literary terms they encounter.

3 **FIRST READ:** Based on the complexity of the passage and your knowledge of your students, you may choose to conduct the first reading in a variety of ways:

- independent reading
- paired reading
- small group reading
- choral reading
- read aloud

Text Complexity
Overall: Very Complex
Lexile: 1230L
Qualitative: Moderate Difficulty
Task: Moderate (Analyze)

4 As students are reading, monitor their progress. Be sure they are engaged with the text and annotating examples of the negation strategy. Evaluate whether the selected reading mode is effective.

5 Based on the observations you made during the first reading, you may want to adjust your reading mode. For example, you may decide for the second reading to read aloud certain complex passages, or you may group students differently.

6 **SECOND READ:** During the second reading, students will be returning to the text to answer the text-dependent comprehension question. You may choose to have students reread and work on the question in a variety of ways:

- independently
- in pairs
- in small groups
- together as a class

ACTIVITY 1.16

Negation Strategy of Definition

LEARNING STRATEGIES: Quickwrite, Marking the Text, Drafting, Substituting

My Notes

Learning Targets

- Examine and analyze examples of the negation strategy of definition.
- Apply the negation strategy to a new topic.

Review of the Negation Strategy

1. Review the negation definition strategy:

Paragraphs using the **negation** strategy explain what something is by showing what it *is not*. Pointing out what the subject *is not* can make what it *is* clearer to the reader. For example, here is an excerpt from a definition of a horse that uses the negation strategy:

> A horse, a zebra and a mule, though alike in many ways, have significant differences. A horse, unlike a zebra, can be tamed and trained. And unlike a mule, which is a sterile beast of burden, a horse is a valued breeder of future generations of racing champions and hard-working ranch animals.

Preview

In this activity, you will read a definition essay about the concept of a "gentleman" and evaluate how the author used the negation strategy.

Setting a Purpose for Reading

- As you read, underline examples of the negation strategy.
- Circle unknown words and phrases. Try to determine the meaning of the words by using context clues, word parts, or a dictionary.

ABOUT THE AUTHOR

John Henry Newman (1801–1890) was a scholar and clergyman who became an influential figure at Oxford College. Newman was a pioneer of the Oxford Movement which sought to inject more Catholic dogma into the Protestant-leaning Church of England. Some of his works, including the seminal *Parochial and Plain Sermons*, helped influence the ideals of the Oxford Movement. In 1845 he converted to Roman Catholicism. Pope Benedict XVI beatified Newman in 2010, which means he was officially bestowed as someone in the church to be glorified and exalted.

Essay

"A Definition of a GENTLEMAN"

by John Henry Newman

(1) The true gentleman in like manner carefully avoids whatever may cause a jar or a jolt in the minds of those with whom he is cast;—all clashing of opinion, or collision of feeling, all restraint, or suspicion, or gloom, or resentment; his great concern being to make everyone at their ease and at home. (2) He has his eyes on all his company; he is tender towards the bashful, gentle towards the distant, and merciful towards the **absurd**; he can recollect

absurd: something that is ridiculous

COMMON CORE STATE STANDARDS

Focus Standards:

RI.8.1: Cite the textual evidence that most strongly supports an analysis of what the text says explicitly as well as inferences drawn from the text.

RI.8.10: By the end of the year, read and comprehend literary nonfiction at the high end of the grades 6–8 text complexity band independently and proficiently.

W.8.3b: Use narrative techniques, such as dialogue, pacing, description, and reflection, to develop experiences, events, and/or characters.

Additional Standards Addressed:

RI.8.4; W.8.2a; W.8.2b; W.8.2c; W.8.10

to whom he is speaking; he guards against unseasonable allusions, or topics which may irritate; he is seldom prominent in conversation, and never **wearisome**. (3) He makes light of favours while he does them, and seems to be receiving when he is conferring. (4) He never speaks of himself except when compelled, never defends himself by a mere retort, he has no ears for **slander** or gossip, is scrupulous in imputing motives to those who interfere with him, and interprets everything for the best. (5) He is never mean or little in his disputes, never takes unfair advantage, never mistakes personalities or sharp sayings for arguments, or **insinuates** evil which he dare not say out. (6) From a long-sighted prudence, he observes the **maxim** of the ancient **sage**, that we should ever conduct ourselves towards our enemy as if he were one day to be our friend.

From *The Idea of a University*, by John Henry Newman, originally delivered as a series of lectures in 1852.

wearisome: causing to be tired

slander: spoken lies about someone

insinuates: implies
maxim: truthful adage
sage: wise person

My Notes

Second Read

- Reread the excerpt to answer these text-dependent questions.
- Write any additional questions you have about the text in your Reader/Writer Notebook.

2. **Craft and Structure:** How does negation make this portrait of a gentleman clearer and more extensive?

By providing negative examples, a definition can set up a contrast between what is and what is not, which explains a definition and makes it clearer. "He never speaks of himself unless compelled" gives a more complete picture of a humble person. RI.8.4

Check Your Understanding

WRITING to SOURCES **Expository Writing Prompt**

Write about what heroism is not. Use the negation strategy to distinguish what heroism is from what it is not. Be sure to:

- Begin with a topic sentence that answers the prompt.
- Provide supporting detail and commentary to develop ideas.
- Cite examples from the texts you have read.
- Use transitions to create coherence.

A true hero is a person who is humble and yet goes beyond what is expected. A hero does not expect reward or recognition for his actions. He runs into a burning building because it is the right thing to do, not because he expects the attention of the media and the praise of the world for his actions. A hero does not give up the quest when the challenge becomes difficult. The hero of the poem "A Man" did not give up when he thought he would only be able to do everything by half when he lost his arm. A hero is not someone whose heroic actions are simply a brave stunt. A hero is not someone who is simply more talented than the next man or woman. A hero is the ordinary man or woman who acts to benefit others, not himself.

INDEPENDENT READING LINK

Read and Recommend

Your independent reading choice can be used as a source in your definition essay. Write about how the protagonist of your reading faced and overcame obstacles and challenges. Then discuss with a classmate why you think this text will be valuable in writing your definition essay. Be sure to provide clear reasons for your recommendation.

ACTIVITY 1.16 continued

7 Have students answer the text-dependent question. If they have difficulty, scaffold the question by rephrasing it or breaking it down into smaller parts. See the Scaffolding the Text-Dependent Questions boxes for suggestions.

Leveled Differentiated Instruction

Students may need extra support for difficult vocabulary in context such as *wearisome* and *insinuates*.

Em Have students complete an **Unknown Word Solver** graphic organizer for a few words they didn't understand.

Ex Have students complete an **Unknown Word Solver** graphic organizer for difficult words independently. Then have partners share their completed organizers to confirm understanding.

8 After students independently respond to the writing prompt, guide them through a revision of their language.

ASSESS

Review student writing to determine if students were able to draft and revise a response that uses the negation strategy and meets the stated criteria.

ADAPT

To support learning, write a model of a negation paragraph in response to the prompt, and/or allow students to co-construct the draft (as a class, in groups, or with a partner).

If students struggle with any aspect of the writing, display and discuss a successful student model.

SCAFFOLDING THE TEXT-DEPENDENT QUESTIONS

2. Craft and Structure (RI.8.4) **How does negation make this portrait of a gentleman clearer and more extensive?** You may want to get students to use negation to define a good teacher or good parent—something they are familiar with in order to make this point.

ACTIVITY 1.17

▶PLAN

Suggested Pacing: 2 50-minute class periods

▶TEACH

TEACHER TO TEACHER

In this activity, have students work in writing/discussion groups in order to make revision and self-evaluation a part of their writing process.

1 Make sure the Definition Essay Scoring Criteria are clear to students; then have them fill in the chart in Student Step 1 with the required skills and concepts.

2 With students, read the information about the parts of an introduction. Check for understanding by having students paraphrase the information orally.

ACTIVITY 1.17

Expository Writing Focus: Organization

LEARNING STRATEGIES: Close Reading, Marking the Text, Note-taking, Collaborative Discussion

My Notes

Learning Targets

- Identify and evaluate the effectiveness of the structural elements of a definition essay.
- Draft a thesis and outline ideas for a definition essay.

Planning a Definition Essay

1. Review the Scoring Criteria for Embedded Assessment 2. What defines a proficient definition essay? List required skills and concepts for each category.

Ideas	– Provides a precise definition of heroism. – Uses definition strategies, supporting details from a variety of sources, and commentary to develop ideas
Organization	– Provides a clear structure: – Introduction with an original definition of heroism (thesis) – Body paragraphs reflecting definition strategies – Conclusion – Uses transitions to create coherence
Language and Conventions	– Maintains a formal style appropriate for an academic essay – Embeds quotations from sources smoothly and correctly – Demonstrates command of conventions (grammar and usage; capitalization; punctuation; spelling)

Introduction

The **introduction** to an essay has three main parts (listed in the order in which they should appear):

I. **The Hook:** If the opening lines are dull or confusing, the reader loses interest right away. Therefore, you must write an opening that grabs the reader's attention. Lure your readers into the piece with a ***hook***—an anecdote, compelling question, a quote, or an intriguing statement (AQQS)—to grab them so firmly that they will want to read on.

- **Anecdote:** Begin with a brief anecdote (a story from real life) that relates to the point of your essay.
- **Question:** Ask a thought-provoking universal question relating to the concept of your thesis, which you will answer in your essay. Don't ask simplistic questions such as "How would you feel if . . .?" or "What would you do if . . .?"

WORD CONNECTIONS

Etymology

The Latin root *-voc-* in ***provocative*** comes from a Latin word meaning "to call." This root appears in words related to a calling, such as *vocation* and *advocate*. The Latin prefix *pro-* means "forth," "before," or "forward."

COMMON CORE STATE STANDARDS

Focus Standards:

W.8.2: Write informative/explanatory texts to examine a topic and convey ideas, concepts, and information through the selection, organization, and analysis of relevant content.

W.8.2a: Introduce a topic or thesis statement clearly, previewing what is to follow; organize ideas, concepts, and information into broader categories; include formatting (e.g., headings), graphics (e.g., charts, tables), and multimedia when useful to aiding comprehension.

W.8.2f: Provide a concluding statement or section that follows from and supports the information or explanation presented.

W.8.4: Produce clear and coherent writing in which the development, organization, and style are appropriate to task, purpose, and audience. (Grade-specific expectations for writing types are defined in standards 1–3.)

© 2017 College Board. All rights reserved.

- **Quote:** Find a quote to state an ordinary idea in an extraordinary or provocative way, or state a provocative idea in an ordinary way. Either will grab the reader's interest. This quote can come from any source: someone you know, someone famous, or a song.
- **Intriguing statement:** Knock down a commonly held assumption or define a word in a new and startling way.

II. The Bridge: This writing represents the content between the hook and the thesis (the controlling idea of the essay). The purpose of the bridge is to make a clear and concise connection between these two parts. The bridge is also the place where a writer provides necessary background information to set the context for the ideas in the essay.

III. The Thesis: Your thesis is your response to the writing prompt, and it includes information about both the topic and your interpretation of it. The thesis is the single most important part of the essay in establishing focus and coherence; all parts of the essay should work to support this idea. Your thesis should be a clear and precise assertion. It should not be an announcement of your intent, nor should it include the first person (*I/my*).

A thesis should show a level of sophistication and complexity of thought. You may want to try to create a complex sentence as your thesis statement. Complex sentences contain a dependent clause that begins with a dependent marker, such as *because, before, since, while, although, if, until, when, after, as, as if.*

Evaluating and Revising Introductions

2. Read the following introductions. For each one, identify, label, and evaluate the three parts of the introduction: hook, bridge, and thesis.

Sample 1

Aristotle said "The beauty of the soul shines out when a man bears with composure one heavy mischance after another, not because he does not feel them, but because he is a man of high and heroic temper." When someone goes though calamity with poise, it is not because they don't feel anything; it is because they are of a heroic nature. Heroism is being brave and helping other people before yourself, but it does not always have a happy ending.

Sample 2

"A hero is no braver than an ordinary man, but he is braver five minutes longer." When heroes keep on going and keep battling a challenge or problem, it makes them that much more heroic. Anyone could just give up, but heroes keep going. Instead of stressing over satisfying everyone, heroes know that their best is good enough, and focus on doing the right thing. Heroism is putting others before yourself and directly facing challenges, but not always saving or satisfying everyone.

My Notes

ACTIVITY 1.17 continued

3 After reviewing the key parts of an introduction, have students independently read and label the parts of each sample introduction.

COMMON CORE STATE STANDARDS

Additional Standards Addressed:

RI.8.1; W.8.2b; W.8.2d; W.8.2e; W.8.5; L.8.4b; L.8.6

4 Put students into writing groups to evaluate and discuss one or both introductions, as assigned. Allow groups time to share evaluations and consider revisions. The goal is to agree upon an evaluation and determine how to revise. Explain that each group member should take turns leading the evaluation and discussion about revising/ editing the paragraph. All students should actively participate by building on others' ideas and expressing their own.

5 Finally, individuals should create a final revised version of one or both introductions based on their writing groups' discussion and decisions.

6 With students, read the information about revising thesis statements to have a complex sentence structure. You may need to briefly review with students dependent markers, dependent clauses, independent clauses, and complex sentences.

Expository Writing Focus: Organization

My Notes

3. Now reread each introductory paragraph, evaluate its effectiveness, and mark it for revision. Use these questions to aid your evaluation:
   - Is the hook engaging?
   - If the hook is a quote, is it integrated smoothly?
   - Is there a bridge that effectively links the hook to the thesis?
   - Is the thesis a clear and precise interpretation of the topic?
   - Is the use of language formal or informal?
   - Is the language effective? Where can it be made clearer, or where can ideas be stated more smoothly?

Check Your Understanding

Revise one of the two paragraphs above based on your evaluation and discussion of how it could benefit by additional content, reworking sentences, and using more precise or formal diction.

Revising Thesis Statements

Examine the model thesis statement below and then see how the statement has been revised to have a complex sentence structure with a beginning dependent clause.

- **Model thesis statement:** Heroism involves selflessness and dedication to a challenge. It means helping others without desire for recognition or stardom.
- **Revised model:** ***Because*** heroism involves selflessness, it requires dedication to a challenge and helping others without desire for recognition or stardom.

4. What is the value of combining the two sentences in this way? How does it improve the communication of ideas in the thesis statement?

5. Now follow the model to revise the remaining thesis statements on the next page. Create a complex sentence structure by using a dependent marker to create a dependent clause at the beginning of the sentence. Revise other elements as needed for smooth expression while still keeping the same ideas.

- **Thesis statement:** Heroism means taking action when you are needed, showing dedication to your quest, and not giving up even when the odds are against you.

  Revised thesis statement: Answers will vary.

  Even when the odds are overwhelmingly against you, heroism means taking action, remaining dedicated to the quest, and not giving up.

- **Thesis statement:** Heroism means putting others before oneself and directly facing challenges, but not always saving or satisfying everyone.

  Revised thesis statement: Answers will vary.

  While it is not possible to always save or satisfy everyone, heroism means putting others before yourself and facing challenges directly.

- **Thesis statement:** Heroism is being brave and helping other people before yourself, but it does not always guarantee a happy ending.

  Revised thesis statement: Answers will vary.

  Though being heroic doesn't always lead to a happy ending, it always means being brave and helping other people before oneself.

Writing a Concluding Paragraph

The **concluding** paragraph in an essay is the last thing your reader takes from your essay. Try to make the reader think in a new way, feel emotional, or feel enlightened. Choose the ending carefully. Avoid clichés or something stale, such as "The end," "That is all I have to say," or "That's my definition of heroism." Make your readers feel that they have arrived somewhere by sharing with them what you have learned, discovered, or realized.

The following are some possible ways to conclude your essay.

- Be genuine. Explain why this topic is important to you and/or important in life.
- If you used a quote as your hook, refer back to it. If you didn't use a quote, use one to guide your conclusion.
- You may finish by reviewing the paper's main point, but with new insight.
- Direct the readers into the future. How does an understanding of this topic relate to future thought or action? What will or should happen in the months or years ahead?

My Notes

WORD CONNECTIONS

Etymology

The word *cliché* is from the French and means "something that is overused." It derives from the French word *clicher*, meaning "to click." which resembled a sound made when using printing plates. One method of creating printing plates was called *stereotype* which could produce the same image repetitively. The word *stereotype* is now used as a synonym of *cliché*.

ACTIVITY 1.17 continued

7 Have students revise the thesis statements by beginning each with a dependent clause. Tell students that they can revise other aspects of the thesis statements' wording as necessary as they revise.

8 **Activate prior knowledge** about writing conclusion paragraphs, and then make sure students understand the function and expectations of a conclusion.

ACTIVITY 1.17 continued

9 Ask students to independently read the sample conclusion paragraphs and determine which of the conclusion techniques was used.

10 Put students into the same **discussion groups** as earlier in this activity. Allow time to evaluate one or both of the sample conclusions and discuss possible revisions. Then have each student revise one or both concluding paragraphs according to the group's decisions. Be sure students address the use of formal style, correct spelling, and precise diction in their revision efforts.

11 Ask one student from each group to read part of their revised conclusion aloud and discuss what was revised and why.

12 Students will now move on to analyzing and revising a body paragraph. In their **discussion groups**, ask students to read the information on body paragraphs and **mark the text** for key details. As students work, circulate to check for understanding and accuracy.

Expository Writing Focus: Organization

My Notes

Evaluating and Revising Conclusions

6. As you read examples of a conclusion, identify which technique the writer used and how effective the conclusion is.

Sample 1

The best heroes out there are those that put others before themselves. How do we know when someone is a hero? When they face challenges with pure determination, but don't save or satisfy everyone in the end. It blows us away every time a hero can fix sticky situations, but it is more important to know that a hero is doing what they're doing for the protection of everyone else. Making mistakes is what makes everything else that they do even more spectacular.

Sample 2

Heroes often look like the normal people we see walking down the street and they might be the plainest form of normal there is. Behind that normal appearance there has been struggle and challenge that has turned into wisdom. Heroes have to not only overcome challenges, but have done it with dignity. Heroes have grown from their experiences and now put a different value on life itself. Heroes are absolutely essential to life, for without heroes we would have no one to admire or set our goals to their standards.

Check Your Understanding

Revise one of the two paragraphs above based on your evaluation and discussion of how it could benefit by additional content, reworking sentences, and using more precise or formal diction.

Writing Body Paragraphs

Body paragraphs are the meat of your essay. Outlined by the thesis, they include the reasons, plus the details and examples, that provide the support for your thesis. Part of the strength of your support is **synthesizing**, or pulling together, examples and details from your experiences and from texts and resources you have read or studied. As you write body paragraphs, be sure to include the following:

- A topic sentence that introduces the focus of the paragraph
- A concluding sentence that follows from the information and explanations presented
- Details and examples relevant and sufficient to make your point
- Commentary that explains why these details and examples are significant

WORD CONNECTIONS

Cognates

The English word *synthesize* has the same meaning as its Spanish cognate *sintetizar*.

- Paraphrases and embedded quotations conveying important details and examples
- Transitions to show your understanding of the content by showing the connections among ideas

Evaluating and Revising Body Paragraphs

7. Read the following body paragraph and evaluate its effectiveness. Look at the transitions, the details and examples, and the commentary, as well as the skill with which paraphrases and embedded quotations are handled.

Heroism is trying your hardest, no matter the obstacles, to go beyond the needs of yourself to help others. A son writes about how his mother, Ana, has an obstacle, but does all that she can to fight it, and does not complain. He says that she fights cancer with a smile and "hasn't let it slow her down, either" (Gandara). This shows that even though she could complain and give up fighting the disease, she tries her hardest, which inspires her loved ones. In addition, in the movie *Mulan*, the main character wants to help her father by enlisting in the army, which is impossible according to Chinese law because she is a girl. Instead of giving up on this, Mulan decides to pretend to be a man and goes to extremes to keep up her charade. This is heroic because her father, being the only male in his family, had to enlist in the army, yet he was too sick to fight and would have undoubtedly died in the conflict. Facing illness or danger with courage for the sake of another is inspiring and heroic.

Check Your Understanding

Return to the texts you have read and studied in this unit. Begin to think about which ones you can use to help support your definition of heroism. Make a list of the texts, the heroes, and the events you may be able to use in your essay. Begin to categorize them as you think of each definition strategy: function, example, and negation.

My Notes

ACTIVITY 1.17 continued

13 Put students into their groups once again to read and evaluate the effectiveness of the sample body paragraph.

14 As an alternative to having students move on to revising this paragraph, conduct a whole-class discussion in which you review the groups' evaluations of the effectiveness of the paragraph.

TEACHER TO TEACHER

This paragraph is a clear example of a proficient body paragraph in its use of detail, examples, commentary, and transitions. Still, it could benefit from another example that supports the function described in the topic sentence—putting others before self. Use this as the prompt to have groups think of another example they could use from their reading to support the idea of this paragraph.

ACTIVITY 1.17 continued

15 Finally, ask students to independently respond to the writing prompt in outline form, using the hints in parentheses as a guide. Make sure they know that this work serves as prewriting for Embedded Assessment 2, and point out that an outline does not require complete sentences; the purpose is to start organizing ideas on paper.

Leveled Differentiated Instruction

In this activity, some students may have difficulty completing every part of this outline. To support learning, have students work with a partner to complete their essay outline.

Em Help students express their ideas by putting them into pairs to ask and answer simple questions about different parts of the essay.

Ex Have students respond to their discussion partners by adding relevant information about different parts of the essay.

Br Have students respond to their discussion partners by adding relevant information and providing useful feedback about different parts of the essay.

▶ASSESS

As students evaluate and revise, be sure they use the Scoring Guide from the Embedded Assessment and the descriptors of effective paragraphs included in the activity. The more familiar and comfortable they are with reviewing, evaluating, and revising work, the more likely they are to do these things in their own writing.

▶ADAPT

The pacing of this activity will be determined by how often your students need direct instruction and support in evaluating and revising the paragraphs. To support learning, model the revision process each time and then assign another paragraph to groups. If your students are able to discuss and revise independently, you may need only to monitor their evaluation and revision work.

Expository Writing Focus: Organization

My Notes

WRITING to SOURCES **Expository Writing Prompt**

Think about people who deserve status as a hero from the past, from the present, from life, and from literature. What defines a hero? Draft an insightful thesis statement using a complex sentence structure. Then, outline ideas for your essay. Remember to return to your work in Activity 1.13 on defining a hero.

Hero Definition Essay Outline

I. **INTRODUCTION**

Hook: (What would make an effective hook?)
Bridge: (background information and connections)
Thesis: (state your original definition)

II. **BODY PARAGRAPH 1** (Function/Example/Negation)

Topic Sentence: (connect to thesis)
Supporting Detail: (list source)
Paraphrase, quotations, examples with commentary
Supporting Detail: (list source)

III. **BODY PARAGRAPH 2** (Function/Example/Negation)

Topic Sentence: (connect to thesis)
Supporting Detail: (list source)
Paraphrase, quotations, examples with commentary
Supporting Detail: (list source)

IV. **BODY PARAGRAPH 3** (Function/Example/Negation)

Topic Sentence: (connect to thesis)
Supporting Detail: (list source)
Paraphrase, quotations, examples with commentary
Supporting Detail: (list source)

V. **CONCLUSION**

(What would make an effective conclusion?)

Independent Reading Checkpoint

Look back at the article about Tristan Segers on page 59. Compare how his life and the life of the hero in your independent reading text fit into the hero's archetype that you have learned about in this unit.

The act of creating a possible list of readings to use is best done first as a small discussion group, then in a large group discussion, so that by the time students get to creating an outline of the essay they will be ready with content. Encourage students to revisit texts and previous activities to generate ideas.

INDEPENDENT READING CHECKPOINT

Have students complete the Independent Reading Checkpoint.

Writing a Definition Essay

EMBEDDED ASSESSMENT 2

Assignment

Think about people who deserve status as heroes—from the past, from the present, from life, and from literature. What defines a hero? Write a multi-paragraph essay that develops your definition of heroism. Be sure to use strategies of definition (function, example, and negation) to guide your writing.

Planning and Prewriting: Take time to make a plan for your essay.

- Which activities and texts have you collected that will help you refine and expand your definition of a hero?
- What prewriting strategies (such as free writing or graphic organizers) could help you brainstorm ideas and organize your examples?

Drafting: Write a multi-paragraph essay that effectively organizes your ideas.

- How will you provide a hook, a bridge, and a thesis in the introduction?
- How will you use the strategies of definition (function, example, negation) in your support paragraphs?
- How will your conclusion demonstrate the significance of heroism and encourage readers to accept your definition?

Evaluating and Revising: Create opportunities to review and revise your work.

- During the process of writing, when can you pause to share and respond with others?
- What is your plan to include suggestions and revision ideas in your draft?
- How can the Scoring Guide help you evaluate how well your draft meets the requirements of the assignment?

Checking and Editing for Publication: Confirm that your final draft is ready for publication.

- How will you proofread and edit your draft to demonstrate command of the conventions of standard English capitalization, punctuation, spelling, grammar, and usage?
- What would be an engaging title for your essay?

Reflection

After completing this Embedded Assessment, think about how you went about accomplishing this task, and respond to the following:

- Explain how the activities in this unit helped prepare you for success in the Embedded Assessment.
- Which activities were especially helpful, and why?

My Notes

EMBEDDED ASSESSMENT 2

Materials: access to website for finding a definition of *heroism*: http://heroicimagination.org/welcome/psychology-and-heroism/

Suggested Pacing: 3 50-minute class periods (depending on homework)

1 Planning and Prewriting: Students should have completed most of their planning and prewriting in the activities leading up to the Embedded Assessment.

2 Drafting: Remind students to consult their outlines to help them draft the essay.

3 Evaluating and Revising: Consider having students meet in writing groups to share and respond to one another's drafts, first focusing on the elements of the thesis statement and the three body paragraphs. Another meeting could be focused on an effective conclusion or introduction.

4 Checking and Editing for Publication: Students need to take responsibility for this important stage of the writing process. You can encourage this by asking students to hand in a typed draft before they hand in a final draft to provide evidence of proofreading and editing.

Reflection: After students have completed this task, remind them to respond to the reflection questions. This is an opportunity to ask students to be reflective about their learning and academic growth.

COMMON CORE STATE STANDARDS

Focus Standards:

W.8.2a: Introduce a topic or thesis statement clearly, previewing what is to follow; organize ideas, concepts, and information into broader categories; include formatting (e.g., headings), graphics (e.g., charts, tables), and multimedia when useful to aiding comprehension.

W.8.2b: Develop the topic with relevant well-chosen facts, definitions, concrete details, quotations, or other information and examples.

W.8.2c: Use appropriate and varied transitions to create cohesion and clarify the relationships among ideas and concepts.

W.8.2d: Use precise language and domain-specific vocabulary to inform about or explain the topic.

W.8.2e: Establish and maintain a formal style.

W.8.2f: Provide a concluding statement or section that follows from and supports the information or explanation presented.

EMBEDDED ASSESSMENT 2 continued

Portfolio Once students have written the reflection about their essays, be sure they add it to their portfolios.

Ask students to reflect on what skills and knowledge they have gained that will help them as they think about their future after high school.

You may want to use this time to have students find, among all their work that you asked them to keep, the pieces that they think represent some of their best, most interesting, or most successful work to keep and reflect on later in the year. They should place these pieces in their portfolios.

SCORING GUIDE

When you score this Embedded Assessment, you may wish to download and print copies of the Scoring Guide from SpringBoard Digital. In this way you can have a copy to mark for each student's work.

EMBEDDED ASSESSMENT 2

Writing a Definition Essay

SCORING GUIDE

Scoring Criteria	Exemplary	Proficient	Emerging	Incomplete
Ideas	The essay • uses all three strategies of definition effectively to define a hero • maintains a precise and original thesis • integrates relevant supporting details and evidence (quotes and paraphrases) with citations and commentary.	The essay • uses strategies of definition (function, example, negation) to define a hero • maintains a clear thesis • includes adequate supporting details and evidence (quotes and paraphrases) with citations and commentary.	The essay • uses insufficient strategies of definition to define a hero • has an unclear or unfocused thesis • includes inadequate supporting details and evidence; may have inconsistent citations and/or weak commentary.	The essay • does not define a hero using strategies of definition • has no discernible thesis • lacks supporting details, citations, and/or commentary.
Structure	The essay • introduces the main idea with an engaging hook, bridge, and thesis • organizes ideas into focused support paragraphs that progress smoothly • creates coherence with the purposeful use of a variety of transitions and topic sentences • provides an insightful conclusion.	The essay • introduces the topic with a hook, bridge, and thesis • organizes ideas into support paragraphs that progress logically • creates coherence with the use of transitions and topic sentences • provides a conclusion that follows from the ideas presented.	The essay • includes an ineffective or partial introduction • has unrelated, undeveloped, or insufficient support paragraphs • uses transitions and topic sentences ineffectively or inconsistently • provides a weak, illogical, or repetitive conclusion.	The essay • lacks an introduction • has minimal, absent, or flawed support paragraphs • uses few or no transitions and topic sentences • lacks a conclusion.
Use of Language	The essay • uses consistent diction and style appropriate for an academic audience • demonstrates command of the conventions of standard English capitalization, punctuation, spelling, grammar, and usage (including complex sentences).	The essay • uses diction and style that is generally appropriate for an academic audience • demonstrates adequate command of the conventions of standard English capitalization, punctuation, spelling, grammar, and usage (including complex sentences).	The essay • uses diction or a style that is basic or inappropriate to an academic audience • demonstrates partial or inconsistent command of the conventions of standard English capitalization, punctuation, spelling, grammar, and usage.	The essay • uses flawed diction • lacks command of the conventions of standard English capitalization, punctuation, spelling, grammar, and usage; frequent errors obscure meaning.

COMMON CORE STATE STANDARDS

Additional Standards Addressed:

W.8.4; W.8.5; W.8.7; W.8.8; W.8.9a; W.8.9b; W.8.10; L.8.2c

ENGLISH LANGUAGE DEVELOPMENT RUBRIC

The Embedded Assessment that the whole class completes can be a useful source of English language development evidence. Use this additional rubric to examine the Embedded Assessment products of English learners. The analysis will help you gain additional information about student learning related to the strands of the English Language Development Standards and identify individual areas for improvement.

Criteria	Emerging	Expanding	Bridging
Interpretive	The student • explains basic ideas based on close readings of texts with substantial support. • expresses inferences and conclusions based on close reading of texts with substantial support.	The student • explains ideas based on close readings of texts with some support. • expresses inferences and conclusions based on close reading of texts with some support.	The student • explains complex ideas based on close readings of texts with little support. • expresses inferences and conclusions based on close reading of texts with some support.
Productive	The student • plans and delivers oral presentations • writes short literary texts collaboratively and independently. • uses general academic vocabulary with domain-specific words to create some precision.	The student • plans and delivers oral presentations • writes longer literary texts collaboratively and independently with appropriate text organization. • uses general academic vocabulary with domain-specific words with precision and an awareness of shades of meaning.	The student • plans and delivers oral presentations • writes longer, more detailed literary texts collaboratively and independently with appropriate text organization. • uses precise, nuanced, vocabulary and figurative language appropriately.
Structuring Cohesive Texts	The student • organizes narrative sequentially, with a beginning, middle and end. • uses basic language resources to make text more cohesive. • uses simple connecting words to link ideas or events in the text.	The student • organizes narrative with a natural event sequence. • uses increasingly complex language resources to make text more cohesive. • uses connecting words or phrases to link ideas or events in the text.	The student • organizes narrative with a clear and natural event sequence. • uses complex language resources to make text more cohesive. • uses a variety of connecting words or phrases to link ideas or events in the text.
Expanding and Enriching Ideas	The student • uses a variety of verbs in different tenses appropriate to narrative text. • uses nouns and noun phrases to add details. • uses simple adverbials to provide details.	The student • uses a variety of verbs in different tenses appropriate to the task, text type, and discipline. • uses a variety of nouns and noun phrases to add rich details. • uses adverbials to provide rich details.	The student • uses a variety of verbs in different tenses, aspects, voices, and moods, appropriate for the task, text type, and discipline. • uses an expanded variety of nouns and noun phrases to add rich details. • uses complex adverbials to provide rich details.
Connecting and Condensing Ideas	The student • connects ideas in compound sentences using simple conjunctions. • condenses ideas by using prepositional phrases to create precise and detailed sentences.	The student • connects ideas in compound and complex sentences using a variety of ways. • condenses ideas in a variety of ways to create precise and detailed sentences.	The student • connects and combines ideas in compound and complex sentences using a variety of ways. • condenses ideas in a variety of complex ways to create precise and detailed sentences.

Embedded Assessment 2
Writing a Definition Essay

ENGLISH LANGUAGE DEVELOPMENT RUBRIC

The Embedded Assessment that the whole class completes can be a useful source of English language development evidence. Use this additional rubric to examine the Embedded Assessment products of English learners. The analysis will help you gain additional information about student learning related to the strands of the English Language Development Standards and identify individual areas for improvement.

Criteria	Emerging	Expanding	Bridging
Interpretive	The student • explains basic ideas based on close readings of texts with substantial support. • expresses inferences and conclusions based on close reading of texts with substantial support. • explains how language supports ideas with substantial support. • analyzes how words produce different effects.	The student • explains ideas based on close readings of texts with some support. • expresses inferences and conclusions based on close reading of texts with some support. • explains how language presents ideas with some support. • analyzes how words produce shades of meaning and the effect on the audience.	The student • explains complex ideas based on close readings of texts with little support. • expresses inferences and conclusions based on close reading of texts with some support. • explains how language presents ideas with little support. • analyzes how words or phrases produce shades of meaning and the effect on the audience.
Productive	The student • writes short literary texts collaboratively and independently. • writes brief summary of text using complete sentences. • uses general academic vocabulary with domain-specific words to create some precision.	The student • writes longer literary texts collaboratively and independently with appropriate text organization. • writes concise summary of text. • uses general academic vocabulary with domain-specific words with precision and an awareness of shades of meaning.	The student • writes longer, more detailed literary texts collaboratively and independently with appropriate text organization. • writes clear and coherent summary of text. • uses precise, nuanced, vocabulary and figurative language appropriately
Structuring Cohesive Texts	The student • organizes writing logically to express ideas. • uses basic language resources to make text more cohesive. • uses simple connecting words to link ideas or events in the text.	The student • organizes writing naturally, logically, and coherently. • uses increasingly complex language resources to make text more cohesive. • uses connecting words or phrases to link ideas or events in the text.	The student • organizes writing in a logical, clear sequence to create cohesion and precision. • uses complex language resources to make text more cohesive. • uses a variety of connecting words or phrases to link ideas or events in the text.
Expanding and Enriching Ideas	The student • uses a variety of verbs in different tenses appropriate to narrative text. • uses nouns and noun phrases to add details. • uses simple adverbials to provide details.	The student • uses a variety of verbs in different tenses appropriate to the task, text type, and discipline. • uses a variety of nouns and noun phrases to add rich details. • uses adverbials to provide rich details.	The student • uses a variety of verbs in different tenses, aspects, voices, and moods, appropriate for the task, text type, and discipline. • uses an expanded variety of nouns and noun phrases to add rich details. • uses complex adverbials to provide rich details.
Connecting and Condensing Ideas	The student • connects ideas in compound sentences using simple conjunctions. • condenses ideas by using prepositional phrases to create precise and detailed sentences.	The student • connects ideas in compound and complex sentences using a variety of ways. • condenses ideas in a variety of ways to create precise and detailed sentences.	The student • connects and combines ideas in compound and complex sentences using a variety of ways. • condenses ideas in a variety of complex ways to create precise and detailed sentences.

Planning the Unit

UNIT 2

Context

This unit gives students a deeper understanding of the world. Through their study of utopian societies, students see that life cannot be perfect, no matter how hard we try, but they also see that without hardships, heroes would not exist. Just as a day is a balance of dark and light, so is life. Through their study of argumentation, students realize they have the power to convince others to do what is right, to make a change, or to see from a new perspective.

Instructional Sequence

In the first half of the unit, students study a novel. Students read to explore the concepts of *utopia* and *dystopia*, deepen their understanding of the Hero's Journey archetype, analyze literary elements, and form responses to literature using the compare/contrast structure to organize ideas. Students apply their understanding by writing an expository essay relating to the concept of *dystopia* or the Hero's Journey archetype.

In the second half, students learn how to develop an effective argument through reading, writing, collaboration, and debate. They learn the importance of understanding one's audience and using research and logic to support a claim. Students apply their understanding by writing a research-based argumentative essay about a controversial topic.

CollegeBoard

AP/College Readiness

In this unit, students will focus on refining these important skills and knowledge areas for AP/College Readiness:

- Analyzing writer's craft (Activities 2.2, 2.3, 2.5, 2.11, 2.13)
- Using textual evidence to support a literary interpretation (Activities 2.4–2.9)
- Applying a literary archetype to literary text (Activities 2.7, 2.8, 2.9)
- Produce expository, analytical, and argumentative texts that introduce a complex idea and develop it with evidence, explanations, and transitions (Activities 2.2, 2.3, 2.5, 2.15, 2.16, 2.17)
- Create and sustain arguments based on readings, research, and/or personal experience (Activities 2.15, 2.16, 2.17)

Unpacked Embedded Assessments

Embedded Assessment 1: Writing an Expository Essay	Embedded Assessment 2: Writing an Argumentative Essay
Skills and Knowledge: • Establish a clear thesis in a focused introduction. • Develop a thesis with relevant details, evidence, and explanations. • Embed and cite direct quotations. • Sequence ideas logically using an appropriate organizational structure. • Use transitions to create coherence. • Provide a relevant conclusion. • Use literary terms and precise language to convey an academic tone. • Demonstrate a command of conventions.	**Skills and Knowledge:** • Gather and synthesize relevant information from credible sources. • Establish a clear claim and support it with valid reasoning, relevant and sufficient evidence, and counterclaims. • Sequence ideas logically and use transitions to create coherence. • Provide a clear and focused introduction and conclusion. • Use diction and language (e.g., persuasive appeals and grammatical mood) to convey an appropriate tone and persuade an audience. • Demonstrate a command of conventions (e.g., when citing textual evidence). • Create an accurate annotated bibliography.

Instructional Activities and Pacing

Total: 35 class periods	Description
2.1–2.2 3 class periods	Students are introduced to the unit's Essential Questions and vocabulary before unpacking Embedded Assessment 1. Next, students develop their expository writing skills by examining the compare/contrast organizational structure and learning how to use transitions to create coherence. Students apply their learning by writing a compare/contrast response to an informational text.
2.3 2 class periods	This activity introduces and distinguishes between the concepts of *utopia* and *dystopia* through the reading of informational and classic literary texts. In two Language and Writer's Craft lessons, students practice embedding direct quotations and using active and passive voice for effect. Students apply their learning by writing a response to literature.
2.4–2.6 6 class periods	The next six activities guide a study of *The Giver* or *Fahrenheit 451*; each novel is chunked into six sections. Before reading, students conduct a close reading of the cover to make predictions about the story. As students progress through the first half of the novel, they examine and make connections among literary elements (e.g., character, setting, conflict, and theme), develop a personal vocabulary list, use reading strategies to comprehend and analyze the text, and prepare for and engage in class discussions (including a Socratic Seminar). In addition, students study grammatical mood to deepen their understanding of character perspective. These activities begin to prepare students for Embedded Assessment 1 by teaching students to think from multiple perspectives and to form and support opinions based on evidence.
2.7–2.9 6 class periods	As students progress through the second half of the novel, they use the Hero's Journey archetype from Unit 1 to structure their analysis. After examining each stage (Departure, Initiation, and Return), students write expository responses that explain the protagonist's journey, and they engage in related discussions. Through this work, students see the transformational nature of the Hero's Journey and its connection to a deeper meaning about life (theme). Finally, in preparation for the Embedded Assessment, students practice writing introductory paragraphs and form an initial response to one of the two essay prompts.
Embedded Assessment 1 4 class periods	Students will now work through the stages of the writing process and collaborate in writing groups to prepare their essay for publication. Once the essay is finalized, students will reflect on their learning.
2.10–2.11 3 class periods	The first activity serves as a transition between the first and second halves of the unit. Students begin by reflecting on their learning in the first half, making connections to the second half, unpacking Embedded Assessment 2, and selecting an independent reading text. Next, students examine elements of argumentation (e.g., claim, evidence, reasoning, and counterclaim) and the connection between purpose, audience, and content in an argument. They apply their understanding by outlining ideas for an argument based on a technology-related topic.

2.12–2.16 8 class periods	Students learn how to use rhetorical appeals (i.e., *logos, pathos,* and *ethos*) for effect, distinguish between effective and faulty *logos*, write debatable claims, analyze an audience to form appropriate counterclaims, conduct and cite research to support a claim, and create annotated bibliographies. As activities progress, students apply their learning by forming and supporting claims using evidence from informational texts and research.
2.17 1 class period	Students complete their research and outline their argumentative essays, then share research and outlines in writing groups to generate feedback.
Embedded Assessment 2 2 class periods	Students will now continue to work through the stages of the writing process and collaborate in writing groups to prepare their essay for publication. Once the essay is finalized, students will reflect on their learning.

Novel Reading Plan

Unit 2 Reading Plan		
Text Chunks	**Corresponding Activity**	**Suggested Treatment of Text**
Chunk 1 *The Giver*: pp. 1–19 *Fahrenheit 451*: pp. 1–21	2.4 Understanding a Society's Way of Life	Begin reading **in class** Complete reading as **homework**
Chunk 2 *The Giver*: pp. 20–49 *Fahrenheit 451*: pp. 21–38	2.5 Contemplating Conflicting Perspectives	Begin reading **in class** Complete reading as **homework**
Chunk 3 *The Giver*: pp. 50–79 *Fahrenheit 451*: pp. 38–60	2.6 Questioning Society	Begin reading **in class** Complete reading as **homework**
Chunk 4 *The Giver*: pp. 80–117 *Fahrenheit 451*: pp. 61–88	2.7 A Shift in Perspective: Beginning the Adventure	Begin reading **in class** Complete reading as **homework**
Chunk 5 *The Giver*: pp. 118–145 *Fahrenheit 451*: pp. 88–123	2.8 Navigating the Road of Trials	Begin reading **in class** Complete reading as **homework**
Chunk 6 *The Giver*: pp. 146–179 *Fahrenheit 451*: pp. 123–158	2.9 The End of the Journey	Begin reading **in class** Complete reading as **homework**

Socratic Seminar Notes
Topic: Rules and Laws in a Utopian/Dystopian Society
Listening to Comprehend
• **Interesting points:** 1. ________________: 2. ________________: 3. ________________: • **My thoughts:** 1. 2. 3.
Listening to Evaluate
• **Speaking:** Strength: Challenge: • **Listening:** Strength: Challenge:
Reflection
• **I did/did not meet my speaking and listening goals. Explanation:** • **I am most proud of:** • **Next time I will:**

Unit Resources at a Glance

Readings	Writing Tasks	Language Skills
"Grant and Lee: A Study in Contrasts," by Bruce Catton "Harrison Bergeron," by Kurt Vonnegut, Jr. *The Giver*, by Lois Lowry *Fahrenheit 451*, by Ray Bradbury "Banned Books Week: Celebrating the Freedom to Read," from ALA "Parents Share Son's Fatal Text Message to Warn Against Texting & Driving," from the Associated Press "The Science Behind Distracted Driving," from KUTV Austin "How the Brain Reacts," by Marcel Just and Tim Keller "Cellphones and driving: As dangerous as we think?" by Matthew Walberg	Quickwrite: Why are books important? Expository Writing Prompts • Compare and contrast • Conflict between needs of society and the individual • How the contrast in characters highlights a conflict • Explain journey in relation to Hero's Journey • Compare and contrast characters in novel Argumentative Writing Prompts • Write a paragraph in support of a claim • State a claim and support with research findings	**Language and Writers Craft** Embedding Direct Quotations Active and Passive Voice Choosing Mood Shifts in Voice and Mood **Grammar and Usage** Using Ellipses and Brackets Conditional Tense Mood Passive Voice
Strategy Introduction	**Speaking and Listening**	**Family Connections**
Socratic Seminar Fishbowl	Socratic Seminar Fishbowl Collaborative Discussion Think Pair Share	Suggestions for Independent Reading Family Letters (English and Spanish) Student Reports

English Language Development	Independent Reading	Assessments
Leveled Differentiated Instruction ELD Graphic Organizers *SpringBoard English Language Development*, Student Edition, Grade 8, Unit 2 *SpringBoard English Language Development*, Teacher Edition Grade 8, Unit 2	Independent Reading Links Independent Reading Checkpoints Independent Reading Log Reader/Writer Notebook Suggestions for Independent Reading	Check Your Understanding Writing Prompts Embedded Assessment One: Writing an Expository Essay Embedded Assessment Two: Writing an Argumentative Essay Short-Cycle Assessments Unit Assessments
SpringBoard Writing Workshop with Grammar Activities, Grade 8	**SpringBoard Close Reading Workshop, Grade 8**	**Routines for Teaching Foundational Skills**
Writing Workshop 1: The Writing Process: Strategies for Writing Writing Workshop 2: Argumentative Writing Writing Workshop 3: Expository Writing: Compare and Contrast Writing Workshop 5: Response to Expository Writing Grammar Activities: Unit 2 Grammar Handbook	Close Reading Workshop 1: Close Reading of Informational/Literary Nonfiction Texts Close Reading Workshop 2: Close Reading of Argumentative Texts	Phonics and Word Recognition Mini-lessons Fluency Mini-lessons

Suggestions for Independent Reading

This list, divided into the categories of **Literature** and **Nonfiction/Informational Text**, comprises titles related to the themes and content of the unit. For their independent reading, students can select from this wide array of titles, which have been chosen based on complexity and interest. You can also encourage students to do their own research and select titles that intrigue them.

Unit 2: The Challenge of Utopia		
Literature		
Author	**Title**	**Lexile**
Ada, Alma	*Love, Amalia*	940L
Asimov, Isaac	*I, Robot*	820L
Bradbury, Ray	*The Martian Chronicles: Something Wicked This Way Comes*	820L
Budhos, Marina	*Ask Me No Questions*	790L
Burg, Ann	*All the Broken Pieces*	680L
Carlson, Lori Marie	*Red Hot Salsa*	N/A
Cisneros, Sandra	*The House on Mango Street*	870L
Collins, Suzanne	*The Hunger Games*	810L
Dayton, Arwen Elys	*Seeker*	800L
Farmer, Nancy	*The House of the Scorpions*	660L
Frank, Pat	*Alas, Babylon*	870L
Heinlein, Robert	*Stranger in a Strange Land*	940L
Huxley, Aldous	*Brave New World*	870L
LeGuin, Ursula	*The Left Hand of Darkness*	970L
Lu, Marie	*Legend*	710L
Meyer, Marissa	*Cinder*	790L
More, Thomas	*Utopia*	1370L
O'Brien, Tim	*The Things They Carried*	880L
Orwell, George	*1984*	1090L
Orwell, George	*Animal Farm*	1170L
Reinhardt, Dana	*A Brief Chapter in My Impossible Life*	N/A
Roth, Veronica	*Divergent*	700L
Salisbury, Graham	*House of the Red Fish*	610L
Verne, Jules	*Twenty Thousand Leagues Under the Sea*	1030L
Wells, H.G.	*The Time Machine*	1070L
Wells, H.G.	*The War of the Worlds*	1040L
Westerfield, Scott	*Uglies*	770L
Yancey, Rick	*The Fifth Wave*	N/A
Yang, Dori Jones	*Daughter of Xanadu*	780L

Nonfiction/Informational Text		
Author	**Title**	**Lexile**
Bausum, Ann	*Denied, Detained, Deported: Stories from the Dark Side of American Immigration*	1170L
Carson, Rachel,	*Silent Spring The Sea Around Us*	1340L
D'Aluisio, Faith and Peter Menzel	*What the World Eats*	1150L
Engle, Margarita	*The Lightening Dreamer: Cuba's Greatest Abolitionists*	N/A
Gore, Al	*Global Warming Is an Immediate Crisis*	N/A
Hatkoff, Juliana and Isabella Hatkoff	*Winter's Tail: How One Little Dolphin Learned to Swim Again*	930L
Hesse, Karen	*Aleutian Sparrow*	N/A
Hoose, Philip	*The Race to Save the Lord God Bird*	1150L
Kalan, Robert	*We Are Not Beasts of Burden*	1150L
Lasky, Kathryn	*John Muir: America's First Environmentalist*	1050L
Markle, Sandra	*How Many Baby Pandas?*	N/A
Pollan, Michael	*In Defense of Food: An Eater's Manifesto*	1390L
Schlosser, Eric	*Fast Food Nation*	1240L
Scholsser, Eric and Wilson, Charles,	*Chew on This: Everything You Don't Want to Know About Fast Food*	1110L
Sivertsen, Linda and Josh Sivertsen	*Generation Green: The Ultimate Teen Guide to Living an Eco-Friendly Life*	N/A
Somervill, Barbara	*Animal Survivors of the Wetlands*	1060L
Stearman, Kaye	*Taking Action Against Homelessness*	N/A
Waters, Alice	*Edible Schoolyard: A Universal Idea*	N/A
Welsbacher, Anne	*Earth-Friendly Design*	N/A

The Challenge of Utopia

Visual Prompt: The perfect society may mean different things to different people. What type of society does each image represent? What does each say about what is important to the people who prefer one over the other?

Unit Overview

We probably all agree that we would like to live in an ideal society where everyone is free and happy, but what does that actually mean, and why do definitions of the ideal society differ so greatly? Some would argue that an ideal life is a life without conflict or problems, but what is a "perfect" life? In this unit, you will read, write, and engage in various types of collaborative discussions to explore these universal questions. Then, you will move from discussion and exposition into debate and effective argumentation as you research and develop a claim about a contemporary issue.

UNIT 2

UNIT OVERVIEW

Read aloud the Unit Overview, asking students to **mark the text** by highlighting words and phrases that help them predict what the unit will be about. Share responses in partner, small-group, or whole-class discussion.

Have students look at the image and respond to the visual prompt. You may want to have students **think-pair-share** to write a short response or discuss their responses as a class.

TEACHER TO TEACHER

You may want to engage students in a preliminary class discussion of what an ideal society would be like. What would it include and not include? Who would live there? Why is an ideal society so difficult to bring about?

ELL Support

ELD Modes and Processes

Collaborative: Students work in groups to explore the meaning of satire and to prepare for a Socratic Seminar. Students also ask and answer questions about texts in pairs or smaller groups.

Interpretive: Students explore the meanings of *utopia* and *dystopia*. Students also evaluate how certain words in a story portray the theme. Students also listen to interpret others' arguments.

Productive: Students explore and use the vocabulary of literary analysis in their writing. Students also write about protagonists in a text and why books are an important part of our society.

Structuring Cohesive Texts: Students explore the structure of argumentative writing.

Connecting and Condensing Ideas: Students will use transitions to generate comparison and contrast statements.

UNIT 2

Have students read the goals for the unit and mark any words that are unfamiliar to them. Have students add these words to the classroom Word Wall, along with definitions.

You may also want to post these goals in a visible place in the classroom for the duration of this unit, allowing you and your students to revisit the goals easily and gauge progress toward achieving goals throughout the unit.

VOCABULARY DEVELOPMENT

Important terms in this unit are divided into Academic Vocabulary (those words that are used in multiple curriculum areas) and Literary Terms, which are specific to the student of literature and language arts.

Adding to vocabulary knowledge is essential for reading fluency. Students will encounter new vocabulary in this course in multiple ways:

- Academic Vocabulary
- Literary Terms
- Vocabulary in Context (unfamiliar terms glossed in text selections)
- Word Connections
- Oral discussions

Continue to expect students to keep a **Reader/Writer Notebook** in which they record new words and their meanings (and pronunciations if needed). Having students use word-study graphic organizers to study key vocabulary terms in depth will greatly enhance their understanding of new words and their connection to unit concepts and to the broader use of academic terms.

See the Resources section at the back of this book for examples of graphic organizers suitable for word study. As students become more familiar with using graphic organizers to explore the meaning of a word, you may want them to create their own graphic organizers.

UNIT 2

The Challenge of Utopia

GOALS:

- To analyze a novel for archetype and theme
- To analyze and evaluate a variety of expository and argumentative texts for ideas, structure, and language
- To develop informative/explanatory texts using the compare/contrast organizational structure
- To understand the use of active voice and passive voice
- To develop effective arguments using logical reasoning, relevant evidence, and persuasive appeals for effect

ACADEMIC VOCABULARY

compare/contrast
perspective
Socratic
seminar
argument
debate
controversy
research
search terms

Literary Terms

antagonist

Contents

Activities

ELL Support continued

English Language Development Standards

ELD.PI.8.1 Bridging* Contribute to class, group, and partner discussions by following turn-taking rules, asking relevant questions, affirming others, adding relevant information and evidence, paraphrasing key ideas, building on responses, and providing useful feedback. **ELD.PI.8.5 Expanding*** Demonstrate active listening in oral presentation activities by asking and answering detailed questions with occasional prompting and moderate support. **ELD.PI.8.6a Bridging*** Explain ideas, phenomena, processes, and text relationships based on close reading of a variety of grade-level texts and viewing of multimedia with light support. **ELD.PI.8.6c Bridging*** Use knowledge of morphology, context, reference materials, and visual cues to determine the meanings, including figurative and connotative meanings, of unknown and multiple-meaning words on a variety of new topics. **ELD.PI.8.7 Expanding*** Explain how well writers and speakers use specific language to

The Challenge of Utopia

UNIT 2

*Texts not included in these materials.

Language and Writer's Craft

- Embedding Direct Quotations (2.3)
- Active and Passive Voice (2.3)
- Choosing Mood (2.5)
- Shifts in Voice and Mood (2.17)

MY INDEPENDENT READING LIST

UNIT 2 continued

LANGUAGE AND WRITER'S CRAFT

Each unit includes Language and Writer's Craft features as well as Grammar & Usage content. You may want students to devote a section of their Reader/Writer Notebooks to their study of language and grammar. Encourage students to make notes about their understanding of specific grammar rules and how to use language in their writing to create specific effects.

CONTENTS

Have the students **skim/scan** the activities and texts to find a Wow (an activity that looks interesting) and a Whoa (an activity that looks challenging). Share responses in partner, small-group, or whole-class discussion.

INDEPENDENT READING

In this half of the unit, while working on creating an expository essay about dystopia or the concept of the Hero's Journey, students will have the opportunity to read on their own. They will choose a societal challenge to research and select a few short informational or narrative nonfiction pieces to read. The Planning Unit section of the Teacher's Edition and the Resources section of the Student Edition contain information, Reading Logs, and Reading Lists to help you and your students find the right readings. While reading a novel for close study, students will not be expected to read an additional novel for Independent Reading.

ELL Support continued

present ideas or support arguments and provide detailed evidence when provided with moderate support. **ELD.PI.8.10a Bridging*** Write longer and more detailed literary and informational texts collaboratively and independently using appropriate text organization and growing understanding of register. **ELD.PI.8.12a Expanding*** Use a growing set of academic words, domain-specific words, synonyms, and antonyms to create precision and shades of meaning while speaking and writing. **ELD.PII.8.1 Bridging*** Apply understanding of the organizational structure

TEACHER TO TEACHER

The SpringBoard program has been designed to allow students to interact with the text by making notes in their books and marking text to facilitate close reading. In addition to making notes in the text, students are expected to use their Reader/Writer Notebooks often: for vocabulary study, answering text-dependent reading comprehension questions, reflections, some writing assignments, notes in response to the Independent Reading Links, capturing thoughts about learning strategies and how to use them, and so on. The Reader/Writer Notebooks are not listed as part of the materials for each activity, but the expectation is that students will have access to them.

ACTIVITY 2.1

▶PLAN

Suggested Pacing: 1 50-minute class period

▶TEACH

1 Read the Making Connections information aloud for students.

2 To **activate prior knowledge,** ask students to **think-write-pair-share** responses to the Essential Questions. Remind students that their understanding of these ideas will grow deeper throughout the unit.

3 Explain that throughout the unit, students should **revisit** their initial responses to the Essential Questions and vocabulary to reflect on their learning and to demonstrate that their learning has progressed (e.g., using a strategy such as QHT).

4 Ask students to independently sort the Academic Vocabulary and Literary Terms.

5 Facilitate a **close reading** of the EA1 assignment. Be sure students understand that each prompt will require a different form of organization–either a traditional expository essay organization or a compare/contrast organization. When looking at the Scoring Guide criteria, focus on the "Proficient" column. Instruct students to **mark the text** by underlining or highlighting key skills (verbs) and knowledge (nouns).

ACTIVITY 2.1

The Challenge of Utopia

LEARNING STRATEGIES: Think-Pair-Share, QHT, Close Reading, Marking the Text, Paraphrasing, Graphic Organizer

Learning Targets

- Preview the big ideas and vocabulary for the unit.
- Identify and analyze the skills and knowledge necessary to be successful in completing Embedded Assessment 1.

Making Connections

In the last unit you studied what it is to be a hero and how heroes test themselves to find their own heroic qualities. In this unit you will read a novel that features a hero who must struggle to combat forces greater than he knows in his quest for an individual sense of freedom and identity.

Essential Questions

The following Essential Questions will be the focus of the unit study. Respond to both questions.

1. To what extent can a perfect or ideal society exist?

2. What makes an argument effective?

My Notes

Vocabulary Development

Create a QHT chart in your Reader/Writer Notebook and sort the Academic Vocabulary and Literary Terms on the Contents page into the columns Q, H, and T. One academic goal would be to move all words to the "T" column by the end of the unit.

Unpacking Embedded Assessment 1

Read the assignment for Embedded Assessment 1: Writing an Expository Essay.

Think about how writers organize and develop ideas in expository writing. Use an expository structure to communicate your understanding of the concept of dystopia and/or the concept of the Hero's Journey. Select one of the prompts below:

- Write an essay that compares and contrasts life in a dystopian society with modern day society.
- Write an essay that explains how the protagonist (hero) changes as a result of conflict with his dystopian society (Road of Trials), and explain how this change connects to the novel's theme (the Crossing, or Return Threshold).

Work with your class to paraphrase the expectations and create a graphic organizer to use as a visual reminder of the required concepts and skills. Once you have analyzed the assignment, go to the Scoring Guide for a deeper look into the requirements of the assignment. Add additional information to your graphic organizer.

INDEPENDENT READING LINK

Read and Research

During this half of the unit, you will read a science fiction novel together as a class. The protagonist in this novel is a hero fighting against a challenge in society. Think about challenges in your own society that interest you. Research news articles, narrative nonfiction pieces, or contemporary short stories that discuss the challenge, and what people are trying to do to fix it. List the pieces you will read in your My Independent Reading List.

ELL Support continued

of different text types to comprehending texts and to writing clear and cohesive arguments, informative/explanatory texts and narratives. **ELD.PII.8.6 Expanding*** Combine clauses in an increasing variety of to make connections between and join ideas, for example, to express a reason or to make a concession.

*The citation reflects the highest level supported. Support is also offered for the lower levels.

COMMON CORE STATE STANDARDS

Focus Standards:

L.8.6: Acquire and use accurately grade-appropriate general academic and domain-specific words and phrases; gather vocabulary knowledge when considering a word or phrase important to comprehension or expression.

Additional Standard Addressed:

RL.8.10; SL.8.1

Expository Writing: Compare/Contrast

ACTIVITY 2.2

Learning Targets

- Analyze and explain how a writer uses the compare/contrast structure to communicate ideas.
- Write a paragraph that demonstrates an ability to use compare/contrast organizational structure.

LEARNING STRATEGIES: Graphic Organizer, QHT, Close Reading, Marking the Text, Summarizing, Rereading, Brainstorming, Drafting

Review of Expository Writing

You have had many experiences writing in the expository mode. Every time you explain something or define a concept or idea, you are writing an expository text. One form of expository writing is **compare/contrast**. This method of organization is an important model of exposition to master and can be used in many different writing situations.

ACADEMIC VOCABULARY
Compare/contrast is a rhetorical strategy and method of organization in which a writer examines similarities and differences between two people, places, ideas, or things.

1. Brainstorm ideas for topics for different school subjects that would require you to write a compare/contrast essay.

   characters in stories

   The Hunger Games vs. *The Last Olympians*

   reptiles vs. mammals

   Alaskan gold rush vs. California gold rush

2. Writers use planning and prewriting to decide how to organize their ideas. The graphic organizer below shows two methods of organizing a compare/contrast essay, using "reptiles vs. mammals" as a topic.

Subject-by-Subject Organization	Feature-by-Feature Organization
Discuss all the features of one subject and then all the features of the other.	Select a feature common to both subjects and then discuss each subject in light of that feature. Then go on to the next feature.
Subject A: Mammals Habitat Reproduction Physiology **Subject B: Reptiles** Habitat Reproduction Physiology	**Habitat** Subject A: Mammals Subject B: Reptiles **Reproduction** Subject A: Mammals Subject B: Reptiles **Physiology** Subject A: Mammals Subject B: Reptiles

3. Why would a writer select one organizational structure over the other?

My Notes

ACTIVITY 2.2

PLAN

Materials: sentence strips
Suggested Pacing: 2 50-minute class periods

TEACH

1 **Activate prior knowledge** by asking students to share what they know about expository and compare/contrast writing. You may want to focus your brainstorming only on ELA topics, though topics from different academic subjects can show the cross-curricular application of this mode of writing.

2 Discuss the logic of the methods of compare/contrast organization outlined in the table. Explain that these two models require identification of features that can be compared for both subjects, as with *habitat*, *reproduction*, and *physiology* for reptiles and mammals.

TEACHER TO TEACHER

It may be helpful to create a large visual display of the two organizational structures and post it in the room for easy reference. Since some of the analytical thinking about the novel study is focused on comparing the fictional society with actual society, you could anticipate this comparison work here by asking students what features they would use to build a comparison of two societies—e.g., education, family, government, social norms, rituals around life and death, etc.

COMMON CORE STATE STANDARDS

Focus Standards:

RI.8.3: Analyze how a text makes connections among and distinctions between individuals, ideas, or events (e.g., through comparisons, analogies, or categories).

W.8.2: Write informative/explanatory texts, including career development documents (e.g., simple business letters and job applications), to examine a topic and convey ideas, concepts, and information through the selection, organization, and analysis of relevant content.

W.8.2a: Introduce a topic or thesis statement clearly, previewing what is to follow; organize ideas, concepts, and information into broader categories; include formatting (e.g., headings), graphics (e.g., charts, tables), and multimedia when useful to aiding comprehension.

Additional Standards Addressed:

RI.8.1; RI.8.2; RI.8.4; RI.8.5; RI.8.10; W.8.2b; W.8.2c; W.8.5; W.8.10; L.8.1c; L.8.4c; L.8.4d; L.8.5a; L.8.5b; L.8.5c; L.8.6

TEACHER TO TEACHER

The focus of this reading is structure. Bruce Catton's essay is a powerful example of effective comparison/contrast writing about two heroic figures in American history. Connecting this reading to students' previous study of heroism and connecting heroic traits to the study of character development in the novel they will be reading will provide a bridge between the learning of the previous unit and that of this unit.

3 Read the Preview and the Setting a Purpose for Reading sections with your students. Help them understand the literary terms they encounter.

4 **FIRST READ:** Based on the complexity of the passage and your knowledge of your students, you may choose to conduct the first reading in a variety of ways:

- independent reading
- paired reading
- small group reading
- choral reading
- read aloud

Expository Writing: Compare/Contrast

My Notes

4. Writers often use a graphic organizer to generate ideas. Explain how the graphic organizer could help you in structuring an essay comparing and contrasting two subjects.

Preview

In this activity, you will read and analyze a text that compares and contrasts two Civil War heroes: Ulysses S. Grant, leader of the Union Army (North), and Robert E. Lee, leader of the Confederate Army (South). You will then think about how these two men connect to your previous study of heroism.

Setting a Purpose for Reading

- As you read, pay attention to the organization of the text. Write the focus of each paragraph in the My Notes section.
- Circle unknown words and phrases. Try to determine the meaning of the words by using context clues, word parts, or a dictionary.
- Underline transitional words and phrases that help you follow the changes in focus.

ABOUT THE AUTHOR

Bruce Catton (1899–1978) was a noted historian and journalist whose books on the Civil War were celebrated for narrative historical style. The third book in a trilogy on the Civil War, *A Stillness at Appomattox,* earned Catton both a Pulitzer Prize and the National Book Award (1954).

SCAFFOLDING THE TEXT-DEPENDENT QUESTIONS

5. Craft and Structure (RI.8.4) **How does Catton use a metaphor to illustrate conflict in paragraph 3?** In this paragraph what are the two generals being compared to as they move toward the great conflict or collision that is the Civil War?

6. Craft and Structure (RI.8.4) **Find the words "aristocratic," "chivalry," "knighthood," and "country squire" in the passage. How are these words related? Make an inference about what the author believes Robert E. Lee embodied.** Reread the sentence in paragraph 5 that begins, "Lee stood for the feeling..." and explain how this statement relates to the ideas embodied in the words.

7. Key Ideas and Details (RI.8.3) **Choose a sentence from paragraphs 5 or 6 and one from paragraphs 7 or 8 showing the greatest contrast between the two generals. Explain your choice.** Carefully reread paragraphs 5–8

Nonfiction Narrative

GRANT AND LEE: A STUDY IN CONTRASTS

by Bruce Catton

My Notes

1 When Ulysses S. Grant and Robert E. Lee met in the parlor of a modest house at Appomattox Court House, Virginia, on April 9, 1865, to work out the terms for the surrender of Lee's Army of Northern Virginia, a great chapter on American life came to a close, and a great new chapter began.

Ulysses S. Grant

2 These men were bringing the Civil War to its virtual finish. To be sure, other armies had yet to surrender, and for a few days the **fugitive** Confederate government would struggle desperately and **vainly**, trying to find some way to go on living now that its chief support was gone. But in effect it was all over when Grant and Lee signed the papers. And the little room where they wrote out the terms was the scene of one of the **poignant**, dramatic contrasts in American History.

fugitive: fleeting; transient

vainly: futilely; unsuccessfully

poignant: passionate; emotional

3 They were two strong men, these oddly different generals, and they represented the strengths of two conflicting currents that, through them, had come into final collision.

4 Back of Robert E. Lee was the notion that the old aristocratic concept might somehow survive and be dominant in American life.

5 Lee was tidewater Virginia, and in his background were family, culture, and tradition . . . the age of chivalry transplanted to a New World which was making its own legends and its own myths. He embodied a way of life that had come down through the age of knighthood and the English country squire. America was a land that was beginning all over again, dedicated to nothing much more complicated than the rather hazy belief that all men had equal rights and should have an equal chance in the world. In such a land Lee stood for the feeling that it was somehow of advantage to human society to have a pronounced inequality in the social structure. There should be a leisure class, backed by ownership of land; in turn, society itself should be tied to the land as the chief source of wealth and influence. It would bring forth (according to this ideal) a class of men with a strong sense of obligation to the community; men who lived not to gain advantage for themselves, but to meet the solemn obligations which had been laid on them by the very fact that they were privileged. From them the country would get its leadership; to them it could look for higher values—of thought, of conduct, or personal **deportment**—to give it strength and virtue.

deportment: behavior

Text Complexity
Overall: Complex
Lexile: 1110L
Qualitative: Moderate Difficulty
Task: Moderate (Analyze)

5 As students are reading, monitor their progress. Be sure they are engaged with the text and annotating as directed. Evaluate whether the selected reading mode is effective.

6 Based on the observations you made during the first reading, you may want to adjust your reading mode. For example, you may decide for the second reading to read aloud certain complex passages, or you may group students differently.

TEACHER TO TEACHER

Paragraph 3 can be considered the thesis. Notice that the last sentence restates this idea. Notice also that transitions of contrast and similarity begin to show up in paragraph 7 with the introduction of Grant.

and underline the descriptions of the two generals. Then choose one for each general that shows them to be opposites.

8. Craft and Structure (RI.8.5) **Which paragraph signals a change from a discussion of the generals' differences to a discussion of their similarities? What transition words help you see this?** In paragraph 13, examine the phrase, "Yet it was not all contrasts..." and think about how it signals a change in the discussion.

Teacher Notes

Expository Writing: Compare/Contrast

My Notes

WORD CONNECTIONS

Etymology

Sanctified comes from the Latin words *facere* ("to make") and *sanctus* ("holy").

tanner: leather worker

sinewy: lean and muscular

reverence: deep respect

obeisance: respectful submission or yielding to the judgment, opinion, will, etc., of another

implicit: implied though not directly stated

GRAMMAR & USAGE

Conditional Tense

Note the usage of the conditional tense in paragraph 9: "If the land was settled . . . he could better himself." How does the use of the conditional support the main idea of this paragraph?

6 Lee embodied the noblest elements of this aristocratic ideal. Through him, the landed nobility justified itself. For four years, the Southern states had fought a desperate war to uphold the ideals for which Lee stood. In the end, it almost seemed as if the Confederacy fought for Lee; as if he himself was the Confederacy . . . the best thing that the way of life for which the Confederacy stood could ever have to offer. He had passed into legend before Appomattox. Thousands of tired, underfed, poorly clothed Confederate soldiers, long since past the simple enthusiasm of the early days of the struggle, somehow considered Lee the symbol of everything for which they had been willing to die. But they could not quite put this feeling into words. If the Lost Cause, sanctified by so much heroism and so many deaths, had a living justification, its justification was General Lee.

Robert E. Lee

7 Grant, the son of a **tanner** on the Western frontier, was everything Lee was not. He had come up the hard way and embodied nothing in particular except the eternal toughness and **sinewy** fiber of the men who grew up beyond the mountains. He was one of a body of men who owed **reverence** and **obeisance** to no one, who were self-reliant to a fault, who cared hardly anything for the past but who had a sharp eye for the future.

8 These frontier men were the precise opposites of the tidewater aristocrats. Back of them, in the great surge that had taken people over the Alleghenies and into the opening Western country, there was a deep, **implicit** dissatisfaction with a past that had settled into grooves. They stood for democracy, not from any reasoned conclusion about the proper ordering of human society, but simply because they had grown up in the middle of democracy and knew how it worked. Their society might have privileges, but they would be privileges each man had won for himself. Forms and patterns meant nothing. No man was born to anything, except perhaps to a chance to show how far he could rise. Life was competition.

9 Yet along with this feeling had come a deep sense of belonging to a national community. The Westerner who developed a farm, opened a shop, or set up in business as a trader could hope to prosper only as his own community prospered—and his community ran from the Atlantic to the Pacific and from Canada down to Mexico. If the land was settled, with towns and highways and accessible markets, he could better himself. He saw his fate in terms of the nation's own destiny. As its horizons expanded, so did his. He had, in other words, an acute dollars-and-cents stake in the continued growth and development of his country.

10 And that, perhaps, is where the contrast between Grant and Lee becomes most striking. The Virginia aristocrat, inevitably, saw himself in relation to his own region. He lived in a static society which could endure almost anything except change. Instinctively, his first loyalty would go to the locality in which that society existed. He would fight to the limit of endurance to defend it, because in defending it he was defending everything that gave his own life its deepest meaning.

Teacher Notes

11 The Westerner, on the other hand, would fight with an equal **tenacity** for the broader concept of society. He fought so because everything he lived by was tied to growth, expansion, and a constantly widening horizon. What he lived by would survive or fall with the nation itself. He could not possibly stand by unmoved in the face of an attempt to destroy the Union. He would combat it with everything he had, because he could only see it as an effort to cut the ground out from under his feet.

12 So Grant and Lee were in complete contrast, representing two diametrically opposed elements in American life. Grant was the modern man emerging; beyond him, ready to come on the stage was the great age of steel and machinery, of crowded cities and a restless **burgeoning** vitality. Lee might have ridden down from the old age of chivalry, lance in hand, silken banner fluttering over his head. Each man was the perfect champion for his cause, drawing both his strengths and his weaknesses from the people he led.

13 Yet it was not all contrast, after all. Different as they were—in background, in personality, in underlying aspiration—these two great soldiers had much in common. Under everything else, they were marvelous fighters. Furthermore, their fighting qualities were really very much alike.

14 Each man had, to begin with, the great virtue of utter tenacity and **fidelity**. Grant fought his way down the Mississippi Valley in spite of acute personal discouragement and profound military handicaps. Lee hung on in the trench at Petersburg after hope born of a fighter's refusal to give up as long as he can still remain on his feet and lift his two fists.

15 Daring and resourcefulness they had, too: the ability to think faster and move faster than the enemy. These were the qualities which gave Lee the dazzling campaigns of Second Manassas and Chancellorsville and won Vicksburg for Grant.

16 Lastly, and perhaps greatest of all, there was the ability, at the end, to turn quickly from the war to peace once the fighting was over. Out of the way these two men behaved at Appomattox came the possibility of peace of reconciliation. It was a possibility not wholly realized, in the year to come, but which did, in the end, help the two sections to become one nation again … after a war whose bitterness might have seemed to make such a reunion wholly impossible. No part of either man's life became him more than the part he played in their brief meeting in the McLean house at Appomattox. Their behavior there put all succeeding generations of Americans in their debt. Two great Americans, Grant and Lee—very different, yet under everything very much alike. Their encounter at Appomattox was one of the great moments of American history.

tenacity: the quality of holding together; remaining persistent

burgeoning: quickly growing or developing; flourishing

WORD CONNECTIONS

Content Connections

Diametrically, in the context of Grant and Lee being opposed, means "completely or directly." Mathematically speaking, *diametrically opposed* refers to "two points directly opposite of each other on a circle or sphere." The mathematic meaning provides a picture of the complete opposite viewpoints and traits we observe in Grant and Lee.

fidelity: strict observance of promises, duties, etc.; loyalty; faithfulness

My Notes

7 **SECOND READ:** During the second reading, students will be returning to the text to answer the text-dependent comprehension questions. You may choose to have students reread and work on the questions in a variety of ways:

- independently
- in pairs
- in small groups
- together as a class

8 Have students answer the text-dependent questions. If they have difficulty, scaffold the questions by rephrasing them or breaking them down into smaller parts. See the Scaffolding the Text-Dependent Questions boxes for suggestions.

9 For the Working from the Text activity, have students work in pairs or individually to use their text **annotations** to determine the structure of the text and to create a brief **outline**.

Expository Writing: Compare/Contrast

My Notes

Second Read

- Reread the passage to answer these text-dependent comprehension questions.
- Write any additional questions you have about the text in your Reader/Writer Notebook.

5. **Craft and Structure:** How does Catton use a metaphor to illustrate conflict in paragraph 3?

History is being represented as a book, with major historical periods as chapters. Catton compares conflict to a current, which is a natural, powerful force. RI.8.4

6. **Craft and Structure:** Find the words "aristocratic," "chivalry," "knighthood," and "country squire" in the passage. How are these words related? Make an inference about what the author believes Robert E. Lee embodied.

The words are related to the traditions of English social ranks and landholding society. According to the author, Robert E. Lee embodied inequality in social structure based on family, land wealth, and tradition. RI.8.4

7. **Key Ideas and Details:** Choose a sentence from paragraphs 5 or 6 and one from paragraphs 7 or 8 showing the greatest contrast between the two generals. Explain your choice.

Answers will vary, but might include the following: "There should be a leisure class, backed by ownership of land: ..." "No man was born to anything, except perhaps to a chance to show how far he could rise." RI.8.3

8. **Craft and Structure:** Which paragraph signals a change from a discussion of the generals' differences to a discussion of their similarities? What transition words help you see this?

Paragraph 13; the paragraph includes transition words that signal both contrast and comparison. RI.8.5

Working from the Text

9. This essay was very carefully organized. Skim the paragraphs, noting the content of the paragraphs and the text you have noted. Then, create a brief outline of the text's organizational structure.

Paragraphs 1–3: introduction about both generals
Paragraphs 4–6: Lee
Paragraphs 7–9: Grant
Paragraphs 10–12: summary contrast
Paragraphs 13–16: similarities

10. What is the central idea or purpose of the text? Provide textual evidence to support your analysis.

Both generals were equally important and shared similarities and differences. Paragraph 3 describes them both as "strong men" and "oddly different generals." Paragraph 13 summarizes, "Different as they were—in background, in personality, in underlying aspiration—these two great soldiers had much in common."

My Notes

Creating Coherence

In Unit 1, you learned that ***coherence*** in writing is the clear and orderly presentation of ideas in a paragraph or essay. One way a writer creates coherence is to use transitional words, phrases, and sentences to link ideas within and between paragraphs. The following chart lists some transitional words and phrases that create coherence in compare/contrast essays.

Transitions That Compare	Transitions That Contrast	
Likewise Similarly In the same way	Although Instead Even though On the other hand On the contrary In contrast	Nevertheless Still However Yet/But Rather Conversely

11. Sort the transitions using the QHT strategy. Then, practice using some of the transitions on a subject that you know about such as *short stories versus poetry*. Write a few sentences in the My Notes section of this page.

Check Your Understanding

WRITING to SOURCES **Expository Writing Prompt**

After reading "Grant and Lee: A Study in Contrasts," write a short compare/contrast paragraph comparing Robert E. Lee and Ulysses S. Grant. Be sure to:

- Explain at least one difference and one similarity of the two subjects.
- Organize ideas logically (subject-by-subject or feature-by-feature). Refer to the chart on page 95 for these organizational structures.
- Create coherence by using transitional words and phrases.
- Support your explanations and ideas with evidence from the text.

© 2017 College Board. All rights reserved.

▶ADAPT

If student responses to the writing prompt indicate confusion relating to features of comparison and/or logically organizing ideas, revisit Catton's text to review how he applies these skills. Then, form mixed-level groups, and ask students to work together to rewrite the second paragraph, or co-construct the second paragraph as a class.

10 Introduce the concept of *coherence*, and read through the transitions that can create coherence in a compare/contrast text. Have students sort transitions in the chart, using **QHT**.

Leveled Differentiated Instruction

For more practice in using transitions, ask students to choose two subjects for comparison and then use an **Idea Connector** graphic organizer to help them generate compare and contrast statements. You may choose to have students share their statements orally or in writing.

Em Have students use basic transitions such as *and*, *but*, and *or* to make connections between ideas.

Ex Encourage students to use a variety of transitions such as *because*, *even though* to make connections between ideas.

11 As a class, discuss how the organizational structures would be applied to the topic in the writing prompt. Choose one structure, and then co-construct the first paragraph. Ask students to complete the essay. Be sure to have them **prewrite** and plan the entire organization prior to **drafting**.

▶ASSESS

Be sure students spend time identifying and evaluating the coherence created by the transitions and the clear organizational structure of the essay. Note that this essay combines both forms of compare/contrast organization. Use sections of this essay as models for students to follow in the next activity.

Paragraphs 1–12 form a complete essay of contrast, while the last four paragraphs emphasize similarities between the leaders and use these to close the essay and to stress the equal importance of both generals to American history.

ACTIVITY 2.3

▶PLAN

Materials: highlighters
Suggested Pacing: 2 50-minute class periods

▶TEACH

1 Introduce the concepts of *utopia* and *dystopia* by **activating prior knowledge** and conducting a **shared reading** of the informational text. Be sure to help students make meaning of difficult vocabulary.

2 Coming to a consensus on values that all societies would consider utopian will help set the context for the novel students will be reading.

3 Read the Preview and the Setting a Purpose for Reading sections with your students. Help them understand the literary terms they encounter.

4 **FIRST READ:** Based on the complexity of the passage and your knowledge of your students, you may choose to conduct the first reading in a variety of ways:

- independent reading
- paired reading
- small group reading
- choral reading
- read aloud

5 Set the context by reading About the Author aloud to students.

ACTIVITY 2.3

Utopian Ideals and Dystopian Reality

LEARNING STRATEGIES: Close Reading, Rereading, Diffusing, Paraphrasing, Marking the Text, Shared Reading, Think Aloud

Learning Targets

- Use direct quotations and correct punctuation for effect.
- Closely read a story and analyze the relationship between character and theme.

The Concept of Utopia

A utopia is an ideal or perfect community or society. It is a real or imagined place considered to be ideal or perfect (politically, socially, economically, technologically, ecologically, religiously, etc.). People in a utopia lead civilized lives filled with peace, fulfillment, and happiness.

The western idea of utopia originates in the ancient world, where legends of an earthly paradise (e.g. Eden in the Old Testament, the mythical Golden Age of Greek mythology), combined with the human desire to create, or re-create, an ideal society, helped form the utopian idea.

The English statesman Sir Thomas More (1478–1535) wrote the book *Utopia* in 1516. Describing a perfect political and social system on an imaginary island named Utopia, the term "utopia" has since entered the English language, meaning any place, state, or situation of ideal perfection.

Both the desire for Eden-like perfection and an attempt to start over in "unspoiled" America led religious and nonreligious groups and societies to set up communities in the United States. These experimental utopian communities were committed to such ideals as simplicity, sincerity, and brotherly love.

Once the idea of a utopia was created, its opposite, the idea of a **dystopia**, was also created. It is the opposite of a utopia. Such societies appear in many works of fiction, particularly in stories set in a speculative future.

WORD CONNECTIONS

Roots and Affixes

The word *utopia* is made from the Greek *ou-*, meaning "no" or "not," and *topos*, meaning "place." But it is also similar to *eutopia*, made from the English prefix *eu-*, meaning "good," and *topos*. This implies that the perfectly "good place" is really "no place."

WORD CONNECTIONS

Roots and Affixes

A **dystopia** is a community or society, usually fictional, that is in some important way undesirable or frightening. The word *dystopia* comes from the Latin prefix *dys-*, meaning "bad, abnormal," and the word *utopia*, which you've already learned means "good place" or "no place."

Preview

In this activity, you will read a story and expand your understanding of the concepts of utopia and dystopia.

Setting a Purpose for Reading

- As you read, take note of the setting and the rules of the community. Underline any sentences that give you this information.
- Circle unknown words and phrases. Try to determine the meaning of the words by using context clues, word parts, or a dictionary.

ABOUT THE AUTHOR

Kurt Vonnegut (1922–2007) was one of the most influential American writers of the 20th century. He wrote such works as *Cat's Cradle* (1963), *Slaughterhouse-Five* (1969), and *Breakfast of Champions* (1973), blending satire, black comedy, and science fiction. He was known for his humanist beliefs and was honorary president of the American Humanist Association.

COMMON CORE STATE STANDARDS

Focus Standards:

RL.8.2: Determine a theme or central idea of a text and analyze its development over the course of the text, including its relationship to the characters, setting, and plot; provide an objective summary of the text.

RL.8.3: Analyze how particular lines of dialogue or incidents in a story or drama propel the action, reveal aspects of a character, or provoke a decision.

W.8.2b: Develop the topic with relevant, well-chosen facts, definitions, concrete details, quotations, or other information and examples.

Additional Standards Addressed:

RL.8.1; RL.8.4; RL.8.6; W.8.2a; W.8.9; W.8.10; L.8.1b; L.8.3a; L.8.4b; L.8.5a; L.8.6

Short Story

Harrison Bergeron

by Kurt Vonnegut, Jr.

1 THE YEAR WAS 2081, and everybody was finally equal. They weren't only equal before God and the law. They were equal every which way. Nobody was smarter than anybody else. Nobody was better looking than anybody else. Nobody was stronger or quicker than anybody else. All this equality was due to the 211th, 212th, and 213th Amendments to the Constitution, and to the **unceasing vigilance** of agents of the United States Handicapper General.

2 Some things about living still weren't quite right, though. April for instance, still drove people crazy by not being springtime. And it was in that clammy month that the H-G men took George and Hazel Bergeron's fourteen-year-old son, Harrison, away.

3 It was tragic, all right, but George and Hazel couldn't think about it very hard. Hazel had a perfectly average intelligence, which meant she couldn't think about anything except in short bursts. And George, while his intelligence was way above normal, had a little mental handicap radio in his ear. He was required by law to wear it at all times. It was tuned to a government transmitter. Every twenty seconds or so, the transmitter would send out some sharp noise to keep people like George from taking unfair advantage of their brains.

4 George and Hazel were watching television. There were tears on Hazel's cheeks, but she'd forgotten for the moment what they were about, as the ballerinas came to the end of a dance.

5 A buzzer sounded in George's head. His thoughts fled in panic, like bandits from a burglar alarm.

6 "That was a real pretty dance, that dance they just did," said Hazel.

7 "Huh," said George.

8 "That dance—it was nice," said Hazel.

9 "Yup," said George. He tried to think a little about the ballerinas. They weren't really very good—no better than anybody else would have been, anyway. They were burdened with sash weights and bags of birdshot, and their faces were masked, so that no one, seeing a free and graceful gesture or a pretty face, would feel like something the cat drug in. George was toying with the vague notion that maybe dancers shouldn't be handicapped. But he didn't get very far with it before another noise in his ear radio scattered his thoughts.

10 George winced. So did two out of the eight ballerinas.

11 Hazel saw him wince. Having no mental handicap herself, she had to ask George what the latest sound had been.

12 "Sounded like somebody hitting a milk bottle with a **ball peen hammer**," said George.

13 "I'd think it would be real interesting, hearing all the different sounds," said Hazel a little envious. "All the things they think up."

WORD CONNECTIONS

Etymology

The verb *to handicap* is a word taken from sports. In the late 19th century, *handicap* meant the extra weight given to a superior race horse to even the odds of winning for other horses. The sports term became generalized over time and came to mean the practice of assigning disadvantage to certain players to equalize the chances of winning. Vonnegut's "Handicapper General" is in charge of dumbing down and disabling citizens who are above average so that all citizens are equal.

unceasing: relentless; persistent; continuous

vigilance: watchfulness; alertness

My Notes

ball-peen hammer: a hammer used in metalworking, distinguished by a hemispherical head

Text Complexity

Overall: Accessible

Lexile: 820L

Qualitative: Moderate Difficulty

Task: Moderate (Analyze)

6 As students are reading, monitor their progress. Be sure they are engaged with the text and annotating as directed. Evaluate whether the selected reading mode is effective.

7 Based on the observations you made during the first reading, you may want to adjust your reading mode. For example, you may decide for the second reading to read aloud certain complex passages, or you may group students differently.

SCAFFOLDING THE TEXT-DEPENDENT QUESTIONS

1. Key Ideas and Details (RL.8.1) **What is George's "little mental handicap radio" and what is it intended to do?** Who or what requires George to wear the handicap radio and who controls the transmitter? Why is this important?

2. Key Ideas and Details (RL.8.1) **Why is the punishment for removing weight from the "handicap bag" so harsh? Find textual evidence to support your answer.** Reread the dialogue in paragraphs 25–35 to determine the effect of removing government handicaps.

3. Key Ideas and Details (RL.8.1) **According to this society, what are the things that make George and his son and people like the ballerinas so dangerous? Cite textual evidence to support your inference.** Examine paragraph 39 that describes the ballerina. What are her handicaps and why does she have them? She

Teacher Notes

Utopian Ideals and Dystopian Reality

My Notes

doozy: something that is unusually good, bad, severe, etc.

14 "Um," said George.

15 "Only, if I was Handicapper General, you know what I would do?" said Hazel. Hazel, as a matter of fact, bore a strong resemblance to the Handicapper General, a woman named Diana Moon Glampers. "If I was Diana Moon Glampers," said Hazel, "I'd have chimes on Sunday—just chimes. Kind of in honor of religion."

16 "I could think, if it was just chimes," said George.

17 "Well—maybe make 'em real loud," said Hazel. "I think I'd make a good Handicapper General."

18 "Good as anybody else," said George.

19 "Who knows better than I do what normal is?" said Hazel.

20 "Right," said George. He began to think glimmeringly about his abnormal son who was now in jail, about Harrison, but a twenty-one-gun salute in his head stopped that.

21 "Boy!" said Hazel, "that was a **doozy**, wasn't it?"

22 It was such a doozy that George was white and trembling, and tears stood on the rims of his red eyes. Two of the eight ballerinas had collapsed to the studio floor, were holding their temples.

23 "All of a sudden you look so tired," said Hazel. "Why don't you stretch out on the sofa, so's you can rest your handicap bag on the pillows, honeybunch." She was referring to the forty-seven pounds of birdshot in a canvas bag, which was padlocked around George's neck. "Go on and rest the bag for a little while," she said. "I don't care if you're not equal to me for a while."

24 George weighed the bag with his hands. "I don't mind it," he said. "I don't notice it any more. It's just a part of me."

25 "You been so tired lately—kind of wore out," said Hazel. "If there was just some way we could make a little hole in the bottom of the bag, and just take out a few of them lead balls. Just a few."

26 "Two years in prison and two thousand dollars fine for every ball I took out," said George. "I don't call that a bargain."

27 "If you could just take a few out when you came home from work," said Hazel. "I mean—you don't compete with anybody around here. You just sit around."

28 "If I tried to get away with it," said George, "then other people'd get away with it—and pretty soon we'd be right back to the dark ages again, with everybody competing against everybody else. You wouldn't like that, would you?"

29 "I'd hate it," said Hazel.

30 "There you are," said George. The minute people start cheating on laws, what do you think happens to *society*?"

31 If Hazel hadn't been able to come up with an answer to this question, George couldn't have supplied one. A siren was going off in his head.

32 "Reckon it'd fall all apart," said Hazel.

33 "What would?" said George blankly.

34 "Society," said Hazel uncertainly. "Wasn't that what you just said?

35 "Who knows?" said George.

introduces Harrison. What descriptions of him show him to be above average?

4. Craft and Structure (RL.8.4) **How does the author use parallel structure for effect in paragraph 51? In paragraph 53?** Why is using a series of adjectives an efficient and effective way to visualize this character of Harrison?

5. Craft and Structure (RL.8.4) **Examine the author's choice of verbs to describe the actions of Harrison and the ballerina in motion. What is the intended effect?** Reread paragraphs 69–74 and notice that the verbs create visual images of energetic physical motion. How does this motion represent freedom?

6. Key Ideas and Details (RL.8.2) **How is the story's theme reflected in the conversation between Hazel and George that concludes the story?** Reread the last dialogue between George and Hazel and notice especially the last 7 lines. Determine what lines of dialogue show how George and Hazel are handicapped.

Teacher Notes

36 The television program was suddenly interrupted for a news bulletin. It wasn't clear at first as to what the bulletin was about, since the announcer, like all announcers, had a serious speech **impediment**. For about half a minute, and in a state of high excitement, the announcer tried to say, "Ladies and Gentlemen."

impediment: a hindrance; a physical defect that prevents normal speech

37 He finally gave up, handed the bulletin to a ballerina to read.

38 "That's all right—" Hazel said of the announcer, "he tried. That's the big thing. He tried to do the best he could with what God gave him. He should get a nice raise for trying so hard."

39 "Ladies and Gentlemen," said the ballerina, reading the bulletin. She must have been extraordinarily beautiful, because the mask she wore was hideous. And it was easy to see that she was the strongest and most graceful of all the dancers, for her handicap bags were as big as those worn by two-hundred pound men.

40 And she had to apologize at once for her voice, which was a very unfair voice for a woman to use. Her voice was a warm, luminous, timeless melody. "Excuse me—" she said, and she began again, making her voice absolutely uncompetitive.

41 "Harrison Bergeron, age fourteen," she said in a **grackle** squawk, "has just escaped from jail, where he was held on suspicion of plotting to overthrow the government. He is a genius and an athlete, is under-handicapped, and should be regarded as extremely dangerous."

grackle: any of several blackbirds smaller than a crow

42 A police photograph of Harrison Bergeron was flashed on the screen—upside down, then sideways, upside down again, then right side up. The picture showed the full length of Harrison against a background calibrated in feet and inches. He was exactly seven feet tall.

43 The rest of Harrison's appearance was Halloween and hardware. Nobody had ever borne heavier handicaps. He had outgrown **hindrances** faster than the H-G men could think them up. Instead of a little ear radio for a mental handicap, he wore a tremendous pair of earphones, and spectacles with thick wavy lenses. The spectacles were intended to make him not only half blind, but to give him whanging headaches besides.

hindrances: obstacles; deterrents; impediments

44 Scrap metal was hung all over him. Ordinarily, there was a certain **symmetry**, a military neatness to the handicaps issued to strong people, but Harrison looked like a walking junkyard. In the race of life, Harrison carried three hundred pounds.

symmetry: balance; arrangement

45 And to offset his good looks, the H-G men required that he wear at all times a red rubber ball for a nose, keep his eyebrows shaved off, and cover his even white teeth with black caps at snaggle-tooth random. "If you see this boy," said the ballerina, "do not—I repeat, do not—try to reason with him."

46 There was the shriek of a door being torn from its hinges.

47 Screams and barking cries of **consternation** came from the television set. The photograph of Harrison Bergeron on the screen jumped again and again, as though dancing to the tune of an earthquake.

consternation: alarm; bewilderment

48 George Bergeron correctly identified the earthquake, and well he might have—for many was the time his own home had danced to the same crashing tune. "My God—" said George, "that must be Harrison!"

49 The realization was blasted from his mind instantly by the sound of an automobile collision in his head.

7. Key Ideas and Details (RL.8.2) **Summarize what happens in this story.** Think again about the conflict of this story between individual freedom and society's control. Which force wins? Does the author agree that this resolution is a positive outcome?

© 2017 College Board. All rights reserved.

Teacher Notes

My Notes

50 When George could open his eyes again, the photograph of Harrison was gone. A living, breathing Harrison filled the screen.

51 Clanking, clownish, and huge, Harrison stood—in the center of the studio. The knob of the uprooted studio door was still in his hand. Ballerinas, technicians, musicians, and announcers cowered on their knees before him, expecting to die.

52 "I am the Emperor!" cried Harrison. "Do you hear? I am the Emperor! Everybody must do what I say at once!" He stamped his foot and the studio shook.

53 "Even as I stand here," he bellowed, "crippled, hobbled, sickened—I am a greater ruler than any man who ever lived! Now watch me become what I can become!"

54 Harrison tore the straps of his handicap harness like wet tissue paper, tore straps guaranteed to support five thousand pounds.

55 Harrison's scrap-iron handicaps crashed to the floor.

56 Harrison thrust his thumbs under the bar of the padlock that secured his head harness. The bar snapped like celery. Harrison smashed his headphones and spectacles against the wall.

57 He flung away his rubber-ball nose, revealed a man that would have awed Thor, the god of thunder.

58 "I shall now select my Empress!" he said, looking down on the cowering people. "Let the first woman who dares rise to her feet claim her mate and her throne!"

59 A moment passed, and then a ballerina arose, swaying like a willow.

60 Harrison plucked the mental handicap from her ear, snapped off her physical handicaps with marvelous delicacy. Last of all he removed her mask.

61 She was blindingly beautiful.

62 "Now—" said Harrison, taking her hand, "shall we show the people the meaning of the word dance? Music!" he commanded.

63 The musicians scrambled back into their chairs, and Harrison stripped them of their handicaps, too. "Play your best," he told them, "and I'll make you barons and dukes and earls."

64 The music began. It was normal at first—cheap, silly, false. But Harrison snatched two musicians from their chairs, waved them like batons as he sang the music as he wanted it played. He slammed them back into their chairs.

65 The music began again and was much improved.

66 Harrison and his Empress merely listened to the music for a while—listened gravely, as though synchronizing their heartbeats with it.

67 They shifted their weights to their toes.

68 Harrison placed his big hands on the girl's tiny waist, letting her sense the weightlessness that would soon be hers.

69 And then, in an explosion of joy and grace, into the air they sprang!

70 Not only were the laws of the land abandoned, but the law of gravity and the laws of motion as well.

71 They reeled, whirled, swiveled, flounced, capered, **gamboled**, and spun.

gamboled: leapt; pranced

72 They leaped like deer on the moon.

73 The studio ceiling was thirty feet high, but each leap brought the dancers nearer to it.

74 It became their obvious intention to kiss the ceiling. They kissed it.

75 And then, neutralizing gravity with love and pure will, they remained suspended in air inches below the ceiling, and they kissed each other for a long, long time.

76 It was then that Diana Moon Glampers, the Handicapper General, came into the studio with a double-barreled ten-gauge shotgun. She fired twice, and the Emperor and the Empress were dead before they hit the floor.

77 Diana Moon Glampers loaded the gun again. She aimed it at the musicians and told them they had ten seconds to get their handicaps back on.

78 It was then that the Bergerons' television tube burned out.

79 Hazel turned to comment about the blackout to George. But George had gone out into the kitchen for a can of beer.

80 George came back in with the beer, paused while a handicap signal shook him up. And then he sat down again. "You been crying," he said to Hazel.

81 "Yup," she said.

82 "What about?" he said.

83 "I forget," she said. "Something real sad on television."

84 "What was it?" he said.

85 "It's all kind of mixed up in my mind," said Hazel.

86 "Forget sad things," said George.

87 "I always do," said Hazel.

88 "That's my girl," said George. He winced. There was the sound of a riveting gun in his head.

89 "Gee—I could tell that one was a doozy," said Hazel.

90 "You can say that again," said George.

91 "Gee—" said Hazel, "I could tell that one was a doozy."

Second Read

- Reread the passage to answer these text-dependent comprehension questions.
- Write any additional questions you have about the text in your Reader/Writer Notebook.

1. **Key Ideas and Details:** What is George's "little mental handicap radio" and what is it intended to do?

The "mental handicap radio" is in George's ear and at regular intervals a noise is transmitted to keep him from thinking too much or too hard. RL.8.1

My Notes

ACTIVITY 2.3 continued

8 **SECOND READ:** During the second reading, students will be returning to the text to answer the text-dependent comprehension questions. You may choose to have students reread and work on the questions in a variety of ways:

- independently
- in pairs
- in small groups
- together as a class

9 Have students answer the text-dependent questions. If they have difficulty, scaffold the questions by rephrasing them or breaking them down into smaller parts. See the Scaffolding the Text-Dependent Questions boxes for suggestions.

© 2017 College Board. All rights reserved.

10 Work with the class to respond to each question in the Working from the Text section with a statement of interpretation and supporting evidence. Give students time to respond to each question in writing before engaging in a class discussion.

Leveled Differentiated Instruction

Students may need more support to understand the ideas of *utopia* and *dystopia*. Put them in groups of four to participate in Round Table Discussions of the concepts.

Em Have students start by completing an **Unknown Word Solver** graphic organizer.

Ex and Br Once students have thought about the concepts of utopia and dystopia, have groups complete a **Round Table Discussion** graphic organizer.

Support Have students write their own definitions of the words *utopia* and *dystopia* and list examples of things they would expect to find in each.

Stretch Have students research and write about references to *utopia* such as Shangri-La, the Garden of Eden, and the Promised Land.

Utopian Ideals and Dystopian Reality

My Notes

2. **Key Ideas and Details:** Why is the punishment for removing weight from the "handicap bag" so harsh? Find textual evidence to support your answer.

   Society "would fall apart." "Pretty soon we would be right back in the dark ages again, with everybody competing against everybody else." RL.8.1

3. **Key Ideas and Details:** According to this society, what are the things that make George and his son and people like the ballerinas so dangerous? Cite textual evidence to support your inference.

   George's son is "a genius," "an athlete," "dangerously under-handicapped." The ballerina is "extraordinarily beautiful," "strong," and "graceful." George has above average intelligence. Any special traits or characteristics are thought to give individuals the ability to take "unfair advantage of their brains." RL.8.1

4. **Craft and Structure:** How does the author use parallel structure for effect in paragraph 51? In paragraph 53?

   "Clanking, clownish, and huge" describes Harrison's outlandish appearance and "crippled, hobbled, sickened" describes the physical and mental effects of the handicapping. RL.8.4

5. **Craft and Structure:** Examine the author's choice of verbs to describe the actions of Harrison and the ballerina in motion. What is the intended effect?

   The verbs the author uses here include *reeled*, *whirled*, *swiveled*, *flounced*, *capered*, *gamboled*, *spun*, and *leaped*. These verbs create a sense of freedom, looseness, and joy. RL.8.4

6. **Key Ideas and Details:** How is the story's theme reflected in the conversation between Hazel and George that concludes the story?

   The conversation showcases George's inability to focus mentally and Hazel's inability to focus emotionally, both of which are caused by the society's repression of individuality. RL.8.2

7. **Key Idea and Details:** Summarize what happens in this story.

Working from the Text

8. Complete the following chart, citing evidence from the text.

© 2017 College Board. All rights reserved.

11 Review how to smoothly embed direct quotations into writing, and connect this learning to a writer's use of ellipsis and brackets.

(a) What "ideal" is the society based upon?	Interpretation: Equality of opportunity; social and economic equality Evidence:
(b) What did the society sacrifice in order to create this "ideal" life?	Interpretation: Individual differences; freedom of individual expression; individual achievement Evidence:
(c) How was this **utopian** ideal transformed into a **dystopian** reality?	Interpretation: The desire to create equality became focused on erasing mental and physical differences rather than eliminating social and economic inequalities. Evidence:
(d) What new problems were created?	Interpretation: A society in which no citizen was allowed to be unique or live up to his or her potential Evidence:

GRAMMAR & USAGE
Conventions

An **ellipsis** is a row of three dots (. . .) that indicates something omitted from within a quoted passage.

Two things to consider:
(1) Using an ellipsis is a form of "editing" the source material, so be certain that the final outcome does not change the original meaning or intent of the quoted passage.
(2) If quoted text ends up with more ellipses than words, consider paraphrasing rather than using direct quotes.

Brackets ([ ]) are most often used to clarify the meaning of quoted material. If the context of your quote might be unclear, you may add a few words to provide clarity. Enclose the added material in brackets.

For example: "They [the other team] played a better game."

Language and Writer's Craft: Embedding Direct Quotations

After writing the controlling idea (thesis) for a paragraph or essay, the writer needs to develop additional ideas to support the thesis. The writer does this by providing specific evidence, such as paraphrased and/or direct quotations and insightful analysis (explanation).

Review the following information about using **direct quotations** in your writing:

- Remember to avoid plagiarism by **paraphrasing** or directly **quoting** evidence. Although it is often easier to paraphrase information, a direct quotation can strengthen ideas if it is selected carefully and embedded smoothly.
- In order to smoothly embed a direct quotation, just remember TLQC format: transition, lead-in, quotation, citation. For example:

  The reader is stunned by Harrison's dramatic death scene, yet Harrison's parents hardly react. **When George realizes Hazel has been crying, he simply says,** "Forget sad things" (Vonnegut 6).
- Using **ellipses and brackets** helps you to include more without writing out long pieces of quoted material. Study how the quoted material below has been added smoothly with the use of ellipses.

  "Harrison tore the straps of his handicap harness like wet tissue paper, tore straps guaranteed to support five thousand pounds. Harrison's scrap-iron handicaps crashed to the floor."

  The reader celebrates the moment when "Harrison tore the straps of his handicap harness like wet tissue paper... [and] scrap-iron handicaps crashed to the floor," allowing him full freedom at last (Vonnegut 104).

My Notes

12 Read over the information on active and passive voice, and help students see the stylistic differences in effect and impact when active voice is used rather than passive voice.

▶PLAN

Ask students to independently respond to the writing prompt, in class or as homework. When students are finished responding to the writing prompt, ask a few volunteers to read their embedded direct quotation; then provide feedback as a class.

▶ADAPT

If students struggle with embedding direct quotations or using syntax and punctuation for effect, display successful student models, use a **think aloud** to explain what makes the examples successful, and ask students to revise their work.

Utopian Ideals and Dystopian Reality

My Notes

Language and Writer's Craft: Active and Passive Voice

Writers use **active and passive voice** to convey certain effects. Be sure you understand and use these voices correctly and deliberately.

- You should generally use active voice because it puts the emphasis on who or what is performing the action of the verb rather than on the verb itself.
- The passive voice contains some form of *be* (*is, was, were, was being, has been,* etc.), plus a past participle of the verb. It is particularly useful (even recommended) in two situations:

1. When it is more important to draw attention to the person or thing being acted upon: *The unidentified victim was struck near her home.*
2. When the actor in the situation is not important: *The eaglet's birth was witnessed in the early morning hours.*

Active voice: Harrison removed his handicaps.

Passive voice: The handicaps were removed by Harrison.

Notice that in the active voice version, the emphasis is on Harrison as the one who takes action. Passive voice is not inherently wrong. However, if you can say the same thing in active voice, you can make your sentences more vibrant and direct. Later in this unit you will learn more about appropriate use of passive voice.

- Most importantly, do not mix active and passive constructions in the same sentence:

"The Handicapper General approved the new handicaps, and a new amendment was added."

should be recast as

"The Handicapper General approved the new handicaps and added the new amendment."

Check Your Understanding

WRITING to SOURCES **Expository Writing Prompt**

How does "Harrison Bergeron" convey the conflict between the needs or ideals of society and the realities of individuals? Be sure to:

- Provide examples from the text and use at least one direct quotation to support your ideas.
- Include a reference to utopia and dystopia.
- Use active voice unless you choose passive voice for a certain effect.

© 2017 College Board. All rights reserved.

Understanding a Society's Way of Life

ACTIVITY 2.4

Learning Targets

- Collaboratively analyze the opening chapters of a fictional text citing text evidence to support your analysis.
- Analyze the significance of specific passages to interpret the relationship between character and setting.

LEARNING STRATEGIES: Visualizing, Questioning the Text, Predicting, Graphic Organizer, Note-taking, Discussion Groups

Questioning the Text

Remember that questioning a text on multiple levels can help you explore its meaning more fully. Read the definitions below and write an example of each type of question, based on texts you have read in this unit.

- A **Level 1** question is **literal** (the answer can be found in the text).
  "Harrison Bergeron": Who calls himself the Emperor?
  "Grant and Lee": What famous historical occasion does the essay highlight?
- A **Level 2** question is **interpretive** (the answer can be inferred based on textual evidence).
  "Harrison Bergeron": Why doesn't George react to the death of his son?
  "Grant and Lee": How are the backgrounds of the two men fundamentally different?
- A **Level 3** question is **universal** (the answer is about a concept or idea beyond the text).
  "Harrison Bergeron": How is society in conflict with the individual?
  "Grant and Lee": How can leaders of such divisive causes create a sense of a peaceful future?

WORD CONNECTIONS

Etymology

Fantasy comes from the Old French word *fantasie* ("fantasy"), the Latin word *phantasia* ("imagination"), and the Ancient Greek word *phantasia*, meaning "apparition." The literary genre of fantasy is imaginative fiction crafted in a setting other than the real world. It involves creatures and events that are improbable or impossible in the world as we know it.

You will be reading a novel that questions whether a utopian society is possible. Such novels generally fit into the genre of science fiction.

1. Read the following text to gather more information about science fiction (from readwritethink.org). As you read, highlight the characteristics of science fiction.

Science fiction is a genre of fiction in which the stories often tell about science and technology of the future. It is important to note that science fiction has a relationship with the principles of science—these stories involve partially true/partially fictitious laws or theories of science. It should not be completely unbelievable with magic and dragons, because it then ventures into the genre of fantasy. The plot creates situations different from those of both the present day and the known past. Science fiction texts also include a human element, explaining what effect new discoveries, happenings and scientific developments will have on us in the future. Science fiction texts are often set in the future, in space, on a different world, or in a different universe or **dimension**. Early pioneers of the genre of science fiction are H. G. Wells (*The War of the Worlds*) and Jules Verne (*20,000 Leagues Under the Sea*). Some well-known 20th-century science fiction texts include *1984* by George Orwell and *Brave New World* by Aldous Huxley.

dimension: a level of existence or consciousness

COMMON CORE STATE STANDARDS

Focus Standards:

RL.8.1: Cite the textual evidence that most strongly supports an analysis of what the text says explicitly as well as inferences drawn from the text.

RL.8.3: Analyze how particular lines of dialogue or incidents in a story or drama propel the action, reveal aspects of a character, or provoke a decision.

Additional Standards Addressed:

RL.8.2; RL.8.4; W.8.2a; W.8.2b; W.8.4; W.8.10; SL.8.1a; L.8.4a; L.8.6

ACTIVITY 2.4

PLAN

Materials: copies of *The Giver* or *Fahrenheit 451*, index cards
Suggested Pacing: 2 50-minute class periods

TEACHER TO TEACHER

The next six activities are intended as a study of *The Giver* or *Fahrenheit 451*. Although you will probably select one novel to read as a class, you might want to assign the other as independent reading.

Each novel has been **chunked** into six sections, and each section should take two days to complete (this includes the reading and the corresponding activity).

This activity represents section one of six and covers the reading assignment below:

- *The Giver*: pp. 1–19
- *Fahrenheit 451*: pp. 1–21

TEACH

1 Review the strategy of questioning the text by writing **Levels of Questions**. The sample responses refer to both "Harrison Bergeron" and the Catton article. During the course of reading the novel, suggest that students routinely pose Level 2 questions and find new vocabulary. Remind students that Level 1 questions need to be significant to the meaning of the story—not simply things like "What is the main character's name?"

2 The information on science fiction as a genre is to set the context of the novel within a certain fictional genre. Ask students why science fiction is a good genre for focusing on the relationship between the individual and society.

The Giver

Text Complexity
Overall: Complex
Lexile: 760L
Qualitative: Moderate Difficulty
Task: Challenging (Create)

ACTIVITY 2.4 continued

Fahrenheit 451

Text Complexity
Overall: Complex
Lexile: 890L
Qualitative: Moderate Difficulty
Task: Challenging (Create)

3 Review key literary terms to set the context for this lesson. As you review each term, ask a student to create and post a Word Wall card.

4 Guide students in a **close reading** of the cover of the book.

TEACHER TO TEACHER

If you are teaching *The Giver*, there are two different versions of the cover. This is a great opportunity for comparison and contrast.

5 As a class, share predictions. Ask students to use evidence to **predict** whether the book is set in a utopian or a dystopian society.

Leveled Differentiated Instruction

In this activity, some students may need more support to review the vocabulary of literary analysis.

Em Have students write to complete an **Unknown Word Solver** graphic organizer for each term.

Ex Guide students to write example sentences using the vocabulary of literary analysis.

6 Discuss expectations for reading. Students should **closely read** to record evidence relating to either the protagonist and/or the setting. Specify how many pieces of evidence you expect and how you want students to record it (e.g., TLQC).

7 Set a purpose for reading by asking half the class to focus on the protagonist and half the class to focus on the setting.

8 Begin Chunk 1 with students using the **shared reading/think aloud** strategies, and **guide reading** by asking students to focus on finding evidence that reveals

Understanding a Society's Way of Life

Literary Terms
An **antagonist** is the opposite of a protagonist and is the character who fights against the hero or main character (the protagonist).

My Notes

Reviewing Vocabulary of Literary Analysis

Theme, or the central message of the story, is revealed through an understanding of and the resolution to the ***conflicts***, both internal and external, that the central ***character*** experiences throughout the story.

Characterization is the method of developing characters through *description* (e.g., appearance, thoughts, feelings), *action*, and *dialogue*. The central character or protagonist is usually pitted against the **antagonist**, his or her enemy, rival, or opponent.

Evidence in analysis includes many different things, such as descriptions of characters and actions, objects, title, dialogue, details of setting, and plot.

Novel Study

Preview the novel you will be reading as a class.

2. The cover art of a novel tries to represent important aspects of the content of the novel. Study the cover of your novel to make predictions about the story. Based on your reading about the genre of science fiction, what might you predict about a science fiction story?
   - **Setting:** a futuristic, technologically advanced society that is somewhat believable
   - **Characters:** positively or negatively affected by society
   - **Plot:** not completely unbelievable; rooted in real life and scientific possibilities
   - **Theme:** based on the effect of new developments on human life

3. Use the graphic organizer to note evidence that reveals important information about the protagonist and setting. Then, make inferences based on the evidence.

Literary Element	Evidence (page #)	Inferences
Protagonist __________ (name)		
Setting (description of the society/the way of life)		

4. In your Reader/Writer Notebook, begin a personal vocabulary list. Identify, record, and define (in context) at least five new words. Plan to do this for every reading assignment.
5. Select and record an interesting quotation—relating to the protagonist or setting—that you think is important to understanding the conflict or theme. Then, analyze the idea and form two thoughtful questions for discussion.

Quotation (page #)
Analysis
Questions Level 1: What is the job of a fireman? (*Fahrenheit 451*) What does it mean to "release" someone? (*The Giver*) Level 2: Why is it important that Montag doesn't know the history of his occupation? (*Fahrenheit 451*) Why is the Ceremony of Twelve so important? (*The Giver*)

My Notes

INDEPENDENT READING LINK

Read and Respond

What challenge are you studying? How did this challenge begin? Who does it affect? What are the opposing sides? Write a summary of what you have learned so far, citing information from a few sources. Write your response in you Reader/Writer Notebook.

Check Your Understanding

Group Discussion

Using the questions you have created for the novel you're reading, participate in a brief discussion about the society the novel presents and the protagonist's role in it.

important information about the protagonist or the setting. You might model this in a **think aloud**.

9 Assign homework: Ask students to finish reading Chunk 1, complete the evidence for the protagonist or setting, and complete the vocabulary list.

Day 2

10 When students return to class use the quotation and questions as the basis for a quick collaborative discussion. During the discussion, students should record evidence and inferences in the graphic organizer and ask questions for clarification. Emphasize the importance of writing thought-provoking questions.
A Level 2 question is based on inference or analysis, and a Level 1 question is based on important factual elements.

11 Encourage students to complete the Independent Reading Link activity, reminding them to record responses in the Reader/Writer Notebook.

ASSESS

Ask mixed-level **discussion groups** to discuss the relationship between the protagonist and his role in society. Limit the discussion to 10–15 minutes.

ADAPT

To monitor the discussion you might consider having the class agree on the questions before they break into groups. In addition, ask the groups to take notes on the responses to their questions.

ACTIVITY 2.5

▶PLAN

Materials: copies of *The Giver* or *Fahrenheit 451*, index cards
Suggested Pacing: 2 50-minute class periods

TEACHER TO TEACHER

This activity represents section two of six and covers the reading assignment below:

The Giver: pp. 20–49

Fahrenheit 451: pp. 21–38

▶TEACH

1 Ask students to complete the questions with a partner or small group. For Question 2, instead of writing out a response, students could add symbols (e.g., lines, hearts) to their lists of names to show characters' relationships.

2 Discuss characters and their relationships as a class to check for understanding.

3 Assign parts to strong readers, and begin reading Chunk 2 as a class. Tell students to take notes on conflicts and perspectives they see emerging. Ask text-dependent questions to set a purpose for a second read.

4 As you read, also ask students to practice forming and supporting statements of comparison and contrast relating to characters and setting.

5 Assign homework: Ask students to finish reading Chunk 2 and complete the perspective **graphic organizer.**

ACTIVITY 2.5

Contemplating Conflicting Perspectives

LEARNING STRATEGIES: Shared Reading, Close Reading, Rereading, Questioning the Text, Note-taking, Discussion Groups

My Notes

ACADEMIC VOCABULARY
Perspective is a point of view or a specific attitude toward something. Your *perspective* describes how you look at or interpret situations or events.

Learning Targets

- Analyze conflicting perspectives within the novel and explain how the author uses this technique to shape readers' understanding of the story.
- Identify and analyze the importance of specific vocabulary to the story.

Novel Study

In this activity, you will look at the different perspectives in the novel you are reading.

1. Other than the protagonist, who are the most important characters so far in the story? What do we know about each of these characters? Make a list of these characters and provide a brief description of each.

2. Which of these characters usually agree with one another? Which of these characters tend to disagree?

3. Conflict among people or between people and society is a result of conflicting **perspectives.** Support this idea by identifying a topic that has created the most important conflict so far in the story and contrast two different perspectives about the topic.

Topic:	
Character 1:	**Character 2:**
Perspective:	**Perspective:**
Textual Evidence (#):	**Textual Evidence (#):**

COMMON CORE STATE STANDARDS

Focus Standards:

RL.8.4: Determine the meaning of words and phrases as they are used in a text, including figurative and connotative meanings; analyze the impact of specific word choices on meaning and tone, including analogies or allusions to other texts.

RL.8.6: Analyze how differences in the points of view of the characters and the audience or reader (e.g., created through the use of dramatic irony) create such effects as suspense or humor.

Additional Standards Addressed:

RL.8.2; W.8.2a; W.8.2b; W.8.4; W.8.5; W.8.9; L.8.1c; L.8.3a; L.8.6

4. Write questions for discussion based on the information you provided in the chart.
   - **Level 1 (literal, factual):**
   - **Level 2 (interpretive):**

5. Which characters are questioning society? How might that tie in to the novel's theme?

6. Continue to add to your personal vocabulary list in your Reader/Writer Notebook. Identify, record, and define (in context) at least five new words. Choose one you think is important to understanding the character, setting, or conflict of the story. Explain why you chose that word.

7. In addition to creating differences in characters' perspectives, authors create differences between the perspectives of the characters and that of the reader. Support this idea by identifying a topic and comparing and contrasting a character's perspective with your own perspective. This time, include the main reason for each perspective and provide evidence from the text for each reason.

Topic:	
Character's Perspective:	**My Perspective:**
Main Reason:	**Main Reason:**
Textual Evidence (page #)	**Textual Evidence (page #)**

My Notes

Day 2

6 Vocabulary: Ask students to star their favorite new word from their reading. Call on five students to teach their word to the class; the class should add these words to their personal vocabulary list. Check to see if there are any Word Wall nominations.

7 Form **discussion groups** of four. Students should discuss Chunk 2, using notes from the graphic organizer as a guide.

8 As a class, select a topic, and work through questions 7 and 8 with each student filling in information based on his or her own perspective.

ACTIVITY 2.5 continued

9 The Language and Writer's Craft review of mood emphasizes the different kinds of verbal moods and their appropriate uses. Review the material with students, and then ask them to work through the exercise individually or in pairs.

10 Review how to organize an expository paragraph (Unit 1) logically. Review how to use transitions to create coherence (Unit 1). Consider asking students to independently respond to the writing prompt as an in-class timed writing.

▶ASSESS

The writing prompt asks students to extend their discussion of perspective by discussing the differing perspectives of two characters. They could also identify how their own perspective differs from one of the characters in the novel, as long as they can connect it to a conflict in the story.

▶ADAPT

This is a challenging writing prompt. If student responses reflect a superficial understanding and/or are underdeveloped, form mixed-level **discussion groups**, allow time for students to discuss the prompt (using their written response as a guide), and then ask students to revise their work to reflect their new, deeper understanding.

ACTIVITY 2.5 continued

Contemplating Conflicting Perspectives

My Notes

Language and Writer's Craft: Choosing Mood

Recall what you learned in the last unit about verbal mood:

- **Indicative Mood:** Verbs that indicate a fact or opinion. *I am too ill to go to school today.*
- **Imperative Mood:** Verbs that express a command or request. *Go to school. Please get up and get dressed.*
- **Interrogative Mood:** Verbs that ask a question. *Are you going to school? Do you feel ill?*
- **Conditional Mood:** Verbs that express something that hasn't happened or something that can happen if a certain condition is met. *I would have gone to school yesterday if I had felt well.*
- **Subjunctive Mood:** Verbs that describe a state that is uncertain or contrary to fact. When using the verb *to be* in the subjunctive, always use *were* rather than *was. I wish my cold were better today. If you were to go to school, what would you learn?*

8. Which of the moods described above would be most suitable for a topic sentence? Identify the mood and then choose the most suitable topic sentence among the examples below.
   - If Harrison and his mother were put in the same room, they would not be able to communicate. (conditional and subjunctive)
   - Arrest Harrison Bergeron immediately. (imperative)
   - Are Harrison and Hazel Bergeron really so different? (interrogative, hook)
   - Harrison and George Bergeron are father and son. (indicative)
   - If Harrison's father were not handicapped, would he be like his son? (subjunctive)
9. Which of the sentences might be a good hook for an introductory paragraph?

Check Your Understanding

WRITING to SOURCES **Expository Writing Prompt**

Identify the perspectives of two different characters and show how the contrast between them highlights a conflict of the story. Be sure to:

- Create a topic sentence indicating the contrasting perspectives.
- Provide examples from the text and at least one direct quotation to support your ideas.
- Logically organize your ideas.

Questioning Society

ACTIVITY 2.6

Learning Targets

- Evaluate specific rules and laws in a fictional society and compare them to present society, referencing the text and notations from additional research and reading materials.
- Contribute analysis and evidence relating to this topic in a Socratic Seminar discussion.

Preview

In this activity, you will read a short article about banned books and make connections to the novel you are reading.

Setting a Purpose for Reading

- As you read this article, underline words and phrases that relate to big concepts you have been thinking about in this unit.
- Circle unknown words and phrases. Try to determine the meaning of the words by using context clues, word parts, or a dictionary.

LEARNING STRATEGIES:
Shared Reading, Marking the Text, Questioning the Text, Socratic Seminar, Fishbowl

My Notes

Article

Banned Books Week:
Celebrating the Freedom to Read

September 30–October 6, 2012

1 Banned Books Week (BBW) is an annual event celebrating the freedom to read and the importance of the First Amendment. Held during the last week of September, Banned Books Week highlights the benefits of free and open access to information while drawing attention to the harms of censorship by spotlighting actual or attempted bannings of books across the United States.

2 Intellectual freedom—the freedom to access information and express ideas, even if the information and ideas might be considered unorthodox or unpopular—provides the foundation for Banned Books Week. BBW stresses the importance of ensuring the availability of unorthodox or unpopular viewpoints for all who wish to read and access them.

3 The books featured during Banned Books Week have been targets of attempted bannings. Fortunately, while some books were banned or restricted, in a majority of cases the books were not banned, all thanks to the efforts of librarians, teachers, booksellers, and members of the community to retain the books in the library collections. Imagine how many more books might be challenged—and possibly banned

WORD CONNECTIONS

Etymology

Censorship comes from the Latin word *censor*. A censor in Rome was responsible for counting citizens and for supervising and regulating their morals. The suffix *-ship* makes the word a noun.

GRAMMAR & USAGE

Mood

Notice the strong **imperative** (command or request) quality of the sentence beginning, "Imagine . . ." Think how this sentence could have been changed to an **interrogative.**

ACTIVITY 2.6

PLAN

Materials: copies of *The Giver* or *Fahrenheit 451*, colored cards or chips, and numbered cards (optional)
Suggested Pacing: 2 50-minute class periods

TEACHER TO TEACHER

This activity represents section three of six and covers the reading assignment below:

The Giver: pp. 50–79

Fahrenheit 451: pp. 38–60

TEACH

1 Read the Preview and the Setting a Purpose for Reading sections with your students. Help them understand the literary terms they encounter.

2 **FIRST READ:** Based on the complexity of the passage and your knowledge of your students, you may choose to conduct the first reading in a variety of ways:

- independent reading
- paired reading
- small group reading
- choral reading
- read aloud

Text Complexity
Overall: Complex
Lexile: 1590L
Qualitative: Low Difficulty
Task: Accessible (Understand)

3 As students are reading, monitor their progress. Be sure they are engaged with the text and annotating as directed. Evaluate whether the selected reading mode is effective.

4 Based on the observations you made during the first reading, you may want to adjust your reading mode. For example, you may decide for the second reading to read aloud certain complex passages, or you may group students differently.

5 As a class, briefly discuss the central idea of this informational text. Share with students the text of the First Amendment to the Constitution:

COMMON CORE STATE STANDARDS

Focus Standards:

SL.8.1: Engage effectively in a range of collaborative discussions (one-on-one, in groups, and teacher-led) with diverse partners on grade 8 topics, texts, and issues, building on others' ideas and expressing their own clearly.

SL.8.1a: Come to discussions prepared, having read or researched material under study; explicitly draw on that preparation by referring to evidence on the topic, text, or issue to probe and reflect on ideas under discussion.

SL.8.1b: Follow rules for collegial discussions and decision-making, track progress toward specific goals and deadlines, and define individual roles as needed.

Additional Standards Addressed:

RL.8.1; RL.8.2; RL.8.4; RL.8.10; RI.8.1; RI.8.2; W.8.9; W.8.10; SL.8.1c; SL.8.1d; SL.8.6; L.8.4a; L.8.6

ACTIVITY 2.6 continued

"Congress shall make no law respecting an establishment of religion, or prohibiting the free exercise thereof; or abridging the freedom of speech, or of the press; or the right of the people peaceably to assemble, and to petition the government for a redress of grievances."

Have students make connections between the First Amendment and the celebration of the freedom to read.

6 **SECOND READ:** During the second reading, students will be returning to the text to answer the text-dependent comprehension question. You may choose to have students reread and work on the questions in a variety of ways:

- independently
- in pairs
- in small groups
- together as a class

7 Have students answer the text-dependent question. If they have difficulty, scaffold the question by rephrasing it or breaking it down into smaller parts. See the Scaffolding the Text-Dependent Questions boxes for suggestions.

8 Have students respond to the **Quickwrite** in Working from the Text. Be sure to address the American value of freedom of expression, and discuss the connection to "danger . . . when restraints are imposed."

9 Now that students understand the issue surrounding the banning of books, transition back into literary analysis. Discuss the connections between setting, character, and theme. Point out that banning books is an example of a "social circumstance."

10 Ask students to begin reading Chunk 3 (in small groups, pairs, or individually). Once they have read part of the chunk, pose some text-dependent questions to guide a second read.

11 Assign homework: Ask students to finish reading Chunk 3 and to complete Student Step 8. Explain that the work is intended to prepare students for a class discussion on the topic of rules or laws.

Questioning Society

or restricted—if librarians, teachers, and booksellers across the country did not use Banned Books Week each year to teach the importance of our First Amendment rights and the power of literature, and to draw attention to the danger that exists when **restraints** are **imposed** on the availability of information in a free society.

restraints: confines; controls
imposed: forced

My Notes

Second Read

- Reread the passage to answer the text-dependent comprehension question.
- Write any additional questions you have about the text in your Reader/Writer Notebook.

1. **Craft and Structure:** What clues in the text help you understand the meaning of the word *banned*?

   Paragraph 2 states, "BBW stresses the importance of ensuring the availability of unorthodox or unpopular viewpoints..." Paragraph 3 follows banned with "or restricted." RI.8.4

Working from the Text

2. **Quickwrite:** Explain why books are an important part of our society. Which values do they symbolize? You may use the informational text to guide your response.

   Books symbolize freedom of expression: "...the freedom to access information and express ideas."

Novel Study

Setting is not simply the time and place in a story. It is also the ***social circumstances*** that create the world in which characters act and make choices. Readers who are sensitive to this world are better able to understand and judge the behavior of the characters and the significance of the action. The social circumstances of a story will often provide insights into the theme of a literary piece.

3. Using "Harrison Bergeron," show how the setting connects to the character and theme.

   Example from "Harrison Bergeron": The society enforces equality by handicapping people who are outside the norm in any way. Harrison rebels and is killed. Society is too powerful for an individual to fight against.

4. How are books viewed in the society of your novel's protagonist?

5. Compare and contrast perspectives relating to banned books. How might this connect to the story's theme?

SCAFFOLDING THE TEXT-DEPENDENT QUESTIONS

1. Craft and Structure (RI.8.4) **What clues in the text help you understand the meaning of the word "banned"?** Note that the title pairs "banned" with "freedom," which could be confusing. The second sentence of the first paragraph pairs the idea of censorship with "bannings of books."

6. Think about the way of life in this society. Which rules and/or laws do you completely disagree with? Take notes below to prepare for a collaborative discussion based on this topic.

State the rule or law (paraphrase or directly quote).	Analyze: Underlying Value	Evaluate: State why you disagree with the rule or law and then form a thoughtful Level 3 question to spark a meaningful conversation with your peers.
1. Books are not part of the ordinary person's life. page(s): ___	Books are dangerous to conformity.	**Response:** Answers will vary. **Level 3 Question:** Are books dangerous to society?
2. Family life is carefully controlled. page(s): ___	Family creates a society. Conformity begins in the family.	**Response:** Answers will vary. **Level 3 Question:** How important are ceremony and ritual in life?
3. page(s): ___		**Response:** **Level 3 Question:**

7. Continue to add to your personal vocabulary list. Identify, record, and define (in context) at least five new words.

Introducing the Strategy: Socratic Seminar

A **Socratic Seminar** is a type of collaborative discussion designed to explore a complex question, topic, or text. Participants engage in meaningful dialogue by asking one another questions and using textual evidence to support responses. The goal is for participants to arrive at a deeper understanding of a concept or idea by the end of the discussion. A Socratic Seminar is not a debate.

ACADEMIC VOCABULARY

The word **Socratic** is an adjective formed from the name of the philosopher Socrates, who was famous for using the question-and-answer method in his search for truth and wisdom. A **seminar** is a term used to describe a small group of students engaged in intensive study.

© 2017 College Board. All rights reserved.

ACTIVITY 2.6 continued

Leveled Differentiated Instruction

In this activity, some students may need help preparing for the Socratic Seminar. It may be useful for students to practice by answering questions about rules and laws in a pair or smaller group.

Em Guide students to work in pairs to answer literal *yes-no* questions about rules and laws, such as *Do rules and laws help a community to be more safe?*

Ex Guide students to work in smaller groups or pairs to discuss literal questions about rules and laws, such as *How do rules and laws help a community to be more safe?*

Br Have students work in smaller groups or pairs to discuss literal and interpretive questions about rules and laws, such as *Which rules and laws are more important than others?* Encourage students to respond to their partners by offering useful feedback.

Support Model a discussion about rules and laws with a student. Have students take notes on the model discussion in order to practice listening to comprehend ideas.

Day 2

12 Ask students to star their favorite new word from their reading. Call on three new students to teach their word to the class; the class should add these words to their personal vocabulary lists.

13 Check to see if there are any Word Wall nominations.

14 Discuss values associated with rules and laws to check for understanding. Students can form Level 3 questions based on these values (e.g., freedom of speech, education, honesty, obeying rules/laws). Ask students to create and post Word Wall cards to reference during the upcoming **Socratic Seminar.**

15 Read aloud Introducing the Strategy: Socratic Seminar to students. Ask for four volunteers with experience to form an inner circle. As you explain each part of

ACTIVITY 2.6 continued

the strategy, ask students to briefly model it. It is important to show students how to build off of others' ideas, transition between ideas, and achieve a balance among speakers.

TEACHER TO TEACHER

During the Socratic Seminar, you might want to use a concrete system to ensure balanced speaking. For example, you could give each student in the inner circle two colored cards (or two poker chips). One color could represent asking a question and one color could represent making a comment. Set the expectations that students use both of their cards during the discussion. Also, once they have used their cards, they must listen the rest of the time to allow others the chance to speak.

16 Ask students to set one speaking and one listening goal before engaging in the Socratic Seminar.

17 Set expectations for **note-taking** in the outer circle. In the "Interesting Points" section, students should write the speaker's name on the line and then **paraphrase** or directly quote the idea.

18 Set up the **fishbowl**, set a timer (approximately 10 minutes), and begin the Socratic Seminar.

Leveled Differentiated Instruction

In this activity, students may need more practice to prepare for the Socratic Seminar.

Em and Ex Have students fill out the **Collaborative Dialogue** graphic organizer while they are in the outer circle. The sheet will help them fill out their Socratic Seminar Notes.

Questioning Society

My Notes

8. You will next participate in a Socratic Seminar. During the Seminar:
   - Challenge yourself to build on others' ideas by asking questions in response to a statement or question. To do this effectively, you will have to listen to comprehend and evaluate.
   - Work to transition between ideas to maintain coherence throughout the discussion.
   - Work to achieve a balance between speaking and listening within a group. Make sure everyone has a chance to speak, and allow quiet time during the discussion so people have a chance to formulate a thoughtful response.
   - Have you heard the expression: "Be a frog, not a hog or a log"? What do you think that means? Set two specific and attainable goals for the discussion:

   Speaking Goal:

   Listening Goal:

Oral Discussion sentence starters:

- I agree with your idea relating to . . . , but it is also important to consider . . .
- I disagree with your idea about . . . , and would like to point out . . .
- You made a point about the concept of . . . How are you defining that?
- On page ___, (a specific character) says . . . I agree/disagree with this because . . .
- On page ___, (a specific character) says . . . This is important because . . .
- On page ____, we learn . . . , so would you please explain your last point about . . . ?
- Add your own:

Introducing the Strategy: Fishbowl

Fishbowl is a speaking and listening strategy that divides a large group into an inner and an outer circle. Students in the inner circle model appropriate discussion techniques as they discuss ideas, while students in the outer circle listen to comprehend ideas and evaluate the discussion process. During a discussion, students have the opportunity to experience both circles.

9. Engage in the Socratic Seminar.
   - When you are in the *inner* circle, you will need your work relating to rules and laws, a pen or pencil, and the novel.
   - When you are in the *outer* circle, you will need a pen or pencil and the note-taking sheet on the next page.

© 2017 College Board. All rights reserved.

Socratic Seminar Notes

Topic: Rules and Laws in a Utopian/Dystopian Society

Listening to Comprehend

- **Interesting points:**
  1. ______________:
  2. ______________:
  3. ______________:
- **My thoughts:**
  1.
  2.
  3.

Listening to Evaluate

- **Speaking:**
  Strength:
  Challenge:
- **Listening:**
  Strength:
  Challenge:

Reflection

- I did/did not meet my speaking and listening goals.
  Explanation:
- I am most proud of:
- Next time I will:

My Notes

TEACHER TO TEACHER

During the Socratic discussion, the teacher's role is to be a facilitator. The goal is to get students to start and maintain the discussion on their own, but the teacher should be prepared to bridge ideas, encourage student speaking, and take the discussion in a new direction. An additional copy of the note-taking graphic organizer can be found on page 90f.

19 In the "My thoughts" section of the note-taking graphic, students should note comments or questions they would have made during the discussion if they were in the inner circle.

20 In the "Listening to Evaluate" section, students can evaluate the whole group, or you can anonymously assign one student in the inner circle to one student in the outer circle (give each student in the outer circle a numbered card that corresponds to a numbered seat). Either way, during the evaluation, students should just state evidence, not use students' names.

ASSESS

Ensure that all students are actively participating in the Socratic discussion, either as speakers or listeners, and that they are taking notes.

After 10–15 minutes of discussion, ask students from the outer circle to share an interesting point, a speaking strength or challenge, and a listening strength or challenge.

Rotate inner and outer circles and repeat the process.

Ask all students to reflect on their participation (in class or as homework).

ADAPT

Students who are uncomfortable speaking in front of the class may choose not to speak during the Socratic Seminar. If this is the case, provide another opportunity to participate, by setting up a small-group discussion (before, during, or after class) and inviting these students to join.

ACTIVITY 2.7

▶PLAN

Materials: copies of *The Giver* or *Fahrenheit 451*, index cards, sticky notes

Suggested Pacing: 2 50-minute class periods

TEACHER TO TEACHER

This activity represents section four of six and covers the reading assignment below:

The Giver: pp. 80–117

Fahrenheit 451: pp. 61–88

▶TEACH

1 Before students respond to the writing prompt, explain how to craft an effective response. First, provide the following sentence frames to model an effective **topic sentence**:

[The protagonist] is [adjective] and [adjective].

[The protagonist] shows [noun] and [noun].

Second, explain that since this is a **quickwrite**, evidence should be specific examples from memory, not direct quotes. Remind students to use a transition (T) and lead-in (L) prior to stating the evidence.

Third, remind students to include a few sentences of analysis or commentary (C) to further support the topic sentence.

2 After students respond to the prompt (approximately 10 minutes), ask a few students to **read aloud** their writing to check for understanding.

3 Quickly review Stage 1 of the Hero's Journey to set the context for the next part of the activity. You might want to reference the chart in Unit 1 on page 16.

4 Distribute sticky notes, and ask students to begin reading Chunk 4 (as a class, in small groups, pairs, or individually). **Guide reading** by asking students to focus on the protagonist's Departure (three steps).

5 Assign homework: Ask students to finish reading Chunk 4, complete the sticky notes for questions 3 and 4, and complete the vocabulary list.

ACTIVITY 2.7

A Shift in Perspective: Beginning the Adventure

LEARNING STRATEGIES: Summarizing, Close Reading, Marking the Text, Skimming/Scanning, Rereading, Drafting

My Notes

Learning Targets

- Analyze and explain how the Hero's Journey archetype provides a framework for understanding the actions of a protagonist.
- Develop coherence by using transitions appropriate to the task.

Novel Study

In this activity, you will reflect on the protagonist in your novel and the journey he or she is on.

1. What can you infer about the protagonist in this story? Make an inference based on relevant *descriptions* (e.g., appearance, thoughts, feelings), *actions*, and/or *dialogue*. Support your inference with evidence from the text. Follow this format:

   Topic Sentence: State an important character trait.

   - **Supporting Detail/Evidence:** Provide a transition, lead-in, and specific example that demonstrates the trait.
   - **Commentary/Analysis:** Explain how the evidence supports the trait.
   - **Commentary/Analysis:** Explain why this character trait is important to the story.

2. In Unit 1 you studied the Hero's Journey archetype. What do you remember about the departure? Provide a brief summary of each of the first three steps and their importance.

   Stage 1: The Departure

Stage and Definition	Connection to the Story
Step 1: The Call to Adventure	
Step 2: Refusal of the Call	
Step 3: The Beginning of the Adventure	

3. The protagonist is considered the hero of the story. Readers most often identify with his or her perspective. While you read, use sticky notes to mark text that could reflect the protagonist's Departure. On each note, comment on the connection to the archetype.
4. Continue to add to your personal vocabulary list in your Reader/Writer Notebook. Identify, record, and define (in context) at least five new words.

COMMON CORE STATE STANDARDS

Focus Standards:

RL.8.9: Analyze how a modern work of fiction draws on themes, patterns of events, or character types from myths, traditional stories, or religious works such as the Bible, including describing how the material is rendered new.

W.8.2c: Use appropriate and varied transitions to create cohesion and clarify the relationships among ideas and concepts.

Additional Standards Addressed:

RL.8.1; RL.8.3; RL.8.4; RI.8.2; W.8.2a; W.8.2b; W.8.4; L.8.1b; L.8.4a; L.8.4b

5. Skim/scan the first half of the story and revisit your sticky notes to determine the beginning of the protagonist's journey, the Departure. It may be easiest to start with Step 3, the Beginning of the Adventure.
   - Remember that the Hero's Journey is organized sequentially, in chronological order (although some steps may occur at the same time or not at all). This means that once you connect a step to the story, the next step in the journey must reflect an event that occurs later in the story.
   - Because this task is based on interpretation, there is more than one correct answer. To convince an audience of your interpretation, you must be able to provide a convincing explanation.
   - Go back to the chart outline above and add connections to the story. Use this information in your response to the Expository Writing Prompt below.

WORD CONNECTIONS

Roots and Affixes

Sequential is the adjective form of the word *sequence*, which comes from the Latin root *sequi*, meaning "to follow."

Chronological order means "time order," reflecting the origin of the word in *chronos*, a Greek word meaning "time."

Check Your Understanding

WRITING to SOURCES **Expository Writing Prompt**

Explain the beginning of the protagonist's journey using the first three steps of the Hero's Journey archetype to guide your explanation. Be sure to:

- Establish a clear controlling idea.
- Develop ideas with relevant and convincing evidence from the text (include at least one direct quotation) and analysis.
- Use appropriate and varied transitions to create coherence and clarify the relationships among ideas (e.g., steps in the Hero's Journey).
- Use the active rather than the passive voice in your analysis, unless there is a specific reason to use the passive.

My Notes

ACTIVITY 2.7 continued

Day 2

6 Ask students to star their favorite new word from their reading. Call on five students to teach their word to the class; the class should add these words to their personal vocabulary lists. Check for Word Wall nominations.

7 Allow time for students to complete question 5 independently.

8 Form small **discussion groups**, and ask students to present and evaluate interpretations of Stage 1. Students should evaluate interpretations by listening for an accurate understanding of the Hero's Journey and convincing support from the text. Encourage students to question one another's ideas, respectfully disagree, and revise their own ideas if they are convinced that another's interpretation is more accurate.

9 As a class, read the writing prompt and brainstorm effective transitions that can be used to link ideas—*first, then, as a result of, next,* etc. Ask a student to create Word Wall cards and display them on the Word Wall next to the transitions used to compare and contrast.

ASSESS

Ask students to independently respond to the writing prompt (in class or as homework). Be sure students don't fall into summary, but rather show how the main character is being characterized and developed as a hero.

ADAPT

If student responses are underdeveloped and/or lack effective transitions, make copies of at least one successful student model. Conduct a **shared reading** and **think aloud** to explain how the writer successfully develops ideas and uses transitions to create cohesion. Students should **mark/annotate** the text(s) to capture the discussion for future reference.

After checking for understanding, give students time to revise their written response.

ACTIVITY 2.8

▶ PLAN

Materials: copies of *The Giver* or *Fahrenheit 451*, index cards, sticky notes
Suggested Pacing: 2 50-minute class periods

TEACHER TO TEACHER

This activity represents section five of six and covers the reading assignment below:
The Giver: pp. 118–145
Fahrenheit 451: pp. 88–123

▶ TEACH

1 You may want to refer students back to page 17 to review the steps and stages of the Hero's Journey. Guide students through the section on The Road of Trials. After students have identified significant trials (conflicts), ask them to categorize the society as utopian or dystopian (this should be very obvious by now). Discuss how the antagonist represents society—the conflict is essentially the individual against society.

2 After connecting the conflicts to The Experience with Unconditional Love, discuss the concept of archetypal characters (e.g., a wise old man gives advice to a confused, disillusioned young man).

Leveled Differentiated Instruction

In this activity, students may need help analyzing how words and phrases in the story portray unconditional love. Provide students with phrases from the story to analyze, such as "give another the experience of sunshine" and "he no longer cared about himself."

Em Have students complete a **Word Choice Analyzer** for each phrase.

Ex Guide students to write to explain how well each phrase supports the idea of unconditional love using the sentence frames. *The phrase ___ shows unconditional love because ___. The effect of this phrase is ___.*

ACTIVITY 2.8

Navigating the Road of Trials

LEARNING STRATEGIES: Close Reading, Rereading, Graphic Organizer, Shared Reading, Marking the Text, Note-taking, Discussion Group

My Notes

Learning Targets

- Analyze conflicts revealed through specific passages of dialogue.
- Contribute analysis and evidence in a small group collaborative discussion.

Novel Study

In this activity, you will continue exploring your protagonist's journey.

1. Review the Initiation stage of the Hero's Journey. What do you remember about:
   Step 4. The Road of Trials

   Step 5. The Experience with Unconditional Love

2. In the previous activity, you interpreted the protagonist's Departure. Now begin your interpretation of the next two steps in the protagonist's journey: the Road of Trials and the Experience with Unconditional Love.
   - List three significant trials (conflicts)—in chronological order—that occur *after* the event you identified as Step 3 of the Hero's Journey.
   - Connect *the experience with unconditional love* to the *trial* (if present).
   - Analyze how the *trial* and the *experience with unconditional love* affect the protagonist.

Trial: (focus on conflicts with other characters and society)	**Experience with Unconditional Love:**	**Effect:** (actions; words; thoughts/ feelings)
1.		
2.		
3.		

COMMON CORE STATE STANDARDS

Focus Standards:

RL.8.3: Analyze how particular lines of dialogue or incidents in a story or drama propel the action, reveal aspects of a character, or provoke a decision.

SL.8.1: Engage effectively in a range of collaborative discussions (one-on-one, in groups, and teacher-led) with diverse partners on grade 8 topics, texts, and issues, building on others' ideas and expressing their own clearly.

SL.8.1a: Come to discussions prepared, having read or researched material under study; explicitly draw on that preparation by referring to evidence on the topic, text, or issue to probe and reflect on ideas under discussion.

Additional Standards Addressed:

RL.8.1; RL.8.2; RL.8.4; W.8.10; SL.8.6; L.8.4a

3. Who is the **antagonist** in the story? How would you describe this character? What does he or she value or believe?

My Notes

4. Prepare for a small group discussion by continuing to focus on the *trials* and *unconditional love* experienced by the protagonist. Use sticky notes for the following:
   - Mark conflicts reflected in dialogue spoken by other characters, and analyze how the dialogue affects the protagonist's perspective on his society, encouraging him to reject their way of life.
   - Mark evidence of *unconditional love* reflected in dialogue spoken by other characters, and analyze how the dialogue affects the protagonist's perspective on his society, encouraging him to reject their way of life.

5. In your Reader/Writer Notebook, continue to add to your personal vocabulary list. Identify, record, and define (in context) at least five new words.

6. Using the notes you have prepared about important dialogue, engage in a small group discussion based on the following prompt.

   Discussion Prompt: Analyze how specific lines of dialogue provoke the protagonist to make the decision to reject his or her dystopian society.

Check Your Understanding

WRITING to SOURCES **Expository Writing Prompt**

In a paragraph, explain how the trials (conflicts) experienced by the main character in your novel and the evidence of unconditional love are representative of the Hero's Journey archetype. Be sure to:

- Include a topic sentence
- Use evidence from the novel
- Show an understanding of the steps of the journey archetype.

ACTIVITY 2.8 continued

3 Distribute sticky notes, and begin reading Chunk 5 as a class. **Guide reading** by asking students to focus on conflicts and unconditional love (as revealed through dialogue), as well as on analyzing the antagonist.

4 As you progress through the reading, stop to complete and discuss sticky-note responses, and ask students to identify and record new vocabulary.

5 Ask students to continue to practice forming and supporting statements of comparison and contrast relating to characters and setting.

6 Ask students to work independently to complete questions 4 and 5, the response for Chunk 5, and their personal vocabulary list. As students work, circulate to check for understanding.

7 Ask students to star their favorite new word from their reading. Call on five students to teach their word to the class; the class should add these words to their personal vocabulary list. Check for Word Wall nominations.

8 After reading the discussion prompt, form **discussion groups**, and set expectations for speaking and listening (e.g., students should listen to comprehend ideas and evaluate interpretations). Groups should start at the beginning of Chunk 5 and work their way to the end. The responses they recorded on sticky notes should guide their discussion.

ASSESS

During the discussion, check that students use specific evidence from the text to support their ideas.

ADAPT

This discussion prompt will demand precise notes and interpretation. If students have a hard time getting started, remaining focused, or maintaining a meaningful discussion, use the **fishbowl** strategy with strong readers and speakers to model the discussion expectations and to inspire the rest of the class to resume their own discussions.

You might also rearrange some discussion groups to ensure that there are strong leaders in each group.

ACTIVITY 2.9

▶PLAN

Materials: copies of *The Giver* or *Fahrenheit 451*, index cards, highlighters
Suggested Pacing: 2 50-minute class periods

TEACHER TO TEACHER

This activity represents section six of six and covers the reading assignment below:
The Giver: pp. 146–179
Fahrenheit 451: pp. 123–158

▶TEACH

1 Guide students through questions 1 and 2.

2 Begin reading Chunk 6 as a class to model the expectations. Assign parts to strong readers, and ask the class to focus on the connection between the protagonist's conflicts with society and his transformation into a hero (Student Step 3). As the class generates related theme subjects, ask students to create and display Word Wall cards.

3 Assign homework: Ask students to finish the book, complete the graphic organizer under question 3, and complete the vocabulary list.

4 Encourage students to complete the Independent Reading Link activity, reminding them to record responses in the Reader/Writer Notebook.

ACTIVITY 2.9

The End of the Journey

LEARNING STRATEGIES: Discussion Groups, Shared Reading, Close Reading, Note-taking, Drafting

Learning Targets

- Analyze the transformational nature of conflicts and the hero's *boon* as it relates to the archetype of the Hero's Journey in the novel.
- Contrast the protagonist with another character.
- Determine and explain the novel's theme in written responses, citing evidence from the text as support.

Novel Study

In this activity, you will reflect on how your protagonist has changed over the course of the novel.

1. Think about the protagonist's Departure into the Hero's Journey (Stage 1) and his *Road of Trials*. How has the character changed as a result of these trials or conflicts? Use the sentence frame below to explain the change, and be sure to provide evidence to support your interpretation.

   In the beginning, the protagonist was ______________, but after ____________________, he becomes ______________.

2. What do you remember about the *boon* in Stage 2, the Initiation of the Hero's Journey?

   Step 6: The Ultimate Boon:

3. How do conflicts with society (including characters who believe in the society's way of life) transform the character into a hero? As you read, take notes in the chart below.

Conflict with Society	Heroic Traits Revealed Through Conflict	Connection to Theme Subjects

My Notes

INDEPENDENT READING LINK
Read and Connect
Find information on a person who is working to fight the challenge you are exploring. Does this person embody the concept of a "hero"? Why or why not? What has this person's journey been? Write your response in your Reader/Writer Notebook.

COMMON CORE STATE STANDARDS

Focus Standards:

RL.8.2: Determine a theme or central idea of a text and analyze its development over the course of the text, including its relationship to the characters, setting, and plot; provide an objective summary of the text.

RL.8.9: Analyze how a modern work of fiction draws on themes, patterns of events, or character types from myths, traditional stories, or religious works such as the Bible, including describing how the material is rendered new.

W.8.9: Draw evidence from literary or informational texts to support analysis, reflection, and research.

W.8.9a: Apply grade 8 Reading standards to literature (e.g., "Analyze how a modern work of fiction draws on themes, patterns of events, or character types from myths, traditional stories, or religious works such as the Bible, including describing how the material is rendered new").

4. Use your Reader/Writer Notebook to continue adding to your personal vocabulary list. Identify, record, and define (in context) at least five new words.

5. Interpret the hero's *boon*: What did the hero achieve through this journey?

6. Which characteristics helped the hero to achieve the *boon*? Explain.

Writing Introductory Paragraphs

7. Read and analyze the samples of introductory paragraphs below. Which one would be used to write an essay structured as compare/contrast? Which would introduce an essay based on a different expository organizational structure?

Sample 1

People say that kids are a lot like their parents, but in Kurt Vonnegut's short story "Harrison Bergeron," this is definitely not the case. Harrison Bergeron, the protagonist, and Hazel Bergeron, Harrison's mother, have close to nothing in common. Hazel is completely average and therefore content, while her son is completely superior and therefore rebellious.

Sample 2

A hero must be willing to take risks and have the courage to go against the norm to help others. "Harrison Bergeron" by Kurt Vonnegut is a story of how society holds back its most talented members in search of the supposed ideal of equality. Harrison Bergeron, the protagonist, is a would-be hero who is struck down before he has the opportunity to begin, much less complete, his hero's journey.

My Notes

© 2017 College Board. All rights reserved.

COMMON CORE STATE STANDARDS

Additional Standards Addressed:

RL.8.1; RL.8.3; RL.8.4; RL.8.6; W.8.2a; W.8.2b; W.8.4; W.8.5; W.8.10; L.8.1b; L.8.1c; L.8.3a; L.8.4a

ACTIVITY 2.9 continued

Day 2

5 Ask students to respond independently to questions 5–6.

6 Form small groups. Ask students to share their answers and to evaluate others' interpretations of the hero's boon. Remind students to use evidence from the text to support or disagree with an interpretation.

7 Debrief as a class to check for understanding.

8 Ask students to revisit Activity 2.4 to determine whether their predictions about the story (based on the cover of the book) were accurate.

9 Conduct a **shared reading** of the sample introductory paragraphs. As you read, students should **mark/annotate** the text for key elements that distinguish the kind of essay organization that is being introduced.

10 Allow time for pairs to share their analyses, and then analyze and evaluate the samples as a class.

11 Note that the writing prompts mirror the kind of writing that the EA will require; then review the Scoring Guide for Ideas, Structure, and Use of Language.

12 Emphasize that the second prompt is asking students to interpret the final stage in the Hero's Journey: Return. The response should not be written in comparison/contrast structure since the prompt asks us to explain how the protagonist's transformation naturally connects to what was learned (theme).

13 Remind students to use specific diction to communicate ideas. Make sure students understand that formal style is created when a writer uses diction, syntax, and ideas appropriate for an academic audience (Unit 1).

▶ASSESS

Because the Embedded Assessment is next, you may elect not to have students write to the writing prompts of this activity. Instead you might consider co-constructing an outline or a paragraph for one or each of the prompts in order to model the thinking and writing of part of an expository essay. Or you may ask students to respond to the writing prompts as part of a collaborative writing group.

▶ADAPT

Depending on time and level of student understanding, consider showing a student exemplar for a literary essay such as the one required for the novel study of *Tangerine* in Grade 7.

If you notice that students are still struggling with certain skills, form mixed-level groups of four and ask students who "get it" to reteach the skill to their group members (using their written response as models).

The End of the Journey

My Notes

Check Your Understanding

WRITING to SOURCES

Analyze the prompts below. Notice that each prompt requires a different organizational structure. Choose one of the prompts and write a response.

Expository Writing Prompt 1: Think about the protagonist's characteristics, what he achieved, and how he changed by the end of the story. Contrast the protagonist with another character from his society. Be sure to:

- Introduce the topic clearly, establishing a clear controlling idea.
- Provide examples from the text (including at least one direct quotation) and analysis to support your ideas.
- Sequence ideas logically using the appropriate compare/contrast structure.
- Choose the appropriate verbal mood for the ideas you want to express.
- Write in active voice unless the passive voice is specifically needed.

Expository Writing Prompt 2: Think about the final stage in the Hero's Journey: the Crossing, or Return Threshold. What does the hero learn about life as a result of the journey (theme)? Be sure to:

- Introduce the topic clearly, establishing a clear controlling idea.
- Provide examples from the text (including at least one direct quotation) and analysis to support your ideas.
- Sequence ideas logically to explain how the protagonist's transformation connects to what he learns.
- Choose the appropriate verbal mood for the ideas you want to express.
- Write in active voice unless the passive voice is specifically needed.

Independent Reading Checkpoint

Discuss the challenge you researched with a partner. Take notes on what your partner says, and hand in your notes at the end of the discussion.

INDEPENDENT READING CHECKPOINT

Put students into pairs to discuss the challenges they researched. Students should take notes on what their partners say, and then hand in the notes at the end of the discussion. As you review their notes, determine whether they did adequate reading on their own topic, and whether they paid attention to what their partners said about their topics.

Leveled Differentiated Instruction

In this activity, students could use a **Venn Diagram for Writing a Comparison** to compare and contrast the protagonist with another character from his society.

Em Help students use the completed graphic organizer to write a comparison using the comparison sentence frames.

Ex Guide students to use the completed graphic organizer to write longer original sentences to compare the protagonist with another character.

Writing an Expository Essay

EMBEDDED ASSESSMENT 1

Assignment

Think about how writers organize and develop ideas in expository writing. Use an expository organizational structure to communicate your understanding of the concept of dystopia or the concept of the Hero's Journey. Select one of the prompts below:

- Write an essay that compares and contrasts life in the dystopian society of the novel you read with our modern-day society.
- Write an essay that explains how the protagonist (hero) changes as a result of conflict with his dystopian society (Road of Trials) and how this change connects to the novel's theme (the Crossing, or Return Threshold).

Planning and Prewriting: Take time to plan your essay.

- Which prompt do you feel best prepared to respond to with examples from literature and real life?
- What prewriting strategies (such as freewriting or graphic organizers) could help you brainstorm ideas and organize your examples?

Drafting: Write a multi-paragraph essay that effectively organizes your ideas.

- How will you introduce the topic clearly and establish a controlling idea (thesis)?
- How will you develop the topic with well-chosen examples and thoughtful analysis (commentary)?
- How will you logically sequence the ideas using an appropriate structure and transitions?
- How will your conclusion support your ideas?

Evaluating and Revising the Draft: Create opportunities to review and revise your work.

- During the process of writing, when can you pause to share and respond with others in order to elicit suggestions and ideas for revision?
- How can the Scoring Guide help you evaluate how well your draft meets the requirements of the assignment?

Checking and Editing for Publication: Confirm your final draft is ready for publication.

- How will you proofread and edit your draft to demonstrate command of the conventions of standard English capitalization, punctuation, spelling, grammar and usage?
- How did you use TLQC (transition/lead-in/quote/citation) to properly embed quotations?
- How did you ensure use of the appropriate voice and mood in your writing?

Reflection

After completing this Embedded Assessment, think about how you went about accomplishing this task, and respond to the following:

- How has your understanding of utopia and dystopia developed through the reading in this unit?

My Notes

COMMON CORE STATE STANDARDS

Focus Standards:

W.8.2a: Introduce a topic or thesis statement clearly, previewing what is to follow; organize ideas, concepts, and information into broader categories; include formatting (e.g., headings), graphics (e.g., charts, tables), and multimedia when useful to aiding comprehension.

W.8.2b: Develop the topic with relevant, well-chosen facts, definitions, concrete details, quotations, or other information and examples.

W.8.2c: Use appropriate and varied transitions to create cohesion and clarify the relationships among ideas and concepts.

W.8.2d: Use precise language and domain-specific vocabulary to inform about or explain the topic.

W.8.2e: Establish and maintain a formal style.

W.8.2f: Provide a concluding statement or section that follows from and supports the information or explanation presented.

EMBEDDED ASSESSMENT 1

Suggested Pacing: 4 50-minute class periods

TEACHER TO TEACHER

Make sure students know that each prompt requires a response using a different expository organization. You may want to specifically require one or the other. The first prompt requires a compare/contrast structure, whereas the second prompt expects students to discuss the changes in the main character using the Hero's Journey as a framework for discussing his or her development.

1 Planning and Prewriting: Direct students to select a prompt and begin prewriting.

2 Drafting: Help students to understand the importance of creating a rough draft by requiring that they create and use it during the **sharing and responding** they will do with a **writing group**. Having them take notes on the draft about possible revisions will give you an idea of the amount of rewriting a student is planning.

3 Evaluating and Revising: Form **discussion groups** for **sharing and responding**. Each student should explain his or her organizational structure and then read one paragraph aloud. Group members should listen to evaluate and respond by providing specific feedback based on Scoring Guide criteria.

4 The goal is to recognize weaknesses and offer concrete solutions so each student leaves the discussion with a revision plan that will help them strengthen their draft.

5 You might want to review revision strategies briefly, such as **adding**, **deleting**, **rearranging**, and **substituting**. Explain that these verbs can be used as stems when providing specific feedback in **discussion groups**. Display the following formula and example:

- **Add** a direct quotation from the text to provide convincing evidence for your interpretation.
- **Substitute** a vague word with a more precise one.

EMBEDDED ASSESSMENT 1 continued

6 Set expectations for sharing work in **discussion groups**, and circulate to check for understanding while students work.

7 **Checking and Editing for Publication:** Provide time for students to **self-** and **peer-edit**.

8 Specify your expectations for formatting, and monitor progress as students work to prepare their final draft.

Reflection After students have handed in their essays, give them time to respond to the reflection questions, and then briefly discuss responses as a class.

Portfolio Be sure students include their reflections as they collect and organize the work of this unit. Ask students to organize and turn in all steps of the writing process:

- Reflection
- Final draft
- Drafts with evidence of revision and editing
- Prewriting

Give students time to organize their work leading up to Embedded Assessment 1 and move it from their Working Folders into their Portfolios. Keeping a portfolio of work during the year is an important strategy for having students go through regular self-evaluations of their academic progress.

SCORING GUIDE

When you score this Embedded Assessment, you may wish to download and print copies of the Scoring Guide from SpringBoard Digital. This way, you can have copies to mark for each student's work.

To identify additional areas where your English learners could use additional support, see the English Language Development Rubric for Embedded Assessment 1 on page 168a.

EMBEDDED ASSESSMENT 1

Writing an Expository Essay

SCORING GUIDE

Scoring Criteria	Exemplary	Proficient	Emerging	Incomplete
Ideas	The essay • maintains a focused thesis in response to one of the prompts • develops ideas thoroughly with relevant supporting details, facts, and evidence • provides insightful commentary and deep analysis.	The essay • responds to one of the prompts with a clear thesis • develops ideas adequately with supporting details, facts, and evidence • provides sufficient commentary to demonstrate understanding.	The essay • has an unclear or unrelated thesis • develops ideas unevenly or with inadequate supporting details, facts, or evidence • provides insufficient commentary to demonstrate understanding.	The essay • has no obvious thesis • provides minimal supporting details, facts, or evidence • lacks commentary.
Structure	The essay • has an engaging introduction • uses an effective organizational structure for a multi-paragraph essay • uses a variety of transitional strategies to create cohesion and unity among ideas • provides an insightful conclusion.	The essay • has a complete introduction • uses an appropriate organizational structure for a multi-paragraph essay • uses transitional strategies to link, compare, and contrast ideas • provides a conclusion that supports the thesis.	The essay • has a weak or partial introduction • uses an inconsistent organizational structure for a multi-paragraph essay • uses transitional strategies ineffectively or inconsistently • provides a weak or unrelated conclusion.	The essay • lacks an introduction • has little or no obvious organizational structure • uses few or no transitional strategies • provides no conclusion.
Use of Language	The essay • conveys a consistent academic voice by using a variety of literary terms and precise language • embeds quotations effectively • demonstrates command of the conventions of standard English capitalization, punctuation, spelling, grammar, and usage (including a variety of syntax).	The essay • conveys an academic voice by using some literary terms and precise language • embeds quotations correctly • demonstrates adequate command of the conventions of standard English capitalization, punctuation, spelling, grammar, and usage (including a variety of syntax).	The essay • uses insufficient language and vocabulary to convey an academic voice • embeds quotations incorrectly or unevenly • demonstrates partial or inconsistent command of the conventions of standard English capitalization, punctuation, spelling, grammar, and usage.	The essay • uses limited or vague language • lacks quotations • lacks command of the conventions of standard English capitalization, punctuation, spelling, grammar, and usage; frequent errors obscure meaning.

COMMON CORE STATE STANDARDS

Additional Standards Addressed:

RL.8.1; RL.8.3; W.8.4; W.8.5; W.8.8; W.8.9; W.8.10; L.8.1b; L.8.1c; L.8.2c; L.8.3a

Previewing Embedded Assessment 2 and Effective Argumentation

ACTIVITY 2.10

LEARNING STRATEGIES: QHT, Close Reading, Paraphrasing, Graphic Organizer

Learning Targets

- Reflect on learning and make connections to new learning specific to vocabulary and concept knowledge introduced thus far.
- Collaboratively analyze and identify the skills and knowledge necessary for success in the Embedded Assessment.

Making Connections

It can be said that writers of fiction, especially dystopian novels, are trying to make a point or criticize some aspect of society. In this part of the unit, you will think about how you can have an impact by creating a well-reasoned argument about a social issue important to you.

Essential Questions

1. Reflect on your understanding of the first Essential Question: *To what extent can a perfect society exist?*

2. How has your understanding of the concept of *utopia* changed over the course of this unit?

3. How would you change your original response to Essential Question 2, *What makes an argument effective?*

Developing Vocabulary

4. Re-sort the Academic and Literary Vocabulary using the **QHT** strategy.

5. Return to your original list sorted at the beginning of the unit. Compare this list with your original. How has your understanding changed?

6. Select a word from the above chart and write a concise statement about your learning. How has your understanding changed over the course of this unit?

My Notes

INDEPENDENT READING LINK

Read and Recommend

In this half of the unit, while working on creating an argumentative essay, you will have the opportunity to read on your own. Argumentative texts (speeches and essays) are recommended. The Resources section of your textbook, your Reading Lists and Logs, and your teacher can hep you with your selections. With your class, brainstorm and recommend argumentative text options.

ACTIVITY 2.10

PLAN

Suggested Pacing: 1 50-minute class period

TEACH

1 Guide students through the process of reflecting on their learning by revisiting the first Essential Question. You might have them use the following sentence frame to guide their thinking: At the beginning of the unit, I thought ________, but at this point of the unit I think ________.

2 To categorize the vocabulary as either **Q, H, or T**, students can simply place letters next to the words. Students can share with a partner or the whole class.

INDEPENDENT READING

In this half of the unit, while working on creating an argumentative essay, students will have the opportunity to read on their own. Argumentative texts (speeches and essays) are recommended, but student choice is paramount. The Planning Unit section of the Teacher's Edition and the Resources section of the Student Edition contain information, Reading Logs, and Reading Lists to help you and your students find the right text.

COMMON CORE STATE STANDARDS

Focus Standards:

L.8.6: Acquire and use accurately grade-appropriate general academic and domain-specific words and phrases; gather vocabulary knowledge when considering a word or phrase important to comprehension or expression.

SL.8.1b: Follow rules for collegial discussions and decision-making, track progress toward specific goals and deadlines, and define individual roles as needed.

Additional Standards Addressed:

RL.8.10; W.8.10

3 Facilitate a **close reading** of the EA 2 assignment and Scoring Guide, focusing on the "Proficient" column. Instruct students to **mark the text** by underlining or highlighting key skills (verbs) and knowledge (nouns).

4 To unpack, you may want to number the Scoring Guide categories (Ideas, Structure, Use of Language, Conventions), form **expert groups**, and assign each group a number (one category).

5 Instruct groups to reread the Scoring Guide descriptors for their assigned category and **paraphrase** skills and knowledge at each level (i.e., exemplary, proficient, emerging, and incomplete) to clarify how one level differs from the others. Assign group roles such as discussion leader, note-taker, diction detective (looks up unknown words), and presenter to hold individuals accountable.

6 As a class, create a large **graphic organizer** with a heading representing each Scoring Guide category (make sure to display it so all students can see). Ask students to create their own copy.

7 As each expert group presents, note the key knowledge and skills on the graphic organizer, under each category. Students should do the same on their own graphic organizer.

8 Make sure to keep the unpacked assessment in a visible place in your classroom so you and your students can refer to specific skills and knowledge before, during, and/or after a daily activity.

9 Use the Scoring Guides for EA 1 and EA 2 to compare and contrast the two writing modes. It is important that students understand that their learning in the first half of the unit applies to the second half.

10 Guide students in the selection of a new independent reading text.

11 To help focus the transition from expository to argumentative writing, ask students to write individual responses, and then **pair-share**. End with a whole-group debrief of their insights.

Previewing Embedded Assessment 2 and Effective Argumentation

My Notes

Unpacking Embedded Assessment 2

Closely read the Embedded Assessment 2 assignment.

> Write an argumentative essay in which you convince an audience to support your claim about a debatable idea. Use your research and experience or observations to support your argument.

Now consult the Scoring Guide and work with your class to paraphrase the expectations. Create a graphic organizer to use as a visual reminder of the required concepts and skills.

After each activity, use this graphic organizer to guide reflection about what you have learned and what you still need to learn in order to be successful in completing the Embedded Assessment.

Looking Ahead to Argumentative Writing

7. Based on your current understanding, how are expository and argumentative writing similar? How are they different?

Similarities:

Differences:

Understanding Elements of Argumentation

ACTIVITY 2.11

Learning Targets

- Evaluate a writer's ideas, point of view, or purpose in an argumentative essay.
- Determine how the writer manages counterclaims.
- Identify and apply the six elements of argumentation.

Preview

In this activity, you will read and analyze part of an eighth-grader's **argumentative** essay.

Setting a Purpose for Reading

- As you read the essay, use three different highlighters to identify the parts of the writer's argument. Mark text evidence with the first color, reasoning with the second color, and counterclaims used to support the claim with the third color.
- Circle unknown words and phrases. Try to determine the meaning of the words by using context clues, word parts, or a dictionary.

LEARNING STRATEGIES:
QHT, Marking the Text, Graphic Organizer

ACADEMIC VOCABULARY
An **argument** is a logical appeal, supported by reasons and evidence, to persuade an audience to take an action or agree with a point of view.

My Notes

Private Eyes

by Brooke Chorlton (an eighth-grader from Washington State)

1 "Private eyes, they're watching you, they see your every move," sang the band Hall and Oates in their 80s hit "Private Eyes." A popular song three decades ago is quite relevant to life today. We do not live very private lives, mainly due to the Internet, whose sole purpose is to help people share everything. But there are still boundaries to what we have to share. Employers should not require access to the Facebook pages of potential or current employees because Facebook is intended to be private, is not intended to be work-related, and employers do not need this medium to make a good hiring decision.

2 It is true that the Internet is not private, and it is also true that Facebook was not created to keep secrets; it is meant for people to share their life with the selected people they choose as their "friends." However, Facebook still has boundaries or some limits, so that members can choose what to share. As a fourteen-year-old girl I know for a fact, because I have seen it, that when you are setting up your Facebook account, you are able to choose the level of security on your page. Some choose to have no security; if someone on Facebook were to search them, they would be able to see all of their friends, photos, and posts. And, according to *Seattle Times* journalists Manuel Valdes and Shannon McFarland, "It has become common for managers to review publically available Facebook Profiles." The key words are "publically available." The owners of these profiles have chosen to have no boundaries, so it is not as big a deal if an employer were to look at a page like this. But others choose to not let the rest of the world in; if you search them, all that would come up would be their name and profile picture. That is all: just a name and a picture. Only the few selected to be that person's friends are allowed into their online world, while the strangers and stalkers are left out in the cold. It is not likely that you would walk up to a stranger and share what you did that weekend. Orin Kerr, a George Washington University law professor and former federal **prosecutor**, states that requiring someone's password to their profile is, "akin to requiring [their] house keys." If we expect privacy in our real world life, shouldn't we be able to have privacy in our online life as well?

COMMON CORE STATE STANDARDS

Focus Standards:

RI.8.5: Analyze in detail the structure of a specific paragraph in a text, including the role of particular sentences in developing and refining a key concept.

RI.8.6: Determine an author's point of view or purpose in a text and analyze how the author acknowledges and responds to conflicting evidence or viewpoints.

Additional Standards Addressed:

RI.8.1; RI.8.2; RI.8.3; W.8.2a; W.8.2b; W.8.4; W.8.5; L.8.6

© 2017 College Board. All rights reserved.

ACTIVITY 2.11

PLAN

Materials: index cards (6), highlighters (3 colors)
Suggested Pacing: 2 50-minute class periods

TEACH

1 Read the Preview and the Setting a Purpose for Reading sections with your students. Help them understand the literary terms they encounter.

2 **FIRST READ:** Based on the complexity of the passage and your knowledge of your students, you may choose to conduct the first reading in a variety of ways:

- independent reading
- paired reading
- small group reading
- choral reading
- read aloud

3 As students are reading, monitor their progress. Be sure they are engaged with the text and annotating as directed. Evaluate whether the selected reading mode is effective.

4 Based on the observations you made during the first reading, you may want to adjust your reading mode. For example, you may decide for the second reading to read aloud certain complex passages, or you may group students differently.

ACTIVITY 2.11 continued

5 **SECOND READ:** During the second reading, students will be returning to the text to answer the text-dependent comprehension questions. You may choose to have students reread and work on the questions in a variety of ways:

- independently
- in pairs
- in small groups
- together as a class

6 Have students answer the text-dependent questions. If they have difficulty, scaffold the questions by rephrasing them or breaking them down into smaller parts. See the Scaffolding the Text-Dependent Questions boxes for suggestions.

7 The Working from the Text questions are intended to have students look closely at the purpose of, structure of, and evidence in the essay.

TEACHER TO TEACHER

The section on Beginning to Construct an Argument begins the parallel instruction leading to writing an argumentative essay. In class, guide students through the process of choosing a topic; creating a claim; and finding, incorporating, and citing evidence. The controversial topic that is suggested is the use of cellphones while driving, and the texts and suggested responses beginning with the next activity all address that topic.

While the class goes through this together, each student needs to be building an argument that he or she can use for the Embedded Assessment. The process is fluid here, but students should be recording ideas in their Reader/Writer Notebooks as they go through the group process in class. In this way, by the last activity of this half of the unit they will have chosen a topic, made a claim, and perhaps done some thinking about what research questions need to be answered and how they will locate sources.

Students will return to the topics **brainstormed** in this activity, so they need to think about what topic they will choose and what claim they

Understanding Elements of Argumentation

prosecutor: a person, especially a public official, who institutes legal proceedings against someone

My Notes

Second Read

- Reread the passage to answer these text-dependent comprehension questions.
- Write any additional questions you have about the text in your Reader/Writer Notebook.

1. **Key Ideas and Details:** What is the writer's purpose? Who is the writer's audience? How do you know? Use textual evidence to support your answer.

   The writer's purpose is to convince the reader that employers should not access private information from a public website. The audience is employers and the general public. I can tell this because she uses persuasive, strong language, like, "If we expect privacy in our real world life, shouldn't we be able to have privacy in our online life as well?" RI.8.1

2. **Key Ideas and Details:** What is the writer's claim? Is it clear to the audience? Use textual evidence to support your answer.

   The writer's claim is that employers should not require employees to grant them access to private online pages. The writer directly states her claim at the end of the opening paragraph. RI.8.1

3. **Craft and Structure:** Paragraph 2 mentions a counterclaim. Restate the counterclaim in your own words. What evidence and reasoning does the writer use to counter or refute the claim?

   The counterclaim makes the point that Facebook is meant to be public and so should be available to employers. The author counters this by saying that if users choose to make their profile public, then employers are welcome; otherwise no one other than "friends" are invited to see. RI.8.6

Working from the Text

4. Based on the thesis, what is the next point the writer will make about the right of employers to ask for access to Facebook?

   Facebook "is not intended to be work-related."

5. Notice that the writer ends the paragraph with an interrogative sentence. Why is this an effective mood to use as a transition to the next major idea of the essay?

Beginning to Construct an Argument

6. Think of a technology-related topic that has two sides that can be argued. Decide which side of the issue you want to argue. Brainstorm possible topics and claims.

   Topics: texting, Facebook, cellphones, Screen Time, video games

SCAFFOLDING THE TEXT-DEPENDENT QUESTIONS

1. Key Ideas and Details (RI.8.1, RI.8.6) **What is the writer's purpose? Who is the writer's audience? How do you know? Use textual evidence to support your answer.** What is the writer's position? What is her purpose for writing? What kind of language does she use? What does this tell us about who she is writing for?

2. Key Ideas and Details (RI.8.1) **What is the writer's claim? Is it clear to the audience? Use textual evidence to support your answer.** Read the opening paragraph closely and note the claim the writer is making.

3. Craft and Structure (RI.8.6) **Paragraph 2 mentions a counterclaim. Restate the counterclaim in your own words. What evidence and reasoning does the writer use to counter or refute the claim?** How does the first sentence of paragraph 2 provide a counterclaim to the writer's claim? What does the writer state she has the power to do as a 14-year-old setting up a Facebook account?

Claims:

Driving while using a cellphone is dangerous.

Texting keeps families more closely connected.

Cellphones are an essential part of a teen's social life.

Teens shouldn't have Facebook accounts until they are 16 years old.

Video games are good for the brain.

Video games are too violent and lead to unhealthy habits.

Check Your Understanding

To convince or persuade someone to share your point of view, you must structure an argument with certain elements in mind. Completing the graphic organizer below will help you structure a convincing argument.

Choose one of the topics you brainstormed and complete the response portion of the graphic organizer.

Element	Definition/Explanation	Response
Purpose	the specific reason(s) for writing or speaking; the goal the writer or speaker wishes to achieve	to convince people that driving and using a cellphone is dangerous
Audience	the specific person or group of people the writer is trying to convince (the opposition); one must consider the audience's values and beliefs before writing the argument	adults and teenagers—anyone who uses a cellphone and can drive
Claim	an assertion of something as true, real, or factual	Using a cellphone while driving is distracting and dangerous.
Evidence	knowledge or data on which to base belief; used to prove truth or falsehood; evidence may include: • testimony from experts and authorities • research-based facts and statistics • analogies (comparisons to similar situations) • references to history, religious texts, and classic literature	own and others' experiences quotes from experts or authorities
Reasoning	logical conclusions, judgments, or inferences based on evidence	Logic: Driving a car is a potentially dangerous activity that requires full concentration. Using a phone while driving is distracting and can lead to accidents.
Counterclaim (Concession/ Refutation)	a claim based on knowledge of the other side of a controversial issue; used to demonstrate understanding of the audience, expertise in the subject, and credibility (ethos) a writer or speaker briefly recognizes and then argues against opposing viewpoints	Counterclaims: Many people are able to multitask and drive safely while talking on their cellphones. Talking on a cellphone while driving is no more dangerous than talking while driving.

writing. Have students complete a **Persuasive/Argument Writing Map** graphic organizer in order to organize their ideas.

Em After students have completed their graphic organizers, ask students basic questions about why persuasive writing is organized in this way.

Ex After students have completed their graphic organizers, ask students to explain why persuasive writing is organized in this way.

Br After students have completed their graphic organizers, ask students to present an argument about why persuasive writing should be organized in this way.

ACTIVITY 2.11 continued

will make for their individual argumentative topic, just as the class has chosen its topic for a class-created example of argument.

You can continue the topic of technology, or think of topics related to the novel students just read. Possible topics relating to the dystopian novel study include banning books, education, media/technology use, marriage, rules/laws, punishments, happiness.

8 To check understanding, consider using one of the brainstormed topics to do a **think aloud** while completing the **graphic organizer** before releasing the students to choose a topic and complete the graphic organizer individually. The suggested responses provided are on the topic of driving while using a cellphone.

9 Once students complete the graphic organizer for their argument, form **discussion groups**, and ask students to **share and respond**. While each student presents his or her argument, group members should listen to comprehend and evaluate. Afterward, group members should provide specific feedback.

ASSESS

Circulate to check for understanding and to clarify confusion. You can collect student work on the graphic organizer to be sure students understand the basic elements of argument.

Ask students to revisit their **QHT** chart to determine how their understanding has grown and to move words to a new column.

ADAPT

This activity serves to review and deepen students' knowledge of argumentation, but you can expect students to feel somewhat comfortable with most of the elements, such as claims, support, reasoning, and counterarguments.

Leveled Differentiated Instruction

In this activity, students may need support to understand the organization of argumentative

ACTIVITY 2.12

▶PLAN

Suggested Pacing: 1 50-minute class period

▶TEACH

1 Now that the foundation has been set, students are ready to practice forming and defending their own arguments.

2 Students should already have been introduced to persuasive appeals. If so, review; if not, use this opportunity to introduce and define terms. Asking students to **visualize** the appeal helps them to conceptualize the idea.

3 Creatively use the Word Wall to help students understand the definitions and purpose of each appeal. Distribute an index card to a student volunteer, and ask him or her to create a Word Wall card during the discussion of each appeal.

4 Ask students to make connections between the elements of argumentation and the appeals. Add the persuasive appeals to the Word Wall to show the connection visually.

5 Explain that **debate** is a speaking and listening strategy designed to engage students in a structured argument that examines both sides of an issue.

6 Provide students with time to complete the Independent Reading Link activity in class. They will need time to complete the exercise and to discuss responses with their peers.

7 Students will next practice using the elements of argument and persuasive appeals by engaging in a debate. As they read the mock news story, students should **mark the text** to indicate whether they agree or disagree with the proposed legislation and then explain their thinking. It will be important to get students thinking about the pro side of this argument since they will probably be against the legislation.

ACTIVITY 2.12

Don't Hate—Debate!

LEARNING STRATEGIES: Visualizing, KWHL, Debate, Brainstorming, Note-taking, Graphic Organizer

Learning Targets

- Identify and analyze persuasive appeals.
- Orally present valid reasoning, well-chosen details, and relevant evidence to support a debatable claim.
- Identify and evaluate arguments as *logos*, *pathos*, and/or *ethos*.
- Assess the soundness of arguments based on reasoning, relevance, and sufficient evidence.

INDEPENDENT READING LINK

Read and Discuss

Choose one essay or speech from your Independent Reading List that contains a compelling claim or argument. What makes the claim or argument effective? Include the author's purpose and any elements of argument you see in the text. Document your response in your Reader/Writer Notebook. You will discuss your response in a small-group setting.

Persuasive Appeals

1. Persuasive appeals are an important part of creating a convincing argument. Read the definitions below to understand how writers or speakers use each type of appeal.

Appeal	Meaning
Logos	an appeal to reason; providing logical reasoning and evidence in the form of *description*, *narration*, and/or *exposition*
Pathos	an appeal to emotions; using descriptive, connotative, and figurative language for effect; providing an emotional anecdote; developing tone
Ethos	an appeal based on trust or character; demonstrating that you understand the audience's point of view; making the audience believe that you are knowledgeable and trustworthy; showing that you have researched your topic by supporting reasons with appropriate, logical evidence and reasoning

2. Create a visual of each type of appeal to help you remember its definition.

ACADEMIC VOCABULARY

A **debate** is an informal or formal discussion in which opposing arguments are put forward. A debate usually focuses on a debatable or controversial issue.

Introducing the Strategy: Debate

A **debate** is an informal or formal argumentation of an issue. Its purpose is to provide an opportunity to collect and orally present evidence supporting the affirmative and negative arguments of a proposition or issue. During a debate, participants follow a specific order of events and often have a time limit for making their points.

Preparing to Debate

A debate provides an opportunity to practice creating a reasoned argument and to identify and use appeals when trying to convince others of your point of view. You will engage in an informal debate on a debatable topic arising from the article below.

3. Read and respond to the following news article, first by circling any words you don't know that you think are important, and next by deciding whether you are for or against the legislation.

COMMON CORE STATE STANDARDS

Focus Standards:

SL.8.3: Delineate a speaker's argument and specific claims, evaluating the soundness of the reasoning and relevance and sufficiency of the evidence and identifying when irrelevant evidence is introduced.

SL.8.4: Present claims and findings, emphasizing salient points in a focused, coherent manner with relevant evidence, sound valid reasoning, and well-chosen details; use appropriate eye contact, adequate volume, and clear pronunciation.

Additional Standards Addressed:

RI.8.1; RI.8.4; W.8.1a; W.8.1b; SL.8.1a; SL.8.1b; SL.8.1c; SL.8.2; SL.8.6; L.8.6

© 2017 College Board. All rights reserved.

Article

Representative Urges Action on the Media

In order to combat what he calls the dangerous increases in teens' harmful media habits, Representative Mark Jenkins has recently introduced legislation that would make it a crime for anyone under the age of 18 to engage with more than two hours of media a day on the weekdays and three hours a day on the weekends. The bill defines "media" as television, radio, commercial magazines, non-school related Internet and any blogs or podcasts with advertising. Penalties for violation can range from **forfeiture** of driver's licenses and media counseling to fines for parents or removal of media tools (TVs, computers, phones, etc.). Monitoring systems will be set up in each Congressional district through the offices of Homeland Security and the National Security Agency. Rep. Jenkins could not be reached for comment because he was appearing on television.

My Notes

forfeiture: the giving up of something as a penalty for wrongdoing

4. Read the debate prompt (always posed as an interrogative sentence).

Debate: Should the government restrict media usage for anyone under the age of 18 to two hours a day on weekdays and three hours a day on weekends?

5. Brainstorm valid reasons for both sides of the issue. Focus on *logos* (logical) appeals, though you may use other appeals to develop your argument. During the debate, you will use these notes to argue your side.

YES, the government should restrict media usage because:		NO, the government should not restrict media usage because:	
Reason 1:	Evidence:	Reason 1:	Evidence:
Reason 2:	Evidence:	Reason 2:	Evidence:

ACTIVITY 2.12 continued

8 Guide students as they assert a claim in response to the question for debate and then build an argument for or against the question by using evidence and appeals.

TEACHER TO TEACHER

Preparing for and conducting the debate can be accomplished in many ways. Consider assigning pro or con to each half of the class and then having them work together in small groups to create effective support for their claim. It will be important for students on either side to be able to anticipate and refute counterclaims.

ACTIVITY 2.12 continued

9 Rearrange the classroom into a **fishbowl**. Half of the students should be in the inside circle and half in the outside circle.

10 Divide the students in the inside circle in half. If you have not already done so, assign sides—*affirmative* (pro) and *negative* (con)—and explain that students must take the side they have been assigned regardless of their true feelings about the topic.

11 Explain that a debate is more formal than a small-group discussion. Encourage students to use the sentence starters to bring up a point or respond to a point. In addition, remind students to use appropriate eye contact, adequate volume, and clear pronunciation when they speak.

▶ASSESS

During the debate, students in the outer circle should listen to evaluate the arguments on both sides, note the use of logic as opposed to *pathos*, and take notes in preparation for their debate. After approximately eight minutes, ask the outer circle to provide feedback, and then switch circles and repeat the process.

Students should independently write responses to the Check Your Understanding questions. Then discuss student responses.

▶ADAPT

Students who are uncomfortable speaking in front of the class may choose not to speak during the debate. If this is the case, provide another opportunity to participate, by setting up a small-group debate (before, during, or after class) and inviting these students to join.

Leveled Differentiated Instruction

In this activity, you may want to have some students complete a different graphic organizer to record ideas from others' arguments.

Em Help students use an **Active Listening Notes** graphic organizer to record words and phrases about others' arguments.

Ex Have students use an **Active Listening Notes** graphic organizer to record complete sentences about others' arguments.

ACTIVITY 2.12 continued

Don't Hate—Debate!

WORD CONNECTIONS

Cognates

A cognate is a word that has the same root meaning as a word in the same or another language. The English word *evaluate* comes from the French verb *evaluer*, which means "to find the value of." It has the same meaning as *evaluar*, a similar word in Spanish. Both *evaluate* and *evaluar* mean "to assess."

My Notes

6. When it is your turn to speak, engage in the debate. Be able to argue either claim. Keep in mind the elements of argument and the different types of appeals. Be sure to use appropriate eye contact, volume, and a clear voice when speaking in a debate.

Sentence Starters

- I agree with your point about . . . , but it is also important to consider . . .
- I disagree with your point about . . . , and would like to counter with the idea that . . .
- You made a good point about . . . , but have you considered . . .
- Your point about . . . is an appeal to emotions and so is not a logical reason/explanation.

7. When it is your turn to listen, evaluate others' arguments for their use of logical appeals. Record notes in the chart below as you identify examples of effective and ineffective *logos*, and provide a brief explanation for each example.

Effective Use of *Logos*	Other Appeals

Check Your Understanding

Reflect on your experience by responding to the following questions:

- What types of persuasive appeals were most effective in supporting the topic during the debate? Why?
- Was any appeal to *logos*, or logic, convincing enough to make you change your mind about the issue? Explain.
- What makes an effective debate? How can the debate strategy help a writer form an effective argument?

Highlighting Logos

ACTIVITY 2.13

Learning Targets

- Identify and evaluate logical reasoning and relevant evidence in an argument.
- Understand the relationship between logic and fallacy.
- Write arguments based on logical reasoning and evidence to support a claim.

Preview

In this activity, you will read two articles about distracted driving and evaluate the logic presented in each.

Setting a Purpose for Reading

- As you read, underline precise adjectives and verbs the writer uses for impact.
- Circle unknown words and phrases. Try to determine the meaning of the words by using context clues, word parts, or a dictionary.

LEARNING STRATEGIES: Marking the Text, Close Reading, Rereading

My Notes

Online Article

Parents Share Son's Fatal Text Message to Warn Against Texting & Driving

1 DENVER (AP) – Alexander Heit's final text cut off in mid-sentence. Before he could send it, police say the 22-year-old University of Northern Colorado student drifted into oncoming traffic, jerked the steering wheel and went off the road, rolling his car.

2 Heit died shortly after the April 3 crash, but his parents and police are hoping the photo of the mundane text on his iPhone will serve as a stark reminder to drivers.

3 The photo, published Wednesday in *The Greeley Tribune*, shows Heit was responding to a friend by typing "Sounds good my man, seeya soon, ill tw" before he crashed.

4 Witnesses told police that Heit appeared to have his head down when he began drifting into the oncoming lane in the outskirts of Greeley, where the University of Northern Colorado is located. According to police, an oncoming driver slowed and moved over just before Heit looked up and jerked the steering wheel.

5 Police say Heit, a Colorado native who loved hiking and snowboarding, had a spotless driving record and wasn't speeding.

6 In a statement released through police, Heit's mother said she doesn't want anyone else to lose someone to texting while driving.

7 "In a split second you could ruin your future, injure or kill others, and tear a hole in the heart of everyone who loves you," Sharon Heit said.

Source: CBS News, © 2013 The Associated Press

ACTIVITY 2.13

PLAN

Materials: highlighters (3 colors), index cards (3)
Suggested Pacing: 1 50-minute class period

TEACH

1 Read the Preview and the Setting a Purpose for Reading sections with your students. Help them understand the terms *logos*, *pathos*, and *ethos*.

2 **FIRST READ:** Based on the complexity of the passage and your knowledge of your students, you may choose to conduct the first reading in a variety of ways:

- independent reading
- paired reading
- small group reading
- choral reading
- read aloud

Text Complexity
Overall: Complex
Lexile: 1360L
Qualitative: Low Difficulty
Task: Challenging (Evaluate)

TEACHER TO TEACHER

If you search for this online article, you can find the actual photo of the boy's cellphone messages.

3 As students are reading, monitor their progress. Be sure they are engaged with the text and annotating as directed. Evaluate whether the selected reading mode is effective.

4 Based on the observations you made during the first reading, you may want to adjust your reading mode. For example, you may decide for the second reading to read aloud certain complex passages, or you may group students differently.

COMMON CORE STATE STANDARDS

Focus Standards:

RI.8.8: Delineate and evaluate the argument and specific claims in a text, assessing whether the reasoning is sound and the evidence is relevant and sufficient; recognize when irrelevant evidence is introduced.

W.8.1b: Support claim(s) with logical reasoning and relevant evidence, using accurate, credible sources and demonstrating an understanding of the topic or text.

Additional Standards Addressed:

RI.8.1; RI.8.2; RI.8.4; RI.8.5; RI.8.10; W.8.1a; W.8.8; SL.8.6; L.8.1b; L.8.2b; L.8.3a; L.8.6

ACTIVITY 2.13 continued

5 **SECOND READ:** During the second reading, students will be returning to the text to answer the text-dependent comprehension questions. You may choose to have students reread and work on the questions in a variety of ways:

- independently
- in pairs
- in small groups
- together as a class

6 Have students answer the text-dependent question. If they have difficulty, scaffold the question by rephrasing it or breaking it down into smaller parts. See the Scaffolding the Text-Dependent Questions boxes for suggestions.

7 Have students respond to the Working from the Text questions individually or in pairs. Then discuss responses as a class. It is important for students to understand that all the appeals in the article overlap and work together to form a convincing argument.

An ineffective argument can be characterized by too much dependence on *pathos* at the expense of logic, resulting in irrelevant *points* and unsound reasoning (i.e., "Only thoughtless and immature people text.").

8 The next section is a brief presentation of valid and sound reasoning in which the ideas of premise, assumption, and conclusion are introduced and discussed. This section can simply be a quick overview of logical reasoning and its connection to effective argumentation.

Highlighting Logos

My Notes

Second Read

- Reread the passage to answer this text-dependent comprehension question.
- Write any additional questions you have about the text in your Reader/Writer Notebook.

1. **Key Ideas and Details:** What kind of appeal does the writer use at the beginning of this article: *logos*, *pathos*, or *ethos*? Why is it effective?

   Pathos engages the reader with an alarming story related to the topic. RI.8.1

Working from the Text

2. What evidence is used to convince others that texting and driving is dangerous? Is this evidence logical, relevant, and convincing?

   The evidence is the retelling of an accidental death. The evidence is relevant and convincing, and it shows a logical relationship between texting and the accident.

3. Now that you have examined and identified the use of the three "appeals" used to convince an audience, explain why *logos* is the most important appeal to be able to use skillfully.

   Building support for a claim with reasoning and evidence allows an argument to stand the test of time and create a strong ethos of credibility.

4. Notice how the different appeals overlap in an argument.

   Logos (fact) and *pathos* (emotion) often overlap; *logos* enhances *ethos*.

What Is Sound Reasoning?

Sound reasoning stems from a valid argument whose conclusion follows from its premises. A **premise** is a statement upon which an argument is based or from which a conclusion is drawn. In other words, a premise is an assumption that something is true.

For example, consider this argument:

Premise: A implies B;

Premise: B implies C;

Conclusion: Therefore, A implies C.

Although we do not know what statements A, B, and C represent, we are still able to judge the argument as valid. We call an argument "sound" if the argument is valid *and* all the statements, including the conclusion, are true.

This structure of **two premises** and **one conclusion** forms the basic argumentative structure. Aristotle held that any logical argument could be reduced to two premises and a conclusion.

Premises: If Socrates is a man, and all men are mortal,

Conclusion: then Socrates is mortal.

A logical fallacy is an error in reasoning that makes an argument invalid or unsound. Common fallacies include:

- claiming too much
- oversimplifying a complex issue
- supporting an argument with abstract generalizations
- false assumptions
- incorrect premises

WORD CONNECTIONS

Multiple Meaning Word

When you hear the word "sound," you probably think of noise, but "sound" has many meanings. It can mean free from error, showing good judgment, or being logically valid, such as in "sound advice" or a "sound argument." A "sound heart" is one free from defects, and a "sound sleep" describes sleep that was deep and undisturbed.

GRAMMAR & USAGE

Conditional Statements

Statements of premises and conclusions, also known as syllogisms, are always formed as **conditional** statements that are finished with a conclusion.

SCAFFOLDING THE TEXT-DEPENDENT QUESTIONS

1. Key Ideas and Details (RI.8.2) **What kind of appeal does the writer use at the beginning of the article: *logos*, *pathos*, or *ethos*? Why is it effective?** Explain the connection between the visuals that begin the reading and the first paragraph. How does this appeal to emotion?

Example: *We need to pass a law that stupid people cannot get a driver's license.* This statement incorrectly equates driving skills with intelligence.

Avoid logical fallacies by being sure you present relevant evidence and logical and sound reasoning—the cornerstones of effective argumentation.

5. Examine this statement of the premises and conclusion of the argument of the article you just read. Is it valid and sound? Explain why or why not.

   Premises: If texting is distracting, and distracted driving can result in an accident,

   Conclusion: then texting can result in an accident.

My Notes

Setting a Purpose for Reading

- As you read this article, underline words and phrases that indicate the science behind the article.
- Circle unknown words and phrases. Try to determine the meaning of the words by using context clues, word parts, or a dictionary.

Online Article

The Science Behind Distracted Driving

from KUTV, Austin

1 Texting while driving can be deadly, but what is it that makes it so dangerous?

2 No longer are people simply talking on their cellphones, they're multi-tasking—checking email, updating social media and texting.

3 "Particularly texting, that seems to be a really hazardous activity, much more dangerous than talking on a cellphone, rising to a level that exceeds what we see with someone who's driving drunk," David Strayer says. He has been studying distracted driving for 15 years.

4 Strayer says we're becoming a nation of distracted drivers. He says that when you take your eyes off the road, hands off the steering wheel, and your mind off driving, it's a deadly mix. "That combination of the three: the visual, the manual, and the cognitive distraction significantly increase the crash risk," says Strayer.

5 With two sophisticated driving **simulators**, an instrumented vehicle, an eye tracker, and a way to measure brain activity, Strayer and his team at the University of Utah have been able to pinpoint what's happening when a person texts while driving. He says, "They're not looking at the road. They're not staying in their lane. They're missing traffic lights," creating a crash risk that is eight times greater than someone giving the road their undivided attention. "That's a really significant crash risk. It's one of the reasons many states have enacted laws to outlaw texting."

6 Thirty-nine states have banned texting while driving.

WORD CONNECTIONS

Roots and Affixes

Distracted comes from the prefix *dis-*, meaning "away" and the Latin root word *tract*, meaning "to drag or pull." "Distracted driving" happens when your attention is being pulled away to something other than driving.

simulators: machines that model certain environmental and other conditions for purposes of training or experimentation

SCAFFOLDING THE TEXT-DEPENDENT QUESTIONS

6. Knowledge and Ideas (RI.8.8) **What is David Strayer's argument? Is it sound? Cite textual evidence in your response.** Paragraph 5 of the article presents scientific evidence of the hazardous effects of driving while texting. How does this make his argument more convincing?

9 After the class reads about logical fallacies, make sure students understand that a writer or speaker loses credibility (*ethos*) if the audience recognizes faulty logic or reasoning in the argument.

Textual Complexity
Overall: Complex
Lexile: 1130L
Qualitative: Low Difficulty
Task: Challenging (Evaluate)

10 Read the Setting a Purpose for Reading section with your students. Help them understand the literary terms they encounter.

11 **FIRST READ:** Based on the complexity of the passage and your knowledge of your students, you may choose to conduct the first reading in a variety of ways:

- independent reading
- paired reading
- small group reading
- choral reading
- read aloud

12 As students are reading, monitor their progress. Be sure they are engaged with the text and annotating as directed. Evaluate whether the selected reading mode is effective.

13 Based on the observations you made during the first reading, you may want to adjust your reading mode. For example, you may decide for the second reading to read aloud certain complex passages, or you may group students differently.

14 **SECOND READ:** During the second reading, students will be returning to the text to answer the text-dependent comprehension questions. You may choose to have students reread and work on the questions in a variety of ways:

- independently
- in pairs
- in small groups
- together as a class

15 Have students answer the text-dependent question. If they have difficulty, scaffold the question by rephrasing it or breaking it down into smaller parts. See the Scaffolding the Text-Dependent Questions boxes for suggestions.

Leveled Differentiated Instruction

In this activity, students may need support to understand Latin roots.

Em Help students complete a **Root and Affixes** graphic organizer for the Latin root *tract* using words they already know, such as *subtract* and *attract*.

Ex Have students complete a **Root and Affixes** graphic organizer for the Latin root *tract* using words they already know and words they find in a dictionary, such as *intractable* and *protracted*. Students should use each new word from the dictionary in a sentence to demonstrate that they understand the word's meaning.

Br Ask students to complete a **Root and Affixes** graphic organizer for the Latin root *tract* using words they find in a dictionary. Students should compare the meanings of the words they find and explain how they are connected to the Latin root *tract*.

Highlighting Logos

7 Strayer's work has been featured at National Distracted Driving summits, used by states to enact no-texting while driving laws, he's even testified in criminal court proceedings—often meeting the families of those killed in distracted driving crashes.

Second Read

- Reread the passage to answer this text-dependent comprehension question.
- Write any additional questions you have about the text in your Reader/Writer Notebook.

6. **Knowledge and Ideas:** What is David Strayer's argument? Is it sound? Cite textual evidence in your response.

   Strayer argues that texting while driving can be hazardous. He presents evidence in the form of the "deadly mix" in paragraph 3 and in the form of testing crash risk in paragraph 5. RI.8.8

Working from the Text

7. Effective arguments use quotes and paraphrased evidence from sources to support claims. For example, David Strayer, who has been studying distracted driving for 15 years, calls texting "hazardous" and "more dangerous than . . . driving drunk." Write a quote and/or paraphrase evidence from the article above.

   "That combination of the three: the visual, the manual, and the cognitive distraction significantly increase the crash risk," says Strayer.

My Notes

Check Your Understanding

WRITING to SOURCES **Writing Prompt**

Choose one quote from each of the articles you have just read to support the claim: *Texting while driving is distracting and increases the risk of crashes.* Use the TLQC format, as you learned in Unit 1 (Activity 1.15), to state the importance of the evidence. Be sure to:

- Use the TLQC format for introducing quoted material.
- Write in the active voice.
- Use ellipses when necessary to show that words have been left out.

▶ASSESS

The writing prompt expects students to have practiced the TLQC format for including quotes in text. (See Unit 1 Actvity 1.15 and Activity 2.3.) It may be a good idea to create an example with students and then ask them in groups to show how seamlessly they can incorporate a quote into their own sentences. Then ask them to do it independently.

▶ADAPT

You may want students to write samples in which they use ellipses to show they are leaving out words. Students need to begin the practice of incorporating parts of quotes to make their points rather than using long, uninterrupted passages. Learning to use ellipses will help them use quoted material more effectively.

Forming and Supporting a Debatable Claim

ACTIVITY 2.14

Learning Targets

- Identify the difference between a debatable and a non-debatable claim.
- Develop an argument to support a debatable claim about a controversial topic, using valid reasons and relevant evidence.

LEARNING STRATEGIES: Summarizing, Brainstorming, Outlining, Freewriting, Marking the Draft

Debatable and Non-Debatable Claims

You have already brainstormed topics and possible claims. It may seem obvious, but it is important to be sure your topic and claim are debatable.

- If a claim is **debatable**, it is **controversial**; that is, two logical people might disagree based on evidence and reasoning used to support the claim. Example: *Using a cellphone while driving puts you and other drivers in danger.*
- If a claim is **non-debatable**, it is a fact and therefore it cannot be argued. Example: *Cellphones are a popular form of modern communication*. This could be an expository topic, but is not suitable for argument.

ACADEMIC VOCABULARY
A **controversy** occurs when there are two sides that disagree with each other.
A *controversial topic* is a topic that can be debated.

1. Summarize the difference between a debatable and a non-debatable claim.

2. Write one debatable and one non-debatable claim relating to each topic below.

Topic: the amount of time teens spend using technology

- **Debatable:** Too much screen time has a negative effect on student performance in school.
- **Non-debatable:** Teenagers and adults use media in many ways.

Topic: the age at which someone should have a social media account

- **Debatable** Teens under 16 shouldn't be allowed to have social media accounts.
- **Non-debatable:** Social media sites such as Facebook are popular with teens.

INDEPENDENT READING LINK

Read and Recommend

Select one essay or speech from your Independent Reading List that provides a clear use of *logos*, *pathos*, or *ethos*. Prepare to give an oral recommendation of this essay or speech by connecting an explanation of the persuasive appeal with specific examples from the text. Document your response in a paragraph in your Reader/Writer Notebook.

My Notes

ACTIVITY 2.14

PLAN

Materials: highlighters
Suggested Pacing: 2 50-minute class periods

TEACH

1 With students, read the definitions and examples of debatable and non-debatable claims. As you discuss claims, encourage students to revisit ideas from the debate in the previous activity.

2 The next activity is designed to show that students understand the difference between a debatable and a non-debatable claim. You might have the students complete this activity with partners and then share their ideas with the rest of the class.

3 Explain that the class will focus on the topic *cellphone use while driving* for the rest of the unit. The remaining activities will use this topic as a model to show students how to prepare an effective argumentative essay. At the same time, students should be completing the same activities based on the topic they have chosen for their own argumentative essay. Make sure that students are completing this preparation either in class or as homework. If students have not yet decided on a topic for their essay or would like to change topics, this is the time.

4 Provide students with time to complete the Independent Reading Link activity in class. They will need time to complete the exercise and to present responses orally.

COMMON CORE STATE STANDARDS

Focus Standards:

W.8.1: Write arguments to support claims with clear reasons and relevant evidence.

W.8.1a: Introduce claim(s), acknowledge and distinguish the claim(s) from alternate or opposing claims, and organize the reasons and evidence logically.

RI.8.8: Delineate and evaluate the argument and specific claims in a text, assessing whether the reasoning is sound and the evidence is relevant and sufficient; recognize when irrelevant evidence is introduced.

Additional Standards Addressed:

W.8.10; L.8.6

ACTIVITY 2.14 continued

5 Guided writing instructions:

Step 1: As a class, **brainstorm** and select two opposing claims relating to **using cellphones while driving.**

Step 2: Assign a claim to each half of the class, or allow students to select the claim they would like to support.

Step 3: Ask students to **freewrite** to create support for the claim about texting that they are arguing. This should be done in class and can be accompanied by sharing and responding in order to add ideas to the initial freewrite. During this freewrite it is not likely that students will bring up many counterclaims. Take no more than 10 minutes for this writing.

Step 4: Analyzing the audience will focus students on recognizing counterclaims and the evidence they will need to refute the counterclaims. After students identify their audience, discuss the importance of analyzing one's audience prior to forming an argument. As you present each question, ask students to consider their audience and record responses to the questions.

Step 5: Remind students that addressing counterclaims shows the audience that you know who they are, what they believe, and why they believe it. This appeals to *ethos*, and an audience is much more likely to agree with you when their beliefs are countered with strong *logos*.

Ask students to identify two counterclaims to address in their argument.

▶ASSESS

As you work with students on the guided writing, evaluate their understanding of the process based on their comments and the questions they ask. Also check their answers to the Check Your Understanding question to ensure they understand the importance of audience to crafting an argument.

▶ADAPT

Have students share their claims to ensure that they are debatable. Some students may need guidance in choosing an appropriate claim.

Forming and Supporting a Debatable Claim

My Notes

Forming and Supporting a Debatable Claim

3. Use the following steps to form and support a debatable claim for the topic you chose in Activity 2.11.

Step 1: Write a debatable claim for each side of an issue relating to the topic.

Texting	
Side 1 **Claim:** Using a cell phone while driving is distracting and dangerous.	**Side 2** **Claim:** Using a cellphone while diving is no more dangerous than talking while driving.

Step 2: Highlight the claim you will support.

Step 3: Freewrite: How can you support the claim you chose? How much logical reasoning can you use? Will you depend on *pathos*? How can you support your claim with evidence and sound reasoning?

Step 4: Identify and analyze your **audience**. Who would support the other side? Be specific! Consider the kind of information, language, and overall approach that will appeal to your audience. Ask yourself the following questions:

- What does the audience know about this topic (through personal experience, research, etc.)?
- What does the audience value related to this topic?
- How might the audience disagree with me? What objections will the audience want me to address or answer?
- How can I best use *logos* to appeal to and convince this audience?
- How will I use language to show I am worth listening to on this subject?

Step 5: Now that you better understand your audience, plan to address at least two counterclaims by identifying potential weaknesses of your argument within opposing reasons, facts, or testimony. Use this format:

My audience might argue___________, so I will counter by arguing or pointing out that ___________.

1. My audience might argue that cellphone use is just one of many tasks experienced while driving, so I will counter by arguing that using cellphones is a deliberate and avoidable distraction.
2. My audience might argue that they can multitask so well that cellphone use is not a distraction, so I will counter by arguing that confidence in multitasking is a false assumption.

Check Your Understanding

Why is it necessary to identify your audience as precisely and accurately as possible?

© 2017 College Board. All rights reserved.

Conducting Effective Research

ACTIVITY 2.15

Learning Targets

- Form effective questions to focus research.
- Identify appropriate sources that can be used to support an argument.

LEARNING STRATEGIES: Skimming/Scanning, Close Reading, Marking the Text, Note-taking

Using the Research Process

Once you have chosen your topic, created a claim, and considered possible counterclaims, you are ready to conduct additional **research** on your topic to find evidence to support your claim and refute counterclaims.

1. What are the steps of the research process? Are the steps logical? Why?

   1. Identify the issue or problem.
   2. Form questions.
   3. Gather evidence.
   4. Interpret information and draw conclusions.
   5. Communicate findings (quote or paraphrase).

ACADEMIC VOCABULARY
Research (*v.*) is the process of locating information from a variety of sources.
Research (*n.*) is the information found from investigated sources.

Writing Research Questions

2. What makes an effective research question?

   open-ended, directly related to claim, and purposeful (the answer will be used to support the argument)

3. How will gathering evidence affect my research questions?

   Gaining a deeper understanding about a topic leads to revising existing questions and generating additional questions.

4. What is an example of an effective research question?

   How does cellphone use affect driving performance?

WORD CONNECTIONS

Etymology

Refute comes from the prefix *re-*, meaning "back/ backward" and the Latin root word *futare*, meaning "to beat." The Latin word *refutare* came to mean "to drive back or rebut." *To refute* now means "to disprove or invalidate." For example, if you refute an argument, you're proving the argument to be false.

Locating and Evaluating Sources

Many people rely on the Internet for their research, since it is convenient and it can be efficient. To find relevant information on the Internet, you need to use effective **search terms** to begin your research. Try to choose terms that narrow your results. For example, searching on the term "driving accidents" will return broad information, whereas searching on the term "distracted driving" will return results more closely in line with that topic.

The Internet has a lot of useful information, but it also has a great deal of information that is not reliable or credible. You must carefully examine the websites that offer information, since the Internet is plagued with unreliable information from unknown sources. Faulty information and unreliable sources undermine the validity of one's argument.

ACADEMIC VOCABULARY
Search terms are the words or phrases entered into an online search engine to find information related to the words or phrases.

COMMON CORE STATE STANDARDS

Focus Standards:

W.8.7: Conduct short research projects to answer a question (including a self-generated question), drawing on several sources and generating additional related, focused questions that allow for multiple avenues of exploration.

W.8.8: Gather relevant information from multiple print and digital sources, using search terms effectively; assess the credibility and accuracy of each source; and quote or paraphrase the data and conclusions of others while avoiding plagiarism and following a standard format for citation.

Additional Standards Addressed:

RI.8.1; RI.8.2; RI.8.4; RI.8.10; W.8.1b; W.8.4; W.8.10; L.8.6

ACTIVITY 2.15

▶PLAN

Materials: research process manipulatives, (optional) access to computers for research
Suggested Pacing: 2 50-minute class periods

▶TEACH

1 Now that the claim, audience, and counterclaims are clear in their minds, students are ready to conduct research to find evidence that is relevant and convincing. Discuss the definition of *research* and then ask students to explain how research strengthens *logos* and *ethos*.

2 You may either **brainstorm** the steps of the research process or create sets of five cards with a step on each card and use them as **manipulatives**. Form small groups and hand each group a set of cards for that order. Ask groups to arrange the steps in logical order and then provide a rationale. Ask students to record the steps and discuss the logic behind the order.

TEACHER TO TEACHER

Like the last activity, class work focuses on the class topic—cellphones. It may be better to go through the whole activity focusing on this topic, reminding students that you are modeling the process of researching and locating support for the claim. Then at the end of the activity, ask students to go through the process again using their own chosen topic, so that by the end of the lesson they have researched their topic and found at least one article they can use to support their claim and refute the counterclaims.

3 Discuss responses to the Writing Research Questions items as a class, and have the students suggest options for an effective research question relating to the class topic of cellphone use while driving. Then give students time to form one or more research questions for their own topic.

4 Guide students in a discussion about search terms and the necessity of evaluating Internet sources for reliability.

5 You might put students in pairs or small groups to fill in the Criteria for Evaluating Websites chart. Students may have difficulty with telling the difference between some of the criteria, such as *accuracy* and *validity*. Read the TE explanations for students as they take notes in the chart.

6 As a class, create questions about cellphone use while driving. Then have students research relevant sources and effective search terms for the cellphones topic. Discuss search terms that should elicit the most relevant information.

7 At this point you may choose to have students go through the process for their chosen topic.

Conducting Effective Research

WORD CONNECTIONS

Multiple Meaning Words

Currency often refers to money or financial exchanges, but it can also mean "the state of being current," such as the *currency of information*, or "general use or acceptance," such as an idea gaining *widespread currency*.

My Notes

5. What do you know about the following criteria that define reliable Internet sites? Fill in the chart with your current knowledge.

Criteria for Evaluating Websites	
Accuracy	the site is free from errors and operates properly; information is consistent with other sources
Validity	information appears to be well researched and/or there is a statement about the purpose of the site, which is educational in nature
Authority	the author appears to be well qualified to write on the subject and/or the site is part of a respected institution (e.g., a college, a museum, a newspaper, a journal)
Currency	the site has been updated recently and/or sources of information are current
Coverage	the site seems to cover the topic fully, other related topics are discussed on the site, and/or there is a resource section with links to other sites

6. What types of websites are reliable and trustworthy? Why?

government sites, sites sponsored by a large institution such as a university or research group; news and newspaper sites

7. Now it is time to find additional evidence from a variety of outside sources to strengthen your argument. First, form two or three research questions that will help you to support your claim:
   - Does any scientific evidence connect cellphone use to accidents?
   - Is talking on a cellphone illegal anywhere and, if so, why?

8. Which types of sources are best for the information you seek? List at least three and explain your choices.

   current newspaper articles, documentaries, research studies, expert testimony (doctors, psychologists)

9. What search terms will you use to narrow your search for sources with relevant information on the topic and claim?

   cellphones while driving, auto accidents and cellphones

Researching and Reading Informational Texts

Much research information is taken from informational texts, which can be challenging to read. An effective strategy for reading these texts is to pay attention to their **text features**.

There are five broad categories of text features found in informational texts:

- **Text organization** identifies text divisions (e.g., chapters, sections, introductions, summaries, and author information).
- **Headings** help readers understand the information (e.g., titles, labels, and subheadings).
- **Graphics** show information visually to add or clarify information (e.g., diagrams, charts and tables, graphs, maps, photographs, illustrations, paintings, timelines, and captions).
- **Format and font size** signal to the reader that certain words are important (e.g., boldface, italics, or a change in font).
- **Layout** includes aids such as insets, bullets, and numbers that point readers to important information.

Preview

In this activity, you will read an article and evaluate its validity.

Setting a Purpose for Reading

- As your read, put a star next to the writer's claim. Underline information you think would be logical evidence to support the claim.
- Circle unknown words and phrases. Try to determine the meaning of the words by using context clues, word parts, or a dictionary.
- Note whether the text features lend the article credibility or not.

ABOUT THE AUTHOR

Marcel Just *is the D.O. Hebb Professor of Psychology and director of the Center for Cognitive Brain Imaging at Carnegie Mellon University.*

Tim Keller *is a senior research psychologist at the center. They are co-authors of the study,* "A Decrease in Brain Activation Associated with Driving When Listening to Someone Speak."

My Notes

ACTIVITY 2.15 continued

8 In order to be efficient researchers, students must develop the ability to evaluate the potential usefulness of a text as a source without having to read the entire text. Remind students of the importance of using text features to determine whether a text will yield useful supporting evidence.

9 The text-dependent questions in the upcoming article point students toward support and counterarguments contained in the article. You might also discuss the use of the images and captions as evidence.

10 Read the Preview and the Setting a Purpose for Reading sections with your students. Help them understand the terms they encounter.

11 **FIRST READ:** Based on the complexity of the passage and your knowledge of your students, you may choose to conduct the first reading in a variety of ways:

- independent reading
- paired reading
- small group reading
- choral reading
- read aloud

Text Complexity
Overall: Complex
Lexile: 1410L
Qualitative: Moderate Difficulty
Task: Moderate (Analyze)

12 As students are reading, monitor their progress. Be sure they are engaged with the text and annotating claims. Evaluate whether the selected reading mode is effective.

13 Based on the observations you made during the first reading, you may want to adjust your reading mode. For example, you may decide for the second reading to read aloud certain complex passages, or you may group students differently.

WORD CONNECTIONS

Content Connections

In general terms, *spatial* means "relating to, occupying, or having the character of space." Scientifically speaking, *spatial* refers to the location of objects and the metric relationships between them. Specific to how the brain reacts, *spatial processing* indicates the brain activity required to engage spatial memory and orientation so that driving can occur.

My Notes

Article

How the Brain Reacts

http://roomfordebate.blogs.nytimes.com/2009/07/18/should-cellphone-use-by-drivers-be-illegal/

1 Behavioral studies have shown that talking on a cellphone diverts the driver's attention and disrupts driving performance. We investigated that question by looking at brain activity that occurs during driving. In our study, using functional magnetic resonance imaging (fMRI), we examined the effect of listening to someone speak on the brain activity associated with simulated driving.

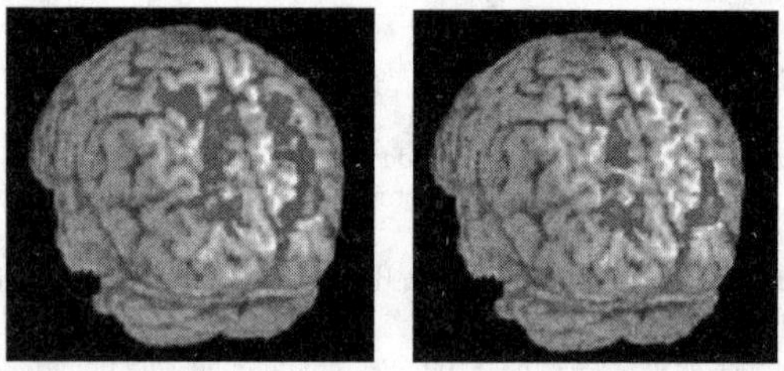

Brain activity associated with spatial processing when driving without distraction (left) and when driving while listening to sentences (right).

Center for Cognitive Brain Imaging, Carnegie Mellon University

2 Participants steered a vehicle along a curving virtual road, either undisturbed or while listening to spoken sentences that they judged as true or false. The parietal lobe activation associated with spatial processing in driving decreased by 37 percent when participants **concurrently** listened to the sentences. We found that listening comprehension tasks drew mental resources away from driving and produced a **deterioration** in driving performance, even though the drivers weren't holding or dialing a phone.

concurrently: occurring at the same time
deterioration: the act or process of becoming worse

3 These brain activation findings show the biological basis for the deterioration in driving performance (in terms of errors and staying in a lane) that occurs when one is also processing language. They suggest that under mentally demanding circumstances, it may be dangerous to combine processing of spoken language with a task like driving a car in demanding circumstances.

4 Our listening experiment did not require the participants to speak, so it was probably less disruptive to driving than an actual two-way conversation might be. It's likely that our study actually underestimates the reduction in driving performance.

5 If listening to sentences degrades driving performance, then probably a number of other common driver activities—including tuning or listening to a radio, eating and drinking, monitoring children or pets, or even conversing with a passenger—would also cause reduced driving performance.

SCAFFOLDING THE TEXT-DEPENDENT QUESTIONS

10. Knowledge and Ideas (RI.8.8) **What evidence do the writers provide to support their claim that spoken language can degrade driving performance?** Note that the title points the reader to the central focus of this study, so that readers should expect some evidence based on brain research.

11. Craft and Structure (RI.8.4) **What transition words do the writers use to navigate the reader through their argument?** Reread the section that begins with "If listening to sentences, and not the transitions..."

6 It would be incorrect, however, to conclude that using a cellphone while driving is no worse than engaging in one of these other activities. First, it's not known how much these other distractions affect driving (though that would be an interesting study).

7 Second, talking on a cellphone is a particular social interaction, with demands different from a conversation with a passenger. Not responding in a cellphone conversation, for instance, can be interpreted as rude behavior.

8 By contrast, a passenger in a car is more likely to be aware of the competing demands for a driver's attention. Indeed there is recent experimental evidence suggesting that passengers and drivers suppress conversation in response to driving demands.

9 Third, with spoken language, a listener cannot willfully stop the processing of a spoken utterance. These considerations suggest that talking on cellphones while driving can be a risky choice, not just for common sense reasons, but because of the way our brains work.

My Notes

Second Read

- Reread the passage to answer these text-dependent comprehension questions.
- Write any additional questions you have about the text in your Reader/Writer Notebook.

10. **Knowledge and Ideas:** What evidence do the writers provide to support their claim that spoken language can degrade driving performance?

Brain activation findings show that "listening" comprehension tasks drew mental resources away from driving resulting in a "deterioration of driving performance." RI.8.8

11. **Craft and Structure:** What transition words do the writers use to navigate the reader through their argument?

Transitions in this article become obvious in the second half of the article when the authors are presenting concessions and refuting them. The concession begins with "However," and the refutations are signaled by "First," "Second," and "Third." RI.8.4

Working from the Text

12. Choose two pieces of relevant and convincing information that support the authors' claim. Quote as much of the original material as is necessary. Write your responses in the My Notes section on this page.

Examples:

- "We found that listening comprehension tasks drew mental resources away from driving and produced a deterioration in driving performance."
- "The parietal lobe activation associated with spatial processing in driving decreased by 37 percent when participants concurrently listened to the sentences."

ACTIVITY 2.15 continued

14 SECOND READ: During the second reading, students will be returning to the text to answer the text-dependent comprehension questions. You may choose to have students reread and work on the questions in a variety of ways:

- independently
- in pairs
- in small groups
- together as a class

15 Have students answer the text-dependent questions. If they have difficulty, scaffold the questions by rephrasing them or breaking them down into smaller parts. See the Scaffolding the Text-Dependent Questions boxes for suggestions.

Leveled Differentiated Instruction

In this activity, students may need the support of an **Idea and Argument Evaluator** to help them analyze the text.

Em Have students work in pairs to answer the following questions using simple phrases: *What is the author's main idea? What ideas support the author's main idea?*

Ex Guide students to work in pairs to identify the author's main idea and list support from the text, offering support as needed.

Br Have students work in pairs to complete the graphic organizer, building on each other's responses in order to understand the author's ideas.

Support Have students work independently to complete the graphic organizer.

▶ASSESS

The writing prompt asking students to incorporate quotes and paraphrases to support the author's claim should be a review of using quoting and paraphrasing as evidence or support in an essay of argumentation. Note students' use of ellipses.

▶ADAPT

After the modeling of this activity, students should be prepared to do research and find a source that they can use to support their claim about the topic of their choice.

Give time in class to do research or assign it as homework with the expectation that students will bring in a copy of the source they have found.

Explain that in the next two activities, students will read two reliable texts about cellphones to practice using research to strengthen an argument.

Conducting Effective Research

My Notes

Check Your Understanding

WRITING to SOURCES **Argumentative Writing Prompt**

Using the examples from question 12, write a paragraph for an argumentative essay in support of the claim. Paraphrase the first piece of information. For the second piece of information, smoothly combine quoting and paraphrasing. Then add your own commentary to explain the quote. Be sure to:

- Carefully paraphase the quote to avoid changing its meaning.
- Choose a relevant quote that fully supports the claim and smoothly incorporate it into your paragraph, citing the author or the article.
- Write insightful commentary that adds your own interpretation and meaning to the evidence and how it supports the claim.

Examples:

1. Paraphrase: Trying to pay attention to and understand a conversation takes the driver's focus away from driving tasks, resulting in a lower level of driving performance.
2. Quote and paraphrase: According to Just and Keller, brain activity involved with driving tasks "decreased by 37 percent when participants concurrently listened to the sentences" and driving. This decrease is enough to impact driving ability, and it shows that trying to carry on a conversation while driving is a significant distraction.

Gathering and Citing Evidence

ACTIVITY 2.16

Learning Targets

- Create annotated bibliography entries and show how to use this information to strengthen an argument.
- Refine research questions to guide the research process.

LEARNING STRATEGIES: Predicting, Graphic Organizer, Summarizing, Paraphrasing, Note-taking, Marking the Text, Questioning the Text

Conducting Research

You have begun to conduct research on a topic and claim of your choice, creating research questions, using effective search terms, and finding appropriate sources from which you can take information to use as evidence.

Citing Sources and Creating a Bibliography

When using information from research in your writing, you should cite the source of the information. In addition to giving credit in your essay, you may also be asked to provide a **Works Cited** page or an **Annotated Bibliography** to document your research and strengthen your ethos. A Works Cited page includes a properly formatted citation for each source you use. An **Annotated Bibliography** includes both the full citation of the source and a summary of information in the source or commentary on the source.

Citation Formats

Works Cited Entry:

Burke, Kenneth. *Language as Symbolic Action: Essays on Life, Literature, and Method. Berkeley*: U of California P, 1966. Print.

In-text Citation:

Human beings have been described as "symbol-using animals" (Burke 3).

1. To practice note-taking and generating a bibliography entry, complete the *research card* below using information from "How the Brain Reacts."

Source Citation:

Just, Marcel and Tim Heller. "How the Brain Reacts." *Room for Debate Blogs. The New York* Times, 18 July 2009. Web. 1 Feb. 2012.

How can this source help you to support your argument?

What makes this source credible?

In this activity, you will read another article about cellphones and driving and connect it to previous texts you have read on the subject.

Setting a Purpose for Reading

- As you read, note conflicting information the writer brings up. Underline words that indicate these transitions.
- Circle unknown words and phrases. Try to determine the meaning of the words by using context clues, word parts, or a dictionary.

My Notes

INDEPENDENT READING LINK

Read and Respond

Choose a text from your Independent Reading List that shows effective research and use of relevant text. List examples from the text to support your opinion in your Reader/Writer Notebook.

ACTIVITY 2.16

▶ PLAN

Materials: a possible source to consult for proper citation formats is http://owl.english.purdue.edu/owl/resource/747/2/

Suggested Pacing: 2 50-minute class periods

▶ TEACH

TEACHER TO TEACHER

Consider citing all of the sources in advance to guide your work with students.

1 Guide students as they complete an annotated bibliography entry for the article in the previous activity. The additional information beyond the proper citation of the article is important when students locate multiple sources and may need to choose among sources.

2 Encourage students to complete the Independent Reading Link activity, reminding them to record responses in the Reader/Writer Notebook.

3 Read the Setting a Purpose for Reading section with your students. Help them understand the terms they encounter.

COMMON CORE STATE STANDARDS

Focus Standards:

W.8.7: Conduct short research projects to answer a question (including a self-generated question), drawing on several sources and generating additional related, focused questions that allow for multiple avenues of exploration.

W.8.8: Gather relevant information from multiple print and digital sources, using search terms effectively; assess the credibility and accuracy of each source; and quote or paraphrase the data and conclusions of others while avoiding plagiarism and following a standard format for citation.

Additional Standards Addressed:

RI.8.1; RI.8.2; RI.8.4; RI.8.8; RI.8.9; RI.8.10; W.8.1a; W.8.1b; W.8.9; L.8.6

ACTIVITY 2.16 continued

Text Complexity
Overall: Very Complex
Lexile: 1410L
Qulaitative: Moderate Difficulty
Task: Moderate (Analyze)

4 **FIRST READ:** Based on the complexity of the passage and your knowledge of your students, you may choose to conduct the first reading in a variety of ways:

- independent reading
- paired reading
- small group reading
- choral reading
- read aloud

5 This text has a high Lexile measure because it has very long sentences. The vocabulary is not unusually difficult, although there are some words that you may want to explain to students or have them diffuse (such as *ordinance*, *consensus*, *prohibition*).

6 As students are reading, monitor their progress. Be sure they are engaged with the text and annotating as directed. Evaluate whether the selected reading mode is effective.

7 Based on the observations you made during the first reading, you may want to adjust your reading mode. For example, you may decide for the second reading to read aloud certain complex passages, or you may group students differently.

Gathering and Citing Evidence

My Notes

ABOUT THE AUTHOR
Matthew Walberg is an investigative reporter for the *Chicago Tribune*, specializing in criminal justice and a wide range of governmental topics.

Article

Cellphones and driving: As dangerous as we think?

Despite calls for cellphone bans, there's no conclusive data on handheld devices and safe driving

March 26, 2012 | By Matthew Walberg, *Chicago Tribune* reporter
Source: http://articles.chicagotribune.com/2012-03-26/news/ct-met-cellphone-safety-studies-20120326_1_handheld-cellphones-cellphone-restrictionscellphone-subscribers

1 A bill pending in Springfield would ban all drivers in Illinois from using handheld cellphones in Illinois. An **ordinance** being considered in Evanston would go further and prohibit motorists in that town from talking on cellphones of any kind—including hands-free.

2 It's a matter of safety, proponents of both measures say.

3 But two decades of research done in the U.S. and abroad have not yielded **conclusive** data about the impact cellphones have on driving safety, it appears. Nor is there a **consensus** that hands-free devices make for safer driving than handheld cellphones.

4 In theory, the effect of cellphones on driver performance should be relatively easy to determine: Compare crash data against phone records of drivers involved in accidents. But phone records are not easily obtained in the United States, forcing researchers in this country to find less direct ways to analyze the danger of cellphone distraction. The issue is further clouded because auto accidents overall have been decreasing, even as cellphones become more common.

5 "The expectation would be that as cellphone use has skyrocketed we would see a correlation in the number of accidents, but that hasn't happened," said Jonathan Adkins, spokesman for the Governors Highway Safety Association.

6 Adkins said the association believes that states should simply enforce their current cellphone laws, if any, and wait for further research to better understand exactly how much of a role cellphone use plays in automobile accidents.

7 "We know it's distracting, we know it increases the likelihood of a crash," Adkins said. "It just hasn't shown up in data in a lot of cases—in other words, it's hard to prove that a crash was caused because someone was on their cellphone."

8 Proponents of cellphone restrictions—whether total bans or **prohibition** of handheld phones—can cite some studies to back up their positions.

9 A 2005 study published in the British Medical Journal looked at crash data for 456 cellphone subscribers in Perth, Australia, who had an auto accident that required medical attention. The study, which essentially confirmed a similar 1997 study

GRAMMAR & USAGE
Passive Voice
Note how the passive voice is used in the second sentence of the first paragraph. Why is it used in this case?

ordinance: statute; law

conclusive: definitive; clear

consensus: general agreement

WORD CONNECTIONS
Roots and Affixes
The word *correlation* is made from the Latin prefix *cor-*, meaning "together; with" and the root word *relation*, meaning "connection."

prohibition: the action of forbidding something, especially by law

SCAFFOLDING THE TEXT-DEPENDENT QUESTIONS

2. Craft and Structure (RI.8.4) **What clues in the text tell you the meaning of the word intoxicated?** Reread paragraph 10 to find the word "intoxicated." How does its association with blood alcohol levels give you a clue about its meaning?

3. Knowledge and Ideas (RI.8.8) **What is the writer's purpose for citing studies? How do you know?** Find the writer's claim about cellphone use causing accidents. How will this claim require that he produce conflicting results from studies about cellphone use and driving?

4. Craft and Structure (RI.8.4) **How does the writer transition between pieces of opposing information? Cite some examples.** Notice that the writer's argument begins with information that supports the idea that though cellphone use is distracting, we don't really know its effects. By paragraph 8 the writer begins with a series of opposing points of view.

conducted in Toronto, concluded that drivers talking on their phones were about four times more likely to be involved in an accident than those who were not on the phone.

10 Another highly publicized 2006 study from the University of Utah concluded that drivers who talked on cellphones were as impaired as drivers who were intoxicated at the legal blood-alcohol limit of 0.08. The study, however, found that using hands-free devices did little to improve drivers' performances.

11 There is some evidence suggesting state and local bans have caused some drivers to talk less while on the road.

12 This month, California's Office of Traffic Safety released the results of a study showing a sharp decrease in the number of accidents caused by cellphone use that resulted in death or injury.

13 Researchers tracked the number of accident reports that listed cellphone use as a factor during the two-year periods before and after the 2008 passage of a statewide ban on handheld devices. The study concluded that while overall traffic **fatalities** of all kinds dropped by 22 percent, fatalities caused by drivers who were talking on a handheld phone at the time of the crash dropped nearly 50 percent. Similar declines were found for drivers using hands-free devices.

14 The study followed the agency's 2011 survey of more than 1,800 drivers that found that only about 10 percent of drivers reported that they regularly talked on the phone while driving—down from 14 percent from the previous year's survey. In addition, the survey saw increases in the number of people who said they rarely or never use their cellphone behind the wheel.

15 Those surveyed, however, overwhelmingly believed that hands-free devices made cellphone use safer, a perception that runs counter to research showing such tools do little to reduce the distraction.

16 "If there is an advantage, it's only because a person may have two hands on the wheel, but most people drive with one hand all the time anyway," said Chris Cochran, spokesman for the Office of Traffic Safety. "In reality, it's the conversation, not the phone itself."

My Notes

fatalities: deaths

Second Read

- Reread the passage to answer these text-dependent comprehension questions.
- Write any additional questions you have about the text in your Reader/Writer Notebook.

2. **Craft and Structure:** What clues in the text tell you the meaning of the word *intoxicated*?

   The association between "legal blood-alcohol" limits and the word *intoxicated* gives enough clues to infer that the word means "drunk." RI.8.4

3. **Knowledge and Ideas:** What is the writer's purpose for citing studies? How do you know?

   The author cites studies in an attempt to provide a more balanced view of cellphones and driving. He spends the first seven paragraphs making the point that there is no conclusive evidence linking cellphone use to driving safety. He then cites conflicting studies to prove his point. RI.8.8

5. Knowledge and Ideas (RI.8.9) **In what way does the writer of this article disagree with the other writers in these activities, on matters of fact or interpretation? Cite textual evidence to support your answer.** What factual data does the author present about the use of cellphones and accidents? Does he interpret the data or does he allow the reader to make judgments?

ACTIVITY 2.16 continued

8 **SECOND READ:** During the second reading, students will be returning to the text to answer the text-dependent comprehension questions. You may choose to have students reread and work on the questions in a variety of ways:

- independently
- in pairs
- in small groups
- together as a class

9 Have students answer the text-dependent questions. If they have difficulty, scaffold the questions by rephrasing them or breaking them down into smaller parts. See the Scaffolding the Text-Dependent Questions boxes for suggestions.

Leveled Differentiated Instruction

In this activity, students may need more interaction with the text for full comprehension.

Em Guide students to work in pairs to answer literal *yes-no* questions about the text, such as *Is it dangerous to use a cellphone while driving?*

Ex Guide students to work in smaller groups or pairs to discuss literal questions about the text, such as *Why is it hard to measure the effect of cellphones on driver performance?*

Br Have students work in smaller groups or pairs to discuss literal and interpretive questions about the text, such as *Do you think there should be laws against using cellphones while driving?* Encourage students to respond to their partners by offering useful feedback.

10 The Working from the Text item again asks students to choose relevant and convincing evidence from the informational source and compose it for use in an essay of argumentation. Discuss when it is best to directly quote textual evidence and when it is best to paraphrase. Again, ask students to experiment with using ellipses.

Leveled Differentiated Instruction

In this activity, students may need support with organizing their argumentative writing. Before writing, students will look closely at the word choices writers can make in order to persuade.

Em Provide students with some persuasive words and phrases such as *we know, we found that,* and *by contrast.* Have students work in pairs to explain how well these words support ideas and arguments.

Ex Provide students with some persuasive words and phrases such as *we investigated, these findings show,* and *correlation.* Have students work in pairs to explain how well these words present ideas or support arguments.

Br Provide students with some persuasive words and phrases such as *it would be incorrect, common sense,* and *overwhelmingly.* Have students work in pairs to explain how well these words present ideas or support arguments.

11 The writing prompt is designed to give students practice including evidence from sources clearly and with convincing commentary. This is something you could co-construct with the class as a model of what they will have to do in their own essay of argumentation.

▶ASSESS

Ask students to complete bibliography entries for the text they just read and annotated or for each quotation that supports their argument.

If you determine students are ready, you might have them use the note cards to cite the sources they have found to use for their chosen topic of argumentation.

▶ADAPT

If you notice citation errors or incomplete responses, use examples of exemplary entries to reinforce expectations. Then, ask struggling students to revise their work to show their new understanding of this skill. Students who already demonstrate understanding could be paired with students who need to revise.

At this point expect students to conduct additional research to find another source for evidence to support the claim they have made about their topic.

Gathering and Citing Evidence

My Notes

4. **Craft and Structure:** How does the writer transition between pieces of opposing information? Cite some examples.

   "It's a matter of safety...but..." "In theory...but..." "The expectation would be... but..." RI.8.4

5. **Knowledge and Ideas:** In what way does the writer of this article disagree with the other writers in these activities on matters of fact or interpretation? Cite textual evidence to support your answer.

   The writer believes that evidence supporting the impact of cellphone use on driving is inconclusive as noted in paragraph 3. He further explains in paragraph 4 that the effect of cellphones on driver performance is "clouded." RI.8.9

Working from the Text

6. Choose two pieces of relevant and convincing information from the article. Then prepare the information to be included in an argumentative essay. Paraphrase the first piece of information. Combine quoting and paraphrasing in the second piece of information, and add your own commentary to it.

   Paraphrase: Jonathan Adkins, a spokesman for the governors' Highway Safety Association, says that even with the huge increase in cellphone use, there has been no significant increase in the number of accidents, suggesting a lack of relationship among cellphones, driving, and accidents.

   Quote and paraphrase: After banning cellphone use while driving, a study concluded that deaths caused by "talking on a handheld phone...dropped nearly 50 percent," while traffic deaths of all kinds dropped by only "22 percent." This study shows a marked relationship between a ban on using cellphones while driving and traffic deaths.

Check Your Understanding

WRITING to SOURCES **Argumentative Writing Prompt**

Based on the research and the evidence you have gathered from reading the sources, write a paragraph that states a claim about cellphone use while driving. Incorporate paraphrased and/or quoted information that supports your claim. Be sure to:

- State your claim.
- Incorporate evidence by paraphrasing and/or quoting.
- Show your reasoning with commentary.

Independent Reading Checkpoint

You have read a variety of sources relating to your topic. Which information supports your claim? Which information counters your claim? How can you use this information to strengthen your argument? Prepare your answers in the form of a brief oral presentation.

INDEPENDENT READING CHECKPOINT

Ask students to complete the Independent Reading Checkpoint as homework. You will check their work at the end of the next activity.

Organizing and Revising Your Argument

ACTIVITY 2.17

Learning Targets

- Use research to support a claim(s) and frame an argument.
- Share and respond to preliminary drafts in a discussion group using questions and comments with relevant evidence, observation, and ideas.
- Use new information to revise an argument to reflect Scoring Guide Criteria.

LEARNING STRATEGIES: Writer's Checklist, Discussion Groups, Oral Reading, Sharing and Responding, Self-Editing/Peer-Editing

Monitor Progress by Creating and Following a Plan

You have gone through a model of the research process and conducted research on your own topic for the argumentative essay you will write for the Embedded Assessment.

Now you will focus on completing your research and finding evidence for your argument. You will also work on organizing and communicating your argument.

1. First, look at the chart below. Where are you in the process of researching for your essay? Check off the steps you have already completed, but remember that you can go back to revise your claim or find additional support for your argument, if necessary. In the third column, add planning notes for completing each step of the process.

My Notes

Research Plan for My Argumentative Essay

Check Progress	Step of Research Process	Notes
	Identify the issue or problem; establish a claim.	
	Form a set of questions that can be answered through research.	
	Locate and evaluate sources. Gather evidence for claims and counterclaims.	
	Interpret evidence.	
	Communicate findings.	

2. Reflect on your research. Which questions have you answered? What do you still need to know? What new questions do you have? You should keep research notes on a computer, on note cards, or in a log such as the one that follows.

ACTIVITY 2.17

PLAN

Suggested Pacing: 1 50-minute class period

TEACH

TEACHER TO TEACHER

By this time students have completed the modeling of the process of building an argumentative essay. This activity is designed to guide students as they prepare for the **Drafting and Revision** stages of writing the essay for the Embedded Assessment.

The **graphic organizers** are intended to be aids for planning and prewriting for the Embedded Assessment. Ideally, students will have chosen a topic, determined their claim, done some **prewriting** about their topic, and located at least one resource from which they can gather evidence to use in their essay.

1 Model filling out the graphic organizer for a research plan. Then ask students to complete the organizer to show their progress on their topic. In this way students can monitor their own progress toward writing an argumentative essay for the Embedded Assessment.

You will need to determine how many sources students will need to find before they can start drafting. Two is probably sufficient, although more may be needed to show the complete range of opinions about the topic.

COMMON CORE STATE STANDARDS

Focus Standards:

SL.8.1b: Follow rules for collegial discussions and decision-making, track progress toward specific goals and deadlines, and define individual roles as needed.

SL.8.1c: Pose questions that connect the ideas of several speakers and respond to others' questions and comments with relevant evidence, observations, and ideas.

SL.8.1d: Acknowledge new information expressed by others and, when warranted, qualify or justify their own views in light of the evidence presented.

Additional Standards Addressed:

RI.8.1; RI.8.2; W.8.1a; W.8.1b; W.8.1c; W.8.1d;W.8.1e; W.8.4; W.8.5; W.8.7; W.8.8; W.8.10; SL.8.1a; L.8.1b; L.8.1c; L.8.1d; L.8.3a; L.8.6

ACTIVITY 2.17 continued

2 The research log can be used to prepare students to create a Works Cited page. The assignment doesn't require this, but you may want to give an example.

3 Based on the prewriting, research, and drafting students have done so far, ask them to prepare an **outline** of the essay they will be writing for the Embedded Assessment.

ACTIVITY 2.17 continued

Organizing and Revising Your Argument

My Notes

Argumentative Essay Research Log

Topic/Issue: ____________________

My claim: ____________________

____

Research Questions:

Works Consulted Source + Citation	**Notes/Examples/Quotes**
Sample citation for a website: Just, Marcel, and Tim Heller. "How the Brain Reacts." *Room for Debate Blogs. The New York Times*, 18 July 2009. Web. 1 Feb. 2012.	

Outlining an Essay

3. A clear organizational structure is essential to a successful essay. Fill in the blank spaces in the following outline with your claim and the reasons and evidence you will use to support it.

I. **Introduction**

A. Attention-getting hook

B. Background information/definition of terms

C. Claim (Thesis):

II. **Body paragraphs**

A. Reason 1:

Evidence:

B. Reason 2:

Evidence:

C. Reason 3:

Evidence:

III. **Conclusion follows from and supports the argument**

A. Restate claim

B. Connect back to hook

C. State specific call to action

My Notes

Sharing and Responding in Writing Groups

4. Prepare for discussion by doing the following:
   - Revisit your outline and think about its organization.
   - Think about your research notes and decide where the information fits in your argument.
   - At the top of your draft, make a list of vocabulary and transitions you might use while discussing your ideas.
   - Determine whether you should revise your claim to reflect the new information.
   - Listen, comprehend, and evaluate as others read their claims.
5. Gather the materials you will need in the discussion group: the draft outline of your argument, your research cards, and a pen or pencil.
6. Set speaking and listening goals for the discussion:

   Speaking: I will ______________________________

   Listening: I will ______________________________

4 Students now have the opportunity to engage in a small **group discussion** to share their arguments in order to generate, clarify, and elaborate upon their ideas and language. This process will help students see what is included in and/or missing from their argument.

TEACHER TO TEACHER

Students should at least write an outline for their essay, but you could also require that they do a first draft of their essay to share in the discussion groups. It all depends on how much you want students to have done before they get to the Embedded Assessment.

5 Review expectations for speaking and listening, as well as expectations for participation. **Sharing and responding** works best in a writing group of three people who are all committed to participating in the discussion.

6 Ask students to gather materials and set goals in preparation for the discussion.

© 2017 College Board. All rights reserved.

ACTIVITY 2.17 continued

7 Before each writer presents his or her **outline** draft aloud, ask groups to assign one area of focus from the **Writer's Checklist** to each student in the writer's audience (ideas, organization, or use of language).

8 While each student **reads** his or her draft **aloud**, group members should listen to comprehend and evaluate, and they should take notes on their section of the Writer's Checklist.

9 After each student has read his or her draft, group members should take turns providing feedback for their area, telling the writer what is *exemplary* or *proficient* (and thus can be checked off), and what is *emerging* or *incomplete* (and thus should be highlighted). The highlighted items will guide the student's revisions.

▶ ASSESS

As students work, listen to feedback to make sure it is specific and accurate. Ask students to reflect upon how they will revise their draft using a variety of resources to ensure quality revision.

▶ ADAPT

If students struggle with revision or editing, provide additional guidance in the process. This is the final activity before Embedded Assessment 2. At this time, students should be ready to continue the writing and research process independently.

INDEPENDENT READING CHECKPOINT

Randomly choose students to summarize responses from their last Independent Reading Checkpoint activity for the class, using their Reader/Writer Notebooks as a reference. You may want to collect the notebooks of those students who did not have the opportunity to share a summary to ensure that independent reading and engagement are occurring.

Organizing and Revising Your Argument

7. When you write your essay for Embedded Assessment 2, use the Writer's Checklist below to get feedback from others in your writing group and to self-edit before finalizing your essay draft. Also, use the Language and Writer's Craft suggestions as you consider revising your essay for effective use of language.

Writer's Checklist

Use this checklist to guide the sharing and responding in your writing group.

IDEAS

- ☐ The writer has a clear claim (thesis).
- ☐ The writer supports his or her claim with logical reasoning and relevant evidence from accurate, credible sources.
- ☐ The writer effectively uses appeals to *logos* and *pathos*.
- ☐ The writer addresses counterclaims effectively.

ORGANIZATION

- ☐ The writer clearly introduces the claim at the beginning of the argument.
- ☐ The writer organizes reasons and evidence logically.
- ☐ The writer effectively uses transitional words, phrases, and clauses to create cohesion and clarify the relationships among ideas.
- ☐ The writer provides a concluding statement or section that follows from and supports the argument presented.

USE OF LANGUAGE

- ☐ The writer effectively and correctly embeds quotations and paraphrases clearly to strengthen evidence and create convincing reasoning.
- ☐ The writer uses a formal style, including proper referencing to sources to express ideas and add interest.
- ☐ The writer uses precise and clear language in the argument rather than vague or imprecise vocabulary.

My Notes

Language and Writer's Craft: Shifts in Voice and Mood

As you write and revise, recognize and correct inappropriate shifts in voice and mood.

Use verbs in active or passive voice and in the conditional and subjunctive mood to achieve particular effects (e.g., emphasizing the actor or the action, expressing uncertainty or a statement contrary to fact).

Check Your Understanding

Summarize the process for researching and presenting an argumentative essay. Include the steps in the research process and descriptions of the elements of an argument.

Writing an Argumentative Essay

EMBEDDED ASSESSMENT 2

Assignment

Write an argumentative essay in which you convince an audience to support your claim about a debatable idea. Use your research and experience or observations to support your argument.

Planning and Prewriting: Take time to make a plan for generating ideas and research questions.

- What prewriting strategies (such as outlining or webbing) can you use to select and explore a controversial idea?
- How will you draft a claim that states your position?
- What questions will guide your research?

Researching: Gather information from a variety of credible sources.

- What types of sources are best for the information you seek?
- What criteria will you use to evaluate sources?
- How will you take notes to gather and interpret evidence?
- How will you create a bibliography or Works Cited page?

Drafting: Convince your audience to support your claim.

- How will you select the best reasons and evidence from your research to support your claim?
- How will you use persuasive appeals (*logos*, *ethos*, *pathos*) in your essay?
- How will you introduce and respond to counterclaims?
- How will you organize your essay logically with an introduction, transitions, and concluding statement?

Evaluating and Revising the Draft: Create opportunities to review and revise your work.

- During the process of writing, when can you pause to share and respond with others in order to elicit suggestions and ideas for revision?
- How can the Scoring Guide help you evaluate how well your draft meets the requirements of the assignment?

Checking and Editing for Publication: Confirm that your final draft is ready for publication.

- How will you proofread and edit your draft to demonstrate command of the conventions of standard English capitalization, punctuation, spelling, grammar, usage, and formal style?
- How did you use TLQC (transition/lead-in/quote/citation) to properly embed quotations?

Reflection

After completing this Embedded Assessment, think about how you went about accomplishing this task, and respond to the following:

- How can you use discussion and/or debate in the future to explore a topic?

My Notes

Technology TIP:

Consider publishing your essay on a website, blog, or online student literary magazine.

EMBEDDED ASSESSMENT 2

Suggested Pacing: 2 50-minute class periods

TEACHER TO TEACHER

The time needed to complete this assessment depends on how much students have done in preparation for this essay and whether you give students the option of choosing a new topic.

1 Planning and Prewriting: If students choose a new controversial topic, they should begin **prewriting** by identifying two sides to the issue, selecting a side, identifying and analyzing the audience, writing counterarguments, and outlining ideas (students should revisit Activity 2.13 for ideas and steps in the process).

2 Researching: Students have begun this process, and you will need to determine how many sources you expect students to locate and use in their argument.

COMMON CORE STATE STANDARDS

Focus Standards:

W.8.1a: Introduce claim(s), acknowledge and distinguish the claim(s) from alternate or opposing claims, and organize the reasons and evidence logically.

W.8.1b: Support claim(s) with logical reasoning and relevant evidence, using accurate, credible sources and demonstrating an understanding of the topic or text.

W.8.1c: Use words, phrases, and clauses to create cohesion and clarify the relationships among claim(s), counterclaims, reasons, and evidence.

W.8.1d: Establish and maintain a formal style.

W.8.1e: Provide a concluding statement or section that follows from and supports the arguments presented.

EMBEDDED ASSESSMENT 2 continued

3 Be sure students understand the importance of finding relevant and convincing evidence to support their claim and refute the counterclaims.

4 **Drafting:** You may want to require an outline to be sure students are in control of the organization of an argumentative essay.

5 **Evaluating and Revising the Draft:** Form **discussion groups** for **sharing and responding.** Students should be able to explain the logic behind their organizational structure and then read one body paragraph aloud. Group members should provide feedback based on Scoring Guide criteria.

6 Set expectations for sharing work in discussion groups, and circulate to check for understanding while students work. As a class, create a **Writer's Checklist** based on feedback that was provided in the groups.

7 **Checking and Editing for Publication:** Provide time to **self-** and **peer-edit.** Encourage students to work with a partner to edit their draft.

8 Provide time to draft the bibliography or Works Cited page if you are requiring one.

9 Specify your expectations for formatting, and monitor progress as students prepare their final draft.

Reflection Have students respond to the reflection question after completing the assignment.

Portfolio Ask students to organize and turn in work from all steps of the writing process.

Before moving on to the next unit, ask students to revisit all the work in their Working Folder and their Reader/Writer Notebook. You may want to ask students to select a few activities they feel have been especially helpful in doing the work of the unit.

SCORING GUIDE

When you score this Embedded Assessment, you may wish to download and print copies of the Scoring Guide from SpringBoard Digital. In this way you can have a copy to mark for each student's work.

EMBEDDED ASSESSMENT 2

Writing an Argumentative Essay

SCORING GUIDE

Scoring Criteria	Exemplary	Proficient	Emerging	Incomplete
Ideas	The essay • supports a claim with compelling, relevant reasoning and evidence • provides extensive evidence of the research process • addresses counterclaim(s) effectively • uses a variety of persuasive appeals.	The essay • supports a claim with sufficient reasoning and evidence • provides evidence of the research process • addresses counterclaim(s) • uses some persuasive appeals (*logos*, *ethos*, *pathos*).	The essay • has an unclear or unfocused claim and/or inadequate support • provides insufficient evidence of the research process • addresses counterclaims ineffectively • uses inadequate persuasive appeals.	The essay • has no claim or claim lacks support • provides little or no evidence of research • does not reference a counterclaim • fails to use persuasive appeals.
Structure	The essay • has an introduction that engages the reader and defines the claim's context • follows a logical organizational structure • uses a variety of effective transitional strategies • contains an insightful conclusion.	The essay • has an introduction that includes a hook and background • follows an adequate organizational structure • uses transitional strategies to link ideas • has a conclusion that supports and follows from the argument.	The essay • has a weak introduction • uses an ineffective or inconsistent organizational strategy • uses basic or insufficient transitional strategies • has an illogical or unrelated conclusion.	The essay • lacks an introduction • has little or no obvious organizational structure • uses few or no transitional strategies • lacks a conclusion.
Use of Language	The essay • uses precise diction and language effectively to convey tone and persuade an audience • demonstrates command of the conventions of standard English capitalization, punctuation, spelling, grammar, and usage • includes an accurate, detailed annotated bibliography.	The essay • uses diction and language to convey tone and persuade an audience • demonstrates adequate command of the conventions of standard English capitalization, punctuation, spelling, grammar, and usage • includes a generally correct and complete annotated bibliography.	The essay • uses basic or weak diction and language • demonstrates partial command of the conventions of standard English capitalization, punctuation, spelling, grammar, and usage; for the most part, errors do not impede meaning • includes an incorrect or insufficient annotated bibliography.	The essay • uses confusing or vague diction and language • lacks command of the conventions of standard English capitalization, punctuation, spelling, grammar, and usage • does not include an annotated bibliography.

COMMON CORE STATE STANDARDS

Additional Standards Addressed:

W.8.4; W.8.5; W.8.6; W.8.7; W.8.8; W.8.9; W.8.10; L.8.2c

ENGLISH LANGUAGE DEVELOPMENT RUBRIC

The Embedded Assessment that the whole class completes can be a useful source of English language development evidence. Use this additional rubric to examine the Embedded Assessment products of English learners. The analysis will help you gain additional information about student learning related to the strands of the English Language Development Standards and identify individual areas for improvement.

Criteria	Emerging	Expanding	Bridging
Collaborative	The student • engages in conversational exchanges by asking and answering questions using simple phrases. • engages and collaborates on short written exchanges with peers. • adapts language choice to setting and audience.	The student • engages in discussion by asking relevant questions and adding relevant information. • engages and collaborates on longer written exchanges with peers. • adapts language choice to purpose, task, and audience.	The student • engages in discussion by asking relevant questions and contributing useful feedback. • engages and collaborates on complex written exchanges with peers. • adapts complex language choice to task, purpose, and audience.
Interpretive	The student • basic ideas based on close readings of texts with substantial support. • expresses inferences and conclusions based on close reading of texts with substantial support. • explains how language supports ideas with substantial support. • analyze how words produce different effects.	The student • explains ideas based on close readings of texts with some support. • expresses inferences and conclusions based on close reading of texts with some support. • explains how language presents ideas with some support. • analyzes how words produce shades of meaning and the effect on the audience.	The student • explains complex ideas based on close readings of texts with little support. • expresses inferences and conclusions based on close reading of texts with some support. • explains how language presents ideas with little support. • analyzes how words or phrases produce shades of meaning and the effect on the audience.
Productive	The student • writes short informational texts collaboratively and independently. • uses general academic vocabulary with domain-specific words to create some precision.	The student • writes longer informational texts collaboratively and independently with appropriate text organization. • uses general academic vocabulary with domain-specific words with precision and an awareness of shades of meaning.	The student • writes longer, more detailed informational texts collaboratively and independently with appropriate text organization. • uses precise, nuanced, vocabulary and figurative language appropriately.
Structuring Cohesive Texts	The student • organizes writing logically to express ideas. • uses basic language resources to make text more cohesive. • uses simple connecting words to link ideas or events in the text.	The student • organizes writing naturally, logically, and coherently. • uses increasingly complex language resources to make text more cohesive. • uses connecting words or phrases to link ideas or events in the text.	The student • organizes writing in a logical, clear sequence to create cohesion and precision. • uses complex language resources to make text more cohesive. • uses a variety of connecting words or phrases to link ideas or events in the text.
Expanding and Enriching Ideas	The student • uses a variety of verbs in different tenses appropriate to narrative text. • uses nouns and noun phrases to add details. • uses simple adverbials to provide details.	The student • uses a variety of verbs in different tenses appropriate to the task, text type, and discipline. • uses a variety of nouns and noun phrases to add rich details. • uses adverbials to provide rich details.	The student • uses a variety of verbs in different tenses, aspects, voices, and moods, appropriate for the task, text type, and discipline. • uses an expanded variety of nouns and noun phrases to add rich details. • uses complex adverbials to provide rich details.
Connecting and Condensing Ideas	The student • connects ideas in compound sentences using simple conjunctions. • condenses ideas by using prepositional phrases to create precise and detailed sentences.	The student • connects ideas in compound and complex sentences using a variety of ways. • condenses ideas in a variety of ways to create precise and detailed sentences.	The student • connects and combines ideas in compound and complex sentences using a variety of ways. • condenses ideas in a variety of complex ways to create precise and detailed sentences.

ELD RUBRIC

Embedded Assessment 2
Writing an Argumentative Essay

ENGLISH LANGUAGE DEVELOPMENT RUBRIC

The Embedded Assessment that the whole class completes can be a useful source of English language development evidence. Use this additional rubric to examine the Embedded Assessment products of English learners. The analysis will help you gain additional information about student learning related to the strands of the English Language Development Standards and identify individual areas for improvement.

Criteria	Emerging	Expanding	Bridging
Interpretive	The student • explains basic ideas based on close readings of texts with substantial support. • expresses inferences and conclusions based on close reading of texts with substantial support. • explains how language supports ideas with substantial support. • analyze how words produce different effects.	The student • explains ideas based on close readings of texts with some support. • expresses inferences and conclusions based on close reading of texts with some support. • explains how language presents ideas with some support. • analyzes how words produce shades of meaning and the effect on the audience.	The student • explains complex ideas based on close readings of texts with little support. • expresses inferences and conclusions based on close reading of texts with some support. • explains how language presents ideas with little support. • analyzes how words or phrases produce shades of meaning and the effect on the audience.
Productive	The student • writes short informational texts collaboratively and independently. • justifies opinions by providing some evidence with substantial support. • expresses opinions using appropriate words or phrases. • uses general academic vocabulary with domain-specific words to create some precision.	The student • writes longer informational texts collaboratively and independently with appropriate text organization. • justifies opinions or persuades other by providing relevant evidence with some support. • expresses opinions using a variety of appropriate expressions or phrases. • uses general academic vocabulary with domain-specific words with precision and an awareness of shades of meaning.	The student • writes longer, more detailed informational texts collaboratively and independently with appropriate text organization. • justifies opinions or persuades others by providing detailed and relevant evidence with little support. • expresses opinions using a variety of nuanced expressions or phrases. • uses precise, nuanced, vocabulary and figurative language appropriately.
Structuring Cohesive Texts	The student • organizes writing logically to express ideas. • uses basic language resources to make text more cohesive. • uses simple connecting words to link ideas or events in the text.	The student • organizes writing naturally, logically, and coherently. • uses increasingly complex language resources to make text more cohesive. • uses connecting words or phrases to link ideas or events in the text.	The student • organizes writing in a logical, clear sequence to create cohesion and precision. • uses complex language resources to make text more cohesive. • uses a variety of connecting words or phrases to link ideas or events in the text.
Expanding and Enriching Ideas	The student • uses a variety of verbs in different tenses appropriate to narrative text. • uses nouns and noun phrases to add details. • uses simple adverbials to provide details.	The student • uses a variety of verbs in different tense appropriate to the task, text type, and discipline. • uses a variety of nouns and noun phrases to add rich details. • uses adverbials to provide rich details.	The student • uses a variety of verbs in different tenses, aspects, voices, and moods, appropriate for the task, text type, and discipline. • uses an expanded variety of nouns and noun phrases to add rich details. • uses complex adverbials to provide rich details.
Connecting and Condensing Ideas	The student • connects ideas in compound sentences using simple conjunctions. • condenses ideas by using prepositional phrases to create precise and detailed sentences.	The student • connects ideas in compound and complex sentences using a variety of ways. • condenses ideas in a variety of ways to create precise and detailed sentences.	The student • connects and combine ideas in compound and complex sentences using a variety of ways. • condenses ideas in a variety of complex ways to create precise and detailed sentences.

Planning the Unit

Context

This unit invites students to study the past as a way to act on their future. By reading narratives from the Holocaust, students will grapple with significant challenges from history and then examine and evaluate current national or global issues by analyzing and synthesizing a multitude of ideas from literature and informational texts in print and online. Through critical reading, collaborative discussion, expository and argumentative writing, students will research, create, and communicate ideas to positively influence others inside the classroom walls and outside in our contemporary world.

Instructional Sequence

The first half of the unit introduces the theme "finding light in the darkness" through a visual prompt, poetry, and novel excerpts. Students will study an allegory and film as a means to move into an in-depth exploration of Holocaust narratives in Literature Circles. Applying close reading strategies and collaborative discussion skills, students build maturity for discussing a sensitive subject. They communicate their new understanding of the Holocaust in Embedded Assessment 1 by conducting a panel discussion in which they explain how the theme or central idea of "finding light in the darkness" is developed in a Holocaust narrative.

The second part of the unit asks students to connect the past to the present by researching challenges in today's society. Students will read print and online informational texts, including news articles, public service announcements, and speeches, to gather information, analyze elements and techniques of an argument, and evaluate how an author integrates multimedia and visual displays to enhance communication. For Embedded Assessment 2, students select an issue of national or global significance and collaboratively create a plan that uses diverse media channels to address a specific audience for the purpose of convincing that audience to take action to make a difference.

CollegeBoard

AP/College Readiness

In this unit, students will focus on refining these important skills and knowledge areas for AP/College Readiness:

- Using strategies of close reading to analyze how a literary text conveys meaning (Activities 3.4, 3.10, 3.12)
- Writing for a variety of purposes (Activities 3.5, 3.8, 3.9, 3.10, 3.15)
- Creating and sustaining arguments based on readings, research, and/or personal experience (Activities 3.15, 3.16, 3.18)
- Controlling tone, establishing and maintaining voice, achieving appropriate emphasis through diction and sentence structure (Activities 3.3, 3.5, 3.7)
- Demonstrating an understanding and mastery of standard written English as well as a stylistic maturity (Activities 3.8, 3.12, 3.14)

Unpacked Embedded Assessments

Embedded Assessment 1: Presenting Voices of the Holocaust	Embedded Assessment 2: Presenting a Multimedia Campaign
Skills and Knowledge: • Present a discussion that explains how literary elements develop a theme. • Use a variety of details and relevant elaboration to support and develop topics of discussion. • Demonstrate evidence of strong collaboration and preparation through original, compelling dramatic interpretation of text. • Follow a logical and smooth organizational structure. • Use precise, academic language to communicate effectively with group members and audience. • Demonstrate a deep command of the conventions of standard English grammar, usage, and language (including active/passive voice).	**Skills and Knowledge:** • Develop a multimedia campaign that addresses the prompt. • Presents a clear claim and addresses counterclaim(s) with relevant reasons and evidence from a variety of accurate sources. • Utilize persuasive appeals and multimedia to support claims. • Organize ideas logically, with an engaging introduction, smoothly sequenced ideas, and concluding call to action. • Demonstrate evidence of strong collaboration and preparation. • Use precise diction and tone appropriate to target audience. • Cite and evaluate sources thoroughly in an annotated bibliography. • Demonstrate a command of the conventions of standard English grammar, usage, and language (including correct mood/voice).

Instructional Activities and Pacing

Total: 36 class periods	Description
3.1 1 class period	Students begin the unit by unpacking the Embedded Assessment assignment so they can understand the reading/writing, speaking and listening, and language expectations of the analytical panel discussion of a narrative text.
3.2–3.3 4 class periods	Students select a Holocaust narrative to read independently during this half of the unit. With their Literature Circle groups, students create a reading schedule and list of due dates for the reading. Students learn the roles in Literature Circles, as well as the use of a double-entry journal to prepare for and participate in their first text-based collaborative discussion. Students will continue using the double-entry journal and Literature Circle roles throughout the unit.
3.4–3.5 3 class periods	These activities are designed to deepen students' understanding of the narrative genre and of the Holocaust and the purpose for studying it. As students continue to read their Holocaust narrative, they analyze an excerpt from an autobiographical narrative and a poem to make and explain the thematic connection between texts. Revisiting the concept of *allegory*, students interpret a children's story and present a dramatic interpretation of a text passage. As a synthesis of these experiences, students respond to an expository writing prompt to analyze how the themes in multiple genres connect.

3.6–3.8 5 class periods	Students study new Holocaust-related vocabulary and conduct research. They explore the historical timeline and events that contributed to the Holocaust by researching information from a website and create talking points to deliver an effective collaborative presentation. In addition, students research a specific Holocaust victim and present a narrative that captures his or her story while applying understanding of active and passive voice. Along with a deepening understanding of the Holocaust, students have opportunities to practice expressive oral reading/speaking when presenting information to others.
3.9–3.12 7 class periods	Students view and read a variety of texts, including film, drama, novel excerpt, and diary entry, to analyze how writers use literary elements to develop theme. Students work collaboratively to present an effective oral reading and transform writing into talking points for discussion. As students finish reading their Holocaust narratives, they apply their analysis by transforming a selection of text into a found poem and present it to practice expressive oral reading.
Embedded Assessment 1 2 class periods	For the EA, students will collaboratively present a panel discussion in front of their peers that explains how the theme or central idea of "finding light in the darkness" is developed in their narrative. Students will move through steps of planning the focus and organization of the discussion and will draft talking points in order to be prepared for rehearsal and final panel discussion presentation. Completion of EA1 prepares students to develop the idea of people taking action to create positive change for others.
3.13 1 class period	The first activity of the second half of the unit guides students to make connections between the lessons of the Holocaust and "taking action." To be clear on learning expectations, students unpack the skills and knowledge needed to complete Embedded Assessment 2 successfully.
3.14–3.15 3 class periods	To begin preparation for developing a multimedia presentation, students study visuals from public service announcements to analyze purpose and effect. By reading images and slogans from various websites, students evaluate how diverse media enhance the presentation of information. Students apply this understanding to an analysis of written texts to discover the purpose, audience, tone, and argumentative elements of a speech. They synthesize their learning by responding to an argumentative writing prompt.
3.16–3.18 5 class periods	The next series of activities is designed to expose students to different topics and a variety of multimedia campaigns they might consider when generating ideas for Embedded Assessment 2. By analyzing informational texts and websites about efforts that have made a difference on a global scale, students explain how specific media types appeal to different target audiences. They apply their understanding of the components of a campaign by creating a Web page and sketching a visual that shows how to use persuasive appeals in different types of media to convince a target audience.
3.19 1 class period	Before students begin Embedded Assessment 2, they conduct a final evaluation of the effectiveness of arguments. By reading an article and online information on the same topic, students will compare and contrast how different mediums use argumentative elements and rhetorical appeals to present ideas.

Embedded Assessment 2 4 class periods	Students will work in collaborative groups to develop a multimedia presentation that informs their peers about an issue of national or global significance and convinces them to take action. After students finish the task, they will reflect on their learning in this unit.

Unit Resources at a Glance

Readings	Writing Tasks	Language Skills
Excerpt from *Night*, by Elie Wiesel "First They Came for the Communists,"by Martin Niemöller *Terrible Things: An Allegory of the Holocaust,* by Eve Bunting *Life Is Beautiful* (film), directed by Roberto Benigni Excerpt from *The Boy in the Striped Pajamas,* by John Boyne Excerpt from *The Diary of a Young Girl*, by Anne Frank Excerpt from Elie Wiesel's Nobel Peace Prize Acceptance Speech Excerpt from *Do Something! A Handbook for Young Activists* "Wangari Maathai" "About Freerice.com" Address by Cesar Chavez	Quickwrites: What did you learn about the Holocaust?; What music might you add to your PSA? Expository Writing Prompts • Explain theme. • Draft a story based on research. • Explain theme as presented in film. • Explain how dialogue reveals character and conflict. • Summarize a selection. • Write a letter to convince.	**Language and Writers Craft** Using Voice and Mood for Effect Reviewing Participial Phrases Reviewing Clauses **Grammar and Usage** Participle Verb Forms Pronoun Antecedents Punctuation Commas Verb Tenses Sentence Fragments
Strategy Introduction	**Speaking and Listening**	**Family Connections**
SOAPSTone	Literature Circles Collaborative Discussion Oral Presentation	Suggestions for Independent Reading Family Letters (English and Spanish) Student Reports
English Language Development	**Independent Reading**	**Assessments**
Leveled Differentiated Instruction ELD Graphic Organizers *SpringBoard English Language Development,* Student Edition, Grade 8, Unit 3 *SpringBoard English Language Development,* Teacher Edition Grade 8, Unit 3	Independent Reading Links Independent Reading Checkpoints Independent Reading Log Reader/Writer Notebook Suggestions for Independent Reading	Check Your Understanding Writing Prompts Embedded Assessment One: Presenting Voices of the Holocaust Embedded Assessment Two: Presenting a Multimedia Campaign Short-Cycle Assessments Unit Assessments

SpringBoard Writing Workshop with Grammar Activities, Grade 8	SpringBoard Close Reading Workshop, Grade 8	Routines for Teaching Foundational Skills
Writing Workshop 1: The Writing Process: Strategies for Writing Writing Workshop 3: Expository Writing: Compare and Contrast Writing Workshop 6: Research Writing Writing Workshop 7: Narrative Nonfiction Grammar Activities: Unit 3 Grammar Handbook	Close Reading Workshop 1: Close Reading of Informational/Literary Nonfiction Texts Close Reading Workshop 2: Close Reading of Argumentative Texts Close Reading Workshop 3: Close Reading of Poetry	Phonics and Word Recognition Mini-lessons Fluency Mini-lessons

Suggestions for Independent Reading

This list, divided into the categories of **Literature** and **Nonfiction/Informational Text**, comprises titles related to the themes and content of the unit. For their independent reading, students can select from this wide array of titles, which have been chosen based on complexity and interest. You can also encourage students to do their own research and select titles that intrigue them.

Unit 3: The Challenge to Make a Difference		
Literature		
Author	**Title**	**Lexile**
Adlington, L. J.	*The Diary of Pelly D.*	770L
Arato, Rona	*The Last Train: A Holocaust Story*	580L
Bergman, Tamar	*Along the Tracks*	650L
Boyne, John	*The Boy in the Striped Pajamas*	1080L
Chotjewitz, David	*Daniel, Half Human: And the Good Nazi,*	740L
Gratz, Alan and Gruener, Ruth	*Prisoner B-3087*	760L
Hesse, Karen	*The Cats in Krasinski Square*	990L
Hoestlandt, Jo	*Star of Fear, Star of Hope*	490L
Boom, Corrie Ten	*The Hiding Place*	900L
Isaacs, Anne	*Torn Thread*	880L
Lowry, Lois	*Number the Stars*	670L
Matas, Carol	Daniel's Story	720L
Drucker, Malka and Halperin, Michael	*Jacob's Rescue*	680L
Matas, Carol	*The Garden*	810L
Mazer, Norma Fox	*Good Night, Maman*	510L
Meminger, Neesha	*Shine, Coconut Moon*	740L
Morpurgo, Michael	*Waiting for Anya*	770L
Na, An	*The Fold*	700L

Literature (continued)		
Author	**Title**	**Lexile**
Napoli, Donna Jo	*Stones in Water*	630L
Nye, Naomi Shihab	*19 Varieties of Gazelle: Poems of the Middle East*	970L
Orgel, Doris	*The Devil in Vienna*	700L
Orlev, Uri	*Run, Boy, Run*	570L
Orlev, Uri	*The Island on Bird Street*	690L
Peacock, Carol Antionette	*Red Thread Sisters*	700L
Polacco, Patricia	*The Butterfly*	430L
Radin, Ruth Yaffe	*Escape to the Forest: Based on a True Story of the Holocaust*	660L
Spinelli, Jerry	*Milkweed*	510L
Venkatraman, Padma	*Climbing the Stairs*	750L
Yep, Laurence	*Golden Mountain Chronicles: Child of the Owl*	920L
Yolen, Jane	*The Devil's Arithmetic*	730L
Zullo, Allan	*We Fought Back: Teen Resisters of the Holocaust*	1070L
Zusak, Markus	*The Book Thief*	730L

Nonfiction/Informational Text		
Author	**Title**	**Lexile**
Bachrach, Susan D.	*Tell Them We Remember: The Story of the Holocaust*	1190L
Bitton-Jackson, Livia	*I Have Lived a Thousand Years: Growing Up in the Holocaust*	720L
Boas, Jacob	*We Are Witnesses: Five Diaries of Teenagers Who Died in the Holocaust*	970L
Deedy, Carmen Agra	*The Yellow Star: The Legend of King Christian X of Denmark*	550L
Frank, Anne	*The Diary of a Young Girl*	1080L
Freedman, Russell	*Kids at Work: Lewis Hine and the Crusade Against Child Labor*	1140L
Gregory, Josh	*Cesar Chavez*	930L
Herman, Gail	*Who Was Jackie Robinson?*	670L
Hoose, Philip	*The Race to Save the Lord God Bird*	1150L
Lobel, Anita	*No Pretty Pictures: A Child of War*	750L
Meltzer, Milton	*Rescue: The Story of How Gentiles Saved Jews in the Holocaust*	1020L
Millman, Isaac	*Hidden Child*	860L
Nir, Yehuda	*The Lost Childhood: A World War II Memoir*	920L
Opdyke, Irene Gut	*In My Hands: Memories of a Holocaust Rescuer*	890L
Perl, Lila and Lazan, Marion Blumenthal	*Four Perfect Pebbles: A Holocaust Story*	1080L
Sender, Ruth Minsky	*The Cage*	500L
Siegal, Aranka	*Upon the Head of the Goat: A Childhood in Hungary 1939–1944*	830L
van de Rol, Rudd and Verhoeven, Rian	*Anne Frank: Beyond the Diary: A Photographic Remembrance*	1030L
Warren, Andrea	*Charles Dickens and the Street Children of London*	1160L
Wiesel, Elie	*Night*	570L

The Challenge to Make a Difference

Visual Prompt: What do you notice about this art? How does the artist use visual techniques for effect? How do you think the arts (artwork, music, literature, etc.) can help change the world?

Unit Overview

The world has dark pages in its history, and at times the challenge of righting such immeasurable wrongs seems impossible. Reading narratives about the Holocaust will reveal the worst in human behavior, but it will also show how individuals can find light in the darkness. In this unit, you will present the voices of fictional or real people who fought the darkness of the Holocaust by helping, hoping, or persevering. You will also apply the lessons of the past to start making a difference today by raising awareness and encouraging people to take action about a significant national or global issue.

UNIT 3

Read aloud the Unit Overview, asking students to **mark the text** by highlighting words and phrases that help them **predict** what the unit will be about. Share responses in partner, small-group, or whole-class discussion.

Have students look at the photograph and respond to the visual prompt. You may want to have students **think-pair-share** to write a short response or discuss their responses as a class.

TEACHER TO TEACHER

You may want to ask students what they know about the Holocaust as preparation for the activities and readings in this unit. You might discuss with students that studying the Holocaust can be disturbing, but that it is necessary in order to learn about that tragic episode in history.

ELL Support

ELD Modes and Processes

Collaborative: Students work together to edit their writing. Students also collaborate to support comprehension by reading a text in chunks and making predictions about a story.

Interpretive: Students draw conclusions and support them with evidence from a text. Students also interpret story elements in a film and analyze author's word choice for tone.

Productive: Students write to record research, opinions, key ideas, and details, and to summarize a text. Students also use academic vocabulary and the vocabulary of persuasion. Additionally, students will write a résumé for a Literature Circle role.

Structuring Cohesive Texts: Students analyze persuasive text structure.

English Language Development Standards

ELD.PI.8.1 Bridging* Contribute to class, group, and partner discussions by following

UNIT 3 continued

Have students read the goals for the unit and mark any words that are unfamiliar to them. Have students add these words to the classroom Word Wall, along with definitions.

You may also want to post these goals in a visible place in the classroom for the duration of this unit, allowing you and your students to revisit the goals easily and gauge progress toward achieving goals throughout the unit.

VOCABULARY DEVELOPMENT

Important terms in this unit are divided into Academic Vocabulary (those words that are used in multiple curriculum areas) and Literary Terms, which are specific to the student of literature and language arts.

Adding to vocabulary knowledge is essential for reading fluency. Students will encounter new vocabulary in this course in multiple ways:

- Academic Vocabulary
- Literary Terms
- Vocabulary in Context (unfamiliar terms glossed in text selections)
- Word Connections
- Oral discussions

Encourage students to keep a Reader/Writer Notebook in which they record new words and their meanings (and pronunciations if needed). Having students use word-study **graphic organizers** to study key vocabulary terms in depth will greatly enhance their understanding of new words and their connection to unit concepts and to the broader use of academic terms.

See the Resources section at the back of this book for examples of graphic organizers suitable for word study. As students become more familiar with using **graphic organizers** to explore the meaning of a word, you may want them to create their own graphic organizers.

UNIT 3

The Challenge to Make a Difference

GOALS:

- To engage effectively in a range of collaborative discussions
- To analyze the development of a theme or central idea of a text
- To research an issue of national or global significance
- To create an informative and persuasive multimedia presentation
- To strengthen writing through the effective use of voice and mood

ACADEMIC VOCABULARY
communication
résumé
euphemism
slogan
media

Literary Terms
found poem

Contents

Activities

ELL Support (continued)

turn-taking rules, asking relevant questions, affirming others, adding relevant information and evidence, paraphrasing key ideas, building on responses, and providing useful feedback. **ELD.PI.8.6b Bridging*** Express inferences and conclusions drawn based on close reading of grade-level texts and viewing of multimedia using a variety of precise academic verbs. **ELD.PI.8.8 Bridging*** Explain how phrasing or different words with similar meanings or figurative language produce shades of meaning, nuances, and different effects on the audience. **ELD.PI.8.9 Expanding*** Plan and deliver longer oral presentations on a variety of topics using details and evidence to support ideas. **ELD.PI.8.10a Bridging*** Write longer and more detailed literary and informational texts collaboratively and independently using appropriate text organization and growing understanding of register. **ELD.PI.8.11a Expanding*** Justify opinions or persuade others by providing relevant textual evidence or

Texts not included in these materials.

Language and Writer's Craft

- Using Voice and Mood for Effect (3.8)
- Reviewing Participial Phrases (3.14)
- Reviewing Clauses (3.15)

MY INDEPENDENT READING LIST

UNIT 3 continued

LANGUAGE AND WRITER'S CRAFT

Each unit includes Language and Writer's Craft features as well as Grammar & Usage content. You may want students to devote a section of their Reader/Writer Notebooks to their study of language and grammar. Encourage students to make notes about their understanding of specific grammar rules and how to use language in their writing to create specific effects.

CONTENTS

Have the students **skim/scan** the activities and texts to find a Wow (an activity that looks interesting) and a Whoa (an activity that looks challenging). Share responses in partner, small-group, or whole-class discussion.

INDEPENDENT READING

In this half of the unit, while reading texts about the Holocaust, students will have the opportunity to read another text. While reading a novel for close study, students will not be expected to read an additional novel for independent reading. You may, however, want to ask students to read informative texts about the central focus of the unit reading. The Planning the Unit section of the Teacher's Edition and the Resources section of the Student Edition contain information, Reading Logs, and Reading Lists to help you and your students find the right narrative.

ELL Support (continued)

relevant background knowledge with moderate support. **ELD.PI.8.11b Bridging*** Express attitude and opinions or temper statements with nuanced modal expressions. **ELD.PI.8.12a Expanding*** Use a growing set of academic words, domain-specific words, synonyms, and antonyms to create precision and shades of meaning while speaking and writing. **ELD.PII.8.1 Bridging*** Apply understanding of the organizational structure of different text types to comprehending texts and to writing clear and cohesive arguments, informative/explanatory texts and narratives.

*The citation reflects the highest level supported. Support is also offered for the lower levels.

the Independent Reading Links, capturing thoughts about learning strategies and how to use them, and so on. The Reader/Writer Notebooks are not listed as part of the materials for each activity, but the expectation is that students will have access to them.

TEACHER TO TEACHER

The SpringBoard program has been designed to allow students to interact with the text by making notes in their books and marking text to facilitate close reading. In addition to making notes in the text, students are expected to use their Reader/Writer Notebooks often: for vocabulary study, answering text-dependent reading comprehension questions, reflections, some writing assignments, notes in response to

ACTIVITY 3.1

▶PLAN

Suggested Pacing: 1 50-minute class period

▶TEACH

1 **Activate prior knowledge** by asking students to **think-pair-share** responses to the Essential Questions.

2 Ask students to independently **sort** the vocabulary and literary terms in the Table of Contents.

3 Explain that throughout the unit, students will revisit their initial responses to the Essential Questions and vocabulary to reflect on their learning and to demonstrate that their learning has progressed.

4 Facilitate a **close reading** of the EA1 assignment and Scoring Guide criteria, focusing on the "Proficient" column. Instruct students to **mark the text** by underlining key skills and knowledge.

5 As a class, create a large **graphic organizer** labeled with the Scoring Guide criteria.

6 During discussions, note the key knowledge and skills on the graphic organizer. Students should do the same on their own graphic organizer.

ACTIVITY 3.1

Previewing the Unit

LEARNING STRATEGIES: Think-Pair-Share, QHT, Close Reading, Marking the Text, Paraphrasing, Graphic Organizer

My Notes

INDEPENDENT READING LINK

You will be reading a narrative related to events preceding and during World War II and the genocide of a people based on their religion. You may want to read an additional novel or nonfiction narrative from the additional titles mentioned in this unit. Book lists are available in the back of this textbook, and you can use book discussions and recommendations from classmates to help you choose. Use your Reader/Writer Notebook and your Independent Reading Logs to keep notes on what you are reading and answer questions that will come up. As you read, look for the thematic focus of this unit: "finding light in the darkness."

Learning Targets

- Examine the big ideas and the vocabulary for the unit.
- Identify the skills and knowledge necessary to be successful in completing the Embedded Assessement.

Making Connections

In the first part of this unit, you will read texts about the Holocaust that show both the tragedy of historical events and the ways in which people reacted to those events. This study will help prepare you to research current issues from around the world and choose one for which to create a persuasive multimedia campaign.

Essential Questions

The following **Essential Questions** will be the focus of the unit study. Respond to both questions.

1. Why is it important to learn about the Holocaust?

2. How can one person make a difference?

Developing Vocabulary

3. Use a QHT chart to sort the Academic Vocabulary and Literary Terms in the Contents.

Unpacking Embedded Assessment 1

Read the assignment for Embedded Assessment 1:

> Present a panel discussion that includes an oral reading of a significant passage from the narrative read by your group. Your discussion should explain how the theme or central idea of "finding light in the darkness" is developed in the entire narrative.

After you closely read the Embedded Assessment 1 assignment and use the Scoring Guide to further analyze the requirements, work with your class to paraphrase the expectations. Create a graphic organizer to use as a visual reminder of the required concepts and skills.

COMMON CORE STATE STANDARDS

Focus Standard:

L.8.6: Acquire and use accurately grade-appropriate general academic and domain-specific words and phrases; gather vocabulary knowledge when considering a word or phrase important to comprehension or expression.

Additional Standards Addressed:

RL.8.10; RI.8.10

Collaborating to Preview Holocaust Narratives

ACTIVITY 3.2

Learning Targets

- Demonstrate effective communication in collaborative discussions.
- Analyze and discuss text in a collaborative group.

LEARNING STRATEGIES: Note-taking, Graphic Organizer, Previewing, Predicting, Summarizing, Discussion Groups

Preparing for Listening and Speaking

1. As a student, you have probably spent years observing teachers and other students who demonstrate both effective and ineffective speaking and listening skills. To help you identify good speaking and listening skills, create two T charts in your Reader/Writer Notebook, one for Listening and one for Speaking. Brainstorm effective and ineffective listening and speaking habits and practices. Add to your chart during the class discussion.
2. Read the following information to learn more about effective **communication** in collaborative groups. All members of a group need to communicate effectively to help the group work smoothly to achieve its goals. Group members should allow opportunities for everyone to participate. To help ensure a successful group experience, follow these guidelines.

ACADEMIC VOCABULARY
Communication is a process of exchanging information between individuals. It can include both verbal (words) and nonverbal (expressions, gestures) language.

As a speaker:

- Come prepared to the discussion, having read or researched the material being studied.
- Organize your thoughts before speaking.
- Ask questions to clarify and to connect to others' ideas.
- Respond to others' questions and comments with relevant evidence, observations, and ideas.
- Use appropriate eye contact, adequate volume, and clear pronunciation.

As a listener:

- Listen to comprehend, analyze, and evaluate others' ideas.
- Avoid barriers to listening such as daydreaming, fidgeting, or having side conversations.
- Take notes to prepare a thoughtful response.

3. On the following page are quotations about the topic of light and darkness. Take turns reading aloud, interpreting, and discussing the meaning and figurative language used in each quotation. Follow the guidelines for effective communication.

My Notes

ACTIVITY 3.2

PLAN

Materials: copies of Holocaust narratives students will read for class Literature Circles, online book reviews (optional), index cards (optional)
Suggested Pacing: 2 50-minute class periods

TEACH

1 Use the **Think-Write-Pair-Share** strategy to **activate prior knowledge** about effective speaking and listening (Student Steps 1–2).

2 Define *communication* and connect it to students' previous knowledge of collaborative work. Add these words to the Word Wall.

3 Read and discuss the information about effective speaking and listening.

COMMON CORE STATE STANDARDS

Focus Standards:

SL.8.1: Engage effectively in a range of collaborative discussions (one-on-one, in groups, and teacher-led) with diverse partners on Grade 8 topics, texts, and issues, building on others' ideas and expressing their own clearly.

SL.8.1a: Come to discussions prepared, having read or researched material under study; explicitly draw on that preparation by referring to evidence on the topic, text, or issue to probe and reflect on ideas under discussion.

SL.8.1b: Follow rules for collegial discussions and decision-making, track progress toward specific goals and deadlines, and define individual roles as needed.

Additional Standards Addressed:

RI.8.1; W.8.10; SL.8.1c; SL.8.1d; SL.8.6; L.8.4b; L.8.5a; L.8.5b; L.8.6

4 Place students in groups of five, and instruct them to assign a different quote to each person. Give them time to interpret and **take notes** in order to lead a discussion about their assigned quote.

5 After the discussion, guide students to reflect on their collaborative experience.

6 When students finish, briefly discuss challenges and goals. Provide feedback relating to the quality of student reflections.

Collaborating to Preview Holocaust Narratives

Quotation	Interpretation
A. "We've all got both light and darkness inside us. What matters is the part we choose to act on. That's who we really are." —J.K. Rowling	
B. "Darkness cannot drive out darkness; only light can do that. Hate cannot drive out hate; only love can do that." —Martin Luther King, Jr.	
C. "It is better to light a candle than curse the darkness." —Eleanor Roosevelt	
D. "Sometimes our light goes out, but is blown into flame by another human being. Each of us owes deepest thanks to those who have rekindled the light." —Albert Schweitzer	
E. "Maybe it's the very presence of one thing—light or darkness—that necessitates the existence of the other. Think about it, people couldn't become legendary heroes if they hadn't first done something to combat darkness. Doctors could do no good if there weren't diseases for them to treat." —Jessica Shirvington	

4. Reflect on your group's discussion of the quotes. Identify challenges and set specific goals for improving your speaking, listening, and reading skills.

	Challenges	Goals
Speaking		
Listening		
Reading		

5. For this activity, you will be reading and discussing Holocaust narratives. In your discussion group, choose a different Holocaust narrative for each group member to preview.

6. Form a new group with other students who are previewing the same Holocaust narrative. Use the graphic organizer below to prepare a book preview.

Title:	Author:
Genre:	Length:
Predictions based on significant imagery from the book cover design:	
Summary of the information provided in the book description or review:	
Information about the author:	
Personal response after reading a passage: This book sounds . . . This book reminds me of . . . Someone who would like this book . . .	

7. Go back to your original discussion group and take turns presenting your book previews. Use the chart on the next page to take notes on each book as you hear it described. If needed, continue on a new page in your Reader/Writer Notebook.

WORD CONNECTIONS

Etymology

The word *holocaust* comes from the Greek words *holos*, meaning "whole" or "entire," and *caustos*, meaning "burn."

During World War II, the mass killing of European Jews, Roma, Slavs, and people with physical or mental disabilities during Hitler's regime was referred to as a *holocaust*. It wasn't until 1957, however, before it became a proper name, *Holocaust*.

My Notes

ACTIVITY 3.2 continued

7 Use the **jigsaw** strategy by placing students in home base groups and giving each group copies of one of the selected narratives. Inform students that today they are only selecting a book to present; later they will have a chance to select a book to read. See the Unit 3 Planning the Unit pages for suggested titles.

TEACHER TO TEACHER

You will need enough titles to split among approximately six or seven groups of five students each (one student for each Literature Circle role). It may be helpful to students if you provide them with copies of book reviews too.

8 Give students time to preview their books and prepare a presentation.

9 Have students return to their home base groups, and introduce the Book Preview Note-Taking graphic organizer. Ask students to record their top three choices on an index card to help you sort them into Literature Circle groups.

10 Create Literature Circle groups, and distribute copies of narratives to each group. Consider forming groups based on each student's interest and skill level as a reader, speaker, and listener.

11 Guide groups as they work to formulate a plan for reading and discussion (Date Assigned, Due Date, Pages to Read). Inform students when they should start reading, when they should be prepared for a discussion, and when they should be finished with the narrative. Explain that they can leave the last two columns blank at this time.

▶ASSESS

Check the reading schedules to be sure that students have met your expectations. Decide how and when you will assess their journals and meeting notes.

▶ADAPT

Some groups may need additional class time to read or prepare for their meetings; others may need to be challenged with supplemental reading material. You may also need to revisit some of the skills and strategies necessary for success in Literature Circles (**Double-Entry Journal, Levels of Questions**, speaking and listening).

Collaborating to Preview Holocaust Narratives

Book Preview Note-Taking Graphic Organizer

Book Title	An Interesting Point Made About the Book	My Thoughts/Comments/Questions

8. Record your top three choices and explain the reasons for your selection.

9. Once you have formed your Literature Circle group, formulate a plan for reading your Holocaust narrative.

Reading Schedule

Title of Book: ______________________________

Author: ______________________

Total Number of Pages: _____

Date Assigned	Date Due	Pages to Read	Role	Number of Journal Entries

Understanding Literature Circle Discussions

ACTIVITY 3.3

Learning Targets

- Analyze Literature Circle role descriptions and communicate an understanding of the qualifications for one role by creating a résumé.
- Apply learning about Literature Circle roles while participating in a text-based collaborative discussion.

LEARNING STRATEGIES: Diffusing, Literature Circles, Questioning the Text, Summarizing, Note-taking, Discussion Groups

Understanding Literature Circle Roles

Read the following information about Literature Circle roles. For each role, think about the skills required and consider your personal strengths.

Discussion Leader

Your job is to develop a list of questions you think your group should discuss about the assigned section of the book. Use your knowledge of Levels of Questions to create thought-provoking interpretive (Level 2) and universal (Level 3) questions that connect to understanding the content and themes of the book. Try to create questions that encourage your group to consider many ideas. Help your group to explore these important ideas and share their reactions. You are in charge of facilitating the day's discussion.

Diction Detective

Your job is to carefully examine the diction (word choice) in the assigned section. Search for words, phrases, and passages that are especially descriptive, powerful, funny, thought-provoking, surprising, or even confusing. List the words or phrases and explain why you selected them. Then, analyze the intended effect, asking and answering questions such as the following: What is the author trying to say? How does the diction help the author achieve his or her purpose? What tone do the words indicate?

Bridge Builder

Your job is to build bridges between the events of the book and other people, places, or events in school, the community, or your own life. Look for connections between the text, yourself, other texts, and the world. Also, make connections between what has happened before and what might happen as the narrative continues. Look for the character's internal and external conflicts and the ways that these conflicts influence his or her actions.

Reporter

Your job is to identify and report on the key points of the reading assignment. Make a list or write a summary that describes how the setting, plot, and characters are developed in this section of the book. Consider character interactions, major events that occur, and shifts in the setting or mood that seem significant. Share your report at the beginning of the group meeting to help your group focus on the key ideas presented in the reading. Like that of a newspaper reporter, your report must be concise, yet thorough.

My Notes

ACTIVITY 3.3

▶PLAN

Materials: children's books about the Holocaust, construction paper or index cards, manila folders (optional)
Suggested Pacing: 2 50-minute class periods

▶TEACH

TEACHER TO TEACHER

This activity will give students practice applying the Literature Circle roles before they begin reading their narratives. This practice can be done with children's books as suggested here, or it can be done with short stories or poems about the Holocaust if you prefer. You may also choose to use one of the narratives included in the unit. See Activity 3.4 or 3.11.

1 As a class, read and **diffuse** the role descriptions to make sure that students understand the expectations of each role. After each role description, ask students to summarize the required skills. Be sure to review **Levels of Questions** (page 109). Explain that these roles are like training wheels: they help students become successful, but eventually they are no longer needed.

COMMON CORE STATE STANDARDS

Focus Standards:

SL.8.1: Engage effectively in a range of collaborative discussions (one-on-one, in groups, and teacher-led) with diverse partners on Grade 8 topics, texts, and issues, building on others' ideas and expressing their own clearly.

SL.8.1a: Come to discussions prepared, having read or researched material under study; explicitly draw on that preparation by referring to evidence on the topic, text, or issue to probe and reflect on ideas under discussion.

SL.8.1b: Follow rules for collegial discussions and decision-making, track progress toward specific goals and deadlines, and define individual roles as needed.

Additional Standards Addressed:

RI.8.1; RI.8.2; W.8.2; W.8.10; SL.8.1c; SL.8.1d; L.8.6

ACTIVITY 3.3 continued

2 After defining *résumé*, ask students to select a role and create a résumé describing the requirements and their related skills and experiences.

Leveled Differentiated Instruction

To support students in creating a résumé, provide the sentence frames below.

Em *I am good for this role because I am good at ___. One experience I've had that helped prepare me for this role is ___.*

Ex *One reason I am good for this role is ___. I have experience with ___, which relates to the role because ___.*

3 Remind students that they will have opportunities to take different roles throughout the unit; then place them in groups of five to "apply for" and assign roles for today's activity.

4 Model the creation of a table tent by folding a piece of construction paper or an index card. Make sure students understand that they should write the role and image on one side and the description and responsibilities on the other.

TEACHER TO TEACHER

You might want to laminate some or all of the table tents to use throughout the unit. Also, consider giving groups a manila folder to store their work and supplies.

5 Introduce a Holocaust narrative by asking students to respond to the questions. Encourage them to make connections to their own lives and to think about how old they were when they first began learning about difficult social issues.

ACTIVITY 3.3 continued

Understanding Literature Circle Discussions

ACADEMIC VOCABULARY
A **résumé** is a brief written account of personal, educational, and professional qualifications and experience, prepared by an applicant for a job.

My Notes

Artist

Your job is to create an illustration to clarify information, communicate an important idea (e.g., about setting, character, conflict, or theme), and/or to add interest to the discussion. It can be a sketch, cartoon, diagram, flow chart, or a piece that uses visual techniques for effect. Show your illustration to the group without any explanation. Ask each group member to respond, either by making a comment or asking a question. After everyone has responded, explain your picture and answer any questions that have not been answered.

Assigning Literature Circle Roles

1. Create a **résumé** using the template below to apply for a role.

Name:
Role (Job Description): Choose one of the roles and summarize the requirements.
Skills: Describe the skills you have that will help you perform this role (e.g., reading, artistic skills, etc.).
Experience: Describe similar experiences you have had and how they will help you in this role.
Activities: Describe any class work or extracurricular activities that have prepared you for the role.

2. Use your résumés to distribute role assignments in your group. Record these assignments on your reading schedule.

3. Create a table tent for your role by folding an index card or construction paper. On the side facing your group, write the role title and a symbolic image. On the side facing you, write a description of your role and bullet points listing the requirements. Be specific so that the next person who has this role will understand what to do.

Practicing Literature Circle Roles

4. Before you begin reading, think about these questions: How old do you think someone should be when they first learn about the Holocaust? Why would someone write a children's book about such a disturbing subject?

5. Create a double-entry journal in your Reader/Writer Notebook, keeping your Literature Circle role in mind. For example, the discussion leader may want to record passages that inspire questions, while the artist might record interesting imagery.

6. After you read, use the notes from your double-entry journal to prepare for your role. When everyone in the group is ready, practice conducting a Literature Circle meeting. As you listen, take notes on interesting ideas presented by group members, and form questions in response.

Discussion Note-Taking Graphic Organizer

An Interesting Point Made by a Member of My Group	My Thoughts/Comments/Questions

7. Reflect on your discussion. Review your responses in the graphic organizer.
   - What contributed most to your understanding or appreciation of the text?
   - What did you learn about the Holocaust through the narrative and discussion?

© 2017 College Board. All rights reserved.

ACTIVITY 3.3 continued

6 Introduce or review the format and purpose of a **double-entry journal**. Set expectations by explaining what makes an effective textual selection and response. Model your expectations with an example from one of the selected children's stories.

7 Select a reading method, and instruct students to read the children's book. If each group has only one copy of the book, ask a strong reader to read the book aloud or have students take turns. If you have multiple copies, you might want to do a shared reading, partner reading, or independent reading. Remind students that they need to listen and **take notes** during reading.

8 When students have finished reading, allow time for them to prepare their roles.

9 Before they begin the discussions, point out the Discussion Note-Taking graphic organizer. When ready, ask the Discussion Leader to begin. As students are discussing the text, circulate and provide assistance and feedback (relating to reading, speaking, and listening) as needed.

TEACHER TO TEACHER

The double-entry journal and Discussion Note-Taking graphic organizer should serve as models. In the future, students should create these in their Reader/Writer Notebooks, or you could make copies from the templates on SpringBoard Online.

10 Based on interest and time, consider using a **jigsaw** after student discussions so students can share what they learned about the Holocaust from their different books.

11 Ask students to independently respond to the reflection questions. Briefly discuss responses as a class.

▶ASSESS

Review students' work to determine how well they met the requirements for participating in a Literature Circle.

▶ADAPT

You may need to revisit the Double-Entry Journal strategy before the students have their first Holocaust narrative Literature Circle meeting. This would be a great time to provide student models from this activity.

Understanding Literature Circle Discussions

My Notes

Check Your Understanding

Using the information from your Literature Circle discussion, create an analytical statement about the theme of the narrative you read. Provide textual evidence to support your analytical statement.

Theme:

Evidence:

© 2017 College Board. All rights reserved.

Making Thematic Connections

ACTIVITY 3.4

Learning Target

- Analyze an excerpt from an autobiographical narrative and a poem.
- Compare the themes of two literary texts in a formal collaborative discussion.

LEARNING STRATEGIES: Choral Reading, Rereading, Close Reading, Questioning the Text, Visualizing, Marking the Text, Discussion Groups

Preview

In this activity, you will read a passage from a memoir and a poem and compare their themes.

Setting a Purpose for Reading

- As you read the passage, underline words and phrases that describe how Moishe changed after returning to Sighet.
- Circle unknown words and phrases. Try to determine the meaning of the words by using context clues, word parts, or a dictionary.

My Notes

ABOUT THE AUTHOR

Elie Wiesel (1928–) was a teenager in 1944 when he and his whole family were taken from their home to the Auschwitz concentration camp and then to Buchenwald. Wiesel wrote his internationally acclaimed memoir *Night* about his experiences in the camps. In addition to writing many other books, Wiesel became an activist who spoke out about injustices in many countries around the world. He was awarded the Nobel Peace Prize in 1986.

Memoir

from **Night**

by Elie Wiesel

1 AND THEN, one day all foreign Jews were expelled from Sighet.[1] And Moishe the Beadle[2] was a foreigner.

2 Crammed into cattle cars by the Hungarian police, they cried silently. Standing on the station platform, we too were crying. The train disappeared over the horizon; all that was left was thick, dirty smoke.

3 Behind me, someone said, sighing, "What do you expect? That's war …"

4 The **deportees** were quickly forgotten. A few days after they left, it was rumored that they were in Galicia,[3] working, and even that they were content with their fate.

deportees: people forced to leave a country by an authority

[1] **Sighet:** a town in Romania
[2] **Beadle:** a minor church official; a caretaker of a synagogue
[3] **Galicia:** a former province of Austria, now in parts of Poland and Ukraine

ACTIVITY 3.4

PLAN

Materials: map of Europe (optional)
Suggested Pacing: 2 50-minute class periods

TEACHER TO TEACHER

Prior to the lesson, **chunk** the excerpt by event. If you plan to use visuals to help students picture the setting and make meaning of the text (e.g., a map), prepare these in advance.

TEACH

1 Read the Preview and the Setting a Purpose for Reading sections with your students. Help them understand what they should annotate for.

2 **FIRST READ:** Based on the complexity of the passage and your knowledge of your students, you may choose to conduct the first reading in a variety of ways:

- independent reading
- paired reading
- small group reading
- choral reading
- read aloud

3 As students are reading, monitor their progress. Be sure they are engaged with the text and annotating about Moishe's return to Sighet. Evaluate whether the selected reading mode is effective.

4 Based on the observations you made during the first reading, you may want to adjust your reading mode. For example, you may decide for the second reading to read aloud certain complex passages, or you may group students differently.

Leveled Differentiated Instruction

In this activity, students may need support drawing a conclusion about how Moishe changed in the story. Have students complete a **Conclusion Builder** graphic organizer as they read.

COMMON CORE STATE STANDARDS

Focus Standards:

RL.8.5: Compare and contrast the structure of two or more texts and analyze how the differing structure of each text contributes to its meaning and style.

RI.8.1: Cite the textual evidence that most strongly supports an analysis of what the text says explicitly as well as inferences drawn from the text.

RI.8.2: Determine a central idea of a text and analyze its development over the course of the text, including its relationship to supporting ideas; provide an objective summary of the text.

Additional Standards Addressed:

RL.8.1; RL.8.2; RL.8.3; RL.8.10; RI.8.3; RI.8.4; RI.8.5; RI.8.6; RI.8.10; W.8.10; SL.8.1a; SL.8.1b; SL.8.1c; SL.8.1d; L.8.4b; L.8.6

© 2017 College Board. All rights reserved.

Em Guide students to analyze the text by providing evidence and modeling how to draw a conclusion about how Moishe changed. Model using the phrases *shows that, based on* to explain conclusions.

Ex Guide students to draw a conclusion about how Moishe changed and support it with text evidence. Have students use the phrases *suggests that, leads to* to explain their conclusions.

Br Have students draw multiple conclusions based on the text and support each conclusion with evidence. Have students use the words *indicates that, influences* to explain their conclusions.

Support Have students support their conclusions with text evidence and then analyze the evidence to determine whether or not the conclusion could be challenged.

Stretch Challenge students to write a script for a collaborative discussion using conclusions, text evidence, and counterstatements.

Text Complexity
Overall: Accessible
Lexile: 630L
Qualitative: Moderate Difficulty
Task: Moderate (Analyze)

TEACHER TO TEACHER

Be sure students know that Elie Weisel and his family were eventually transported to a concentration camp in 1944. This excerpt, the poem, and the later reading of Eve Bunting's book *Terrible Things: An Allegory of the Holocaust* move from the specific and personal to a more general and universal application of the same idea—that inaction and passivity create a dangerous environment and precedent that allow tyranny to grow.

Making Thematic Connections

5 Days went by. Then weeks and months. Life was normal again. A calm, reassuring wind blew through our homes. The shopkeepers were doing good business, the students lived among their books, and the children played in the streets.

synagogue: a building that houses Jewish religious services

6 One day, as I was about to enter the **synagogue**, I saw Moishe the Beadle sitting on a bench near the entrance.

7 He told me what had happened to him and his companions. The train with the deportees had crossed the Hungarian border and, once in Polish territory, had been taken over by the Gestapo.[4] The train had stopped. The Jews were ordered to get off and onto waiting trucks. The trucks headed toward a forest. There everybody was ordered to get out. They were forced to dig huge trenches. When they had finished their work, the men from the Gestapo began theirs. Without passion or haste, they shot their prisoners, who were forced to approach the trench one by one and offer their necks. Infants were tossed in the air and used as targets for the machine guns. This took place in the Galician forest, near Kolomay. How had he, Moishe the Beadle, been able to escape? By a miracle. He was wounded in the leg and left for dead …

Kabbalah: a Jewish religious tradition that strives to explain how the universe works

insinuated: implied; hinted at

8 Day after day, night after night, he went from one Jewish house to the next, telling his story and that of Malka, the young girl who lay dying for three days, and that of Tobie, the tailor who begged to die before his sons were killed.

9 Moishe was not the same. The joy in his eyes was gone. He no longer sang. He no longer mentioned either God or **Kabbalah**. He spoke only of what he had seen. But people not only refused to believe his tales, they refused to listen. Some even **insinuated** that he only wanted their pity, that he was imagining things. Others flatly said that he had gone mad.

10 As for Moishe, he wept and pleaded:

11 "Jews, listen to me! That's all I ask of you. No money. No pity. Just listen to me!" he kept shouting in the synagogue, between the prayer at dusk and the evening prayer.

12 Even I did not believe him. I often sat with him, after services, and listening to his tales, trying to understand his grief. But all I felt was pity.

13 "They think I'm mad," he whispered, and tears, like drops of wax, flowed from his eyes.

14 Once, I asked him the question: "Why do you want people to believe you so much? In your place I would not care whether they believed me or not …"

15 He closed his eyes, as if to escape time.

16 "You don't understand," he said in despair. "You cannot understand. I was saved miraculously. I succeeded in coming back. Where did I get my strength? I wanted to return to Sighet to describe to you my death so you might ready yourselves while there is still time. Life? I no longer care to live. I am alone. But I wanted to come back to warn you. Only no one is listening to me …"

17 This was toward the end of 1942.

18 Thereafter life seemed normal once again. London radio, which we listened to every evening, announced encouraging news: the daily bombings of Germany and Stalingrad, the preparation of the Second Front. And so we, the Jews of Sighet, waited for better days that surely were soon to come.

GRAMMAR & USAGE
Participle Verb Forms

The participle forms of verbs can be used as adjectives. There are two participial forms: present (ending in *-ing*) and past (usually ending in *-d*). Note the use of these participles as adjectives:

"… **reassuring** wind …" (paragraph 5)

"… **waiting** trucks …" (paragraph 7)

A participle may occur in a participial phrase, which includes the participle plus any complements and modifiers. The whole phrase serves as an adjective. For example:

"**Crammed into cattle cars by the Hungarian police**, they …" (paragraph 2)

An introductory participial phrase must modify the noun or pronoun that follows it. In the example above, the phrase modifies "they."

[4] **Gestapo:** the secret police in Nazi Germany

SCAFFOLDING THE TEXT-DEPENDENT QUESTIONS

1. Craft and Structure (RI.8.4) **Who are the people represented by the pronouns "they" and "we" in paragraph 2? What is the intended effect?** What group of people is mentioned in paragraph 1? What is happening to them? Are they referred to as "they" or "we" in paragraph 2? Does using "they" and "we" make the people to which they are referring seem like one group or separate groups?

2. Craft and Structure (RI.8.4) **What is the intended effect of the following line from paragraph 7: "Infants were tossed in the air and used as targets for the machine guns"?** What are machine guns used for? How does it make you feel reading that Gestapo officers fired them at infants?

Second Read

- Reread the passage to answer these text-dependent questions.
- Write any additional questions you have about the text in your Reader/Writer Notebook.

1. **Craft and Structure:** Who are the people represented by the pronouns "they" and "we" in paragraph 2? What is the intended effect?

2. **Craft and Structure:** What is the intended effect of the following line from paragraph 7: "Infants were tossed in the air and used as targets for the machine guns"?

3. **Key Ideas and Details:** Why did the Jews of Sighet refuse "to believe his tales, and refused to listen"?

4. **Key Ideas and Details:** What are the two main events of this narrative? What is Wiesel's purpose in focusing on these two events?

Setting a Purpose for Reading

- As you read the poem, underline words and phrases that identify what the author is not.
- Circle unknown words and phrases. Try to determine the meaning of the words by using context clues, word parts, or a dictionary.

My Notes

3. Key Ideas and Details (RI.8.2) **Why did the Jews of Sighet refuse "to believe his tales, and refused to listen"?** Reread paragraph 9. Why would people not want to hear what Moishe was saying? Why didn't they think his story could be possible?

4. Key Ideas and Details (RI.8.2) **What are the two main events of this narrative? What is Wiesel's purpose in focusing on these two events?** What event happens to Moishe in paragraphs 1 through 7? What event happens to Moishe in paragraphs 8 through 18? What attitudes do other people express toward Moishe in both events?

5 **SECOND READ:** During the second reading, students will be returning to the text to answer the text-dependent comprehension question. You may choose to have students reread and work on the question in a variety of ways:

- independently
- in pairs
- in small groups
- together as a class

6 Have students answer the text-dependent question. If they have difficulty, scaffold the question by rephrasing it or breaking it down into smaller parts. See the Scaffolding the Text-Dependent Questions boxes for suggestions.

7 Review the Setting the Purpose for Reading section with your students. Help them understand any terms they encounter.

8 **FIRST READ:** Based on the complexity of the passage and your knowledge of your students, you may choose to conduct the first reading in a variety of ways:

- independent reading
- paired reading
- small group reading
- choral reading
- read aloud

9 As students are reading, monitor their progress. Be sure they are engaged with the text and annotating what the author is saying he is not. Evaluate whether the selected reading mode is effective.

10 Based on the observations you made during the first reading, you may want to adjust your reading mode. For example, you may decide to select four students to read. Each student should read one stanza, and all students should read the final stanza together. Explain that this is an example of **choral reading**, which is often used to present a dramatic interpretation of a text.

11 **SECOND READ:** During the second reading, students will be returning to the text to answer the text-dependent comprehension question. You may choose to have students reread and work on the question in a variety of ways:

- independently
- in pairs
- in small groups
- together as a class

12 Have students answer the text-dependent question. If they have difficulty, scaffold the question by rephrasing it or breaking it down into smaller parts. See the Scaffolding the Text-Dependent Questions boxes for suggestions.

13 Discuss the root of *communism*. Ask a student to explain the difference between *communism* and *democracy*.

Making Thematic Connections

WORD CONNECTIONS

Roots and Affixes

The Latin root *-commun-* in ***communist*** means "common." There are a few distinctions in the definition of *common*. In this case it refers to something that is shared or owned together by several people or groups. In communism, land and factories are owned by the community. This root occurs in *communal, communicate,* and *communion*.

The word ***democrat*** contains the Greek root *demo-*, which means "people," and the Greek suffix *-crat*, which means "rule." Democracy is a government run by the people.

My Notes

ABOUT THE AUTHOR

Martin Niemöller (1892–1984) was a German Protestant pastor. During World War II, he opposed Hitler's religious policies and was sent to concentration camps. He survived and, after the war, joined the World Peace Movement. This poem is his response to the question "How could it happen?"

Poetry

FIRST THEY CAME FOR THE COMMUNISTS

by Martin Niemöller

When the Nazis came for the communists,
I remained silent;
I was not a communist.

When they locked up the social democrats,
I remained silent;
I was not a social democrat.

When they came for the trade unionists,
I did not speak out;
I was not a trade unionist.

When they came for the Jews,
I did not speak out;
I was not a Jew.

When they came for me,
there was no one left to speak out.

Second Read

- Reread the poem to answer these text-dependent questions.
- Write any additional questions you have about the text in your Reader/Writer Notebook.

5. **Key Ideas and Details:** How does each stanza contribute to a developing sense of doom?

5. Key Ideas and Details (RI.8.2) **How does each stanza contribute to a developing sense of doom?** What is happening in each stanza? How many people are left at the end of the poem? How does a sense of doom develop through each stanza?

Working from the Text

6. Work collaboratively to apply each of the different Literature Circle roles to the autobiographical narrative and the poem. Use the Text-Dependent Questions, as well as questions you develop during your discussion, to compare and analyze these texts.
7. How is the autobiographical narrative's theme similar to and different from the poem's theme?
8. Use the graphic organizer that follows as a reminder of the roles and to guide your thinking for your Literature Circle discussion of both texts.

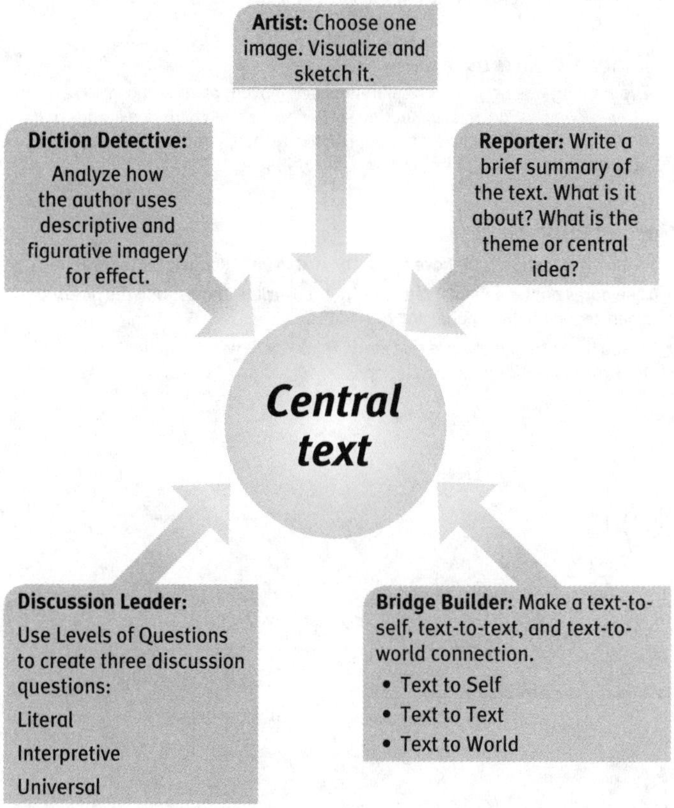

Check Your Understanding

Quickwrite: What did you learn about the Holocaust through your discussion of these texts? Which text is more powerful? Explain using at least one quote from the text you chose as part of your explanation.

My Notes

© 2017 College Board. All rights reserved.

ACTIVITY 3.4 continued

14 Point out the **graphic organizer** illustrating the Literature Circle roles. Have students work in groups to analyze and discuss the texts using the Literature Circle roles as a guide. During the discussion, students should record responses in the **graphic organizer** for future reference.

15 Be sure that students are able to distinguish between a topic (*prejudice*) and a theme (*prejudice will spread if it is allowed to thrive*).

16 Once the class has analyzed the poem and the narrative, ask them to consider how they might use pauses, emphasis, volume, and tone to convey important ideas in an oral reading of a section of the personal narrative or the poem.

17 Ask student volunteers to read passages from the narrative or the poem aloud, using the class suggestions to inform the reading.

TEACHER TO TEACHER

Many students have a very limited interpretation of what the "Artist" role can be in Literature Circles. Review options such as sketching, creating a figurative representation of an important concept, creating an illustrated timeline, and using visual techniques for effect.

18 Come together as a class; discuss responses from a variety of groups. Focus discussion on the similarities and differences between the texts, guiding students to an understanding of how similar subjects and themes can be represented by different genres and specific circumstances.

▶ASSESS

Monitor student discussions to see how well students understand and are able to apply each of the different roles. For example, make sure they can correctly distinguish between the different **Levels of Questions.**

▶ADAPT

If students are struggling with any of the roles, consider modeling again with another Holocaust poem. The anthology *Holocaust Poetry*, compiled by Hilda Schiff, has excellent selections.

ACTIVITY 3.5

▶PLAN

Materials: *Terrible Things* by Eve Bunting, copies of sections of *Terrible Things*
Suggested Pacing: 1 50-minute class period

▶TEACH

TEACHER TO TEACHER

At the end of the activity, students will work in groups to plan and present a dramatic interpretation of a passage. There will be eight groups and four passages from the story. Groups will be paired so they can view another interpretation of the same passage.

Chunk *Terrible Things* by events; select four chunks (beginning, middle, middle, and end); then select one passage per chunk for dramatic interpretation.

1 Review the definition of *allegory*, and briefly discuss examples that students may be familiar with. See the Glossary in the Resources section or Activity 1.14 for review.

2 Read the Preview and the Setting a Purpose for Reading sections with your students. Help them understand what they will listen for and take notes on.

3 **FIRST READ:** Model a dramatic reading as you read the story aloud.

4 As you are reading, be sure students are engaged with the text and taking notes.

5 **SECOND READ:** As you read the text again, pause after each **chunk** to give students time to complete the **graphic organizer** notes for that event.

6 Have students share any questions they have about the story.

ACTIVITY 3.5

Analyzing an Allegory

LEARNING STRATEGIES: Oral Interpretation, Think-Pair-Share, Graphic Organizer

My Notes

Learning Targets

- Present an oral dramatic interpretation of a passage from the text.
- Analyze how the themes in multiple genres are connected.

Preview

In this activity, you will be read a children's story and analyze it as an allegory of the Holocaust.

Setting a Purpose for Reading

- As you hear the story, listen for all the different types of animals.
- Write down unknown words and phrases. Try to determine the meaning of the words by using context clues, word parts, or a dictionary.

ABOUT THE AUTHOR

Eve Bunting was born in 1928 in Ireland and moved to California in 1958. After taking a writing class, Bunting started to get her children's stories and books published. Several of her books have received awards. Bunting has also taught many classes of her own on writing.

Second Read

- Write any questions you have about the text in your Reader/Writer Notebook.
- Take notes on the animals' reactions to the Terrible Things. Use the graphic organizer on the next pages for your notes.
- As you listen to and discuss this story, think about why a children's story of the Holocaust is best told as an allegory.

COMMON CORE STATE STANDARDS

Focus Standards:

RL.8.2: Determine a theme or central idea of a text and analyze its development over the course of the text, including its relationship to the characters, setting, and plot; provide an objective summary of the text.

SL.8.1a: Come to discussions prepared, having read or researched material under study; explicitly draw on that preparation by referring to evidence on the topic, text, or issue to probe and reflect on ideas under discussion.

SL.8.4: Present claims and findings (e.g., argument, narrative, response to literature presentations), emphasizing salient points in a focused, coherent manner with relevant evidence, sound valid reasoning, and well-chosen details; use appropriate eye contact, adequate volume, and clear pronunciation.

Additional Standards Addressed:

RL.8.1; RL.8.3; RL.8.4; RL.8.5; RL.8.6; W.8.2a; W.8.2b; W.8.2e; W.8.9a; W.8.9b; W.8.10; SL.8.1c; SL.8.1d; SL.8.6; L.8.6

© 2017 College Board. All rights reserved.

How do the other animals respond to the demand of the Terrible Things?	How do the other animals respond after the Terrible Things have taken the animals?
When the Terrible Things come for "every creature with feathers on its back"	
Frogs, squirrels, porcupines, rabbits, fish:	Porcupine, squirrels:
	Little Rabbit:
	Big Rabbit:
When the Terrible Things come for "every bushy-tailed creature"	
Frogs, porcupines, fish, rabbits:	Little Rabbit:
	Big Rabbit:

Teacher Notes

7 As a class, discuss characteristics of fluent and dramatic reading.

8 Assign a chunk to each group. Make enough copies so each student has a copy of the group's assigned passage.

Analyzing an Allegory

How do the other animals respond to the demand of the Terrible Things?	How do the other animals respond after the Terrible Things have taken the animals?
When the Terrible Things come for "every creature that swims"	
Rabbits, porcupines:	Little Rabbit:
	Big Rabbit:
When the Terrible Things come for "every creature that sprouts quills"	
Rabbits:	Little Rabbit:
	Big Rabbit:
When the Terrible Things come for "any creature that is white"	
	Little Rabbit:

Working from the Text

1. Why would authors choose to use an allegory to tell a story?

2. After listening and taking notes, meet with your Literature Circle groups and, using your notes and insights, discuss how this text connects to the previous two texts you have read. Discuss the three different genres presented and why they are effective and appropriate for the topic, audience, and purpose.

3. Work collaboratively to plan and perform a dramatic interpretation of your assigned passage. Mark the text for pauses, emphasis, volume, and tone to convey important ideas and to add interest.

4. Rehearse your interpretation, and then present to the other group that shares your passage.

5. Reflect on your group's dramatic interpretation. What did your group do well? What will you do differently next time?

Check Your Understanding

WRITING to SOURCES **Expository Writing Prompt**

How is the theme of this story similar to the theme of Wiesel's excerpt and the Neimöller poem? Be sure to:

- Begin with a topic sentence that responds to the prompt and states a theme.
- Provide textual evidence from the texts and commentary for support.
- Use precise diction to inform or explain.

My Notes

ACTIVITY 3.5 continued

9 In **Literature Circle** groups, have students discuss the Working from the Text discussion topic and prepare for a dramatic reading of their section.

10 As students plan their dramatic interpretation, circulate to check for understanding and to provide feedback about the quality and accuracy of the interpretations.

11 When students are ready, pair groups with the same passage, and ask them to present to each other. Circulate to assess the level of effectiveness in presentations.

12 Monitor student understanding to determine how well they can explain the concepts of *theme, dramatic interpretation*, and *reflection*.

ASSESS

Ask students to independently respond to the writing prompt, either as homework or as an in-class writing activity.

ADAPT

If students struggle with explaining *theme*, share and display student models that meet and exceed expectations. Ask a successful group to present their dramatic interpretation in front of the class as a model.

Leveled Differentiated Instruction

In this activity, offer support to students who have difficulty writing to the expository writing prompt.

Em Have students take turns with a partner asking and answering the following questions to check their writing. *Is your writing organized? Did you use topic sentences? Did you include evidence from the text? Did you use transition words? Did you write in complete sentences? Did you use correct spelling?*

Ex Guide partners to look at the **Peer-Editing** checklist and discuss each of the checklist items in relation to their writing.

Br Have students work with a partner to create their own **Peer-Editing** checklist and use it to revise their paragraph.

ACTIVITY 3.6

▶PLAN

Materials: dictionaries, visuals of Holocaust vocabulary (optional—see http://www.ushmm.org/wlc/en/article.php?ModuleId=10005151)
Suggested Pacing: 1 50-minute class period

▶TEACH

1 Review *diction, connotation,* and *denotation*, and then introduce *euphemism*. Add it to the Word Wall.

2 Have students look up *relocation* in the dictionary and paraphrase or copy the definition. Discuss the connotation in the context of the Holocaust. Ask students to **pair-share** the difference in meanings, and then have them work in small groups to complete the chart.

Leveled Differentiated Instruction

In this activity, some students may need more support to review the meanings of *euphemism*.

Em Guide students to complete an **Unknown Word Solver** for *euphemism*. You can also prompt them with the following questions: *What does* euphemism *mean? What image comes to mind when you think about the word* euphemism? Then provide more examples such as euphemisms for vomiting ("tossing your cookies") or dying ("kicking the bucket").

Ex Guide students to write sentences explaining the meaning of the word *euphemism*. Ask students to include other examples of *euphemisms* in their sentences.

3 Discuss the effect and significance of Nazi euphemisms. Point out the time difference between the start of the Holocaust and the start of U.S. involvement in World War II. Ask students to make connections between the use of euphemisms and the world's slow response to intervention.

ACTIVITY 3.6

Dangerous Diction

LEARNING STRATEGIES: Graphic Organizer, Discussion Groups

Learning Target

- Understand the Holocaust-related diction of euphemism and explain new learning about the Holocaust using new vocabulary words.

Understanding Euphemism

The Nazis deliberately used **euphemisms** to disguise the true nature of their crimes. Euphemisms replace disturbing words using diction with more positive connotations.

ACADEMIC VOCABULARY
A **euphemism** is an inoffensive expression that is a substitute for one that is considered too harsh or blunt.

1. Work with a small group to analyze how the Nazis manipulated language to disguise the horror of their policies. Research the term *euphemism* and its use in Nazi Germany. If doing an online search, use an effective search term to find the true meanings of the terms below.

Euphemism	Denotation (Literal Definition)	Meaning in Context of the Holocaust	Analyze the Difference in Connotation
Relocation			
Disinfecting or Delousing Centers			
Camp			
The Final Solution			

WORD CONNECTIONS

Etymology

Euphemism contains the Greek prefix *eu-*, meaning "well" or "pleasing," and the Greek root *-pheme-*, which has the meaning of "speak." A person who uses a euphemism speaks with pleasing words.
People in ancient Greece were superstitious about using certain words in religious ceremonies. Euphemisms were used instead to be more pleasing.

2. To discuss the Holocaust, you will need to be familiar with Holocaust-related diction. In your Literature Circle groups, use a dictionary or other resource to find a definition or explanation for each of the terms in the list on the next page.

COMMON CORE STATE STANDARDS

Focus Standard:

L.8.4c: Consult general and specialized reference materials (e.g, dictionaries, glossaries, thesauruses), both print and digital, to find the pronunciation of a word or determine or clarify its precise meaning or its part of speech or trace the etymology of words.

Additional Standards Addressed:

RL.8.4; RI.8.4; W.8.7; SL.8.1a; SL.8.1b; L.8.4a; L.8.4b; L.8.4d; L.8.5c; L.8.6

Holocaust Vocabulary	Definition/Explanation
Antisemitism	
Concentration Camp	
Death Camp	
Genocide	
Gestapo	
Holocaust	
Nazi	
Persecution	
Propaganda	
SS *(Schutzstaffel)*	
Star of David	

Check Your Understanding

In two or three sentences, use at least six new words to explain what you have learned about the Holocaust. Read your explanation to a partner to practice fluency.

As you discover more vocabulary and euphemisms in your Holocaust narrative, copy them down to share, define, and discuss with your class.

WORD CONNECTIONS

Roots and Affixes

Genocide comes from the Greek word *genos*, which means "race" or "line of descent." The root *-gen-* occurs in such words as *gene*, *genesis*, and *genus*.

The suffix *-cide* forms nouns with the meaning of "kill" or "causing death," as in *homicide* and *pesticide*.

ACTIVITY 3.6 continued

4 Instruct students to work in small groups to define the list of Holocaust vocabulary.

5 As a class, discuss each Holocaust vocabulary term as you begin a Holocaust Word Wall. Students should continue to add to this list as they encounter new words in their narratives and activities. Students should use this vocabulary to strengthen their reading, writing, and speaking.

TEACHER TO TEACHER

Provide as many visuals of the terms as you can to increase comprehension and add interest.

Independent Reading: By now students should be well into their independent reading. Confirm that students are on track and following their reading plans, and help them to make adjustments to the plan if necessary.

ASSESS

Review student work to determine students' ability to successfully use Holocaust vocabulary to explain what they have learned.

ADAPT

To further expand students' Holocaust vocabulary, ask students to record unfamiliar vocabulary as they explore the Holocaust Museum website in the next activity; then have them work online in pairs or small groups to define the terms. These words should be posted on the Word Wall.

ACTIVITY 3.7

▶PLAN

Materials: computers with Internet access or copies of Web pages from the Holocaust Learning Site, a bulletin board with Holocaust dates posted in chronological order, index cards
Suggested Pacing: 2 50-minute class periods

▶TEACH

TEACHER TO TEACHER

Post the years from 1933–1945 on a bulletin board prior to this activity, leaving space under each year for index cards.

1 Give students a chance to **think-pair-share** responses to Question 1, and then discuss the importance of setting in a Holocaust narrative. Explain that they will conduct guided research in order to develop a better understanding of the context for their narratives.

TEACHER TO TEACHER

Rather than a research experience in which students discover and evaluate their own sources, this guided research provides a safe and accessible overview of the Holocaust by allowing them to navigate within a reliable website. This avoids the risk of confronting propaganda about the Holocaust that students may not yet have the skills and knowledge to evaluate. Students will have the opportunity to do more extended research in other activities at this level.

ACTIVITY 3.7

Exploring the Museum

LEARNING STRATEGIES: Oral Reading, Note-taking, Discussion Groups, Graphic Organizer, Summarizing

My Notes

Learning Targets

- Summarize information from a Holocaust website and contribute events to a historical timeline.
- Create and organize talking points and deliver an effective collaborative presentation.

Researching the Holocaust

1. Setting (time and place) is important in any story, but why is it especially important in a Holocaust narrative?

2. The United States Holocaust Memorial Museum in Washington, D.C., has a large collection of artifacts and educational displays about the events and people of the Holocaust. Work collaboratively to research and take notes on your assigned topics by exploring the museum's website, starting with the page "The Holocaust: A Learning Site for Students."
3. Each of the topics on the Learning Site links to a different webpage. Visit the website to explore your topics. Take notes on a graphic organizer like the one below in order to prepare your talking points for a presentation on the Holocaust. Your talking points should contain interesting information that leads to an exploration of the theme, or central idea.

On the next page is a list of topics about the Holocaust. Your teacher will assign each group a topic (column) and individual subjects within that topic to research. As you research, neatly copy your key dates and events onto individual index cards to add to the collaborative timeline after your presentation.

My Group's Topic:	
Topic 1:	**Topic 2:**
Notes for Talking Points:	**Notes for Talking Points:**
Summaries and Dates of Key Events:	**Summaries and Dates of Key Events:**

COMMON CORE STATE STANDARDS

Focus Standards:

SL.8.4: Present claims and findings (e.g., argument, narrative, response to literature presentations), emphasizing salient points in a focused, coherent manner with relevant evidence, sound valid reasoning, and well-chosen details; use appropriate eye contact, adequate volume, and clear pronunciation.

Additional Standards Addressed:

RI.8.1; RI.8.2; W.8.2a; W.8.2b; W.8.2c; W.8.2e; W.8.2f; W.8.7; W.8.8; SL.8.1a; SL.8.3

4. Mark the chart to indicate your assignment by circling the title of your group's topic (column) and highlighting or placing a check mark by the topics you are responsible for.

Nazi Rule	Jews in Prewar Germany	The "Final Solution"	Nazi Camp System	Rescue and Resistance
• Hitler Comes to Power • The Nazi Terror Begins • SS Police State • Nazi Propaganda and Censorship • Nazi Racism • World War II in Europe • The Murder of the Handicapped • German Rule in Occupied Europe	• Jewish Life in Europe Before the Holocaust • Antisemitism • The Boycott of Jewish Businesses • The Nuremberg Race Laws • The "Night of Broken Glass" • The Evian Conference • Voyage of the *St. Louis* • Locating the Victims	• Ghettos in Poland • Life in the Ghettos • Mobile Killing Squads • The Wannsee Conference and the "Final Solution" • At the Killing Centers • Deportations • Auschwitz	• Prisoners of the Camps • "Enemies of the State" • Forced Labor • Death Marches • Liberation • The Survivors • The Nuremberg Trials	• Rescue in Denmark • Jewish Partisans • The Warsaw Ghetto Uprising • Killing Center Revolts • The War Refugee Board • Resistance Inside Germany

Source: Copyright © United States Holocaust Memorial Museum, Washington, D.C.

5. Present your talking points to your peer group, and then prepare a collaborative presentation based on your group's most interesting or important talking points. Each person in your group should prepare and present at least one talking point. Use the outline that follows to organize your presentation. Draft an introduction and conclusion, arrange the order of talking points into broader categories, and assign a speaker to each part of the presentation.

© 2017 College Board. All rights reserved.

ACTIVITY 3.7 continued

2 Divide the class into five groups, and assign each group a column from the chart. Instruct them to assign at least two topics from their column to each person in the group.

3 Model finding the link for one topic and preparing a talking point on that topic by **taking notes** and summarizing key dates and events. Remind students that the goal is to use the information to analyze a theme, or central idea.

4 Give students the web address of the Learning Site [http://www.ushmm.org/outreach/en/] and access to computers with Internet access if possible. If this is not possible, print out copies of the Web page for each topic. You may want to laminate these for future use.

5 Have students **take notes** to prepare their talking points. Students should recreate the organizer on the previous page for their note-taking.

ACTIVITY 3.7 continued

6 After students present their talking points to their group, the group will prepare a collaborative presentation for the class. Make sure students understand all aspects of the outline.

7 Explain what is meant by "arrange the order of talking points into broader categories," and discuss how to transition between talking points. Provide specific models of transitions to clarify understanding.

8 As the students view the presentations, have them **take notes** in their Reader/Writer Notebooks, using a chart like the one shown in Student Step 8.

9 After each presentation, remind the presenters to add their index cards to the collaborative timeline.

10 Ask students to reflect on their learning to determine what they understand and what they still need to learn before Embedded Assessment 1.

11 Allow students time to analyze the completed timeline in a gallery walk. Discuss their observations and reflections.

12 Students should continue to add to this timeline throughout the unit as they expand their knowledge of the Holocaust. For example, when they view film clips from *Life Is Beautiful*, you could add significant dates related to Italy.

▶ASSESS

Review the Scoring Guide and check for understanding during rehearsal of the presentations.

▶ADAPT

If students struggle with preparing individual talking points or organizing and delivering collaborative presentations, provide a successful student model from this activity and continue to reinforce these skills in future activities.

Students will have an additional opportunity to practice preparing a collaborative presentation in an upcoming activity, as well as multiple opportunities to practice speaking and listening skills.

ACTIVITY 3.7 continued

Exploring the Museum

Organization of Presentation	Assignment
Introduction: Begin with a dramatic interpretation of a startling fact, statistic, or anecdote from the site and preview what is to follow in the presentation.	Dramatic Interpretation: Preview:
Transition: **Talking Point 1:** Topic:	
Transition: **Talking Point 2:** Topic:	
Transition: **Talking Point 3:** Topic:	
Transition: **Talking Point 4:** Topic:	
Conclusion: Summarize the main points of your discussion and end with a thoughtful question or thematic connection.	Brief Summary: Question or Connection:

My Notes

6. As you rehearse your presentation, turn to the Scoring Guide criteria on page 197 and use it to evaluate yourself and the rest of your group.
7. Deliver your presentation and add the information from your index cards to the collaborative timeline.
8. As you view the other presentations, take notes in your Reader/Writer Notebook. Use a chart like the one below, drawing a line under each new presentation.

Presentation Topic and Speaker Names	Facts and Information About the Topic	My Opinion and Evaluation of the Talking Points

9. Reflect on your group's collaborative presentation:
   - What did your group do well?
   - What will you do differently next time?

Check Your Understanding

Analyze the collaborative timeline created by your class. What inferences can you make about the Holocaust?

Leveled Differentiated Instruction

In this activity, students may need support to present research. Have students work in pairs as they complete their research.

Em Guide students to write short sentences to prepare talking points on their individual topics.

Provide the sentence frame, *One thing that I learned in my research is that ____.*

Ex Guide students to write more detailed sentences to prepare talking points on their individual topics. Tell students to include direct quotes from their research if possible to support their talking points.

Presenting Voices

ACTIVITY 3.8

Learning Targets

- Research a specific Holocaust victim and present a narrative that captures his or her story.
- Apply an understanding of active and passive voice, by using voice for effect.

Researching the Holocaust

1. During the Holocaust, many people fit into one of the following categories based on either their circumstances or decisions that they made. Try to think of individual examples of each from your reading, research, and/or prior knowledge. Which group do you think was the largest? Which was the smallest?

Victims:

Perpetrators:

Rescuers:

Bystanders:

2. Choose an ID card from the Holocaust Museum website. Take notes on each section of your card, using the chart to organize information.

Name: **Date of Birth:** **Place of Birth:**
Biographical Background:
Experiences from 1933–1939:
War Years:
Future and Fate:

LEARNING STRATEGIES: Note-taking, Graphic Organizer, Drafting, Adding, Substituting, Oral Reading

WORD CONNECTIONS

Roots and Affixes

Perpetrator contains the Latin root *-petrare-*, which means "to bring about." It derives from *pater*, which means "father," as seen in *paternity* and *patriarch*. Adding the suffix *-or*, which means "one that performs a specific action," makes *perpetrator* refer to the person who brings about, or commits, a certain action. It is commonly associated with doing something wrong or illegal.

INDEPENDENT READING LINK

Read and Respond

Find a few instances in the narrative you are reading independently where the author uses the active voice and the passive voice. Rewrite each sentence in the other voice.

My Notes

ACTIVITY 3.8

PLAN

Materials: computers with Internet access or printed copies of Holocaust ID Cards from the Holocaust Memorial Museum site, sentence strips

Suggested Pacing: 2 50-minute class periods

TEACH

1 Help students **brainstorm** different examples of victims, perpetrators, rescuers, and bystanders. Guide them to understand that the bystanders were the largest group, and discuss the implication of this fact.

TEACHER TO TEACHER

In the last activity, students got an overview or "big picture" of the Holocaust. In this activity, they will narrow their focus to one Holocaust victim. The ID cards they will use are the ones that visitors to the U.S. Holocaust Memorial Museum are given in order to put a personal perspective on the tragedy. Victims include survivors as well as people who died; they also include people from a variety of religions, nationalities, genders, and ages. If you print the cards, you might consider laminating them for future use and/or color coding them by gender.

2 Have students select a card and **take notes** as they research their subject.

COMMON CORE STATE STANDARDS

Focus Standards:

W.8.3: Write narratives to develop real or imagined experiences or events using effective technique, relevant descriptive details, and well-structured event sequences.

W.8.3a: Engage and orient the reader by establishing a context and point of view and introducing a narrator and/or characters; organize an event sequence that unfolds naturally and logically.

L.8.1b: Form and use verbs in the active and passive voice.

Additional Standards Addressed:

RI.8.1; RI.8.2; W.8.3b; W.8.3c; W.8.3d; W.8.3e; W.8.5; W.8.7; W.8.10; SL.8.1a; SL.8.4; SL.8.6; L.8.1c; L.8.1d; L.8.3a; L.8.4b; L.8.6

Leveled Differentiated Instruction

In this activity, students may need support to prepare their presentations. Have students pair up to complete an **Active Listening Feedback** graphic organizer. Each partner will present his or her narrative and then respond to the other partner's. You might ask students to add the criteria from the chart to the graphic organizer.

Em Guide students to write short sentences on the graphic organizer.

Ex Guide students to write more detailed feedback on the graphic organizer.

Br Have students record feedback on the graphic organizer and then write a paragraph to summarize their comments.

3 The Language and Writer's Craft section models the use of active and passive voice and conditional and subjunctive mood. Create additional models as a class.

4 After briefly reviewing the elements of effective narrative writing, ask students to respond to the writing prompt independently.

Presenting Voices

My Notes

Language and Writer's Craft: Using Voice and Mood for Effect

Active Versus Passive Voice

When writing or speaking, active voice is usually preferred to passive voice. However, skilled writers and speakers use voice for effect, so sometimes it is more powerful to use the passive voice. Study the model below. How is the effect different in each sentence?

Passive: Relocation camps were used to destroy whole villages.
Active: The Nazis used the camps to empty whole villages of their citizens.

Active voice names the destroyers, passive voice hides the destroyers. Do you as a writer want to show responsibility or hide responsibility?

Mood

You learned in earlier units that conditional mood expresses a hypothetical situation while the subjunctive mood describes a state contrary to fact. When using the verb *to be* in the subjunctive, always use *were* rather than *was*.
For example:

Conditional Mood: *I would have spoken out against the Nazis if I had been alive then.*

Subjunctive Mood: *If I were a prisoner in a concentration camp, would I survive?*

As a class, create additional model sentences relating to the Holocaust. Use passive and active voice and conditional and subjunctive mood effectively and correctly.

Passive:

Active:

Conditional:

Subjunctive:

WRITING to SOURCES **Narrative Writing Prompt**

Think about the research you did on the experiences of one victim of the Holocaust. Draft one victim's story using information from all four sections of the ID card. Be sure to:

- Use narrative technique (dialogue, pacing, description, and reflection) to develop experiences, events, and/or characters.
- Establish a context and use first person point of view.
- Sequence events logically and naturally using your notes as a guide.
- Use voice and mood effectively.

3. Revise your writing to show your understanding of voice and mood by adding or substituting for effect. Also, be sure you have included transitions to convey sequence, signal shifts, and connect the relationships among experiences and events. Reflect on your editing: How does using voice and mood for effect strengthen your writing?

WORD CONNECTIONS

Roots and Affixes

Both *pronounce* and *enunciate* contain the Latin root *-nuntius-* which means "messenger." There is a delicate distinction between the two words. To *pronounce* means to say words correctly. To *enunciate* means to say words clearly as you are pronouncing them.

Presenting the Narrative

4. Before you prepare an oral reading of your narrative, examine the criteria for evaluation below. These criteria also apply to speaking.

Element of Expressive Oral Reading/Speaking	Proficient	Emerging
Enunciation: Pronunciation of words	Enunciation is clear, correct, and effective throughout the reading and enhances the listener's understanding.	Mumbling, incorrect, or indistinct pronunciation hinders the listener's understanding.
Pitch: Vocal highs and lows	Variety in vocal highs and lows enhances the listener's understanding of the passage.	Mostly monotone
Volume: Variety in volume	Variety in volume enhances the listener's understanding of the passage.	Too quiet
Tempo: Appropriate pacing (fast or slow)	Appropriate pacing enhances the listener's understanding of the passage.	Too fast or too slow
Phrasing: Pausing at appropriate points and for emphasis	Pauses and emphasis enhance the listener's understanding of the passage.	No pauses or emphasized words

5. Prepare and present an oral reading of your revised narrative to a small group of your peers. Use the chart above to provide feedback about each speaker's strengths and weaknesses.

WORD CONNECTIONS

Roots and Affixes

The word *monotone* includes the prefix *mono-*, meaning "one," as in *monologue*, *monomania*, and *monocle*. Thus *monotone* means "one tone," or "without inflection."

Check Your Understanding

How did the process of researching a person from the Holocaust and assuming that person's identity add to your understanding of the Holocaust?

ACTIVITY 3.8 continued

5 Ask students to edit their narratives for voice and mood. You may then want students to copy—onto a sentence strip—a sentence for you to review. Display strong examples for future reference. After students respond to the reflection question, briefly discuss as a class to check for understanding.

6 As a class, discuss criteria for expressive oral reading and speaking. Read the information in the chart.

7 After students model proficient and emerging reading for each element, ask them to prepare their oral reading.

8 As students present in their small groups, choose one or two students to perform their oral reading for the whole class.

9 Asking students to reflect on their strengths and goals for improvement will keep them focused on the skills needed for the Embedded Assessment.

ASSESS

In their response to the narrative writing prompt, check that students understand the moods presented and how to use active and passive voice for effect.

ADAPT

If students need more practice with oral reading, have them select a passage to rehearse and read for their next Literature Circle meeting.

If students need more practice distinguishing between active and passive voice, revisit a text from a previous activity and conduct a **close reading** for this skill.

ACTIVITY 3.9

▶PLAN

Materials: DVD: *Life Is Beautiful*, directed by Roberto Benigni
Suggested Pacing: 2 50-minute class periods

▶TEACH

1 Set up the film clips by explaining that *Life Is Beautiful* is about a father and son trying to survive in a concentration camp in Italy during World War II. The clips begin when they are on a truck being transported to the train station. The mother is not Jewish, so she has not been taken and is not on the truck.

TEACHER TO TEACHER

If you prefer, you can use another film about the Holocaust in this activity. There are many to choose from, including *The Devil's Arithmetic and The Boy in the Striped Pajamas.*

2 Read the brief summary introducing the film, and have students **pair-share** their **predictions**.

ACTIVITY 3.9

Finding Light in Film

LEARNING STRATEGIES:
Predicting, Graphic Organizer, Drafting, Oral Reading, Discussion Groups

Learning Targets

- Explain how screenwriters use literary elements such as setting, character, plot, and mood to develop a theme.
- Present an effective oral reading and transform a written draft into talking points for discussion.

Finding Light in the Darkness

1. Return to Activity 3.2 and reread the quotes. Notice that each speaker uses the imagery of light and darkness to express his or her ideas about good and evil, love and hatred, hope and depression—all of which are opposites. How do you think this conflict between opposites might be portrayed in film?

Life Is Beautiful is a fictional story about a family in Italy that is sent to a concentration camp. The father and son are Jewish, but the mother is not. The father tries to protect his son from the ugly realities of the Holocaust by making it seem as if they are playing a game whose prize is a real tank.

2. Based on the information above, predict conflicts that the father might encounter as he tries to convince his son that the concentration camp is just a game.

3. Work in groups of four to take notes on setting, character, plot, and mood in each film clip. Share notes and trade jobs after each clip to complete the graphic organizer on the next page.

My Notes

COMMON CORE STATE STANDARDS

Focus Standards:

SL.8.1: Engage effectively in a range of collaborative discussions (one-on-one, in groups, and teacher-led) with diverse partners on Grade 8 topics, texts, and issues, building on others' ideas and expressing their own clearly.

SL.8.1a: Come to discussions prepared, having read or researched material under study; explicitly draw on that preparation by referring to evidence on the topic, text, or issue to probe and reflect on ideas under discussion.

Additional Standards Addressed:

W.8.2a; W.8.2b; W.8.2e; W.8.5; W.8.10; SL.8.1b; SL.8.1c; SL.8.2; SL.8.4; SL.8.6

Setting	Character(s)	Plot	Mood
Clip 1 A father and son are on a truck, and then at a train station, in Italy during the Holocaust.	The father, Guido, tries to cheer up his son. The son, Joshua, is confused. The mother, Dora, wants to be with her family.	The son asks his father what is happening. The mother joins them.	The mood is nervous and a little hysterical, and then becomes serious and desperate.
Clip 2			
Clip 3			
Clip 4			

© 2017 College Board. All rights reserved.

ACTIVITY 3.9 continued

3 Divide students into groups of four, and assign each group to take notes on one literary element during the first clip. After each clip, discuss literary elements to check for understanding before asking students to rotate columns.

Leveled Differentiated Instruction

In this activity, some students may benefit from using sentence frames to complete the graphic organizer.

Em *The setting is ___. The characters in the clip are ___. The plot in this clip is ___. The mood is ___.*

Ex *The clip takes place ___. The character ___ is ___. The character ___ feels ___. The character ___ wants ___. What happens in the clip is ___. The mood is ___ and then it becomes ___.*

ACTIVITY 3.9 continued

4 Have students co-construct a response to the writing prompt and then present an oral reading to another pair for feedback.

Leveled Differentiated Instruction

In this activity, students may need support building and expressing an opinion. Have students complete an **Opinion Builder** graphic organizer to gather reasons for their opinion.

Em Prompt students to find support for their opinions using the following questions: *What evidence from the film influenced your opinion? Have you had any life experiences that influenced your opinion?*

Ex Tell students to use film evidence and relevant background knowledge to support their opinion. Offer support to students as necessary while they identify reasons that support their opinion.

5 Instruct students to work in their groups to prepare talking points for a class discussion. Based on experience, students should distinguish between effective and ineffective talking points. Use examples from previous activities to support this discussion.

6 After the class discussion, have students independently prepare talking points for a small-group discussion based on the discussion prompts provided.

7 During discussion, make sure students **take notes**. Circulate to assess the quality of ideas and provide specific feedback about ways to improve. Select a few student models to share with the class.

8 Ask students to independently reflect on how literary texts can help one better understand real-life events from history.

▶ASSESS

Review student work to determine the level of theme analysis and the quality of written responses.

▶ADAPT

If students provide superficial theme analysis or create ineffective talking points, display and discuss successful student models.

ACTIVITY 3.9 continued

Finding Light in Film

My Notes

WRITING to SOURCES **Expository Writing Prompt**

How is the theme "finding light in the darkness" expressed in the film? Write a draft that explains how setting, characters, and/or plot are used to develop theme. Be sure to:

- Begin with a topic sentence that responds to the prompt.
- Provide textual evidence and commentary for support.
- Use precise diction to inform or explain.

Prepare and present an oral reading of your written draft. Use the chart in the previous activity to guide your preparation. Present your response to another pair of students. Provide feedback about ideas and oral reading.

Check Your Understanding

Work with your group to transform your draft into talking points to guide a class discussion about the theme. After your class discussion, prepare talking points for a small group discussion on at least two of the following prompts. Be sure to include textual evidence from the film to support your opinion. During your small group discussion, create and use a graphic organizer like the one on page 179 to record and respond to the other speakers' talking points.

Discussion Prompts:

A. Is it disrespectful to make a film about the Holocaust that has so much comedy in it?

B. What aspects of the Holocaust, as portrayed in the film, are similar to or different from what you learned in your research?

C. How and when did the mood change during the film clips, and what settings, characters, or events caused those shifts?

Dramatic Tone Shifts

ACTIVITY 3.10

Learning Target

- Analyze how dialogue is used in a play to develop character and plot, convey tone, and reveal theme.

Preview

In this activity, you will read part of a play. Pay attention to the tone at the beginning of the scene and at the end.

Setting a Purpose for Reading

- As you read the dialogue, underline words and phrases that indicate the tone of how the characters are feeling.
- Circle unknown words and phrases. Try to determine the meaning of the words by using context clues, word parts, or a dictionary.
- Actors often highlight their lines when they get a new script. The beginning of the passage lists the characters involved in the scene. Choose one and highlight each instance they speak.

LEARNING STRATEGIES: Skimming/Scanning, Marking the Text, Close Reading, Rereading, Oral Reading, Discussion Groups, Drafting, Adding

My Notes

ABOUT THE AUTHOR
Frances Goodrich (1891–1984) and Albert Hackett (1900–1995) were both writers and actors who married in 1931. Together they wrote numerous plays and film screenplays. In 1955 they adapted Anne Frank's *The Diary of a Young Girl* for the stage, where it received several Tony Award nominations, including a win for Best Play. The play also was awarded the Pulitzer Prize for Drama in 1956.

INDEPENDENT READING LINK
Read and Connect
Find an instance in the narrative you are reading independently where the tone shifts dramatically. How is it similar to or different than the tone shift in the play in Activity 3.10?

Drama

from
The Diary of **Anne Frank**

by Frances Goodrich and Albert Hackett

Families living in the hidden attic:
Mr. Frank and Mrs. Frank: Anne and Margot Frank's parents
Margot and Anne: sisters, 18 and 13 years old
Mr. van Daan and Mrs. van Daan: Mr. van Daan worked with Otto Frank in Amsterdam
Peter van Daan: their son
Mr. Dussel: older; dentist who also lives in the attic
Others:
Miep Gies: close friend of the Frank family
Eisenhower: the voice of the American general
Scene: Anne, Mr. Dussel, Mr. van Daan, Mr. Frank, Mrs. van Daan, Mrs. Frank, Margot, Peter, Miep, Eisenhower

(Night. Everyone is asleep. Suddenly, Mrs. Frank sits up in bed.)

Mrs. Frank: *(In a whisper.)* Otto. Listen. The rat!

ACTIVITY 3.10

PLAN

Materials: DVD: *The Diary of Anne Frank* (optional)
Suggested Pacing: 2 50-minute class periods

TEACH

1 Read the Preview and the Setting a Purpose for Reading sections with your students. Help them understand what they will be annotating in the scene.

2 **FIRST READ:** Based on the complexity of the passage and your knowledge of your students, you may choose to conduct the first reading in a variety of ways:

- independent reading
- paired reading
- small group reading
- choral reading
- read aloud

3 As students are reading, monitor their progress. Be sure they are engaged with the text and annotating instances that reveal the tone of the scene. Evaluate whether the selected reading mode is effective.

4 Based on the observations you made during the first reading, you may want to adjust your reading mode. For example, you may decide for the second reading to read aloud certain complex passages, or you may group students differently.

COMMON CORE STATE STANDARDS

Focus Standards:

RL.8.2: Determine a theme or central idea of a text and analyze its development over the course of the text, including its relationship to the characters, setting, and plot; provide an objective summary of the text.

RL.8.3: Analyze how particular lines of dialogue or incidents in a story or drama propel the action, reveal aspects of a character, or provoke a decision.

Additional Standards Addressed:

RL.8.1; RL.8.4; W.8.2a; W.8.4; W.8.5; W.8.9a; SL.8.1a; L.8.1b; L.8.1c; L.8.2a; L.8.2b; L.8.3a; L.8.6

ACTIVITY 3.10 continued

TEACHER TO TEACHER

If you have a copy of the DVD of *The Diary of Anne Frank*, use this scene as a visual prompt before reading. Each student should focus on the role he or she will play and **take notes** on how the actor delivers those lines.

Leveled Differentiated Instruction

Some students may benefit from analyzing the key ideas and details as they read in order to be sure they understand the drama.

Em Guide students to complete a **Key Ideas and Details Chart** graphic organizer as they read to help them understand the text.

Ex Guide students to write notes about the key ideas and details from the text using the sentence frames. *The key idea of the drama is ____. One supporting detail is ____. Another supporting detail is ____.*

Br Have students write independently about the key ideas and details from the text as they read.

Support Have students list details from the drama and write about how each detail affects the tone of the story.

ACTIVITY 3.10 continued

Dramatic Tone Shifts

gnawing: biting or chewing

My Notes

Mr. Frank: Edith, please. Go back to sleep. *(He turns over. Mrs. Frank gets up, quietly creeps to the main room, standstill. There is a tiny crunching sound. In the darkness, a figure is faintly illuminated, crouching over,* **gnawing** *on something. Mrs. Frank moves closer, turns on the light. Trembling, Mr. van Daan jumps to his feet. He is clutching a piece of bread.)*

Mrs. Frank: My God, I don't believe it! The bread! He's stealing the bread! *(Pointing at Mr. van Daan.)* Otto, look!

Mr. van Daan: No, no. Quiet.

Mr. Frank: *(As everyone comes into the main room in their nightclothes.)* Hermann, for God's sake!

Mrs. van Daan: *(Opening her eyes sleepily.)* What is it? What's going on?

Mrs. Frank: It's your husband. Stealing our bread!

Mrs. van Daan: It can't be. Putti, what are you doing?

Mr. van Daan: Nothing.

Mr. Dussel: It wasn't a rat. It was him.

Mr. van Daan: Never before! Never before!

Mrs. Frank: I don't believe you. If he steals once, he'll steal again. Every day I watch the children get thinner. And he comes in the middle of the night and steals food that should go to them!

Mr. van Daan: *(His head in his hands.)* Oh my God. My God.

Mr. Frank: Edith. Please.

Margot: Mama, it was only one piece of bread.

Mr. van Daan: *(Putting the bread on the table. In a panic.)* Here. *(Mrs. Frank swats the bread away.)*

Mr. Frank: Edith, he couldn't help himself! It could happen to any one of us.

Mrs. Frank: *(Quiet.)* I want him to go.

Mrs. van Daan: Go? Go where?

Mrs. Frank: Anywhere.

Mrs. van Daan: You don't mean what you're saying.

Mr. Dussel: I understand you, Mrs. Frank. But it really would be impossible for them—

Mrs. Frank: They have to! I can't take it with them here.

Mr. Frank: Edith, you know how upset you've been these past—

Mrs. Frank: That has nothing to do with it.

Mr. Frank: We're all living under terrible strain. *(Looking at Mr. van Daan.)* It won't happen again.

Mr. van Daan: Never. I promise.

Mrs. Frank: I want them to leave.

Mrs. van Daan: You'd put us out on the street?

SCAFFOLDING THE TEXT-DEPENDENT QUESTIONS

1. Key Ideas and Details (RL.8.1) **Quote a line of dialogue that expresses Mrs. Frank's anger and explain why she is so angry.** Read Mrs. Frank's first several lines of dialogue. Why is she angry at Mr. van Daan? What does she say about him to express her anger?

2. Key Ideas and Details (RL.8.3) **Examine Mr. Frank's dialogue in this scene. How does it show his role in the family and in this particular scene?** What does Mr. Frank say to his wife after his wife yells at Mr. van Daan? What is his attitude toward the situation?

3. Key Ideas and Details (RL.8.2) **How does Miep's news of the invasion change the tone of the scene? Characterize the new tone and explain how it has changed.** How are the characters acting before Miep brings the news? What news does Miep bring when she arrives in the attic? How do the other characters react when she brings this news?

Mrs. Frank: There are other hiding places. Miep will find something. Don't worry about the money. I'll find you the money.

Mrs. van Daan: Mr. Frank, you told my husband you'd never forget what he did for you when you first came to Amsterdam.

Mrs. Frank: If my husband had any **obligation** to you, it's paid for.

obligation: legal or moral duty or commitment

Mr. Frank: Edith, I've never seen you like this, for God's sake.

Anne: You can't throw Peter out! He hasn't done anything.

Mrs. Frank: Peter can stay.

Peter: I wouldn't feel right without Father.

Anne: Mother, please. They'll be killed on the street.

Margot: Anne's right. You can't send them away.

Mrs. Frank: They can stay till Miep finds them a place. But we're switching rooms. I don't want him near the food.

Mr. Dussel: Let's divide it up right now.

Margot: *(As he gets a sack of potatoes.)* We're not going to divide up some rotten potatoes.

Mr. Dussel: *(Dividing the potatoes into piles.)* Mrs. Frank, Mr. Frank, Margot, Anne, Peter, Mrs. van Daan, Mr. van Daan, myself… Mrs. Frank, Mr. Frank…

Margot: *(Overlapping.)* Mr. Dussel, please. Don't! No more. No more, Mr. Dussel! I beg you. I can't bear it. *(Mr. Dussel continues counting nonstop. In tears.)* Stop! I can't take it …

Mrs. Frank: All this … all that's happening …

Mr. Frank: Enough! Margot. Mr. Dussel. Everyone—back to your rooms. Come, Edith. Mr. Dussel, I think the potatoes can wait. *(Mr. Dussel goes on counting. Tearing the sack from Mr. Dussel, the potatoes spilling.)* Just let them wait! *(He holds out his hand for Mrs. Frank. They all go back to their rooms. Peter and Mrs. van Daan pick up the scattered potatoes. Not looking at each other, Mr. and Mrs. van Daan move to their separate beds. The buzzer rings frantically, breaking the silence.)* Miep? At this hour? *(Miep runs up the stairs, as everyone comes back into the main room.)*

Miep: *(Out of breath.)* Everyone … everyone … the most wonderful, incredible news!

Mr. Frank: What is it?

Miep: *(Tears streaming down her cheeks.)* The invasion. The invasion has begun! *(They stare at her, unable to grasp what she is telling them.)* Did you hear me? Did you hear what I said? The invasion! It's happening—right now! *(As Mrs. Frank begins to cry.)* I rushed to tell you before the workmen got here. You can feel it in the streets—the excitement! This is it. They've landed on the coast of Normandy.

Peter: The British?

Miep: British, Americans … everyone! More than four thousand ships! Look—I brought a map. *(Quickly she unrolls a map of Normandy on the table.)*

Mr. Frank: *(Weeping, embracing his daughters.)* For over a year we've hoped for this moment.

GRAMMAR & USAGE
Pronoun Antecedents

A pronoun takes the place of a noun or another pronoun, called its **antecedent.** Mrs. Frank speaks the sentence "They have to!" To whom is she referring? The preceding part of the play indicates that Mrs. Frank is referring to the van Daans. How confusing would this be, however, if you did not know the antecedent (the van Daans in this example)?

When using pronouns in your writing, make sure you have clearly stated the nouns to which your pronouns refer. As you read, look for other examples of antecedents.

My Notes

TEACHER TO TEACHER

To illustrate the uses of different punctuation marks, point out the following examples:

Ellipses: "Everyone ... everyone ..."

Colon: "Mr. Frank: What is it?"

Exclamation point: "Enough!"

Dash: "Look—I brought a map."

Parentheses: "*(Out of breath.)*"

5 **SECOND READ:** During the second reading, students will be returning to the text to answer the text-dependent comprehension questions. You may choose to have students reread and work on the questions in a variety of ways:

- independently
- in pairs
- in small groups
- together as a class

6 Have students answer the text-dependent questions. If they have difficulty, scaffold the questions by rephrasing them or breaking them down into smaller parts. See the Scaffolding the Text-Dependent Questions boxes for suggestions.

Dramatic Tone Shifts

GRAMMAR & USAGE
Punctuation

Punctuation helps to clarify meaning in sentences. Notice the varied punctuation on these pages.

Ellipses (...) are used to show pauses or to show that words are omitted.

A **colon** (:) is used in a script to follow the name of the speaker. It is also used to introduce a list of a second clause that explains or expands on the first.

An **exclamation point** (!) is used to show excitement.

A **dash** (—) is used to set off or emphasize content.

Parentheses ( ) set off comments or additional information in a sentence.

convulsive: marked by violent shaking

WORD CONNECTIONS

Word Relationships

Concerted and *conjunction* are similar in meaning. *Concerted* describes the combined efforts of people or groups that work together to achieve a goal. Think of a concert where musicians and singers perform together to make music. You could also say these musicians are working in *conjunction*, meaning they are working together at the same time to put on a great show.

Miep: *(Pointing.)* Cherbourg. The first city. They're fighting for it right now.

Mr. Dussel: How many days will it take them from Normandy to the Netherlands?

Mr. Frank: *(Taking Mrs. Frank in his arms.)* Edith, what did I tell you?

Mr. Dussel: *(Placing the potatoes on the map to hold it down as he checks the cities.)* Cherbourg. Caen. Pont L'Eveque. Paris. And then … Amsterdam! *(Mr. van Daan breaks into a* ***convulsive*** *sob.)*

Mrs. van Daan: Putti.

Mr. Frank: Hermann, didn't you hear what Miep said? We'll be free … soon. *(Mr. Dussel turns on the radio. Amidst much static, Eisenhower's voice is heard from his broadcast of June 6, 1944.)*

Eisenhower: *(Voice-over.)* People of Western Europe, a landing was made this morning on the coast of France by troops of the Allied Expeditionary Force. This landing is part of the concerted United Nations plan for the liberation of Europe …

Mr. Frank: *(Wiping tears from his eyes.)* Listen. That's General Eisenhower. *(Anne pulls Margot down to her room.)*

Eisenhower: *(Voice-over, fading away.)* … made in conjunction with our great Russian allies. I have this message for all of you. Although the initial assault may not have been made in your own country, the hour of your liberation is approaching. All patriots …

Anne: *(Hugging Margot.)* Margot, can you believe it? The invasion! Home. That means we could be going home.

Margot: I don't even know what home would be like anymore. I can't imagine it—we've been away for so long.

Anne: Oh, I can! I can imagine every little detail. And just to be outside again. The sky, Margot! Just to walk along the canal!

Margot: *(As they sit down on Anne's bed.)* I'm afraid to let myself think about it. To have a real meal—*(They laugh together.)* It doesn't seem possible! Will anything taste the same? Look the same? *(Growing more and more serious.)* I don't know if anything will ever feel normal again. How can we go back … really?

Second Read

- Reread the scene to answer these text-dependent questions.
- Write any additional questions you have about the text in your Reader/Writer Notebook.

1. **Key Ideas and Details:** Quote a line of dialogue that expresses Mrs. Frank's anger and explain why she is so angry.

"Every day I watch the children get thinner." Mrs. Frank is so angry because everyone is short of food, and Mr. van Daan has taken food that should have been shared by the group. RL.8.1

2. **Key Ideas and Details:** Examine Mr. Frank's dialogue in this scene. How does it show his role in the family and in this particular scene?

   Mr. Frank says things like: "Edith, he couldn't help himself. It could happen to any one of us." "We're all living under terrible strain." Mr Frank is trying to be understanding and mitigate Mrs. Frank's anger. He tries to soften her outrage. RL.8.3

3. **Key Ideas and Details:** How does Miep's news of the invasion change the tone of the scene? Characterize the new tone and explain how it has changed.

   Miep's news changes the tone from despair, anger, and hopelessness to a sense of hope and possibilities for a future. RL.8.2

My Notes

Working from the Text

4. In your group, assign roles for an oral reading of the scene.
5. Prepare for an oral reading by skimming/scanning the scene independently, marking and annotating your character's lines:
   - Mark connotative diction and label the tone you intend to use in speaking lines of dialogue.
   - Mark words of the dialogue that you will emphasize with a shift in volume or pitch.
   - Place slash marks in places where you will pause for effect.
6. Conduct an oral reading in your group, using your marks and annotations as a guide.
7. Discuss how and when the tone shifted in the play. Did setting, character, or plot cause the shift in tone? Everyone is on edge from living so closely together for so long and fearing capture. When they hear the radio announcement that the war may soon end, they become excited and hopeful about being free again. This tone shift is caused by character, specifically Miep and General Eisenhower.

Check Your Understanding

WRITING to SOURCES **Expository Writing Prompt**

Think about the characters in the scene from *The Diary of Anne Frank*. How does their dialogue reveal the characters and the conflicts of the story and increase the reader's understanding of an aspect of the Holocaust experience? Draft a response that explains how specific dialogue is used to develop character(s) or plot and to reveal theme. Be sure to:

- Begin with a topic sentence that responds to the prompt.
- Provide textual evidence and commentary for support.
- Use variety in sentence mood and voice.

Revise your writing to add transitions to clarify the relationships among ideas and concepts.

© 2017 College Board. All rights reserved.

ACTIVITY 3.10 continued

7 Divide students into large groups of 9–12. Instruct them to assign roles for the first scene. Larger groups may need to share roles, while in smaller groups students may need to take multiple roles.

8 Model **marking/annotating** the text for tone, volume, pitch, and phrasing. Instruct students to **skim/scan** for their lines and **mark the text** accordingly.

9 After groups conduct an oral reading of the scene, analyze tone shifts as a class.

10 Ask students to think about and share successes and challenges relating to reading and analyzing the scene. Based on the discussion, set class goals for reading and speaking.

11 Discuss tone shifts and the events, characters, or lines of dialogue that facilitate those shifts. Provide examples from texts such as *Life Is Beautiful* or *Terrible Things*.

12 If you have the time, ask students to repeat the process, reading different characters for the second reading. Observe reading and speaking to determine successes and challenges and to identify improvement.

13 Instruct students to respond to the writing prompt independently and then revise and reflect on their writing.

ASSESS

Review student work to assess the level of analysis and explanation and to assess understanding of voice and transitions.

ADAPT

If skills are emerging in some areas, model a successful student response to the writing prompt. Then, ask students to respond to the same or a similar prompt in response to the text in the next activity.

ACTIVITY 3.11

▶PLAN

Suggested Pacing: 2 50-minute class periods

TEACHER TO TEACHER

Prior to the lesson, chunk the text into natural sections to facilitate discussion.

Leveled Differentiated Instruction

Support students' comprehension by asking them to make predictions as they read the story.

Em Guide students to work with a partner to write their predictions after reading paragraph 15 using the sentence frames. *After Shmuel left his home, I think that ___. Bruno's family probably ___.* Have students note clues about what is happening as they read. Then have students revisit their predictions after reading using the sentence frames. *I predicted that ___. In the story ___.*

Ex Have students work with a partner to make a prediction about what will happen in the story after reading paragraph 15. Student pairs should revisit their prediction after reading and compare it to what actually happened.

▶TEACH

1 Read the Preview and the Setting a Purpose for Reading sections with your students. Help them understand what they should annotate.

2 **FIRST READ:** Based on the complexity of the passage and your knowledge of your students, you may choose to conduct the first reading in a variety of ways:

- independent reading
- paired reading
- small group reading
- choral reading
- read aloud

ACTIVITY 3.11

The Wrong Side of the Fence

LEARNING STRATEGIES: Marking the Text, Note-taking, Graphic Organizer, Close Reading, Outlining, Summarizing, Rehearsal

My Notes

Learning Targets

- Analyze an excerpt of a Holocaust narrative and prepare talking points to present in a panel discussion.
- Deliver an oral reading and orally explain the thematic focus of a passage.

Preview

In this activity, you will read about two boys with different perspectives of the Holocaust.

Setting a Purpose for Reading

- As you read the passage, underline words and phrases that describe the setting.
- Draw squiggly lines under words and phrases that describe the boys' characters.
- Circle unknown words and phrases. Try to determine the meaning of the words by using context clues, word parts, or a dictionary.

ABOUT THE AUTHOR

John Boyne (1971–) is an Irish writer who began his writing career creating short stories. He published *The Boy in the Striped Pajamas* in 2006, and this novel proceeded to win multiple international awards. The novel also was made into a film.

Fiction

from

The Boy in the Striped Pajamas

by John Boyne

1 Two boys were sitting on opposite sides of a fence.

2 "All I know is this," began Shmuel. "Before we came here I lived with my mother and father and my brother Josef in a small flat above the store where Papa makes his watches. Every morning we ate our breakfast together at seven o'clock and while we went to school, Papa mended the watches that people brought to him and made new ones too. I had a beautiful watch that he gave me but I don't have it anymore. It had a golden face and I wound it up every night before I went to sleep and it always told the right time."

3 "What happened to it?" asked Bruno.

4 "They took it from me," said Shmuel.

5 "Who?"

6 "The soldiers of course," said Shmuel as if it was the most obvious thing in the world.

COMMON CORE STATE STANDARDS

Focus Standards:

RL.8.1: Cite the textual evidence that most strongly supports an analysis of what the text says explicitly as well as inferences drawn from the text.

W.8.9: Draw evidence from literary or informational texts to support analysis, reflection, and research.

W.8.9a: Apply *Grade 8 Reading standards* to literature (e.g., "Analyze how a modern work of fiction draws on themes, patterns of events, or character types from myths, traditional stories, or religious works such as the Bible, including describing how the material is rendered new").

SL.8.1: Engage effectively in a range of collaborative discussions (one-on-one, in groups, and teacher-led) with diverse partners

7 "And then one day things started to change," he continued. "I came home from school and my mother was making armbands for us from a special cloth and drawing a star on each one. Like this." Using his finger he drew a design in the dusty ground beneath him.

The star of David. 

8 "And every time we left the house, she told us we had to wear one of these armbands."

9 "My father wears one too," said Bruno. "On his uniform. It's very nice. It's bright red with a black-and-white design on it." Using his finger he drew another design in the dusty ground on his side of the fence.

A swastika. 

10 "Yes, but they're different, aren't they?" said Shmuel.

11 "No one's ever given me an armband," said Bruno.

12 "But I never asked to wear one," said Shmuel.

13 "All the same," said Bruno, "I think I'd quite like one. I don't know which one I'd prefer though, your one or father's."

14 Shmuel shook his head and continued with his story. He didn't often think about these things anymore because remembering his old life above the watch shop made him very sad.

15 "We wore the armbands for a few months," he said. "And then things changed again. I came home one day and Mama said we couldn't live in our home any more."

16 "That happened to me too!" said Bruno, delighted that he wasn't the only boy who'd been forced to move. "The Fury came for dinner, you see, and the next thing I knew we moved here. And I *hate* it here," he added. "Did he come to your house and do the same thing?"

17 "No, but when we were told we couldn't live in our house we had to move to a different part of Cracow, where the soldiers built a big wall and my mother and father and my brother and I all had to live in one room."

18 "All of you?" asked Bruno. "In one room?"

"And not just us," said Shmuel. "There was another family there and the mother and father were always fighting with each other and one of the sons was bigger than me and hit me even when I did nothing wrong."

19 "You can't have all lived in the one room," said Bruno. "That doesn't make any sense."

20 "All of us," said Shmuel. "Eleven in total."

Bruno opened his mouth to **contradict** him again—he didn't really believe that eleven people could live in the same room together—but changed his mind.

My Notes

contradict: to express an opposite thought

ACTIVITY 3.11 continued

Text Complexity
Overall: Accessible
Lexile: 700L
Qualitative: Moderate Difficulty
Task: Moderate (Analyze)

3 As students are reading, monitor their progress. Be sure they are engaged with the text and annotating words and phrases that establish the passage's setting. Evaluate whether the selected reading mode is effective.

4 Based on the observations you made during the first reading, you may want to adjust your reading mode. For example, you may decide for the second reading to read aloud certain complex passages, or you may group students differently.

COMMON CORE STATE STANDARDS

on Grade 8 topics, texts, and issues, building on others' ideas and expressing their own clearly.

SL.8.1a: Come to discussions prepared, having read or researched material under study; explicitly draw on that preparation by referring to evidence on the topic, text, or issue to probe and reflect on ideas under discussion.

Additional Standards Addressed:
RL.8.2; RL.8.3; RL.8.4; RL.8.10; W.8.2a; W.8.2c; W.8.10; SL.8.1b; SL.8.3; SL.8.4; SL.8.6

Teacher Notes

The Wrong Side of the Fence

My Notes

21 "We lived there for some more months," continued Shmuel, "all of us in that one room. There was one small window in it but I didn't like to look out of it because then I would see the wall and I hated the wall because our real home was on the other side of it. And this part of town was a bad part because it was always noisy and it was impossible to sleep. And I hated Luka, who was the boy who kept hitting me even when I did nothing wrong."

22 "Gretel hits me sometimes," said Bruno. "She's my sister," he added. "And a Hopeless Case. But soon I'll be bigger and stronger than she is and she won't know what's hit her then."

23 "Then one day the soldiers all came with huge trucks," continued Shmuel, who didn't seem all that interested in Gretel. "And everyone was told to leave the houses. Lots of people didn't want to and they hid wherever they could find a place but in the end I think they caught everyone. And the trucks took us to a train and the train …" He hesitated for a moment and bit his lip. Bruno thought he was going to start crying and couldn't understand why.

24 "The train was horrible," said Shmuel. "There were too many of us in the carriages for one thing. And there was no air to breathe. And it smelled awful."

25 "That's because you all crowded onto one train," said Bruno, remembering the two trains he had seen at the station when he left Berlin. "When we came here, there was another one on the other side of the platform but no one seemed to see it. That was the one we got. You should have got on it too."

26 "I don't think we would have been allowed," said Shmuel, shaking his head. "We weren't able to get out of our carriage."

27 "The door's at the end," explained Bruno.

28 "There weren't any doors," said Shmuel.

29 "Of course there were doors," said Bruno with a sigh. "They're at the end," he repeated. "Just past the **buffet** section."

buffet: a counter or table where food is served

30 "There weren't any doors," insisted Shmuel. "If there had been, we would have gotten off."

31 Bruno mumbled something under his breath along the lines of "Of course there were," but he didn't say it very loud so Shmuel didn't hear.

32 "When the train finally stopped," continued Shmuel, "we were in a very cold place and we all had to walk here."

33 "We had a car," said Bruno, out loud now.

34 "And Mama was taken away from us, and Papa and Josef and I were put into the huts over there and that's where we've been since."

35 Shmuel looked very sad when he told this story and Bruno didn't know why; it didn't seem like such a terrible thing to him, and after all much the same thing happened to him.

36 "Are there many other boys over there?" asked Bruno.

37 "Hundreds," said Shmuel.

38 Bruno's eyes opened wide. "Hundreds?" he said, amazed. "That's not fair at all. There's no one to play with on this side of the fence. Not a single person."

WORD CONNECTIONS

Multiple Meaning Words

The word *carriage* can refer to many things, all stemming from its root meaning "carry." We know it as a wheeled vehicle drawn by a horse, a device to transport babies (a baby carriage), or any general support frame to carry a heavy object (like a car's undercarriage). The British use it specifically to refer to a railroad passenger car. It can also be used to describe a person's bearing, or the manner in which they move their head and body.

SCAFFOLDING THE TEXT-DEPENDENT QUESTIONS

1. Key Ideas and Details (RL.8.3) **Analyze the description and dialogue. Why is the watch so important to Shmuel? What does it symbolize for him?** Read paragraphs 2 through 6. What happened to Shmuel's watch? What connection does it have to the home that he has lost?

2. Key Ideas and Details (RL.8.3) **What does Bruno not seem to understand about their different situations, as shown in the conversation about the armbands?** How do the armbands discussed in paragraphs 7 through 9 symbolize the differences between Bruno and Shmuel?

3. Key Ideas and Details (RL.8.1) **What inferences can you make about the setting? Provide details that help form your inferences.** What are some details in the story that indicate

Teacher Notes

My Notes

39 "We don't play," said Shmuel.

40 "Don't play? Why ever not?"

41 "What would we play?" he asked, his face looking confused at the idea of it.

42 "Well, I don't know," said Bruno. "All sorts of things. Football, for example. Or exploration. What's the exploration like over there anyway? Any good?"

43 Shmuel shook his head and didn't answer. He looked back towards the huts and turned back to Bruno then. He didn't want to ask the next question but the pains in his stomach made him.

44 "You don't have any food on you, do you?" he asked.

45 "Afraid not," said Bruno. "I meant to bring some chocolate but I forgot."

46 "Chocolate," said Shmuel very slowly, his tongue moving out from behind his teeth. "I've only ever had chocolate once."

47 "Only once? I love chocolate. I can't get enough of it although Mother says it'll rot my teeth."

48 "You don't have any bread, do you?"

49 Bruno shook his head. "Nothing at all," he said. "Dinner isn't served until half past six. What time do you have yours?"

50 Shmuel shrugged his shoulders and pulled himself to his feet. "I think I'd better get back," he said.

51 "Perhaps you can come to dinner with us one evening," said Bruno, although he wasn't sure it was a very good idea.

52 "Perhaps," said Shmuel, although he didn't sound convinced.

53 "Or I could come to you," said Bruno. "Perhaps I could come and meet your friends," he added hopefully. He had hoped that Shmuel would suggest this himself but there didn't seem to be any sign of that.

54 "You're on the wrong side of the fence though," said Shmuel.

55 "I could crawl under," said Bruno, reaching down and lifting the wire off the ground. In the centre, between two wooden telegraph poles, it lifted quite easily and a boy as small as Bruno could easily fit through.

SCAFFOLDING THE TEXT-DEPENDENT QUESTIONS

what kind of fence is separating the boys? Which boy is on which side of the fence?

4. Craft and Structure (RL.8.4) **Examine paragraph 16 that talks about "The Fury." Who is this and why does Bruno call him "The Fury"?** In paragraph 16 Bruno mentions "The Fury." Who is Bruno referring to that has a title that sounds similar to "The Fury"?

5. Key Ideas and Details (RL.8.1) **Quote one or more lines of dialogue that show how Bruno's perspective lacks an understanding of Shmuel's situation and explain why.** How do paragraphs 17 through 20 indicate that Bruno lacks understanding of Shmuel's situation?

6. Craft and Structure (RL.8.4) **What specifically are the carriages mentioned in paragraph 24?** Read paragraph 24. Does "carriages" refer to the individual train cars or the whole train?

5 **SECOND READ:** During the second reading, students will be returning to the text to answer the text-dependent comprehension questions. You may choose to have students reread and work on the questions in a variety of ways:

- independently
- in pairs
- in small groups
- together as a class

6 Have students answer the text-dependent questions. If they have difficulty, scaffold the questions by rephrasing them or breaking them down into smaller parts. See the Scaffolding the Text-Dependent Questions boxes for suggestions.

The Wrong Side of the Fence

My Notes

56 Shmuel watched him do this and backed away nervously. "I have to get back," he said.

57 "Some other afternoon then," said Bruno.

58 "I'm not supposed to be here. If they catch me I'll be in trouble."

59 He turned and walked away and Bruno noticed again how small and skinny this new friend was. He didn't say anything about this because he knew only too well how unpleasant it was being criticized for something as silly as your height, and the last thing he wanted to do was be unkind to Shmuel.

60 "I'll come back tomorrow," shouted Bruno to the departing boy and Shmuel said nothing in reply; in fact he started to run off back to the camp, leaving Bruno all on his own.

Second Read

- Reread the passage to answer these text-dependent questions.
- Write any additional questions you have about the text in your Reader/Writer Notebook.

1. **Key Ideas and Details:** Analyze the description and dialogue. Why is the watch so important to Shmuel? What does it symbolize for him?

   The watch symbolizes Shmuel's home and the happy life that he has lost. RL.8.3

2. **Key Ideas and Details:** What does Bruno not seem to understand about their different situations, as shown in the conversation about the armbands?

   Bruno doesn't understand that Shmuel is a prisoner at the camp. RI.8.3

3. **Key Ideas and Details:** What inferences can you make about the setting? Provide details that help form your inferences.

   The boys are on opposite sides of the fence of a concentration camp during World War II. The imagery of an armband, a swastika, and a Star of David, along with the opening line of the story, are clues to the setting. RL.8.1

4. **Craft and Structure:** Examine paragraph 16 that talks about "The Fury." Who is this and why does Bruno call him "The Fury"?

   The Führer—Adolf Hitler. This misunderstanding of Hitler's title is perhaps an indication of Bruno's naïveté and youth. He may not have come to Shmuel's house, but he forced them to move too. RL.8.4

5. **Key Ideas and Details:** Quote one or more lines of dialogue that show Bruno's perspective lacks an understanding of Shmuel's situation and explain why.

   Talking about armbands, Bruno says, "I think I'd quite like one. I don't know which one I'd prefer though, your one or father's." Bruno doesn't realize Shmuel has to wear his to identify him as a Jew. Then Bruno says, "You can't have all lived in the one room. That doesn't make any sense," again showing he doesn't realize Shmuel is forced to do these things. RL.8.1

SCAFFOLDING THE TEXT-DEPENDENT QUESTIONS

7. Craft and Structure (RL.8.4) **The conversation about train travel between Bruno and Shmuel uses the phrases "said Shmuel, shaking his head" and "said Bruno with a sigh." How do these phrases reveal what both boys are feeling?** Read paragraphs 25 through 30. Why would someone shake their head or sigh when they are speaking? Does it seem like Bruno or Shmuel understands what the other is saying?

8. Key Ideas and Details (RL.8.3) **How does the following dialogue reveal theme: "You're on the wrong side of the fence though"?** How does being "on the wrong side of the fence" affect Bruno? How does it affect Shmuel?

© 2017 College Board. All rights reserved.

6. **Craft and Structure:** What specifically are the carriages mentioned in paragraph 24?

   Carriages are the individual cars that make up the whole train. RL.8.4

7. **Craft and Structure:** The conversation about train travel between Bruno and Shmuel uses the phrases "said Shmuel, shaking his head" and "said Bruno with a sigh." How do these phrases reveal what both boys are feeling?

   These phrases indicate that each boy is frustrated that the other doesn't understand what he is trying to say. RL.8.4

8. **Key Ideas and Details:** How does the following dialogue reveal theme: "You're on the wrong side of the fence though"?

   Bruno is on the "wrong side of the fence" to be able to understand Shmuel and his situation, and Shmuel is literally "on the wrong side of the fence" as a prisoner. RL.8.3

My Notes

Working from the Text

9. How does the theme "finding light in the darkness" connect to the passage about Shmuel and Bruno?

   Despite being separated by a fence, both boys have each other to talk to and pass the time.

10. Why would an author write a Holocaust narrative from a child's perspective? How would that change a reader's understanding of the story?

    There is an innocence about the children who don't fully understand why these events are happening. It can also be more emotional to see children suffering.

ACTIVITY 3.11 continued

7 Have students respond to Working from the Text steps 9 and 10. Have them **pair-share** after each response.

8 Explain that since this text is an excerpt, it contains only one event. Students should use the **graphic organizer** to take notes on the beginning, middle, and end of the event.

9 Explain that students have practiced developing talking points in previous activities, but now expectations will get more specific. Point out that the thematic focus is "finding light in the darkness," but they can connect the text to other themes as well.

10 Form small groups, and ask them to work collaboratively to prepare talking points. As students work, circulate to check for understanding and to provide feedback relating to relevant Embedded Assessment 1 scoring criteria.

The Wrong Side of the Fence

Character 1:	Character 2:	Setting:
Plot		
Beginning:	**Middle:**	**End:**
Theme:		

My Notes

11. Fill in the graphic organizer above with information from the passage. Use your notes to prepare talking points that will guide a meaningful discussion of the text. Be sure to:
    - Discuss how an individual (character), event (plot), or place (setting) contributes to the development of a theme.
    - Include details from text, commentary (analysis), and questions to spark discussion.

12. Work collaboratively to prepare the content of your panel discussion. Use the outline to organize your presentation. Draft an introduction and conclusion, select and arrange talking points into broader categories, and assign a speaker to each part of the presentation. This time, have at least two people present the dramatic interpretation of the text.

Organization of Presentation	Assignment
Introduction: Begin with a dramatic interpretation of an important section of the narrative, and preview what is to follow in the presentation.	**Dramatic Interpretation:** **Preview:**
Transition: **Talking Point 1:** Topic:	
Transition: **Talking Point 2:** Topic:	
Conclusion: Summarize the main points of your discussion. Connect the story to the theme of "finding light in the darkness."	**Brief Summary:** **Connection to Theme:**

13. Review the criteria from the Scoring Guide on page 218 to prepare the delivery of your panel discussion.

14. After rehearsing your panel discussion, present it to another group. Use the Scoring Guide to provide specific feedback and suggestions for improvement (focus on the quality of speakers' interpretation and evidence).

Check Your Understanding

WRITING to SOURCES **Expository Writing Prompt**

Write a short, objective summary of the excerpt from *The Boy in the Striped Pajamas*, including its theme and how the characters, setting, and plot relate to the theme. Be sure to:

- Include a topic sentence that includes a statement of theme.
- Include details and quotes from the text in the summary.
- Explain how characters, setting, and plot relate to the theme.

My Notes

ACTIVITY 3.11 continued

11 As a class, share a few talking points and then review expectations for the panel discussion, using the outline as a guide.

12 Ask groups to work collaboratively to prepare the panel discussion. As students work, circulate to check for understanding and to provide feedback relating to relevant Embedded Assessment 1 scoring criteria.

13 As a class, share a few ideas for the introduction and conclusion, and then review expectations for language and for speaking and listening.

14 After groups **rehearse**, combine two groups and ask them to present their panel discussion and provide specific feedback for each other.

15 Have students complete the Check Your Understanding prompt as an exit slip or for homework.

TEACHER TO TEACHER

This would be a good time to set clear expectations for the length of panel discussions.

ASSESS

Evaluate the outlines and panel discussions to be sure students are prepared for Embedded Assessment 1.

ADAPT

If you have concerns about any elements of the presentations, consider providing more practice with the Holocaust narratives or alternative texts.

ACTIVITY 3.12

▶PLAN

Suggested Pacing: 1 50-minute class period

▶TEACH

1 Read the Preview and the Setting a Purpose for Reading sections with your students. Help them understand any literary terms they encounter.

2 **FIRST READ:** Based on the complexity of the passage and your knowledge of your students, you may choose to conduct the first reading in a variety of ways:

- independent reading
- paired reading
- small group reading
- choral reading
- read aloud

3 As students are reading, monitor their progress. Be sure they are engaged with the text and annotating words and phrases that indicate why Anne is upset. Evaluate whether the selected reading mode is effective.

4 Based on the observations you made during the first reading, you may want to adjust your reading mode. For example, you may decide for the second reading to read aloud certain complex passages, or you may group students differently.

ACTIVITY 3.12

Creating a Memorable Opening

LEARNING STRATEGIES: Rereading, Close reading, Oral Reading, Choral Reading, Discussion Groups

My Notes

Learning Targets

- Transform a prose selection into a "found poem."
- Orally present a dramatic interpretation.

Preview

In this activity, you will read an excerpt from Anne Frank's diary and create a found poem.

Setting a Purpose for Reading

- As you read the diary entry, underline words and phrases that indicate why Anne is so upset.
- Circle unknown words and phrases. Try to determine the meaning of the words by using context clues, word parts, or a dictionary.

ABOUT THE AUTHOR

Anne Frank (1929–1945) is one of the Holocaust's most famous victims. The Frank family fled Germany for Amsterdam, but eventually the Nazis also occupied the Netherlands. The family spent two years in hiding, during which Anne wrote of her thoughts and feelings to her imaginary friend, Kitty. The German authorities found the family's hiding place and sent them to concentration camps, where Anne perished at age 15. Her diary was found years later, and it continues to be read today as a moving narrative from the Holocaust.

Diary

from The Diary of a Young Girl

Wednesday, 13 January, 1943

by Anne Frank

Dear Kitty,

1 Everything has upset me again this morning, so I wasn't able to finish a single thing properly.

2 It is terrible outside. Day and night more of those poor miserable people are being dragged off, with nothing but a rucksack and a little money. On the way they are deprived even of these possessions. Families are torn apart, the men, women, and children all being separated. Children coming home from school find that their parents have disappeared. Women return from shopping to find their homes shut up and their families gone.

3 The Dutch people are anxious too, their sons are being sent to Germany. Everyone is afraid.

4 And every night hundreds of planes fly over Holland and go to German towns, where the earth is plowed up by their bombs, and every hour hundreds and thousands of people are killed in Russia and Africa. No one is able to keep out of it, the whole globe is waging war and although it is going better for the allies, the end is not yet in sight.

COMMON CORE STATE STANDARDS

Focus Standards:

RL.8.5: Compare and contrast the structure of two or more texts and analyze how the differing structure of each text contributes to its meaning and style.

W.8.9: Draw evidence from literary or informational texts to support analysis, reflection, and research.

W.8.9b: Apply *Grade 8 Reading standards* to literary nonfiction (e.g., "Delineate and evaluate the argument and specific claims in a text, assessing whether the reasoning is sound and the evidence is relevant and sufficient; recognize when irrelevant evidence is introduced").

SL.8.6: Adapt speech to a variety of contexts and tasks, demonstrating command of formal English when indicated or appropriate.

Additional Standards Addressed:

RL.8.1; RL.8.2; RL.8.4; RI.8.10; W.8.9a; W.8.10; L.8.6

5 And as for us, we are fortunate. Yes, we are luckier than millions of people. It is quiet and safe here, and we are, so to speak, living on **capital**. We are even so selfish as to talk about "after the war," brighten up at the thought of having new clothes and new shoes, whereas we really ought to save every penny, to help other people, and save what is left from the wreckage after the war.

capital: wealth kept after paying expenses

6 The children here run about in just a thin blouse and clogs; no coat, no hat, no stockings, and no one helps them. Their tummies are empty; they chew an old carrot to **stay** the pangs, go from their cold homes out into the cold street and, when they get to school, find themselves in an even colder classroom. Yes, it has even got so bad in Holland that countless children stop the passers-by and beg for a piece of bread. I could go on for hours about all the suffering the war has brought, but then I would only make myself more dejected. There is nothing we can do but wait as calmly as we can till the misery comes to an end. Jews and Christians wait, the whole earth waits, and there are many who wait for death.

stay: to delay or postpone

Yours,

Anne

My Notes

Second Read

- Reread the diary entry to answer these text-dependent questions.
- Write any additional questions you have about the text in your Reader/Writer Notebook.

1. **Key Ideas and Details:** Why does Anne feel that she is fortunate?

   Anne feels that she is fortunate because she and her family are together, and they have food and a place where they are safer than some others. RL.8.2

2. **Craft and Structure:** Based on the mood Anne portrays in this passage, what does she mean in paragraph 6 by "more dejected"?

   Anne will become sadder and more depressed. RL.8.4

Literary Terms
A **found poem** is verse that is created from a prose text by using the original words, phrases, images, and/or sentences, but manipulating them and reformatting them into poetic lines.

Working from the Text

3. In a previous activity, you read a play based on Anne Frank's diary. What could you learn from her diary that you could not learn from the play?

   Her diary entry describes how families were separated and taken away. This indicates why her family is living in hiding in an attic.

4. The opening two paragraphs of the diary entry have been transformed into a model of a **found poem**. With a partner, conduct an oral reading using choral reading for effect.

"Wednesday, 13 January, 1943"

Everyone is afraid:

It is terrible outside.
Day and night
more of those poor miserable people
are being dragged off.

INDEPENDENT READING LINK
Read and Respond
Choose a passage from the Holocaust narrative you are reading independently to transform into a found poem. Perform an oral reading of your poem at the final literature circle meeting.

SCAFFOLDING THE TEXT-DEPENDENT QUESTIONS

1. Key Ideas and Details (RL.8.2) **Why does Anne feel that she is fortunate?** What examples does Anne give in paragraph 5 for why she feels more fortunate than many other people?

2. Craft and Structure (RL.8.4) **Based on the mood Anne portrays in this passage, what does she mean in paragraph 6 by "more dejected"?** How would you describe Anne's mood in paragraph 6? What does "dejected" mean if Anne is afraid of becoming "more dejected"?

© 2017 College Board. All rights reserved.

ACTIVITY 3.12 continued

Text Complexity
Overall: Complex
Lexile: 990L
Qualitative: Moderate Difficulty
Task: Moderate (Analyze)

5 **SECOND READ:** During the second reading, students will be returning to the text to answer the text-dependent comprehension questions. You may choose to have students reread and work on the questions in a variety of ways:

- independently
- in pairs
- in small groups
- together as a class

6 Have students answer the text-dependent questions. If they have difficulty, scaffold the questions by rephrasing them or breaking them down into smaller parts. See the Scaffolding the Text-Dependent Questions boxes for suggestions.

7 Help students distinguish between the two genres—diary and play—in which Anne Frank's diary is presented in this unit.

8 Remind students that Anne kept a detailed diary while she was in hiding during WWII. Point out that Anne Frank named her diary Kitty, and ask students to consider why Anne might have wanted to pretend that her diary was a friend.

9 After defining *found poem* and connecting it to the opening of the panel discussion, ask students to work with a partner to plan a dramatic reading of the found poem based on this diary entry. Be sure that students understand that the words of a found poem come verbatim from the original source. Some lines may be repeated or omitted, but none may be added.

10 Combine pairs to form small groups, and have pairs present to each other.

ACTIVITY 3.12 continued

11 Ask students to work collaboratively to analyze the form and effect of the poem. Briefly discuss responses as a class to check for understanding. Be sure to discuss how the author uses poetic elements such as repetition and stanzas for effect.

12 Ask students to transform passages from the rest of the diary entry into a found poem and then to plan and present a dramatic interpretation. Students should keep their found poems short.

Leveled Differentiated Instruction

In this activity, students may need support to plan a dramatic interpretation of the text. Have students work in pairs to highlight the words, phrases, and images they think are important.

Em Help students express and record their ideas about the important parts of the poem with their partner by using a **Collaborative Dialogue** graphic organizer.

Ex Have students respond to their partner's ideas about the important parts of the poem by adding relevant information and paraphrasing key ideas. Encourage students to take notes based on the discussion.

Br Have students respond to their discussion partners by adding relevant information, paraphrasing key ideas, and providing useful feedback. Encourage students to take notes based on the discussion.

▶ASSESS

After reviewing the criteria for expressive oral reading/speaking in Activity 3.8, ask students to use it to provide specific feedback after a dramatic interpretation.

▶ADAPT

This is the last activity before Embedded Assessment 1. At this point, students should feel confident about meeting the expectations of "Presenting the Voices of the Holocaust" using the fictional or nonfiction narrative they read and analyzed together in Literature Circle groups.

If students express uncertainty about one or more of the Embedded Assessment 1 requirements, consider building in one more lesson, using an excerpt from the graphic novel *Maus II*, by Art Spiegelman. Students might be inspired to use a visual to add interest to their dramatic performance, and they can practice creating talking points and planning a panel discussion.

Creating a Memorable Opening

My Notes

Families are torn apart.
Children coming home from school
find that their parents
have disappeared.

Women
return from shopping to find
their homes shut up and
their families gone.

The Dutch people,
their sons are being sent
to Germany.
Everyone is afraid ...

5. The author of the found poem selected particular lines from the text and then transformed them into poetry. How does this transformation change the power of the language?
   By transforming the prose to poetic lines, the author creates a sharper emphasis on the feelings and images represented by the words.

6. How does the structure of the lines in the found poem transform the text from prose to poetry? Which lines stand out? Why?
   The found poem is restructured into stanzas that group images to create more emphasis. The author has made the lines "Everyone is afraid" stand out by beginning and ending the poem with this imagery of fear.

7. How would a dramatic interpretation of this found poem successfully open a panel discussion about the Holocaust?
   A dramatic interpretation of this found poem would set the context of a discussion about the Holocaust by emphasizing the historical date and the idea that everyone is afraid. The imagery of people being "dragged off" or "their homes shut up and their families gone" adds to the context of fear.

Check Your Understanding

Reread the diary entry again, highlighting words, phrases, and images you think are important. Then, transform the text into a found poem and plan a dramatic interpretation (i.e., oral reading) of the text. Present your oral reading to a partner, and listen and provide feedback to your partner's oral reading.

Independent Reading Checkpoint

Respond to the first Reflection question in Embedded Assessment 1 as it relates to the independent reading narrative you have read: How was the theme or central idea of "finding light in the darkness" developed in the narrative you read independently?

INDEPENDENT READING CHECKPOINT

Have students respond to the first Reflection question in Embedded Assessment 1 as it relates to the independent reading narrative they chose: How was the theme or central idea of "finding light in the darkness" developed in the narrative you read independently?

Presenting Voices of the Holocaust

EMBEDDED ASSESSMENT 1

Assignment

Present a panel discussion that includes an oral reading of a significant passage from the narrative read by your group. Your discussion should explain how the theme or central idea of "finding light in the darkness" is developed in the entire narrative.

Planning: Discuss your ideas with your group to prepare a focus for your panel discussion.

- How was the theme or central idea of "finding light in the darkness" developed in your Holocaust narrative?
- How did supporting details such as character, plot, and setting contribute to the theme?
- How will you find a significant passage for your oral reading that will help communicate the idea of "finding light in the darkness"?
- How will you assign talking points to each group member to include an introduction, at least two supporting details, and a conclusion?

Drafting: Write a draft of your talking point(s) that includes details from the text, commentary (analysis), and discussion questions.

- How will the introductory talking point present a hook, summary of the text, and thematic statement?
- How will the supporting talking points explain how an individual, event, or place contributed to theme?
- How will the concluding talking point restate the theme, summarize the main points of the discussion, and elicit textual connections (text to self, text, or world) from the entire group?

Rehearsing: Rehearse and revise your panel discussion to improve the final presentation.

- How will you prepare notes to constructive feedback and build on ideas and questions presented by other group members?
- How will your group create smooth transitions between speakers?
- How will you include your oral reading as you introduce and develop your explanation?
- How will you use precise diction in order to establish and maintain a formal style?
- How will you use eye contact, volume, and pronunciation to express your ideas clearly?

Reflection

After completing this Embedded Assessment, think about how you went about accomplishing this task, and respond to the following:

- How was the theme or central idea of "finding light in the darkness" developed in the different Holocaust narratives that you heard about in the panel discussions?
- What did you learn from studying and discussing narratives about the Holocaust that you can apply to your own life?

My Notes

Technology TIP:

If possible, consider projecting an outline of your panel discussion to provide your audience with an "agenda" to follow.

EMBEDDED ASSESSMENT 1

Suggested Pacing: 2 50-minute class periods

1 Planning: Remind students that they have been practicing preparing for and conducting a panel presentation during the previous activities.

2 Review the Scoring Guide to be sure students understand each of the analytical, written, oral, and collaborative components of this task.

- Include a dramatic presentation of a passage.
- Present talking points about how narrative elements contribute to a theme.
- Provide sufficient and relevant evidence to support claim.
- Include an introduction and conclusion.

3 Drafting: Suggest that students use the **graphic organizers** from Activities 3.7 and 3.11 as they draft their talking points and transitions.

4 Rehearsing: Remind students of the oral presentation evaluation criteria in Activity 3.8 as they rehearse their panel presentations. Suggest that they use peer responding to evaluate the need for further practice and revision to create and maintain a smooth, formal presentation.

Reflection The first reflection question could be turned into a short literary analysis essay that gives students a chance to develop the concept of "finding light in the darkness."

COMMON CORE STATE STANDARDS

Focus Standards:

SL.8.1a: Come to discussions prepared, having read or researched material under study; explicitly draw on that preparation by referring to evidence on the topic, text, or issue to probe and reflect on ideas under discussion.

SL.8.1b: Follow rules for collegial discussions and decision-making, track progress toward specific goals and deadlines, and define individual roles as needed.

SL.8.1c: Pose questions that connect the ideas of several speakers and respond to others' questions and comments with relevant evidence, observations, and ideas.

SL.8.1d: Acknowledge new information expressed by others, and, when warranted, qualify or justify their own views in light of evidence presented.

SL.8.3: Delineate a speaker's argument and specific claims, evaluating the soundness of the reasoning and relevance and sufficiency of

EMBEDDED ASSESSMENT 1 continued

Portfolio Students should have kept their work for this Embedded Assessment in their Reader/Writer Notebook and in a Working Folder. Now is the time for them to collect, review, and create a Table of Contents for the work leading to Embedded Assessment 1. Each student needs to be responsible for gathering all the work he or she has done during the literature discussions, preparation, drafting, and presenting of this Embedded Assessment. Once they have reviewed their work and answered the reflection questions, be sure they add it to their portfolios.

SCORING GUIDE

When you score this Embedded Assessment, you may wish to download and print copies of the Scoring Guide from SpringBoard Digital. In this way, you can have a copy to mark for each student's work.

To identify additional areas where your English learners could use additional support, see the English Language Development Rubric for Embedded Assessment 1 on page 246a.

EMBEDDED ASSESSMENT 1

Presenting Voices of the Holocaust

SCORING GUIDE

Scoring Criteria	Exemplary	Proficient	Emerging	Incomplete
Ideas	The discussion • includes an effective oral reading of a significant text passage • presents a variety of significant ideas to explain how literary elements contribute to the development of a theme • provides relevant elaboration to develop the topic, including textual evidence, details, commentary, and questions.	The discussion • includes an oral reading of a text passage • presents adequate ideas to explain how literary elements in a narrative contribute to the development of a theme • provides sufficient elaboration to develop the topic, including textual evidence, details, commentary, and questions.	The discussion • includes an ineffective passage or reading of a passage • presents unfocused or undeveloped ideas to explain how literary elements in a narrative contribute to the development of a theme • provides insufficient or weak elaboration to develop the topic.	The discussion • does not include an oral reading of a passage • does not explain how literary elements in a narrative contribute to the development of a theme • provides minimal or irrelevant elaboration.
Structure	The discussion • demonstrates strong evidence of effective collaboration and preparation • follows a logical and smooth organizational structure • uses transitional strategies effectively and purposefully.	The discussion • demonstrates sufficient evidence of collaboration and preparation • follows an adequate organizational structure • uses transitional strategies to create cohesion and clarify relationships.	The discussion • demonstrates insufficient evidence of collaboration and preparation • follows an uneven or ineffective organizational structure • uses transitional strategies inconsistently.	The discussion • demonstrates little or no collaboration and/or preparation • lacks any obvious organizational structure • does not use transitional strategies.
Use of Language	The speaker • communicates effectively with group members and the audience • uses consistently precise diction and academic language • demonstrates deep command of the conventions of standard English grammar, usage, and language (including active/passive voice).	The speaker • communicates appropriately with group members and the audience • uses sufficiently precise diction and academic language • demonstrates adequate command of the conventions of standard English grammar, usage, and language (including active/passive voice).	The speaker • communicates inappropriately or inconsistently with group members and/or the audience • uses insufficiently precise diction and academic language • demonstrates partial command of the conventions of standard English grammar, usage, and language.	The speaker • does not communicate well with the group of audience • uses flawed, confusing, or basic diction and language • has frequent errors in standard English grammar, usage, and language.

COMMON CORE STATE STANDARDS

the evidence and identifying when irrelevant evidence is introduced.

SL.8.4: Present claims and findings (e.g. argument narrative, response to literature presentations), emphasizing salient points in a focused, coherent manner with relevant evidence, sound valid reasoning, and well-chosen details; use appropriate eye contact, adequate volume, and clear pronunciation.

SL.8.6: Adapt speech to a variety of contexts and tasks, demonstrating command of formal English when indicated or appropriate. (See Grade 8 Language standards 1 and 3 for specific expectations.)

Additional Standards Addressed:

RL.8.1; RL.8.2; RL.8.3; RL.8.10; W.8.2a; W.8.2b; W.8.2d; W.8.2e; W.8.2f; W.8.4; W.8.10

Previewing Embedded Assessment 2 and Looking at Multimedia

ACTIVITY 3.13

Learning Targets

- Reflect on and make connections between the lessons of the Holocaust and "taking action."
- Analyze the skills and knowledge needed to complete Embedded Assessment 2 successfully.

LEARNING STRATEGIES: QHT, Close Reading, Paraphrasing, Graphic Organizer

Making Connections

During your study of narratives of the Holocaust, you were asked to think about the concept of "finding the light in the darkness." This idea is developed further in the last half of the unit by building on the idea of people taking action to create positive change in their communities and the world.

INDEPENDENT READING LINK

To support your learning in the second half of the unit, select a fiction or nonfiction narrative about someone who made a difference in the world or who tried to confront social injustice.

Essential Questions

Reflect on your understanding of the relationship between the first Essential Question *(Why is it important to learn about the Holocaust?)* and the second Essential Question *(How can one person make a difference?)*.

Developing Vocabulary

Return to the **Academic Vocabulary** and **Literary Terms** at the beginning of the unit. Using the QHT strategy, re-sort the words based on your new learning.

1. Compare this sort with your original sort. How has your understanding changed?

2. Select a word from the chart (or a Holocaust-related term) and write a concise statement about your learning. How has your understanding of this word changed over the course of this unit?

My Notes

Unpacking Embedded Assessment 2

Closely read the Embedded Assessment 2 Assignment and the Scoring Guide.

> Develop a multimedia presentation that informs your peers about an issue of national or global significance and convinces them to take action. Work collaboratively to conduct and synthesize research into an engaging campaign that challenges your audience to make a difference.

Work with your class to paraphrase the expectations and create a graphic organizer to use as a visual reminder of the required concepts (what you need to know) and skills (what you need to do).

After each activity, use this graphic organizer to guide reflection about what you have learned and what you still need to learn in order to be successful in the Embedded Assessment.

COMMON CORE STATE STANDARDS

Focus Standard:

L.8.6: Acquire and use accurately grade-appropriate general academic and domain-specific words and phrases; gather vocabulary knowledge when considering a word or phrase important to comprehension or expression.

Additional Standards Addressed:

RL.8.10; RI.8.10; W.8.10; L.8.5b

ACTIVITY 3.13

PLAN

Suggested Pacing: 1 50-minute class period

TEACH

1 After students have thought and written about the Essential Questions, ask them to share what they have learned. Use this as a basis for a whole-class discussion about "taking action and making a difference" and how they relate to the first half of the unit.

2 Before they re-sort the vocabulary, remind them to review their original sort to compare and determine what more they can learn.

3 Guide students through the process of reflecting on their learning.

4 Facilitate a **close reading** of the Embedded Assessment 2 Assignment and Scoring Guide criteria, focusing on the "Proficient" column. Instruct students to **mark the text** by underlining or highlighting key skills (verbs) and knowledge (nouns).

5 Determine an effective way to make a visual reminder of the skills and knowledge required by the Embedded Assessment. As a class, create a large **graphic organizer** that reflects the criteria of the Scoring Guide. Ask students to create their own copy in their Reader/Writer Notebooks.

6 To help students get a clear sense of your expectations for the Embedded Assessment, you might have them particularly note the requirements at the proficient level on the Scoring Guide.

7 Make sure to keep the unpacked assessment in a visible place in your classroom so you and your students can refer to specific skills and knowledge before, during, and/or after each daily activity.

8 Using the Scoring Guides for Embedded Assessment 1 and Embedded Assessment 2, compare and contrast the two presentations. It is important that students understand that their learning in the first half of the unit applies to the second half.

ACTIVITY 3.13 continued

9 Have students work in pairs to respond to the questions about multimedia and to analyze how they use multimedia.

10 Guide students in the selection of a new independent reading text.

TEACHER TO TEACHER

You might want to schedule a visit to your school library or a series of book talks in which you, the librarian, parent volunteers, and/or students share ideas for independent reading.

▶ASSESS

Review student work to determine what students know at this point in the unit and what they still need to work on.

▶ADAPT

Be sure students understand the relationship between the two halves of the unit. During the second half of this unit they will encounter many informational texts and be expected to conduct research, especially on the Internet. If Internet connections are not available, you may want to furnish students with screen shots of public service announcements or public service campaigns that have taken action to make a difference, such as of those relating to seat belt use, smoking, and texting while driving.

INDEPENDENT READING

In this half of the unit, while preparing to present a multimedia campaign, students will have the opportunity to read another text about someone who made a difference in the world or fought for a cause. The Planning the Unit section of the Teacher's Edition and the Resources section of the Student Edition contain information, Reading Logs, and Reading Lists to help you and your students find the right book.

Previewing Embedded Assessment 2 and Looking at Multimedia

My Notes

3. How would you define *multimedia*? Think of the meanings of each part of the word: *multi-* and *media*. What is the connection between the words *medium* and *media*?

Multimedia means using several forms of media to present information, such as video, audio, websites, graphics, etc. *Medium* is singular and *media* is plural.

4. Work with a partner to create a web showing the different types of media that you use.

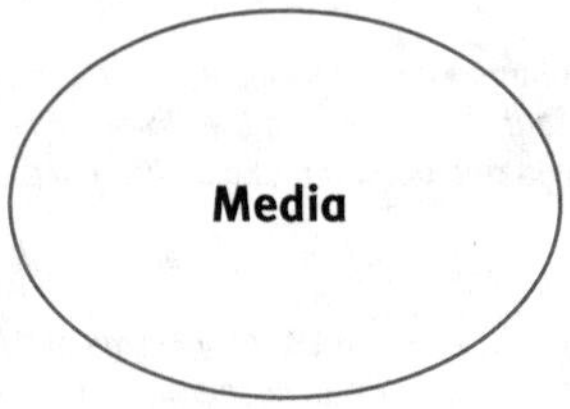

5. Explain how you use the different types of media and for what purposes.

© 2017 College Board. All rights reserved.

Making a Difference

ACTIVITY 3.14

Learning Targets

- Analyze imagery and slogans in public service announcements for purpose and effect.
- Evaluate how diverse media enhance presentations of information.

LEARNING STRATEGIES:
Discussion Groups

Communicating with Visuals

1. How effective are visuals in making a point about a significant issue? How do they compare with other media channels: speeches, articles, videos, radio announcements, and so on?

ACADEMIC VOCABULARY
A **slogan** is a memorable phrase or motto used to identify or promote a product or group.

2. Look at the two images below. Each is intended as a "call to action" as part of a public service campaign to make a difference. Examine each of the visuals and determine its purpose. Note also that each image has text, including a **slogan**. How does a slogan help promote a goal?

3. Evaluate the effectiveness of the imagery and the slogan. Each image is associated with a website. What can you tell about the sponsors of the visuals by their Web addresses? In groups, explore the websites and find other images, text, and perhaps video associated with the campaigns.

ACTIVITY 3.14

PLAN

Materials: Internet access
Suggested Pacing: 1 50-minute class period

TEACH

1 **Activate prior knowledge** by asking students what they know about public service campaigns.

2 Create small groups to complete Student Steps 1–3 and examine the visuals closely. Students should read as much of the text as they can and determine what the slogan of each visual is.

3 As students explore the effectiveness of each ad, encourage them to think about the use of visual techniques for effect (e.g. framing, angles, color).

TEACHER TO TEACHER

At this point consider forming the groups for the Embedded Assessment so that students' work can inform their multimedia campaign planning.

COMMON CORE STATE STANDARDS

Focus Standards:

RI.8.5a: Analyze the use of text features (e.g. graphics, headers, captions) in consumer materials.

RI.8.7: Evaluate the advantages and disadvantages of using different mediums (e.g., print or digital text, video, multimedia) to present a particular topic or idea.

SL.8.2: Analyze the purpose of information presented in diverse media and formats (e.g., visually, quantitatively, orally) and evaluate the motives (e.g., social, commercial, political) behind its presentation.

Additional Standards Addressed:

W.8.8; W.8.10; SL.8.1b; L.8.1a; L.8.6

© 2017 College Board. All rights reserved.

ACTIVITY 3.14 continued

4 In groups, have students explore the government website and the websites listed in the **graphic organizer.** After group discussion and evaluation of each site, the recorder should fill in the graphic organizer.

5 Have students respond to the **quickwrite** and then briefly **brainstorm** the effect of music in making a call to action memorable.

6 Review participial phrases with students.

TEACHER TO TEACHER

You may want to create a bulletin board for students to post inspirational quotes and/or song lyrics throughout the unit (i.e., that contain a call to action). Also, you might want to create a playlist of songs that encourage people to make a difference and play one each day at the start or end of class or as they research. Possible titles include the following:

- "If I Had a Hammer" by Peter, Paul, and Mary
- "Man in the Mirror" or "Heal the World" by Michael Jackson
- "Change" by Taylor Swift
- "Today I'm Going to Try and Change the World" by Johnny Reid
- "Make a Difference" by Blind Melon
- "Change the World" by Eric Clapton
- "Who Will I Be" by Demi Lovato
- "Waiting on the World to Change" by John Mayer
- "Let It Be Me" by Indigo Girls

▶ASSESS

Have students turn in their notes on the website investigation. Check that they analyzed the purpose and effectiveness of the imagery.

▶ADAPT

Students will be able to explore more websites to examine public service announcement campaigns in later activities.

Making a Difference

My Notes

4. In addition to the websites on the previous page, explore the following government site, which has PSA (public service announcement) images and videos: https://www.dhs.gov/see-something-say-something. As you explore each website, analyze the purpose of the information presented. In your groups, discuss and evaluate the purpose or purposes of the information. Is it presented for social, commercial, public safety, or political purposes?

5. Choose a recorder to capture the insights and conclusions of your group discussion.

Poster	Visit the website and take notes about the images, slogans, and additional media formats present. Describe how the purpose is enhanced by the media format.	Why has this visual been created? Is it for social, commercial, public safety, or political purposes?
1	**http://www.nature.org/photosmultimedia/psas/index.htm**	
2	**https://www.dhs.gov/see-something-say-something**	
3	Search wfp.org	

6. **Quickwrite:** What kind of music would you combine with these campaigns to make them memorable?

Language and Writer's Craft: Reviewing Participial Phrases

The **participle** forms of verbs can be used as adjectives. There are two participial forms: present (ending in *-ing*) and past (usually ending in *-d* or *-ed*). Look at these examples of participles used as adjectives.

rising world concern

widely *used* medium

A participle may occur in a participial phrase, which includes the participle plus any complements and modifiers. The whole phrase then serves as an adjective.

Located 275 miles north of San Francisco, Arcata is ....

An introductory participial phrase must modify the noun or pronoun that follows it.

Never Forget, Never Again

ACTIVITY 3.15

Learning Targets

- Analyze the purpose, audience, and tone of a speech.
- Analyze a speech for the elements of argumentation.

LEARNING STRATEGIES: SOAPSTone, Close Reading, Discussion Groups, Drafting, Rehearsal, Oral Reading

Preview

In this activity, you will read a speech by Elie Wiesel and think about its audience and tone.

Setting a Purpose for Reading

- As you read the speech, underline words and phrases that help set the tone of the speech.
- Circle unknown words and phrases. Try to determine the meaning of the words by using context clues, word parts, or a dictionary.

My Notes

ABOUT THE AUTHOR

The Nobel Committee called Elie Wiesel a "messenger to mankind," stating that through his struggle to come to terms with "his own personal experience of total humiliation and of the utter contempt for humanity shown in Hitler's death camps," as well as his "practical work in the cause of peace," Wiesel had delivered a powerful message "of peace, atonement and human dignity" to humanity.

WORD CONNECTIONS

Etymology

The word *deportation* derives from an Old French word meaning "to carry off." When first used, it referred to the way a person behaved or acted. In the 1640s people began using it to mean "banishment."

Speech

from The Nobel Acceptance Speech Delivered by Elie Wiesel

in Oslo on December 10, 1986

1 I am moved, deeply moved by your words, Chairman Aarvik. And it is with a profound sense of **humility** that I accept the honor—the highest there is—that you have chosen to bestow upon me. I know your choice transcends my person.

2 Do I have the right to represent the multitudes who have perished? Do I have the right to accept this great honor on their behalf? I do not. No one may speak for the dead, no one may interpret their **mutilated** dreams and visions. And yet, I sense their presence. I always do—and at this moment more than ever. The presence of my parents, that of my little sister. The presence of my teachers, my friends, my companions …

3 This honor belongs to all the survivors and their children and, through us, to the Jewish people with whose destiny I have always identified.

4 I remember: it happened yesterday, or eternities ago. A young Jewish boy discovered the Kingdom of Night. I remember his bewilderment, I remember his **anguish**. It all happened so fast. The ghetto. The **deportation**. The sealed cattle car. The fiery altar upon which the history of our people and the future of mankind were meant to be sacrificed.

5 I remember he asked his father: "Can this be true? This is the twentieth century, not the Middle Ages. Who would allow such crimes to be committed? How could the world remain silent?"

humility: modesty
mutilated: damaged beyond repair
anguish: agonizing pain
deportation: removal to another country

ACTIVITY 3.15

PLAN

Materials: downloaded podcast from www.ushmm.org (search the term "Antisemitism Voices") (optional), highlighters, models of annotated bibliographies (from Unit 2)
Suggested Pacing: 2 50-minute class periods

TEACH

1 Read the Preview and the Setting a Purpose for Reading sections with your students. Help them understand literary terms they encounter.

2 **FIRST READ:** Based on the complexity of the passage and your knowledge of your students, you may choose to conduct the first reading in a variety of ways:

- independent reading
- paired reading
- small group reading
- choral reading
- read aloud

3 As students are reading, monitor their progress. Be sure they are engaged with the text and annotating words or phrases that help set the tone. Evaluate whether the selected reading mode is effective.

4 Based on the observations you made during the first reading, you may want to adjust your reading mode. For example, you may decide for the second reading to read aloud certain complex passages, or you may group students differently.

Leveled Differentiated Instruction

Students may need support analyzing certain words for tone. As students begin to read, point out the word *transcend*.

Em Guide students to complete a **Word Choice Analyzer** for the word *transcend*.

Ex Guide students to complete a **Word Choice Analyzer** for the word *transcend*. Then ask students to name another way to say *transcend*. Then ask students to explain how this word affects the tone of the writing.

COMMON CORE STATE STANDARDS

Focus Standards:

RI.8.1: Cite the textual evidence that most strongly supports an analysis of what the text says explicitly as well as inferences drawn from the text.

RI.8.2: Determine a central idea of a text and analyze its development over the course of the text, including its relationship to supporting ideas; provide an objective summary of the text.

SL.8.3: Delineate a speaker's argument and specific claims, evaluating the soundness of the reasoning and relevance and sufficiency of the evidence and identifying when irrelevant evidence is introduced.

Additional Standards Addressed:

RI.8.3; RI.8.4; RI.8.5; RI.8.6; RI.8.8; W.8.1a; W.8.1b; W.8.8; W.8.9a; SL.8.1a; SL.8.1b; SL.8.1c; SL.8.2; SL.8.5; SL.8.6; L.8.1c; L.8.3a; L.8.6

Br Have students think about the word *transcend* and then present analysis of the author's word choice to the class.

Text Complexity
Overall: Complex
Lexile: 830L
Qualitative: Moderate Difficulty
Task: Challenging (Evaluate)

5 **SECOND READ:** During the second reading, students will be returning to the text to answer the text-dependent comprehension questions. You may choose to have students reread and work on the questions in a variety of ways:

- independently
- in pairs
- in small groups
- together as a class

6 Have students answer the text-dependent questions. If they have difficulty, scaffold the questions by rephrasing them or breaking them down into smaller parts. See the Scaffolding the Text-Dependent Questions boxes for suggestions.

7 Remind students that they were introduced to Wiesel in a previous activity. He is the author of the Holocaust autobiography *Night*. He received the Nobel Peace Prize for his "practical work in the cause of peace."

8 Conduct a **shared reading** of the speech, using Key Ideas and Details and **SOAPSTone** to guide student analysis. Consider **diffusing** unfamiliar or challenging vocabulary.

9 After reading, review *call to action*, and have students respond to the question about the last sentence of Wiesel's speech.

Never Forget, Never Again

My Notes

naïve: simple; unsophisticated
jeopardy: peril; danger

integrity: adherence to an ethical code
dissident: one who disagrees

6 And now the boy is turning to me. "Tell me," he asks, "what have you done with my future, what have you done with your life?" And I tell him that I have tried. That I have tried to keep memory alive, that I have tried to fight those who would forget. Because if we forget, we are guilty, we are accomplices.

7 And then I explain to him how **naïve** we were, that the world did know and remained silent. And that is why I swore never to be silent whenever wherever human beings endure suffering and humiliation. We must take sides. Neutrality helps the oppressor, never the victim. Silence encourages the tormentor, never the tormented. Sometimes we must interfere. When human lives are endangered, when human dignity is in **jeopardy**, national borders and sensitivities become irrelevant. Wherever men and women are persecuted because of their race, religion, or political views, that place must—at that moment—become the center of the universe.

8 There is so much injustice and suffering crying out for our attention: victims of hunger, of racism and political persecution—in Chile, for instance, or in Ethiopia—writers and poets, prisoners in so many lands governed by the Left and by the Right.

9 Human rights are being violated on every continent. More people are oppressed than free. How can one not be sensitive to their plight? Human suffering anywhere concerns men and women everywhere.

10 There is so much to be done, there is so much that can be done. One person—a Raoul Wallenberg, an Albert Schweitzer, Martin Luther King, Jr.—one person of **integrity**, can make a difference, a difference of life and death. As long as one **dissident** is in prison, our freedom will not be true. As long as one child is hungry, our life will be filled with anguish and shame. What all these victims need above all is to know that they are not alone; that we are not forgetting them, that when their voices are stifled we shall lend them ours, that while their freedom depends on ours, the quality of our freedom depends on theirs.

11 This is what I say to the young Jewish boy wondering what I have done with his years. It is in his name that I speak to you and that I express to you my deepest gratitude as one who has emerged from the Kingdom of Night. We know that every moment is a moment of grace, every hour an offering; not to share them would mean to betray them.

12 Our lives no longer belong to us alone; they belong to all those who need us desperately.

Second Read

- Reread the speech to answer these text-dependent questions.
- Write any additional questions you have about the text in your Reader/Writer Notebook.

1. **Craft and Structure:** What can you infer about the meaning of "bestow" in paragraph 1?

   It means to present an award or title to honor someone. RI.8.4

2. **Key Ideas and Details:** In paragraphs 2–5, Elie Wiesel makes reference to or alludes to what central event? Why does he use fragments to evoke the memory?

   Wiesel alludes to the Holocaust. The fragments represent the images that are seared in his memory. RI.8.3

SCAFFOLDING THE TEXT-DEPENDENT QUESTIONS

1. Craft and Structure (RI.8.4) **What can you infer about the meaning of "bestow" in paragraph 1?** In paragraph 1, how does Wiesel feel about receiving the Nobel Prize? Based on this feeling, what can you infer about the meaning of the word "bestow"?

2. Key Ideas and Details (RI.8.3) **In paragraphs 2–5, Elie Wiesel makes reference to or alludes to what central event? Why does he use fragments to evoke the memory?** In paragraphs 2 through 5, what event that you've been reading about in this unit is Wiesel remembering? In paragraph 4, Wiesel states some of his memories in fragments. What impact does this have on them?

3. Craft and Structure (RI.8.4) **What does Wiesel mean when he says that human dignity is "in jeopardy" in paragraph 7?** In paragraph 7

3. **Craft and Structure:** What does Wiesel mean when he says that human dignity is "in jeopardy" in paragraph 7?

He means that human dignity is in danger, or that it could be taken away from people. RI.8.4

4. **Key Ideas and Details:** Closely examine paragraphs 6 and 7. What is Wiesel saying about memory and silence?

Forgetting and silence are ways we become accomplices in injustice and suffering. RI.8.3

Working from the Text

5. The purpose of "a call to action" is to provide a concluding statement or section that supports the argument by making clear to the audience what the writer or speaker wants them to think or do. How is Wiesel's last sentence a "call to action"?

With this sentence, Wiesel attempts to persuade the audience that many people are desperate for help and we all have a responsibility.

6. You will be assigned a specific element from the SOAPSTone strategy below. Annotate the speech for this element.

Introducing the Strategy: SOAPSTone

SOAPSTone stands for Speaker, Occasion, Audience, Purpose, Subject, and Tone. It is a reading and writing tool for analyzing the relationship among a writer, his or her purpose, and the target audience of the text. SOAPSTone guides you in asking questions to analyze a text or to plan for writing a composition.

- **Speaker:** The speaker is the voice that tells the story.
- **Occasion:** The occasion is the time and place of the story; it is the context that prompted the writing.
- **Audience:** The audience is the person or persons to whom the piece is directed.
- **Purpose:** The purpose is the reason behind the text or what the writer wants the audience to think as a result of reading the text.
- **Subject:** The subject is the focus of the text.
- **Tone:** Tone is the speaker's attitude toward the subject.

My Notes

ACTIVITY 3.15 continued

10 While previewing the **SOAPSTone** strategy, be sure to define *call to action.*

11 Assign elements of SOAPSTone so that every student has one element as a focus for his or her reading. Students should continually add to their analysis of each element while they read.

TEACHER TO TEACHER

Some questions have been added to the SOAPSTone analysis to facilitate analysis of an argument.

SCAFFOLDING THE TEXT-DEPENDENT QUESTIONS

Wiesel refers to human dignity being "in jeopardy." What is happening to human dignity? What do you think "in jeopardy" means?

4. Key Ideas and Details (RI.8.3) **Closely examine paragraphs 6 and 7. What is Wiesel saying about memory and silence?** In paragraphs 6 and 7, what is Wiesel cautioning against? Why does he feel this is important?

© 2017 College Board. All rights reserved.

12 Read over the information on the **SOAPSTone** strategy as students follow along and **mark the text** for key elements.

13 Model filling in the first two rows of the **SOAPSTone** graphic organizer with students (see the Resources section for a SOAPSTone graphic organizer). Then put students in small groups of 3–4 to complete the rest of the chart on their own. Remind them to use their notes and to reread the text as necessary.

Never Forget, Never Again

7. Use your annotations of the speech and take notes on analyzing the argument in a SOAPSTone graphic organizer like the one below. Refer to the Resources section of your book for a SOAPSTone graphic organizer that you can copy and use for your analysis. The questions in the Analysis column below should help guide your analysis of the speech.

Element	Analysis	Textual Evidence
Speaker	Who is the speaker?	
Occasion	What event(s) or situation(s) prompted the creation of this text?	
Audience	Who is the intended audience?	
Purpose	What is the speaker's claim? What is the speaker's reason for creating this text? What is the speaker's call to action?	
Subject	How does the speaker appeal to *logos* (i.e., how does the speaker use facts, examples, statistics, research, and logical reasoning for effect)? How does the speaker use counterclaims or concession and rebuttal? How does the speaker appeal to *pathos* (emotion)?	
Tone	What is the speaker's attitude toward the subject? How does the speaker use connotative diction and/or imagery to create tone?	

Check Your Understanding

In discussion groups, analyze and evaluate Wiesel's argument:

- What is Wiesel's motive for writing his speech? Is it social, commercial, for public safety, or political? Provide textual evidence to support your response.
- How effective are Wiesel's appeals to *logos* (i.e., reasoning and evidence)? Provide textual evidence to support your response.
- How effective are Wiesel's appeals to *pathos*? Provide textual evidence to support your response.

LEARNING STRATEGIES: Think-Pair-Share, Marking the Text, Metacognitive Markers, Questioning the Text, Rereading, Close Reading, Discussion Groups, Socratic Seminar, Drafting

Language and Writer's Craft: Reviewing Clauses

A **clause** is a group of words with both a subject and verb. Common clauses include adverbial and adjectival clauses.

Adverbial: An adverbial clause is a dependent clause that functions as an adverb. It modifies another clause in the sentence. The writer can place the adverbial clause in different parts of the sentence, depending on where it best adds to the desired effect. An adverbial clause begins with a subordinating conjunction (such as *if, when, although, because, as*).

Example: "Experience is what you get *when you didn' t get what you wanted.*" (Randy Pausch, "The Last Lecture," 2008)

Adjectival: An adjectival clause is a dependent clause that is used as an adjective in a sentence. Since the adjectival clause modifies a noun, it cannot be moved around. An adjectival clause generally begins with a relative pronoun (*that, which, who, whom, whose*).

Example: "He *who can no longer pause to wonder and stand rapt in awe* is as good as dead." (Albert Einstein)

My Notes

Argumentative Writing Prompt: Think about what you learned in the first half of the unit, and what you learned from the text in this activity. Why should students continue to learn about the Holocaust? Draft a speech or a letter to convince the school board that this is an important subject to study in school. Be sure to:

- Assert a clear claim and address a counterclaim.
- Support your claim by using evidence from texts you have read.
- Use subjunctive and conditional mood for effect, as well as adverbial and adjectival clauses.

To support your writing, create a visual to clarify information, strengthen claims and evidence, and/or add interest. Then, rehearse and present an oral reading of your speech or letter a partner, displaying your visual for effect. Evaluate your partner's speech and visual to provide feedback relating to ideas, language, and oral presentation.

As a last step, create an annotated bibliography (see page 149) that includes (a) a statement about the main argument(s) in the text and the connection to your argument, and (b) a statement about the credibility of the source.

INDEPENDENT READING LINK

Read and Respond

Explain how the subject of your biography or autobiography has chosen an issue and hopes to make a difference in the lives of others who might be suffering.

ACTIVITY 3.15 continued

14 Have groups engage in **collaborative discussion** and complete the analysis and evaluation questions. When finished, discuss responses as a class.

15 Review with students the information on adverbial and adjectival clauses.

16 Ask students to respond independently to the writing prompt and to draft a visual to support ideas, like those in Activity 3.14.

17 Remind students to use evidence from at least two sources from the first half of the unit to support their ideas.

18 After reviewing expectations for speaking (appropriate eye contact, adequate volume, and clear pronunciation), form pairs, and ask students to rehearse and present their speech or letter.

19 Ask students to practice creating an annotated bibiliograpy (see Activity 2.16, page 149) using three different types of Holocaust texts from this unit. (Students can do this even if they did not include all three texts in their draft—it is just for practice.)

Leveled Differentiated Instruction

In this activity, students may need support with organizing their argumentative letter. Have students complete a **Persuasive/ Argument Writing Map** in order to organize their ideas.

Em After students have completed their organizers, ask students basic questions about why persuasive writing is organized in this way, such as *What is the purpose of including a summary or conclusion at the end of your letter?*

Ex After students have completed their organizers, ask students to explain why persuasive writing is organized in this way.

Br After students have completed their organizers, ask students to present an argument about why persuasive writing should be organized in this way.

▶ASSESS

Review speeches/letters (oral delivery and in writing) and annotated bibliographies to determine student understanding of argumentation and presentation, and identify any gaps before Embedded Assessment 2.

▶ADAPT

Have students conduct independent research on victims of injustice, suffering, human rights violations, genocide, or oppression in the world today in order to bring these issues to "the center of the universe" as Wiesel encourages. This research could help generate topics for Embedded Assessment 2. Suggest a website such as globalissues.org as a starting point for their research, and have students create an informational flyer to present to the class.

ACTIVITY 3.16

▶PLAN

Materials: computers with Internet access
Suggested Pacing: 2 50-minute class periods

TEACHER TO TEACHER

You may wish to spend some time exploring the website DoSomething.org to determine specific guidelines you might want to set regarding which issues students may select for Embedded Assessment 2.

Also, the website has a campanion book titled *Do Something: A Guidebook for Young Activists* that would be an excellent classroom resource for your students.

▶TEACH

1 Define *campaign* and distinguish it from a *multimedia campaign*.

2 Read the Preview and the Setting a Purpose for Reading sections with your students.

3 **FIRST READ:** Based on the complexity of the passage and your knowledge of your students, you may choose to conduct the first reading in a variety of ways:

- independent reading
- paired reading
- small group reading
- choral reading
- read aloud

4 As students are reading, monitor their progress. Be sure they are engaged with the text and annotating how young people are making a difference. Evaluate whether the selected reading mode is effective.

5 Based on the observations you made during the first reading, you may want to adjust your reading mode. For example, you may decide for the second reading to read aloud certain complex passages, or you may group students differently.

ACTIVITY 3.16

Students Taking Action

LEARNING STRATEGIES: Predicting, Marking the Text, Summarizing, Brainstorming, Graphic Organizer, Note-taking

ACADEMIC VOCABULARY
Media is the plural of *medium*, which is a means of expression or communication.

My Notes

WORD CONNECTIONS

Etymology

Campaign comes from a French word meaning "open country," and it referred to military engagement in open fields. It later came to denote any large-scale military operation, and now it is used to refer to any involved pursuit of a goal. You may be familiar with its use in political campaigns and fundraising campaigns.

Learning Targets

- Evaluate a variety of multimedia campaigns.
- Generate ideas for research in preparation for creating an original campaign.

Preview

In this activity, you will read and evaluate an informational text about taking action.

Setting a Purpose for Reading

- As you read the excerpt, underline words and phrases that are targeted for a youthful audience.
- Circle unknown words and phrases. Try to determine the meaning of the words by using context clues, word parts, or a dictionary.

Informational Text

from

Do Something!

A Handbook for Young Activists

Listen up! You don't have to be a rock star or the president or even have a driver's license to change the world. You can do something important right now—like, before your head hits the pillow tonight—that can make a difference in someone's life, change something for the better, or fix an important problem.

Young people rocking change isn't just possible; it's happening every day. Like the 12-year-old who registered over 10,000 people to donate bone marrow for people with cancer. Or the 7-year-old who taught other kids to swim. Or the 10-year-old who raised $30 by selling lemonade—and it was enough to buy dog food at a shelter for one night. If they can do it, so can you.

▶ Facts About DoSomething.org in 2012

1. 2.4 million young people took action through our campaigns in 2012.
2. We have 1,666,208 members doing stuff to improve their communities and the world.
3. Our 977,781 mobile subscribers take action and text us all about it.
4. We gave young people $240,000 in scholarships in 2012.
5. Our members collected 1,020,041 pairs of jeans for homeless youth through our Teens for Jeans campaign.
6. Our members recycled over 1.2 million aluminum cans through our 50 Cans campaign.
7. Our members donated 316,688 books to school libraries through our Epic Book Drive.
8. 67,808 members stood up to bullying through our Bully Text campaign.

COMMON CORE STATE STANDARDS

Focus Standards:

RI.8.1: Cite the textual evidence that most strongly supports an analysis of what the text says explicitly as well as inferences drawn from the text.

RI.8.5a: Analyze the use of text features (e.g. graphics, headers, captions) in consumer materials.

SL.8.2: Analyze the purpose of information presented in diverse media and formats (e.g., visually, quantitatively, orally) and evaluate the motives (e.g., social, commercial, political) behind its presentation.

Additional Standards Addressed:

RI.8.4; RI.8.6; W.8.7; SL.8.1a; SL.8.1b; SL.8.1c; SL.8.1d; SL.8.6; L.8.2a; L.8.6

Second Read

- Reread the excerpt to answer these text-dependent questions.
- Write any additional questions you have about the text in your Reader/Writer Notebook.

1. **Craft and Structure:** How effective is the diction of the piece in appealing to the target audience? Cite examples in your explanation.

   It is clear that this piece is targeting young people. "You don't have to be a rock star" links youth with their possible idols. "Or even have a driver's license" identifies with a situation they might also be in. "Rocking change" is the slang youth might use. RI.8.4

Working from the Text

2. Mark the text of the following campaign summaries to identify the what, why, and how of each issue.
   - What is the issue or problem the student wanted to do something about?
   - Why did the student care about this issue?
   - How did the student make a difference?

Student 1: Sarah Cronk **State:** IA **Issue:** Disability Rights

Sarah watched her older brother Charlie struggle to fit in during high school because of his disabilities. He was depressed and anxious, until the captain of the swim team invited him to join. Suddenly the cool kids welcomed him, and he found a new group of friends. Inspired by Charlie, Sarah co founded the first high school–based inclusive cheerleading squad in the nation. Today, the Sparkle Effect has generated 26 squads in 15 states and South Africa, encouraging a culture of acceptance in every community.

Student 2: Danny Mendoza **State:** CA **Issue:** Foster Care

While in college, Danny learned that his 9-year-old cousin, Roger, was living in a car. After lots of maneuvering, Danny helped him move from the Honda to a house, but he was deeply disturbed by how little control Roger had over his own situation. Danny took action and created Together We Rise, a youth-led organization dedicated to running programs that not only bring a sense of normalcy and stability to children in foster care, but also allow foster children to make their own choices. Through programs like music lessons, mentoring, sports and athletics, résumé building, and job readiness, Together We Rise provides the resources for foster kids to prepare for success at age 18, when they are kicked out of the foster care system and left to fend for themselves. Together, Danny and Together We Rise have reached 3,000 foster care youth through these programs, providing a better opportunity for long-term success.

My Notes

ACTIVITY 3.16 continued

Text Complexity
Overall: Accessible
Lexile: 820L
Qualitative: Low Difficulty
Task: Accessible (Understand)

6 **SECOND READ:** During the second reading, students will be returning to the text to answer the text-dependent comprehension question. You may choose to have students reread and work on the question in a variety of ways:

- independently
- in pairs
- in small groups
- together as a class

7 Have students answer the text-dependent question. If they have difficulty, scaffold the question by rephrasing it or breaking it down into smaller parts. See the Scaffolding the Text-Dependent Questions boxes for suggestions.

8 As a class, begin a Media Word Wall. Add the heading "Media Types," and then create a card for each type of media students have encountered in this unit (e.g., books, art, songs, speeches, podcasts, websites, etc.). Students should continue to add to this list throughout the rest of the unit as they encounter types of media that they could incorporate into Embedded Assessment 2.

9 Later in this activity, students will explore various campaigns independently on the Do Something! website. Prepare them for this by leading a guided exploration of the what, why, and how of the sample campaigns.

SCAFFOLDING THE TEXT-DEPENDENT QUESTIONS

1. Craft and Structure (RI.8.4) **How effective is the diction of the piece in appealing to the target audience? Cite examples in your explanation.** Who is the target audience of this text? How do phrases like "You don't have to be a rock star," "have a driver's license," and "rocking change" appeal to that audience?

TEACHER TO TEACHER

You may want to show students how to locate these campaigns on the DoSomething.org website by using the website search. The profiles have photographs, and some include brief video profiles.

© 2017 College Board. All rights reserved.

10 Ask students to summarize and form a personal response to check for understanding.

11 After giving students a few minutes to **brainstorm** national or global issues, place them with partners or in small groups to work with for the rest of the activity. Have them share their ideas, and encourage them to keep an open mind about which issues they want to explore further, as some of the most interesting and important issues can also be the ones that are not common knowledge.

12 Explain the difference between a *cause* and an *issue*.

13 Provide students with a list of the causes to choose from as a starting point for their exploration. Have each group select a different cause. These are listed under the "Causes" tab at DoSomething.org.

14 On the Web page for each cause, there is a list of issues related to that cause. Be sure that each student in the group selects a different issue related to their group cause.

Students Taking Action

GRAMMAR & USAGE
Commas

A comma after an introductory element in a sentence indicates a pause before the main part of the sentence. Look at these examples.

Introductory participial phrase: **Inspired by Charlie, . . .**

Introductory adverbial phrase: **While in college, . . .**

Introductory prepositional phrase: **At age 14, . . .**

Look for introductory elements like these as you write, and use a comma to punctuate them.

My Notes

Student 3: Jordan Coleman **State:** NJ **Issue:** Education

Jordan was angry when he learned that fewer than half of African American boys graduate from high school. He's an actor, so he decided to make a movie called *Say It Loud* (at age 13) to raise awareness about the importance of education. He toured with the film to spread his message to young people in community centers and schools around the country. He even got to speak at an education rally during the Presidential Inauguration in 2009!

Student 4: Evan Ducker **State:** NY **Issue:** Discrimination

Evan was born with a large birthmark on his face. At age 14, he decided to educate the public about the medical and psychological issues facing kids born with these kinds of birthmarks through his book, *Buddy Booby's Birthmark*, and his annual International *Buddy Booby's Birthmark* Read-Along for Tolerance and Awareness.

3. In the My Notes section, summarize the kinds of kids that are featured and how they have made a difference.
4. Form a personal response to connect to the text by answering these questions:
   - To which student do you most relate? Why?
   - Which student do you most respect? Why?
5. Create a web to brainstorm issues of community, national, and global significance that you are aware of and/or care about.
6. Choose a cause from the website dosomething.org to explore as a group.

   Our Cause: Animals, Violence, Disasters, Discrimination, Education, Environment, Poverty, Human Rights, Our Troops, Health
7. Have each person in your group focus on a different issue related to your cause. For example, if your cause is "Animals," you can have one person research animal testing, another animal cruelty, and a third animal homelessness. (You will find links to different issues under each cause.)

   My Issue:
   - Complete the first row of the graphic organizer on the next page by taking notes on the what, why, and how of your issue. Add your own ideas as well as the ones you find on the website.
   - Present your issue to your group members. As group members present their issues, take notes in the graphic organizer.

WORD CONNECTIONS
Word Relationships

Cause and *issue* are two related words. *Cause* is used to refer to an often broad area of concern that needs to be addressed. An *issue* refers to a specific item under that cause. For example, global warming, overpopulation, and pollution are all issues within the cause of helping the environment.

8. Reflect on your research: Is there an issue that stands out to your group as a potential subject for your multimedia campaign? If so, where can you find more information about it?

"Do Something" Graphic Organizer

WHAT is the issue or problem? List informative and compelling facts.	**WHY should you care?** Record appeals to *logos*, *pathos*, and *ethos*.	**HOW can you make a difference?** Record a clear and reasonable call to action.
Issue: ________________		
Issue: ________________		
Issue: ________________		

Our cause:

© 2017 College Board. All rights reserved.

ASSESS

Direct students to work independently to complete the research, notes, and reflection. Review student work to be sure that students can recognize the informative and persuasive aspects of a campaign as well as the call to action.

ADAPT

Discuss possible strategies for continued research, and discuss the importance of using relevant evidence from a variety of accurate, credible sources. If you feel that students need to do more exploration in order to generate subjects for Embedded Assessment 2, have them visit other websites, such as www.globalissues.org or www.causes.com.

ACTIVITY 3.17

▶PLAN

Materials: computers with Internet access (optional), index cards
Suggested Pacing: 2 50-minute class periods

▶TEACH

1 Read the Preview and the Setting a Purpose for Reading sections with your students. Help them understand what they should be annotating.

2 **FIRST READ:** Based on the complexity of the passage and your knowledge of your students, you may choose to conduct the first reading in a variety of ways:

- independent reading
- paired reading
- small group reading
- choral reading
- read aloud

3 As students are reading, monitor their progress. Be sure they are engaged with the text and annotating what steps are being taken to make a difference. Evaluate whether the selected reading mode is effective.

4 Based on the observations you made during the first reading, you may want to adjust your reading mode. For example, you may decide for the second reading to read aloud certain complex passages, or you may group students differently.

ACTIVITY 3.17

From Vision to Action

LEARNING STRATEGIES: Metacognitive Markers, Diffusing, Rereading, Summarizing, Discussion Groups, Graphic Organizer, Drafting

Learning Targets

- Analyze informational texts about efforts that have made a difference on a global scale.
- Create a Web page to represent a campaign to make a difference.

Preview

In this activity, you will read about two ways that people can make a difference in the world. Then you will think about how you can make a difference for an issue you care about.

Setting a Purpose for Reading

- As you read the informational texts, underline verbs that describe what the activists are doing, or trying to do, to solve a problem.
- Circle unknown words and phrases. Try to determine the meaning of the words by using context clues, word parts, or a dictionary.

WORD CONNECTIONS

Content Connections

Deforestation and *desertification* are terms learned in both social studies and science. *Deforestation* is the large scale removal of trees and forest. *Desertification* is the transformation of habitable land to desert. Desertification sometimes happens after an area has been deforested.

Informational Text

Wangari Maathai

Wangari Maathai rose to prominence fighting for those most easily marginalized in Africa—poor women.

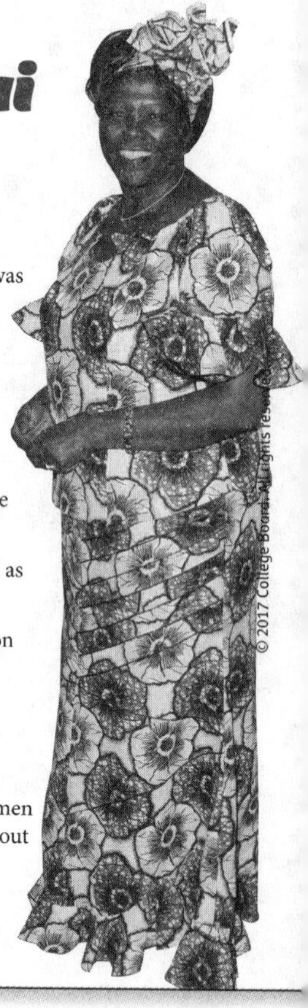

My Notes

1 The first African woman to win the Nobel Peace Prize (2004) was praised by the awarding committee as "a source of inspiration for everyone in Africa fighting for sustainable development, democracy and peace."

2 A pioneering academic, her role as an environmental campaigner began after she planted some trees in her back garden.

3 This inspired her in 1977 to form an organization—primarily of women—known as the Green Belt Movement aiming to **curtail** the **devastating** effects of deforestation and desertification.

4 Her desire was to produce sustainable wood for fuel use as well as combating soil **erosion**.

5 Her campaign to mobilize poor women to plant some 30 million trees has been copied by other countries.

6 Speaking as recently as Wednesday on the BBC's Africa Live program, she said her tree planting campaign was not at all popular when it first began.

7 "It took me a lot of days and nights to convince people that women could improve their environment without much technology or without much financial resources."

8 The Green Belt Movement went on to campaign on education, nutrition, and other issues important to women.

curtail: to cut short
devastating: highly destructive
erosion: the process of wearing away

COMMON CORE STATE STANDARDS

Focus Standards:

RI.8.1: Cite the textual evidence that most strongly supports an analysis of what the text says explicitly as well as inferences drawn from the text.

SL.8.2: Analyze the purpose of information presented in diverse media and formats (e.g., visually, quantitatively, orally) and evaluate the motives (e.g., social, commercial, political) behind its presentation.

Additional Standards Addressed:

RI.8.2; RI.8.3; RI.8.5a; W.8.1a; W.8.1e; W.8.4; W.8.6; W.8.8; W.8.10; SL.8.1a

Political role

9 Mrs. Maathai has been arrested several times for campaigning against deforestation in Africa.

10 In the late 1980s, she became a prominent opponent of a skyscraper planned for the middle of the Kenyan capital's main park—Uhuru Park.

11 She was **vilified** by Kenyan President Daniel arap Moi's government but succeeded in **thwarting** the plans.

12 More recently, she evolved into a leading campaigner on social matters.

13 Once she was beaten unconscious by heavy-handed police. On another occasion she led a demonstration of naked women.

14 In 1997, she ran for president against Mr. Moi but made little impact.

Esteem

15 But in elections in 2002, she was elected as MP with 98% of the votes as part of an opposition **coalition** which swept to power after Mr. Moi stepped down.

16 She was appointed as a deputy environment minister in 2003.

17 Mrs. Maathai says she usually uses a biblical analogy of creation to stress the importance of the environment.

18 "God created the planet from Monday to Friday. On Saturday he created human beings.

19 "The truth of the matter is … if man was created on Tuesday, I usually say, he would have been dead on Wednesday, because there would not have been the essential elements that he needs to survive," she told the BBC.

20 The Nobel Peace Prize committee praised her for taking "a **holistic** approach to **sustainable** development that embraces democracy, human rights and women's rights in particular."

21 She thinks globally and acts locally, they said.

22 She was born in 1940 and has three children.

23 Her former husband, whom she divorced in the 1980s, was said to have remarked that she was "too educated, too strong, too successful, too stubborn and too hard to control."

vilified: subjected to vicious statements
thwarting: preventing

coalition: an alliance of people or groups

holistic: emphasizing the whole of something, as opposed to its parts
sustainable: able to be maintained

My Notes

Text Complexity
Overall: Complex
Lexile: 1190L
Qualitative: Moderate Difficulty
Task: Moderate (Analyze)

Leveled Differentiated Instruction

Students may need support to understand the sequence of events in "Wangari Maathai." Have students use a **Sequence of Events Timeline** to take notes as they read the text.

Em Guide students to read the text with a partner and stop to talk about the sequence of events after each paragraph. Provide the sentence frames: *This paragraph is about ___. The events in this paragraph happened before/after ___.*

Ex Have students read the text with a partner and stop to ask and answer questions about the sequence of events after each paragraph such as, *What happened in this paragraph? Where does this paragraph fit in the sequence of events?*

Br Have students read the text and take notes about the sequence of events using the graphic organizer.

SCAFFOLDING THE TEXT-DEPENDENT QUESTIONS

1. Key Ideas and Details (RI.8.1) **What were some of the obstacles Wangari Maathai struggled against in creating and campaigning for the Green Belt Movement?** Read paragraphs 7 through 13. How did people resist Maathai's efforts?

2. Key Ideas and Details (RI.8.2) **Why do you think the Nobel Peace Prize committee praised Wangari Maathai for thinking globally and acting locally?** In paragraphs 20 and 21, how did the Nobel Peace Prize committee praise Maathai? Why do you think it was important to help people in her community first instead of all over the world?

Text Complexity
Overall: Complex
Lexile: 970L
Qualitative: Low Difficulty
Task: Moderate (Analyze)

5 Read the informational text about Freerice.com. To engage students, you might want to allow them to access the Freerice.com site and begin donating rice while improving their vocabulary.

Text Complexity
Overall: Complex
Lexile: 1240L
Qualitative: Low Difficulty
Task: Moderate (Analyze)

My Notes

Informational Text

About Freerice.com

1 Freerice is a nonprofit website that is owned by and supports the United Nations World Food Programme. Freerice has two goals:

- Provide education to everyone for free.
- Help end world hunger by providing rice to hungry people for free.

2 Whether you are CEO of a large corporation or a street child in a poor country, improving your education can improve your life. It is a great investment in yourself.

3 Perhaps even greater is the investment your donated rice makes in hungry human beings, enabling them to function and be productive. Somewhere in the world, a person is eating rice that you helped provide.

Informational Text

Free Rice Online Quiz Game

4 Freerice is an online internet game that donates 20 grains of rice to the World Food Programme (WFP) for every word that is correctly defined. WFP, the United Nations frontline organization fighting hunger, distributes the rice to the hungry. WFP uses the donations from the site to purchase rice locally, both feeding people in need and **stimulating** local economies.

5 Already, the site has raised enough rice to feed over 1.5 million people for a day. The game has been embraced by young and old alike, proving to be an excellent tool for prepping for the SATs or to brush up on vocabulary words. Teachers have been using the game to teach both vocabulary and the value of helping others in need.

stimulating: causing increased activity in

INDEPENDENT READING LINK
Read and Respond
Think about the cause or issue that the person is fighting for in your independent reading book. What personal, political, or social connections exist between that cause or issue and the person?

SCAFFOLDING THE TEXT-DEPENDENT QUESTIONS

3. Key Ideas and Details (RI.8.2) **How does the game on Freerice.com achieve its two goals?** Read paragraph 1 and describe the two goals Freerice.com hopes to achieve. How is each goal met when people play the online game described in paragraphs 4 and 5?

© 2017 College Board. All rights reserved.

Second Read

- Reread the informational texts to answer these text-dependent questions.
- Write any additional questions you have about the text in your Reader/Writer Notebook.

1. **Key Ideas and Details:** What were some of the obstacles Wangari Maathai struggled against in creating and campaigning for the Green Belt Movement?

   Maathai was beaten and arrested and also had to work to convince people that they could make a difference. RI.8.1

2. **Key Ideas and Details:** Why do you think the Nobel Peace Prize committee praised Wangari Maathai for thinking globally and acting locally?

   She approached global environmental problems by taking action in her local area. RI.8.2

3. **Key Ideas and Details:** How does the game on freerice.com achieve its two goals?

   Answering the quiz questions helps educate people, and rice is donated to help end hunger each time a question is answered correctly. RI.8.2

Working from the Text

4. What is the meaning of the slogan "Think Globally, Act Locally"?

   Think about an issue that affects the whole world and then try to help change it in your local community.

5. Wangari Maathai and Freerice.com each made a difference on a global scale by organizing their goals around a specific mission and taking action. Use the chart on the next page to evaluate different elements from the homepages of their websites.

My Notes

ACTIVITY 3.17 continued

6 **SECOND READ:** During the second reading, students will be returning to the text to answer the text-dependent comprehension questions. You may choose to have students reread and work on the questions in a variety of ways:

- independently
- in pairs
- in small groups
- together as a class

7 Have students answer the text-dependent questions. If they have difficulty, scaffold the questions by rephrasing them or breaking them down into smaller parts. See the Scaffolding the Text-Dependent Questions boxes for suggestions.

8 After defining *slogan*, have students **think-pair-write-share** responses to the question.

9 Briefly discuss their responses as a class, asking them to think of ways they might "act locally" to confront a global issue, such as turning out lights when they leave a room to save energy and cut down on pollution and global warming.

10 Define other common campaign features. Ask students to think about how each one can be used for effect in a campaign. Remind students that they will need to think through these features for their own campaign in Embedded Assessment 2.

11 Create the heading "Campaign Diction" and the subheading "Features" on the Word Wall. Ask students to create and display cards for these features.

12 Help students **diffuse** the text. Ask students to add selected words to the Word Wall under the heading "Campaign Diction."

© 2017 College Board. All rights reserved.

13 Have students access the home pages of Wangari Maathai's Green Belt Movement and Freerice.com, which is sponsored by the World Food Programme. Have them use the **graphic organizer** to analyze the specified elements of each organization's home page.

14 Have students work in pairs, using the information in the chart to evaluate the elements of an effective organization home page.

15 For independent practice, either during class or as homework, have students design their own Web pages including these elements.

▶ASSESS

Review student work to determine student understanding of campaign features and how to use them for effect.

▶ADAPT

If needed, work as a class to analyze additional examples of articles about or websites for organizations that are making a difference on a global scale.

From Vision to Action

My comments:	Wangari Maathai	World Food Programme
Organization Name	The Green Belt Movement	World Food Programme Freerice
Logo	the green belt movement international	FREE Rice
Slogan	"A values-driven society of people who consciously work for continued improvement of their livelihoods and a greener, cleaner world."	Hunger: The World's Greatest Solvable Problem
Mission Statement	"We strive for better environmental management, community empowerment, and livelihood improvement using tree-planting as an entry point."	Freerice has two goals: Provide education to everyone for free. Help end world hunger by providing rice to hungry people for free.
Call to Action	International Tree Planting Campaign: Plant a tree anywhere in your own neighborhood and mark it on an interactive map.	"Somewhere in the world, a person is eating rice that you helped provide."

Check Your Understanding

Draft a website home page for the issue you researched in the previous activity. Use campaign features (organization name, logo, slogan, mission statement) for effect, and be sure to include a clear and reasonable call to action.

© 2017 College Board. All rights reserved.

Examining Media Campaigns

ACTIVITY 3.18

Learning Targets

- Identify and explain how specific media types appeal to different target audiences.
- Evaluate the effectiveness of specific elements of multimedia campaigns.
- Create a visual that shows how to use persuasive appeals in different types of media to convince a target audience to take action.

Preview

In this activity, you will read about multimedia campaigns and think about how to create your own.

Setting a Purpose for Reading

- As you read the informational text, underline words and phrases that describe what public service announcements (PSAs) are like.
- Circle unknown words and phrases. Try to determine the meaning of the words by using context clues, word parts, or a dictionary.

LEARNING STRATEGIES: Graphic Organizer, Note-taking, Discussion Groups, Sketching

WORD CONNECTIONS

Word Relationships

You can see that *commercial* derives from the word *commerce*, which is the buying and selling of goods. As a noun a *commercial* refers to an advertisement on television or radio. As an adjective, it describes a business or enterprise where the main goal is to make money and earn profits.

Informational Text

Public Service Announcements

1 Broadcast media—radio and television—are required by the Federal Communications Commission (FCC) to serve "in the public interest." Most stations use PSAs as one of the ways they meet this requirement. While they aren't required to donate a fixed percentage of air time per day to PSAs, stations do have to state in their licensing and renewal applications how much air time they plan to devote to PSAs. Most stations donate about a third of their commercial spots to non-commercial causes; in other words, if a station has 18 minutes of commercials in a given hour, six minutes of that will probably be devoted to PSAs.

2 Public service announcements, or PSAs, are short messages produced on film, videotape, DVD, CD, audiotape, or as a computer file and given to radio and television stations. Generally, PSAs are sent as ready-to-air audio or video tapes, although radio stations sometimes prefer a script that their announcers can read live on the air.

3 Since World War II, public service announcements (PSAs) have informed and attempted to persuade the public about a variety of issues.

4 If people find an ad or PSA entertaining enough, they might talk about it with a friend or share it online. When this happens, many more people will receive the intended message.

INDEPENDENT READING LINK

Read and Discuss

Suppose you were to help the subject of your independent reading narrative make a PSA to promote his or her cause. Discuss with a classmate who the target audience of the PSA would be. What words or phrases would you use to appeal to that audience?

ACTIVITY 3.18

▶PLAN

Materials: downloaded audio/video PSAs from http://knowhow2go.acenet.edu/
computers with Internet access
Suggested Pacing: 1 50-minute class period

▶TEACH

1 Define *PSA*, and ask a student to add a Word Wall card underneath the heading "Media Types/Channels." The brief informational article about PSAs is intended to give a bit more information about a form of multimedia campaign students might want to create.

Text Complexity
Overall: Accessible
Lexile: 1290L
Qualitative: Low Difficulty
Task: Low (Understand)

2 Read the Preview and the Setting a Purpose for Reading sections with your students.

3 **FIRST READ:** Based on the complexity of the passage and your knowledge of your students, you may choose to conduct the first reading in a variety of ways:

- independent reading
- paired reading
- small group reading
- choral reading
- read aloud

4 As students are reading, monitor their progress. Be sure they are engaged with the text and annotating parts that provide key information about PSAs. Evaluate whether the selected reading mode is effective.

5 Based on the observations you made during the first reading, you may want to adjust your reading mode. For example, you may decide for the second reading to read aloud certain complex passages, or you may group students differently.

COMMON CORE STATE STANDARDS

Focus Standards:

RI.8.7: Evaluate the advantages and disadvantages of using different mediums (e.g., print or digital text, video, multimedia) to present a particular topic or idea.

W.8.8: Gather relevant information from multiple print and digital sources, using search terms effectively; assess the credibility and accuracy of each source; and quote or paraphrase the data and conclusions of others while avoiding plagiarism and following a standard format for citation.

SL.8.2: Analyze the purpose of information presented in diverse media and formats (e.g., visually, quantitatively, orally) and evaluate the motives (e.g., social, commercial, political) behind its presentation.

Additional Standards Addressed:

RI.8.1; RI.8.2; RI.8.3; RI.8.4; RI.8.6; RI.8.8; W.8.4; W.8.6; SL.8.5; L.8.6

ACTIVITY 3.18 continued

6 **SECOND READ:** During the second reading, students will be returning to the text to answer the text-dependent comprehension question. You may choose to have students reread and work on the question in a variety of ways:

- independently
- in pairs
- in small groups
- together as a class

7 Have students answer the text-dependent question. If they have difficulty, scaffold the question by rephrasing it or breaking it down into smaller parts. See the Scaffolding the Text-Dependent Questions boxes for suggestions.

8 In groups, pairs, or individually, students should locate and identify at least three public service campaigns that they find appealing. Students will then use the **graphic organizer** as they evaluate each PSA in terms of the elements given. You might analyze one PSA together as a class to model expectations. Make sure to examine the use of visual techniques for effect (framing, angles, color), and how language is used for effect (e.g., diction, syntax, imagery).

9 Guide students as they analyze and evaluate the use of persuasive appeals in the campaigns they have selected.

Examining Media Campaigns

My Notes

Second Read

- Reread the informational text to answer these text-dependent questions.
- Write any additional questions you have about the text in your Reader/Writer Notebook.

1. **Key Ideas and Details:** What evidence in this text suggests that public service announcements are not intended for commercial purposes?
   PSAs are not advertisements for products or services that require people to buy them. They may, however, encourage people to take actions, such as getting a flu shot, that may require a payment to the provider. RI.8.2

Working from the Text

2. Brainstorm types of media you could use to raise awareness and encourage action about an issue of national or global significance.
   Television, Internet, Facebook, Twitter, newspapers, magazines, radio, YouTube, billboard, blog, podcast
3. What is meant by a target audience? How does audience affect how an argument is developed and presented?
   A target audience is the group of people whom you want to receive your message. Different tactics can be used in delivering the message depending on the audience.
4. Research examples of public service announcements and campaigns. You might use the Internet, listen to radio, watch television, or look at newpaper or magazine ads to find examples. Find at least three examples that appeal to you, and **evaluate** them for the clarity of their messages, use of visuals and multimedia elements, and effectiveness.

Description of PSA	Clarity of Message	Use of Visuals/ Multimedia Elements	Effectiveness
Name: **Purpose:** **Audience:** **Content:**			
Name: **Purpose:** **Audience:** **Content:**			
Name: **Purpose:** **Audience:** **Content:**			

SCAFFOLDING THE TEXT-DEPENDENT QUESTIONS

1. Key Ideas and Details (RI.8.2) **What evidence in this text suggests that public service announcements are not intended for commercial purposes?** Review the Word Connection box about the word "commercial." What parts of the text, particularly in paragraph 3, suggest that PSAs do not contain a commercial message?

5. Analyze the campaigns' use of persuasive appeals for effect. How did each campaign use *pathos*, *ethos*, and *logos* to convince the target audience to take action? Give examples from your research. For a quick review of persuasive appeals, see Activity 2.12.

   Pathos: Example: It used humor to make the audience feel good. It also showed people who felt good about their accomplishments.

   Ethos: Example: The students portrayed in the campaign were all successful in their fields, but they also seemed real and accessible.

   Logos: Example: The message contained a clear "if/then" message: "If you want to go to college, then you should be prepared."

6. Of the different media and appeals used, which would you use in your own multimedia campaign? Who is your target audience? Which type of media would appeal to them? What type of ads would you create (magazine, newspaper, poster, billboard, Web banner), and where would you put them in order to reach your target audience?

Check Your Understanding

Choose one of the public service campaigns you researched and identify the various types of media it uses to get the word out. For each type of media used in the campaign, analyze the use of persuasive appeals for effect. Do the various ads in this campaign appeal to *pathos*, *ethos*, *logos*, or a combination of these? Are these appeals effective?

Public Service Announcement Campaign:		
Sponsor Organization:		
Volunteer Agency:		
Type of Media	**Target Audience**	**Types of Appeals Used/ Effectiveness**

7. Revisit the target audiences and types of media you are considering for your campaign. How can you use persuasive appeals in different types of media to convince your target audience to take action? Sketch a visual to show your thinking. Think about these guidelines for creating a PSA:
   - Aim for a sticky slogan.
   - Use one powerful image.
   - Use one shocking statistic.
   - Search for images by idea or create your own images.
   - Include a "Works Cited" or "Credits" slide for images as well as content. Please document with this text: "This image is used under a CC license from [insert URL back to image]."

My Notes

ACTIVITY 3.18 continued

10 Have students work individually to complete the analysis and respond to Student Steps 5 and 6 and the Check Your Understanding.

11 Instruct students to continue planning for Embedded Assessment 2. As a class, share ideas and provide feedback.

ASSESS

Review students' work to be sure they have a clear idea how to use different types of media and persuasive appeals to convince target audiences to take action.

ADAPT

If students need additional practice with these skills and concepts, conduct another guided exploration of a PSA campaign.

ACTIVITY 3.19

▶PLAN

Suggested Pacing: 1 50-minute class period

▶TEACH

1 Read the Preview and the Setting a Purpose for Reading sections with your students. Help them understand what they will be annotating.

2 **FIRST READ:** Based on the complexity of the passage and your knowledge of your students, you may choose to conduct the first reading in a variety of ways:

- independent reading
- paired reading
- small group reading
- choral reading
- read aloud

3 As students are reading, monitor their progress. Be sure they are engaged with the text and annotating instances of *logos* and *pathos*. Evaluate whether the selected reading mode is effective.

4 Based on the observations you made during the first reading, you may want to adjust your reading mode. For example, you may decide for the second reading to read aloud certain complex passages, or you may group students differently.

ACTIVITY 3.19

Raising Awareness

LEARNING STRATEGIES: Diffusing, Graphic Organizer, Note-taking, Collaborative Discussion

Learning Target

- Evaluate the effectiveness of arguments in print texts.

Preview

In this activity, you will read part of a speech and think about how to make an argument effectively.

Setting a Purpose for Reading

- As you read the speech, mark with *L* words and phrases that use *logos* (facts) to support the argument, and mark with *P* words and phrases that use *pathos* (emotion).
- Circle unknown words and phrases. Try to determine the meaning of the words by using context clues, word parts, or a dictionary.

My Notes

ABOUT THE AUTHOR

Cesar Chavez (1927–1993) was born in Yuma, Arizona, to a family that worked as migrant farm workers. As a migrant worker himself in 1962, he founded the National Farm Workers Association (NFWA). This group led strikes throughout California against agricultural businesses, including grape growers and lettuce growers. The NFWA changed its name to the United Farm Workers of America, and Chavez continued to campaign for fair labor practices and worker safety with nonviolent protests. A year after his death, Chavez was awarded the Presidential Medal of Freedom.

WORD CONNECTIONS

Content Connections

Neuroblastoma is a tumor that affects young children. It commonly begins in the abdomen and develops from tissues in the part of the nervous system that controls body functions.

GRAMMAR & USAGE

Verb Tenses

The present progressive verb tense describes an ongoing action that is happening at the same time the statement is written. This tense is formed by using *am, is,* or *are* with the verb form ending in *-ing*. For example, look at the first sentence in paragraph 10: "In McFarland ... **are being reported.**" The words "are being reported" show that the action was happening when the writer wrote this article.

Speech

ADDRESS BY

CAESAR CHAVEZ,

PRESIDENT, UNITED FARM WORKERS OF AMERICA, AFL-CIO

Pacific Lutheran University
March 1989, Tacoma, Washington

1 What is the worth of a man or a woman? What is the worth of a farm worker? How do you measure the value of a life?

2 Ask the parents of Johnnie Rodriguez.

3 Johnnie Rodriguez was not even a man; Johnnie was a five year old boy when he died after a painful two year battle against cancer.

4 His parents, Juan and Elia, are farm workers. Like all grape workers, they are exposed to pesticides and other agricultural chemicals. Elia worked in the table grapes around Delano, California until she was eight months pregnant with Johnnie.

5 Juan and Elia cannot say for certain if pesticides caused their son's cancer. But neuroblastoma is one of the cancers found in McFarland, a small farm town only a few miles from Delano, where the Rodriguezes live.

6 "Pesticides are always in the fields and around the towns," Johnnie's father told us. "The children get the chemicals when they play outside, drink the water or when they hug you after you come home from working in fields that are sprayed.

COMMON CORE STATE STANDARDS

Focus Standard:

RI.8.8: Delineate and evaluate the argument and specific claims in a text, assessing whether the reasoning is sound and the evidence is relevant and sufficient; recognize when irrelevant evidence is introduced.

Additional Standards Addressed:

RI.8.1; RI.8.2; RI.8.3; RI.8.4; RI.8.5; RI.8.6; W.8.7; SL.8.2; L.8.6

7 "Once your son has cancer, it's pretty hard to take," Juan Rodriguez says. "You hope it's a mistake, you pray. He was a real nice boy. He took it strong and lived as long as he could."

8 I keep a picture of Johnnie Rodriguez. He is sitting on his bed, hugging his Teddy bears. His sad eyes and cherubic face stare out at you. The photo was taken four days before he died.

9 Johnnie Rodriguez was one of 13 McFarland children diagnosed with cancer in recent years; and one of six who have died from the disease. With only 6,000 residents, the rate of cancer in McFarland is 400 percent above normal.

10 In McFarland and in Fowler childhood cancer cases are being reported in excess of expected rates. In Delano and other farming towns, questions are also being raised.

11 The chief source of **carcinogens** in these communities are **pesticides** from the vineyards and fields that encircle them. Health experts believe the high rate of cancer in McFarland is from pesticides and nitrate-containing fertilizers **leaching** into the water system from surrounding fields.

****

12 Farm workers and their families are exposed to pesticides from the crops they work. The soil the crops are grown in. Drift from sprays applied to adjoining fields—and often to the very field where they are working.

13 The fields that surround their homes are heavily and repeatedly sprayed. Pesticides pollute irrigation water and groundwater.

14 Children are still a big part of the labor force. Or they are taken to the fields by their parents because there is no child care.

15 Pregnant women labor in the fields to help support their families. **Toxic** exposure begins at a very young age—often in the womb.

16 What does acute pesticide poisoning produce?

17 Eye and respiratory irritations. Skin rashes. Systemic poisoning.

18 Death.

19 What are the chronic effects of pesticide poisoning on people, including farm workers and their children, according to scientific studies?

20 Birth defects. Sterility. Still births. Miscarriages. Neurological and neuropsychological effects. Effects on child growth and development.

21 Cancer.

22 Do we feel deeply enough the pain of those who must work in the fields every day with these poisons? Or the anguish of the families that have lost loved ones to cancer? Or the heartache of the parents who fear for the lives of their children? Who are raising children with deformities? Who agonize the outcome of their pregnancies?

My Notes

carcinogen: a substance that causes cancer
pesticides: chemicals used to kill insects
leaching: draining
toxic: poisonous

GRAMMAR & USAGE
Sentence Fragments

In almost all cases, incomplete sentences are incorrect. There are instances, however, where they can be used for effect. Look at paragraphs 17 and 18. These are incomplete sentences because they have no verbs. Paragraph 16, though, asks about the effects of pesticide poisoning. By following with a set of sentence fragments, each danger is emphasized more than it would be in a regular sentence separated with commas.

Think about how sentence fragments might help emphasize a point in your writing.

Text Complexity
Overall: Very Complex
Lexile: 1350L
Qualitative: Moderate Difficulty
Task: Challenging (Evaluate)

SCAFFOLDING THE TEXT-DEPENDENT QUESTIONS

1. Craft and Structure (RI.8.5) **What can you predict about this article given the opening question of the speech? Is the question intended to appeal to *logos, pathos,* or *ethos*? Explain.** Read the questions posed in paragraph 1. How do you think those questions will be answered throughout the speech? Do the questions require logical, emotional, or ethical answers?

2. Key Ideas and Details (RI.8.3) **The speaker opens his speech with an anecdote. What kind of persuasive appeal is he using and what effect does it have?** Read the anecdote about Johnnie Rodriguez in paragraphs 3 through 8. How does this anecdote make you feel? Is this effective in making you concerned about the case Chavez is making?

3. Key Ideas and Details (RI.8.2) **What is the claim Cesar Chavez is making?** Read paragraphs 9 through 13. What link is Chavez

5 SECOND READ: During the second reading, students will be returning to the text to answer the text-dependent comprehension questions. You may choose to have students reread and work on the questions in a variety of ways:

- independently
- in pairs
- in small groups
- together as a class

6 Have students answer the text-dependent questions. If they have difficulty, scaffold the questions by rephrasing them or breaking them down into smaller parts. See the Scaffolding the Text-Dependent Questions boxes for suggestions.

plague: a highly fatal epidemic affliction

wanton: immoral and excessive

My Notes

23 Who ask in fear, 'where will this deadly **plague** strike next?'

24 Do we feel their pain deeply enough?

25 I didn't. And I was ashamed.

26 I studied this **wanton** abuse of nature. I read the literature, heard from the experts about what pesticides do to our land and our food.

27 I talked with farm workers, listened to their families, and shared their anguish and their fears. I spoke out against the cycle of death.

28 But sometimes words come too cheaply. And their meaning is lost in the clutter that so often fills our lives.

29 That is why, in July and August of last year, I embarked on a 36-day unconditional, water-only fast.

30 The fast was first and foremost directed at myself. It was something I felt compelled to do to purify my own body, mind and soul.

31 The fast was an act of penance for our own members who, out of ignorance or need, cooperate with those who grow and sell food treated with toxins.

32 The fast was also for those who know what is right and just. It pains me that we continue to shop without protest at stores that offer grapes; that we eat in restaurants that display them; that we are too patient and understanding with those who serve them to us.

33 The fast, then, was for those who know that they could or should do more—for those who, by not acting, become bystanders in the poisoning of our food and the people who produce it.

34 The fast was, finally, a declaration of noncooperation with supermarkets that promote, sell, and profit from California table grapes. They are as culpable as those who manufacture the poisons and those who use them.

35 It is my hope that our friends everywhere will resist in many nonviolent ways the presence of grapes in the stores where they shop.

Second Read

- Reread the speech to answer these text-dependent questions.
- Write any additional questions you have about the text in your Reader/Writer Notebook.

1. **Craft and Structure:** What can you predict about this article given the opening question of the speech? Is the question intended to appeal to *logos*, *pathos*, or *ethos*? Explain.

   The speech will be about how people are being treated unjustly. The opening question sets the context in the ethical realm of the value of a human life. RI.8.5

SCAFFOLDING THE TEXT-DEPENDENT QUESTIONS

making between the use of pesticides and high incidences of cancer and illness?

4. Key Ideas and Details (RI.8.2) **Summarize the logic of Chavez's argument about the relationship between human health and pesticides. How has the author depended on logical reasoning and relevant evidence (*logos*)?** How does Chavez use facts and evidence in paragraphs 9 and 10 to support his claim?

5. Key Ideas and Details (RI.8.2) **How does Cesar Chavez satisfy the call to action part of the argument he is making?** In paragraph 29 what action does Chavez take to support his cause? What reasons does he give in paragraphs 30 through 34 for doing this? How does Chavez encourage others to take action in the last paragraph?

2. **Key Ideas and Details:** The speaker opens his speech with an anecdote. What kind of persuasive appeal is he using and what effect does it have?

The opening anecdote is an appeal to *pathos* in that it tells the story of one family's tragedy of losing a son to cancer that may have been caused by pesticides. RI.8.3

3. **Key Ideas and Details:** What is the claim Cesar Chavez is making?

Chavez's claim is that pesticides are responsible for the higher incidence of systemic poisoning of farmworkers, resulting in various sicknesses and especially cancer. RI.8.2

4. **Key Ideas and Details:** Summarize the logic of Chavez's argument about the relationship between human health and pesticides. How has the author depended on logical reasoning and relevant evidence (*logos*)?

Chavez argues that workers who spend hours each day working on the crops are exposed to the harmful pesticides. The families also live near the fields and drink the water into which the pesticides seep and become poisonous. Chavez states that the cancer rate in MacFarland is 400% higher than average, and that new cases are being reported more often than in the past. RI.8.2

5. **Key Ideas and Details:** How does Cesar Chavez satisfy the call to action part of the argument he is making?

Chavez himself participated in a fast to bring awareness to the issue. He also urged others to boycott the markets selling grapes from the polluted fields. RI.8.2

Working from the Text

6. Who is the article's target audience? How do you know?

The audience would be members of the UFW and supporters of the cause of the United Farm Workers. These are the people who would be following Chavez's fast and are concerned with the fate of farm workers.

7. Based on the target audience, use your analysis to evaluate each element of the authors' argument.

The argument engages with a rhetorical question that appeals to *ethos*, then moves to an anecdote that appeals to *pathos*. Chavez then goes on to establish a logical relationship between pesticides and various human ailments. He concludes with a call to action—don't buy grapes.

8. Overall, is the argument effective? Why or why not?

Yes, the argument focuses on creating awareness and presents a specific call to action.

My Notes

INDEPENDENT READING LINK

Read and Research

Go online to research another person who supported the same cause as the person in your independent reading narrative. How were their actions similar or different than your subject's?

ACTIVITY 3.19 continued

7 Have students respond to the Working from the Text questions as a **think-pair-share** and then report their conclusions in a class discussion.

ACTIVITY 3.19 continued

8 The website http://www.beyondpesticides.org/ provides helpful information on how to avoid dangerous pesticides. It details various issues related to pesticides and informs users how they can address legislators and affect policy. Instruct students to analyze the site's use of *logos* and *pathos* for effect. Briefly discuss as a class to check for understanding.

If for some reason you are unable to show students the websites, consider finding another example of a nonprint argument, such as a video or speech.

9 Add newspaper and magazine articles as well as photo essays and videos to the Word Wall under "Media Types."

▶ASSESS

Use the article analysis as a formative assessment of student understanding of the elements of an argument and target audience. The website analysis can provide further assessment of students' readiness for success on Embedded Assessment 2.

▶ADAPT

If students need additional practice, find another print or nonprint text about an issue of global or national significance, and have students analyze it for the elements of argumentation.

INDEPENDENT READING CHECKPOINT

Have students complete the Independent Reading Checkpoint

Raising Awareness

My Notes

9. Find an online site (probably a site that ends in ".org") that advocates for the use of safe pesticides and the protection of the environment, for instance: http://www.beyondpesticides.org/. Use the organizer below to take notes on the website you find and the elements of a multimedia campaign to create change.

Logos Facts used to help me understand the issue.	**Pathos** Images used to create emotion and to convince me to act.

Check Your Understanding

How does the text use *ethos* to raise awareness of the use of pesticides in farming. How can you use *ethos* in your own multimedia campaign?

Independent Reading Checkpoint

You are going to participate in book talks in small groups to share insights into the narratives you have each read. You should consider the challenge to society presented in your independent reading book and how that challenge was confronted. What did it take for one person to address that challenge, and how was that person successful? How has he or she left a positive impact on our society or on the world?

Presenting a Multimedia Campaign

EMBEDDED ASSESSMENT 2

Assignment

Develop a multimedia presentation that informs your peers about an issue of national or global significance and convinces them to take action. Work collaboratively to conduct and synthesize research into an engaging campaign that challenges your audience to make a difference.

Planning and Researching: Collaborate with a group of peers to select and gather information on an issue for your campaign.

- Which of the issues from the list your class has developed are of interest to you?
- Where could you look online to find out about more issues of national or global significance?
- How will you evaluate the credibility and timeliness of sources?
- How will you investigate what others are doing about your issue in order to evaluate possible solutions to incorporate into your call to action?
- How will you give credit for information found in your sources and prepare a Works Cited page or an Annotated Bibliography?

Drafting: Collaborate with your group to design a multimedia campaign.

- How will you use rhetorical appeals (*pathos*, *logos*, and *ethos*) to persuade your audience to care?
- How can you raise awareness by informing your peers about compelling facts related to your issue?
- What will be your group's name, mission statement, logo, and/or slogan?
- What media channels will you use in your presentation, such as presentation tools, audio/visual components, social media, or others?
- How will you organize talking points to inform your audience about the issue, convince them to care, and provide a call to action (what, why, and how)?

Rehearsing and Presenting: Use effective speaking and listening to prepare, present, and observe.

- How can you use feedback from a dress rehearsal to improve your presentation?
- How will you use the scoring guide to provide feedback on your own and others' presentations?
- How will you listen and take notes on the what, why, and how of each multimedia presentation?

Reflection

After completing this Embedded Assessment, think about how you went about accomplishing this task, and respond to the following:

- Which presentations were effective in convincing you to care about the issue, and why?
- What were the most effective media channels you observed, and what were the strengths of each?

My Notes

Technology TIP:

Using a presentation tool such as Prezi or PowerPoint can help organize your presentation, but be careful to focus on your audience instead of the screen. Using note cards can help you maintain eye contact instead of reading directly from your slides.

EMBEDDED ASSESSMENT 2

Materials: computers with Internet access

Suggested Pacing: 4 50-minute class periods

1 Planning and Researching: Since this is a collaborative task, it is important to have groups working together in the activities leading up to the Embedded Assessment. You may want to assign working groups early in this half of the unit so that they can make preliminary decisions and begin research.

2 This project will require time on the Internet to search for and examine multimedia campaigns. If working on the Internet is not possible, you could create screen shots of campaigns or ask students to look for PSAs on television and in magazines.

3 Drafting: Be sure students understand the components of a multimedia campaign. Videos, Prezi, and PowerPoint are effective media channels for presentation. Students could also present a low-tech version of a campaign with posters, scripted scenes, music selections, etc.

4 Rehearsing and Presenting: Remind students that every person should have a presenting responsibility. Consider scheduling a dress rehearsal with two groups so they can give each other focused feedback.

5 Decide how you will have students share and respond to presentations. For example, the final presentations could be in the form of stations around the room. Students could do peer evaluations based on the Scoring Guide and/or take notes on their classmates' campaigns.

Reflection These questions could be used as part of a peer or self-evaluation.

COMMON CORE STATE STANDARDS

Focus Standards:

W.8.1a: Introduce claim(s), acknowledge and distinguish the claim(s) from alternate or opposing claims, and organize the reasons and evidence logically.

W.8.1b: Support claim(s) with logical reasoning and relevant evidence, using accurate, credible sources and demonstrating an understanding of the topic or text.

W.8.1c: Use words, phrases, and clauses to create cohesion and clarify the relationships among claim(s), counterclaims, reasons, and evidence.

W.8.1e: Provide a concluding statement or section that follows from and supports the argument presented.

W.8.4: Produce clear and coherent writing in which the development, organization, and style are appropriate to task, purpose, and audience. (Grade-specific expectations for writing types are defined in standards 1–3.)

EMBEDDED ASSESSMENT 2 continued

Portfolio Ask students to collect and organize their work and create a Table of Contents for the work leading up to Embedded Assessment 2.

Be sure they add their response to the reflection questions to their Portfolios. They should also include their response to the reflection from the end of Embedded Assessment 1.

Once they have finished organizing their work in this unit and now that you are more than halfway through the year, you may want to ask students to pause and reflect on their growth and learning so far.

SCORING GUIDE

When you score this Embedded Assessment, you may wish to download and print copies of the Scoring Guide from SpringBoard Digital. In this way, you can have a copy to mark for each student's work.

EMBEDDED ASSESSMENT 2

Presenting a Multimedia Campaign

SCORING GUIDE

Scoring Criteria	Exemplary	Proficient	Emerging	Incomplete
Ideas	The presentation • supports a clear claim and addresses counterclaim(s) with relevant reasons and evidence from a variety of accurate sources • uses persuasive appeals effectively • integrates engaging multimedia and campaign features to clarify ideas.	The presentation • supports a claim and addresses counterclaim(s) with sufficient reasons and evidence from reliable sources • uses persuasive appeals (*logos*, *pathos*, and *ethos*) • includes adequate multimedia and campaign features to clarify ideas.	The presentation • has an unclear or unsupported claim, addresses counterclaim(s) ineffectively, and/or uses research from insufficient or unreliable sources • uses persuasive appeals unevenly • includes inadequate multimedia and campaign features.	The presentation • has no claim or counterclaim, and/or shows little or no evidence of research • does not use persuasive appeals • lacks multimedia or campaign features.
Structure	The presentation • demonstrates extensive evidence of collaboration and preparation • has an introduction that engages and informs the audience • sequences ideas and quotations smoothly with transitions • concludes with a clear call to action.	The presentation • demonstrates adequate evidence of collaboration and preparation • has an introduction that informs and orients the audience • sequences ideas and embeds quotations with transitions • includes a conclusion with a call to action.	The presentation • demonstrates insufficient or uneven collaboration and/or preparation • has a weak introduction • uses flawed or illogical sequencing; quotations seem disconnected • includes a weak or partial conclusion.	The presentation • demonstrates a failure to collaborate or prepare • lacks an introduction • has little or no evidence of sequencing or transitions • lacks a conclusion.
Use of Language	The speaker • communicates to a target audience with a persuasive tone and precise diction • demonstrates command of the conventions of standard English grammar, usage, and language (including correct mood/voice) • cites and evaluates sources thoroughly in an annotated bibliography.	The speaker • communicates to a target audience with appropriate tone and some precise diction • demonstrates adequate command of the conventions of standard English grammar, usage, and language (including correct mood/voice) • cites and evaluates sources in an annotated bibliography.	The speaker • communicates to a target audience inappropriately; may use basic diction • demonstrates partial command of the conventions of standard English grammar, usage, and language • begins to cite and/or evaluate sources in an annotated bibliography; may use improper format.	The speaker • does not communicate clearly; uses vague or confusing diction • has frequent errors in standard English grammar, usage, and language • lacks an annotated bibliography.

W.8.6: Use technology, including the Internet, to produce and publish writing and present the relationships between information and ideas efficiently as well as to interact and collaborate with others.

W.8.7: Conduct short research projects to answer a question (including a self-generated question), drawing on several sources and generating additional related, focused questions that allow for multiple avenues of exploration.

W.8.8: Gather relevant information from multiple print and digital sources, using search terms effectively; assess the credibility and accuracy of each source; and quote or paraphrase the data and conclusions of others while avoiding plagiarism and following a standard format for citation.

Additional Standards Addressed:

RL.8.10; W.8.5; W.8.10; SL.8.1a; SL.8.1d; SL.8.2; SL.8.3; SL.8.4–6; L.8.1c; L.8.3a

© 2017 College Board. All rights reserved.

ENGLISH LANGUAGE DEVELOPMENT RUBRIC

The Embedded Assessment that the whole class completes can be a useful source of English language development evidence. Use this additional rubric to examine the Embedded Assessment products of English learners. The analysis will help you gain additional information about student learning related to the strands of the English Language Development Standards and identify individual areas for improvement.

Criteria	Emerging	Expanding	Bridging
Collaborative	The student • engages in conversational exchanges by asking and answering questions using simple phrases. • engages and collaborates on short written exchanges with peers. • adapts language choice to setting and audience.	The student • engages in discussion by asking relevant questions and adding relevant information. • engages and collaborates on longer written exchanges with peers. • adapts language choice to purpose, task, and audience.	The student • engages in discussion by asking relevant questions and contributing useful feedback. • engages and collaborates on complex written exchanges with peers. • adapts complex language choice to task, purpose, and audience.
Interpretive	The student • demonstrates active listening by asking and answering basic questions with support. • explains basic ideas of texts with substantial support. • expresses inferences and conclusions with substantial support. • analyzes how words produce different effects.	The student • demonstrates active listening by asking and answering detailed questions with some support. • explains ideas of texts with some support. • expresses inferences and conclusions with some support. • analyzes how words produce shades of meaning and effect the audience.	The student • demonstrates active listening by asking and answering basic questions with little support. • explains complex ideas based on close readings of texts with little support. • expresses inferences and conclusions with little support. • analyzes how words or phrases produce shades of meaning and effect the audience.
Productive	The student • plans and delivers brief informational oral presentations. • writes short informational texts collaboratively and independently. • uses general academic vocabulary with domain-specific words to create some precision.	The student • plans and delivers longer informational oral presentations. • writes longer informational texts collaboratively and independently with appropriate text organization. • uses precise general academic vocabulary with domain-specific words.	The student • plans and delivers complex informational oral presentations. • writes longer, more detailed informational texts collaboratively and independently with appropriate text organization. • uses precise, nuanced, vocabulary.
Structuring Cohesive Texts	The student • organizes writing logically to express ideas. • uses basic language resources to make text more cohesive. • uses simple connecting words to link ideas or events in the text.	The student • organizes writing naturally, logically, and coherently. • uses increasingly complex language resources to make text more cohesive. • uses connecting words or phrases to link ideas or events in the text.	The student • organizes writing in a logical, clear sequence to create cohesion and precision. • uses complex language resources to make text more cohesive. • uses a variety of connecting words or phrases to link ideas or events in the text.
Expanding and Enriching Ideas	The student • uses a variety of verbs. • uses nouns and noun phrases to add details. • uses simple adverbials to provide details.	The student • uses a variety of verbs in different tenses. • uses a variety of nouns and noun phrases to add rich details. • uses adverbials to provide rich details.	The student • uses a variety of verbs in different tenses, aspects, voices, and moods. • uses an expanded variety of nouns and noun phrases to add rich details. • uses complex adverbials to provide rich details.
Connecting and Condensing Ideas	The student • connects ideas in compound sentences using simple conjunctions. • condenses ideas by using prepositional phrases.	The student • connects ideas in compound and complex sentences using a variety of ways. • condenses ideas in a variety of ways.	The student • connects and combines ideas in compound and complex sentences using a variety of ways. • condenses ideas in a variety of complex ways.

Embedded Assessment 2: Presenting a Multimedia Campaign

ENGLISH LANGUAGE DEVELOPMENT RUBRIC

The Embedded Assessment that the whole class completes can be a useful source of English language development evidence. Use this additional rubric to examine the Embedded Assessment products of English learners. The analysis will help you gain additional information about student learning related to the strands of the English Language Development Standards and identify individual areas for improvement.

Criteria	Emerging	Expanding	Bridging
Collaborative	The student • engages in conversational exchanges by asking and answering questions using simple phrases. • engages and collaborates on short written exchanges with peers using technology as appropriate. • adapts language choice to setting and audience.	The student • engages in discussion by asking relevant questions and adding relevant information. • engages and collaborates on longer written exchanges with peers using technology as appropriate. • adapts language choice to purpose, task, and audience.	The student • engages in discussion by asking relevant questions and contributing useful feedback. • engages and collaborates on complex written exchanges with peers using technology as appropriate. • adapts complex language choice to task, purpose, and audience.
Interpretive	The student • demonstrates active listening by asking and answering basic questions with support. • explains basic ideas of texts with substantial support. • expresses inferences and conclusions with substantial support. • analyzes how words produce different effects.	The student • demonstrates active listening by asking and answering detailed questions with some support. • explains ideas of texts with some support. • expresses inferences and conclusions with some support. • analyzes how words produce shades of meaning and effect the audience.	The student • demonstrates active listening by asking and answering basic questions with little support. • explains complex ideas based on close readings of texts with little support. • expresses inferences and conclusions with little support. • analyzes how words or phrases produce shades of meaning and effect the audience.
Productive	The student • plans and delivers brief informational oral presentations. • writes short informational texts collaboratively and independently. • uses general academic vocabulary with domain-specific words to create some precision.	The student • plans and delivers longer informational oral presentations. • writes longer informational texts collaboratively and independently with appropriate text organization. • uses precise general academic vocabulary with domain-specific words.	The student • plans and delivers complex informational oral presentations. • writes longer, more detailed informational texts collaboratively and independently with appropriate text organization. • uses precise, nuanced, vocabulary.
Structuring Cohesive Texts	The student • organizes basic informational texts logically. • uses basic language resources to make text more cohesive. • uses simple connecting words to link ideas or events in the text.	The student • organizes informational texts with a natural event sequence. • uses increasingly complex language resources to make text more cohesive. • uses connecting words or phrases to link ideas or events in the text.	The student • organizes informational texts with a clear and natural event sequence. • uses complex language resources to make text more cohesive. • uses a variety of connecting words or phrases to link ideas or events in the text.
Expanding and Enriching Ideas	The student • uses a variety of verbs. • uses nouns and noun phrases to add details. • uses simple adverbials to provide details.	The student • uses a variety of verbs in different tenses. • uses a variety of nouns and noun phrases to add rich details. • uses adverbials to provide rich details.	The student • uses a variety of verbs in different tenses, aspects, voices, and moods. • uses an expanded variety of nouns and noun phrases to add rich details. • uses complex adverbials to provide rich details.
Connecting and Condensing Ideas	The student • connects ideas in compound sentences using simple conjunctions. • condenses ideas by using prepositional phrases	The student • connects ideas in compound and complex sentences using a variety of ways. • condenses ideas in a variety of ways	The student • connects and combines ideas in compound and complex sentences using a variety of ways. • condenses ideas in a variety of complex ways

Planning the Unit

UNIT 4

Context

Students have learned that overcoming challenges is not easy, but they have also experienced that finding humor in life can help along the way. In Unit 4, students identify and analyze the elements commonly found in humorous writing and visual media. Students will examine the ways authors create humor for effect and will demonstrate their understanding by writing an expository essay analyzing a humorous text and by analyzing and performing scenes from a Shakespeare comedy.

Instructional Sequence

The first half of the unit introduces comedy as a genre for study. Students explore how authors create humor, and they use comedic vocabulary to discuss humor. To further develop critical analysis skills, students identify and analyze levels of comedy and elements of humor. Finally, to synthesize their understanding of humorous texts and to create a model for Embedded Assessment 1, students work collaboratively to write and revise a multiparagraph expository analysis of a humorous text.

In the second half of the unit, students study the humor in William Shakespeare's comedy *A Midsummer Night's Dream*. After an introduction to Shakespeare and his play, students learn to make meaning of the text through close reading and comparative analysis of film. Working in collaborative groups, students interpret and perform a scene from the play for Embedded Assessment 2.

CollegeBoard

AP/College Readiness

In this unit, students will focus on refining these important skills and knowledge areas for AP/College Readiness:

- Reading to make careful observations of textual detail and draw an interpretive conclusion about the meaning and value of a piece of writing (Activities 4.4, 4.5, 4.8)
- Reading to become aware of how stylistic effects are achieved by a writer (Activities 4.8, 4.9, 4.14)
- Analyzing literature using the language of literary analysis (Activities 4.4, 4.5, 4.10)
- Applying effective strategies and techniques in own writing (Activities 4.2, 4.4, 4.11)
- Controlling tone, establishing and maintaining voice, achieving appropriate emphasis through diction and sentence structure (Activities 4.4, 4.14, 4.16)

Unpacked Embedded Assessments

Embedded Assessment 1: Writing an Analysis of a Humorous Text	Embedded Assessment 2: Performing Shakespearean Comedy
Skills and Knowledge: • Write a multiparagraph literary analysis essay that addresses the prompt. • Develop a topic with textual evidence. • Use insightful commentary to analyze the effect of humorous elements. • Organize an essay with an engaging beginning, transitions to smoothly connected ideas, and a satisfying conclusion. • Use precise academic language to maintain formal style. • Demonstrate a command of the conventions of standard English capitalization, punctuation, spelling, grammar, and usage. • Work through all stages of the writing process.	**Skills and Knowledge:** • Demonstrate a deep understanding of Shakespeare's humor. • Use a variety of effective performance elements (staging, set design, lighting, sound, props) for comic effect. • Show evidence of extensive collaboration, planning, rehearsal, and reflection. • Provide context in an engaging introduction and deliver a satisfying conclusion for the audience. • Deliver lines from memory for comic effect and to convey meaning (through tone, pronunciation, inflection, facial expressions, gestures, movement, and blocking). • Use punctuation cues consistently and naturally to inform vocal delivery.

Instructional Activities and Pacing

Total: 42 class periods	Description
4.1–4.3 4 class periods	Students begin the unit by unpacking the Embedded Assessment so that they understand the task ahead. They are introduced to the complexity of humor by reading closely and writing an objective summary of an informational text. They will also learn about and discuss the diction and the levels of comedy, high and low, that are used to analyze and create humor. The unit's first Language and Writer's Craft lesson addresses using verbals and asks students to apply this new learning to their writing to add variety. These activities introduce students to the concepts and vocabulary that will help them analyze complex texts and humor throughout the unit.
4.4–4.6 7 class periods	Through close reading of film and literary texts, students continue to examine comedy by analyzing how speakers and authors use anecdote and satire to create humor. Using the close reading, writing, and collaborative strategies questioning the text, TWIST, and Socratic Seminar, students explain how an author conveys universal truths (theme) through humor. They continue their study of verbals in a second Language and Writer's Craft lesson and are asked to review and apply transitional strategies to an analytical paragraph to create coherence in writing.
4.7–4.10 8 class periods	These lessons are designed to strengthen students' understanding of comedy by introducing the specific elements of comic characters and caricatures, comic situations, hyperbole, and wordplay. Through close reading of texts from diverse genres, such as television show scenes, short story, film, novel excerpt, poetry, and comedic skit, students work collaboratively to define, recognize, and analyze these elements and their comedic effect. Students also respond to expository writing prompts to practice literary analysis.
4.11 3 class periods	As students near the Embedded Assessment, they practice analyzing the effect of the humorous elements they have studied so far by using a graphic organizer that will aid them in composing an analytical essay about a humorous text. They then evaluate a sample student essay in order to analyze its effectiveness and work in a writing group to collaboratively revise a component of it. This activity guides students through a group practice experience to prepare for the reading and writing tasks of Embedded Assessment 1.
Embedded Assessment 1 3 class periods	Students will write an analytical essay on a humorous text. This experience prepares students to continue thinking and learning about comedy as it applies to Shakespeare, in the second half of the unit.
4.12 1 class period	Students begin the second half of the unit by reflecting on learning and making connections between studying humor as a writer and reader and studying humor as a performer. To clarify learning expectations, students identify the knowledge and skills needed to complete Embedded Assessment 2 successfully.

4.13–4.14 4 class periods	To begin preparing for performing a comedic Shakespearean scene in Embedded Assessment 2, students conduct research to build background knowledge about Shakespeare and to establish context for the play *A Midsummer Night's Dream*. Students conduct a close reading of quotes to practice making meaning of Shakespeare's language, and they prepare and perform the quotes with attention to proper inflection, tone, gestures, and movement.
4.15–4.16 3 class periods	The next set of activities continues to develop effective collaborative groups. First, students collaborate as a class to read and make meaning of a specific scene from *A Midsummer Night's Dream* using summary and visualization. After creating group norms, students form acting companies. Each acting company engages in a close reading of the specific scenes they will perform for the Embedded Assessment. Acting companies plan roles, discuss the humor to be exaggerated or created, analyze blocking, and begin rehearsal.
4.17–4.20 6 class periods	As students get close to the Embedded Assessment, they will respond to an informational text about performance challenges and begin memorization of lines. Students will analyze aspects of their own role (character) and conduct a comparative analysis of different film adaptations and evaluate their own choices for performance. Acting companies participate in a dress rehearsal, and individuals reflect on and plan to address their strengths and challenges as performers.
Embedded Assessment 2 3 class periods	For the Embedded Assessment, students will have planned and conducted initial rehearsals for their performance that will demonstrate their understanding of Shakespeare's text and its elements of comedy. After students finish the task, they will reflect on the successes and challenges of performing a comic scene.

Unit Resources at a Glance

Readings	Writing Tasks	Language Skills
"Made You Laugh," by Marc Tyler Nobleman "I've Got a Few Pet Peeves about Sea Creatures," by Dave Barry "Underfunded Schools Forced To Cut Past Tense from Language Programs," from *The Onion* "The Open Window," by Saki "A Day's Work" from *The Adventures of Tom Sawyer*, by Mark Twain "They Have Yarns," by Carl Sandburg "Mooses," by T Hughes "El Chicle," by Ana Castillo	Quickwrites: How is a comedian able to create laughter?; Reaction to humor in a story; Describe norms for working collaboratively; Challenges to performing? Expository Writing Prompts • Explain your sense of humor. • Explain humor or a cartoon or comic strip. • Explain humor the author creates. • How does Barry use humor to convey truth? • How is satire used to expose folly?	**Language and Writers Craft** Verbals Using Verbals **Grammar and Usage** Subject-Verb Agreement Active and Passive Voice Participial Phrases Punctuation: Comma, Question Mark, Semicolon, Exclamation Point, Apostrophe

Readings (continued)	Writing Tasks (continued)	Language Skills (continued)
"Is Traffic Jam Delectable?" by Jack Prelutsky "Who's on First?" by Bud Abbott and Lou Costello "The Power of Pets," by Isha Sharma Excerpts from *A Midsummer Night's Dream*, by William Shakespeare A *Midsummer Night's Dream* (film)	• How does Twain convey a universal truth through humor? • How does writer use comic language? Narrative Writing Prompts • Write an original humorous scenario.	

Strategy Introduction	Speaking and Listening	Family Connections
RAFT TWIST	Performance	Suggestions for Independent Reading Family Letters (English and Spanish) Student Reports

English Language Development	Independent Reading	Assessments
Leveled Differentiated Instruction ELD Graphic Organizers *SpringBoard English Language Development*, Student Edition, Grade 8, Unit 4 *SpringBoard English Language Development*, Teacher Edition Grade 8, Unit 4	Independent Reading Links Independent Reading Checkpoints Independent Reading Log Reader/Writer Notebook Suggestions for Independent Reading	Check Your Understanding Writing Prompts Embedded Assessment One: Writing an Analysis of a Humorous Text Embedded Assessment Two: Performing Shakespearean Comedy Short-Cycle Assessments Unit Assessments

SpringBoard Writing Workshop with Grammar Activities, Grade 8	SpringBoard Close Reading Workshop, Grade 8	Routines for Teaching Foundational Skills
Writing Workshop 1: The Writing Process: Strategies for Writing Writing Workshop 2: Argumentative Writing Writing Workshop 3: Expository Writing: Compare and Contrast Writing Workshop 4: Narrative Writing: Short Story Writing Workshop 8: Poetry Writing Workshop 9: Script Writing Grammar Activities: Unit 4 Grammar Handbook	Close Reading Workshop 1: Close Reading of Informational/Literary Nonfiction Texts Close Reading Workshop 3: Close Reading of Poetry Close Reading Workshop 4: Close Reading of Shakespeare	Phonics and Word Recognition Mini-lessons Fluency Mini-lessons

Suggestions for Independent Reading

This list, divided into the categories of **Literature** and **Nonfiction/Informational Text**, comprises titles related to the themes and content of the unit. For their independent reading, students can select from this wide array of titles, which have been chosen based on complexity and interest. You can also encourage students to do their own research and select titles that intrigue them.

Unit 4: The Challenge of Comedy

Literature

Author	Title	Lexile
Adams, Douglas	*The Hitchhiker's Guide to the Galaxy*	1000L
Alexie, Sherman	*The Absolutely True Diary of a Part-Time Indian*	600L
Allison, Jennifer	*Gilda Joyce, Psychic Investigator: A Mystery*	1000L
Dahl, Roald	*The Wonderful Story of Henry Sugar: And Six More*	850L
Eliott, Rob	*Laugh Out Loud Jokes for Kids*	N/A
Healey, Christopher	*Hero's Guide to Saving Your Kingdom Series*	750L
Kindl, Patrice	*Keeping the Castle*	1050L
Kinney, Jeff	*Diary of a Wimpy Kid*	900L
Kipling, Rudyard	*Just So Stories*	1190L
Korman, Gordon	*Don't Care High*	920L
Leavitt, Lindsey	*Princess for Hire*	670L
McAlpine, Gordon	*The Tell-Tale Start: The Misadventures of Edgar & Allan Poe (series)*	850L
McCloskey, Robert	*Homer Price*	1000L
Paulsen, Gary	*Molly McGinty Has a Really Good Day*	960L
Pilkey, Dav	*Captain Underpants Collection*	800L
Scieszka, Jon	*Frank Einstein and the Antimatter Motor*	730L
Snicket, Lemony	*The Bad Beginning*	1010L
Snicket, Lemony	*The Grim Grotto*	1120L
Sparknotes	*No Fear Shakespeare Graphic Novels*	N/A
Swift, Jonathan	*A Modest Proposal*	1520L
Twain, Mark	*The Celebrated Jumping Frog and Other Stories*	1000L
Vonnegut, Kurt	*Cat's Cradle*	790L

Nonfiction/Informational Text

Author	Title	Lexile
Crutcher, Chris	*King of the Mild Frontier: An Ill-Advised Autobiography*	1180L
Dahl, Roald	*Boy*	1090L
Fey, Tina	*Bossypants*	950L
Kimmel, Haven	*A Girl Named Zippy*	1010L
Martin, Steve	*Born Standing Up: A Comic's Life*	N/A
Mayfield, Katherine	*Acting A to Z: The Young Person's Guide to a Stage or Screen Career*	1030L

The Challenge of Comedy

Visual Prompt: What makes people laugh?

Unit Overview

If laughter is truly the best medicine, then a study of challenges would not be complete without a close examination of the unique elements of comedy. Overcoming challenges is often easier when we are able to look at the humorous side of life. However, finding humor is not always easy; it can be a challenge in itself. In this unit, you will learn how authors create humor and how they use humor to reveal a universal truth (theme).

UNIT 4

Read aloud the Unit Overview, asking students to **mark the text** by highlighting words and phrases that help them predict what the unit will be about. Share responses in partner, small-group, or whole-class discussion.

Have students look at the photograph and respond to the visual prompt. You may want to have students **think-pair-share** to write a short response or discuss their responses as a class.

TEACHER TO TEACHER

Ask students if they can think of times when humor has helped them to overcome a challenge. Why does humor make it easier to deal with life's challenges?

ELL Support

ELD Modes and Processes

Collaborative: Students work together to analyze an essay and to understand idioms. Students also collaborate to evaluate class performances and to exchange information about creating and evaluating class performances.

Interpretive: Students demonstrate active listening to analyze a comedy. Students also analyze the language in a poem.

Productive: Students write to analyze humor in essays and stories and to compare films. Students also write to summarize a story and to analyze the key idea and details in an informational text.

Structuring Cohesive Texts: Students examine the structure of expository writing. Students also work to add transitions to their writing.

Expanding and Enriching Ideas: Students expand sentences using adverbs and adverb phrases.

UNIT 4

Have students read the goals for the unit and mark any words that are unfamiliar to them. Have students add these words to the classroom Word Wall, along with definitions.

You may also want to post these goals in a visible place in the classroom for the duration of this unit, allowing you and your students to revisit the goals easily and gauge progress toward achieving goals throughout the unit.

VOCABULARY DEVELOPMENT

Important terms in this unit are divided into Academic Vocabulary (those words that are used in multiple curriculum areas) and Literary Terms, which are specific to the student of literature and language arts.

Adding to vocabulary knowledge is essential for reading fluency. Students will encounter new vocabulary in this course in multiple ways:

- Academic Vocabulary
- Literary Terms
- Academic Vocabulary in Context (unfamiliar terms glossed in text selections)
- Word Connections
- Oral discussions

By now, the **Reader/Writer Notebook** should be a familiar tool that students use as they study key vocabulary terms in depth. The Reader/Writer Notebooks are not listed as part of the materials for each activity, but the expectation is that students will have access to them. Encourage students to continue their study of new words and their connection to unit concepts and to the broader use of academic terms. Remind students that the Reader/Writer Notebook may also be used for Independent Reading questions and observations.

Because students have become more familiar with using graphic organizers to explore the meaning of a word, you may want them to create their own graphic organizers as they near the end of the year.

LANGUAGE & WRITER'S CRAFT

Each unit includes Language and Writer's Craft features as well as Grammar & Usage content. Encourage

UNIT 4

The Challenge of Comedy

GOALS:

- To analyze how a variety of authors create humor in print and nonprint texts
- To analyze how humor is used to reveal a universal truth (theme)
- To write a well-developed analysis of a humorous text
- To analyze and perform a scene from a Shakespearean comedy
- To understand verbals and how they are used in writing

ACADEMIC VOCABULARY
juxtaposition
derision
denounce
caricature

Literary Terms
persona
satire
irony
dialect
hyperbole
yarn
alliteration

Contents

Activities:

ELL Support (continued)

English Language Development Standards

ELD.PI.8.1 Bridging* Contribute to class, group, and partner discussions by following turn-taking rules, asking relevant questions, affirming others, adding relevant information and evidence, paraphrasing key ideas, building on responses, and providing useful feedback. **ELD.PI.8.5 Expanding*** Demonstrate active listening in oral presentation activities by asking and answering detailed questions with occasional prompting and moderate support. **ELD.PI.8.8 Expanding*** Explain how phrasing or different words with similar meanings or figurative language produce shades of meaning and different effects on the audience. **ELD.PI.8.10a Bridging*** Write longer and more detailed literary and informational texts collaboratively and independently using appropriate text organization and growing understanding of register. **ELD.PI.8.10b Bridging*** Write clear and coherent summaries of texts and experiences using complete and

© 2017 College Board. All rights reserved.

*Texts not included in these materials.

Language and Writer's Craft
- Verbals (4.2)
- Using Verbals (4.4)

MY INDEPENDENT READING LIST

ELL Support (continued)

concise sentences and key words. **ELD.PII.8.1 Bridging*** Apply understanding of the organizational structure of different text types to comprehending texts and to writing clear and cohesive arguments, informative/explanatory texts and narratives. **ELD.PII.8.2b Bridging*** Apply increasing understanding of how ideas, events, or reasons are linked throughout a text using an increasing variety of academic connecting and transitional words or phrases to comprehending and writing texts with increasing cohesion. **ELD.PII.8.5 Expanding*** Expand sentences with adverbials to provide details about a familiar or new activity or process.

*The citation reflects the highest level supported. Support is also offered for the lower levels.

UNIT 4 continued

students to make notes about their understanding of specific grammar rules and how to use language in their writing to create specific effects in their Reader/Writer Notebooks.

CONTENTS

Have the students **skim/scan** the activities and texts to find a Wow (an activity that looks interesting) and a Whoa (an activity that looks challenging). Share responses in partner, small-group, or whole-class discussion.

INDEPENDENT READING

In this half of the unit, students will have the opportunity to read humorous texts in addition to classroom reading. Humorous essays, poems, and short stories are recommended. The Planning the Unit section of the Teacher's Edition and the Resources section of the Student Edition contain information, Reading Logs, and Reading Lists to help you and your students make a selection. Independent Reading Links in the Student Edition will prompt students to actively respond to their reading, and responses will be recorded in their Reader/Writer Notebook or Reading Logs. Independent Reading Checkpoints have been placed prior to each embedded assessment to provide formative check-ins.

TEACHER TO TEACHER

The SpringBoard program has been designed to allow students to interact with the text by making notes in their books and marking text to facilitate close reading. In addition to making notes in the text, students are expected to use their Reader/Writer Notebooks often: for vocabulary study, answering text-dependent reading comprehension questions, reflections, some writing assignments, notes in response to the Independent Reading Links, capturing thoughts about learning strategies and how to use them, and so on. The Reader/Writer Notebooks are not listed as part of the materials for each activity, but the expectation is that students will have access to them.

ACTIVITY 4.1

▶PLAN

Suggested Pacing: 1 50-minute class period

▶TEACH

1 Take an informal poll to see what kinds of things students find funny. Ask them to think about the last time they laughed and to share a quick story with a partner.

2 **Activate prior knowledge** by asking students to **think-pair-share** responses to the Essential Questions.

3 Ask students to independently sort the Academic Vocabulary and Literary Terms in the Table of Contents.

4 Ask students to conduct a **close reading** of the EA1 assignment and the Scoring Guide criteria, focusing on the "Proficient" column. Instruct students to **mark the text** by underlining or highlighting key skills (verbs) and knowledge (nouns).

5 As a class, create and display a large **graphic organizer** labeled with the Scoring Guide criteria. Ask students to create their own copy in their Reader/Writer Notebooks.

6 Make sure to keep the unpacked assessment in a visible place in your classroom so you and your students can refer to specific skills and knowledge before, during, and/or after each daily activity.

7 Assist students in the selection of independent reading texts for the unit. Review expectations as noted in the Independent Reading Link. Include a deadline by which selections should be made and reading should begin.

▶ASSESS

Have students work individually or in small groups to unpack the Embedded Assessment assignment and Scoring Guide. Check to see how independently they can do this important work.

▶ADAPT

Monitor students' discussions about the skills and knowledge they will need for Embedded Assessment 1. Guide understanding as needed.

ACTIVITY 4.1

Previewing the Unit

LEARNING STRATEGIES: Think-Pair-Share, QHT, Close Reading, Marking the Text, Paraphrasing, Graphic Organizer

My Notes

Learning Targets

- Preview the big ideas in the unit and make predictions about the topics of study.
- Demonstrate an understanding of the skills and knowledge needed to complete Embedded Assessment 1 successfully.

Making Connections

In the final unit you will encounter the challenging task of appreciating humorous texts and Shakespearean texts. You will use all your collaborative, speaking and listening, reading, and writing skills as you examine the ways in which authors create humor.

Essential Questions

Based on your current knowledge, respond to the following Essential Questions:

1. How do writers and speakers use humor to convey truth?

2. What makes an effective performance of a Shakespearean comedy?

Developing Vocabulary

Use a QHT chart to sort the terms on the Contents page. Remember, one academic goal is to move all words to the "T" column by the end of the unit.

Unpacking Embedded Assessment 1

Closely read the assignment for Embedded Assessment 1.

Write an essay that explains how an author creates humor for effect and uses it to communicate a universal truth.

Then, find the Scoring Guide and work with your class to paraphrase the expectations. Create a graphic organizer to use as a visual reminder of the required concepts (what you need to know) and skills (what you need to do).

After each activity, use this graphic to guide reflection about what you have learned and what you still need to learn in order to be successful in the Embedded Assessment.

INDEPENDENT READING LINK

Read and Respond

For your outside reading for this unit, choose texts by writers whom you find humorous. You might look for humorous short stories as well as narrative essays and poetry. Create a list of titles in your Independent Reading List of at least five texts based on recommendations from your teacher as well as your own research.

COMMON CORE STATE STANDARDS

Focus Standards:

L.8.6: Acquire and use accurately grade-appropriate general academic and domain-specific words and phrases; gather vocabulary knowledge when considering a word or phrase important to comprehension or expression.

Additional Standards Addressed:

RL.8.10; RI.8.10

Understanding the Complexity of Humor

ACTIVITY 4.2

Learning Targets

- Write an objective summary of an informational text.
- Demonstrate understanding of the denotations and connotations of words related to humor.

LEARNING STRATEGIES: Skimming/Scanning, Predicting, Close Reading, Marking the Text, Summarizing, Revisiting Prior Work, Discussion Groups

Preview

In this activity, you will read an essay on the topic of humor. As you read, think about your own sense of humor and what makes you laugh.

Setting a Purpose for Reading

- As you read, underline key words and phrases that explain the main idea of each section.
- Circle unknown words and phrases. Try to determine the meaning of the words by using context clues, word parts, or a dictionary.

My Notes

ABOUT THE AUTHOR

Marc Tyler Nobleman (b. 1972) has written more than 70 books. His current writing interest is picture books for readers of all ages. He is also a cartoonist whose work has been published in numerous well-known publications, including *The Wall Street Journal, Forbes, The Saturday Evening Post*, and *New York Daily News*.

Essay

Made You Laugh

by Marc Tyler Nobleman

1 Would you like to know a language everyone in the world understands? You already do—because you laugh. Any two people from vastly different cultures who don't speak a word of the other's language still know exactly what is meant when the other person laughs.

2 Think of laughter as the unofficial language of Earth. Yet how much do any of us really understand about humor?

On the Laugh Track

3 What makes things funny? READ asked John Ficarra, the editor of MAD magazine. After all, he should know. Here's what he said: "Monkeys. They're unbeatable. For example, show a photo of

ACTIVITY 4.2

PLAN

Materials: dictionaries or online references, index cards
Suggested Pacing: 2 50-minute class periods

TEACH

Text Complexity
Overall: Accessible
Lexile: 900L
Qualitative: Low Difficulty
Task: Accessible (Understand)

1 Read the Preview and the Setting a Purpose for Reading sections with your students. Help them understand any new terms they encounter.

2 **FIRST READ:** Based on the complexity of the passage and your knowledge of your students, you may choose to conduct the first reading in a variety of ways:

- independent reading
- paired reading
- small group reading
- choral reading
- read aloud

COMMON CORE STATE STANDARDS

Focus Standards:

RI.8.2: Determine a central idea of a text and analyze its development over the course of the text, including its relationship to supporting ideas; provide an objective summary of the text.

W.8.2d: Use precise language and domain-specific vocabulary to inform about or explain the topic.

L.8.5c: Distinguish among the connotations (associations) of words with similar denotations (definitions) (e.g., bullheaded, willful, firm, persistent, resolute).

Additional Standards Addressed:

RI.8.1; RI.8.3; RI.8.4; RI.8.6; RI.8.8; RI.8.10; W.8.2a; W.8.2b; W.8.4; W.8.5; W.8.9b; W.8.10; L.8.1a; L.8.5b; L.8.6

© 2017 College Board. All rights reserved.

3 As students are reading, monitor their progress. Be sure they are engaged with the text and annotating the main ideas from each section. Evaluate whether the selected reading mode is effective. If necessary, use the **think aloud** strategy with the first two paragraphs of the text to demonstrate how to **summarize** the main ideas.

4 Based on the observations you made during the first reading, you may want to adjust your reading mode. For example, you may decide for the second reading to read aloud certain complex passages, or you may group students differently.

Understanding the Complexity of Humor

GRAMMAR & USAGE
Subject-Verb Agreement

A verb form must agree in number (singular or plural) with its subject. When the subject is plural, the verb of the sentence must also be plural. For example:

Singular: "His **comedy is** funny ..."

Plural: "**Comedians have** their own theories ..."

The words *each, each one, either, neither, everyone, everybody, anybody, anyone, nobody, somebody, someone,* and *no one* are singular subjects and thus require a singular verb form. Do not be confused by words that appear between the subject and the verb. For example:

"**Everyone** who writes comedy **needs** to know the audience."

My Notes

a dentist—not funny. Show a photo of a dentist with a monkey in his chair, and it's comedy gold. Try this theory out on a few of your family photos, and you'll see." OK, so monkeys are funny. What else? How about this?

4 Two hunters were in the woods, when one collapsed. He didn't seem to be breathing. The other called the emergency number and said, "My friend is dead! What can I do?" The operator said, "Calm down, I can help. First, let's make sure he's dead." After a second of silence on the hunter's end, the operator heard a gunshot. The hunter came back on the phone and said, "OK, now what?"

5 If you laughed, you're not alone. In the year 2001, that joke was voted the funniest in the world as part of a project called LaughLab. Psychologist Richard Wiseman's goal was to determine what makes people laugh and what is found to be funny among men and women, older and younger people, and people from different countries. His research team tested people in person and asked others to submit opinions online using a "Giggleometer," which ranked jokes on a scale of 1–5. More than 40,000 jokes were tested.

6 You may be saying to yourself, "Studying jokes? Is that science?" But plenty of smart people say yes. Laughter is a biological function. It has a certain rhythm; laughter syllables build, then trail off, and they come out in a repetitive, not random, sequence. For example, "ha-ha-ho-ho-he" is typical, but "ha-ho-ha-ho-ha" or "he-ho-he" just doesn't happen.

7 Babies begin to laugh instinctively when they're about four months old, perhaps to form a connection with parents. Those born blind and deaf also laugh, so laughter is not dependent on sight and hearing. Other animals, notably chimps, exhibit laugh-like behavior when playing with one another. Even rats, when tickled, make high-pitched squeals that can be interpreted as laughter. (As you might guess, only a dedicated few know this firsthand.)

Comedy Is Serious Stuff

8 Comics know that the same jokes are not funny to everyone everywhere. Ed Hiestand, a writer for comedy great Johnny Carson, told READ, "Everyone who writes comedy needs to know the audience. On the Carson show, everybody would laugh on a Friday night. Nobody would laugh on a Monday." Even within one state or town or family, senses of humor are as varied as the people are. Professional comics do not assume a 10 p.m. audience will like a joke because a 7 p.m. audience did.

9 Comedians who test jokes for a living say it's hit or miss. "It's a tough gig, and you have to have a large threshold for pain," said stand-up Jay Nog. Performers whose jokes get a two-second laugh consider that a significant accomplishment.

10 Timing is critical. Starting stand-up Zubair Simonson said he's learning the hard way that "good timing can cause a weak joke to soar, while poor timing can cause a strong joke to falter." Authors and film actors do not often get immediate public feedback. But comics do.

11 What keeps the funny guys going? The laughs and after-effects. "The best humor has some sort of layer to it; it makes a statement of some kind or comment," said Margy Yuspa, a director at Comedy Central. "An example is [Dave] Chappelle. His comedy is funny on the surface and also often comments on race or social issues."

Funny You Said That

12 Comedians have their own theories about humor. "What makes us laugh is a surprise change in perspective that connects an unknown with a known idea in a

SCAFFOLDING THE TEXT-DEPENDENT QUESTIONS

1. Key Ideas and Details (RI.8.3) **Why does laughter seem to qualify as a biological function? What might be the biological function of laughter?** Read paragraphs 6 and 7. What does the author mean when he says "biological function"? Young people, older people, babies, and animals are all different, but how does laughter create common ground?

2. Craft and Structure (RI.8.4) **In paragraph 7, what purpose does the sentence in parentheses serve?** Read paragraph 7, paying attention to the sentence immediately before the one in parentheses. What question comes to mind as you read this sentence? How does the sentence in parentheses address this question?

Teacher Notes

unique manner," said Ronald P. Culberson, a humorist at FUNsulting.com. "For instance, a three-legged dog walks into an Old West saloon and says, "I'm looking for the man who shot my paw."

13 Ask an average person why humans laugh, and he or she would probably say, "Because something was funny." But comics need to know what gives the giggles; their livelihood depends on it.

14 Comedian Anthony DeVito told READ that "people tend to laugh at things that reinforce what they already believe. Comedy tells them they're right."

15 Gary Gulman, a finalist in Last Comic Standing, a reality TV show and comedy competition, gave specifics. "Sometimes it's a keen observation about something you thought you lived through. Sometimes it's a **juxtaposition** of words. Sometimes it's a gesture or a sound. An encyclopedia couldn't do this question justice."

My Notes

ACADEMIC VOCABULARY
Juxtaposition, a technique used by artists and writers, places normally unassociated ideas, words, and phrases next to one another for effect (e.g., surprise or wit).

What Are You Laughing At?

16 Yet laughter is not always a planned response to a joke. One study found that 80 percent of the time, we laugh at something that just happens. People often laugh just because someone else does. Like a yawn, a laugh is contagious. That's why some sit-coms use laugh tracks.

17 Laughter is also social, a way to bond with others. After all, how often do you laugh alone? When two or more people laugh at the same thing, it is as if nature reminds them of what they have in common.

18 Behavioral neuroscientist Robert R. Provine conducted a 10-year experiment in which he eavesdropped on 2,000 conversations in malls, at parties, and on city sidewalks. He found that the greatest guffaws did not follow intentionally funny statements; people laughed hardest at everyday comments that seemed funny only in a certain social context.

19 "Do you have a rubber band?" is not in and of itself humorous, but it is if it's said in response to "I like Amelia so much. I wish I could get her attention."

Theories of Funniness

20 There are three main theories about humor.

21 **Release theory**—Humor gives a break from tension. In a horror movie, as a character creeps through a dark house (often idiotically) to follow an eerie noise, he might open a door to find a cat playing with a squeeze toy. The audience laughs in relief. Humor also lets us deal with unpleasant or forbidden issues, such as death and violence. People are often more comfortable laughing at something shocking said by someone else, though they would never say it themselves. Comedian Keenen Ivory Wayans once said, "Comedy is the flip side of pain. The worst things that happen to you are hysterical—in retrospect. But a comedian doesn't need retrospect; he realizes it's funny while he's in the eye of the storm."

22 **Superiority theory**—Audience members laugh at those who appear to be more stupid than they judge themselves to be. Slapstick humor, such as seeing a guy slip on a banana peel, often falls into this category. This theory dates back to Plato in ancient Greece and was prominent in the Middle Ages, when people with deformities were often employed as court jesters.

23 Some comedians exploited this theory by building a routine—or even a **persona**—around the idea that they were losers who couldn't catch a break. Larry David, David Letterman, and Woody Allen are comedians who have done this, each in his own way.

Literary Terms
A **persona** is the voice or character speaking or narrating a story.

3. Key Ideas and Details (RI.8.3) **As discussed in paragraphs 16–19, why is unplanned humor often funnier than planned humor?** Read paragraphs 16–19. In paragraph 18, what does the author mean by "social context"? How do unplanned humor and social context work together to create a funny situation?

4. Craft and Structure (RI.8.4) **What context clues in paragraph 21 help you understand the meaning of the word "retrospect"?** Read paragraph 21. Keenen Ivory Wayans explains that when bad things happen to us, at what point in time do we find humor in them? If someone is "in the eye of the storm," does that refer to past, present, or future?

Teacher Notes

Understanding the Complexity of Humor

WORD CONNECTIONS

Roots and Affixes

Superiority has the Latin root *super*, which means "placed above." This root is found in many English words, including *superb, superlative, supreme, supervise, superintendent*, and *supernatural*.

An ***incongruity*** happens when things do not match as they are expected to. The word *incongruity* has the root *-congru-*, which means "to come together," "to agree," or "to "coincide." The prefix *in-* means "not" or "without."

Literary Terms

Satire is a form of comedy that uses humor, irony, or exaggeration to expose and criticize issues in society or people's weaknesses.

My Notes

24 **Incongruity theory**—People laugh when things that are not normally associated with each other are put together. Many comedy duos, from Laurel and Hardy to David Spade and Chris Farley, feature a thin man and a fat man, a visual contrast.

25 People also laugh when there is a difference between what they expect to happen and what actually occurs. They are being led in a certain direction, and then that direction abruptly changes, and the unpredictability makes them laugh. Children see birds all the time without reaction, but if one flies into their classroom through an open window, they will probably explode in giggles.

Got Laughs?

26 What we laugh at changes as we age. Here are some examples.

Audience	Often Likes
Young children	Slapstick, or silly **physical humor**
Elementary-school children	**Puns,** simple jokes that play off the sound rather than the meaning of a word, such as "Lettuce all go to the salad bar"
Teens	**Jokes** about topics that authority figures would consider rebellious, a way to use humor to deal with nerve-racking subjects
Adults, particularly well-educated ones	**Satire,** which makes fun of the weaknesses of people and society

27 Generally, children laugh more than adults. One study found that adults laugh 20 times a day, while children laugh 200 times!

The Secrets of Humor

28 Certain comedic devices turn up again and again in jokes, comic strips, and filmed entertainment—because they succeed.

29 "There were tricks," said Hiestand of his days writing for *The Tonight Show* hosted by Johnny Carson, "things you would see, certain things always got laughs." One of the most popular is often called the rule of threes. That is a pattern in which two nonfunny elements are followed by a third that is funny (yet still makes sense within the context). Many jokes start off with a list of three, such as "A rabbi, a lawyer, and a duck walk into a bar." As the joke unfolds, the rabbi says something straightforward, then the lawyer does as well, but the duck finishes with something witty or absurd.

30 Three guys were stranded on an island. An antique lamp washed ashore. When the guys touched it, a genie came out. "I'll grant each of you one wish," the genie said. The first guy said, "I want to go home," then disappeared. The second guy said, "I also want to go home," and he too disappeared. The third man suddenly looked sad. He said, "I want my two friends back to keep me company."

31 Certain concepts seem to be more amusing than others. If you tell any joke involving an animal, and it doesn't matter which one you use, think Donald and Daffy. In the LaughLab experiment, scientists determined that the funniest animal is the duck. (It's not arbitrary that a duck was used in the rule-of-threes joke.)

5. Key Ideas and Details (RI.8.3) **Based on paragraphs 26–27, what distinction can you make between what makes children laugh and what makes adults laugh? Why might children laugh more often than adults?** Read paragraphs 26–27 and think of examples of "silly, physical humor" and humor that is based on sounds. How frequently do children encounter these situations? What are some examples of adult humor and how often do you think adults are exposed to this type of humor?

Do Tell—But Do It Right

32 There are also known techniques for telling jokes well.

- **Keep it short**—Don't include any details that are not necessary to bring you to the punch line. In the genie joke, there was no need to specify it was a tropical island or to name the castaways. The quicker you tell a joke, the funnier it will be.
- **Be specific**—Some comedians swear that a joke is funnier if you say "Aquafresh" instead of "toothpaste." The attention to detail makes the story seem more real.
- **Keep a straight face**—Deliver the joke deadpan, or without emotion. That way, any strangeness in the joke will seem even stranger because the person telling it doesn't seem to notice.
- **Don't laugh at your own joke**—Let your audience decide whether it is funny or foolish—or both.

33 Theories and techniques aside, much about humor remains a mystery. According to Hiestand, Carson many times said, "I don't understand what makes comedy a sure thing. There's no 100-percent surefire formula." Meanwhile, for most of us, laughter is never a problem. It does not need to be solved, just enjoyed.

My Notes

Second Read

- Reread the essay to answer these text-dependent questions.
- Write any additional questions you have about the text in your Reader/Writer Notebook.

1. **Key Ideas and Details:** Why does laughter seem to qualify as a biological function? What might be the biological function of laughter?

   In paragraphs 6 and 7, the author explains that all people laugh, and some animals do too. The function of laughter might be to form a connection. RI.8.3

ACTIVITY 4.2 continued

5 SECOND READ: During the second reading, students will be returning to the text to answer the text-dependent comprehension questions. You may choose to have students reread and work on the questions in a variety of ways:

- independently
- in pairs
- in small groups
- together as a class

6 Have students answer the text-dependent questions. If they have difficulty, scaffold the questions by rephrasing them or breaking them down into smaller parts. See the Scaffolding the Text-Dependent Questions boxes for suggestions.

6. Key Ideas and Details (RI.8.3) **There are four techniques for telling jokes well as explained in paragraph 32. How do the first two techniques relate to narrative writing?** Read paragraph 32. Why might excessive details hamper effective narrative writing? When would specific details be important?

7. Knowledge and Ideas (RI.8.8) **What is the author's argument in this essay? Cite specific evidence from the text in your response.** Read paragraphs 1 and 2. Who is affected by laughter? How does each section compare and contrast what makes people laugh?

Teacher Notes

Understanding the Complexity of Humor

My Notes

2. **Craft and Structure:** In paragraph 7, what purpose does the sentence in parentheses serve?

   The sentence provides additional information and humor, addressing a question that arises in the reader's mind, "Since when would anyone tickle a rat?" RI.8.4

3. **Key Ideas and Details:** As discussed in paragraphs 16–19, why is unplanned humor often funnier than planned humor?

   Unplanned humor is funnier because it is based on a shared context. RI.8.3

4. **Craft and Structure:** What context clues in paragraph 21 help you understand the meaning of the word "retrospect"?

   Keenen Ivory Wayans describes a common situation: something terrible happens, and we are only able to find the humor in it afterwards, "in retrospect." His quote that follows, "But a comedian doesn't need retrospect; he realizes it's funny while he's in the eye of the storm," confirms that retrospect speaks to the past as "the eye of the storm" speaks to the present. RI.8.4

5. **Key Ideas and Details:** Based on paragraphs 26–27, what distinction can you make between what makes children laugh and what makes adults laugh? Why might children laugh more often than adults?

   Children like more physical humor and humor based on sounds, whereas adult humor is more intellectual. Physical humor and sounds happen naturally and more frequently than intellectual humor, and so we can conclude that children laugh more than adults. RI.8.3

6. **Key Ideas and Details:** There are four known techniques for telling jokes well as explained in paragraph 32. How do the first two techniques relate to narrative writing?

   Keeping to the point and knowing when to use details are also rules in narrative writing. RI.8.3

7. **Knowledge and Ideas:** What is the author's argument in this essay? Cite specific evidence from the text in your response.

   The author's argument as presented in the first paragraph is that while laughter is universal, the reasons we laugh vary. Answers that support his argument include the following: how the LaughLab project examined what makes different groups of people laugh, how babies laugh from instinct, how timing affects humor, how different comedians use different approaches, and how people laugh the hardest at everyday comments. RI.8.8

Working from the Text

8. Referring back to the words and phrases you've underlined, write an objective summary of a section of the text by putting the main points into your own words. Remember that a summary is a broad overview of the text; stick to the main points by writing about big ideas and excluding smaller details.

Using Precise Diction to Analyze Humor

9. To analyze a text carefully, one must use specific words to describe the humor and explain the intended effect. Work collaboratively to define terms and to understand the nuances of words with similar denotations (definitions). You have already encountered some of these words.

Words to Describe Humor	Denotation	Connotations
amusing		
cute		
facetious		
hysterical		
ironic		
irreverent		
laughable		
light-hearted		
ludicrous		
mocking		
sarcastic		
satirical		
witty		

My Notes

7 To complete the Working from the Text section, you might ask students to summarize sections individually and then share with a group to be sure all students have all the information. Students could then revise their first effort to hand in. Or students could work with a partner to summarize the text.

8 Review the meaning and importance of *nuance* (Unit 1), and then ask students to preview the lists of words in the chart and put a checkmark next to ones they are familiar with.

9 Next, form small groups, and give each group at least one thesaurus and dictionary. Split the class in half, assigning one half of the class the words to describe humor and the other half the words to describe responses. Each group should work as a team to define as many terms as they can in ten minutes.

10 When the time is up, pair students with a partner from the opposite side of the room to share definitions and connotations of each term. During this discussion, students should record or revise any notes they have already taken.

11 Encourage students to demonstrate or act out the more difficult terms when they are working in their pairs.

12 Next, begin a "Comedy" section on the Word Wall. As a class, select half of the words from each list to display. Distribute index cards to individuals or pairs.

13 Direct students to write their assigned word in large letters on the front of their card and define the word on the back.

14 You may want students to draw an image for the given word. This image should depict something that would create the humor or response.

15 The creator of each Word Wall card should hand the card to another student, who will place the word on the Word Wall under an appropriate heading in a position that represents the nuance of the word (in relation to the other words).

16 The Language and Writer's Craft provides an opportunity to practice verbals: gerund, participial, and infinitive forms of verbs used as nouns, adjectives, or adverbs.

After going over the explanations and examples with students, have them work individually or in pairs to identify the verbals in the four items given. You might also challenge students to come up with original examples of sentences with verbals.

Understanding the Complexity of Humor

My Notes

Words to Describe Response Humor	Denotation	Connotations
chuckle		
giggle		
groan		
guffaw		
snort		
scoff		
smile		
smirk		
snicker		
titter		

Language and Writer's Craft: Verbals

A **verbal** is a word (or words) that functions as a verb. Verbals include participles, infinitives, and gerunds.

Each of the verbs above has a **participial** form in both the present and the past tense:

- Present participle: *smirking, smiling, guffawing*
- Past participle: *smirked, smiled, guffawed*

Each verb also has an **infinitive** form, or "to" form:

- Infinitive: *to smirk, to smile, to guffaw*

As you know, verbs may be used simply to **show action** in sentences.

John **smirked** at the joke; Doris was **giggling**.

Verb forms may also be used as **nouns, adjectives**, and **adverbs**. When used this way, they are called verbals because they look like verbs but are used as other parts of speech. Look at the examples below. Is each of the boldfaced verbals used as a noun, an adjective, or an adverb?

Example: **Smirking**, John handed the **wrapped** gift to Ted, who wanted **to open** it right away.

Smirking is an adjective describing John, **wrapped** is an adjective describing the gift, and **to open** is a noun used as the object of the verb "wanted."

Identify the verbals in the following sentences and tell whether they are used as nouns, adjectives, or adverbs.

- Giggling and snorting, the crowd of students watched the comic video.
- To laugh is my greatest pleasure.
- Hiding his snickering behind a raised hand, Henry bent forward with a side-splitting outburst of laughter.
- Scoffing at the attempted joke, Mark refused to look at the giggling child.

Expository Writing Prompt: Create a detailed paragraph that uses precise diction to explain your sense of humor. Use at least two words from each chart to explain what does and does not make you laugh and how you typically respond to humorous texts. Be sure to:

- Use precise diction to describe humor.
- Begin with a clear thesis statement.
- Include details and examples.
- Include at least three verbals.

My Notes

Leveled Differentiated Instruction

Students may need support writing to explain their sense of humor.

Em Pair students off to fill out a **Conversation for Quickwrite** graphic organizer. After students have completed their organizers, ask students basic questions about why expository writing is organized in this way, such as *What is the purpose of including details and examples?*

Ex Pair students off to fill out a **Conversation for Quickwrite** graphic organizer. After students have completed their organizers, ask students to explain why expository writing is organized in this way.

Br Have students work in pairs to discuss their sense of humor before they begin writing.

ASSESS

The writing prompt asks students to create a detailed paragraph that uses precise diction to explain their sense of humor. Emphasize that they should use precise diction to describe humor and their response to it. This begins the practice students will need as they gain confidence in analyzing humor in texts and performances.

ADAPT

To support learning, use a **think aloud** to explain your own response to the **writing prompt**. If the students' diction is inaccurate or unnatural, select and share successful student models, and provide opportunities to revise language.

ACTIVITY 4.3

▶PLAN

Materials: a variety of humorous comic strips and political cartoons
Suggested Pacing: 1 50-minute class period

▶TEACH

1 **Activate prior knowledge** by asking students to think about how they would classify different types of comedy.

2 After students read and **mark the text**, form pairs and ask them to work collaboratively to complete the charts.

ACTIVITY 4.3

Classifying Comedy

LEARNING STRATEGIES: Marking the Text, Graphic Organizer, Note-taking, Discussion Groups, Brainstorming, RAFT, Drafting

Learning Targets

- Categorize humorous texts into levels of comedy.
- Write an analysis of how an artist creates humor.

Understanding Levels of Comedy

Comedy occurs in different ways.

1. Read and mark the text to indicate information that is new to you.

WORD CONNECTIONS

Cognates

The English word *comedy* comes from the Latin word *comoedia*, meaning "an amusing play or performance." It has the same meaning as the Spanish word, *comedia*.

Low comedy refers to the type of humor that is focused primarily on the situation or series of events. It includes such things as physical mishaps, humor concerning the human body and its functions, coincidences, and humorous situations. With low comedy, the humor is straightforward and generally easy to follow and understand.

Since the primary purpose of most low comedy is to entertain, the action is frequently seen as hilarious or hysterical and the effect is often side-splitting laughter and guffaws. Many times, the characters are exaggerated caricatures rather than fully developed characters. These caricatures are often caught in unlikely situations or they become victims of circumstances seemingly beyond their control. Thus, the plot takes priority over the characters. Examples of low comedy might include *Madea's Family Reunion, Meet the Parents,* and *America's Funniest Home Videos*. Shakespeare's comedies, such as *A Midsummer Night's Dream* and *Twelfth Night*, are full of low comedy.

High comedy refers to the type of humor that is focused primarily on characters, dialogue, or ideas. It includes such things as clever wordplay, wit, and pointed remarks regarding larger issues. Many times, high comedy takes an irreverent or unconventional look at serious issues.

Sometimes the humor of high comedy is not immediately obvious; it can take a bit of reflection in order to realize the humorous intent. Frequently, the purpose of high comedy is to express an opinion, to persuade, or to promote deeper consideration of an idea. Often described as amusing, clever, or witty, high comedy typically results in chuckles, grins, and smiles rather than loud laughter. Clever use of language and interesting characters receive more attention than the circumstances that surround them. Examples of high comedy include *Modern Family*, *The Middle*, and, at times, *The Simpsons*. Shakespeare's tragedies, such as *Hamlet* and *Romeo and Juliet*, also include instances of high comedy.

My Notes

2. Why do we distinguish between different kinds of comedy?

We distinguish between different kinds of comedy so we can understand how and why authors create humor.

3. With a partner, take notes to complete each chart on the next page. Brainstorm a strong example at each level of comedy.

COMMON CORE STATE STANDARDS

Focus Standards:

W.8.2: Write informative/explanatory texts to examine a topic and convey ideas, concepts, and information through the selection, organization, and analysis of relevant content.

W.8.2a: Introduce a topic clearly, previewing what is to follow; organize ideas, concepts, and information into broader categories; include formatting (e.g., headings), graphics (e.g., charts, tables), and multimedia when useful to aiding comprehension.

W.8.9: Draw evidence from literary or informational texts to support analysis, reflection, and research.

W.8.9a: Apply *Grade 8 Reading standards* to literature (e.g., "Analyze how a modern work of fiction draws on themes, patterns of events, or character types from myths, traditional stories, or religious works such as the Bible, including describing how the material is rendered new").

Low Comedy

Purpose	Common Subjects	Emphasis	Descriptions	Intended Responses
to entertain to make the audience laugh without having to think about the humor	physical mishaps bodily functions coincidences humorous situations (e.g. unlikely)	situation or plot (series of events)	humor is straightforward/ easy to follow action is seen as hilarious or hysterical Laughter: "riotous" "side-splitting" hysterical ludicrous	guffaws outburst

High Comedy

Purpose	Common Subjects	Emphasis	Descriptions	Intended Responses
to express an opinion to persuade to promote a deeper consideration of an idea to entertain	larger social issues current events	characters; dialogue clever use of language characters take priority over plot social/political/ racial issues	wordplay witty/clever/ amusing satire/irony irreverent not obvious: requires thinking	chuckles grins smiles (not loud laughter)

Check Your Understanding

4. Write a concise statement that shows you understand the difference between the two levels of comedy.

ACTIVITY 4.3 continued

3 Add *levels of comedy* to the Word Wall. As a class, share examples of low and high comedy, and be sure to discuss the following: Levels of comedy are frequently studied as rungs on a comedy ladder. Within the major levels of low and high, there are other areas that students might hear about in the future. Also, it is important to point out that while individual segments of texts can be identified as either low or high comedy, humorous texts often contain features of both levels.

4 Check Your Understanding asks students to independently write their statement that shows they understand the main differences between the levels of comedy. Call on a variety of students to share with the class.

COMMON CORE STATE STANDARDS

L.8.6: Acquire and use accurately grade-appropriate general academic and domain-specific words and phrases; gather vocabulary knowledge when considering a word or phrase important to comprehension or expression.

Additional Standards Addressed:

RL.8.1; RL.8.5; RI.8.1; RI.8.2; RI.8.4; W.8.2b; W.8.2d; W.8.4; W.8.10; SL.8.6

ACTIVITY 4.3 continued

5 After **activating prior knowledge** about two types of humorous texts—comic strips and political cartoons—preview the **RAFT** strategy, and use it twice: first to model the analysis of a humorous comic strip and then the analysis of a political cartoon.

6 Encourage students to complete their Independent Reading Link exercise, reminding them to write their responses in their Reader/Writer Notebook.

TEACHER TO TEACHER

Use a comic strip that contains more than one panel and has a beginning, middle, and end. Project the comic onto the wall. Make sure to choose a comic strip or cartoon that deals with issues of interest to students. You may ask students to bring their own examples of comic strips or political cartoons to analyze.

Leveled Differentiated Instruction

To support learning, have students work together to sort the comic strips and cartoons into high comedy and low comedy.

Em Have students work in small groups or pairs to complete the RAFT graphic organizer using short words and phrases.

Ex Have students work in small groups or pairs to complete the RAFT graphic organizer using more detailed sentences. After completing the organizer, have students discuss the question, *What details in the comic strips and cartoons helped you understand the difference between high and low comedy?*

Classifying Comedy

My Notes

Analyzing Humorous Texts

5. Brainstorm what you already know about comic strips and political cartoons. Think about format, audience, topics, descriptions of humor, intended effects, etc.

   Comic Strips:

   Political Cartoons:

6. Read and mark the text of the following definitions for information that is new to you:

   Comic strips are meant primarily to entertain. They have a beginning and middle that lead to a humorous ending. They tend to be a low-level comedy that is easily understood by a wide audience.

   Political cartoons deal with larger issues and are often meant to communicate a particular political or social message. They often have a single panel with a powerful statement to reinforce humor displayed through a picture (characters or symbols). They tend to be high-level comedy, appealing to a smaller population that is well-informed about a specific topic.

Introducing the Strategy: RAFT

RAFT is an acronym that stands for role, audience, format, and topic. RAFT is a strategy that can be used for responding to and analyzing a text by identifying and examining its role, audience, format, and topic.

7. Use the graphic organizer and the RAFT strategy on the next page to analyze the humor in comics and political cartoons based on the previous definitions.

INDEPENDENT READING LINK

Read and Respond

Analyze one of the humorous texts you are reading. Does the text reflect high comedy or low comedy? Cite specific examples from the text to support your answer, and record your responses in your Reader/Writer Notebook.

Title ____________________

Role	Comics:	Political Cartoon:
Role Who is the author? Where is this cartoon or political cartoon found? What is the attitude (tone) of the author toward the topic? How can you tell?		
Audience Who does this comic or political cartoon target? How do you know?		
Format Describe the use of print and non-print techniques (dialogue, narration frames, and angles) used for effect.		
Topic What is this comic/cartoon about? Who are the characters? What is happening? How would you describe the humor? What is the intended effect?		

Check Your Understanding

WRITING to SOURCES **Expository Writing Prompt**

Think about your selected cartoon or comic. How does the artist create humor? Draft a response and use specific details of the cartoon or comic to describe the humor and explain the intended effect. Be sure to:

- Establish a controlling idea that describes the humor and intended effect.
- Organize ideas into broader categories.
- Use precise diction to describe humor.

My Notes

ASSESS

After you review elements of effective expository writing to check for understanding, ask students to analyze independently a comic or cartoon and respond to the writing prompt. Students should be sure that their topic sentence uses the language of humor analysis and attempts to interpret the effect.

ADAPT

You might assist students by modeling a controlling idea and using a **think aloud** to explore ways to organize content. Review student writing to identify strengths and weaknesses relating to the criteria. To reinforce skills, read and analyze one or two successful student models as a class. Students will have several more opportunities to strengthen their writing prior to EA1.

ACTIVITY 4.4

▶PLAN

Materials: DVD: *Carlos Oscar: Life Is Crazy Good* or Jerry Seinfeld's *I'm Telling You for the Last Time (optional)*
Suggested Pacing: 3 50-minute class periods

▶TEACH

1 Before having students look at the page, activate prior knowledge by asking if anyone can define the term *anecdote*. Read aloud the information about *anecdote* at the top of the page and in the signal box. Add this term to the Word Wall under the heading "Humorous Genres."

2 Ask students to **think-pair-share** about family anecdotes.

TEACHER TO TEACHER

You could ask a fellow faculty member or professional actor to perform an anecdote for the class. Alternatively, there are many examples of professional comedians performing anecdotes to entertain an audience. Consider showing one or more of the following filmed performances.

Carlos Oscar: Life Is Crazy Good—Play the opening clip of his show (0:2:11–0:10:28). This clip contains Oscar's monologue about his overprotective parents. The anecdote covers the topics of parents being "cheap," holidays and Halloween, and superstitions.

Jerry Seinfeld: I'm Telling You for the Last Time—Seinfeld's monologue on the subject of Halloween is excellent (Chapter 5: 0:16:26–0:22:40). Students may have viewed it in previous levels. He discusses children's obsession with candy and gives a humorous account of his childhood Halloween experiences. Seinfeld also published this anecdote in a picture book called *Halloween*. Viewing a text repeatedly can serve many purposes.

3 After the performance, ask students to describe the comedian's persona and the people, places, and events mentioned in the anecdote.

ACTIVITY 4.4

Humorous Anecdotes

LEARNING STRATEGIES: Graphic Organizer, Discussion Groups, Rereading, Close Reading, Marking the Text, Brainstorming, TWIST, Oral Reading

Learning Targets

- Analyze how authors convey humor in speech and writing.
- Write and present an oral reading of an original anecdote.
- Analyze the effect of verbals in a humorous text.

Humorous Anecdotes

1. Read the following information to see how the use of anecdotes applies to a study of humor.

   An **anecdote** is a brief, entertaining account of an incident or event. Often, anecdotes are shared because of their humorous nature, but anecdotes can also help illustrate larger ideas and concepts. Families sometimes share anecdotes about the humorous things family members have done. Frequently, the stories become more and more absurd as the details are exaggerated with each retelling.

WORD CONNECTIONS

Etymology

The word *anecdote* comes from the Greek word *anekdota*, meaning "things unpublished." Think about the connotation this brings to the modern word.

2. Do you or your family have a humorous anecdote that is shared over and over? What is it? Why is it retold? Who tells it? How does it change over time?

Viewing a Humorous Monologue

The following monologue provides humorous accounts of somewhat ordinary events. Finding and describing the humor in the people, places, and events you encounter can enrich your conversations as well as your writing.

3. As you watch the clip for the first time, listen for different topics in the monologue and take notes.

My Notes

COMMON CORE STATE STANDARDS

Focus Standards:

RI.8.1: Cite the textual evidence that most strongly supports an analysis of what the text says explicitly as well as inferences drawn from the text.

W.8.3: Write narratives to develop real or imagined experiences or events using effective technique, relevant descriptive details, and well-structured event sequences.

W.8.3a: Engage and orient the reader by establishing a context and point of view and introducing a narrator and/or characters; organize an event sequence that unfolds naturally and logically.

L.8.1: Demonstrate command of the conventions of standard English grammar and usage when writing or speaking.

L.8.1a: Explain the function of verbals (gerunds, participles, infinitives) in general and their function in particular sentences.

Comedian's Persona	People	Places	Events

4. The second time you view the clip, pay attention to *how* the comedian delivers the anecdote. Take notes on your assigned section.

1. Describe the comedian's delivery. What is the effect on the audience? Tone: Facial Expressions: Gestures: Volume: Pacing: Inflection (emphasis): Effect:	2. Record the comedian's transitions between topics within his anecdote. What words or phrasing does he use?
3. Desribe the imagery the comedian uses. List details that describe a person, place, or event. Why does the comedian include these specific details? Topic: Descriptive Details: Figurative Language:	4. Does the speaker's tone shift? Record his attitude about the topic at the beginning of the monologue and if his attitude changes. How does he communicate this shift?

ACTIVITY 4.4 continued

4 If you can view the performance a second time, number students off by fours to indicate students' areas of focus on the **graphic organizer**. That is, assign 1's to focus on the first column, etc.

5 After the performance, ask one expert group at a time (e.g., all the 1's) to share their observations and analysis. Students should listen to comprehend and **take notes** in the appropriate section of the **graphic organizer.**

COMMON CORE STATE STANDARDS

Additional Standards Addressed:

RI.8.2; RI.8.3; RI.8.4; W.8.2a; W.8.2b; W.8.2d; W.8.3e; W.8.4; W.8.5; W.8.9a; W.8.10; SL.8.1a; SL.8.2; SL.8.6; L.8.4b; L.8.6

ACTIVITY 4.4 continued

6 Check for understanding by asking students to complete the **Quickwrite** and then engage in the collaborative discussion.

7 Read the Preview and the Setting a Purpose for Reading sections with your students. Help them understand any literary terms they encounter.

8 **FIRST READ:** Based on the complexity of the passage and your knowledge of your students, you may choose to conduct the first reading in a variety of ways:

- independent reading
- paired reading
- small group reading
- choral reading
- read aloud

9 As students are reading, monitor their progress. Be sure they are engaged with the text and annotating words and phrases from the text that remind them of their own experiences. Evaluate whether the selected reading mode is effective.

10 Based on the observations you made during the first reading, you may want to adjust your reading mode. For example, you may decide for the second reading to read aloud certain complex passages, or you may group students differently.

Humorous Anecdotes

My Notes

Check Your Understanding

5. **Quickwrite:** How is the comedian able to create laughter in the audience by telling such simple anecdotes?

6. Discuss how you would describe the humor the comedian uses. What do you think is the intended response? During your discussion, be sure to:
   - Use precise diction to describe the humor.
   - Provide examples from the text to support your analysis.

Preview

In this activity, you will read a humorous essay and think about any funny memories you've had related to a road trip or riding in a car.

Setting a Purpose for Reading

- As you read the essay, underline words and phrases that make you think of your own experiences and memories.
- Circle unknown words and phrases. Try to determine the meaning of the words by using context clues, word parts, or a dictionary.

ABOUT THE AUTHOR
Jon Scieszka (b. 1954) is the oldest of six brothers in his family. He became an elementary school teacher and found that his students liked the funny stories that he enjoyed telling. He has since published a number of children's books, which are illustrated by his friend Lane Smith. In 2008, the Librarian of Congress named him National Ambassador for Young People's Literature.

Essay

from Brothers

by Jon Scieszka

1 Brothers are the guys you stick with and stick up for.

2 The Scieszka brothers are scattered all over the country now, but we still get together once a year to play a family golf tournament. We named it after our dad, Lou, and his favorite car—his old Cadillac Coupe de Ville. It is the Coupe de Lou Classic. We all grew up playing golf, because Dad Lou, an elementary

SCAFFOLDING THE TEXT-DEPENDENT QUESTIONS

7. Craft and Structure (RI.8.4) **How does the author use dashes and parentheses for comic effect?** Read paragraph 3. What information about the cat is in parentheses and why is this information humorous? Read paragraph 5 and explain why the information in parentheses creates comic effect. Read paragraph 6. How does the author's decision to use dashes emphasize comic effect?

school principal, taught Junior Golf and gave us lessons during summers off. And I'm sure my brothers would want me to point out the amazing fact that I am the winner of both the very first Coupe de Lou 1983 and the latest Coupe de Lou 2004.

3 But of all the Scieszka brother memories, I believe it was a family car trip that gave us our finest moment of brotherhood. We were driving cross-country from Michigan to Florida, all of us, including the family cat (a guy cat, naturally), in the family station wagon. Somewhere mid-trip we stopped at one of those Stuckey's rest-stop restaurants to eat and load up on Stuckey's candy.

4 We ate lunch, ran around like maniacs in the warm sun, then packed back into the station wagon—Mom and Dad up front, Jim, Jon, Tom, Gregg, Brian, Jeff, and the cat in back. Somebody dropped his Stuckey's Pecan Log Roll® on the floor. The cat found it and must have scarfed every bit of it, because two minutes later we heard that awful ack ack ack sound of a cat getting ready to barf.

5 The cat puked up the pecan nut log. Jeff, the youngest and smallest (and closest to the floor) was the first to go. He got one look and whiff of the pecan nut cat yack and blew his own sticky lunch all over the cat. The puke-covered cat jumped on Brian, Brian barfed on Gregg. Gregg upchucked on Tom. Tom burped a bit of Stuckey lunch back on Gregg. Jim and I rolled down the windows and hung out as far as we could, yelling in group puke horror.

6 Dad Lou didn't know what had hit the back of the car. No time to ask questions. He just pulled off to the side of the road. All of the brothers—Jim, Jon, Tom, Gregg, Brian, and Jeff—spilled out of the puke wagon and fell in the grass, gagging and yelling and laughing until we couldn't laugh anymore.

7 What does it all mean? What essential guy wisdom did I learn from this?

8 Stick with your brothers. Stick up for your brothers. And if you ever drop a pecan nut log in a car with your five brothers and your cat ... you will probably stick to your brothers.

My Notes

Second Read

- Reread the essay to answer these text-dependent questions.
- Write any additional questions you have about the text in your Reader/Writer Notebook.

7. **Craft and Structure:** How does the author use dashes and parentheses for comic effect?

   Scieszka uses dashes and parentheses to add details and emphasis to already humorous situations. RI.8.4

8. **Key Ideas and Details:** How are the golf tournament and the road trip incident connected?

   The golf tournament and the road trip incident are connected as they represent events and memories shared by Scieszka and his brothers and both the tournament and road trip are linked with a car. RI.8.3

8. Key Ideas and Details (RI.8.3) **How are the golf tournament and the road trip incident connected?** Read paragraphs 2 and 3. Who are the participants in both the golf tournament and the road trip? Did these two events occur in the past or present?

© 2017 College Board. All rights reserved.

ACTIVITY 4.4 continued

Text Complexity
Overall: Complex
Lexile: 1110L
Qualitative: Low Difficulty
Task: Moderate (Analyze)

11 SECOND READ: During the second reading, students will be returning to the text to answer the text-dependent comprehension questions. You may choose to have students reread and work on the questions in a variety of ways:

- independently
- in pairs
- in small groups
- together as a class

12 Have students answer the text-dependent questions. If they have difficulty, scaffold the questions by rephrasing them or breaking them down into smaller parts. See the Scaffolding the Text-Dependent Questions boxes for suggestions.

TEACHER TO TEACHER

While reading this selection, you may want to note the syntactical variety within the text: the use of parallelism, many active verbs, a variety of moods (look to the last paragraph, which uses the imperative mood), and verbals, (a grammatical form introduced in the Language and Writer's Craft exercise in this activity).

ACTIVITY 4.4 continued

13 While you conduct a shared reading of the text, ask students to mark the text for connections.

14 Introduce the **TWIST** strategy. Emphasize to students how all the elements work together. Imagery and word choice, or diction, create the humorous tone. Style is the most complex element, and here refers to the deliberate use of language to create effect. The thematic statement becomes the interpretive statement upon which to build an analysis.

15 Form small groups, and ask students to use the TWIST strategy to analyze the text. Students may use the graphic organizer, or for more of a challenge, write the analysis as a paragraph after taking notes on the organizer.

Leveled Differentiated Instruction

Offer students support with reading and comprehension by having them read the essay in pairs.

Em Instruct students to stop after they read each paragraph to paraphrase the key ideas that they have read so far.

Ex As pairs finish each paragraph, have them work together to answer the question, *What is the central idea of this paragraph?*

Br After each paragraph, students should take turns asking each other questions about what they have read so far. Remind students to build on each other's responses to the questions and provide useful feedback about their answers.

Support Have students pause after paragraph 2 and paragraph 5 to summarize what they have read so far.

Stretch Challenge students to look at each instance of humor in the text and discuss how the humor was effective.

Humorous Anecdotes

My Notes

Working from the Text

9. Review the essay and make connections between the essay and your own experiences. Also think about other humorous texts you have read and how the essay connects to those texts. Finally, make connections between the essay and the world around you. Use the following symbols to mark the text.
   E/S = Essay to Self
   E/T = Essay to other Texts
   E/W =Essay to World

Introducing the Strategy: TWIST

TWIST is an acronym for tone, word choice, imagery, style, and theme. This writing strategy helps a writer analyze each of these elements in a text in order to write a response to an analytical writing prompt about the text.

10. Reread the excerpt from "Brothers," and use the TWIST strategy to guide your analysis of the text.

Acronym	Text: "Brothers" by Jon Scieszka
Tone *What is the author's attitude about the topic?*	Humor; tries to convey the incident as hysterical; side-splitting
Word choice *What specific diction does the author use for effect?*	Slangy and colloquial (the language of kids) "cat yack" "Scarfed," "ack, ack, ack," "barf" "Puke," "upchuck," "burp"
Imagery *What specific descriptive details and figurative language does the author use for effect?*	"Pecan log" "... blew his own sticky lunch all over the cat. The puke-covered cat jumped on Brian, Brian barfed on Gregg. Gregg upchucked on Tom. Tom burped a bit of Stuckey lunch back on Gregg."

Style *How does the author use language to create humor?* *What is the intended response the author hopes to achieve?*	Family language—"Coupe de Lou Classic" Exaggeration—"ran around like maniacs in the warm sun," "spilled out of the puke wagon and fell in the grass, gagging and yelling and laughing until we couldn't laugh anymore." Slangy language—scarfed, ack, ack, ack, barf, puke, upchucked, burped
Theme *What is the central idea of this text? What idea about life is the author trying to convey through humor?*	"family car trip that gave us our finest moment of brotherhood" Stick with your brothers. Stick up for your brothers. ... stick to your brothers.

13. Once you have found textual evidence from the text "Brothers," and made an inference about the theme, you are ready to write an analytical topic sentence. State the title, author, and genre (TAG) in your thesis or topic sentence. For example:

Jon Scieszka's anecdote "Brothers" is a low-level comedy that uses a comic situation, exaggeration, and comic diction to reveal a universal truth about how brothers who laugh together stick together.

Practice writing a topic sentence about the stand-up comedy using the TAG format.

My Notes

16 Once students feel comfortable using TAG, ask them to create an analytical topic sentence independently. Review student work to determine if students are meeting the specified expectations.

17 Have students write their anecdotes and share them in groups to revise and refine. The oral reading is excellent practice for the performance in the second half.

18 The examples in the Scieszka text can be augmented by brainstorming common gerunds, participles, and infinitives to show students they use verbals all the time.

- Gerunds: *Swimming, golfing, hunting* are examples of *-ing* forms commonly used as nouns.
- Participles: *Carrying* a 20 pound backpack, I was quickly exhausted.
- Infinitives as nouns, adjectives, and adverbs: *To cry* was a great release. Meg is the one *to see* about the job. They came to my house *to study.*

19 Have students explain the humor behind an anecdote. After students have drafted a response, you might ask them to highlight the verbals they have included so you can quickly check for understanding. The draft could be an exit slip, with the final drafting as a homework assignment.

Humorous Anecdotes

My Notes

Writing and Presenting Your Own Anecdote

12. Use the TWIST graphic organizer below to plan your own anecdote.

Subject of Humorous Memory:	People/Places/Events:
Tone: *What is your attitude about the topic? How will you convey that attitude?*	
Word Choice: *What specific diction can you use for effect?*	
Imagery: *What specific descriptive and figurative language can you use for effect?*	
Style: *How can you use language (diction and syntax) to create humor?* *What is the intended response you hope to achieve?*	
Theme: *What idea about life are you trying to convey through humor?*	

13. Draft your anecdote. Be sure to include a beginning, middle, and end. As you write your draft, think about using verbals. Study the material below to learn about using verbals.
14. Present an oral reading of your draft to a partner. After your partner presents, provide feedback relating to his or her ideas, organization, language, and the humorous effect.

Language and Writer's Craft: Using Verbals

You have learned that verbals are verb forms that function in a sentence as a noun or a modifier (adjective or adverb) rather than as a verb. Types of verbals include infinitives, gerunds, and participles. It is important to remember that although a verbal is formed from a verb, it does not function as a verb.

Writers add verbals to their writing for variety and effect. Jon Scieszka uses verbals in his anecdote "Brothers" to exaggerate the brothers' reactions to the "pecan log" incident. Look at these examples from the text:

- **Gerunds** are verbals that end in *-ing* and function as nouns.
  Example: ***Playing golf** is an activity that the Scieszka family enjoyed.*
- **Participles** are verbals (*-ing* and *-ed* forms of verbs) that function as adjectives.
  Example: "All of the brothers—Jim, Jon, Tom, Gregg, Brian, and Jeff—spilled out of the puke wagon and fell in the grass, ***gagging and yelling and laughing*** until we couldn't laugh anymore."
- **Infinitives** are verbals (usually preceded by the particle *to*) that function as nouns, adjectives, or adverbs.
  Example: "We still get together once a year **to play** a family golf tournament."

Check Your Understanding

WRITING to SOURCES **Expository Writing Prompt**

Select an anecdote in an audio or visual format or the print anecdote you read in this activity. Explain the humor the author creates and its intended response. Be sure to:

- Establish a clear controlling idea relating the elements of humor to the anecdote.
- Use specific examples from the text to support your analysis.
- Use precise diction.
- Incorporate verbals into your writing.

My Notes

Leveled Differentiated Instruction

In this activity, students may need support incorporating verbals into their writing.

Em Help students write a sentence that begins with *Giggling madly ...* to explain the anecdote.

Ex Provide students with a list of gerunds, participles, or infinitives to explain the anecdote, such as *laughing loudly, waving madly, to remember.* Remind students that verbals must function as nouns, adjectives, or adverbs in a sentence.

Br Have students work together to add gerunds, participles, or infinitives to their writing.

ASSESS

Both the original anecdote that students write and the writing prompt that asks students to analyze an anecdote will be excellent assessments of students' understanding of the use of anecdote for humorous effect.

ADAPT

Students will have additional opportunities to craft analytical paragraphs before EA1. See what they can do, and note trends in your class to address as you encounter future writing prompts.

For the expository writing activity, encourage students to choose a fresh example of an anecdote to analyze.

ACTIVITY 4.5

▶PLAN

Suggested Pacing: 2 50-minute class periods

▶TEACH

Text Complexity
Overall: Complex
Lexile: 1210L
Qualitative: Moderate Difficulty
Task: Moderate (Analyze)

1 Read the Preview and the Setting a Purpose for Reading sections with your students. Introduce the essay by reading the About the Author information. Help students understand any unfamiliar terms.

2 **FIRST READ:** Based on the complexity of the passage and your knowledge of your students, you may choose to conduct the first reading in a variety of ways:

- independent reading
- paired reading
- small group reading
- choral reading
- read aloud

3 As students are reading, monitor their progress. Be sure they are engaged with the text and annotating words and phrases intended to be humorous and those speaking to a universal truth. Evaluate whether the selected reading mode is effective.

4 Based on the observations you made during the first reading, you may want to adjust your reading mode. For example, you may decide for the second reading to read aloud certain complex passages, or you may group students differently.

ACTIVITY 4.5

Finding Truth in Comedy

LEARNING STRATEGIES: Think-Pair-Share, Marking the Text, Metacognitive Markers, Questioning the Text, Rereading, Close Reading, Discussion Groups, Socratic Seminar, Drafting

Learning Targets

- Collaborate to analyze a humorous essay in a Socratic Seminar.
- Write to explain how an author conveys universal truths through humor.

Preview

In this activity, you will read a humorous essay and think about how people use comedy to discuss serious or important topics.

Setting a Purpose for Reading

- As you read the essay, underline words and phrases that are intended to be humorous.
- Circle unknown words and phrases. Try to determine the meaning of the words by using context clues, word parts, or a dictionary.
- Place an exclamation point by text that deals with a universal truth.

ABOUT THE AUTHOR
Dave Barry (b. 1947) was a humor columnist for the *Miami Herald* until 2005. His work there won him the Pulitzer Prize for Commentary in 1988. He has also written novels and children's books and continues to write articles for a variety of magazines. Much of Barry's work provides humorous commentary on current social issues.

My Notes

Essay

i've got a few pet peeves about sea creatures

by Dave Barry

Chunk 1

1 Pets are good, because they teach children important lessons about life, the main one being that, sooner or later, life kicks the bucket.

2 With me, it was sooner. When I was a boy, my dad, who worked in New York City, would periodically bring home a turtle in a little plastic tank that had a little plastic island with a little plastic palm tree, as is so often found in natural turtle habitats. I was excited about having a pet, and I'd give the turtle a fun pet name like Scooter. But my excitement was not shared by Scooter, who, despite residing in a tropical paradise, never did anything except mope around.

3 Actually, he didn't even mope "around": He moped in one place without moving, or even blinking, for days on end, displaying basically the same vital signs as an ashtray. Eventually I would realize—it wasn't easy to tell—that Scooter had passed on to that

COMMON CORE STATE STANDARDS

Focus Standards:

W.8.2: Write informative/explanatory texts to examine a topic and convey ideas, concepts, and information through the selection, organization, and analysis of relevant content.

W.8.2a: Introduce a topic clearly, previewing what is to follow; organize ideas, concepts, and information into broader categories; include formatting (e.g., headings), graphics (e.g., charts, tables), and multimedia when useful to aiding comprehension.

W.8.2d: Use precise language and domain-specific vocabulary to inform about or explain the topic.

SL.8.1: Engage effectively in a range of collaborative discussions (one-on-one, in groups, and teacher-led) with diverse partners on Grade 8 topics, texts, and issues, building on others' ideas and expressing their own clearly.

Additional Standards Addressed:

RI.8.1; RI.8.2; RI.8.4; RI.8.5; RI.8.6; RI.8.10; W.8.2c; W.8.2e; W.8.4; W.8.9b; SL.8.1a; SL.8.1b; SL.8.1c; SL.8.6; L.8.5a

Big Pond in the Sky, and I'd bury him in the garden, where he'd decompose and become food for the zucchini, which in turn would be eaten by my dad, who would in turn go to New York City, where, compelled by powerful instincts that even he did not understand, he would buy me another moping death turtle. And so the cycle of life would repeat.

Chunk 2

4 I say all this to explain why I recently bought fish for my 4-year-old daughter, Sophie. My wife and I realized how badly she wanted an animal when she found a beetle on the patio and declared that it was a pet, named Marvin. She put Marvin into a Tupperware container, where, under Sophie's loving care and feeding, he thrived for maybe nine seconds before expiring like a little six-legged parking meter. Fortunately, we have a beetle-intensive patio, so, unbeknownst to Sophie, we were able to replace Marvin with a parade of stand-ins of various sizes ("Look! Marvin has grown bigger!" "Wow! Today Marvin has grown smaller!"). But it gets to be tedious, going out early every morning to wrangle patio beetles. So we decided to go with fish.

5 I had fish of my own, years ago, and it did not go well. They got some disease like Mongolian Fin Rot, which left them basically just little pooping torsos. But I figured that today, with all the technological advances we have such as cellular phones and "digital" things and carbohydrate-free toothpaste, modern fish would be more reliable.

6 So we got an aquarium and prepared it with special water and special gravel and special fake plants and a special scenic rock so the fish would be intellectually stimulated and get into a decent college. When everything was ready I went to the aquarium store to buy fish, my only criteria being that they should be 1) hardy digital fish; and 2) fish that looked a LOT like other fish, in case God forbid we had to Marvinize them. This is when I discovered how complex fish society is. I'd point to some colorful fish and say, "What about these?" And the aquarium guy would say, "Those are great fish but they do get aggressive when they mate." And I'd say, "Like, how aggressive?" And he'd say, "They'll kill all the other fish."

7 This was a recurring theme. I'd point to some fish, and the aquarium guy would inform me that these fish could become aggressive if there were fewer than four of them, or an odd number of them, or it was a month containing the letter "R," or they heard the song "Who Let the Dogs Out." It turns out that an aquarium is a powder keg that can explode in deadly violence at any moment, just like the Middle East, or junior high school.

Chunk 3

8 TRUE STORY: A friend of mine named David Shor told me that his kids had an aquarium containing a kind of fish called African cichlids, and one of them died. So David went to the aquarium store and picked out a replacement African cichlid, but the aquarium guy said he couldn't buy that one, and David asked why, and the guy said: "Because that one is from a different lake."

9 But getting back to my daughter's fish: After much thought, the aquarium guy was able to find me three totally pacifist fish-Barney Fife fish, fish so nonviolent that, in the wild, worms routinely beat them up and steal their lunch money. I brought these home, and so far they have not killed each other or died in any way. Plus, Sophie LOVES them. So everything is working out beautifully. I hope it stays that way, because I hate zucchini.

Second Read

- Reread the essay to answer these text-dependent questions.
- Write any additional questions you have about the text in your Reader/Writer Notebook.

My Notes

ACTIVITY 4.5 continued

5 **SECOND READ:** During the second reading, students will be returning to the text to answer the text-dependent comprehension questions. You may choose to have students reread and work on the questions in a variety of ways:

- independently
- in pairs
- in small groups
- together as a class

6 Have students answer the text-dependent questions. If they have difficulty, scaffold the questions by rephrasing them or breaking them down into smaller parts. See the Scaffolding the Text-Dependent Questions boxes for suggestions.

Leveled Differentiated Instruction

In this activity, it may be helpful for students to keep track of humor in the essay by taking notes using the following sentence frames and questions.

Em Provide the following sentence frames to help students write personal responses/commentary: *The description of Scooter reminds me of ... This sentences about the beetle named Marvin made me feel ...*

Ex Ask the following questions to guide students' responses. *What does this description remind you of? How does the description make you feel?*

Br Have students add details to their personal response/commentary by asking the following questions. *Which words from the passage are the most important in creating the humor? How do they support the humor in the passage?*

SCAFFOLDING THE TEXT-DEPENDENT QUESTIONS

1. Craft and Structure (RI.8.4) **What is the effect of the repetition of "a little plastic" in paragraph 2?** Read paragraph 2. Would the humorous impact be lessened if the author did not repeat "a little plastic" so many times? Why?

2. Key Ideas and Details (RI.8.1) **What is the effect of the juxtaposed ideas "grown bigger" and "grown smaller" in paragraph 4?** Who do you think is being quoted in paragraph 4? Why are these exclamations humorous? How frequently are the beetles being replaced and why?

7 Have students read and respond to the quote, and discuss their responses.

Finding Truth in Comedy

My Notes

1. **Craft and Structure:** What is the effect of the repetition of "a little plastic" in paragraph 2?

   The repetition makes the turtle habitat seem ridiculous and is juxtaposed to "natural habitats" for ironic effect. RI.8.4

2. **Key Ideas and Details:** What is the effect of the juxtaposed ideas "grown bigger" and "grown smaller" in paragraph 4?

   The juxtaposed ideas create a comic effect of incongruity, showing in a funny way how often the beetle dies and also how the parents try to protect the child. RI.8.1

3. **Craft and Structure:** What is the impact of the phrase "little pooping torsos" in paragraph 5?

   "Little pooping torsos" creates comedic imagery and plays on the stereotypical behavior associated with fish. RI.8.4

4. **Key Ideas and Details:** What specific details does the author include in paragraph 7 in order to have a comic effect?

   Instead of saying "loud music," he names a specific song that upsets the fish. RI.8.1

Working from the Text

5. Read and respond to the following quote.

Quote by George Bernard Shaw	Interpretation	Personal Commentary
"The power of comedy is to make people laugh, and when they have their mouths open and they least expect it—you slip in the truth."		

3. Craft and Structure (RI.8.4) **What is the impact of the phrase, "little pooping torsos" in paragraph 5?** Read paragraph 5. What activities are fish in general well known for doing? What does the phrase "little pooping torsos" help you visualize relative to the Mongolian Fin Disease? How does the author's choice of words lighten the tone?

4. Key Ideas and Details (RI.8.1) **What specific details does the author include in paragraph 7 in order to have a comic effect?** Why does the author choose detailed scenarios to explain how the fish are provoked? Why do you think he chose a specific song, for example? Why is it humorous that the author compares "deadly violence" to the Middle East or junior high?

6. How would you classify this essay (high or low comedy)? Explain.

   High, based on verbal wordplay; less about circumstance than about the way it is conveyed; irreverent (death of pets)

7. How would you describe the humor? What is the author's intended response? Use precise diction in your response.

   The author is using high comedy to express a universal theme that all parents can relate to. The author intends readers to respond with "chuckles, grins, and smiles."

8. How does the author use language (diction, syntax, imagery) to create a humorous tone?

   clever wordplay ("same vital signs as an ashtray," "wrangle patio beetles"); pointed remarks; amusing, clever, or witty

9. How does the author appeal to the audience's emotions, interests, values, and/or beliefs?

   Barry seeks to engage the audience in identifying with a common experience of having a pet, and pets dying.

10. What is the universal truth (theme) of the text? How does the author develop the idea through humorous characters and plot?

    Parents will go to great lengths to create good pet experiences for their children. His father was "compelled by powerful instincts that even he did not understand" to buy him another turtle.

11. Develop Levels of Questions based on your analysis to prepare for a Socratic Seminar discussion. Remember to maintain a formal style in your speaking during the Socratic Seminar. Be sure to:
    - Use precise verbs such as *communicates, creates, emphasizes,* or *illustrates* when discussing the author's purpose.
    - Use the author's last name: "Barry creates humor by ..."
    - Cite textual evidence to support your opinion.

Levels of Questioning	"I've got a few pet peeves about sea creatures"
Level 1: Literal	What are the two times Barry mentions zucchini?
Level 2: Interpretive	What is the significance of zucchini to him? Why can this be classified as high comedy, while "Brothers" may be considered low comedy?
Level 3: Universal (thematic)	Is caring for a pet a good experience for kids?

My Notes

ACTIVITY 4.5 continued

8 Form **collaborative discussion** groups and ask students to respond to the Working from the Text questions. Remind students that analytical questions require **rereading** and **close reading.**

9 Briefly discuss responses as a class to check for understanding. Direct students to revise responses to indicate new learning.

10 In preparation for the Socratic Seminar, ask students to write 2–3 questions for each Level of Questions.

11 Discuss the information on maintaining a formal style in Student Step 11. Using a formal style is important to academic discussions and writing. Help students **brainstorm** more tips and provide examples before commencing the seminar.

12 Before beginning a **Socratic Seminar**, review the procedure and norms (Unit 2). Set up a **fishbowl** (inner and outer circles) so that only half of your class is discussing at a time. After 10 minutes, switch the inner and outer circles so that everyone has an opportunity to discuss.

13 Provide students with time to complete the Independent Reading Link activity in class. They will need time to complete the exercise and to discuss themes with their peers.

▶ASSESS

The seminar serves as an opportunity to generate ideas relating to humor analysis prior to writing. During the discussion, make sure students are able to cite textual evidence to support their analysis, use precise diction to explain the humor, and articulate a theme (universal truth) revealed through the humor.

The writing prompt is another opportunity to practice writing an analysis of a humorous text. Be sure students come to the writing task with a topic sentence about the truth Barry is communicating.

▶ADAPT

Consider supporting students with a list of possible topics that Barry is commenting upon. Barry's writing anticipates the parody and satire of the next activity.

Finding Truth in Comedy

My Notes

12. Brainstorm other precise verbs that will help in your discussion. Do you have any other tips for using formal language?

13. Use your analysis and questions to engage in a Socratic Seminar discussion.

Check Your Understanding

WRITING to SOURCES **Expository Writing Prompt**

How does Barry use humor to convey a truth about life? Be sure to:

- Establish a clear controlling idea about conveying a truth.
- Use transitions to create cohesion and clarify relationships among ideas and concepts.
- Use precise diction to describe humorous effects.
- Cite specific evidence from the text.

INDEPENDENT READING LINK

Read and Discuss

For independent practice, choose one of the humorous texts from your list and explain the theme using specific evidence for support. Write several Levels of Questions for a specific section of reading in your Reader/Writer Notebook. Use the Level 3 questions to have a discussion about themes with your peers.

© 2017 College Board. All rights reserved.

Satirical Humor

ACTIVITY 4.6

Learning Targets

- Analyze satire in print and nonprint texts.
- Write an analytical paragraph that includes appropriate and varied transitions.

LEARNING STRATEGIES: Marking the Text, Discussion Groups, Rereading, Revisiting, Adding, Substituting

1. You will next view a film clip your teacher shows and take notes on the satire you observe.

This clip is from:	
TOPIC (vice or folly exposed)	SATIRE (examples of irony, sarcasm, or ridicule used)

ACADEMIC VOCABULARY
Satiric comedy is not always funny. Sometimes it mocks or derides the subject. This kind of **derision** allows a satirist to **denounce** or express strong disapproval of an attitude or topic.

Preview

In this activity, you will read a satirical article and think about how the author uses satire to express disapproval on a particular topic.

Setting a Purpose for Reading

- As you read the article, underline words and phrases that make you laugh or that you recognize as humor.
- Circle unknown words and phrases. Try to determine the meaning of the words by using context clues, word parts, or a dictionary.
- Place a * by any words or phrases that indicate irony, sarcasm, or ridicule.

My Notes

Article

Underfunded Schools Forced to Cut Past Tense from Language Programs

from *The Onion*

1 WASHINGTON—Faced with ongoing budget crises, underfunded schools nationwide are increasingly left with no option but to cut the past tense—a grammatical construction traditionally used to relate all actions and states that have transpired at an earlier point in time—from their standard English and language arts programs.

2 A part of American school curricula for more than 200 years, the past tense was deemed by school administrators to be too expensive to keep in primary and secondary education.

ACTIVITY 4.6

PLAN

Materials: satirical TV show clip, highlighters
Suggested Pacing: 2 50-minute class periods

TEACH

1 Before reading, direct students to work with a partner to define the term *satire*.

TEACHER TO TEACHER

To engage students and give them a clearer understanding of comic satire, consider showing a clip from a satirical news show such as *The Daily Show with Jon Stewart* or *The Colbert Report*. Choose one that is appropriate for and relevant to your students and current issues. Show a short clip (no longer than 5 minutes).

2 Show a satirical scene and have students **take notes** on the **satire** they observe. Discuss observations as a class. Allow students to discuss other shows that make use of satire, such as *The Simpsons*. Be sure students discuss satire as high comedy.

3 Read the Preview and the Setting a Purpose for Reading sections with your students. Help them understand any unfamiliar terms they encounter.

4 **FIRST READ:** Based on the complexity of the passage and your knowledge of your students, you may choose to conduct the first reading in a variety of ways:

- independent reading
- paired reading
- small group reading
- choral reading
- read aloud

5 As students are reading, monitor their progress. Be sure they are engaged with the text and annotating words and phrases they understand as humorous as well as those they recognize as showing irony, sarcasm, or ridicule. Evaluate whether the selected reading mode is effective.

COMMON CORE STATE STANDARDS

Focus Standards:

W.8.2c: Use appropriate and varied transitions to create cohesion and clarify the relationships among ideas and concepts.

RI.8.4: Determine the meaning of words and phrases as they are used in a text, including figurative, connotative and technical meanings; analyze the impact of specific word choices on meaning and tone, including analogies of allusions to other texts.

Additional Standards Addressed:

RL.8.1; RL.8.4; RI.8.3; W.8.2a; W.8.2b; W.8.2d; W.8.2e; W.8.4; W.8.5; W.8.9a; L.8.1d; L.8.5a; L.8.5b; L.8.5c; L.8.6

Text Complexity
Overall: Very Complex
Lexile: 1410L
Qualitative: Moderate Difficulty
Task: Moderate (Analyze)

6 Based on the observations you made during the first reading, you may want to adjust your reading mode. For example, you may decide for the second reading to read aloud certain complex passages, or you may group students differently.

Satirical Humor

My Notes

3 "This was by no means an easy decision, but teaching our students how to conjugate verbs in a way that would allow them to describe events that have already occurred is a luxury that we can no longer afford," Phoenix-area high school principal Sam Pennock said.

4 "With our current budget, the past tense must unfortunately become a thing of the past."

5 In the most dramatic display of the new trend yet, the Tennessee Department of Education decided Monday to remove "-ed" endings from all of the state's English classrooms, saving struggling schools an estimated $3 million each year. Officials say they plan to slowly phase out the tense by first eliminating the past perfect; once students have adjusted to the change, the past progressive, the past continuous, the past perfect progressive, and the simple past will be cut. Hundreds of school districts across the country are expected to follow suit.

6 "This is the end of an era," said Alicia Reynolds, a school district director in Tuscaloosa, AL. "For some, reading and writing about things not immediately taking place was almost as much a part of school as history class and social studies."

7 "That is, until we were forced to drop history class and social studies a couple of months ago," Reynolds added.

8 Nevertheless, a number of educators are coming out against the cuts, claiming that the embattled verb tense, while outmoded, still plays an important role in the development of today's youth.

9 "Much like art and music, the past tense provides students with a unique and consistent outlet for self-expression," South Boston English teacher David Floen said. "Without it I fear many of our students will lack a number of important creative skills. Like being able to describe anything that happened earlier in the day."

10 Despite concerns that cutting the past tense will prevent graduates from communicating effectively in the workplace, the home, the grocery store, church, and various other public spaces, a number of lawmakers, such as Utah Sen. Orrin Hatch, have welcomed the cuts as proof that the American school system is taking a more forward-thinking approach to education. "Our tax dollars should be spent preparing our children for the future, not for what has already happened," Hatch said at a recent press conference. "It's about time we stopped wasting everyone's time with who 'did' what or 'went' where. The past tense is, by definition, outdated." Said Hatch, "I can't even remember the last time I had to use it."

11 Past-tense instruction is only the latest school program to face the chopping block. School districts in California have been forced to cut addition and subtraction from their math departments, while nearly all high schools have reduced foreign language courses to only the most basic phrases, including "May I please use the bathroom?" and "No, I do not want to go to the beach with Maria and Juan." Some legislators are even calling for an end to teaching grammar itself, saying that in many inner-city school districts, where funding is most lacking, students rarely use grammar at all.

12 Regardless of the recent upheaval, students throughout the country are learning to accept, and even embrace, the change to their curriculum.

13 "At first I think the decision to drop the past tense from class is ridiculous, and I feel very upset by it," said David Keller, a seventh-grade student at Hampstead School in Fort Meyers, FL. "But now, it's almost like it never happens."

GRAMMAR & USAGE
Active and Passive Voice

Active voice emphasizes who or what is doing the action.

Active voice: The past tense provides students with a unique and consistent outlet for self-expression.

Passive voice contains some form of the verb *to be* and the past participle of the verb. It is best used if the person or thing being acted upon is important or if the actor in the situation is unknown or not important.

Passive voice: School districts in California have been forced to cut addition and subtraction from their math departments.

INDEPENDENT READING LINK

Read and Connect

Choose a humorous text from your list that demonstrates satire. Create a graphic organizer to explore the satire and compare your results to the graphic organizer you completed in exercise 6. List the similarities and differences in your Reader/Writer Notebook.

SCAFFOLDING THE TEXT-DEPENDENT QUESTIONS

2. Craft and Structure (RL.8.4) **What role does the first paragraph play in the structure of this article?** Read paragraph 1. What institution is being impacted by the budget cuts? From where is the article being reported?

3. Key Ideas and Details (RL.8.1) **How do quotes from specific people throughout the article add to the development of ideas?** List the credentials of the people being quoted. Does the author use names? When you read a news article with known speakers being quoted, how do the quotations affect your perception of the article?

© 2017 College Board. All rights reserved.

Second Read

- Reread the article to answer these text-dependent questions.
- Write any additional questions you have about the text in your Reader/Writer Notebook.

2. **Craft and Structure:** What role does the first paragraph play in the structure of this article?

   The first sentence identifies the current issue and institution being satirized by the article. RL.8.4

3. **Key Ideas and Details:** How do quotes from specific people throughout the article add to the development of ideas?

   The quotes make the article seem more realistic. RL.8.1

4. **Key Ideas and Details:** How does the use of present tense in the last quote in paragraph 13 emphasize the satire?

   It shows how ridiculous a person sounds when he or she is unable to use the past tense. RL.8.1

Working from the Text

5. Work collaboratively to diffuse and paraphrase the definition of satire.

   Satire, a form of high comedy, is the use of irony, sarcasm, and/or ridicule in exposing, denouncing, and/or deriding human vice and folly.

   Irony – opposite of what is meant or expected

   Sarcasm – a bitter or cutting remark that mocks or taunts

   Ridicule – to make fun of

   Denouncing – to condemn; express strong disapproval

   Deriding – to mock; taunt

   Vice – immoral or evil habit or practice

   Folly – foolish action; an absurdity

   Paraphrase: making fun of something or someone to criticize an idea or issue

My Notes

SCAFFOLDING THE TEXT-DEPENDENT QUESTIONS

4. Key Ideas and Details (RL.8.1) **How does the use of present tense in the last quote in paragraph 13 emphasize the satire?** Read paragraph 13. What is the correct tense that should be used? What point does the use of the present tense make in this sentence?

ACTIVITY 4.6 continued

7 **SECOND READ:** During the second reading, students will be returning to the text to answer the text-dependent comprehension questions. You may choose to have students reread and work on the questions in a variety of ways:

- independently
- in pairs
- in small groups
- together as a class

8 Have students answer the text-dependent questions. If they have difficulty, scaffold the questions by rephrasing them or breaking them down into smaller parts. See the Scaffolding the Text-Dependent Questions boxes for suggestions.

9 Have students read the text another time individually; they should circle the highly connotative diction and gauge its effect. Model annotating with the first two paragraphs.

10 Have students read the text another time individually; they should place an exclamation mark by the highly connotative diction and gauge its effect. Model annotating with the first two paragraphs if necessary.

11 After students finish reading, check that students comprehend the passage and understand the source of its satire. Ask them to circle their reaction to the text. Have them form partner groups or triads with peers who circled a different reaction word. This is an attempt to group students who have varying responses to the satire to explore different points of view.

12 Have students work in their new groups to have a **collaborative discussion** about the humor in the text created by connotative words and to complete the **graphic organizer.**

13 Encourage students to complete their Independent Reading Link on page 278, recording their responses in their Reader/Writer Notebooks.

Satirical Humor

My Notes

6. Reread the text and place an exclamation point by the highly connotative diction that stands out to you. Note the effect of those words in the My Notes space.

7. Circle and explain your response to this text. I think this text is:

   hilarious funny clever ridiculous because ...

   Discuss the parts of the text that made you laugh, and describe how the connotative words help create the humor.

8. Collaboratively, use the graphic organizer to explore the satire.

The vice or folly exposed in the text:	**Textual Evidence:**
The loss of basic subject matter taught in schools associated with the reduction in school funding	**Irony:** The student quote all in present tense **Sarcasm:** "It's about time we stopped wasting everyone's time with who 'did' what or 'went' where." **Ridicule:** "... students rarely use grammar at all."

Writing an Analytical Paragraph

When writing about texts, use the "literary present" (e.g., "The article *states* ...," not "The article *stated* ...").

Also, remember to maintain coherence in your writing. Using a well-chosen transition word or phrase can help show the relationship (connection) between the ideas in your writing. The following is a list of commonly used transitional words and phrases.

© 2017 College Board. All rights reserved.

Purpose	Example
Add	*and, again, and then, besides, equally important, finally, further, furthermore, nor, too, next, lastly, what's more, moreover, in addition, first (second, etc.)*
Compare	*whereas, but, yet, on the other hand, however, nevertheless, on the contrary, by comparison, where, compared to, up against, balanced against, but, although, conversely, meanwhile, after all, in contrast, although this may be true*
Prove	*because, for, since, for the same reason, obviously, evidently, furthermore, moreover, besides, indeed, in fact, in addition, in any case, that is*
Show Exception	*yet, still, however, nevertheless, in spite of, despite, of course, once in a while, sometimes*
Show Time	*immediately, thereafter, soon, after a few hours, finally, then, later, previously, formerly, first (second, etc.), next, and then*
Repeat	*in brief, as I have said, as I have noted, as has been noted, to reiterate*
Emphasize	*definitely, extremely, obviously, in fact, indeed, in any case, absolutely, positively, naturally, surprisingly, always, forever, perennially, eternally, never, emphatically, unquestionably, without a doubt, certainly, undeniably, without reservation*
Show Sequence	*first, second, third, next, then, following this, at this time, now, at this point, after, afterward, subsequently, finally, consequently, previously, before this, simultaneously, concurrently, thus, therefore, hence, next, and then, soon*
Give an Example	*for example, for instance, in this case, in another case, on this occasion, in this situation, take the case of, to demonstrate, to illustrate, as an illustration, to illustrate*
Summarize or Conclude	*in brief, on the whole, summing up, to conclude, in conclusion, as I have shown, as I have said, hence, therefore, accordingly, thus, as a result, consequently*

WRITING to SOURCES **Expository Writing Prompt**

Analyze how the text about underfunded schools uses satirical humor to expose human vice or folly. Be sure to:

- Establish and support a controlling idea.
- Use transitions to create cohesion and clarify the relationships among ideas and concepts.
- Use precise diction and maintain a formal style.
- Support your analysis with evidence from the text.

My Notes

ACTIVITY 4.6 continued

14 To prepare for the analytical writing prompt, have students read the information about analytical writing and the use of transitional words and phrases.

ASSESS

Have students respond to the writing prompt by analyzing the satirical text they have just read. Remind students to use the TLQC [transition word + lead-in + quote + citation] structure to explain and embed textual evidence smoothly into a sentence. Also, remind students that commentary is analysis. Students should never use "I think" statements in an analytical paragraph/essay since a formal style is required. Check that, in responding to the writing prompt, students are following the "Be sure to" statements.

Leveled Differentiated Instruction

In this activity, have students create a bank of additional transitions to add to their writing and use an **Idea Connector** graphic organizer to connect ideas in the two sentences.

Em Guide students to add transition words from their list to their organizer, such as *at the end, next.* Work with students to write a combined sentence using the transitions.

Ex Guide students to add a variety of transition words and phrases from their list to their organizer such as *for example, as a result, on the other hand.*

Br Have students add a variety of transition words and phrases from their list to their organizer such as *for instance, in addition, consequently.*

ADAPT

Ask students to revisit their draft to check for the use of the literary present and appropriate transitions to create cohesion.

The texts in future activities are also examples of satire. Challenge students to find the elements of satire—irony, sarcasm, and ridicule—in upcoming texts.

ACTIVITY 4.7

▶PLAN

Materials: *The Simpsons* (opening credits clip), sample drawings or images of caricatures, audio recording of "The Open Window" (optional)
Suggested Pacing: 2 50-minute class periods

▶TEACH

TEACHER TO TEACHER

Prior to the activity, find examples or have students bring to class examples of caricatures from newspapers, magazines, comic books, and/or stories.

1 Have students read the definitions of *caricature* and *characterization*. Lead students in a discussion of caricatures in movies, television programs, books, and cartoons. Use the examples you and students brought in to guide the discussion.

2 Help students understand that comedies often achieve humorous effects with caricatures. For example, a cartoonist may imply that a politician is a liar by drawing him with a long nose like Pinocchio. Discuss the two-dimensional nature of caricature. Rather than being true representations, they present a narrow view of a person.

3 Use *The Simpsons* to illustrate caricature, not just in the visual, but in the stereotyping. Show the opening clip of any episode and ask students how each family member is a caricature. Discuss what truth (theme) the caricatures convey. Model how to complete the first row of the **graphic organizer** with Bart Simpson, using a **think aloud** to analyze the text. Then, direct students to view the clip and **take notes** themselves on the organizer. Have students share their responses in **discussion groups**.

If you cannot use a clip from *The Simpsons*, you might show a political cartoon or another visual that uses caricature.

ACTIVITY 4.7

Elements of Humor: Comic Characters and Caricatures

LEARNING STRATEGIES:
Graphic Organizer, Note-taking, Diffusing, Marking the Text, Visualizing, Discussion Groups, Rehearsal

ACADEMIC VOCABULARY
To use a **caricature** or to **caricaturize** someone is to exaggerate or imitate certain characteristics to create a comic or distorted idea of a person.

My Notes

Learning Targets

- Define and recognize comic characters and caricatures.
- Collaborate to analyze characters and caricatures in a literary text.

Comic Caricatures and Characters

Characterization is the way a writer reveals a character's personality through what the character says, thinks, and feels or through how the character looks, acts, or interacts with others.

A **caricature** is a pictorial, written, and/or acted representation of a person who exaggerates characteristics or traits for comic effect. Caricatures are often used in cartoon versions of people's faces and usually exaggerate features for comic effect.

1. You will next view some comic scenes. As you view the opening sequence, take notes in the graphic organizer.

Characters Sketch the caricature.	**Details** Describe the characterization.	**Interpretation** What idea is conveyed through the characterization?
Bart	Bart is repetitively writing sentences on the board that say ...	He is the stereotype of the bad kid in the classroom.
Homer		
Marge		
Lisa		
Family		

COMMON CORE STATE STANDARDS

Focus Standards:

RL.8.3: Analyze how particular lines of dialogue or incidents in a story or drama propel the action, reveal aspects of a character, or provoke a decision.

Additional Standards Addressed:

RL.8.1; RL.8.2; RL.8.4; RL.8.6; RL.8.10; W.8.10; SL.8.1a; SL.8.6; L.8.4a; L.8.6

2. With your discussion group, discuss what truth about life the author is conveying through humor. Cite specific examples from the graphic organizer.

Preview

In this activity, you will read a short story and think about the author's use of characterization.

Setting a Purpose for Reading

- As you read the short story, underline words and phrases that reveal something about Nuttel and the niece.
- Circle unknown words and phrases. Try to determine the meaning by using context clues, word parts, or a dictionary.

ABOUT THE AUTHOR

Hector Hugh Munro (1870–1916), better known by the pen name Saki, was a British writer and satirist known for his masterful short stories poking fun at Edwardian society. His witty and intelligent stories are considered among the best the genre has to offer.

Short Story

The Open Window

by Saki (H. H. Munro)

1 "My aunt will be down presently, Mr. Nuttel," said a very self-possessed young lady of fifteen; "in the meantime you must try and put up with me."

2 Framton Nuttel endeavoured to say the correct something which should **duly** flatter the niece of the moment without unduly discounting the aunt that was to come. Privately he doubted more than ever whether these formal visits on a succession of total strangers would do much towards helping the nerve cure which he was supposed to be undergoing.

3 "I know how it will be," his sister had said when he was preparing to migrate to this rural retreat; "you will bury yourself down there and not speak to a living soul, and your nerves will be worse than ever from moping. I shall just give you letters of introduction to all the people I know there. Some of them, as far as I can remember, were quite nice."

4 Framton wondered whether Mrs. Sappleton, the lady to whom he was presenting one of the letters of introduction, came into the nice division.

5 "Do you know many of the people round here?" asked the niece, when she judged that they had had sufficient silent communion.

My Notes

duly: properly or fittingly

ACTIVITY 4.7 continued

Text Complexity
Overall: Complex
Lexile: 1070L
Qualitative: Moderate Difficulty
Task: Moderate (Analyze)

4 Read the Preview and the Setting a Purpose for Reading sections with your students. Help them understand any unfamiliar terms they encounter.

5 **FIRST READ:** Based on the complexity of the passage and your knowledge of your students, you may choose to conduct the first reading in a variety of ways:

- independent reading
- paired reading
- small group reading
- choral reading
- read aloud

TEACHER TO TEACHER

Be sure to point out the About the Author section so students know that Saki is British and thus the text will contain British spellings of some words. Students should also come to the story with some expectation of its challenging vocabulary. If possible, use an audio recording of the text.

Leveled Differentiated Instruction

Some students may need support to read the short story independently. Have students complete a **Notes for Reading Independently** graphic organizer while they are reading to help them understand the story. Students should use the organizer to summarize the text.

Em Help students write a brief summary of the text using complete sentences and key words. Provide sentence frames such as *Framton Nuttel is visiting ___. Mrs. Sappleton's niece Vera tells him ___. When Mrs. Sappleton's husband and brothers return ___.*

SCAFFOLDING THE TEXT-DEPENDENT QUESTIONS

3. Key Ideas and Details (RL.8.3) **Why is it significant that Framton Nuttel is described as undergoing a "nerve cure" in paragraph 2? Predict how this detail could be used for humorous effect.** Read paragraph 2. What does Nuttle struggle to do? What type of personality does he appear to have? What does the author mean by "nerve cure"?

4. Craft and Structure (RL.8.4) **What phrase in paragraph 3 helps you understand what "moping" means?** Read paragraph 3. What does Nuttel's sister say he will do once he arrives in the countryside?

5. Craft and Structure (RL.8.4) **What is the meaning of the word "habitation" in paragraph 9? What clues in the text leading up to and including paragraph 9 support your response?** Based on paragraph 1, where do you think Nuttle and the niece are while they are conversing? Are you familiar with the word "habitat"? What do you think it means? What specifically in paragraph 9 suggests "masculine habitation"?

Ex Help students write a more concise summary of the text using complete sentences and key words. Ask questions to guide their writing such as *Who is Framton Nuttel visiting? What does Mrs. Sappleton's niece Vera tell him? What happens when Mrs. Sappleton's husband and brothers return?*

Br Have students write clear and coherent summaries of the text using complete and concise sentences and key words. Remind students to include the main events of the story in their details.

6 As students are reading, monitor their progress. Be sure they are engaged with the text and annotating characteristic details about Nuttel and the niece. Evaluate whether the selected reading mode is effective.

7 Based on the observations you made during the first reading, you may want to adjust your reading mode. For example, you may decide for the second reading to read aloud certain complex passages, or you may group students differently.

Elements of Humor: Comic Characters and Caricatures

rectory: the house in which a parish priest or minister lives

moor: boggy grassland

My Notes

6 "Hardly a soul," said Framton. "My sister was staying here, at the **rectory**, you know, some four years ago, and she gave me letters of introduction to some of the people here."

7 He made the last statement in a tone of distinct regret.

8 "Then you know practically nothing about my aunt?" pursued the self-possessed young lady.

9 "Only her name and address," admitted the caller. He was wondering whether Mrs. Sappleton was in the married or widowed state. An undefinable something about the room seemed to suggest masculine habitation.

10 "Her great tragedy happened just three years ago," said the child; "that would be since your sister's time."

11 "Her tragedy?" asked Framton; somehow in this restful country spot tragedies seemed out of place.

12 "You may wonder why we keep that window wide open on an October afternoon," said the niece, indicating a large French window that opened on to a lawn.

13 "It is quite warm for the time of the year," said Framton; "but has that window got anything to do with the tragedy?"

14 "Out through that window, three years ago to a day, her husband and her two young brothers went off for their day's shooting. They never came back. In crossing the **moor** to their favourite snipe-shooting ground they were all three engulfed in a treacherous piece of bog. It had been that dreadful wet summer, you know, and places that were safe in other years gave way suddenly without warning. Their bodies were never recovered. That was the dreadful part of it." Here the child's voice lost its self-possessed note and became falteringly human. "Poor aunt always thinks that they will come back some day, they and the little brown spaniel that was lost with them, and walk in at that window just as they used to do. That is why the window is kept open every evening till it is quite dusk. Poor dear aunt, she has often told me how they went out, her husband with his white waterproof coat over his arm, and Ronnie, her youngest brother, singing 'Bertie, why do you bound?' as he always did to tease her, because she said it got on her nerves. Do you know, sometimes on still, quiet evenings like this, I almost get a creepy feeling that they will all walk in through that window—"

15 She broke off with a little shudder. It was a relief to Framton when the aunt bustled into the room with a whirl of apologies for being late in making her appearance.

16 "I hope Vera has been amusing you?" she said.

17 "She has been very interesting," said Framton.

18 "I hope you don't mind the open window," said Mrs. Sappleton briskly; "my husband and brothers will be home directly from shooting, and they always come in this way. They've been out for snipe in the marshes to-day, so they'll make a fine mess over my poor carpets. So like you men-folk, isn't it?"

19 She rattled on cheerfully about the shooting and the scarcity of birds, and the prospects for duck in the winter. To Framton it was all purely horrible. He made a desperate but only partially successful effort to turn the talk on to a less ghastly topic; he was conscious that his hostess was giving him only a fragment of her attention, and her eyes were constantly straying past him to the open window and the lawn beyond. It was certainly an unfortunate coincidence that he should have paid his visit on this tragic anniversary.

20 "The doctors agree in ordering me complete rest, an absence of mental excitement, and avoidance of anything in the nature of violent physical exercise," announced Framton,

6. Key Ideas and Details (RL.8.3) **What tone does the niece convey with her description of the "tragedy" in paragraph 14? What effect might this precise detail have on her guest?** Read paragraph 14. The niece repeats two different words in paragraph 14. What are they, and what tone do they suggest? Based on the personality type you believe Nuttle to be, how might he respond to the niece's tale?

7. Craft and Structure (RL.8.4) **What context clues tell you the meaning of the word "bog" in paragraph 14?** Read paragraph 14. Review the definition of "moor." What does "engulfed" mean? When the author describes the bog as "treacherous," what does he mean?

8. Key Ideas and Details (RL.8.3) **Why is it "horrible" for Framton to listen to Mrs. Sappleton in paragraph 19?** Read paragraph 19. How is Mrs. Sappleton described in the first sentence? To what does Nuttle attribute her behavior?

9. Craft and Structure (RL.8.4) **What is the meaning of the word "ailments" in paragraph 20? What clues in the text support**

who **laboured under** the tolerably wide-spread **delusion** that total strangers and chance acquaintances are hungry for the least detail of one's ailments and infirmities, their cause and cure. "On the matter of diet they are not so much in agreement," he continued.

laboured under: be misled by a mistaken belief
delusion: a persistent false belief

21 "No?" said Mrs. Sappleton, in a voice which only replaced a yawn at the last moment. Then she suddenly brightened into alert attention—but not to what Framton was saying.

22 "Here they are at last!" she cried. "Just in time for tea, and don't they look as if they were muddy up to the eyes!"

23 Framton shivered slightly and turned towards the niece with a look intended to convey sympathetic comprehension. The child was staring out through the open window with dazed horror in her eyes. In a chill shock of nameless fear Framton swung round in his seat and looked in the same direction.

24 In the deepening twilight three figures were walking across the lawn towards the window; they all carried guns under their arms, and one of them was additionally burdened with a white coat hung over his shoulders. A tired brown spaniel kept close at their heels. Noiselessly they neared the house, and then a hoarse young voice chanted out of the dusk: "I said, Bertie, why do you bound?"

25 Framton grabbed wildly at his stick and hat; the hall-door, the gravel-drive, and the front gate were dimly-noted stages in his headlong retreat. A cyclist coming along the road had to run into the hedge to avoid an imminent collision.

26 "Here we are, my dear," said the bearer of the white **mackintosh**, coming in through the window; "fairly muddy, but most of it's dry. Who was that who bolted out as we came up?"

mackintosh: raincoat

27 "A most extraordinary man, a Mr. Nuttel," said Mrs. Sappleton; "could only talk about his illnesses, and dashed off without a word of good-bye or apology when you arrived. One would think he had seen a ghost."

28 "I expect it was the spaniel," said the niece calmly; "he told me he had a horror of dogs. He was once hunted into a cemetery somewhere on the banks of the Ganges by a pack of pariah dogs, and had to spend the night in a newly dug grave with the creatures snarling and grinning and foaming just above him. Enough to make anyone lose their nerve."

29 Romance at short notice was her speciality.

My Notes

Second Read

- Reread the short story to answer these text-dependent questions.
- Write any additional questions you have about the text in your Reader/Writer Notebook.

3. **Key Ideas and Details:** Why is it significant that Framton Nuttel is described as undergoing a "nerve cure" in paragraph 2? Predict how this detail could be used for humorous effect.

   Nuttel will be much more susceptible to the effects of the girl's active imagination. Her story is just eerie enough to send a man with a nervous condition into a panic. His undue nervousness or sensitivity moves his characterization into caricature that builds humor. RL.8.3

4. **Craft and Structure:** What phrase in paragraph 3 helps you understand what "moping" means?

   "you will bury yourself down there and not speak to a living soul,..." RL.8.4

ACTIVITY 4.7 continued

8 SECOND READ: During the second reading, students will be returning to the text to answer the text-dependent comprehension questions. You may choose to have students reread and work on the questions in a variety of ways:

- independently
- in pairs
- in small groups
- together as a class

9 Have students answer the text-dependent questions. If they have difficulty, scaffold the questions by rephrasing them or breaking them down into smaller parts. See the Scaffolding the Text-Dependent Questions boxes for suggestions.

your response? Read paragraph 20. Describe what instructions Nuttle's doctors have given him. What are "cause and cure" referring to?

10. Key Ideas and Details (RL.8.1) **What does the author tell the reader in his narration that makes Framton Nuttel appear silly and pathetic in paragraph 20? Why?** Review paragraph 20. What is Nuttle's delusion? What does this tell you about his character? Does this paragraph create sympathy towards Nuttel?

11. Key Ideas and Details (RL.8.3) **Why is Nuttel's reaction to the return of the men in paragraph 25 comic rather than appropriate?** Read paragraph 25. How does Nuttel's reaction fit what you know of his character? Why does he react this way? What do you know that he doesn't?

12. Key Ideas and Details (RL.8.3) **What aspects of the niece's character are revealed in her last line of dialogue in paragraph 28?** Read paragraph 28. What is humorous about the niece's dialogue? How does her dialogue in this paragraph mimic the niece's interaction with Nuttle?

Teacher Notes

Elements of Humor: Comic Characters and Caricatures

My Notes

5. **Craft and Structure:** What is the meaning of the word "habitation" in paragraph 9? What clues in the text leading up to and including paragraph 9 support your response?

   Habitation refers to a living area. We know from paragraph 1 that Nuttel is waiting in an area for Mrs. Sappleton. In paragraph 9, the author references "something about the room." RL.8.4

6. **Key Ideas and Details:** What tone does the niece convey with her description of the "tragedy" in paragraph 14? What effect might this precise detail have on her guest?

   The niece conveys a mysterious and pitying tone; Nuttel is probably feeling uncomfortable since he is already of a very nervous disposition, and he came to the home expecting an ordinary, boring encounter with a country lady. RL.8.3

7. **Craft and Structure:** What context clues tell you the meaning of the word "bog" in paragraph 14?

   Answers include "crossing the moor," "engulfed," "dreadful wet summer," "places that were safe...gave way suddenly without warning." RL.8.4

8. **Key Ideas and Details:** Why is it "horrible" for Framton to listen to Mrs. Sappleton as noted in paragraph 19?

   Mrs. Sappleton sounds happy and excited about something Nuttel thinks is a figment of her imagination. RL.8.3

9. **Craft and Structure:** What is the meaning of the word "ailments" in paragraph 20? What clues in the text support your response?

   "Ailments" refers to disease or sickness. Nuttle has just shared what his doctors have required of him, and the text references "infirmities," "cause," and "cure." RL.8.4

10. **Key Ideas and Details:** What does the author tell the reader in his narration that makes Framton Nuttel appear silly and pathetic in paragraph 20? Why?

    He tells the reader that Nuttel thinks others "are hungry for the last detail" about his illnesses. This makes him less sympathetic, so the niece's joke seems more amusing than cruel. RL.8.1

11. **Key Ideas and Details:** Why is Nuttel's reaction to the return of the men in paragraph 25 comic rather than appropriate?

    He doesn't get the joke that has been played on him, because he takes himself so seriously, but the reader has begun to suspect the joke. RL.8.3

12. **Key Ideas and Details:** What aspects of the niece's character are revealed in her last line of dialogue in paragraph 28?

    The reader knows she loves to spin imaginative stories, or romances. RL.8.3

Working from the Text

13. For each unfamiliar word you circled, write a synonym in My Notes.
14. **Quickwrite** using a 3–2–1 reflection.
    3 – Describe three things you notice about the author's use of humor in the story.
    2 – Describe two characters you can picture most vividly.
    1 – Share one question you have.
15. Use the graphic organizer to express ideas you have about the characters and humor in this text.

Details How does the author develop the character? (actions, words, thoughts)	Characters Describe the character using precise adjectives. Would any of them be considered a caricature?	Interpretation What truth about life is revealed through the comic character?
Framton Nuttel	Self-absorbed; gullible; nervous; conventional; loner; uncomfortable; anxious; socially inept	Self-absorbed, nervous, social misfits are easy to take advantage of.
Mrs. Sappleton	Cheerful; conventional; self-absorbed; preoccupied; social; matter of fact; bored by Nuttel	Conventional sorts are often unaware of the more imaginative types in their midst.
The niece	Imaginative; mischievous; unconventional; a joker; self-assured	Unconventional, imaginative types can easily take advantage of the stolid and unimaginative types.

Elements of Humor

Explaining why something is funny can be a challenge, but there are some common things authors do that usually make people laugh. Writers create humor by focusing on descriptions and actions that make characters funny, comic situations, and comic language. Humor often depends on some combination of these three elements.

16. Preview the Elements of Humor graphic organizer in Activity 4.11 and add notes about the comic characters and caricatures you explored in this activity. After you explore each new element of humor in the upcoming activities, return to this graphic organizer to add notes about new learning.

My Notes

Check Your Understanding

Explain whether you think the story by Saki is low or high comedy and why. Was any part of the story unexpected? Explain.

ACTIVITY 4.7 continued

10 Direct students to complete the 3–2–1 reflection to prepare to discuss the story. Hold a class discussion.

11 Next, have students further analyze the character they were assigned, using the **graphic organizer**. After students have completed the chart for their assigned character, ask them to share with the class or in a small-group **jigsaw**.

12 Explain that in upcoming activities, students will learn how to recognize other elements of humor in a variety of humorous texts. Direct students to the **graphic organizer** at the start of Activity 4.11. Read aloud the information defining each element of humor, asking students to use prior knowledge to begin to add examples and make predictions about the level of comedy. As they learn about new elements of humor and encounter humorous texts in this unit, they should return to the graphic organizer to add more examples.

ASSESS

Check students' annotations on the graphic organizer to verify that they are able to make inferences about their characters and justify why they are comedic; they should be able to relate exaggeration and irony to the characters.

Use the Check Your Understanding to determine whether students can identify this short story as high comedy.

ADAPT

Challenge students to find the comic characters and caricatures independently in texts they are reading outside of class.

ACTIVITY 4.8

▶PLAN

Materials: Youtube clip from *I Love Lucy* – "Lucy's Famous Chocolate Scene"
Suggested Pacing: 2 50-minute class periods

▶TEACH

TEACHER TO TEACHER

Film clips are optional here, but they can be an engaging and instructional method of introducing literary concepts and devices. The degree to which you use film clips is up to you as you assess your students' needs.

1 Read aloud the information about comic situations. You will continue to illustrate this idea of situational comedy with the following film portion of this activity.

2 Provide context for the film clip: *I Love Lucy* is a well-known classic American television sitcom starring Lucille Ball (Lucy), Desi Arnaz (Ricky), Vivian Vance (Ethel), and William Frawley (Fred). The black-and-white series originally ran from 1951 to 1957 on CBS. In this clip, Ricky and Fred get upset about the women's spending, so Lucy and Ethel go to work in a candy factory while the men do the housework.

3 Play the *I Love Lucy* video clip once without note taking and a second time so students can write down what they think is most funny. Allow students to share reactions.

4 Discuss the clip(s), and check for understanding of the humorous situation.

ACTIVITY 4.8

Elements of Humor: Comic Situations

LEARNING STRATEGIES: Graphic Organizer, Note-taking, Think-Pair-Share, Marking the Text, Discussion Groups

Learning Targets

- Investigate how humor is created by comic situations.
- Analyze comic situations in a literary text collaboratively.
- Determine the impact of word choice on meaning and tone in a comic situation.

Literary Terms
Irony is a literary device that plays on readers' expectations by portraying events in a way that is actually different from reality.

Comic situations can be created in many different ways:

- by placing a character in an unlikely situation in which he or she obviously does not belong
- by portraying characters as victims of circumstances who are surprised by unusual events and react in a comical way
- by creating **situational irony** where there is contrast between what characters or readers might reasonably expect to happen and what actually happens

1. While you watch a film clip, think about how the situation contributes to the humor.
2. As you view the clip a second time, take notes using the graphic organizer below.

Clip:	Director:	
Comic Character ______________	**Comic Situation**	**Film Techniques That Help Create Humor**
Appearance/Facial Expressions:	Setting:	Framing:
Actions:	Humorous Events:	Angles:
Words:		Sound:

COMMON CORE STATE STANDARDS

Focus Standards:

RL.8.4: Determine the meaning of words and phrases as they are used in a text, including figurative and connotative meanings; analyze the impact of specific word choices on meaning and tone, including analogies or allusions to other texts.

RL.8.6: Analyze how differences in the points of view of the characters and the audience or reader (e.g., created through the use of dramatic irony) create such effects as suspense or humor.

W.8.9: Draw evidence from literary or informational texts to support analysis, reflection, and research.

W.8.9a: Apply *Grade 8 Reading standards* to literature (e.g., "Analyze how a modern work of fiction draws on themes, patterns of events, or character types from myths, traditional stories,

Preview

In this activity, you will read an excerpt from a novel and think about the author's use of irony to create comic situations.

Setting a Purpose for Reading

- As you read the excerpt, underline words and phrases that explain what is happening in the plot.
- Circle unknown words and phrases. Try to determine the meaning of the words by using context clues, word parts, or a dictionary.
- Place a "D" by examples of dialect.

Literary Terms
Dialect is a regional or social variety of a language distinguished by pronunciation, grammar, or vocabulary. This section of the story includes a depiction of Tom's and Jim's dialects.

ABOUT THE AUTHOR
Born Samuel Langhorne Clemens, Mark Twain (1835–1910) was an American author and humorist. He is noted for his novels *The Adventures of Huckleberry Finn* (1885), called "the Great American Novel," and *The Adventures of Tom Sawyer* (1876). He has been lauded as the "greatest American humorist of his age," and William Faulkner called Twain "the father of American literature."

My Notes

Novel

FROM The Adventures of TOM SAWYER

by Mark Twain

"A DAY'S WORK"

Chunk 1

1 SATURDAY morning was come, and all the summer world was bright and fresh, and brimming with life. There was a song in every heart; and if the heart was young the music issued at the lips. There was cheer in every face and a spring in every step. The locust-trees were in bloom and the fragrance of the blossoms filled the air. Cardiff Hill, beyond the village and above it, was green with vegetation and it lay just far enough away to seem a Delectable Land, dreamy, reposeful, and inviting.

Chunk 2

2 Tom appeared on the sidewalk with a bucket of whitewash and a long-handled brush. He surveyed the fence, and all gladness left him and a deep melancholy settled down upon his spirit. Thirty yards of board fence nine feet high. Life to him seemed hollow, and existence but a burden. Sighing, he dipped his brush and passed it along the topmost plank; repeated the operation; did it again; compared the insignificant whitewashed streak with the far-reaching continent of unwhitewashed fence, and sat down on a tree-box discouraged. Jim came skipping out at the gate with a tin pail, and singing Buffalo Gals. Bringing water from the town pump had always been hateful

WORD CONNECTIONS

Multiple Meaning Words
The word *whitewash* has come to have a second meaning. In this story, *whitewash* means "a whitening mixture used on fences and walls." The word has also come to mean "to conceal or cover up crimes, scandals, flaws, or failures." You can see how this usage comes from the idea of using whitewash to cover up something bad.

TEACHER TO TEACHER

Feel free to substitute other film clips that include comic situations in which characters are the victims of unlikely circumstances, for example, *Monsters, Inc.* (Scene 11: 0:22:00–0:25:09) in which a child scares a monster.

Many other films contain comic situations. *Elf*, directed by Jon Favreau, 2003; and *Night at the Museum*, directed by Shawn Levy, 2006 are two. Clips from many of these films can be found on Youtube or Teachertube.

5 Discuss the meaning of dialect.

Text Complexity
Overall: Complex
Lexile: 910L
Qualitative: Moderate Difficulty
Task: Moderate (Analyze)

6 Read the Preview and the Setting a Purpose for Reading sections with your students. Help them understand any literary terms they encounter.

7 **FIRST READ:** Based on the complexity of the passage and your knowledge of your students, you may choose to conduct the first reading in a variety of ways:

- independent reading
- paired reading
- small group reading
- choral reading
- read aloud

8 As students are reading, monitor their progress. Be sure they are engaged with the text and annotating words and phrases that identify the plot as well as examples of dialect. Evaluate whether the selected reading mode is effective.

COMMON CORE STATE STANDARDS

or religious works such as the Bible, including describing how the material is rendered new").

Additional Standards Addressed:

RL.8.1; RL.8.2; RL.8.3; W.8.2a; W.8.2b; W.8.2c; W.8.2d; W.8.2e; W.8.4; W.8.5; SL.8.1b; L.8.1a; L.8.5a; L.8.6

SCAFFOLDING THE TEXT-DEPENDENT QUESTIONS

3. Craft and Structure (RL.8.4) **What does the word "reposeful" mean in paragraph 1? What clues in the text help you understand the meaning of the word?** Read paragraph 1. What is the author's tone? What feelings do the following words and phrases create as you read them: "song in every heart," "locust-trees in bloom," "fragrance of the blossom," "far away, dreamy?"

9 Based on the observations you made during the first reading, you may want to adjust your reading mode. For example, you may decide for the second reading to read aloud certain complex passages, or you may group students differently.

My Notes

work in Tom's eyes, before, but now it did not strike him so. He remembered that there was company at the pump. White, mulatto, and negro boys and girls were always there waiting their turns, resting, trading playthings, quarrelling, fighting, skylarking. And he remembered that although the pump was only a hundred and fifty yards off, Jim never got back with a bucket of water under an hour—and even then somebody generally had to go after him. Tom said:

Chunk 3

3 "Say, Jim, I'll fetch the water if you'll whitewash some."

4 Jim shook his head and said:

5 "Can't, Mars Tom. Ole missis, she tole me I got to go an' git dis water an' not stop foolin' roun' wid anybody. She say she spec' Mars Tom gwine to ax me to whitewash, an' so she tole me go 'long an' 'tend to my own business—she 'lowed SHE'D 'tend to de whitewashin.'"

6 "Oh, never you mind what she said, Jim. That's the way she always talks. Gimme the bucket—I won't be gone only a minute. SHE won't ever know."

7 "Oh, I dasn't, Mars Tom. Ole missis she'd take an' tar de head off'n me. 'Deed she would."

8 "SHE! She never licks anybody—whacks 'em over the head with her thimble—and who cares for that, I'd like to know. She talks awful, but talk don't hurt—anyways it don't if she don't cry. Jim, I'll give you a marvel. I'll give you a **white alley**!"

white alley: a kind of marble

9 Jim began to waver.

10 "White alley, Jim! And it's a bully taw."

11 "My! Dat's a mighty gay marvel, I tell you! But Mars Tom I's powerful 'fraid ole missis—"

12 "And besides, if you will I'll show you my sore toe."

13 Jim was only human—this attraction was too much for him. He put down his pail, took the white alley, and bent over the toe with absorbing interest while the bandage was being unwound. In another moment he was flying down the street with his pail and a tingling rear, Tom was whitewashing with vigor, and Aunt Polly was retiring from the field with a slipper in her hand and triumph in her eye.

WORD CONNECTIONS

Word Relationships

The words "great" and "magnificent" may seem similar; however, Twain uses **magnificent** to mean "splendid; impressive," while **great**, in this context, means important. Twain uses both words to inform the reader that a pivotal change is about to occur in the story because of Tom's idea.

14 But Tom's energy did not last. He began to think of the fun he had planned for this day, and his sorrows multiplied. Soon the free boys would come tripping along on all sorts of delicious expeditions, and they would make a world of fun of him for having to work—the very thought of it burnt him like fire. He got out his worldly wealth and examined it—bits of toys, marbles, and trash; enough to buy an exchange of WORK, maybe, but not half enough to buy so much as half an hour of pure freedom. So he returned his **straitened** means to his pocket, and gave up the idea of trying to buy the boys. At this dark and hopeless moment an inspiration burst upon him! Nothing less than a great, magnificent inspiration.

straitened: characterized by poverty

Chunk 4

15 He took up his brush and went tranquilly to work. Ben Rogers hove in sight presently—the very boy, of all boys, whose ridicule he had been dreading. Ben's gait was the hop-skip-and-jump—proof enough that his heart was light and his anticipations high. He was eating an apple, and giving a long, melodious whoop, at intervals, followed by a deep-toned ding-dong-dong, ding-dong-dong, for he was personating a steamboat. As he drew near, he slackened speed, took the middle of the street, leaned far over to starboard and rounded to ponderously and with laborious pomp and circumstance—

SCAFFOLDING THE TEXT-DEPENDENT QUESTIONS

4. Craft and Structure (RL.8.4) **What does the word "melancholy" mean in paragraph 2? What clues in the text help you understand the meaning of the word?** Read paragraph 2. What has caused "all gladness" to leave Tom? How does the author describe Tom's view on life?

5. Craft and Structure (RL.8.4) **One of the notable characteristics of Twain's style is his use of verbals. Examine paragraph 2 and highlight all the verbals in the passage.** Review paragraph 2. What words do you see that end in *-ing* or *-ed*? Which of these words function as adjectives, nouns, or adverbs?

Teacher Notes

My Notes

for he was personating the *Big Missouri*, and considered himself to be drawing nine feet of water. He was boat and captain and engine-bells combined, so he had to imagine himself standing on his own hurricane-deck giving the orders and executing them:

16 "Stop her, sir! Ting-a-ling-ling!" The headway ran almost out, and he drew up slowly toward the sidewalk.

17 "Ship up to back! Ting-a-ling-ling!" His arms straightened and stiffened down his sides.

18 "Set her back on the stabboard! Ting-a-ling-ling! Chow! ch-chow-wow! Chow!" His right hand, mean-time, describing stately circles—for it was representing a forty-foot wheel.

19 "Let her go back on the labboard! Ting-a-ling-ling! Chow-ch-chow-chow!" The left hand began to describe circles.

20 "Stop the stabboard! Ting-a-ling-ling! Stop the labboard! Come ahead on the stabboard! Stop her! Let your outside turn over slow! Ting-a-ling-ling! Chow-ow-ow! Get out that head-line! LIVELY now! Come—out with your spring-line—what're you about there! Take a turn round that stump with the bight of it! Stand by that stage, now—let her go! Done with the engines, sir! Ting-a-ling-ling! SH'T! S'H'T! SH'T!" (trying the gauge-cocks).

21 Tom went on whitewashing—paid no attention to the steamboat. Ben stared a moment and then said: "Hi-YI! YOU'RE up a stump, ain't you!"

Chunk 5

22 No answer. Tom surveyed his last touch with the eye of an artist, then he gave his brush another gentle sweep and surveyed the result, as before. Ben ranged up alongside of him. Tom's mouth watered for the apple, but he stuck to his work. Ben said:

23 "Hello, old chap, you got to work, hey?"

24 Tom wheeled suddenly and said:

25 "Why, it's you, Ben! I warn't noticing."

26 "Say—I'm going in a-swimming, I am. Don't you wish you could? But of course you'd druther WORK—wouldn't you? Course you would!"

27 Tom contemplated the boy a bit, and said:

28 "What do you call work?"

29 "Why, ain't THAT work?"

30 Tom resumed his whitewashing, and answered carelessly:

31 "Well, maybe it is, and maybe it ain't. All I know, is, it suits Tom Sawyer."

32 "Oh come, now, you don't mean to let on that you LIKE it?"

33 The brush continued to move.

34 "Like it? Well, I don't see why I oughtn't to like it. Does a boy get a chance to whitewash a fence every day?"

35 That put the thing in a new light. Ben stopped nibbling his apple. Tom swept his brush daintily back and forth—stepped back to note the effect—added a touch here and there—criticized the effect again—Ben watching every move and getting more and more interested, more and more absorbed. Presently he said:

36 "Say, Tom, let ME whitewash a little."

37 Tom considered, was about to consent; but he altered his mind:

6. Key Ideas and Details (RL.8.1) **How does Tom try to get Jim to help him in Chunk 3? Why does he fail?** Read paragraph 3. What does Tom offer to do if Jim will whitewash? Read paragraph 8. How does Tom attempt to bribe Jim? Read paragraph 13. Why does Jim finally give in to Tom? What happens to cause Jim to leave?

7. Craft and Structure: **How does Twain use steamboat jargon for effect in chunk 4?** What is some of the jargon Twain uses? What do these words make you think about? How do these words make the text "sound"?

8. Key Ideas and Details (RL.8.3) **Tom tries to manipulate his friends into doing whitewashing for him. How does he change his plan in Chunk 5 after Jim's refusal to help?** Read paragraph 31. What is Tom referring to when he says "it"? Tom is trying to convince Ben of what in paragraph 34? Why?

10 **SECOND READ:** During the second reading, students will be returning to the text to answer the text-dependent comprehension questions. You may choose to have students reread and work on the questions in a variety of ways:

- independently
- in pairs
- in small groups
- together as a class

11 Have students answer the text-dependent questions. If they have difficulty, scaffold the questions by rephrasing them or breaking them down into smaller parts. See the Scaffolding the Text-Dependent Questions boxes for suggestions.

Elements of Humor: Comic Situations

My Notes

GRAMMAR & USAGE
Dennotation and Connotation

When Ben enters the fence scene, he's described as "...eating an apple." As he weighs Tom's explanation of how special painting the fence is, Ben "stopped nibbling his apple." "Nibbling" rather than "eating" implies that Ben had become distracted with Tom's speech. Once Ben starts to paint and surrenders his apple to Tom, Tom "munched his apple..." "Munched" carries a deliberately noisy enjoyment of the apple, emphasizing how happy Tom is with himself.

38 "No—no—I reckon it wouldn't hardly do, Ben. You see, Aunt Polly's awful particular about this fence—right here on the street, you know—but if it was the back fence I wouldn't mind and SHE wouldn't. Yes, she's awful particular about this fence; it's got to be done very careful; I reckon there ain't one boy in a thousand, maybe two thousand, that can do it the way it's got to be done."

39 "No—is that so? Oh come, now—lemme just try. Only just a little—I'd let YOU, if you was me, Tom."

40 "Ben, I'd like to, honest injun; but Aunt Polly—well, Jim wanted to do it, but she wouldn't let him; Sid wanted to do it, and she wouldn't let Sid. Now don't you see how I'm fixed? If you was to tackle this fence and anything was to happen to it—"

41 "Oh, shucks, I'll be just as careful. Now lemme try. Say—I'll give you the core of my apple."

42 "Well, here—No, Ben, now don't. I'm afeard—"

43 "I'll give you ALL of it!"

Chunk 6

44 Tom gave up the brush with reluctance in his face, but alacrity in his heart. And while the late steamer *Big Missouri* worked and sweated in the sun, the retired artist sat on a barrel in the shade close by, dangled his legs, munched his apple, and planned the slaughter of more innocents. There was no lack of material; boys happened along every little while; they came to jeer, but remained to whitewash. By the time Ben was fagged out, Tom had traded the next chance to Billy Fisher for a kite, in good repair; and when he played out, Johnny Miller bought in for a dead rat and a string to swing it with—and so on, and so on, hour after hour. And when the middle of the afternoon came, from being a poor poverty-stricken boy in the morning, Tom was literally rolling in wealth. He had besides the things before mentioned, twelve marbles, part of a jews-harp, a piece of blue bottle-glass to look through, a spool cannon, a key that wouldn't unlock anything, a fragment of chalk, a glass stopper of a decanter, a tin soldier, a couple of tadpoles, six fire-crackers, a kitten with only one eye, a brass door-knob, a dog-collar—but no dog—the handle of a knife, four pieces of orange-peel, and a dilapidated old window sash.

Second Read

- Reread the excerpt to answer these text-dependent questions.
- Write any additional questions you have about the text in your Reader/Writer Notebook.

3. **Craft and Structure:** What does the word "reposeful" mean in paragraph 1? What clues in the text help you understand the meaning of the word?

   Reposeful means calm and peaceful. Words and phrases that provide clues to its meaning include "morning," "song in every heart," "locust-trees were in bloom," "fragrance of the blossoms," and "dreamy." RL.8.4

4. **Craft and Structure:** What does the word "melancholy" mean in paragraph 2? What clues in the text helped you understand the meaning of the word?

   Melancholy means sadness. "All gladness left him." The melancholy is described as "deep" and settling down on him. Life is described as "hollow" and existence a burden. Tom is described as sighing. RL.8.4

9. Craft and Structure (RL.8.4) **What does the word "alacrity" mean in paragraph 44? Cite the text to support your response.** Read the first sentence in paragraph 44. Throughout the excerpt, what has been the contrast between how Tom acts and how he genuinely feels? What does the author mean when he describes Tom as having "reluctance on his face"? What is the opposite of reluctance or being reluctant?

10. Key Ideas and Details (RL.8.1) **What is the effect of listing Tom's "treasures" in such great detail in paragraph 44?** Read paragraph 44. What are some of the items Tom receives in trade? What is humorous about this list of items and the author's description of Tom as "literally rolling in wealth"?

5. **Craft and Structure:** One of the notable characteristics of Twain's style is his use of verbals. Examine paragraph 2 and highlight all the verbals.

   Verbals in paragraph 2 include the following: "long-handled," "sighing," "whitewashed," "far-reaching," "unwhitewashed," "discouraged," "skipping," and "bringing." RL.8.4

6. **Key Ideas and Details:** How does Tom try to get Jim to help him in Chunk 3? Why does he fail?

   Tom offers to do Jim's job, and then offers to give him a marble and to show him his sore toe. He fails because Aunt Polly arrives. RL.8.1

7. **Craft and Structure:** How does Twain use steamboat jargon for effect in Chunk 4?

   Twain has Ben emphasize his impersonation of a steamboat captain by using the jargon of that trade ("stabboard," "labboard," "head-line," "spring-line"). RL.8.4

8. **Key Ideas and Details:** Tom tries to manipulate his friends into doing whitewashing for him. How does he change his plan in Chunk 5 after Jim's refusal to help?

   Rather than offering a simple exchange of goods, as he had done with Jim, Tom acts like he wants to paint the fence so that Ben will be jealous. RL.8.3

9. **Craft and Structure:** What does the word "alacrity" mean in paragraph 44? Cite the text to support your response.

   "Alacrity" means willingness. There is a contrast in how Tom is acting versus how he is feeling. We can conclude this charade continues when he gives up the brush with "reluctance on his face but alacrity in his heart." It's clear that "alacrity" means the opposite of "reluctance." RL.8.4

10. **Key Ideas and Details:** What is the effect of listing Tom's "treasures" in such great detail in paragraph 44?

   The details themselves are humorous: "a kitten with only one eye" and "four pieces of orange peel" are not things that one would normally consider "wealth." RL.8.1

My Notes

© 2017 College Board. All rights reserved.

12 In Working from the Text, use the **graphic organizer** as the basis for a whole-class discussion about the text. Encourage students to be creative, for example, by using colored pencils on blank white paper to draw their pictures. Perhaps display the graphic organizers in the classroom after the activity.

Elements of Humor: Comic Situations

My Notes

Working from the Text

11. Review the definition of **dialect** on page 289. Referencing the words and phrases you have already marked with a "D," try to paraphrase a few lines of dialogue in My Notes.
12. Prepare for a collaborative discussion by annotating and reviewing the text as follows:
    - Review what you have already underlined as the plot and make changes as needed. Be prepared to **paraphrase** (retell in your own words) the plot.
    - Place a question mark next to any word or idea you would like to **clarify** (discuss to remove confusion).
    - Place a star next to any part of the text you would like to **analyze** (share an inference, assumption, prediction based on the text).
13. On a separate piece of paper or in your Reader/Writer Notebook, create a graphic organizer like the one below to answer comprehension questions about the story.

Tom is like a ... (create a simile)	It is ironic that ...
The part of the story that stands out in my head is ... (draw a picture) This is a comedic situation because ...	I wonder ...

14. What is the level of comedy of this text? What is a universal truth, or theme, of this text? Write a thematic statement. Be sure to support your ideas with textual evidence.

Twain – "All in a Day's Work"
Level of Comedy: High
Theme subject(s): Work
Theme statement: Work that is shared is always easier.
Getting others to do your work is always a joyful experience.

My Notes

Check Your Understanding

WRITING to SOURCES **Expository Writing Prompt**

Explain how Mark Twain uses comic characters and situations to convey a universal truth through humor. Be sure to:

- Establish a controlling idea and support it with textual evidence and commentary.
- Use transitions to create cohesion and clarify the relationships among ideas and concepts.
- Use precise diction and maintain a formal style.
- Use verbals.

Elements of Humor

Add your notes about comic situations to the Elements of Humor graphic organizer in Activity 4.11.

INDEPENDENT READING LINK

Read and Research

Research other humorous works by Mark Twain. Choose one of these works and create a one-paragraph summary of a comic situation in your Reader/Writer Notebook. Note the level of comedy and identify the theme statement.

© 2017 College Board. All rights reserved.

Br Ask students to be sure they answered the prompt completely by checking the following items. Did you use evidence from Mark Twain's writing to explain how he uses comic characters and situations? Did you add commentary about how Twain's writing conveys a universal truth?

ACTIVITY 4.8 continued

13 Ask students to use **think-pair-write-share** for Student Step 14; this will promote collaborative discussion and diverse ideas.

14 Then guide students to participate in a class discussion about the humorous text they enjoyed most and how the elements of humor contributed to the text's overall effect.

15 Direct students to respond to the expository writing prompt.

16 Prompt students to complete the Independent Reading Link, reminding them to record responses in their Reader/Writer Notebook.

ASSESS

In looking at students' graphic organizers, note whether they are able to visualize and explain the comedic situation using the information from the beginning of the activity.

As they answer the writing prompt, check that students are able to analyze the text for a universal truth by looking at their graphic organizer responses and use of textual evidence to defend their ideas. The controlling idea or topic sentence needs to be about Tom's ability to get others to do work for him.

ADAPT

Challenge students to find the comic situations in the texts they are reading independently.

Leveled Differentiated Instruction

In the upcoming expository writing prompt , students may need help with supporting their controlling idea.

Em Have students use the **Paragraph Frame for Conclusions** with a partner in order to organize the evidence that supports their controlling idea before writing.

Ex Have students use the **Paragraph Frame** for Conclusions with a partner in order to organize the evidence that supports their controlling idea before writing. Have students replace the transitions in the paragraph frame with a variety of transition words and phrases from the list they made in Activity 4.6.

ACTIVITY 4.9

▶PLAN

Materials: sticky notes
Suggested Pacing: 2 50-minute class periods

▶TEACH

1 Begin the activity by using hyperbolic language. With a serious expression and tone, tell students they will have 5,000 things to do today and a thousand pages of reading to do for homework. After the groans and laughter subside, ask students how they knew you weren't serious.

2 The definition of *hyperbole* can be found on the Elements of Humor chart in Activity 4.11. Work with the class to finish the lines using hyperbolic language. Explain that writers use hyperbole to create a variety of effects, not just humor.

3 Read the Preview and the Setting a Purpose for Reading sections with your students. Help them understand any unfamiliar terms they encounter.

4 **FIRST READ:** Based on the complexity of the passage and your knowledge of your students, you may choose to conduct the first reading in a variety of ways:

- independent reading
- paired reading
- small group reading
- choral reading
- read aloud

5 As students are reading, monitor their progress. Be sure they are engaged with the text and annotating words and phrases that demonstrate hyperbole as well as words and phrases that students find humorous or strange. Evaluate whether the selected reading mode is effective.

6 Based on the observations you made during the first reading, you may want to adjust your reading mode. For example, you may decide for the second reading to read aloud certain complex passages, or you may group students differently.

ACTIVITY 4.9

Elements of Humor: Hyperbole

LEARNING STRATEGIES: Note-taking, Marking the Text, Skimming/Scanning, Discussion Groups

Learning Targets

- Analyze the effect of hyperbole in poetry.
- Identify hyperbole in previously studied print and nonprint texts.

Understanding Hyperbole

1. Finish the lines using hyperbolic language. The first line is shown as an example.
   - My dog is so big, he beeps when he backs up.
   - I'm so hungry, I could eat a ______________________.
   - My cat is so smart that ______________________.
   - She was so funny that ______________________.

Literary Terms
Hyperbole describes the literary technique of extreme exaggeration for emphasis, often used for comic effect.

Preview

In this activity, you will read poems and think about the authors' use of hyperbole.

Setting a Purpose for Reading

- As you read the poem, underline words and phrases that demonstrate hyperbole.
- Circle unknown words and phrases. Try to determine the meaning of the words by using context clues, word parts, or a dictionary.
- Mark lines you find humorous or strange with an exclamation point.

My Notes

ABOUT THE AUTHOR
Carl Sandburg (1878–1967) was a journalist who also wrote poetry, novels, and historical books. He is perhaps best known as a poet, although his biography *Abraham Lincoln: The War Years* won a Pulitzer Prize.

Literary Terms
A **yarn** is a long, often involved story, usually telling of incredible or fantastic events; an entertaining tale; a tall tale.

Poetry

"They Have Yarns"

by Carl Sandburg

They have yarns
Of a skyscraper so tall they had to put hinges
On the two top stories so to let the moon go by,
Of one corn crop in Missouri when the roots

Went so deep and drew off so much water
The Mississippi riverbed that year was dry,
Of pancakes so thin they had only one side,
Of "a fog so thick we shingled the barn and six feet out on the fog,"
Of Pecos Pete straddling a cyclone in Texas and riding it to the west coast where
"it rained out under him,"

COMMON CORE STATE STANDARDS

Focus Standards:

L.8.5: Demonstrate understanding of figurative language, word relationships, and nuances in word meanings.

L.8.5a: Interpret figures of speech (e.g., verbal irony, puns) in context.

Additional Standards Addressed:

RL.8.1; RL.8.4; RL.8.9; RL.8.10; W.8.10; SL.8.1a; SL.8.1c; SL.8.2; SL.8.6; L.8.1a; L.8.6

Of the man who drove a swarm of bees across the Rocky Mountains and the Desert
"and didn't lose a bee,"
Of a mountain railroad curve where the engineer in his cab can touch the caboose
and spit in the conductor's eye,
Of the boy who climbed a cornstalk growing so fast he would have starved to death
if they hadn't shot biscuits up to him,
Of the old man's whiskers: "When the wind was with him his whiskers
arrived a day before he did,"
Of the hen laying a square egg and cackling, "Ouch!" and of hens laying eggs with
the dates printed on them,

Of the ship captain's shadow: it froze to the deck one cold winter night,
Of mutineers on that same ship put to chipping rust with rubber hammers,
Of the sheep counter who was fast and accurate: "I just count their feet and divide
by four,"
Of the man so tall he must climb a ladder to shave himself,
Of the runt so teeny-weeny it takes two men and a boy to see him,

Of mosquitoes: one can kill a dog, two of them a man,
Of a cyclone that sucked cookstoves out of the kitchen, up the chimney flue, and on
to the next town,
Of the same cyclone picking up wagon-tracks in Nebraska and dropping them over
in the Dakotas,
Of the hook-and-eye snake unlocking itself into forty pieces, each piece two inches
long, then in nine seconds flat snapping itself together again,
Of the watch swallowed by the cow—when they butchered her a year later the
watch was running and had the correct time,

Of horned snakes, hoop snakes that roll themselves where they want to go, and
rattlesnakes carrying bells instead of rattles on their tails,
Of the herd of cattle in California getting lost in a giant redwood tree that had
hollowed out,
Of the man who killed a snake by putting its tail in its mouth so it swallowed itself,
Of railroad trains whizzing along so fast they reach the station before the whistle,
Of pigs so thin the farmer had to tie knots in their tails to keep them from crawling
through the cracks in their pen,

Of Paul Bunyan's big blue ox, Babe, measuring between the eyes forty-two
ax-handles and a plug of Star tobacco exactly,
Of John Henry's hammer and the curve of its swing and his singing of it as
"a rainbow round my shoulder."

WORD CONNECTIONS

Content Connections

One of the fantastic events in this poem deals with an event common to meteorology: a cyclone. A cyclone is a large, powerful, and destructive storm with high winds turning in an area of low pressure.

GRAMMAR & USAGE

Participial Phrases

A **participial phrase** is a group of words beginning with a participle and used as an adjective. For example:
"laying a square egg"
"growing so fast"
"chipping rust with rubber hammers"

My Notes

TEACHER TO TEACHER

You might have students visualize and draw an illustration of one of the hyperbolic statements in the poem.

Leveled Differentiated Instruction

In this activity, ask students to visualize a scene from "They Have Yarns" based on their close reading. Then ask students to draw a sketch of the scene they visualized.

Em Ask students to pair up and write words from the text that relate to their sketch. Then have them discuss with each other how the words contributed to the scene.

Ex Have students form pairs or small groups and write sentences about how well certain words in the text led them to visualize the scene using the sentence frame. *The word ___ helped me picture ___.*

SCAFFOLDING THE TEXT-DEPENDENT QUESTIONS

2. Knowledge and Ideas (RL.8.9) **Reference the text and choose three of the yarns. Identify the real things they exaggerate. Provide examples of hyperbole related to these real things by citing the text.** What three everyday items does the author describe in the first two paragraphs? How does the author describe each of these items in a way that is unbelievable or exaggerated?

3. Key Ideas and Details (RL.8.1) **What allusions does the author use? How might this add to the humor?** In the second and last paragraphs, the author refers to which famous characters from folklore? What is comical about how the author describes these characters?

© 2017 College Board. All rights reserved.

7 **SECOND READ:** During the second reading, students will be returning to the text to answer the text-dependent comprehension questions. You may choose to have students reread and work on the questions in a variety of ways:

- independently
- in pairs
- in small groups
- together as a class

8 Have students answer the text-dependent questions. If they have difficulty, scaffold the questions by rephrasing them or breaking them down into smaller parts. See the Scaffolding the Text-Dependent Questions boxes for suggestions.

9 In Working from the Text, have students use their **metacognitive markers** in a class discussion of the text.

10 Read the Preview and the Setting a Purpose for Reading sections with your students. Help them understand any unfamiliar terms they encounter.

Elements of Humor: Hyperbole

My Notes

Second Read

- Reread the poem to answer these text-dependent questions.
- Write any additional questions you have about the text in your Reader/Writer Notebook.

2. **Knowledge and Ideas:** Reference the text and choose three of the yarns. Identify the real things they exaggerate. Provide examples of hyperbole related to these real things by citing the text.

   Answers include the following: skyscraper: "so tall they had to put hinges on the top two stories so to let the moon go by..."; pancakes: "of pancakes so thin they only had one side"; fog: "so thick we shingled the barn..." RL.8.9

3. **Key Ideas and Details:** What allusions does the author use? How might this add to the humor?

   The allusions to the tall tales and exaggerated figures of American folklore—such as Paul Bunyan, John Henry, and Pecos Pete—set the tone for humorous exaggeration. The details are all exaggerated stories of impossibilities and make the yarns more hyperbolic and vivid. RL.8.1

Working from the Text

4. Review the definitions of hyperbole and yarn on page 296. Based on Sandburg's poem, how might a yarn relate to a hyperbole?
5. In a collaborative discussion, share the lines you underlined as demonstrating hyperbole, the unknown words and phrases you circled, and the lines you marked as funny or strange.
6. Using the My Notes section on page 297, add a line or two to Sandburg's poem, using hyperbolic language and a participial adjective phrase. Consider using an allusion for humorous effect. Note how each line of hyperbole begins the same way.
7. Place a "V" next to lines in the text containing use of verbals.

Setting a Purpose for Reading

- As you read the poem, underline words and phrases that demonstrate hyperbole.
- Circle unknown words and phrases. Try to determine the meaning of the words by using context clues, word parts, or a dictionary.
- Mark lines you find humorous or strange with an exclamation point.

© 2017 College Board. All rights reserved.

ABOUT THE AUTHOR
Ted Hughes (1930–1998) is considered to be one of the twentieth century's greatest poets. He wrote almost 90 books during his long career and won numerous prizes and fellowships. In 1984, he was appointed England's poet laureate.

Literary Terms
Alliteration is the repetition of consonant sounds at the beginnings of words that are close together.

Poetry

"Mooses"

by Ted Hughes

The goofy Moose, the walking house frame,
Is lost
In the forest. He bumps, he blunders, he stands.

With massy bony thoughts sticking out near his ears—
Reaching out palm upwards, to catch whatever might be
falling from heaven—
He tries to think,
Leaning their huge weight
On the lectern of his front legs.
He can't find the world!
Where did it go? What
does a world look like?

The Moose
Crashes on, and crashes into a
lake, and stares at the
mountain and cries:
'Where do I belong? This is no place!'

He turns dragging half the lake out after him
And charges the crackling underbrush

He meets another Moose
He stares, he thinks: 'It's only a mirror!'
Where is the world?' he groans. 'O my lost world!

And why am I so ugly?
'And why am I so far away from my feet?'

My Notes

8. Craft and Structure (RL.8.4) **Look for examples of parallel structure and repetition in the poem. How do these stylistic choices make the moose appear "goofy"?** Identify the two uses of parallel structure in the first and third paragraphs. How does the author's use of parallel structure contribute to the "goofy" image of the moose?

9. Key Ideas and Details (RL.8.1) **Is this poem high or low comedy? How do you know?** Review the chart explaining high and low comedy on page 243. Based on your understanding of high and low comedy, which level best describes this poem?

© 2017 College Board. All rights reserved.

ACTIVITY 4.9 continued

11 **FIRST READ:** Based on the complexity of the passage and your knowledge of your students, you may choose to conduct the first reading in a variety of ways:

- independent reading
- paired reading
- small group reading
- choral reading
- read aloud

12 As students are reading, monitor their progress. Be sure they are engaged with the text and annotating words and phrases that demonstrate hyperbole as well as those that students find humorous or strange. Evaluate whether the selected reading mode is effective.

13 Based on the observations you made during the first reading, you may want to adjust your reading mode. For example, you may decide for the second reading to read aloud certain complex passages, or you may group students differently.

14 **SECOND READ:** During the second reading, students will be returning to the text to answer the text-dependent comprehension questions. You may choose to have students reread and work on the questions in a variety of ways:

- independently
- in pairs
- in small groups
- together as a class

15 Have students answer the text-dependent questions. If they have difficulty, scaffold the questions by rephrasing them or breaking them down into smaller parts. See the Scaffolding the Text-Dependent Questions boxes for suggestions.

TEACHER TO TEACHER

It is important that students understand that a style analysis essay requires analysis of an author's ideas, organization, and language. This will be the focus of the Text-Dependent Questions, as well as the Working from the Text questions.

16 To do the Working from the Text assignment, ask students to revisit the texts they have read in this unit to hunt for hyperbole. Distribute several sticky notes to pairs, and have them **mark the text** to identify hyperbole and flag the page with a sticky note.

17 Next, combine partners into small groups, and direct them to discuss how hyperbole creates a humorous effect in the text. During the discussion, students should go to the texts, mark additional examples, and take notes in the My Notes section.

18 Monitor students as they hunt for hyperbole from previously read texts to make sure they are able to accurately identify examples. Also listen to their collaborative discussions to determine whether they are using precise diction from the unit.

19 Instruct students to add specific examples of hyperbole to the Elements of Humor **graphic organizer** they have started (Activity 4.11).

Elements of Humor: Hyperbole

My Notes

He weeps.
Hopeless drops drip from his droopy lips.
The other Moose just stands there doing the same.
Two dopes of the deep woods.

Second Read

- Reread the poem to answer these text-dependent questions.
- Write any additional questions you have about the text in your Reader/Writer Notebook.

8. **Craft and Structure:** Look for examples of parallel structure and repetition in the poem. How do these stylistic choices make the moose appear "goofy"?

   Parallel structure in lines like "He bumps, he blunders, he stands" and "Crashes on, and crashes" make the moose's clumsiness seem repetitive and clownish. RL.8.4

9. **Key Ideas and Details:** Is this poem high or low comedy? How do you know?

   Low comedy. The poem features a series of events and physical mishaps. The action is entertaining as the moose appears caught in a situation he cannot control. RL.8.1

Working from the Text

10. Cite the text to illustrate how the author uses hyperbole for effect.

    The effect of the lines "He can't find the world!" and "Why am I so far away from my feet?" exaggerate the moose's oversensitive awareness of being out of place; i.e., being a misfit.

11. What words and phrases show how the speaker's tone shifts throughout the poem?

    The tone begins in a gently comical way, describing the moose's "goofy" appearance. It then turns sadder, more rueful, and pathetic as shown in the moose's plaintive cry, "Why am I so ugly?" "He weeps."

12. How does Hughes's use of verbals, especially participial phrases, contribute to the hyperbole in the poem? Quote specific lines and analyze the use of verbals and hyperbole.

    The verbals "walking house frame," "reaching out palm upward," and "dragging half the lake" create an exaggerated visual image of the physical being of the moose, which is goofy and comical.

© 2017 College Board. All rights reserved.

Setting a Purpose for Reading

- As you read the poem, underline words and phrases that demonstrate hyperbole.
- Circle unknown words and phrases. Try to determine the meaning of the words by using context clues, word parts, or a dictionary.
- Mark lines you find humorous or strange with an exclamation point.

WORD CONNECTIONS

Cognates

Chicle is a gummy substance obtained from trees and used to manufacture chewing gum. In Spanish, *el chicle*, means "gum."

ABOUT THE AUTHOR

Ana Castillo is a celebrated Chicana poet, activist, novelist, and translator. Her commitment to human rights, free expression, and cultural exchange has shaped her career as a writer and scholar. Castillo's work in poetry and prose is highly innovative and is based on oral and literary traditions.

My Notes

Poetry

El Chicle

by Ana Castillo

Mi'jo and I were
laughing
ha, ha, ha—
when the gum he
chewed
fell out of his mouth
and into my hair
which, after I clipped
it,
flew in the air,
on the back
of a dragonfly
that dipped in the
creek
and was snapped
fast by a turtle
that reached high
and swam deep.
Mi'jo wondered
what happened to

20 To prepare for reading "El Chicle," **activate prior knowledge** about the title by discussing the Word Connection/Cognates feature. Read About the Author to introduce the poem.

21 Read the Preview and the Setting a Purpose for Reading sections with your students. Help them understand any new terms.

22 **FIRST READ:** Based on the complexity of the passage and your knowledge of your students, you may choose to conduct the first reading in a variety of ways:

- independent reading
- paired reading
- small group reading
- choral reading
- read aloud

TEACHER TO TEACHER

You might have students visualize and draw an illustration of one of the hyperbolic statements in the poem during the reading.

13. Craft and Structure (RL.8.4): **Who do you think "Mi'jo" refers to? What clues in the poem support your answer?** Do you think "Mi'jo" refers to a person's name or a type of family member? Why? Based on what happened with Mi'jo's gum and the reason he becomes worried, what can you conclude about his age?

14. Key Ideas and Details (RI.8.1) **What is the central event of the poem? How do you know?** What event happens early in the poem that leads to a chain reaction of other events? Why is this early event important?

23 **SECOND READ:** During the second reading, students will be returning to the text to answer the text-dependent comprehension questions. You may choose to have students reread and work on the questions in a variety of ways:

- independently
- in pairs
- in small groups
- together as a class

24 Have students answer the text-dependent questions. If they have difficulty, scaffold the questions by rephrasing them or breaking them down into smaller parts. See the Scaffolding the Text-Dependent Questions boxes for suggestions.

Elements of Humor: Hyperbole

My Notes

that gum,
worried that it stuck
to the back of my
seat
and Mami will be
mad
when she can't get it
out.
Meanwhile, the turtle
in the pond
that ate the dragonfly
that carried the hair
with the gum
swam south on
Saturday
and hasn't been seen
once since.

Second Read

- Reread the poem to answer these text-dependent questions.
- Write any additional questions you have about the text in your Reader/Writer Notebook.

13. **Craft and Structure:** Who do you think "Mi'jo" refers to? What clues in the poem support your answer?

"Mi'jo" is short for "mi hijo," meaning "my son." Another feasible assumption could be "child" based on the following phrases: "out of his mouth and into my hair," "after I clipped it," "worried that it stuck to the back of my seat, and Mami will be mad." RL.8.4

14. **Key Ideas and Details:** What is the central event of the poem? How do you know?

The central event of the poem is the gum falling out and getting stuck in the author's hair. This event is the catalyst for all other actions in the poem. RL.8.1

Working from the Text

15. What is the consistent tone of the poem, and who is the intended audience? Cite words or phrases from the poem to support your response.

Check Your Understanding

Most of the texts you have read so far depend on exaggeration and hyperbole to make readers smile, chuckle, and laugh. Return to the humorous print texts you have read in this unit and identify examples of hyperbole. In a collaborative discussion, share the examples you locate and discuss how hyperbole creates a humorous effect. Use precise diction in your discussion. Record examples shared by your peers in the graphic organizer.

Hyperbole

Title: Example:	Title: Example:
Title: Example:	Title: Example:

My Notes

INDEPENDENT READING LINK

Read and Connect

Research humorous texts in which the author uses hyperbole for effect. Choose a text that exemplifies the use of hyperbole, tone, and verbals. Cite examples to support your choice in your Reader/Writer Notebook. Include a brief summary explaining why this humorous text appeals to you. You will use your notes to recommend the text to your peers in a small group setting.

ASSESS

Use the Check Your Understanding as a formative assessment. Instruct students to add specific examples to the hyperbole **graphic organizer.** On the organizer, check that students use quotation marks correctly. You could also require that they include a commentary statement about each example.

ADAPT

To extend learning, ask students to draft an illustrated anecdote or poem to demonstrate what they know about creating humor through hyperbole.

Illustrations should contain the written hyperbole as well as a drawing that shows the absurdity of the statement. Display the strongest examples in the classroom.

25 Allow time for students to complete the Independent Reading Link activity on page 303. They will need time to complete the activity and to present their recommendations in a small group setting.

ACTIVITY 4.10

▶PLAN

Materials: examples of wordplay you enjoy (your favorite joke, one-liner, and pun), "Who's on First?" by Abbott and Costello (print and audio or video), children's book(s) (optional)
Suggested Pacing: 2 50-minute class periods

▶TEACH

1 Read the Preview and the Setting a Purpose for Reading sections with your students. Help them understand any terms they don't already know.

2 **FIRST READ:** Based on the complexity of the passage and your knowledge of your students, you may choose to conduct the first reading in a variety of ways:

- independent reading
- paired reading
- small group reading
- choral reading
- read aloud

ACTIVITY 4.10

Elements of Humor: Comic Wordplay

LEARNING STRATEGIES:
Marking the Text, Discussion Groups, RAFT

Learning Targets

- Interpret the use of wordplay in poetry and drama.
- Collaborate to explore wordplay in previously studied texts.
- Create a visual representation of a pun.

Preview

In this activity, you will read a poem and think about the author's use of wordplay, specifically puns.

Setting a Purpose for Reading

- As you read the poem, underline words and phrases that demonstrate the author's use of puns.
- Circle unknown words and phrases. Try to determine the meaning of the words by using context clues, word parts, or a dictionary.
- Draw a question mark next to any puns that you do not understand.

ABOUT THE AUTHOR
Jack Prelutsky (b. 1940) says that he has always enjoyed playing with language, although he did not always like poetry. He rediscovered poetry in his twenties, when he began writing humorous verse for children. Since then, he has written more than fifty poetry collections. His poems are sometimes silly, sometimes playful, sometimes frightening, but always entertaining. In 2006, the Poetry Foundation named him the first-ever Children's Poet Laureate. Prelutsky also studied music, and he has set several of his poems to music for the audio versions of his poetry anthologies.

My Notes

Poetry

Is Traffic Jam Delectable?

by Jack Prelutsky

Is traffic jam delectable,
does jelly fish in lakes,
does tree bark make a racket,
does the clamor rattle snakes?

Can salmon scale a mountain,
does a belly laugh a lot,
do carpets nap in flower beds
or on an apricot?
Around my handsome bottleneck,

WORD CONNECTIONS

Roots and Affixes
The word ***clamor*** comes from a Latin word meaning "to call out." The root *-clam-*, also spelled *-claim-*, appears in *exclaim* and *exclamation*, *proclaim* and *proclamation*, and *acclaim* and *acclamation*.

COMMON CORE STATE STANDARDS

Focus Standards:

RL.8.4: Determine the meaning of words and phrases as they are used in a text, including figurative and connotative meanings; analyze the impact of specific word choices on meaning and tone, including analogies or allusions to other texts.

L.8.5: Demonstrate understanding of figurative language, word relationships, and nuances in word meanings.

L.8.5a: Interpret figures of speech (e.g., verbal irony, puns) in context.

Additional Standards Addressed:

RL.8.1; W.8.2a; W.8.2b; W.8.2c; W.8.2d; W.8.4; W.8.5; W.8.9a; SL.8.1a; SL.8.6; L.8.1a; L.8.6

© 2017 College Board. All rights reserved.

I wear a railroad tie,
my treasure chest puffs up a bit,
I blink my private eye.
I like to use piano keys
to open locks of hair,

then put a pair of brake shoes on
and dance on debonair.
I hold up my electric shorts
with my banana belt,
then sit upon a toadstool

and watch a tuna melt.
I dive into a car pool,
where I take an onion dip,
then stand aboard the tape deck
and sail my penmanship.

I put my dimes in riverbanks
and take a quarterback,
and when I fix a nothing flat
I use a lumberjack.
I often wave my second hand

to tell the overtime,
before I take my bull pen up
to write a silly rhyme.

My Notes

Second Read

- Reread the poem to answer these text-dependent questions.
- Write any additional questions you have about the text in your Reader/Writer Notebook.

1. **Craft and Structure:** How does Prelutsky's understanding of children influence his choice of words? What is the result for the reader? Cite examples from the text to support your answer.

Prelutsky chooses questions and statements that children might pose based on their limited understanding of words and phrases. The result is humorous as the reader understands why a child would ask such questions or make such statements, but also understands the resultant humor. Answers include, "does tree bark make a racket?" "sit upon a toadstool," "take an onion dip." RL.8.4

SCAFFOLDING THE TEXT-DEPENDENT QUESTIONS

1. Craft and Structure (RL.8.4) **How does Prelutsky's understanding of children influence his choice of words? What is the result for the reader? Cite examples from the text to support your answer.** What type of vocabulary does Prelutsky use? Read the first two lines of text. How might these lines appeal to children more than adults?

ACTIVITY 4.10 continued

3 As students are reading, monitor their progress. Be sure they are engaged with the text and annotating words and phrases that demonstrate the author's use of puns as well as any puns they do not understand. Evaluate whether the selected reading mode is effective.

4 Based on the observations you made during the first reading, you may want to adjust your reading mode. For example, you may decide for the second reading to read aloud certain complex passages, or you may group students differently.

5 **SECOND READ:** During the second reading, students will be returning to the text to answer the text-dependent comprehension questions. You may choose to have students reread and work on the questions in a variety of ways:

- independently
- in pairs
- in small groups
- together as a class

6 Have students answer the text-dependent questions. If they have difficulty, scaffold the questions by rephrasing them or breaking them down into smaller parts. See the Scaffolding the Text-Dependent Questions boxes for suggestions.

Leveled Differentiated Instruction

In this activity, students may need support diffusing and paraphrasing the meaning of the idiomatic expressions. Have students discuss the meaning of several idiomatic expressions with a partner and record ideas from the discussion.

Em Point out the idiomatic expressions in the poem, *make a racket, scale a mountain,* and *belly laugh.* Help students express their ideas by asking and answering simple questions about the idiomatic expressions such as *What does this phrase remind you of? What do you think the phrase means?* Help students record ideas from the discussion using a **Collaborative Dialogue** graphic organizer.

Ex Have students respond to their discussion partners by adding relevant information and paraphrasing idioms and multiple-meaning words. Encourage students to take notes based on the discussion.

Br Have partners choose a few particularly silly lines or images based on the idioms and explain how the author uses them to create an effect. Have students respond to their discussion partners by adding relevant information, paraphrasing key ideas, and providing useful feedback. Encourage students to take notes based on the discussion.

Support Have students point out any words or expressions in the poem that are difficult to understand and discuss them as a class.

Stretch Challenge students to write their own poem, using idiomatic expressions as Prelutsky has done and share them with the class.

7 When you finish reading, form groups of two or three students. Have students work collaboratively to complete the Working from the Text questions. In observing collaborative discussions, check to hear that students are able to identify and analyze the effect of wordplay using precise humor diction.

8 Review rhythm and ask students how the rhythm of Prelutsky's poem adds to the humorous effect.

9 Have students create and share sketches that illustrate one of the puns from the poem.

10 Direct students to revisit the Elements of Humor graphic organizer in Activity 4.11 and add specific examples of wordplay, puns, and one-liners.

Elements of Humor: Comic Wordplay

My Notes

2. **Key Ideas and Details:** Puns depend on an audience's understanding of both possible meanings of a word or phrase. Why might someone older be more likely to understand what a "tape deck" or "brake shoes" are? What does this indicate about the level of comedy involved in puns?

   Puns are high-level comedy because the reader usually has to access prior knowledge in order to understand the humor. "Tape decks" would be familiar to someone who was alive before the '90s and "brake shoes" is a term recognizable to someone who is old enough to drive. RL.8.1

Working from the Text

3. Referencing the text as an example, define *pun* and create some examples of your own.

   A pun is the humorous use of a word or words to suggest another word with the same sound or a different meaning. Examples:

   "Don't let Cinderella play baseball. She always runs away from the ball."

   Two vultures board an airplane, each carrying two dead raccoons. The stewardess looks at them and says, "I'm sorry, gentlemen, only one carrion allowed per passenger."

   Did you hear that NASA recently put a bunch of Holsteins into low earth orbit? They called it the herd shot 'round the world.

4. Mark the text by highlighting at least three humorous puns that you can visualize.
5. Sketch at least one of the puns in the margin of the poem or on a separate piece of paper.
6. In your discussion groups, share your sketches and read aloud the corresponding pun. Explain the two meanings of the word or phrase that creates the pun. Be sure to use precise diction and discuss how the author uses puns for humorous effect.
7. As a group, review the poem and discuss the puns that you notated with question marks. Try to collaborate to make meaning of these.

Analyzing a Humorous Skit

You will next read and/or listen to the skit "Who's on First?" by Abbott and Costello.

8. Based on the title of the skit, what do you think is the subject?

SCAFFOLDING THE TEXT-DEPENDENT QUESTIONS

2. Key Ideas and Details (RL.8.1) **Puns depend on an audience's understanding of both possible meanings of a word or phrase. Why might someone older be more likely to understand what a "tape deck" or "brake shoes" are? What does this indicate about the level of comedy involved in puns?** Why would someone have to be older to understand what a "tape deck is?" What knowledge would someone have to have to know what "brake shoes" are? What makes a pun high comedy?

9. Sketch a baseball diamond on a separate piece of paper. As you read the skit, try to fill in the names of each of the players mentioned.

10. Write answers to the following questions about "Who's on First?" and compare them with a peer.

- Why are Abbott and Costello having difficulty understanding each other?

- How does the wordplay create humor at a high level of comedy ?

11. Add your notes about comic language (hyperbole and wordplay) to the Elements of Humor graphic organizer in Activity 4.11.

My Notes

Check Your Understanding

WRITING to SOURCES **Expository Writing Prompt**

Choose one of the texts from this or the previous activity. Explain how the writer uses comic language (hyperbole and/or wordplay) to convey a universal truth. Be sure to:

- Establish a controlling idea and support it with textual evidence (quotes from the text) and commentary explaining the humor.
- Use transitions to create cohesion and clarify the relationships among ideas and concepts.
- Use verbals and precise diction, including the correct use of humorous elements.

© 2017 College Board. All rights reserved.

ACTIVITY 4.10 continued

11 Search the Internet to find the text of the skit "Who's on First?" by Abbott and Costello. Provide copies for your students or have them view it online. Depending on time, you may also find the radio broadcast of Abbott and Costello performing the skit and play part of it for students. In addition, Youtube includes several videos of the duo performing the skit. Use the title of the skit as the search term.

12 Before reading, watching, or listening to Abbot and Costello, ask students to **pair-share** to explore any prior knowledge they have about this skit. If possible, listen to a recording of the skit before reading the skit aloud as a class. During reading, **role playing** will help students see how the lines of dialogue play off each other for comic effect. After students read the skit, have them answer the analysis questions and compare responses with a peer.

ASSESS

The writing prompt gives students an opportunity to practice writing analysis. Be sure to remind them about effective topic sentences and incorporating quotations smoothly and effectively into their own sentences. Commentary on textual evidence needs to be relevant and precise. Students should independently complete this writing either as an in-class writing prompt or as homework. It can later be used as part of the evidence for their Embedded Assessment analysis.

ADAPT

Challenge students to write an in-class analysis of the comic characters, situation, and wordplay of any of the previous texts that might be appropriate (Twain, Barry, Abbott and Costello) as practice for timed writing and as a draft for the Embedded Assessment.

ACTIVITY 4.11

▶PLAN

Materials: chart paper for posters
Suggested Pacing: 3 50-minute class periods

▶TEACH

1 Remind students that they will be required to identify and analyze elements of humor as they analyze a humorous text in Embedded Assessment 1.

2 Ask students to revisit the Elements of Humor graphic organizer and self-assess how comfortable they are with the elements. Students should have already made notes on this graphic organizer for each element of humor. Ask them to teach each other what they know to clarify any confusion.

3 You may want to have students create and display a poster that visually represents the humorous element assigned to them. The poster should include the element and its definition.

4 Ask students to select and read a humorous text from this unit, or choose another you would like students to practice analyzing.

ACTIVITY 4.11

Planning and Revising an Analysis of a Humorous Text

LEARNING STRATEGIES: Graphic Organizer, Marking the Text, Note-taking, Drafting, Discussion Groups

Learning Targets

- Draft and revise an essay analyzing a humorous short story.
- Evaluate a sample student essay.

Identifying and Analyzing the Elements of Humor

1. Review the Elements of Humor graphic organizer below and rank how comfortable you are at understanding the elements (#1 being most comfortable, #2 being second most, etc.).

Elements of Humor			
Humorous Element	**Definition**	**Level of Comedy**	**Examples from Texts**
Comic Characters and Caricatures	A caricature is a pictorial, written, or acted representation of a person that exaggerates characteristics or traits for comic effect.		
Comic Situations and Situational Irony	Comic situations are when characters are in an unlikely situation or are victims of circumstances and react in a comical way. Situational irony involves a contrast between what characters or readers might reasonably expect to happen and what actually happens.		
Comic Language: Hyperbole	Hyperbole is extreme exaggeration used for emphasis, often used for comic effect.		
Comic Language: Wordplay • **One-liners** • **Puns**	A one-liner is a short joke or witticism expressed in a single sentence. A pun is the humorous use of a word or words to suggest another word with the same sound or different meaning.		

2. Your teacher will assign a text for you to analyze.
   - Closely read (or reread) the text.
   - Mark the text by highlighting evidence of humorous elements.
   - Annotate the text using precise diction to describe the intended humor and humorous effect.

My Notes

COMMON CORE STATE STANDARDS

Focus Standards:

W.8.2: Write informative/explanatory texts to examine a topic and convey ideas, concepts, and information through the selection, organization, and analysis of relevant content.

W.8.2a: Introduce a topic clearly, previewing what is to follow; organize ideas, concepts, and information into broader categories; include formatting (e.g., headings), graphics (e.g., charts, tables), and multimedia when useful to aiding comprehension.

W.8.9: Draw evidence from literary or informational texts to support analysis, reflection, and research.

W.8.9a: Apply *Grade 8 Reading standards* to literature (e.g., "Analyze how a modern work of fiction draws on themes, patterns of events, or character types from myths, traditional stories, or religious works such as the Bible, including describing how the material is rendered new").

3. Collaborate with your group to complete the graphic organizer below and on the next pages.

Title: ______________________ **Author:** ______________

Humorous Element	Examples from Text	Comedic Effect
Comic Characters and Caricatures		
Comic Situations and Situational Irony		
Comic Language: **Hyperbole**		
Comic Language: Wordplay • **One-liners** • **Puns**		

COMMON CORE STATE STANDARDS

Additional Standards Addressed:

RL.8.1; RL.8.4; RI.8.1; RI.8.2; RI.8.3; RI.8.4; RI.8.5; W.8.2b; W.8.2c; W.8.2f; W.8.4; W.8.5; L.8.5a

TEACHER TO TEACHER

To allow for class discussions and mini-lessons, consider assigning the same text to all students, such as "The Ransom of Red Chief" by O. Henry or "Charles" by Shirley Jackson. You might also choose a previously studied text or another Dave Barry essay.

5 Remind students to **mark/annotate the text** when they identify techniques used to create a humorous effect.

6 Use the graphic organizer as a formative assessment of students' knowledge of the elements of humor, the levels of comedy, and their ability to find humor and explain it. The ability to identify and explain is the foundation of successful analysis.

ACTIVITY 4.11 continued

7 Make sure students classify the text as low or high comedy. Students should **mark** evidence to support their interpretation.

8 Form mixed-level groups, and ask them to complete the **graphic organizers** and share their analysis with the class.

ACTIVITY 4.11 continued

Planning and Revising an Analysis of a Humorous Text

Level of Comedy	Explanation	Evidence

Description of Humor and Intended Effect	Examples from Text	Explanation (Commentary)

Universal Truth (Theme)	Evidence from Text

Reading and Analyzing a Sample Essay

An effective essay includes a clear introduction to the topic, body paragraphs that expand on the thesis and provide evidence and commentary to support it, and a conclusion that provides closure for the topic.

Introduction

- Begin with a **hook**.
- Set the **context** for the essay.
- Establish a **controlling idea** (**thesis** statement) that directly responds to the prompt.

Body Paragraphs

- Begin with a **topic sentence** related to the thesis.
- Include **evidence** from the text (paraphrased and directly quoted).
- Provide **commentary** that uses precise diction to describe humor and the intended effect.
- Use a variety of **transitions** to connect ideas and create coherence.

Concluding Paragraph

- Discuss the universal truth revealed through the text.
- Evaluate the effectiveness of the author's use of humor to communicate this truth.

Setting a Purpose for Reading

- As you read the expository essay, underline precise diction and academic vocabulary, especially humorous vocabulary.
- Circle unknown words and phrases. Try to determine the meaning of the words by using context clues, word parts, or a dictionary.
- Place a question mark by any sentences or sections that you think need to be revised.

My Notes

9 Read the Reading and Analyzing a Sample Essay and Setting a Purpose for Reading sections with your students. Help them understand any unfamiliar terms they encounter.

10 **FIRST READ:** Based on the complexity of the passage and your knowledge of your students, you may choose to conduct the first reading in a variety of ways:

- independent reading
- paired reading
- small group reading
- choral reading
- read aloud

11 As students are reading, monitor their progress. Be sure they are engaged with the text and annotating precise diction and academic vocabulary, especially humorous vocabulary as well as sentences or sections they believe need to be revised. Evaluate whether the selected reading mode is effective.

12 Based on the observations you made during the first reading, you may want to adjust your reading mode. For example, you may decide for the second reading to read aloud certain complex passages, or you may group students differently.

Planning and Revising an Analysis of a Humorous Text

My Notes

Student Expository Essay

"The Power of Pets"

by Isha Sharma (an eighth-grade student)

1 Every child has gone through a phase in life when they have a sudden fixation with getting a pet, and parents often have to go through a lot of trouble in order to appease the child, at least until the obsession is replaced with another. In the light-hearted essay, "I've got a few pet peeves about sea creatures," Dave Barry uses hyperbole and verbal irony to show how a parent will often go through great lengths to satisfy his child, often hoping that the child will learn something in the process.

2 To point out the often ridiculous experiences parents go through for their children, Barry uses hyperbole to emphasize how complicated getting a pet fish can be. For example, he explains first how a "pet" beetle under his daughter's "loving care and feeding ... thrived for maybe nine seconds before expiring like a little six legged parking meter" (1). The additional use of simile and the exaggerated amount of time adds to the humor, as in any case, one's "loving care and feeding" should not cause the death of anything so quickly, no matter how terrible the "care" could actually be. The explanation of the parents replacing each beetle with another shows how willing parents are to support their children no matter how ridiculous the circumstances. Furthermore, Barry calls the fish he bought "so nonviolent that in the wild, worms routinely beat them up and steal their lunch money" (2). As known to all people, it is fish that eat worms and not the other way around. This is hyperbolic because worms are not known for "beating fish up" and animals do not have money, lunch money included. This also ties back to a metaphor/analogy Barry made that "an aquarium is a powder keg that can explode in deadly violence at any moment just like ... junior high" (2). Both of these situations are highly exaggerated. Through the use of hyperbole, Barry is able to convey how parents often feel about their struggle even in simple situations, to which a child might react to them as being overdramatic.

3 Also, Barry uses verbal irony/sarcasm to vent and display his frustration, which proves furthermore the lengths he is going to help his daughter. For instance, when complaining about the aggressive nature of fish, he says they could become aggressive if "it was a month containing the letter 'R', of if they hear the song "Who Let the Dogs Out"" (2). Months and songs are all aspects of human life, it is unlikely that fish will ever have fish months or fish songs. This adds to the sarcastic tone of the writer, which shows that even through his frustrations, he is struggling to find the right choice for his daughter, no matter how much of a nuisance it is to make it. Also, Barry uses sarcasm when explaining the variety of needs for a fish tank so that "the fish would be intellectually stimulated and get into a decent college" (1). The author, as with most intellectual people, knows that fish do not have colleges, and seeing

SCAFFOLDING THE TEXT-DEPENDENT QUESTIONS

4. Craft and Structure (RI.8.4) **Identify and write the hook, context, and controlling idea or thesis in the introduction.** Read paragraph 1. What statement does the writer make that has universal appeal? What two types of comic language does Barry use? What does he hope to accomplish?

5. Craft and Structure (RI.8.5) **In each paragraph, identify the topic sentence, supporting detail, commentary, and transitions, and write your responses below.** Read paragraph 2. What is the main idea of the paragraph? What examples are used to support the main idea? What is the main idea of paragraph 3? What examples are used to support the main idea? What transition words are used to introduce examples? What conclusions does the writer draw in each paragraph?

that their intelligence capacity is smaller than a human's, they cannot be "intellectually stimulated." The author uses this verbal irony to point out that even though the needs of a fish are not as significant as the needs of a human, caring for them still requires a lot of effort. Clearly, the author chooses to go through this effort for his daughter. The usage of verbal irony in this piece further points out the "struggles" of a father to appease his child.

4 Even in the most trivial instances, the parent will go though many obstacles to help his child, often in the hope that the child will learn something along the way. Whether or not the child actually learns this is questionable, yet the parent's effort should not go unnoticed.

My Notes

Second Read

- Reread the expository essay to answer these text-dependent questions.
- Write any additional questions you have about the text in your Reader/Writer Notebook.

4. **Craft and Structure:** Identify and write the hook, context, and controlling idea or thesis in the introduction.

   Hook: "Every child has gone through a phase in life when they have a sudden fixation with getting a pet ..." Controlling idea (thesis): "... Dave Barry uses hyperbole and verbal irony to show how a parent will often go through great lengths to satisfy his child, often hoping that the child will learn something in the process." RI.8.4

5. **Craft and Structure:** In each paragraph, identify the topic sentence, supporting detail, commentary, and transitions and write your responses below.

   Paragraph 2 topic sentence: "... Barry uses hyperbole to emphasize how complicated getting a pet fish can be." Supporting detail with commentary and transitions: "Furthermore, Barry calls the fish he bought 'so nonviolent that in the wild, worms routinely beat them up and steal their lunch money' (2). As known to all people, it is fish that eat worms and not the other way around. This is hyperbolic because worms are not known for 'beating fish up' and animals do not have money, lunch money included." Paragraph 3 topic sentence: "... Barry uses verbal irony/sarcasm to vent and display his frustration ..." Supporting detail with commentary and transitions: "For instance, when complaining about the aggressive nature of fish, he says they would become aggressive if 'it was a month containing the letter 'R'..."; "... it is unlikely that fish will have fish months or fish songs." RI.8.5

13 **SECOND READ:** During the second reading, students will be returning to the text to answer the text-dependent comprehension questions. You may choose to have students reread and work on the questions in a variety of ways:

- independently
- in pairs
- in small groups
- together as a class

14 Have students answer the text-dependent questions. If they have difficulty, scaffold the questions by rephrasing them or breaking them down into smaller parts. See the Scaffolding the Text-Dependent Questions boxes for suggestions.

6. Key Ideas and Details (RI.8.2) **In the concluding paragraph, identify and write the universal truth.** Read paragraph 4. Which sentence restates the controlling idea or thesis of the essay? Summarize this idea or thesis in your own words.

ACTIVITY 4.11 continued

15 Direct groups to work collaboratively to revise one or more paragraphs of the student essay.

16 Explain that although students are working together, each student should make his or her own copy of the revised paragraph.

17 The peer review process may be challenging for students. Support learning by providing the class with models of constructive suggestions for revision. Discuss the models, and set the expectation that responses will be thoughtful and courteous. Have the groups affirm positive features of each paper they read to further support students who are hesitant about sharing. You may want to review the roles and responsibilities of writing group members from Activity 1.8.

18 When the writing groups are finished revising, pair small writing groups with another group and have them share the revisions. After reading the revised paragraphs aloud, they should also discuss the strengths and challenges.

19 Reunite original writing groups, and allow them time to make revisions.

20 Direct students to use the group writing experience to reflect individually and to plan for the Embedded Assessment by listing three specific writing goals they have for Embedded Assesment 1.

▶ASSESS

Have students respond to the Check Your Understanding. Evaluate students' responses to ensure that they have a firm grasp of each element of the essay.

▶ADAPT

Coconstruct or corevise a paragraph as a class, or repeat this process with another text if students struggle with any aspect of the essay.

INDEPENDENT READING CHECKPOINT

During class, allow students to use their Reader/Writer Notebooks and their independent reading material to complete the Independent Reading Checkpoint. Have students hand in their work.

ACTIVITY 4.11 continued

Planning and Revising an Analysis of a Humorous Text

My Notes

6. **Key Ideas and Details:** In the concluding paragraph, identify and write the universal truth.

   The universal truth is that "the parent will go though many obstacles to help his child." RI.8.2

Working from the Text

7. Referring back to the question marks you notated in the text, create revision suggestions for each. Write your responses in the My Notes space next to the text.
8. Work with your writing group to revise the student essay. You may want to review the roles and responsibilities of writing group members in Activity 1.8. Select one or more of the following:
   - Write a new introduction.
   - Write a third support paragraph.
   - Write a new conclusion.

Check Your Understanding

- Analyze the effectiveness of this essay by evaluating each element: introduction, body paragraphs, and conclusion.
- Review verb mood and voice from Unit 1, Activity 1.8.
- Evaluate the verb mood and voice in the original essay and compare it to your revision.
- Ensure that your verb mood and voice are consistent with the original.

Independent Reading Checkpoint

Consider the connections you made while reading humorous texts. In one paragraph, summarize one message (theme) a particular author tried to convey to the reader through humor. Briefly describe the level of comedy and the elements of humor used by the author.

Writing an Analysis of a Humorous Text

EMBEDDED ASSESSMENT 1

Assignment

Write an essay that explains how an author creates humor for effect and uses it to communicate a universal truth.

Planning and Prewriting: Take time to make a plan for your essay.

- What reading strategies (such as marking or diffusing the text) will help you take notes on the author's use of humor as you read the text?
- How can you correctly identify the level of comedy, elements of humor, and intended comedic effect on the reader?
- What prewriting strategies (such as outlining or graphic organizers) could help you explore, focus, and organize your ideas?

Drafting: Write a multiparagraph essay that effectively organizes your ideas.

- What elements of an effective introductory paragraph will you use in your writing?
- How will you develop support paragraphs with well-chosen examples (evidence) and thoughtful analysis (commentary) about at least two elements of humor?
- How will you use transitions to create cohesion?
- How will your conclusion support your ideas, identify and analyze the level(s) of comedy, and evaluate the author's effectiveness at communicating a universal truth?

Evaluating and Revising the Draft: Create opportunities to review and revise your work.

- During the process of writing, when can you pause to share and respond with others in order to elicit suggestions and ideas for revision?
- How can the Scoring Guide help you evaluate how well your draft meets the requirements of the assignment?
- How can you use a precise vocabulary of humor to enhance your critical analysis?

Checking and Editing for Publication: Confirm your final draft is ready for publication.

- How will you proofread and edit your draft to demonstrate command of the conventions of standard English capitalization, punctuation, spelling, grammar, and usage?
- Did you effectively use verbals?
- Did you establish and maintain a formal style?

Reflection

After completing this Embedded Assessment, think about how you went about accomplishing this task, and respond to the following:

- How has your understanding of how humor is created developed during this unit?
- Do you think your sense of humor will change as you mature? Explain.

My Notes

Technology TIP:

Consider using an approved social media channel such as Edmodo or Wikispaces to collaboratively discuss your text online before drafting your essay.

EMBEDDED ASSESSMENT 1

▶PLAN

Suggested Pacing: 3 50-minute class periods

1 Make copies of a humorous short story or essay for your students to analyze on their own. Be mindful of challenges of language in older stories, such as those by O. Henry or Mark Twain. This is an opportunity for you to differentiate instruction.

2 **Planning and Prewriting:** Review the assignment prompt to be sure students understand all the criteria. Distribute copies of the story you have chosen. Tell students that they are to work on their own to write an analysis like the one they revised in Activity 4.11.

3 Give students time to read the story. You may wish to have them read it for homework or allow class time. Remind students to refer to all their work and notes from this unit and apply those concepts in this essay.

4 **Drafting:** You may want to provide a revised version of the student sample as a model for the drafting of the essay. Remind students to check for organization and sentence variety.

5 **Evaluating and Revising the Draft:** You may want to arrange to have students meet in their writing groups to share and respond to each other's drafts.

6 **Checking and Editing for Publication:** This is where students could use a checklist to be sure they have incorporated new learning about grammar and usage into their essays. Checklist items might include:

- Mood and voice
- The use of verbals
- Dangling and misplaced modifiers
- Pronoun agreement

COMMON CORE STATE STANDARDS

Focus Standards:

W.8.2a: Introduce a topic clearly, previewing what is to follow; organize ideas, concepts, and information into broader categories; include formatting (e.g., headings), graphics (e.g., charts, tables), and multimedia when useful to aiding comprehension.

W.8.2b: Develop the topic with relevant, well-chosen facts, definitions, concrete details, quotations, or other information and examples.

W.8.2c: Use appropriate and varied transitions to create cohesion and clarify the relationships among ideas and concepts.

W.8.2d: Use precise language and domain-specific vocabulary to inform about or explain the topic.

W.8.2e: Establish and maintain a formal style.

W.8.2f: Provide a concluding statement or section that follows from and supports the information or explanation presented.

EMBEDDED ASSESSMENT 1 continued

7 As a class, create and display a large graphic organizer with a heading representing each Scoring Guide category. Ask students to create a copy in their Reader/Writer Notebooks.

Reflection Be sure students compile their responses to the reflection questions with the responses they have made in the earlier units.

Portfolio This is the last unit of the year. In order to plan for an end-of-the-year self-evaluation, students should begin to cull through their Portfolios and keep the work they think best represents their growth in learning over time. The reflection questions can give students a review of their thinking over the course of the year.

SCORING GUIDE

Students should use the Scoring Guide as they draft and revise their writing.

Consider asking students to staple a copy of the Scoring Guide onto their final draft before turning it in so you can use it to comment on their writing.

To identify additional areas where your English learners could use additional support, see the English Language Development Rubric for Embedded Assessment 1 on page 242a.

EMBEDDED ASSESSMENT 1

SCORING GUIDE

Scoring Criteria	Exemplary	Proficient	Emerging	Incomplete
Ideas	The essay • establishes and fully maintains a clearly focused controlling idea about the use of humor to convey a universal truth • develops the topic with relevant details, examples, and textual evidence • uses insightful commentary to analyze the effect of humorous elements.	The essay • establishes and maintains a controlling idea about the use of humor to convey a universal truth • develops the topic with adequate details, examples, and textual evidence • uses sufficient commentary to analyze the effect of humorous elements.	The essay • establishes and unevenly maintains a controlling idea that may be unclear or unrelated to the use of humor to convey a universal truth • develops the topic with inadequate details, examples, and textual evidence • uses insufficient commentary to analyze the humor.	The essay • lacks a controlling idea • fails to develop the topic with details, examples, and textual evidence • does not provide commentary or analysis.
Structure	The essay • introduces the topic and context in an engaging manner • uses a well-chosen organizational structure that progresses smoothly to connect ideas • uses a variety of effective transitional strategies • provides a satisfying conclusion.	The essay • introduces the topic and context clearly • uses an organizational structure that progresses logically to connect ideas • uses appropriate transitions to create cohesion and link ideas • provides a logical conclusion.	The essay • provides a weak or partial introduction • uses a flawed or inconsistent organizational structure • uses inappropriate, repetitive, or basic transitions • provides a weak or disconnected conclusion.	The essay • lacks an introduction • has little or no obvious organizational structure • uses few or no transitions • lacks a conclusion.
Use of Language	The essay • uses precise diction and language to maintain an academic voice and formal style • demonstrates command of the conventions of standard English capitalization, punctuation, spelling, grammar, and usage.	The essay • uses some precise diction to maintain a generally appropriate voice and style • demonstrates adequate command of the conventions of standard English capitalization, punctuation, spelling, grammar, and usage.	The essay • uses diction that creates an inappropriate voice and style • demonstrates partial or inconsistent command of the conventions of standard English capitalization, punctuation, spelling, grammar, and usage.	The essay • uses vague or confusing language • lacks command of the conventions of standard English capitalization, punctuation, spelling, grammar, and usage.

COMMON CORE STATE STANDARDS

Additional Standards Addressed:

RL.8.1; RL.8.2; RL.8.4; RL.8.6; RL.8.10; RI.8.1; RI.8.2; RI.8.3; RI.8.4; RI.8.5; W.8.4; W.8.5; W.8.6; W.8.9a; W.8.9b; W.8.10; SL.8.1a; SL.8.1b; SL.8.1c; SL.8.1d; L.8.1a; L.8.2c; L.8.5a

© 2017 College Board. All rights reserved.

Previewing Embedded Assessment 2

ACTIVITY 4.12

Learning Targets

- Reflect on learning and make connections.
- Demonstrate an understanding of the skills and knowledge needed to complete Embedded Assessment 2 successfully.

LEARNING STRATEGIES: QHT, Close Reading, Paraphrasing, Graphic Organizer

Making Connections

You have written an analysis of a humorous text, which required you to know and understand how a writer uses words, characters, and situations to create a humorous effect. Now you will have an opportunity to understand humor from a different perspective—that of a performer.

My Notes

Essential Questions

1. Reflect on your understanding of the first Essential Question from Activity 4:1: How do writers and speakers use humor to convey a truth? How has your understanding of humor changed over the course of this unit?

2. Think about the second Essential Question from Activity 4:1 and respond to it: What makes an effective performance of a Shakespearean comedy?

Developing Vocabulary

3. Reflect on and list all the new humor-related vocabulary you have learned. Use the My Notes section for additional space if needed.

4. Re-sort the unit Academic Vocabulary and Literary Terms using the QHT strategy.

Q (unfamiliar)	H (familiar)	T (very familiar)

COMMON CORE STATE STANDARDS

Focus Standards:

W.8.10: Write routinely over extended time frames (time for research, reflection, and revision) and shorter time frames (a single sitting or a day or two) for a range of discipline-specific tasks, purposes, and audiences.

L.8.6: Acquire and use accurately grade-appropriate general academic and domain-specific words and phrases; gather vocabulary knowledge when considering a word or phrase important to comprehension or expression.

Additional Standard Addressed:

RL.8.10

© 2017 College Board. All rights reserved.

ACTIVITY 4.12

PLAN

Suggested Pacing: 1 50-minute class period

TEACH

1 Guide students through the process of reflecting on their learning and making connections, and then have them respond to the items about the unit Essential Questions.

2 Ask students to share what they have learned by comparing the previous word sort with the new one. Students can share with a partner or the whole class.

3 Facilitate a close reading of the EA2 assignment and the Scoring Guide criteria, focusing on the "Proficient" column. Instruct students to mark the text by underlining or highlighting key skills (verbs) and knowledge (nouns).

TEACHER TO TEACHER

The suggestion below presents one way to unpack the Embedded Assessment. However you decide to do it, it is important to preview the Embedded Assessment and create a graphic to keep track of learning over the course of the unit.

4 Number the Scoring Guide categories, form expert groups, and assign each group a number (one category).

5 Instruct groups to reread the Scoring Guide descriptors for their assigned category and paraphrase skills and knowledge at each level (i.e., exemplary, proficient, emerging, and incomplete) to clarify how one level differs from the others. Assign group roles such as discussion leader, note-taker, diction detective (look up unknown words), and presenter to hold individuals accountable.

6 As a class, create and display a large graphic organizer with a heading representing each Scoring Guide category. Ask students to create a copy in their Reader/Writer Notebooks.

7 As each expert group presents, note the key knowledge and skills in the appropriate category on the graphic organizer. Students should do the same on their own graphic organizer.

8 Make sure to keep the unpacked assessment in a visible place in your classroom so you and your students can refer to specific skills and knowledge before, during, and/or after each daily activity.

9 Use the Scoring Guides for EA1 and EA2 to compare and contrast the two assessments. Stress to students that their learning in the first half of the unit applies to the second half.

INDEPENDENT READING

In this half of the unit, as they interpret and prepare to perform a scene from *A Midsummer Night's Dream*, students will have the opportunity to read other humorous texts independently. Students are asked to read an excerpt from one other comedy by Shakespeare via an Independent Reading Link. Other humorous essays, poems, and short stories are also recommended. The Planning the Unit section of the Teacher's Edition and the Resources section of the Student Edition contain information, Reading Logs, and Reading Lists to help you guide students in the selection of a new independent reading text.

▶ASSESS

Monitor student understanding of and contributions to the discussion of the Embedded Assessment assignment.

▶ADAPT

Reinforce needed skills and knowledge for the Embedded Assessment as students proceed through the activities scaffolding that assessment.

Previewing Embedded Assessment 2

My Notes

5. Compare your resorted terms with your original list. How has your understanding changed?

6. Select a word from the chart and write a **concise** statement about your learning. How has your understanding changed over the course of this unit?

Unpacking Embedded Assessment 2

Closely read the Embedded Assessment 2 assignment:

> Present your assigned scene in front of your peers to demonstrate your understanding of Shakespeare's text, elements of comedy, and performance.

Then, using the Scoring Guide on page 316, work with your class to paraphrase the expectations and create a graphic organizer to use as a visual reminder of the required concepts and skills. Copy the graphic organizer for future reference.

After each activity, use this graphic to guide reflection about what you have learned and what you still need to learn in order to be successful in completing the Embedded Assessment.

Selecting a Text for Independent Reading

To support your learning in the second half of the unit, you might choose another Shakespearean comedy to read on your own. This will help you become more familiar with Shakespeare's language and the sources of his comedy. Suggestions include *The Comedy of Errors, Love's Labours Lost*, and *Much Ado About Nothing*.

INDEPENDENT READING LINK

Read and Discuss

In this half of the unit, you will prepare to perform a scene from one of Shakespeare's plays. You will have the chance to read other humorous texts independently. Gather in a small group and discuss other humor writers you know about, and other comedies by Shakespeare. Prepare a reading list.

© 2017 College Board. All rights reserved.

Creating Context for Shakespearean Comedy

ACTIVITY 4.13

Learning Targets

- Research to build knowledge about Shakespeare.
- Collaborate to build and share knowledge about Shakespeare.
- Make connections to establish context for the play *A Midsummer Night's Dream*.

LEARNING STRATEGIES:
Note-taking, Marking the Text, Skimming/Scanning, Discussion Groups

Drama Study

1. Complete the sentence starters about William Shakespeare in the first column below. Support your responses to the statements, and note any questions you have about him.

Who Is Shakespeare?	How Do I Know This?	Questions I Have
Shakespeare was an author of plays and poetry.	I have seen a movie based on one of his plays, called *Romeo and Juliet*.	How many of his other works have been made into movies?
Shakespeare lived ...		
Shakespeare accomplished ...		
Shakespeare ...		

ACTIVITY 4.13

PLAN

Materials: images of Shakespeare or related art to display, a brief summary of the play *A Midsummer Night's Dream*
Suggested Pacing: 3 50-minute class period

TEACH

1 Explain that students now have some understanding of comedy and the elements of humor that will help them to appreciate the comedy of Shakespeare. The activities in this part of the unit introduce Shakespeare and *A Midsummer Night's Dream*. The goal is for students to recognize the elements of humor and to plan a performance that will demonstrate their understanding of the comedy in the play.

Students will not read the entire play, unless you have the time and the inclination to do so. It will be helpful to give students a brief summary of the play.

2 Direct students to complete the **graphic organizer** to **activate prior knowledge** about Shakespeare.

3 Form small groups in which students share their responses, add information, and try to answer any of the questions others have noted.

4 Ask groups to share their information with the class. Keep track of their responses on the board, and ask students to **take notes** on new information about Shakespeare.

TEACHER TO TEACHER

As students are working, have a picture of Shakespeare or any art relating to Shakespeare displayed. Folger.edu is probably the most authoritative site for information about Shakespeare. The British Museum also has extensive information (britishmuseum.org). There are innumerable sites about Shakespeare where you and your students can access information. Be sure to preview websites before students access them.

COMMON CORE STATE STANDARDS

Focus Standards:

W.8.7: Conduct short research projects to answer a question (including a self-generated question), drawing on several sources and generating additional related, focused questions that allow for multiple avenues of exploration.

Additional Standards Addressed:

RL.8.2; W.8.3a; W.8.3b; W.8.3d; W.8.4; W.8.5; W.8.10; L.8.6

ACTIVITY 4.13 continued

5 Students will have encountered Shakespearean drama in both Grade 6 and Grade 7 SpringBoard and may have a wide range of interesting information or opinions about Shakespeare; this is a good time to fill in some gaps in information and to address questions. If questions remain unanswered, this is a good research opportunity for students. You might want to assign brief research topics:

- Early life
- Life as a playwright
- His tragedies
- His comedies
- His theater and acting company
- *A Midsummer Night's Dream*—brief synopsis and different film versions of the play

6 Have students **quickwrite** and then discuss Lysander's quote.

7 Ask students to read each scenario and determine how they would respond to its challenges. Explain that these are the challenges faced by the characters in *A Midsummer Night's Dream*. To gain various perspectives, invite students to **think-write-pair-share** their thoughts.

8 Remind students that although the scenarios seem tragic, the play is a comedy. Define Shakespearean comedy by explaining that Shakespeare's comedies may have serious subjects, but they all have a happy resolution. Ask students to explain, with this information in mind, why this play is considered a comedy. Then, in a **reflective quickwrite**, ask students to predict elements of humor in the play that might elicit a humorous response from the audience.

ACTIVITY 4.13 continued

Creating Context for Shakespearean Comedy

My Notes

Understanding Plot

2. Read these scenarios to determine how you would respond. Make notes about your reactions in the My Notes space.

Scenario One

The person you are in love with has invited you to your high school dance. Your parents, who disapprove of this person, lay down the law, saying, "You are absolutely not allowed to attend the dance with this person. If you wish to attend, you may go with *X*. Your choices are to go to the dance with *X* or not go at all." You are now faced with a dilemma. You are forbidden to go to the dance with the person you love, but you are permitted to attend with *X*, who has been in love with you forever and whom your parents adore.

Consider this: Would you still go to the dance under these conditions? Why or why not?

Scenario Two

Since you were forbidden by your parents to attend the dance with the person you love, the two of you devise a plan to sneak out and attend the dance anyway. All of a sudden you notice that your love is nowhere in sight. You begin to search the room for her/him. Eventually, you find her/him in the corner of the room talking with your best friend. You happily interrupt the conversation only to be horrified to discover that your love is confessing her/his love to your best friend.

Consider this: What would you do if you saw your girlfriend/boyfriend confessing her/his love to your best friend? How would you feel?

Scenario Three

You confront your love after seeing her/him kiss your best friend. Your girlfriend/boyfriend loudly announces that she/he is no longer interested in you and no longer wants anything to do with you. Your best friend seems confused about the situation as she/he has always been in love with your boyfriend or girlfriend, but the feeling was never shared.

Consider this: What would you do if your girlfriend/boyfriend treated you this way? Would you be mad at your best friend?

Connection to the Play

In Shakespeare's comedy *A Midsummer Night's Dream*, four characters—Lysander, Hermia, Helena, and Demetrius—are entangled in a very complicated love relationship that leaves them open to all sorts of comical mishaps.

3. Using the following information about the key characters from the play, create a visual that shows the relationship among the characters listed below. Practice pronouncing the characters' names. Study the pronunciation of the names, noting the long and short vowel sounds and silent letters as a guide to facilitate your oral pronunciation.

Character's Name	Pronunciation	I am ...	I love ...
Hermia	Hér-me-uh	The daughter of a wealthy nobleman	Lysander
Lysander	Lie-sánd-er	A prominent businessman	Hermia
Demetrius	De-mé-tree-us	Hermia's father's choice for her husband	Hermia too!
Helena	Héll-en-uh	Hermia's best friend	Demetrius

Visual Representation of Characters' Relationships

Check Your Understanding

WRITING to SOURCES **Narrative Writing Prompt**

Using the information from the three scenarios, write your own scenario for the four key characters described above. Be sure to:

- Incorporate an element of comedy examined earlier in this unit.
- Provide detail about the situation.
- Use precise diction.

ACTIVITY 4.13 continued

9 Provide students with a brief summary of the entire play, focusing on the subplot of the lovers. It would be helpful to show students visuals of the setting, characters, and subplots.

10 Invite students to work with a partner to create a visual explaining the relationships among these four characters.

ASSESS

In looking at students' character visualizations, check to see that they are accurately beginning to comprehend the play. The writing prompt is an opportunity to imagine how the story of these four lovers might provide mishaps and complications to prove Lysander's words: "The course of true love never did run smooth."

ADAPT

Consider posting in your classroom each character's name, picture (perhaps from a movie version of the play), and the phonetic spelling of the names. Engage eager students to help with this project.

ACTIVITY 4.14

▶PLAN

Materials: dictionaries (including Internet access to online Shakespeare dictionaries and glossaries), thesauruses, index cards
Suggested Pacing: 1 50-minute class period

▶TEACH

1 Ask students to brainstorm about insults. Then, give them the following information:

- Shakespeare is noted for the insults his characters deliver.
- An effective insult is clever, witty, and funny.
- An effective insult requires proper inflection.
- An effective insult is delivered with purposeful gestures and facial expressions.

2 Inform students that they are to deliver insulting comments with passion. They must choose an insult and study it to determine its meaning and tone.

3 Model a **close reading** of Shakespeare's vivid language to enable students to conduct a similar close reading independently. Do a **think aloud** by displaying for the entire class the lines under "Decoding Shakespeare's Language," from *A Midsummer Night's Dream.* Read the lines, circling unfamiliar words. Remind students that even words that look familiar may mean something different in this context. Define these words.

4 Read the lines again, substituting familiar synonyms for unfamiliar words. Then, **paraphrase** the line in modern English.

5 Put a box around each punctuation mark. Discuss what the punctuation indicates to a person speaking these words.

6 Ask students to interpret the speaker's tone of voice and identify the words that convey this tone. Then, have students describe gestures and facial expressions appropriate for the delivery of the insult. Deliver the insult.

7 Direct students to the insults on this page. Form small groups, and have them interpret the insults.

ACTIVITY 4.14

Insulting Language

LEARNING STRATEGIES: Brainstorming, Close Reading, Marking the Text, Rehearsal, Role Playing

Learning Targets

- Read closely to understand the meaning of Shakespeare's language.
- Prepare a dramatic text with proper inflection, tone, gestures, and movement.

Decoding Shakespeare's Language

Note that punctuation marks signal tone of voice, a crucial element of performance.

"Hang off, thou cat, thou burr! Vile thing, let loose,
Or I will shake thee from me like a serpent."

1. Use close reading to understand the meaning of each line below. Then, write a paraphrase of your interpretation.

Character	Quote/Insult	Paraphrase (Modern English)
Lysander says to Hermia ...	"Get you gone, you *dwarf*, You *minimus* of *hind'ring knotgrass* made ..."	Leave me, you midget, you little nothing made of weeds.
Helena says to Hermia ...	"I will not trust you, Nor longer stay in your *curst* company."	I don't trust you, and I won't stay anywhere near your disgusting self.
Lysander says to Hermia ...	"Out, *tawny Tartar*, out! Out, *loathed medicine*! O, *hated*, *potion*, hence!"	Get away, you dirty enemy, go! Get away you horrible, disgusting poison, leave!
Hermia says to Helena ...	"You *juggler*, you *canker-blossom*! You *thief of love*! What, have you come by night And stol'n my love's heart from him?	You deceiver, you worm, you thief! Have you crept up at night and stolen away his love for me?
Helena says to Hermia ...	"Fie, fie! You *counterfeit, you puppet, you!"*	Ugh! Ugh, you faker, you dummy, you!

COMMON CORE STATE STANDARDS

Focus Standards:

SL.8.6: Adapt speech to a variety of contexts and tasks, demonstrating command of formal English when indicated or appropriate.

L.8.4: Determine or clarify the meaning of unknown and multiple-meaning words and phrases based on *Grade 8 reading* and content, choosing flexibly from a range of strategies.

L.8.4a: Use context (e.g., the overall meaning of a sentence or paragraph; a word's position or function in a sentence) as a clue to the meaning of a word or phrase.

Additional Standards Addressed:

RL.8.2; RL.8.4; W.8.10; SL.8.1a; L.8.6

2. Once you have determined the meaning of the lines, select one and complete the chart below. Rehearse your line in preparation for a performance. Then, role play by becoming that character and feeling that emotion. Move throughout the room and deliver your insult with flair. Be sure to allow time for peers to react to your delivery.

Write the insult you have chosen below.	What inflection will you use? What words will you stress when you speak your lines?	How will you alter your tone when you deliver your line?	What gestures/ movements will you use to enhance your line?

3. What tone of voice do people usually use when delivering an insult? What emotions might someone be feeling when they insult another person, and why?

Check Your Understanding

Reflect on the process of reading Shakespeare's language and understanding of the text. Respond to the following questions:

- What resources might you use to help interpret his language?
- Was your preparation to perform Shakespeare's lines effective?
- Did you deliver your lines as effectively as you planned? Explain.
- What might you do next time to improve your delivery?

GRAMMAR & USAGE
Punctuation

Punctuation gives clear clues as to how lines should be performed, particularly in poetry and plays.

An *exclamation point* shows surprise or extreme happiness or anger.

A *question mark* shows confusion on the part of the speaker or shows that the speaker is questioning another character's actions.

A *comma* marks a pause, usually for dramatic effect.

A *semicolon* marks a pause, usually one that is longer than a comma pause, without the finality of a period.

ACTIVITY 4.14 continued

8 Ask each group to select an insult and prepare to deliver it, using the graphic organizer. Since students are working with only one line, challenge students to memorize it. If they are unable to do so, they could use an index card to prompt their delivery. Ask students to practice a smooth delivery with appropriate inflection, facial expressions, gestures, and movement.

9 When students finish **rehearsing** their lines, instruct them to move throughout the room and deliver their insults with flair to other students.

10 Ask students to reflect on the process of delivering Shakespearean language. Since students have pronounced Shakespeare's names and words, their writing should reflect an understanding of the relationship between spoken sounds and written language.

ASSESS

While observing students delivering their insults, check to see how accurately they are speaking the lines, if they are able to memorize, and how confident their acting is. Use this evidence for future planning for acting groups. The Check Your Understanding will help you assess how ready students are to independently take on the task of performing Shakespeare's language.

ADAPT

To **support** ELL students, coach them in pronouncing the lines for their performance. Provide ongoing opportunities for students to practice the pronunciation of new words and sounds, focusing on long and short vowels, silent letters, and consonant clusters.

© 2017 College Board. All rights reserved.

ACTIVITY 4.15

▶PLAN

Materials: dictionaries (including Internet access to online Shakespeare dictionaries and glossaries), thesauruses, highlighters, colored pencils for marking the text
Suggested Pacing: 1 50-minute class period

▶TEACH

1 Place Act 3, Scene 2 into context for students with a brief summary of the events leading up to it: Hermia picks a fight with Helena because she thinks Helena has stolen Lysander's love from her.

2 Read the Preview and the Setting a Purpose for Reading sections with your students. Help them understand any unfamiliar terms they encounter.

3 **FIRST READ:** Based on the complexity of the passage and your knowledge of your students, you may choose to conduct the first reading in a variety of ways:

- independent reading
- paired reading
- small group reading
- choral reading
- read aloud

4 As students are reading, monitor their progress. Be sure they are engaged with the text and annotating words and phrases where the author uses punctuation to convey or emphasize meaning. Evaluate whether the selected reading mode is effective.

5 Based on the observations you made during the first reading, you may want to adjust your reading mode. For example, you may decide for the second reading to read aloud certain complex passages, or you may group students differently.

6 **SECOND READ:** During the second reading, students will be returning to the text to answer the text-dependent comprehension question. You may choose to have students reread and work on the question in a variety of ways:

- independently
- in pairs
- in small groups
- together as a class

ACTIVITY 4.15

Close Reading of a Scene

LEARNING STRATEGIES: Skimming/Scanning, Diffusing, Paraphrasing, Close Reading, Summarizing, Rereading, Visualizing

Learning Targets

- Collaborate to make meaning of a scene.
- Summarize and visualize the text to demonstrate understanding.

Preview

In this activity, you will read a scene from a Shakespearean play and think about its meaning.

Setting a Purpose for Reading

- As you read the scene, underline words and phrases that are meant to be insults.
- Circle unknown words and phrases. Try to determine the meaning of the words by using context clues, word parts, or a dictionary.

ABOUT THE AUTHOR
Little is known about the early life of William Shakespeare (1564–1616) except that he was born and grew up in Stratford-on-Avon in England. What is known is that he went to London as a young man and became an actor and playwright. He wrote 37 plays (comedies, tragedies, and histories) and is considered one of the greatest playwrights who ever lived. Performances of his plays occur regularly in theaters around the world.

My Notes

GRAMMAR & USAGE
Apostrophe
Just as an **apostrophe** is used in modern English to mark the absence of a letter, so it was used in Shakespeare's time.
Example: "Fine, i'faith!"
Translation: "Fine, **in** faith!"

Drama

from a midsummer night's dream

Act 3, Scene 2, Lines 282–305

by William Shakespeare

HERMIA
Oh me! you juggler! you canker-blossom!
You thief of love! What, have you come by night
And stolen my love's heart from him?

HELENA
Fine, i'faith!
Have you no modesty, no maiden shame,
No touch of bashfulness? What, will you tear
Impatient answers from my gentle tongue?
Fie, fie! you counterfeit, you puppet, you!

HERMIA
Puppet? Why so? Ay, that way goes the game.
Now, I perceive that she hath made compare
Between our statures; she hath urged her height;

COMMON CORE STATE STANDARDS

Focus Standards:

RL.8.1: Cite the textual evidence that most strongly supports an analysis of what the text says explicitly as well as inferences drawn from the text.

RL.8.2: Determine a theme or central idea of a text and analyze its development over the course of the text, including its relationship to the characters, setting, and plot; provide an objective summary of the text.

RL.8.6: Analyze how differences in the points of view of the characters and the audience or reader (e.g., created through the use of dramatic irony) create such effects as suspense or humor.

Additional Standards Addressed:

RL.8.4; RL.8.10; W.8.10; SL.8.1a; SL.8.6; L.8.4a; L.8.4c; L.8.4d; L.8.6

© 2017 College Board. All rights reserved.

And with her personage, her tall personage,
Her height, **forsooth**, she hath prevail'd with him.
And are you grown so high in his esteem;
Because I am so dwarfish and so low?
How low am I, thou painted maypole? speak;
How low am I? I am not yet so low
But that my nails can reach unto thine eyes.

HELENA I pray you, though you mock me, gentlemen,
Let her not hurt me: I was never curst;
I have no gift at all in shrewishness;
I am a right maid for my cowardice:
Let her not strike me. You perhaps may think,
Because she is something lower than myself,
That I can match her.

HERMIA Lower! hark, again.

forsooth: indeed; used to express surprise or indignation

INDEPENDENT READING LINK

Read and Connect

Read an excerpt from another Shakespearean play classified as a comedy. Compare and contrast the use of punctuation in your reading to the excerpt from *A Midsummer Night's Dream*. Note the similarities and differences in your Reader/Writer Notebook.

Second Read

- Reread the scene to answer these text-dependent question.
- Write any additional questions you have about the text in your Reader/Writer Notebook.

1. **Key Ideas and Details:** What details in the text should a director consider when casting Helena and Hermia?

   In lines 288–295, Shakespeare provides clues that Hermia is much shorter than Helena, referring to: "her tall personage" and to herself as "so dwarfish." RL.8.1

Working from the Text

2. Refer to the unknown words or phrases you circled and use reference books or online reference sources to define the words in context. Next to each word you circled, write a synonym or create a paraphrase in modern English.
3. Write a summary of this scene.
4. Reread the text orally with your group.
5. As you listen to the text being read a third time, visualize how the characters would be moving, gesturing, and speaking. Write comments, draw pictures, or stand to act what you are visualizing.

Check Your Understanding

Explain how this scene is intended to be comical on stage. What elements of comedy are represented?

My Notes

SCAFFOLDING THE TEXT-DEPENDENT QUESTIONS

1. Key Ideas and Details (RL.8.1) **What details in the text should a director consider when casting Helena and Hermia?** What does the text say about Helena's appearance? What does the text say about Hermia's appearance?

© 2017 College Board. All rights reserved.

ACTIVITY 4.15 continued

7 Have students answer the text-dependent question. If they have difficulty, scaffold the question by rephrasing it or breaking it down into smaller parts. See the Scaffolding the Text-Dependent Questions boxes for suggestions.

8 Select two students to read the lines aloud again. Ask the rest of the class to visualize how these characters would be moving, gesturing, and speaking. Ask students to describe what they "see" and what this performance might look like on stage. Students should support their ideas with lines from the text.

9 Remind students to complete the Independent Reading Link, writing responses in their Reader/Writer Notebook.

TEACHER TO TEACHER

For further practice on using punctuation to guide performance, you might ask students to find another example of Shakespeare's use of an apostrophe in this passage and translate it (prevail'd = prevailed). You might also ask them to do this with future passages.

Emphasize this relationship between the written form of Shakespeare's language and the pronunciation of words such as "curst" and "i'faith."

This is also an opportunity to review the archaic verb and pronoun forms.

ASSESS

The Working from the Text section and Check Your Understanding summary and responses will give you the opportunity to assess students' understanding of the scene.

ADAPT

You may want to consider supplementing your interpretive work with the class by showing a filmed version of this scene.

ACTIVITY 4.16

▶PLAN

Materials: chart or poster paper for norms of collaboration, copies of selected scenes from *A Midsummer Night's Dream* (one per student)
Suggested Pacing: 2 50-minute class periods

▶TEACH

1 Before assigning students to groups and scenes, spend time with the class discussing norms of collaboration. Ask students to **quickwrite**, and then as a class, coconstruct a list of norms. Turn the list into a poster that can serve as a class display for the remainder of the unit.

TEACHER TO TEACHER

Be thoughtful about grouping and scene assignment. No group needs more than four members.

2 Form groups that will be called "acting companies" and will work collaboratively to perform a comedic scene for Embedded Assessment 2. Inform students that one person in each group will be both an actor and director. In Shakespeare's time, actors were called "players."

TEACHER TO TEACHER

Because students are acting out scenes from *A Midsummer Night's Dream*, they will not need the entire play. However, they will need copies of the scenes to use as "acting scripts" and "director's scripts" that they can annotate for performance. It would be best if you can make copies of the scenes you assign for students. Each student should hand in his or her script to show the level of care and study the student has put into making meaning of and memorizing the scene.

ACTIVITY 4.16

Acting Companies and Collaborative Close Reading

LEARNING STRATEGIES: Close Reading, Skimming/Scanning, Rereading, Paraphrasing, Summarizing, Marking the Text, Rehearsing

My Notes

Learning Targets

- Establish and follow collaborative norms.
- Analyze and rehearse a dramatic scene collaboratively.

Analyzing a Dramatic Scene

1. **Quickwrite:** Describe the attitudes and behaviors (norms) of a positive and productive member of an acting group.

   Listen respectfully to one another's ideas.

   Take responsibility for the success of the task.

   Share responsibilities.

   Attend group meetings and be prepared.

2. In the spaces below, write the names of the members of your acting company for the roles they will play. Write the scene you will perform, the names of the characters, and who will play each character.

   Acting Company Members

   Director:

   Actors:

   Scene:

   Characters:

COMMON CORE STATE STANDARDS

Focus Standards:

SL.8.1b: Follow rules for collegial discussions and decision-making, track progress toward specific goals and deadlines, and define individual roles as needed.

SL.8.6: Adapt speech to a variety of contexts and tasks, demonstrating command of formal English when indicated or appropriate. (See Grade 8 Language standards 1 and 3 for specific expectations.)

Additional Standards Addressed:

RL.8.1; RL.8.2; RL.8.4; W.8.5; W.8.10; SL.8.1a; SL.8.6; L.8.4a; L.8.4c; L.8.4d; L.8.5a

Rehearsing a Dramatic Scene

3. You will next be assigned a scene from *A Midsummer Night's Dream* that your acting group will perform. Work collaboratively in your acting group to make meaning of the text. Follow these steps to guide your close reading and annotation of the text. You will be responsible for taking notes on your script and for using this script and notes as you plan and rehearse your scene.

- Skim/scan the text and circle unfamiliar words. Use a dictionary or thesaurus to replace each unfamiliar word with a synonym.
- Reread the scene and paraphrase the lines in modern English.
- Summarize the action. What is happening in the scene?
- Reread the scene and mark the text to indicate elements of humor (caricature, situation, irony, wordplay, hyperbole).
- Mark the punctuation, and determine how the punctuation affects the spoken lines. Discuss tone of voice and inflection.
- Analyze the movement in your scene:
  What is each character doing?
  When should characters enter and exit?
  How should characters enter and exit?
  What could you do to exaggerate the humor or create a humorous spin?
- Analyze the blocking in your scene, that is, the movement and placement of characters as they speak:
  Where is each character standing?
  To whom is each spoken line addressed?

4. Divide lines equally between group members. You may have to be more than one character. One person in your group will be both a player (actor) and the director.

Player (student's name)	Acting As (character's name)
Director:	

ACTIVITY 4.16 continued

3 Assign a different scene to each group, and review text features of a drama (acts, scenes, line numbers, stage directions, etc.).

4 Direct students to conduct a **close reading**. Eight scenes are suggested; group your students and assign scenes based on what is best for your class.

- Group 1: Act 1, Scene 1, lines 20–90 (Egeus, Theseus, Hermia)
- Group 2: Act 1, Scene 1, lines 111–179 (Theseus, Lysander, Hermia)
- Group 3: Act 1, Scene 1, lines 180–217 (Hermia, Helena) / Act 2, Scene 1, lines 146–182 (Oberon, Puck)
- Group 4: Act 2, Scene 1, lines 188–256 (Demetrius, Helena, Oberon, Puck)
- Group 5: Act 2, Scene 2, lines 43–91 (Lysander, Hermia, Puck)
- Group 6: Act 2, Scene 2, lines 92–164 (Helena, Demetrius, Lysander, Hermia)
- Group 7: Act 3, Scene 2, lines 305–344 (Hermia, Helena, Lysander, Demetrius)
- Group 8: Act 3, Scene 2, lines 345–405 (Oberon, Puck, Lysander)

TEACHER TO TEACHER

The first reading of the scene should simply be an **oral reading** going around the group. No one need take parts—this is a read-through to get a sense of what the scene will require in terms of language—i.e., fluency, inflection, tone, volume, etc.

5 Students should begin to **annotate** and **mark their texts** during this and the many more readings they will do of the pages of the scene, which have now become their "acting script," or "director's script."

6 Once groups have made meaning of their texts, have them divide lines equally among group members. Point out that students may have to play more than one character.

ACTIVITY 4.16 continued

Leveled Differentiated Instruction

In this activity, students may need additional support to analyze their scene. As students work in groups to make meaning of the text, they should complete a **Round Table Discussion** graphic organizer to record each group member's ideas.

Em Provide the sentence frames to support the group discussion. *According to the dictionary, the word ___ means ___. The line ___ means ___ in modern English. The action in the scene shows ___.*

Ex Provide the sentence frames to support the group discussion. *A synonym for ___ is ___. I interpreted ___ to mean ___. The character ___ is ___.*

7 Have groups **rehearse** their scene, focusing on the inflection and correct pronunciation of words as well as on facial expression and gestures.

8 Encourage students to read the text independently at first, marking the text with a strategy of their choice, before reading it in acting companies. Suggest that they find a mentor/homework helper (an adult or older peer or sibling) who will listen to the student read and explain his or her scene.

▶ASSESS

In observing acting companies while they **close read**, look for and listen for students working collaboratively to make meaning and for accurate summaries of their scene. Ensure they are marking the text for tone and inflection. It would be a good idea to collect these scripts to assess the level of marking and annotating the text.

▶ADAPT

Support students by providing them with an additional text (written summary, junior adaptation, comic book rendition, side-by-side edition) that will allow them to build background knowledge about the plot of the scene and the characters involved in it.

ACTIVITY 4.16 continued

Acting Companies and Collaborative Close Reading

My Notes

5. Rehearse your scene. To accurately portray your character and achieve your intended comic effect, be sure to focus on the following:
   - tone and inflection
   - correct pronunciation of words
   - facial expression and gesture

Check Your Understanding

Reflect on the process of reading your scene and determining the meaning of the text, as well as your preparation for and rehearsal of the scene.

- What went well? What will you want to replicate in future rehearsals and in your performance?
- What is a revision or something new you plan to do as you continue to rehearse?

Facing the Challenge of Performance

ACTIVITY 4.17

LEARNING STRATEGIES: Marking the Text, Discussion Groups, Note-taking, Rehearsal

Learning Targets

- Read and respond to an informational text about performance challenges.
- Memorize and rehearse lines for performance.

Preview

In this activity, you will read an informational text about performing and think about how these tips can help you prepare for your performance.

Setting a Purpose for Reading

- As you read the informational text, underline words and phrases that identify the main idea of each section.
- Circle unknown words and phrases. Try to determine the meaning of the words by using context clues, word parts, or a dictionary.
- Place an exclamation point by the tips you think most apply to you.

ABOUT THE AUTHOR
Gary Guwe is an award-winning speaker, entrepreneur, and public speaking trainer, specializing in effective communication. He has trained and helped more than 12,500 people.

My Notes

Informational Text

Adapted from

Fear Busters

10 Tips to Overcome Stage Fright!

by Gary Guwe

F – Focus on your most powerful Experience

Think about your most memorable and powerful experience when you accomplished a goal—maybe a time you worked extremely hard on a project or did well on a test. Reflect on your most powerful experience and remember the feeling of confidence; think about everything you did to create that feeling and how proud you felt after doing something challenging.

E – Energize Yourself

You have adrenaline pumping through your veins. Your heart is racing and your muscles are all tensed up. Your eyes are shifty and you are unsettled. You are ready to bolt for the door ... or are you?

An adrenaline rush is a built-in defense mechanism for human beings. It is a natural response mechanism that allows us to fight or take flight in the event of danger. That explains the heightened sensitivity we have when we are nervous and excited.

ACTIVITY 4.17

PLAN

Materials: copies of selected scenes from *A Midsummer Night's Dream* (one per student), whiteboards (optional)
Suggested Pacing: 1 50-minute class period

TEACH

1 Point out to students that being nervous is normal and that even professional actors get nervous. Have students read the text on overcoming fears, and then ask them to think about how they might use these suggestions in their own performances.

2 Read the Preview and the Setting a Purpose for Reading sections with your students. Help them understand any unfamiliar terms.

3 **FIRST READ:** Based on the complexity of the passage and your knowledge of your students, you may choose to conduct the first reading in a variety of ways:

- independent reading
- paired reading
- small group reading
- choral reading
- read aloud

4 As students are reading, monitor their progress. Be sure they are engaged with the text and annotating the main idea in each section as well as notating those tips that most apply to them. Evaluate whether the selected reading mode is effective.

5 Based on the observations you made during the first reading, you may want to adjust your reading mode. For example, you may decide for the second reading to read aloud certain complex passages, or you may group students differently.

COMMON CORE STATE STANDARDS

Focus Standards:

SL.8.6: Adapt speech to a variety of contexts and tasks, demonstrating command of formal English when indicated or appropriate. (See Grade 8 Language standards 1 and 3 for specific expectations.)

Additional Standards Addressed:

RI.8.1; RI.8.2; RI.8.4; W.8.10; SL.8.1a; SL.8.1c

SCAFFOLDING THE TEXT-DEPENDENT QUESTIONS

1. Key Ideas and Details (RI.8.2) **Refer to the words and phrases you underlined and summarize the main idea of each section.** What are the sections? What are they called? What words and phrases did you think were important?

Text Complexity
Overall: Accessible
Lexile: 900L
Qualitative: Low Difficulty
Task: Accessible (Understand)

Leveled Differentiated Instruction

Some students may benefit from analyzing the key idea and details as they read in order to be sure they understand the informational text.

Em Have students complete a **Key Idea and Details** graphic organizer as they read to help them understand the text.

Ex Guide students to write notes about the key idea and details from the text using the sentence frames. *The key idea of the text is ___. One supporting detail is ___. Another supporting detail is ___.*

Br Have students write independently about the key idea and details from the text as they read.

ACTIVITY 4.17

Facing the Challenge of Performance

My Notes

Harness this nervous energy and make it work for you! One way we harness this nervous energy is to move around. Your character will at some point move and gesture. Use the times when your character can move and react as opportunities to dissipate your nervous energy.

A – Acknowledge Your Fears

It is said that fear is here to protect us, not paralyze us. Don't run away from being afraid. Acknowledge it as being part of you ... use it to identify the possible pitfalls, then work to think about how you can avoid the pitfalls or how you can adjust or adapt if something goes wrong during your performance.

R – Relax ... breathe!

Take deep breaths and regulate your breathing. Let the breathing regulate and calm your heart rate. Practice breathing when you rehearse.

B – Believe in Yourself

Know that your performance has the potential for being a powerful and memorable moment in your life. You will feel a huge sense of accomplishment and pride when you successfully perform your scene. Be knowledgeable about your part and prepared with your lines, and you will be ready to execute with confidence.

U – Understand the Audience

Understand that the audience is here to see you succeed. They know how it feels to perform, and they're not here to sabotage you, or poke fun at you ... they're here to learn from you, to laugh, and to be entertained.

S – Smile!

Changing one's physiology can impact one's mental state.

Before your performance, when your character allows, and immediately afterwards—smile. Soon enough, your body will tell your brain that you're happy ... and before you know it, any fear you have will melt away.

T – Talk to Yourself

Many people will begin telling themselves various reasons why they will not be able to perform well. Counter that.

Tell yourself that you will be able to do a good job and remind yourself of the reasons why you can ("I am prepared." "I will have fun." "I know my peers will laugh when ... ").

E – Enjoy yourself

Get out on the stage and seek to have fun!

R – Rejoice!

Many people begin visualizing their worst case scenario as they ready themselves to perform.

Visualize yourself victorious at the end of the performance. Think of the amount of effort you will have put into preparing and think about the smiles and laughter which you will create and the skills and concepts you will have practiced and mastered.

SCAFFOLDING THE TEXT-DEPENDENT QUESTIONS

2. Craft and Structure (RI.8.4) **How is the text structured? Why do you think the author structured the text in this way?** What does the word acronym mean? How are acronym's useful?

Second Read

- Reread the informational text to answer these text-dependent questions.
- Write any additional questions you have about the text in your Reader/Writer Notebook.

1. **Key Ideas and Details:** Refer to the words and phrases you underlined and summarize the main idea of each section.

   F: Think about a time you did well to remind yourself of that feeling.
   E: Convert your nervous energy into positive energy.
   A: Identify your fears.
   R: Regulate and practice your breathing.
   B: Prepare for your part and be confident.
   U: Remember why the audience is watching: to learn, to laugh, and to be entertained.
   S: Smile whenever fitting; smiling will help your brain remove fears.
   T: Encourage and reassure yourself. Drown out negative thoughts.
   E: Have fun!
   R: Visualize a successful performance and learning experience. RI.8.2

2. **Craft and Structure:** How is the text structured? Why do you think the author structured the text in this way?

   The text is structured as an acronym, which facilitates memorization of the ten steps. RI.8.4

Working from the Text

3. **Quickwrite:** What is the biggest challenge you face when it comes to performing your comic scene?

4. Refer to the text and write your personal response to each tip in the My Notes space. Use them as a guide for a collaborative discussion.

5. Discuss the ten tips with your acting group. Which tips did you notate as applying most to you? How will you use this advice?

My Notes

ACTIVITY 4.17 continued

6 **SECOND READ:** During the second reading, students will be returning to the text to answer the text-dependent comprehension questions. You may choose to have students reread and work on the questions in a variety of ways:

- independently
- in pairs
- in small groups
- together as a class

7 Have students answer the text-dependent questions. If they have difficulty, scaffold the questions by rephrasing them or breaking them down into smaller parts. See the Scaffolding the Text-Dependent Questions boxes for suggestions.

8 Have students **quickwrite** about their greatest challenges relating to performance. Ask if any student would like to share their response. Tell students they are going to read a text suggesting ideas for overcoming performance challenges using the acronym FEARBUSTER.

9 Be sure acting companies discuss the usefulness of the acronym FEARBUSTER as a technique for dealing with the very common experience of stage fright.

10 Next, engage students in reading Memorization Tips individually. Allow them time to ask clarification questions and to add their own tips. For Tip 2, if a whiteboard is not available, have students write each word or a few of the words of the line on an index card or sticky note and remove one word at a time.

11 Give students time to apply the ideas and tips for overcoming performance challenges as they **rehearse** a line of their scene. Allow students to partner with a student of their choosing (even if not in their acting company). With this partner, they should explain the idea from FEARBUSTERS they are thinking about and try a memorization tip.

12 Last, have students respond to the reflection and planning portion of the activity to articulate their next steps.

▶ASSESS

Observe students practicing, and check to hear that they are talking about an idea to overcome challenges and using a memorization strategy.

Check students' reflection and planning to see that they are able to articulate what they plan to do. Use this information to support and check in on their progress.

▶ADAPT

As with the previous activity, you might assign memorization practice as homework and ask students to have a mentor/homework helper provide a signature as verification.

As you proceed through the remainder of the activities, also consider allowing time each day for focused memorization practice.

Facing the Challenge of Performance

My Notes

INDEPENDENT READING LINK

Read and Discuss

Think about the play you are reading independently. Which of your friends or family members would you cast in the lead roles? Why? Come up with your cast and justify your choices based on personality, appearance, or other characteristics.

Memorization Tips

Memorizing lines is a key part of delivering a good performance. Think about school plays you may have seen. Characters who deliver their lines clearly and without hesitation perform well.

Tip 1: Repeat, Repeat, Repeat, Repeat

Say the line over and over, but do it one word at a time, returning to the beginning of the line each time.

Example: Line 108 from Scene 5: "If we offend, it is with our good will." "If." "If we." "If we offend." "If we offend, it." "If we offend, it is." "If we offend, it is with." "If we offend, it is with our." "If we offend, it is with our good." "If we offend, it is with our good will."

Tip 2: Recite and Erase

Write your line(s) on a whiteboard, and then practice the words.

- Recite the line.
- Erase a word or phrase, and recite the missing piece from memory.
- Repeat the process until all the words have disappeared and you are saying the line(s) from memory.

6. Discuss other tips your peers may have for memorizing lines. Then, select your hardest line to memorize and use the memorization tips to work on it.

Check Your Understanding

Describe at least three strategies you can use to overcome stage fright. How will you remind yourself of those strategies on the day of the performance?

Working with Acting Companies and Focus Groups

ACTIVITY 4.18

Learning Targets

- Analyze a dramatic character to inform a performance.
- Collaborate to draft and implement a performance plan.

LEARNING STRATEGIES: Rereading, Close reading, Note-taking, Discussion Groups, Rehearsal

Character Focus Groups

1. **Players:** Reread your lines, using the graphic organizer to guide a close reading and analysis of your character.

   Meet in a focus group, whose members are all acting as the same character, and work collaboratively to interpret what the lines reveal about your character. Take turns sharing your indivudual analysis and add new insights to the graphic organizer.

I am playing: ______________________________

Aspects of Characterization	Detail from Text	Interpretation *What does this reveal about the character?*
Appearance		
Actions		
Words		
Thoughts/Feelings		

ACTIVITY 4.18

PLAN

Suggested Pacing: 2 50-minute class periods

TEACH

1 Create character focus groups by asking students to group together by like character. Because some students may be playing more than one character or are serving as both an actor and director, allow students to move from one group to another as necessary. The purpose of this activity is for students to work collaboratively to analyze the characteristics of and become experts on the character(s) they are going to portray.

2 Direct focus groups to use the **graphic organizer** to guide their discussion and analysis. Focus group members should then take turns applying their analysis to **rehearsing** lines and providing feedback for each other.

3 During this time, work with each group to make sure students are on the right track. The directors should start assuming a leadership role and may need some guidance. Take this opportunity to work with them to help them plan the action on stage and to address any other concerns.

COMMON CORE STATE STANDARDS

Focus Standards:

RL.8.3: Analyze how particular lines of dialogue or incidents in a story or drama propel the action, reveal aspects of a character, or provoke a decision.

SL.8.1b: Follow rules for collegial discussions and decision-making, track progress toward specific goals and deadlines, and define individual roles as needed.

Additional Standards Addressed:

RL.8.1; RL.8.4; RL.8.10; W.8.10; SL.8.1a; SL.8.1d; SL.8.4; SL.8.5; SL.8.6

ACTIVITY 4.18 continued

4 After students have become experts in their roles, ask them to return to their acting companies. Each character should share his or her findings with the group and discuss the implications of each character's words and actions. The director should convey his or her concept for the scene.

5 Review student work in graphic organizers to check that students are able to cite textual evidence and write an interpretation. Then observe if students are able to demonstrate their analysis through an improved commitment to their character as they **rehearse**.

ACTIVITY 4.18 continued

Working with Acting Companies and Focus Groups

Others' Reactions		
Comedic Actions/Words		

2. Take turns reading your character's lines. Practice making the analysis of your character come to life through your tone, inflection, facial expression, and gestures.
3. **Directors:** Select key action sequences and consider possible stage directions to determine how these scenes might be performed on stage.

Key Action Sequences	Stage Directions and Movement on Stage	What This Reveals About the Overall Scene (Comedic Effect)

Acting Groups

4. Return to your acting group and share your analysis in the order that your character speaks during your scene. Discuss the implications of each character's words and actions.
5. Develop a detailed performance plan by consulting the Scoring Guide.

   After reviewing the Scoring Guide criteria, I need to ...

6. Work with your acting company to complete the chart below and outline your performance plan.

Performance Plan				
Character	**Played By**	**Contribution to Set Design**	**Prop(s)**	**Costume**
Hermia	Susie	Plastic tree	Heart with Lysander's name on it	Dress Flowers for hair

6 Set the context for the performance plan by directing students to review the Embedded Assessment 2 Scoring Criteria and create a list of "be sure to" items in their own words.

© 2017 College Board. All rights reserved.

ACTIVITY 4.18 continued

7 Encourage students to thoughtfully complete all parts of the performance plan in preparation for EA2. Have them take into consideration *all* aspects of their performance: costumes, props, and sets, as well as oral delivery, movements, and gestures.

8 In collaboration with the actors, directors should complete the sentence starters in preparation for the performance.

9 Direct acting companies to **rehearse**, using the performance plan to strengthen the performance.

10 Finally, have students reflect on this rehearsal as a means to set goals for future performance.

▶ASSESS

Be sure to monitor student performance plans. You may want to have acting companies turn in their scripts and performance plans along with this first reflection on rehearsal so you can gauge the progress of the groups toward a successful performance. Check to see that they are writing details and suggestions that are relevant to and will improve the effectiveness of their performance.

▶ADAPT

To **support** learning, provide a successful model of a completed performance plan before students begin work on their own.

Consider allowing focus groups to meet at least one more time prior to the EA if some students could benefit from the support of peers who are playing the same character.

Working with Acting Companies and Focus Groups

7. Individually, synthesize all the details of your performance plan.

Element of Performance	Ideas for Character	Explanation
Blocking		
Movements Enter/Exit		
Gestures		
Facial Expression(s)		
Emotion		
Comedic Emphasis		

My Notes

8. Complete this section if you are the director. Share your plan with the members of your acting company.

   We want to create a ______ mood. To accomplish this goal, we will ...

   I will introduce the acting company and scene by ...

   The scene will end when ______ so the audience will be left with a feeling of ...

   We will focus on the comic effects listed below to ensure that ...

9. Use your performance plan to rehearse your scene to accurately portray your character and achieve your intended comic effect. Be sure to focus on the following:
   - tone and inflection
   - correct pronunciation of words
   - gestures and movement

Check Your Understanding

Reflect on the process of planning for and rehearsing your scene.

- What went well? What will you want to replicate in future rehearsals and in your performance?
- What part of your performance do you need to work on?
- What part of the performance does the group need to work on?

Same Text, Different Text

ACTIVITY 4.19

Learning Targets

- Analyze film and text in order to compare/contrast and evaluate the director's choices.
- Generate and evaluate performance choices.

LEARNING STRATEGIES: Discussion Groups, Note-taking, Brainstorming, Rehearsal

Viewing Shakespeare on Film

1. Unlike comparing novels to film versions, turning a play script into a movie allows the viewer to make a close comparison. Think about the extent to which the film scripts adhere to or stray from the original Shakespeare scene and how the actors make the lines come alive through their voices, expressions, and movements.
2. As you view the film or a scene from *A Midsummer Night's Dream*, take notes on what you observe. Use the graphic organizer for either "Actors" or "Directors."

Actors:

Version of *A Midsummer Night's Dream* (Director/Year)	Physical Gestures and Movements	Costume and Makeup	Interpretive Choices in the Delivery of Lines
Film 1:			
Film 2:			

COMMON CORE STATE STANDARDS

Focus Standards:

RL.8.7: Analyze the extent to which a filmed or live production of a story or drama stays faithful to or departs from the text or script, evaluating the choices made by the director or actors.

Additional Standards Addressed:

RL.8.2; RL.8.10; W.8.10

ACTIVITY 4.19

▶PLAN

Materials: DVD: film versions of *A Midsummer Night's Dream* (see Planning the Unit for possibilities)
Suggested Pacing: 2 50-minute class periods

▶TEACH

1 Before viewing a film version of scenes from A *Midsummer Night's Dream*, have students sit with their acting companies to **think-pair-share** their thoughts about books that have been transformed into films and the benefits and challenges of taking the written word and filming it. How might it be different in transforming a play into a film?

2 The purpose here is to help students visualize details of performance and to understand and analyze the effect of different choices made by actors and directors in a performance of *A Midsummer Night's Dream.*

3 Direct students to record their observations on the **graphic organizer** as they view the film versions of their scene.

ACTIVITY 4.19 continued

4 After showing all the scenes, have players and directors compare notes in their acting companies. Then, have each group member respond individually to the questions that follow the **note-taking** graphic. Conduct a class discussion. It is important for students to see how actors suit the action to the words.

Leveled Differentiated Instruction

In this activity, students could use a **Venn Diagram for Writing a Comparison** to contrast the two films.

Em Pair off students to complete the Venn diagram with details. This will prepare them to write a comparison using the comparison sentence frames.

Ex Guide students to use the completed Venn diagram to write longer original sentences to compare the two films.

Same Text, Different Text

My Notes

Actors' Questions

3. To what extent do these films stay faithful to or depart from the original script? Why might these particular choices have been made, and what effect do these choices have on the viewers' understanding of the scene?

4. How do your character's gestures, movements, and language achieve a comical effect? What elements of humor did you see?

Directors:

Version of *A Midsummer Night's Dream* (Director/Year)	Placement of Actors in Relationship to Props, Scenery, Each Other	Music or Other Sound Effects	Set Design, Lighting, Props
Film 1:			
Film 2:			

© 2017 College Board. All rights reserved.

Directors' Questions

5. How has the director stayed faithful to or departed from the scene as written by Shakespeare? What effects do certain staging and technical choices have on the viewers' understanding of the scene?

6. How do the staging, set design, lighting, sound, and props achieve a comical effect? What elements of humor did you see?

Check Your Understanding

Why would a film director choose to portray a scene differently than the way the author wrote it? What effects might the director be trying to achieve?

INDEPENDENT READING LINK

Read and Research

See if there is a modern-day retelling of the play you are reading independently. Watch it and fill out a similar graphic organizer for it.

My Notes

5 Next, post the following questions on the board as students brainstorm new ideas for their performance and begin to plan and rehearse with their company.

- Who is on stage? (character)
- How do the characters enter and exit? (movement)
- What are they doing, and why? (movement)
- What gestures create comedic effect? (movement)
- Where are characters standing in relation to each other? (blocking)
- To whom is each of the lines spoken? (blocking)

6 Have students complete the Independent Reading Link outside of class.

ASSESS

You may want directors to do a formal writing to respond to Question 5, which asks students to analyze how a director or actor's interpretation departs from or stays faithful to Shakespeare's scene.

ADAPT

Consider pausing the film intermittently to allow students to write and discuss the film throughout the viewing. If possible, each acting company could view its individual scene as a small group, rather than as a whole class. You might also conduct alternate "viewing parties" during an open period or before and after school to support students' comprehension of their character and scene.

ACTIVITY 4.20

▶PLAN

Materials: rehearsal space
Suggested Pacing: 1 50-minute class period

▶TEACH

1 Explain that this is the students' last chance to perfect their performance before Embedded Assessment 2.

2 Pair acting companies for dress rehearsal and peer feedback, and set expectations.

3 **Preview** the Scoring Guide criteria and the feedback question stems for the feedback conversation. Allow groups ample time for dress rehearsal.

Leveled Differentiated Instruction

Students may need support to participate in the feedback conversation.

Em Provide the sentence stems. I thought it was effective when ___. *I thought it was funny when ___. Why did you choose to ___?*

Ex Provide the sentence stems. *The audience seemed to ___ when ___. I found the part when ___ to be ___. I don't understand why ___.*

▶ASSESS

Direct students to complete the Dress Rehearsal Reflection. As students rehearse and provide feedback, listen to assess the quality of performance and comments. Redirect when necessary.

▶ADAPT

At this point, students should be completely ready to perform. If there are any lingering issues, help individual students or groups problem solve.

INDEPENDENT READING

Either pair students off or listen to their modern paraphrases of their independent reading.

ACTIVITY 4.20

Dress Rehearsal

LEARNING STRATEGIES: Rehearsal

My Notes

Learning Targets

- Participate in a dress rehearsal of a dramatic scene.
- Reflect on strengths and challenges as a performer.

Dress Rehearsal

1. Participate in a dress rehearsal in which you perform your scene in front of another group. This rehearsal will help you determine what works well in your performance and what does not.
2. When you are in the role of a small group audience, use the Scoring Guide criteria to provide constructive feedback to enable the acting company to adjust its performance.
3. Consider using these questions to start your feedback conversation:
   - What elements of humor do you think you were most successful at using? Least successful?
   - Can you explain why you made the choice to ...
   - When did you feel the audience was most with you?
   - When did you feel the audience was least connected to your performance?
   - Did you ever have to adapt or adjust differently than you had planned? Explain. How did it work out?

Dress Rehearsal Reflection

4. What went well? What will you want to replicate in your performance?

5. What is the most significant thing you are going to do differently? How will you prepare?

Independent Reading Checkpoint

Choose a short part of the play you have been reading independently and rewrite it in modern English. Read it out loud to your teacher or a partner.

COMMON CORE STATE STANDARDS

Focus Standards:

SL.8.4: Present claims and findings, emphasizing salient points in a focused, coherent manner with relevant evidence, sound valid reasoning, and well-chosen details; use appropriate eye contact, adequate volume, and clear pronunciation.

SL.8.6: Adapt speech to a variety of contexts and tasks, demonstrating command of formal English when indicated or appropriate. (See Grade 8 Language standards 1 and 3 for specific expectations.)

Additional Standards Addressed:
W.8.10; SL.8.1a; SL.8.1d

© 2017 College Board. All rights reserved.

Performing Shakespearean Comedy

EMBEDDED ASSESSMENT 2

Assignment

Present your assigned scene in front of your peers to demonstrate your understanding of Shakespeare's text, elements of comedy, and performance.

Planning: As an acting company, prepare to perform your scene.

- How will you collaborate as a group on a performance plan that demonstrates an understanding of Shakespeare's humor?
- Does each member of the acting company understand the scene's meaning as well as his or her role?
- What elements of humor will your company focus on in performance?
- How will you emphasize these elements through the delivery of lines, characterization, gestures, movements, props, and/or setting?
- How will you mark your script to help you pronounce words correctly, emphasize words appropriately, and remember your lines and deliver them smoothly?
- How will you use blocking and movement to interact onstage and emphasize elements of humor?

Rehearsing: Rehearse and revise your performance with your acting company.

- How will you show how characters, conflicts, and events contribute to a universal idea?
- How will you introduce and conclude the scene?
- How can the Scoring Guide help you evaluate how well your performance meets the requirements of the assignment?
- How can you give and receive feedback about your use of eye contact, volume, and inflection in order to improve your own and others' performances?

Performing and Listening: Perform your scene and participate as an audience member:

- How will you convey ideas and emotions through your performance?
- How will you take notes on the elements of humor emphasized in other performances?

Reflection

After completing this Embedded Assessment, think about how you went about accomplishing this task, and respond to the following:

- How did different performers emphasize the elements of humor in their scenes?
- Which performances were successful in eliciting a humorous response from the audience, and what made them effective?

My Notes

Technology TIP:

As part of the rehearsal process, consider video recording your performance. Also, consider using a musical recording to introduce and/or conclude your performance.

EMBEDDED ASSESSMENT 2

▶PLAN

Suggested Pacing: 3 50-minute class periods

1 By this time, students should have created a fairly specific performance plan and done some performance rehearsal.

2 **Planning:** You should expect to see a copy of the performance plan and the script of every student during rehearsals. The scripts should show evidence of planning with marking and annotation.

3 **Rehearsing:** It is important that you set aside some days for rehearsal. This can happen before Activity 2.20 and during the Embedded Assessment assignment time.

4 Both actors and directors should note new ideas as they occur during rehearsals.

5 **Performing and Listening:** Set aside a day for performances, and have each group perform its scene in the proper sequence in the play.

Reflection You may wish to have students turn in their post-performance reflections before they include them in their Portfolios.

TEACHER TO TEACHER

Consider videotaping rehearsals so students can use the information for reviewing and revising performance choices. Acting companies could take responsibility for this and could add it to their collection of evidence of analysis and rehearsal in preparation for performance. In addition, you might want to videotape final performances so you can have models of exceptional student work for next year's students.

COMMON CORE STATE STANDARDS

Focus Standards:

RL.8.4: Determine the meaning of words and phrases as they are used in a text, including figurative and connotative meanings; analyze the impact of specific word choices on meaning and tone, including analogies or allusions to other texts.

RL.8.6: Analyze how differences in the points of view of the characters and the audience or reader (e.g., created through the use of dramatic irony) create such effects as suspense or humor.

RL.8.7: Analyze the extent to which a filmed or live production of a story or drama stays faithful to or departs from the text or script, evaluating the choices made by the director or actors.

RL.8.10: By the end of the year, read and comprehend literature, including stories, dramas and poems, at the high end of grades 6–8

Portfolio Give students an opportunity to reflect on their learning this year and revisit, review, and self-evaluate the work they did as evidence of growth in skills and knowledge during the year.

Be sure students have kept all their Embedded Assessments. They provide excellent evidence of growth over time and are reminders of the processes and reflections students have experienced during the year.

It would be best if students had an opportunity to present their body of work to their parents, you, or another adult in the school community. You may want to have students select their best work, write a cover letter, and use the Portfolio as a "Letter of Introduction" to their high school English teacher.

SCORING GUIDE

When you score this Embedded Assessment, you may wish to download and print copies of the Scoring Guide from SpringBoard Digital. In this way, you can have a copy to mark for each student's work.

You might consider having acting companies evaluate another performance based on the Scoring Guide. Give this peer evaluation and your evaluation to the student performers after they have presented their scene.

EMBEDDED ASSESSMENT 2

Performing Shakespearean Comedy

SCORING GUIDE

Scoring Criteria	Exemplary	Proficient	Emerging	Incomplete
Ideas	The performance • demonstrates a deep understanding of Shakespeare's intended humor • uses a variety of effective performance elements (staging, set design, lighting, sound, props) for comic effect • shows evidence of extensive planning, rehearsal, and reflection.	The performance • demonstrates an adequate understanding of Shakespeare's intended humor • uses some performance elements (staging, set design, lighting, sound, props) for comic effect • shows evidence of sufficient planning, rehearsal, and reflection.	The performance • demonstrates a partial or uneven understanding of Shakespeare's intended humor • uses disconnected or basic performance elements (staging, set design, lighting, sound, props) • shows evidence of ineffective or insufficient planning, rehearsal, and reflection.	The performance • demonstrates little or no understanding of Shakespeare's intended humor • lacks performance elements • does not show evidence of planning, rehearsal, and reflection.
Structure	The performance • demonstrates extensive evidence of collaboration • provides context in an engaging introduction • communicates a satisfying ending to the audience.	The performance • demonstrates adequate evidence of collaboration • provides context in an appropriate introduction • communicates an ending to the audience.	The performance • demonstrates uneven or ineffective collaboration • provides a partial or weak introduction • communicates an abrupt or illogical ending to the audience.	The performance • demonstrates a failure to collaborate • provides no introduction • does not communicate an ending to the audience.
Use of Language	The performer • makes effective interpretive choices to deliver lines for comic effect and to convey meaning (including tone, pronunciation, inflection, facial expressions, gestures, movement, and blocking) • uses punctuation cues consistently and naturally to inform vocal delivery • memorizes lines fully and accurately.	The performer • makes appropriate interpretive choices to deliver lines for comic effect and to convey meaning (including tone, pronunciation, inflection, facial expressions, gestures, movement, and blocking) • uses some punctuation cues to inform vocal delivery • demonstrates an adequate ability to memorize lines.	The performer • makes undeveloped or inappropriate interpretive choices to deliver lines (including tone, pronunciation, inflection, facial expressions, gestures, movement, and blocking) • uses punctuation cues unevenly or inconsistently • demonstrates insufficient ability to memorize lines.	The performer • makes undeveloped or inappropriate interpretive choices to deliver lines • does not recognize punctuation cues or use them incorrectly • does not have any lines memorized.

text complexity band independently and proficiently.

SL.8.1a: Come to discussions prepared, having read or researched material under study; explicitly draw on that preparation by referring to evidence on the topic, text, or issue to probe and reflect on ideas under discussion.

SL.8.1b: Follow rules for collegial discussions and decision-making, track progress toward specific goals and deadlines, and define individual roles as needed.

SL.8.5: Integrate multimedia and visual displays into presentations to clarify information, strengthen claims and evidence, and add interest.

SL.8.6: Adapt speech to a variety of contexts and tasks, demonstrating command of formal English when indicated or appropriate. (See Grade 8 Language standards 1 and 3 for specific expectations.)

Additional Standards Addressed:

SL.8.1c; SL.8.1d; SL.8.4; L.8.4c; L.8.5a

Embedded Assessment 1: Writing an Expository Essay

ENGLISH LANGUAGE DEVELOPMENT RUBRIC

The Embedded Assessment that the whole class completes can be a useful source of English language development evidence. Use this additional rubric to examine the Embedded Assessment products of English learners. The analysis will help you gain additional information about student learning related to the strands of the English Language Development Standards and identify individual areas for improvement.

Criteria	Emerging	Expanding	Bridging
Interpretive	The student • Explains basic ideas based on close readings of texts with substantial support. • Expresses inferences and conclusions based on close reading of texts with substantial support. • Explains how language supports ideas with substantial support. • Analyzes how words produce different effects.	The student • Explains ideas based on close readings of texts with some support. • Expresses inferences and conclusions based on close reading of texts with some support. • Explains how language presents ideas with some support. • Analyzes how words produce shades of meaning and the effect on the audience.	The student • Explains complex ideas based on close readings of texts with little support. • Expresses inferences and conclusions based on close reading of texts with some support. • Explains how language presents ideas with little support. • Analyzes how words or phrases produce shades of meaning and the effect on the audience.
Productive	The student • Writes short literary texts collaboratively and independently. • Uses general academic vocabulary with domain-specific words to create some precision.	The student • Writes longer literary texts collaboratively and independently with appropriate text organization. • Uses general academic vocabulary with domain-specific words with precision and an awareness of shades of meaning.	The student • Writes longer, more detailed literary texts collaboratively and independently with appropriate text organization. • Uses precise, nuanced, vocabulary and figurative language appropriately.
Structuring Cohesive Texts	The student • Organizes writing logically to relay basic information. • Uses basic language resources to make text more cohesive. • Uses simple connecting words to link ideas or events in the text.	The student • Organizes writing logically to relay information clearly and coherently. • Uses increasingly complex language resources to make text more cohesive. • Uses connecting words or phrases to link ideas or events in the text.	The student • Organizes writing logically to relay information naturally, clearly, and coherently. • Uses complex language resources to make text more cohesive. • Uses a variety of connecting words or phrases to link ideas or events in the text.
Expanding and Enriching Ideas	The student • Uses a variety of verbs in different tenses appropriate to narrative text. • Uses nouns and noun phrases to add details. • Uses simple adverbials to provide details.	The student • Uses a variety of verbs in different tenses appropriate to the task, text type, and discipline. • Uses a variety of nouns and noun phrases to add rich details. • Uses adverbials to provide rich details.	The student • Uses a variety of verbs in different tenses, aspects, voices, and moods, appropriate for the task, text type, and discipline. • Uses an expanded variety of nouns and noun phrases to add rich details. • Uses complex adverbials to provide rich details.
Connecting and Condensing Ideas	The student • Connects ideas in compound sentences using simple conjunctions. • Condenses ideas by using prepositional phrases to create precise and detailed sentences.	The student • Connects ideas in compound and complex sentences using a variety of ways. • Condenses ideas in a variety of ways to create precise and detailed sentences.	The student • Connects and combines ideas in compound and complex sentences using a variety of ways. • Condenses ideas in a variety of complex ways to create precise and detailed sentences.

Embedded Assessment 2: Performing Shakespearean Comedy

ENGLISH LANGUAGE DEVELOPMENT RUBRIC

The Embedded Assessment that the whole class completes can be a useful source of English language development evidence. Use this additional rubric to examine the Embedded Assessment products of English learners. The analysis will help you gain additional information about student learning related to the strands of the English Language Development Standards and identify individual areas for improvement.

Criteria	Emerging	Expanding	Bridging
Collaborative	The student • engages in conversational exchanges by asking and answering questions using simple phrases. • engages and collaborates on short written exchanges with peers. • adapts language choice to setting and audience.	The student • engages in discussion by asking relevant questions and adding relevant information. • engages and collaborates on longer written exchanges with peers. • adapts language choice to purpose, task, and audience.	The student • engages in discussion by asking relevant questions and contributing useful feedback. • engages and collaborates on complex written exchanges with peers. • adapts complex language choice to task, purpose, and audience.
Interpretive	The student • listens actively in oral presentation by asking and answering basic questions with prompts or support. • expresses inferences and conclusions based on close reading of texts with substantial support. • analyzes how words produce different effects.	The student • listens actively in oral presentation by asking and answering detailed questions with some prompting and support. • expresses inferences and conclusions based on close reading of texts with some support. • analyzes how words produce shades of meaning and the effect on the audience.	The student • listens actively in oral presentation by asking and answering detailed questions with little support. • expresses inferences and conclusions based on close reading of texts with some support. • analyzes how words or phrases produce shades of meaning and the effect on the audience.
Productive	The student • plans and delivers oral presentations.	The student • plans and delivers detailed oral presentations.	The student • plans and delivers complex oral presentations.
Structuring Cohesive Texts	The student • applies understanding of text structure organization to aid in comprehending text. • applies knowledge of language resources to aid in comprehending text. • applies understanding of basic connecting words to aid in text comprehension.	The student • applies understanding of text structure organization and features to aid in comprehending text. • applies knowledge of growing language resources to aid in comprehending text. • applies understanding of connecting words to aid in comprehending how events or ideas are linked.	The student • applies understanding of complex text structure organization and features to aid in comprehending text. • applies knowledge of complex language resources to aid in comprehending text. • applies understanding of connecting and linking words and phrases to aid in comprehending how events or ideas are linked.

Resources

Correlation of SpringBoard English Language Arts, Grade 8 to the California Common Core State Standards

	Standard Code	Standard	Where Addressed
LITERATURE			
Key Ideas and Details	RL.8.1	Cite the textual evidence that most strongly supports an analysis of what the text says explicitly as well as inferences drawn from the text.	**Focus Standard:** Unit 1: Activity 1.5 (pp. 15–21); Unit 2: Activity 2.4 (pp. 119–121); Unit 3: Activity 3.11 (pp. 206–213); Unit 4: Activity 4.15 (pp. 324–325) Unit 1: Activity 1.3 (pp. 8–10), 1.4 (pp. 11–14), 1.6 (pp. 22–30), 1.7 (pp. 31–40), 1.9 (pp. 47–55), 1.14 (pp. 75–83); Unit 2: Activity 2.3 (pp. 110–118), 2.6 (pp. 125–129), 2.7 (pp. 130–131), 2.8 (pp. 132–133), 2.9 (pp. 134–136), Embedded Assessment 1 (pp. 137–138); Unit 3: Activity 3.3 (pp. 177–180), 3.4 (pp. 181–185), 3.5 (pp. 186–189), 3.10 (pp. 201–205), 3.12 (pp. 214–216), Embedded Assessment 1 (pp. 217–218); Unit 4: Activity 4.3 (pp. 260–263), 4.6 (pp. 277–281), 4.7 (pp. 282–287), 4.8 (pp. 288–295), 4.9 (pp. 296–303), 4.10 (pp. 304–307), 4.11 (pp. 308–314), Embedded Assessment (pp. 315–316), 4.16 (pp. 326–328), 4.18 (pp. 333–336)
	RL.8.2	Determine a theme or central idea of a text and analyze its development over the course of the text, including its relationship to the characters, setting, and plot; provide an objective summary of the text.	**Focus Standard:** Unit 1: Activity 1.12 (pp. 62–68); Unit 2: Activity 2.3 (pp. 110–118), 2.9 (pp. 134–136); Unit 3: Activity 3.5 (pp. 186–189), 3.10 (pp. 201–205); Unit 4: Activity 4.15 (pp. 324–325) Unit 1: Activity 1.3 (pp. 8–10), 1.5 (pp. 15–21), 1.6 (pp. 22–30), 1.7 (pp. 31–40), 1.9 (pp. 47–55); Unit 2: Activity 2.4 (pp. 119–121), 2.5 (pp. 122–124), 2.6 (pp. 125–129), 2.8 (pp. 132–133); Unit 3: Activity 3.3 (pp. 177–180), 3.4 (pp. 181–185), 3.12 (pp. 214–216), Embedded Assessment 1 (pp. 217–218); Unit 4: Activity 4.7 (pp. 282–287), 4.8 (pp. 288–295), Embedded Assessment (pp. 315–316), 4.13 (pp. 319–321), 4.14 (pp. 322–323), 4.16 (pp. 326–328), 4.19 (pp. 337–339)

	Standard Code	Standard	Where Addressed
Key Ideas and Details	RL.8.3	Analyze how particular lines of dialogue or incidents in a story or drama propel the action, reveal aspects of a character, or provoke a decision.	**Focus Standard:** Unit 1: Activity 1.6 (pp. 22–30), 1.7 (pp. 31–40), 1.9 (pp. 47–55); Unit 2: Activity 2.3 (pp. 110–118), 2.4 (pp. 119–121), 2.8 (pp. 132–133); Unit 3: Activity 3.10 (pp. 201–205); Unit 4: Activity 4.7 (pp. 282–287), 4.18 (pp. 333–336) Unit 1: Activity 1.2 (pp. 5–7), 1.5 (pp. 15–21), 1.8 (pp. 41–46), 1.12 (pp. 62–68); Unit 2: Activity 2.7 (pp. 130–131), 2.9 (pp. 134–136), Embedded Assessment 1 (pp. 137–138); Unit 3: Activity 3.4 (pp. 181–185), 3.5 (pp. 186–189), 3.11 (pp. 206–213), Embedded Assessment 1 (pp. 217–218); Unit 4: Activity 4.8 (pp. 288–295)
Craft and Structure	RL.8.4	Determine the meaning of words and phrases as they are used in a text, including figurative and connotative meanings; analyze the impact of specific word choices on meaning and tone, including analogies or allusions to other texts. **(See grade 8 Language standards 4–6 for additional expectations.) CA**	**Focus Standard:** Unit 1: Activity 1.2 (pp. 5–7), 1.3 (pp. 8–10); Unit 2: Activity 2.5 (pp. 122–124); Unit 4: Activity 4.8 (pp. 288–295), 4.10 (pp. 304–307), Embedded Assessment 2 (pp. 341–342) Unit 1: Activity 1.6 (pp. 22–30), 1.7 (pp. 31–40), 1.9 (pp. 47–55), 1.12 (pp. 62–68), 1.14 (pp. 75–83); Unit 2: Activity 2.3 (pp. 110–118), 2.4 (pp. 119–121), 2.6 (pp. 125–129), 2.7 (pp. 130–131), 2.8 (pp. 132–133), 2.9 (pp. 134–136), 3.5 (pp. 186–189), 3.6 (pp. 190–191), 3.10 (pp. 201–205), 3.11 (pp. 206–213), 3.12 (pp. 214–216); Unit 4: Activity 4.6 (pp. 277–281), 4.7 (pp. 282–287), 4.9 (pp. 296–303), 4.11 (pp. 308–314), Embedded Assessment (pp. 315–316), 4.14 (pp. 322–323), 4.15 (pp. 324–325), 4.16 (pp. 326–328), 4.18 (pp. 333–336)
	RL.8.5	Compare and contrast the structure of two or more texts and analyze how the differing structure of each text contributes to its meaning and style.	**Focus Standard:** Unit 1: Activity 1.12 (pp. 62–68); Unit 3: Activity 3.4 (pp. 181–185), 3.12 (pp. 214–216) Unit 3: Activity 3.5 (pp. 186–189); Unit 4: Activity 4.3 (pp. 260–263)
	RL.8.6	Analyze how differences in the points of view of the characters and the audience or reader (e.g., created through the use of dramatic irony) create such effects as suspense or humor.	**Focus Standard:** Unit 2: Activity 2.5 (pp. 122–124); 2.11 (pp. 141–146); Unit 4: Activity 4.8 (pp. 288–295), 4.15 (pp. 324–325), Embedded Assessment 2 (pp. 341–342) Unit 2: Activity 2.3 (pp. 110–118), 2.9 (pp. 134–136); Unit 3: Activity 3.5 (pp. 186–189); Unit 4: Activity 4.7 (pp. 282–287), Embedded Assessment (pp. 315–316)

	Standard Code	Standard	Where Addressed
Integration of Knowledge and Ideas	RL.8.7	Analyze the extent to which a filmed or live production of a story or drama stays faithful to or departs from the text or script, evaluating the choices made by the director or actors.	**Focus Standard:** Unit 1: Activity 1.5 (pp. 15–21); Unit 3: Activity 3.18 (pp. 237–239); Unit 4: Activity 4.19 (pp. 337–339), Embedded Assessment 2 (pp. 341–342)
	RL.8.8	(Not applicable to literature)	
	RL.8.9	Analyze how a modern work of fiction draws on themes, patterns of events, or character types from myths, traditional stories, or religious works such as the Bible, including describing how the material is rendered new.	**Focus Standard:** Unit 2: Activity 2.7 (pp. 130–131), 2.9 (pp. 134–136) Unit 1: Activity 1.5 (pp. 15–21); Unit 4: Activity 4.9 (pp. 296–303)
Range of Reading and Text Complexity	RL.8.10	By the end of the year, read and comprehend literature, including stories, dramas, and poems, at the high end of grades 6–8 text complexity band independently and proficiently.	**Focus Standard:** Unit 2: Activity 2.10 (139–140); Unit 4: Embedded Assessment 2 (pp. 341–342) Unit 1: Activity 1.1 (p. 4), 1.2 (pp. 5–7), 1.3 (pp. 8–10), 1.6 (pp. 22–30), 1.7 (pp. 31–40), 1.9 (pp. 47–55), 1.12 (pp. 62–68), 1.13 (pp. 69–74), 1.14 (pp. 75–83); Unit 2: Activity 2.1 (pp. 102), 2.6 (pp. 125–129); Unit 3: Activity 3.1 (p. 172), 3.4 (pp. 181–185), 3.11 (pp. 206–213), Embedded Assessment 1 (pp. 217–218), 3.13 (pp. 219–220), Embedded Assessment 2 (pp. 245–246); Unit 4: Activity 4.1 (p. 250), 4.7 (pp. 282–287), 4.9 (pp. 296–303), Embedded Assessment (pp. 315–316), 4.12 (pp. 317–318), 4.15 (pp. 324–325), 4.18 (pp. 333–336), 4.19 (pp. 337–339)
		INFORMATIONAL TEXT	
Key Ideas and Details	RI.8.1	Cite the textual evidence that most strongly supports an analysis of what the text says explicitly as well as inferences drawn from the text.	**Focus Standard:** Unit 1: Activity 1.16 (pp. 88–89); Unit 3: Activity 3.4 (pp. 181–185), 3.15 (pp. 223–227), 3.16 (pp. 229–231), 3.17 (pp. 232–236); Unit 4: Activity 4.4 (pp. 264–271) Unit 1: Activity 1.12 (pp. 62–68), 1.13 (pp. 69–74), 1.14 (pp. 75–83), 1.17 (pp. 90–96); Unit 2: Activity 2.2 (pp. 103–109), 2.6 (pp. 125–129), 2.10 (139–140), 2.12 (pp. 144–146), 2.13 (pp. 147–150), 2.15 (pp. 153–158), 2.16 (pp. 159–162), 2.17 (pp. 163–166); Unit 3: Activity 3.2 (pp. 173–176), 3.7 (pp. 192–194), 3.8 (pp. 195–197), 3.18 (pp. 237–239), 3.19 (pp. 240–244); Unit 4: Activity 4.2 (pp. 251–259), 4.3 (pp. 260–263), 4.5 (pp. 272–276), 4.11 (pp. 308–314), Embedded Assessment (pp. 315–316), 4.17 (pp. 329–332)

	Standard Code	Standard	Where Addressed
Key Ideas and Details	RI.8.2	Determine a central idea of a text and analyze its development over the course of the text, including its relationship to supporting ideas; provide an objective summary of the text.	**Focus Standard:** Unit 1: Activity 1.13 (pp. 69–74); Unit 3: Activity 3.4 (pp. 181–185), 3.15 (pp. 223–227); Unit 4: Activity 4.2 (pp. 251–259) Unit 1: Activity 1.14 (pp. 75–83); Unit 2: Activity 2.2 (pp. 103–109), 2.6 (pp. 125–129), 2.7 (pp. 130–131), 2.10 (139–140), 2.13 (pp. 147–150), 2.15 (pp. 153–158), 2.16 (pp. 159–162), 2.17 (pp. 163–166); Unit 3: Activity 3.7 (pp. 192–194), 3.8 (pp. 195–197), 3.17 (pp. 232–236), 3.18 (pp. 237–239), 3.19 (pp. 240–244); Unit 4: Activity 4.3 (pp. 260–263), 4.4 (pp. 264–271), 4.5 (pp. 272–276), 4.11 (pp. 308–314), Embedded Assessment (pp. 315–316), 4.17 (pp. 329–332)
	RI.8.3	Analyze how a text makes connections among and distinctions between individuals, ideas, or events (e.g., through comparisons, analogies, or categories).	**Focus Standard:** Unit 1: Activity 1.13 (pp. 69–74), 1.14 (pp. 75–83); Unit 2: Activity 2.2 (pp. 103–109) Unit 1: Activity 1.12 (pp. 62–68), 1.14 (pp. 75–83); Unit 2: Activity 2.10 (139–140); Unit 3: Activity 3.4 (pp. 181–185), 3.15 (pp. 223–227), 3.17 (pp. 232–236), 3.18 (pp. 237–239), 3.19 (pp. 240–244); Unit 4: Activity 4.2 (pp. 251–259), 4.4 (pp. 264–271), 4.6 (pp. 277–281), 4.11 (pp. 308–314), Embedded Assessment (pp. 315–316)
Craft and Structure	RI.8.4	Determine the meaning of words and phrases as they are used in a text, including figurative, connotative, and technical meanings; analyze the impact of specific word choices on meaning and tone, including analogies or allusions to other texts. **(See grade 8 Language standards 4–6 for additional expectations.) CA**	**Focus Standard:** Unit 4: Activity 4.6 (pp. 277–281) Unit 1: Activity 1.12 (pp. 62–68), 1.13 (pp. 69–74), 1.16 (pp. 88–89); Unit 2: Activity 2.2 (pp. 103–109), 2.12 (pp. 144–146), 2.13 (pp. 147–150), 2.15 (pp. 153–158), 2.16 (pp. 159–162); Unit 3: Activity 3.4 (pp. 181–185), 3.6 (pp. 190–191), 3.15 (pp. 223–227), 3.16 (pp. 229–231), 3.18 (pp. 237–239), 3.19 (pp. 240–244); Unit 4: Activity 4.2 (pp. 251–259), 4.3 (pp. 260–263), 4.4 (pp. 264–271), 4.5 (pp. 272–276), 4.11 (pp. 308–314), Embedded Assessment (pp. 315–316), 4.17 (pp. 329–332)
	RI.8.5	Analyze in detail the structure of a specific paragraph in a text, including the role of particular sentences in developing and refining a key concept.	**Focus Standard:** Unit 2: Activity 2.10 (139–140) Unit 1: Activity 1.12 (pp. 62–68), 1.13 (pp. 69–74), 1.14 (pp. 75–83); Unit 2: Activity 2.2 (pp. 103–109), 2.13 (pp. 147–150); Unit 3: Activity 3.4 (pp. 181–185), 3.15 (pp. 223–227), 3.19 (pp. 240–244), 4.5 (pp. 272–276), 4.11 (pp. 308–314), Embedded Assessment (pp. 315–316)

	Standard Code	Standard	Where Addressed
Craft and Structure	**RI.8.5a**	**Analyze the use of text features (e.g., graphics, headers, captions) in consumer materials. CA**	**Focus Standard:** Unit 3: Activity 3.14 (pp. 221–222), 3.16 (pp. 229–231) Unit 3: Activity 3.17 (pp. 232–236)
	RI.8.6	Determine an author's point of view or purpose in a text and analyze how the author acknowledges and responds to conflicting evidence or viewpoints.	**Focus Standard:** Unit 2: Activity 2.10 (139–140) Unit 1: Activity 1.12 (pp. 62–68); Unit 3: Activity 3.4 (pp. 181–185), 3.15 (pp. 223–227), 3.16 (pp. 229–231), 3.18 (pp. 237–239), 3.19 (pp. 240–244); Unit 4: Activity 4.2 (pp. 251–259), 4.5 (pp. 272–276)
Integration of Knowledge and Ideas	RI.8.7	Evaluate the advantages and disadvantages of using different mediums (e.g., print or digital text, video, multimedia) to present a particular topic or idea.	**Focus Standard:** Unit 3: Activity 3.14 (pp. 221–222) Unit 3: Activity 3.16 (pp. 228–231), Activity 3.17 (pp. 232–236), Activity 3.18 (pp. 237–239)
	RI.8.8	Delineate and evaluate the argument and specific claims in a text, assessing whether the reasoning is sound and the evidence is relevant and sufficient; recognize when irrelevant evidence is introduced.	**Focus Standard:** Unit 2: Activity 2.13 (pp. 147–150), 2.14 (pp. 151–152); Unit 3: Activity 3.19 (pp. 240–244) Unit 2: Activity 2.16 (pp. 159–162); Unit 3: Activity 3.15 (pp. 223–227), 3.18 (pp. 237–239); Unit 4: Activity 4.2 (pp. 251–259)
	RI.8.9	Analyze a case in which two or more texts provide conflicting information on the same topic and identify where the texts disagree on matters of fact or interpretation.	Unit 2: Activity 2.16 (pp. 159–162) Workshops: Writing Workshop 2 (pp. 15–24) Close Reading Workshop 2 (pp. 17–36)
Range of Reading and Text Complexity	RI.8.10	By the end of the year, read and comprehend literary nonfiction at the high end of the grades 6–8 text complexity band independently and proficiently.	**Focus Standard:** Unit 1: Activity 1.16 (pp. 88–89) Unit 1: Activity 1.10 (pp. 58–59), 1.12 (pp. 62–68), 1.13 (pp. 69–74), 1.14 (pp. 75–83); Unit 2: Activity 2.2 (pp. 103–109), 2.13 (pp. 147–150), 2.15 (pp. 153–158), 2.16 (pp. 159–162); Unit 3: Activity 3.1 (p. 172), 3.4 (pp. 181–185), 3.13 (pp. 219–220); Unit 4: Activity 4.1 (p. 250), 4.2 (pp. 251–259), 4.5 (pp. 272–276)
		WRITING	
Text Types and Purposes	W.8.1	Write arguments to support claims with clear reasons and relevant evidence.	**Focus Standard:** Unit 2: Activity 2.14 (pp. 151–152), Embedded Assessment 2 (pp. 167–168); Unit 3: Embedded Assessment 2 (pp. 245–246) Unit 2: Activity 2.12 (pp. 144–146), 2.13 (pp. 147–150), 2.16 (pp. 159–162), 2.17 (pp. 163–166); Unit 3: Activity 3.15 (pp. 223–227), 3.17 (pp. 232–236)

	Standard Code	Standard	Where Addressed
Text Types and Purposes	W.8.1a	Introduce claim(s), acknowledge and distinguish the claim(s) from alternate or opposing claims, and organize the reasons and evidence logically.	**Focus Standard:** Unit 2: Activity 2.14 (pp. 151–152), Embedded Assessment 2 (pp. 167–168); Unit 3: Embedded Assessment 2 (pp. 245–246) Unit 2: Activity 2.12 (pp. 144–146), 2.13 (pp. 147–150), 2.16 (pp. 159–162), 2.17 (pp. 163–166); Unit 3: Activity 3.15 (pp. 223–227), 3.17 (pp. 232–236)
	W.8.1b	Support claim(s) with logical reasoning and relevant evidence, using accurate, credible sources and demonstrating an understanding of the topic or text.	**Focus Standard:** Unit 2: Activity 2.13 (pp. 147–150), Embedded Assessment 2 (pp. 167–168); Unit 3: Embedded Assessment 2 (pp. 245–246) Unit 2: Activity 2.12 (pp. 144–146), 2.15 (pp. 153–158), 2.16 (pp. 159–162), 2.17 (pp. 163–166); Unit 3: Activity 3.15 (pp. 223–227)
	W.8.1c	Use words, phrases, and clauses to create cohesion and clarify the relationships among claim(s), counterclaims, reasons, and evidence.	**Focus Standard:** Unit 2: Embedded Assessment 2 (pp. 167–168); Unit 3: Embedded Assessment 2 (pp. 245–246) Unit 2: Activity 2.17 (pp. 163–166)
	W.8.1d	Establish and maintain a formal style.	**Focus Standard:** Unit 2: Embedded Assessment 2 (pp. 167–168) Unit 2: Activity 2.17 (pp. 163–166); Unit 3: Activity 3.17 (pp. 232–236)
	W.8.1e	Provide a concluding statement or section that follows from and supports the argument presented.	**Focus Standard:** Unit 2: Embedded Assessment 2 (pp. 167–168); Unit 3: Embedded Assessment 2 (pp. 245–246) Unit 2: Activity 2.17 (pp. 163–166)
	W.8.2	Write informative/explanatory texts, **including career development documents (e.g., simple business letters and job applications),** to examine a topic and convey ideas, concepts, and information through the selection, organization, and analysis of relevant content. **CA**	**Focus Standard:** Unit 1: Activity 1.4 (pp. 11–14), 1.17 (pp. 90–96); Unit 2: Activity 2.2 (pp. 103–109); Unit 4: Activity 4.3 (pp. 260–263), 4.5 (pp. 272–276), 4.11 (pp. 308–314) Unit 3: Activity 3.3 (pp. 177–180)

	Standard Code	Standard	Where Addressed
Text Types and Purposes	W.8.2a	Introduce a topic **or thesis statement** clearly, previewing what is to follow; organize ideas, concepts, and information into broader categories; include formatting (e.g., headings), graphics (e.g., charts, tables), and multimedia when useful to aiding comprehension. **CA**	**Focus Standard:** Unit 1: Activity 1.17 (pp. 90–96), Embedded Assessment 2 ; Unit 2: Activity 2.2 (pp. 103–109), Embedded Assessment 1 (pp. 137–138); Unit 4: Activity 4.3 (pp. 260–263), 4.5 (pp. 272–276), 4.11 (pp. 308–314), Embedded Assessment (pp. 315–316) Unit 1: Activity 1.4 (pp. 11–14), 1.13 (pp. 69–74), 1.14 (pp. 75–83), 1.16 (pp. 88–89); Unit 2: Activity 2.3 (pp. 110–118), 2.4 (pp. 119–121), 2.5 (pp. 122–124), 2.7 (pp. 130–131), 2.9 (pp. 134–136), 2.10 (139–140); Unit 3: Activity 3.5 (pp. 186–189), 3.7 (pp. 192–194), 3.9 (pp. 198–200), 3.10 (pp. 201–205), 3.11 (pp. 206–213), Embedded Assessment 1 (pp. 217–218); Unit 4: Activity 4.2 (pp. 251–259), 4.4 (pp. 264–271), 4.6 (pp. 277–281), 4.8 (pp. 288–295), 4.10 (pp. 304–307)
	W.8.2b	Develop the topic with relevant, well-chosen facts, definitions, concrete details, quotations, or other information and examples.	**Focus Standard:** Unit 1: Activity 1.15 (pp. 84–87), Embedded Assessment 2 ; Unit 2: Activity 2.3 (pp. 110–118), Embedded Assessment 1 (pp. 137–138); Unit 4: Embedded Assessment (pp. 315–316) Unit 1: Activity 1.4 (pp. 11–14), 1.13 (pp. 69–74), 1.14 (pp. 75–83), 1.16 (pp. 88–89), 1.17 (pp. 90–96); Unit 2: Activity 2.2 (pp. 103–109), 2.4 (pp. 119–121), 2.5 (pp. 122–124), 2.7 (pp. 130–131), 2.9 (pp. 134–136), 2.10 (139–140); Unit 3: Activity 3.5 (pp. 186–189), 3.7 (pp. 192–194), 3.9 (pp. 198–200), Embedded Assessment 1 (pp. 217–218); Unit 4: Activity 4.2 (pp. 251–259), 4.3 (pp. 260–263), 4.4 (pp. 264–271), 4.6 (pp. 277–281), 4.8 (pp. 288–295), 4.10 (pp. 304–307), 4.11 (pp. 308–314)
	W.8.2c	Use appropriate and varied transitions to create cohesion and clarify the relationships among ideas and concepts.	**Focus Standard:** Unit 1: Activity 1.15 (pp. 84–87), Embedded Assessment 2 ; Unit 2: Activity 2.7 (pp. 130–131), Embedded Assessment 1 (pp. 137–138); Unit 4: Activity 4.6 (pp. 277–281), Embedded Assessment (pp. 315–316) Unit 1: Activity 1.13 (pp. 69–74), 1.16 (pp. 88–89); Unit 2: Activity 2.2 (pp. 103–109); Unit 3: Activity 3.7 (pp. 192–194), 3.11 (pp. 206–213); Unit 4: Activity 4.5 (pp. 272–276), 4.8 (pp. 288–295), 4.10 (pp. 304–307), 4.11 (pp. 308–314)

	Standard Code	Standard	Where Addressed
Text Types and Purposes	W.8.2d	Use precise language and domain-specific vocabulary to inform about or explain the topic.	**Focus Standard:** Unit 1: Embedded Assessment 2; Unit 2: Embedded Assessment 1 (pp. 137–138); Unit 4: Activity 4.2 (pp. 251–259), 4.5 (pp. 272–276), Embedded Assessment (pp. 315–316) Unit 1: Activity 1.13 (pp. 69–74), 1.14 (pp. 75–83), 1.17 (pp. 90–96); Unit 3: Embedded Assessment 1 (pp. 217–218); Unit 4: = Activity 4.3 (pp. 260–263), 4.4 (pp. 264–271), 4.6 (pp. 277–281), 4.8 (pp. 288–295), 4.10 (pp. 304–307)
	W.8.2e	Establish and maintain a formal style.	**Focus Standard:** Unit 1: Embedded Assessment 2 ; Unit 2: Embedded Assessment 1 (pp. 137–138); Unit 4: Embedded Assessment (pp. 315–316) Unit 1: Activity 1.14 (pp. 75–83), 1.17 (pp. 90–96); Unit 3: Activity 3.5 (pp. 186–189), 3.7 (pp. 192–194), 3.9 (pp. 198–200), Embedded Assessment 1 (pp. 217–218); Unit 4: Activity 4.5 (pp. 272–276), 4.6 (pp. 277–281), 4.8 (pp. 288–295)
	W.8.2f	Provide a concluding statement or section that follows from and supports the information or explanation presented.	**Focus Standard:** Unit 1: Activity 1.17 (pp. 90–96), Embedded Assessment 2; Unit 2: Embedded Assessment 1 (pp. 137–138); Unit 4: Embedded Assessment (pp. 315–316) Unit 3: Activity 3.7 (pp. 192–194), Embedded Assessment 1 (pp. 217–218); Unit 4: Activity 4.11 (pp. 308–314)
	W.8.3	Write narratives to develop real or imagined experiences or events using effective technique, relevant descriptive details, and well-structured event sequences.	**Focus Standard:** Unit 1: Activity 1.6 (pp. 22–30), 1.7 (pp. 31–40); Unit 3: Activity 3.8 (pp. 195–197); Unit 4: Activity 4.4 (pp. 264–271)
	W.8.3a	Engage and orient the reader by establishing a context and point of view and introducing a narrator and/or characters; organize an event sequence that unfolds naturally and logically.	**Focus Standard:** Unit 1: Activity 1.6 (pp. 22–30), 1.7 (pp. 31–40), Embedded Assessment 1 (pp. 56–57); Unit 3: Activity 3.8 (pp. 195–197); Unit 4: Activity 4.4 (pp. 264–271) Unit 1: Activity 1.9 (pp. 47–55); Unit 4: Activity 4.13 (pp. 319–321)
	W.8.3b	Use narrative techniques, such as dialogue, pacing, description, and reflection, to develop experiences, events, and/or characters.	**Focus Standard:** Unit 1: Embedded Assessment 1 (pp. 56–57), 1.16 (pp. 88–89) Unit 1: Activity 1.6 (pp. 22–30), 1.7 (pp. 31–40), 1.9 (pp. 47–55); Unit 3: Activity 3.8 (pp. 195–197); Unit 4: Activity 4.13 (pp. 319–321)

	Standard Code	Standard	Where Addressed
Text Types and Purposes	W.8.3c	Use a variety of transition words, phrases, and clauses to convey sequence, signal shifts from one time frame or setting to another, and show the relationships among experiences and events.	**Focus Standard:** Unit 1: Embedded Assessment 1 (pp. 56–57) Unit 1: Activity 1.7 (pp. 31–40), 1.9 (pp. 47–55); Unit 3: Activity 3.8 (pp. 195–197)
	W.8.3d	Use precise words and phrases, relevant descriptive details, and sensory language to capture the action and convey experiences and events.	**Focus Standard:** Unit 1: Activity 1.3 (pp. 8–10), 1.6 (pp. 22–30), 1.7 (pp. 31–40), Embedded Assessment 1 (pp. 56–57) Unit 1: Activity 1.9 (pp. 47–55); Unit 3: Activity 3.8 (pp. 195–197); Unit 4: Activity 4.13 (pp. 319–321)
	W.8.3e	Provide a conclusion that follows from and reflects on the narrated experiences or events.	**Focus Standard:** Unit 1: Activity 1.9 (pp. 47–55), Embedded Assessment 1 (pp. 56–57) Unit 3: Activity 3.8 (pp. 195–197); Unit 4: Activity 4.4 (pp. 264–271)
Production and Distribution of Writing	W.8.4	Produce clear and coherent writing in which the development, organization, and style are appropriate to task, purpose, and audience. (Grade-specific expectations for writing types are defined in standards 1–3 above.)	**Focus Standard:** Unit 1: Activity 1.17 (pp. 90–96); Unit 3: Embedded Assessment 2 (pp. 245–246) Unit 1: Activity 1.6 (pp. 22–30), 1.7 (pp. 31–40), 1.9 (pp. 47–55), Embedded Assessment 1 (pp. 56–57), 1.13 (pp. 69–74), 1.14 (pp. 75–83), 1.15 (pp. 84–87), Embedded Assessment 2 ; Unit 2: Activity 2.4 (pp. 119–121), 2.5 (pp. 122–124), 2.7 (pp. 130–131), 2.9 (pp. 134–136), Embedded Assessment 1 (pp. 137–138), 2.10 (139–140), 2.15 (pp. 153–158), 2.17 (pp. 163–166), Embedded Assessment 2 (pp. 167–168): Unit 3: Activity 3.10 (pp. 201–205), Embedded Assessment 1 (pp. 217–218), 3.17 (pp. 232–236), 3.18 (pp. 237–239); Unit 4: Activity 4.2 (pp. 251–259), 4.3 (pp. 260–263), 4.4 (pp. 264–271), 4.5 (pp. 272–276), 4.6 (pp. 277–281), 4.8 (pp. 288–295), 4.10 (pp. 304–307), 4.11 (pp. 308–314), Embedded Assessment (pp. 315–316), 4.13 (pp. 319–321)

	Standard Code	Standard	Where Addressed
Production and Distribution of Writing	W.8.5	With some guidance and support from peers and adults, develop and strengthen writing as needed by planning, revising, editing, rewriting, or trying a new approach, focusing on how well purpose and audience have been addressed. (Editing for conventions should demonstrate command of Language standards 1–3 up to and including grade 8.)	**Focus Standard:** Unit 1: Activity 1.8 (pp. 41–46) Unit 1: Activity 1.3 (pp. 8–10), 1.9 (pp. 47–55), Embedded Assessment 1 (pp. 56–57), 1.13 (pp. 69–74), 1.15 (pp. 84–87), 1.17 (pp. 90–96), Embedded Assessment 2; Unit 2: Activity 2.2 (pp. 103–109), 2.5 (pp. 122–124), 2.9 (pp. 134–136), Embedded Assessment 1 (pp. 137–138), 2.10 (139–140), 2.17 (pp. 163–166), Embedded Assessment 2 (pp. 167–168); Unit 3: Activity 3.8 (pp. 195–197), 3.9 (pp. 198–200), 3.10 (pp. 201–205), Embedded Assessment 2 (pp. 245–246); Unit 4: Activity 4.2 (pp. 251–259), 4.4 (pp. 264–271), 4.6 (pp. 277–281), 4.8 (pp. 288–295), 4.10 (pp. 304–307), 4.11 (pp. 308–314), Embedded Assessment (pp. 315–316), 4.13 (pp. 319–321), 4.16 (pp. 326–328)
	W.8.6	Use technology, including the Internet, to produce and publish writing and present the relationships between information and ideas efficiently as well as to interact and collaborate with others.	**Focus Standard:** Unit 3: Embedded Assessment 2 (pp. 245–246) Unit 1: Embedded Assessment 1 (pp. 56–57); Unit 2 Embedded Assessment 2 (pp. 167–168); Unit 3: Activity 3.17 (pp. 232–236), 3.18 (pp. 237–239); Unit 4: Embedded Assessment (pp. 315–316)
Research to Build and Present Knowledge	W.8.7	Conduct short research projects to answer a question (including a self-generated question), drawing on several sources and generating additional related, focused questions that allow for multiple avenues of exploration.	**Focus Standard:** Unit 2: Activity 2.15 (pp. 153–158), 2.16 (pp. 159–162); Unit 3: Embedded Assessment 2 (pp. 245–246); Unit 4: Activity 4.13 (pp. 319–321) Unit 1: Activity 1.13 (pp. 69–74), Embedded Assessment 2 ; Unit 2: Activity 2.17 (pp. 163–166), Embedded Assessment 2 (pp. 167–168); Unit 3: Activity 3.6 (pp. 190–191), 3.7 (pp. 192–194), 3.8 (pp. 195–197), 3.16 (pp. 229–231), 3.19 (pp. 240–244)
	W.8.8	Gather relevant information from multiple print and digital sources, using search terms effectively; assess the credibility and accuracy of each source; and quote or paraphrase the data and conclusions of others while avoiding plagiarism and following a standard format for citation.	**Focus Standard:** Unit 2: Activity 2.15 (pp. 153–158), 2.16 (pp. 159–162); Unit 3: Activity 3.18 (pp. 237–239), Embedded Assessment 2 (pp. 245–246) Unit 1: Activity 1.15 (pp. 84–87), Embedded Assessment 2 ; Unit 2: Embedded Assessment 1 (pp. 137–138), 2.13 (pp. 147–150), 2.17 (pp. 163–166), Embedded Assessment 2 (pp. 167–168); Unit 3: Activity 3.7 (pp. 192–194), 3.14 (pp. 221–222), 3.15 (pp. 223–227), 3.17 (pp. 232–236)

	Standard Code	Standard	Where Addressed
Research to Build and Present Knowledge	W.8.9	Draw evidence from literary or informational texts to support analysis, reflection, and research.	**Focus Standard:** Unit 1: Activity 1.14 (pp. 75–83); Unit 2: Activity 2.9 (pp. 134–136); Unit 3: Activity 3.11 (pp. 206–213), 3.12 (pp. 214–216); Unit 4: Activity 4.3 (pp. 260–263), 4.8 (pp. 288–295), 4.11 (pp. 308–314) Unit 2: Activity 2.3 (pp. 110–118), 2.5 (pp. 122–124), 2.6 (pp. 125–129), Embedded Assessment 1 (pp. 137–138), 2.16 (pp. 159–162), Embedded Assessment 2 (pp. 167–168)
	W.8.9a	Apply *grade 8 Reading standards* to literature (e.g., "Analyze how a modern work of fiction draws on themes, patterns of events, or character types from myths, traditional stories, or religious works such as the Bible, including describing how the material is rendered new").	**Focus Standard:** Unit 1: Activity 1.14 (pp. 75–83); Unit 2: Activity 2.9 (pp. 134–136); Unit 3: Activity 3.11 (pp. 206–213); Unit 4: Activity 4.3 (pp. 260–263), 4.8 (pp. 288–295), 4.11 (pp. 308–314) Unit 1: Embedded Assessment 2; Unit 3: Activity 3.5 (pp. 186–189), 3.10 (pp. 201–205), 3.12 (pp. 214–216), 3.15 (pp. 223–227); Unit 4: Activity 4.4 (pp. 264–271), 4.6 (pp. 277–281), 4.10 (pp. 304–307), Embedded Assessment (pp. 315–316)
	W.8.9b	Apply *grade 8 Reading standards* to literary nonfiction (e.g., "Delineate and evaluate the argument and specific claims in a text, assessing whether the reasoning is sound and the evidence is relevant and sufficient; recognize when irrelevant evidence is introduced").	**Focus Standard:** Unit 1: Activity 1.14 (pp. 75–83); Unit 3: Activity 3.12 (pp. 214–216) Unit 1: Embedded Assessment 2; Unit 3: Activity 3.5 (pp. 186–189); Unit 4: Activity 4.2 (pp. 251–259), 4.5 (pp. 272–276), Embedded Assessment (pp. 315–316)
Range of Writing	W.8.10	Write routinely over extended time frames (time for research, reflection, and revision) and shorter time frames (a single sitting or a day or two) for a range of discipline-specific tasks, purposes, and audiences.	**Focus Standard:** Unit 2: Activity 2.10 (139–140); Unit 4: Activity 4.12 (pp. 317–318) Unit 1: Activity 1.2 (pp. 5–7), 1.3 (pp. 8–10), 1.4 (pp. 11–14), 1.6 (pp. 22–30), 1.8 (pp. 41–46), Embedded Assessment 1 (pp. 56–57), 1.12 (pp. 62–68), 1.13 (pp. 69–74), 1.14 (pp. 75–83), 1.16 (pp. 88–89), Embedded Assessment 2; Unit 2: Activity 2.2 (pp. 103–109), Activity 2.3 (pp. 110–118), 2.4 (pp. 119–121), 2.6 (pp. 125–129), 2.8 (pp. 132–133), 2.9 (pp. 134–136), Embedded Assessment 1 (pp. 137–138), 2.14 (pp. 151–152), 2.15 (pp. 153–158), 2.17 (pp. 163–166), Embedded Assessment 2 (pp. 167–168); Unit 3: Activity 3.2 (pp. 173–176), 3.3 (pp. 177–180), 3.4 (pp. 181–185), 3.5 (pp. 186–189), 3.8 (pp. 195–197), 3.9 (pp. 198–200), 3.11 (pp. 206–213), 3.12 (pp. 214–216), Unit 3: Embedded Assessment 1 (pp. 217–218),

	Standard Code	Standard	Where Addressed
Range of Writing			3.13 (pp. 219–220), 3.14 (pp. 221–222), 3.17 (pp. 232–236), Embedded Assessment 2 (pp. 245–246); Unit 4: Activity 4.2 (pp. 251–259), 4.3 (pp. 260–263), 4.4 (pp. 264–271), 4.7 (pp. 282–287), 4.9 (pp. 296–303), Embedded Assessment (pp. 315–316), 4.13 (pp. 319–321), 4.14 (pp. 322–323), 4.15 (pp. 324–325), 4.16 (pp. 326–328), 4.17 (pp. 329–332), 4.18 (pp. 333–336), 4.19 (pp. 337–339), 4.20 (p. 340)
		SPEAKING AND LISTENING	
Comprehension and Collaboration	SL.8.1	Engage effectively in a range of collaborative discussions (one-on-one, in groups, and teacher-led) with diverse partners on *grade 8 topics, texts, and issues*, building on others' ideas and expressing their own clearly.	**Focus Standard:** Unit 1: Activity 1.2 (pp. 5–7); Unit 2: Activity 2.6 (pp. 125–129), 2.8 (pp. 132–133); Unit 3: Activity 3.2 (pp. 173–176), 3.3 (pp. 177–180), 3.9 (pp. 198–200), 3.11 (pp. 206–213); Unit 4: Activity 4.5 (pp. 272–276) Unit 2: Activity 2.1 (pp. 102)
	SL.8.1a	Come to discussions prepared, having read or researched material under study; explicitly draw on that preparation by referring to evidence on the topic, text, or issue to probe and reflect on ideas under discussion.	**Focus Standard:** Unit 2: Activity 2.6 (pp. 125–129), 2.8 (pp. 132–133); Unit 3: Activity 3.2 (pp. 173–176), 3.3 (pp. 177–180), 3.5 (pp. 186–189), 3.9 (pp. 198–200), 3.11 (pp. 206–213), Embedded Assessment 1 (pp. 217–218); Unit 4: Embedded Assessment 2 (pp. 341–342) Unit 1: Activity 1.2 (pp. 5–7), 1.8 (pp. 41–46); Unit 2: Activity 2.4 (pp. 119–121), 2.12 (pp. 144–146), 2.17 (pp. 163–166); Unit 3: Activity 3.4 (pp. 181–185), 3.6 (pp. 190–191), 3.7 (pp. 192–194), 3.8 (pp. 195–197), 3.10 (pp. 201–205), 3.15 (pp. 223–227), 3.16 (pp. 229–231), 3.17 (pp. 232–236), Embedded Assessment 2 (pp. 245–246); Unit 4: Activity 4.4 (pp. 264–271), 4.5 (pp. 272–276), 4.7 (pp. 282–287), 4.9 (pp. 296–303), 4.10 (pp. 304–307), Embedded Assessment (pp. 315–316), 4.14 (pp. 322–323), 4.15 (pp. 324–325), 4.16 (pp. 326–328), 4.17 (pp. 329–332), 4.18 (pp. 333–336), 4.20 (p. 340)

	Standard Code	Standard	Where Addressed
Comprehension and Collaboration	SL.8.1b	Follow rules for collegial discussions and decision-making, track progress toward specific goals and deadlines, and define individual roles as needed.	**Focus Standard:** Unit 2: Activity 2.6 (pp. 125–129), 2.10 (139–140), 2.17 (pp. 163–166); Unit 3: Activity 3.2 (pp. 173–176), 3.3 (pp. 177–180), Embedded Assessment 1 (pp. 217–218); Unit 4: Activity 4.16 (pp. 326–328), 4.18 (pp. 333–336), Embedded Assessment 2 (pp. 341–342) Unit 1: Activity 1.8 (pp. 41–46); Unit 2: Activity 2.12 (pp. 144–146); Unit 3: Activity 3.4 (pp. 181–185), 3.6 (pp. 190–191), 3.9 (pp. 198–200), 3.11 (pp. 206–213), 3.14 (pp. 221–222), 3.15 (pp. 223–227); Unit 4: Activity 4.5 (pp. 272–276), 4.8 (pp. 288–295), Embedded Assessment (pp. 315–316)
	SL.8.1c	Pose questions that connect the ideas of several speakers and respond to others' questions and comments with relevant evidence, observations, and ideas.	**Focus Standard:** Unit 2: Activity 2.17 (pp. 163–166); Unit 3: Embedded Assessment 1 (pp. 217–218) Unit 1: Activity 1.8 (pp. 41–46); Unit 2: Activity 2.6 (pp. 125–129), 2.12 (pp. 144–146); Unit 3: Activity 3.2 (pp. 173–176), 3.3 (pp. 177–180), 3.4 (pp. 181–185), 3.5 (pp. 186–189), 3.9 (pp. 198–200), 3.15 (pp. 223–227), 3.16 (pp. 229–231); Unit 4: Activity 4.5 (pp. 272–276), 4.9 (pp. 296–303), 4.9 (pp. 296–303), Embedded Assessment (pp. 315–316), 4.17 (pp. 329–332), Embedded Assessment 2 (pp. 341–342)
	SL.8.1d	Acknowledge new information expressed by others, and, when warranted, qualify or justify their own views in light of the evidence presented.	**Focus Standard:** Unit 2: Activity 2.17 (pp. 163–166); Unit 3: Embedded Assessment 1 (pp. 217–218) Unit 1: Activity 1.8 (pp. 41–46); Unit 2: Activity 2.6 (pp. 125–129); Unit 3: Activity 3.2 (pp. 173–176), 3.3 (pp. 177–180), 3.4 (pp. 181–185), 3.5 (pp. 186–189), 3.16 (pp. 229–231), Embedded Assessment 2 (pp. 245–246); Unit 4: Activity 4.18 (pp. 333–336), 4.20 (p. 340), Embedded Assessment 2 (pp. 341–342)
	SL.8.2	Analyze the purpose of information presented in diverse media and formats (e.g., visually, quantitatively, orally) and evaluate the motives (e.g., social, commercial, political) behind its presentation.	**Focus Standard:** Unit 3: Activity 3.14 (pp. 221–222), 3.16 (pp. 229–231), 3.17 (pp. 232–236), 3.18 (pp. 237–239) Unit 1: Activity 1.4 (pp. 11–14); Unit 2: Activity 2.12 (pp. 144–146); Unit 3: Activity 3.9 (pp. 198–200), 3.15 (pp. 223–227), 3.19 (pp. 240–244), Embedded Assessment 2 (pp. 245–246); Unit 4: Activity 4.4 (pp. 264–271), 4.9 (pp. 296–303)

	Standard Code	Standard	Where Addressed
Comprehension and Collaboration	SL.8.3	Delineate a speaker's argument and specific claims, evaluating the soundness of the reasoning and relevance and sufficiency of the evidence and identifying when irrelevant evidence is introduced.	**Focus Standard:** Unit 2: Activity 2.12 (pp. 144–146); Unit 3: Embedded Assessment 1 (pp. 217–218), 3.15 (pp. 223–227) Unit 3: Activity 3.7 (pp. 192–194), 3.11 (pp. 206–213), Embedded Assessment 2 (pp. 245–246)
Presentation of Knowledge and Ideas	SL.8.4	Present claims and findings **(e.g., argument, narrative, response to literature presentations)**, emphasizing salient points in a focused, coherent manner with relevant evidence, sound valid reasoning, and well-chosen details; use appropriate eye contact, adequate volume, and clear pronunciation. **CA**	**Focus Standard:** Unit 2: Activity 2.12 (pp. 144–146); Unit 3: Activity 3.7 (pp. 192–194), Embedded Assessment 1 (pp. 217–218); Unit 4: Activity 4.20 (p. 340) Unit 1: Activity 1.2 (pp. 5–7), 1.11 (pp.60–61); Unit 3: Activity 3.8 (pp. 195–197), 3.9 (pp. 198–200), 3.11 (pp. 206–213), Embedded Assessment 2 (pp. 245–246); Unit 4: Activity 4.18 (pp. 333–336), Embedded Assessment 2 (pp. 341–342)
	SL.8.4a	**Plan and present a narrative that: establishes a context and point of view, presents a logical sequence, uses narrative techniques (e.g., dialogue, pacing, description, sensory language), uses a variety of transitions, and provides a conclusion that reflects the experience. CA**	**Focus Standard:** Unit 1: Embedded Assessment 1 (pp. 56–57) Unit 2: Activity 2.4 (pp. 119–121), Embedded Assessment 2 (pp. 245–246)
	SL.8.5	Integrate multimedia and visual displays into presentations to clarify information, strengthen claims and evidence, and add interest.	**Focus Standard:** Unit 4: Embedded Assessment 2 (pp. 341–342) Unit 1: Activity 1.2 (pp. 5–7); Unit 3: Activity 3.15 (pp. 223–227), 3.18 (pp. 237–239), Embedded Assessment 2 (pp. 245–246); Unit 4: Activity 4.18 (pp. 333–336)
	SL.8.6	Adapt speech to a variety of contexts and tasks, demonstrating command of formal English when indicated or appropriate. (See grade 8 Language standards 1 and 3 for specific expectations.)	**Focus Standard:** Unit 3: Activity 3.12 (pp. 214–216), Embedded Assessment 1 (pp. 217–218); Unit 4: Activity 4.14 (pp. 322–323), 4.16 (pp. 326–328), 4.17 (pp. 329–332), 4.20 (p. 340), Embedded Assessment 2 (pp. 341–342) Unit 1: Activity 1.2 (pp. 5–7), Activity 1.11 (pp. 60–61); Unit 2: Activity 2.6 (pp. 125–129), 2.8 (pp. 132–133), 2.12 (pp. 144–146), 2.13 (pp. 147–150); Unit 3: Activity 3.2 (pp. 173–176), 3.5 (pp. 186–189), 3.8 (pp. 195–197), 3.9 (pp. 198–200), 3.11 (pp. 206–213), 3.15 (pp. 223–227), 3.16 (pp. 229–231), Embedded Assessment 2 (pp. 245–246);

	Standard Code	Standard	Where Addressed
Presentation of Knowledge and Ideas			Unit 4: Activity 4.3 (pp. 260–263), 4.4 (pp. 264–271), 4.5 (pp. 272–276), 4.7 (pp. 282–287), 4.9 (pp. 296–303), 4.10 (pp. 304–307), 4.15 (pp. 324–325), 4.16 (pp. 326–328), 4.18 (pp. 333–336)
		LANGUAGE	
Conventions of Standard English	L.8.1	Demonstrate command of the conventions of standard English grammar and usage when writing or speaking.	**Focus Standard:** Unit 4: Activity 4.4 (pp. 264–271) Unit 1: Activity 1.8 (pp. 41–46), 1.9 (p. 48), Embedded Assessment 1 (pp. 56–57), Embedded Assessment 2 (pp. 97–98), 1.12 (p. 65); Unit 2: Activity 2.3 (p. 117), Embedded Assessment 1 (pp. 137–138), Embedded Assessment 2 (pp. 167–168); Unit 4: Embedded Assessment 1 (pp. 315–316)
	L.8.1a	Explain the function of verbals (gerunds, participles, infinitives) in general and their function in particular sentences.	**Focus Standard:** Unit 4: Activity 4.4 (pp. 264–271) Unit 3: Activity 3.14 (pp. 221–222), 3.16 (pp. 229–231); Unit 4: Activity 4.2 (pp. 251–259), 4.8 (pp. 288–295), 4.9 (pp. 296–303), 4.10 (pp. 304–307), Embedded Assessment (pp. 315–316)
	L.8.1b	Form and use verbs in the active and passive voice.	**Focus Standard:** Unit 3: Activity 3.8 (pp. 195–197) Unit 2: Activity 2.3 (pp. 110–118), 2.7 (pp. 130–131), 2.9 (pp. 134–136), Embedded Assessment 1 (pp. 137–138), 2.13 (pp. 147–150), 2.17 (pp. 163–166); Unit 3: Activity 3.10 (pp. 201–205)
	L.8.1c	Form and use verbs in the indicative, imperative, interrogative, conditional, and subjunctive mood.	Unit 1: Activity 1.8 (pp. 41–46), Embedded Assessment 1 (pp. 56–57); Unit 2: Activity 2.2 (pp. 103–109), 2.5 (pp. 122–124), 2.9 (pp. 134–136), Embedded Assessment 1 (pp. 137–138), 2.17 (pp. 163–166); Unit 3: Activity 3.8 (pp. 195–197), 3.10 (pp. 201–205), 3.15 (pp. 223–227), Embedded Assessment 2 (pp. 245–246)
	L.8.1d	Recognize and correct inappropriate shifts in verb voice and mood.*	Unit 1: Activity 1.8 (pp. 41–46); Unit 2 Activity 2.17 (pp. 163–166); Unit 3: Activity 3.8 (pp. 195–197); Unit 4: Activity 4.6 (pp. 277–281)

	Standard Code	Standard	Where Addressed
Conventions of Standard English	L.8.2	Demonstrate command of the conventions of standard English capitalization, punctuation, and spelling when writing.	Unit 1: Activity 1.8 (pp. 41–46), Embedded Assessment 1 (pp. 56–57), Embedded Assessment 2 (pp. 97–98); Unit 2: Embedded Assessment 1 (pp. 137–138), Activity 2.13 (pp. 147–150), Embedded Assessment 2 (pp. 167–168); Unit 3: Activity 3.10 (pp. 201–205); Unit 4: Embedded Assessment (pp. 315–316)
	L.8.2a	Use punctuation (comma, ellipsis, dash) to indicate a pause or break.	Unit 1: Activity 1.5 (p. 15); Unit 2: Activity 2.3 (pp. 110–118); Unit 3: Activity 3.10 (pp. 201–205); Unit 4: Activity 4.14 (pp. 322– 23), Activity 4.14 (p. 325), 4.16 (pp. 326–328)
	L.8.2b	Use an ellipsis to indicate an omission.	Unit 2: Activity 2.3 (p. 117), 2.13 (pp. 147–150); Unit 3: Activity 3.10 (pp. 201–205)
	L.8.2c	Spell correctly.	Unit 1: Activity 1.8 (pp. 41–46), Embedded Assessment 1 (pp. 56–57), Embedded Assessment 2 (pp. 97–98); Unit 2: Embedded Assessment 1 (pp. 137–138), Embedded Assessment 2 (pp. 167–168); Unit 4: Embedded Assessment (pp. 315–316)
Knowledge of Language	L.8.3	Use knowledge of language and its conventions when writing, speaking, reading, or listening.	Unit 2: Activity 2.3 (pp. 110–118), 2.5 (pp. 122–124), 2.9 (pp. 134–136), Embedded Assessment 1 (pp. 137–138), 2.13 (pp. 147–150), 2.17 (pp. 163–166); Unit 3: Activity 3.8 (pp. 195–197), 3.10 (pp. 201–205), 3.15 (pp. 223–227), Embedded Assessment 2 (pp. 245–246)
	L.8.3a	Use verbs in the active and passive voice and in the conditional and subjunctive mood to achieve particular effects (e.g., emphasizing the actor or the action; expressing uncertainty or describing a state contrary to fact).	Unit 2: Activity 2.3 (pp. 110–118), 2.5 (pp. 122–124), 2.9 (pp. 134–136), Embedded Assessment 1 (pp. 137–138), 2.13 (pp. 147–150), 2.17 (pp. 163–166); Unit 3: Activity 3.8 (pp. 195–197), 3.10 (pp. 201–205), 3.15 (pp. 223–227), Embedded Assessment 2 (pp. 245–246)

	Standard Code	Standard	Where Addressed
Vocabulary Acquisition and Use	L.8.4	Determine or clarify the meaning of unknown and multiple-meaning words or phrases based on *grade 8 reading and content*, choosing flexibly from a range of strategies.	**Focus Standard:** Unit 3: Activity 3.6 (pp. 190–191); Unit 4: Activity 4.14 (pp. 322–323) Unit 1: Activity 1.6 (pp. 22–30), Activity 1.7 (pp. 31–40), 1.9 (pp. 47–55), 1.12 (pp. 62–68), 1.15 (pp. 84–87), 1.17 (pp. 90–96); Unit 2: Activity 2.2 (pp. 103–109), 2.3 (pp. 110–118), 2.7 (pp. 130–131), 2.6 (pp. 125–129), 2.7 (pp. 130–131), 2.8 (pp. 132–133), 2.9 (pp. 134–136); Unit 3: Activity 3.6 (pp. 190–191); Unit 4: Activity 4.7 (pp. 282–287), 4.15 (pp. 324–325), 4.16 (pp. 326–328), Embedded Assessment 2 (pp. 341–342)
	L.8.4a	Use context (e.g., the overall meaning of a sentence or paragraph; a word's position or function in a sentence) as a clue to the meaning of a word or phrase.	**Focus Standard:** Unit 4: Activity 4.14 (pp. 322–323) Unit 1: Activity 1.6 (pp. 22–30), 1.12 (pp. 62–68); Unit 2: Activity 2.6 (pp. 125–129), 2.7 (pp. 130–131), 2.8 (pp. 132–133), 2.9 (pp. 134–136); Unit 3: Activity 3.6 (pp. 190–191); Unit 4: Activity 4.7 (pp. 282–287), 4.15 (pp. 324–325), 4.16 (pp. 326–328)
	L.8.4b	Use common, grade-appropriate Greek or Latin affixes and roots as clues to the meaning of a word (e.g., *precede, recede, secede*).	Unit 1: Activity 1.7 (pp. 31–40), 1.9 (pp. 47–55), 1.15 (pp. 84–87), 1.17 (pp. 90–96); Unit 2: Activity 2.3 (pp. 110–118), 2.7 (pp. 130–131); Unit 3: Activity 3.2 (pp. 173–176), 3.4 (pp. 181–185), 3.6 (pp. 190–191), 3.8 (pp. 195–197); Unit 4: Activity 4.4 (pp. 264–271)
	L.8.4c	Consult general and specialized reference materials (e.g., dictionaries, glossaries, thesauruses), both print and digital, to find the pronunciation of a word or determine or clarify its precise meaning or its part of speech **or trace the etymology of words. CA**	**Focus Standard:** Unit 3: Activity 3.6 (pp. 190–191) Unit 1: Activity 1.6 (pp. 22–30), 1.11 (pp. 60–61); Unit 2: Activity 2.2 (pp. 103–109); Unit 4: Activity 4.15 (pp. 324–325), 4.16 (pp. 326–328), Embedded Assessment 2 (pp. 341–342)
	L.8.4d	Verify the preliminary determination of the meaning of a word or phrase (e.g., by checking the inferred meaning in context or in a dictionary).	Unit 1: Activity 1.11 (pp. 60–61); Unit 2: Activity 2.2 (pp. 103–109); Unit 3: Activity 3.6 (pp. 190–191); Unit 4: Activity 4.15 (pp. 324–325), 4.16 (pp. 326–328)
	L.8.5	Demonstrate understanding of figurative language, word relationships, and nuances in word meanings.	**Focus Standard:** Unit 4: Activity 4.9 (pp. 296–303), 4.10 (pp. 304–307) Unit 1: Activity 1.3 (pp. 8–10), 1.12 (p. 63), 1.13 (p. 74); Unit 4: Activity 4.2 (pp. 251–259), 4.4 (pp. 264–271)

	Standard Code	Standard	Where Addressed
Vocabulary Acquisition and Use	L.8.5a	Interpret figures of speech (e.g. verbal irony, puns) in context.	**Focus Standard:** Unit 4: Activity 4.9 (pp. 296–303), 4.10 (pp. 304–307) Unit 1: Activity 1.12 (pp. 62–68), 1.14 (pp. 75–83); Unit 2: Activity 2.2 (pp. 103–109), 2.3 (pp. 110–118); Unit 3: Activity 3.2 (pp. 173–176); Unit 4: Activity 4.5 (pp. 272–276), 4.6 (pp. 277–281), 4.8 (pp. 288–295), 4.11 (pp. 308–314), Embedded Assessment (pp. 315–316), 4.16 (pp. 326–328), Embedded Assessment 2 (pp. 341–342)
	L.8.5b	Use the relationship between particular words to better understand each of the words.	**Focus Standard:** Unit 1: Activity 1.11 (pp. 60–61) Unit 1: Activity 1.14 (pp. 75–83); Unit 2: Activity 2.2 (pp. 103–109); Unit 3: Activity 3.2 (pp. 173–176), 3.13 (pp. 219–220); Unit 4: Activity 4.2 (pp. 251–259), 4.6 (pp. 277–281)
	L.8.5c	Distinguish among the connotations (associations) of words with similar denotations (definitions) (e.g., *bullheaded, willful, firm, persistent, resolute*).	**Focus Standard:** Unit 1: Activity 1.11 (pp. 60–61); Unit 4: Activity 4.2 (pp. 251–259) Unit 1: Activity 1.13 (pp. 69–74), 1.14 (pp. 75–83); Unit 2: Activity 2.2 (pp. 103–109); Unit 3: Activity 3.6 (pp. 190–191); Unit 4: Activity 4.6 (pp. 277–281)
Vocabulary Acquisition and Use	L.8.6	Acquire and use accurately grade-appropriate general academic and domain-specific words and phrases; gather vocabulary knowledge when considering a word or phrase important to comprehension or expression.	**Focus Standard:** Unit 1: Activity 1.1 (p. 4), 1.4 (pp. 11–14), 1.10 (pp. 58–59), 1.13 (pp. 69–74); Unit 2: Activity 2.1 (pp. 102), 2.10 (139–140); Unit 3: Activity 3.1 (p. 172), 3.13 (pp. 219–220); Unit 4: Activity 4.1 (p. 250), 4.3 (pp. 260–263), 4.12 (pp. 317–318) Unit 1: Activity 1.3 (pp. 8–10), 1.5 (pp. 15–21), 1.7 (pp. 31–40), 1.9 (pp. 47–55), 1.11 (pp. 60–61), 1.12 (pp. 62–68), 1.14 (pp. 75–83), 1.15 (pp. 84–87), 1.17 (pp. 90–96); Unit 2: Activity 2.2 (pp. 103–109), 2.3 (pp. 110–118), 2.4 (pp. 119–121), 2.5 (pp. 122–124), 2.6 (pp. 125–129), 2.12 (pp. 144–146), 2.13 (pp. 147–150), 2.14 (pp. 151–152), 2.15 (pp. 153–158), 2.16 (pp. 159–162), 2.17 (pp. 163–166); Unit 3: Activity 3.2 (pp. 173–176), 3.3 (pp. 177–180), 3.4 (pp. 181–185), 3.5 (pp. 186–189), 3.6 (pp. 190–191), 3.8 (pp. 195–197), 3.10 (pp. 201–205), 3.12 (pp. 214–216), 3.14 (pp. 221–222), 3.15 (pp. 223–227), 3.16 (pp. 229–231), 3.18 (pp. 237–239), 3.19 (pp. 240–244); Unit 4: Activity 4.2 (pp. 251–259), 4.4 (pp. 264–271), 4.6 (pp. 277–281), 4.7 (pp. 282–287), 4.8 (pp. 288–295), 4.9 (pp. 296–303), 4.10 (pp. 304–307), 4.13 (pp. 319–321), 4.14 (pp. 322–323), 4.15 (pp. 324–325)

Independent Reading Log

NAME ____________________ DATE ____________

Directions: This log is a place to record your progress and thinking about your independent reading during each unit. Add your log pages to your Reader/Writer Notebook or keep them as a separate place to record your reading insights.

Unit ____________________

Independent Reading Title ____________________

Author(s) ____________________ Text Type ____________

Pages read: from ________ to ________

Independent Reading Title ____________________

Author(s) ____________________ Text Type ____________

Pages read: from ________ to ________

Independent Reading Title ____________________

Author(s) ____________________ Text Type ____________

Pages read: from ________ to ________

Unit

Independent Reading Title

Author(s) Text Type

Pages read: from to

Independent Reading Title

Author(s) Text Type

Pages read: from to

Independent Reading Title

Author(s) Text Type

Pages read: from to

Independent Reading Title

Author(s) Text Type

Pages read: from to

SpringBoard Learning Strategies

READING STRATEGIES

STRATEGY	DEFINITION	PURPOSE
Chunking the Text	Breaking the text into smaller, manageable units of sense (e.g., words, sentences, paragraphs, whole text) by numbering, separating phrases, drawing boxes	To reduce the intimidation factor when encountering long words, sentences, or whole texts; to increase comprehension of difficult or challenging text
Close Reading	Accessing small chunks of text to read, reread, mark, and annotate key passages, word-for-word, sentence-by-sentence, and line-by-line	To develop comprehensive understanding by engaging in one or more focused readings of a text
Diffusing	Reading a passage, noting unfamiliar words, discovering meaning of unfamiliar words using context clues, dictionaries, and/or thesauruses, and replacing unfamiliar words with familiar ones	To facilitate a close reading of text, the use of resources, an understanding of synonyms, and increased comprehension of text
Double-Entry Journal	Creating a two-column journal (also called Dialectical Journal) with a student-selected passage in one column and the student's response in the second column (e.g., asking questions of the text, forming personal responses, interpreting the text, reflecting on the process of making meaning of the text)	To assist in note-taking and organizing key textual elements and responses noted during reading in order to generate textual support that can be incorporated into a piece of writing at a later time
Graphic Organizer	Using a visual representation for the organization of information from the text	To facilitate increased comprehension and discussion
KWHL Chart	Setting up discussion that allows students to activate prior knowledge by answering "What do I know?"; sets a purpose by answering "What do I want to know?"; helps preview a task by answering "How will I learn it?"; and reflects on new knowledge by answering "What have I learned?"	To organize thinking, access prior knowledge, and reflect on learning to increase comprehension and engagement
Marking the Text	Selecting text by highlighting, underlining, and/or annotating for specific components, such as main idea, imagery, literary devices, and so on	To focus reading for specific purposes, such as author's craft, and to organize information from selections; to facilitate reexamination of a text
Metacognitive Markers	Responding to text with a system of cueing marks where students use a ? for questions about the text; a ! for reactions related to the text; and an * for comments ,about the text and underline to signal key ideas	To track responses to texts and use those responses as a point of departure for talking or writing about texts
OPTIC	**O** (Overview): Write notes on what the visual appears to be about. **P** (Parts): Zoom in on the parts of the visual and describe any elements or details that seem important. **T** (Title): Highlight the words of the title of the visual (if one is available). **I** (Interrelationships): Use the title as the theory and the parts of the visual as clues to detect and specify how the elements of the graphic are related.	To analyze graphic and visual images as forms of text

STRATEGY	DEFINITION	PURPOSE
OPTIC (continued)	**C** (Conclusion); Draw a conclusion about the visual as a whole. What does the visual mean? Summarize the message of the visual in one or two sentences.	
Predicting	Making guesses about the text by using the title and pictures and/or thinking ahead about events which may occur based on evidence in the text	To help students become actively involved, interested, and mentally prepared to understand ideas
Previewing	Making guesses about the text by using the title and pictures and/or thinking ahead about events which may occur based on evidence in the text	To gain familiarity with the text, make connections to the text, and extend prior knowledge to set a purpose for reading
QHT	Expanding prior knowledge of vocabulary words by marking words with a Q, H, or T (Q signals words students do not know; H signals words students have heard and might be able to identify; T signals words students know well enough to teach to their peers)	To allow students to build on their prior knowledge of words, to provide a forum for peer teaching and learning of new words, and to serve as a prereading exercise to aid in comprehension
Questioning the Text* The AP Vertical Teams Guide for English (109–112)	Developing levels of questions about text; that is, literal, interpretive, and universal questions that prompt deeper thinking about a text	To engage more actively with texts, read with greater purpose and focus, and ultimately answer questions to gain greater insight into the text; helps students to comprehend and interpret
Paraphrasing	Restating in one's own words the essential information expressed in a text, whether it be narration, dialogue, or informational text	To encourage and facilitate comprehension of challenging text.
RAFT	Primarily used to generate new text, this strategy can also be used to analyze a text by examining the role of the speaker (R), the intended audience (A), the format of the text (F), and the topic of the text (T).	To initiate reader response; to facilitate an analysis of a text to gain focus prior to creating a new text
Rereading	Encountering the same text with more than one reading.	To identify additional details; to clarify meaning and/or reinforce comprehension of texts
SIFT* The AP Vertical Teams Guide for English (17–20)	Analyzing a fictional text by examining stylistic elements, especially symbol, imagery, and figures of speech in order to show how all work together to reveal tone and theme	To focus and facilitate an analysis of a fictional text by examining the title and text for symbolism, identifying images and sensory details, analyzing figurative language and identifying how all these elements reveal tone and theme
Skimming/Scanning	Skimming by rapid or superficial reading of a text to form an overall impression or to obtain a general understanding of the material; scanning focuses on key words, phrases, or specific details and provides speedy recognition of information	To quickly form an overall impression prior to an in-depth study of a text; to answer specific questions or quickly locate targeted information or detail in a text
SMELL* The AP Vertical Teams Guide for English (138–139)	• Sender-receiver relationship—What is the sender-receiver relationship? Who are the images and language meant to attract? Describe the speaker of the text. • Message—What is the message? Summarize the statement made in the text.	To analyze a persuasive speech or essay by focusing on five essential questions

STRATEGY	DEFINITION	PURPOSE
SMELL* (continued)	• Emotional Strategies—What is the desired effect? • Logical Strategies—What logic is operating? How does it (or its absence) affect the message? Consider the logic of the images as well as the words. • Language—What does the language of the text describe? How does it affect the meaning and effectiveness of the writing? Consider the language of the images as well as the words.	
SOAPSTone*	Analyzing text by discussing and identifying Speaker, Occasion, Audience, Purpose, Subject, and Tone	To facilitate the analysis of specific elements of non-fiction literary and informational texts and show the relationship among the elements to an understanding of the whole
Summarizing	Giving a brief statement of the main points or essential information expressed in a text, whether it be narration, dialogue, or informational text	To facilitate comprehension and recall of a text
Think Aloud	Talking through a difficult passage or task by using a form of metacognition whereby the reader expresses how he/she has made sense of the text	To reflect on how readers make meaning of challenging texts and facilitate comprehension
TP-CASTT* The AP Vertical Teams Guide for English (94–99)	Analyzing a poetic text by identifying and discussing Title, Paraphrase, Connotation, Attitude, Shift, Theme, and Title again	To facilitate the analysis of specific elements of a literary text, especially poetry. To show how the elements work together to create meaning
Visualizing	Forming a picture (mentally and/or literally) while reading a text	To increase reading comprehension and promote active engagement with text
Word Maps	Using a clearly defined graphic organizer such as concept circles or word webs to identify and reinforce word meanings	To provide a visual tool for identifying and remembering multiple aspects of words and word meanings

***Delineates AP strategy**

WRITING STRATEGIES

STRATEGY	DEFINITION	PURPOSE
Adding	Making conscious choices to enhance a text by adding additional words, phrases, sentences, or ideas	To refine and clarify the writer's thoughts during revision and/or drafting
Brainstorming	Using a flexible but deliberate process of listing multiple ideas in a short period of time without excluding any idea from the preliminary list	To generate ideas, concepts, or key words that provide a focus and/or establish organization as part of the prewriting or revision process
Deleting	Providing clarity and cohesiveness for a text by eliminating words, phrases, sentences, or ideas	To refine and clarify the writer's thoughts during revision and/or drafting
Drafting	Composing a text in its initial form	To incorporate brainstormed or initial ideas into a written format

STRATEGY	DEFINITION	PURPOSE
Free writing	Write freely without constraints in order to capture thinking and convey the writer's purpose	To refine and clarify the writer's thoughts, spark new ideas, and/or generate content during revision and/or drafting
Generating Questions	Clarifying and developing ideas by asking questions of the draft. May be part of self-editing or peer editing	To clarify and develop ideas in a draft; used during drafting and as part of writer response
Graphic Organizer	Organizing ideas and information visually (e.g., Venn diagrams, flowcharts, cluster maps)	To provide a visual system for organizing multiple ideas, details, and/or textual support to be included in a piece of writing
Looping	After free writing, one section of a text is circled to promote elaboration or the generation of new ideas for that section. This process is repeated to further develop ideas from the newly generated segments	To refine and clarify the writer's thoughts, spark new ideas, and/or generate new content during revision and/or drafting
Mapping	Creating a graphic organizer that serves as a visual representation of the organizational plan for a written text	To generate ideas, concepts, or key words that provide a focus and/or establish organization during the prewriting, drafting, or revision process
Marking the Draft	Interacting with the draft version of a piece of writing by highlighting, underlining, color-coding, and annotating to indicate revision ideas	To encourage focused, reflective thinking about revising drafts
Note-taking	Making notes about ideas in response to text or discussions; one form is the double-entry journal in which textual evidence is recorded on the left side and personal commentary about the meaning of the evidence on the other side.	To assist in organizing key textual elements and responses noted during reading in order to generate textual support that can be incorporated into a piece of writing at a later time. Note-taking is also a reading and listening strategy.
Outlining	Using a system of numerals and letters in order to identify topics and supporting details and ensure an appropriate balance of ideas.	To generate ideas, concepts, or key words that provide a focus and/or establish organization prior to writing an initial draft and/or during the revision process
Quickwrite	Writing for a short, specific amount of time in response to a prompt provided	To generate multiple ideas in a quick fashion that could be turned into longer pieces of writing at a later time (May be considered as part of the drafting process)
RAFT	Generating a new text and/or transforming a text by identifying and manipulating its component parts of Role, Audience, Format, and Topic	To generate a new text by identifying the main elements of a text during the prewriting and drafting stages of the writing process
Rearranging	Selecting components of a text and moving them to another place within the text and/or modifying the order in which the author's ideas are presented	To refine and clarify the writer's thoughts during revision and/or drafting
Self-Editing/Peer Editing	Working individually or with a partner to examine a text closely in order to identify areas that might need to be corrected for grammar, punctuation, spelling	To facilitate a collaborative approach to generating ideas for and revising writing.

STRATEGY	DEFINITION	PURPOSE
Sharing and Responding	Communicating with another person or a small group of peers who respond to a piece of writing as focused readers (not necessarily as evaluators)	To make suggestions for improvement to the work of others and/or to receive appropriate and relevant feedback on the writer's own work, used during the drafting and revision process
Sketching	Drawing or sketching ideas or ordering of ideas. Includes storyboarding, visualizing	To generate and/or clarify ideas by visualizing them. May be part of prewriting
Substituting / Replacing	Replacing original words or phrases in a text with new words or phrases that achieve the desired effect	To refine and clarify the writer's thoughts during revision and/or drafting
TWIST* The AP Vertical Teams Guide for English 167–174	Arriving at a thesis statement that incorporates the following literary elements: tone, word choice (diction), imagery, style and theme	To craft an interpretive thesis in response to a prompt about a text
Webbing	Developing a graphic organizer that consists of a series of circles connected with lines to indicate relationships among ideas	To generate ideas, concepts, or key words that provide a focus and/or establish organization prior to writing an initial draft and/or during the revision process
Writer's Checklist	Using a co-constructed checklist (that could be written on a bookmark and/or displayed on the wall) in order to look for specific features of a writing text and check for accuracy	To focus on key areas of the writing process so that the writer can effectively revise a draft and correct mistake
Writing Groups	A type of discussion group devoted to sharing and responding of student work	To facilitate a collaborative approach to generating ideas for and revising writing.

SPEAKING AND LISTENING STRATEGIES

STRATEGY	DEFINITION	PURPOSE
Choral Reading	Reading text lines aloud in student groups and/or individually to present an interpretation	To develop fluency; differentiate between the reading of statements and questions; practice phrasing, pacing, and reading dialogue; show how a character's emotions are captured through vocal stress and intonation
Note-taking	Creating a record of information while listening to a speaker or reading a text	To facilitate active listening or close reading ; to record and organize ideas that assist in processing information
Oral Reading	Reading aloud one's own text or the texts of others (e.g., echo reading, choral reading, paired readings)	To share one's own work or the work of others; build fluency and increase confidence in presenting to a group
Rehearsal	Encouraging multiple practices of a piece of text prior to a performance	To provide students with an opportunity to clarify the meaning of a text prior to a performance as they refine the use of dramatic conventions (e.g., gestures, vocal interpretations, facial expressions)
Role Playing	Assuming the role or persona of a character	To develop the voice, emotions, and mannerisms of a character to facilitate improved comprehension of a text

COLLABORATIVE STRATEGIES

STRATEGY	DEFINITION	PURPOSE
Discussion Groups	Engaging in an interactive, small group discussion, often with an assigned role; to consider a topic, text or question	To gain new understanding of or insight into a text from multiple perspectives
Think-Pair-Share	Pairing with a peer to share ideas; before sharing ideas and discussion with a larger group	To construct meaning about a topic or question; to test thinking in relation to the ideas of others; to prepare for a discussion with a larger group

Web Organizer

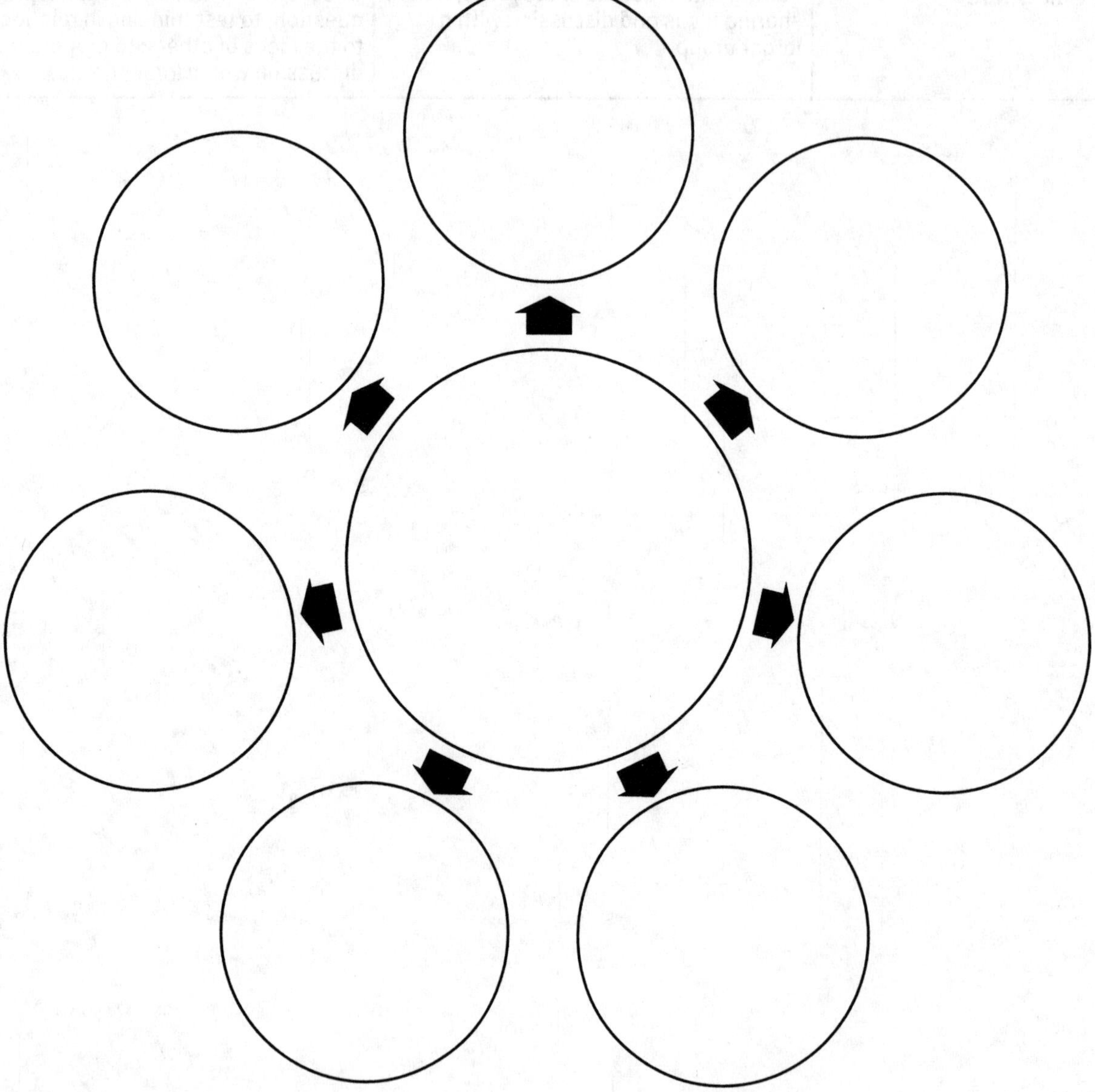

Word Map

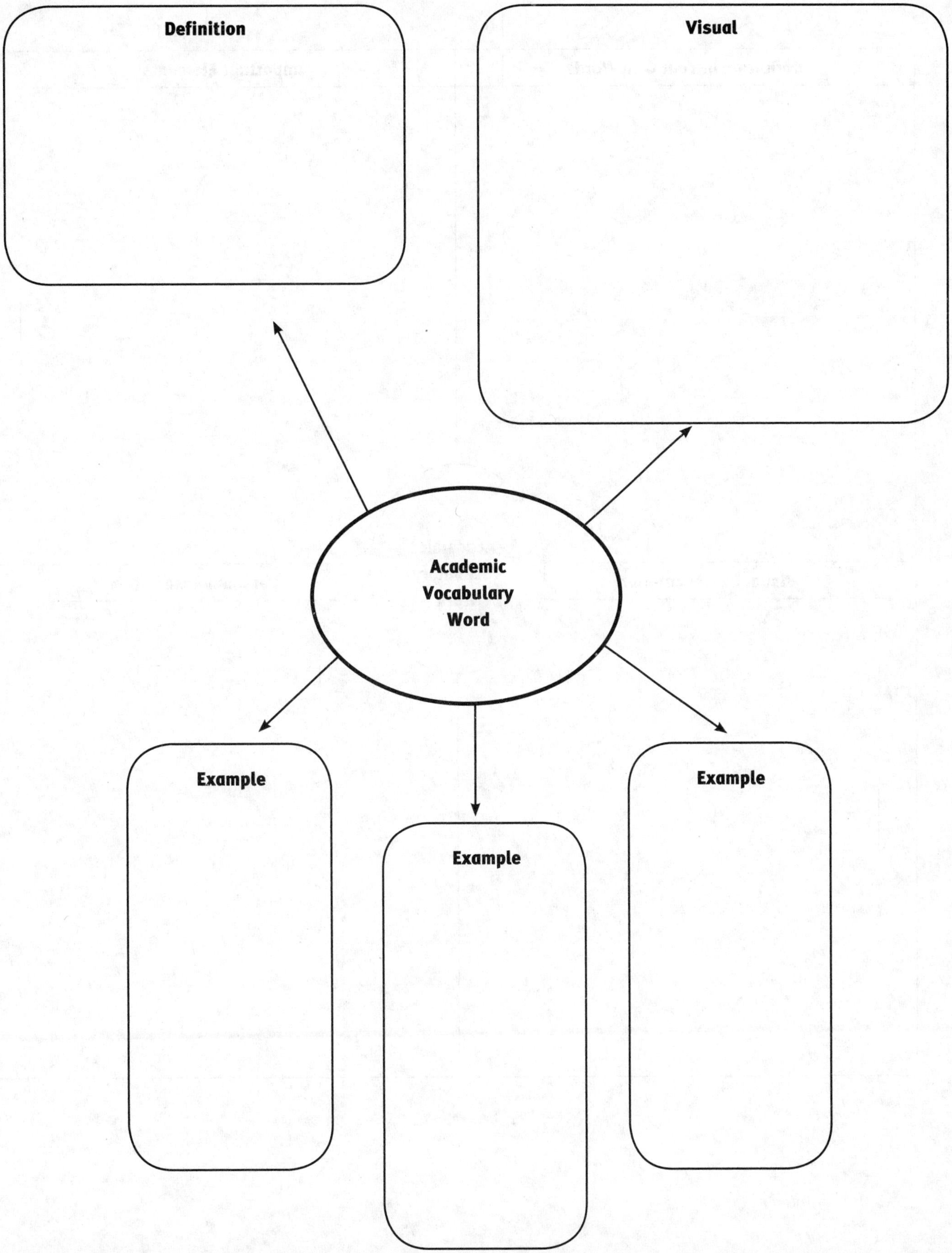
Definition
Visual
Academic
Vocabulary
Word
Example
Example
Example

Verbal & Visual Word Association

Definition in Your Own Words	Important Elements
Visual Representation	**Personal Association**

Academic Vocabulary Word

Academic Vocabulary Tree

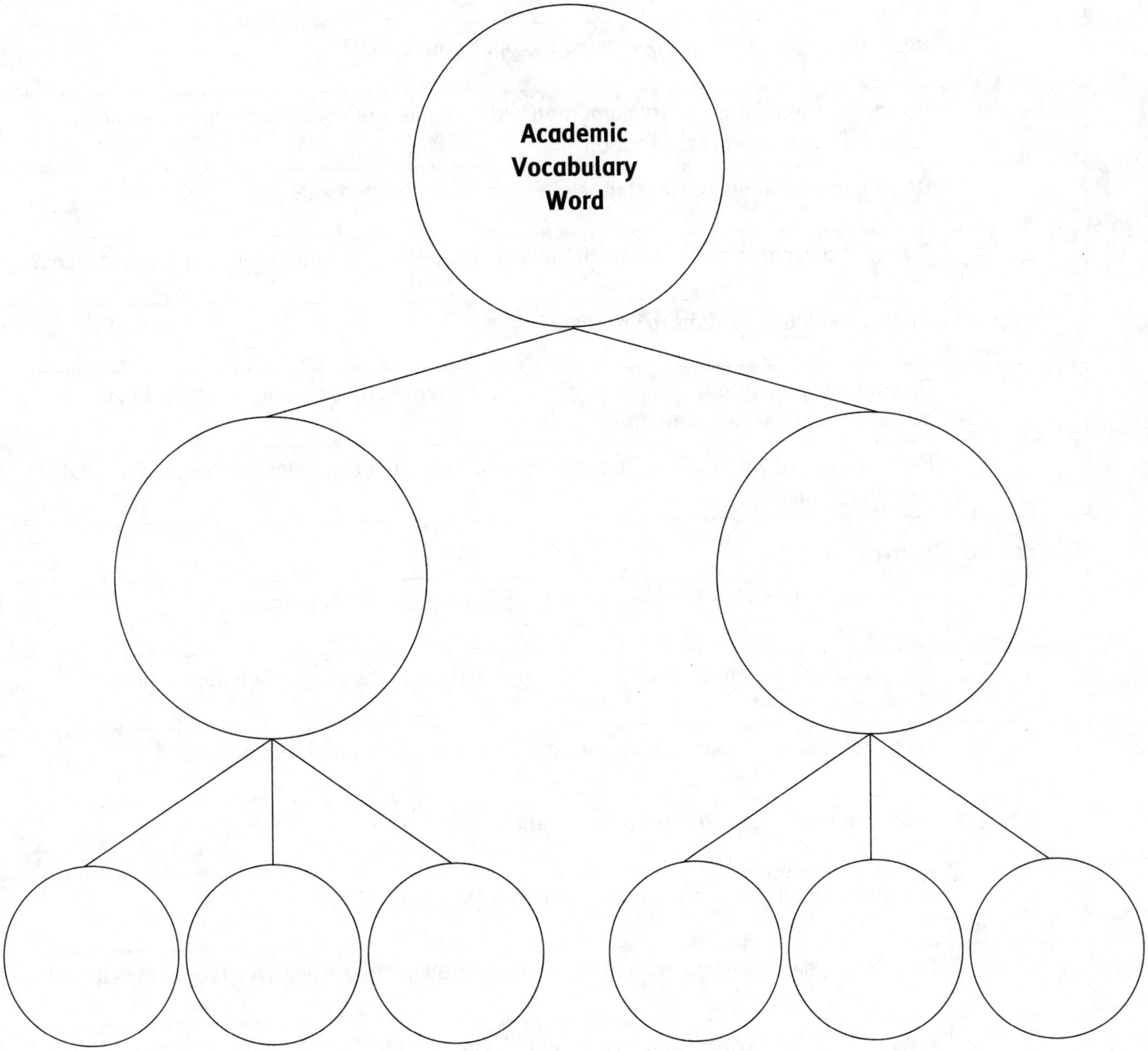

Editor's / Writer's Checklist

Organizational Elements

	Does your title express the topic and engage the reader?
	Do you have an engaging hook or lead to open your essay?
	Do you end your introductory paragraph with a thesis statement that states an opinion on a topic and suggests an organization?
	Do you have topic sentences that relate to the thesis statement?
	Do your body paragraphs contain detail and commentary to support your topic sentences?
	Do you include transitions to link ideas?
	Do your body paragraphs contain concluding sentences that also act as transitional statements to the next paragraph?
	Have you ended your essay with a strong conclusion that comments on the significance of your thesis ideas?

Sentence Elements

	Have you revised to make sure all sentences are complete sentences?
	Do your sentences contain vivid verbs and descriptive adjectives when appropriate?
	Is the verb tense of your writing consistent? Do the subject and verb agree?
	Is pronoun use appropriate and consistent?
	Is parallel structure used to advantage and when appropriate?
	Do you vary sentence beginnings? Have you started sentences with a subordinate clause?
	Are your sentence types (simple, compound, complex) and lengths varied for interest and emphasis?
	Have you tried to include figurative and sensory language for effect?
	Have you used appositives when appropriate?
	Have you checked punctuation use for correctness, especially for appositives, complex sentences and parallel structure?
	Have you incorporated and punctuated quoted material correctly?

Double-Entry Journal Graphic Organizer

Passage from Text	Page #	Personal Response/Commentary

Venn Diagram

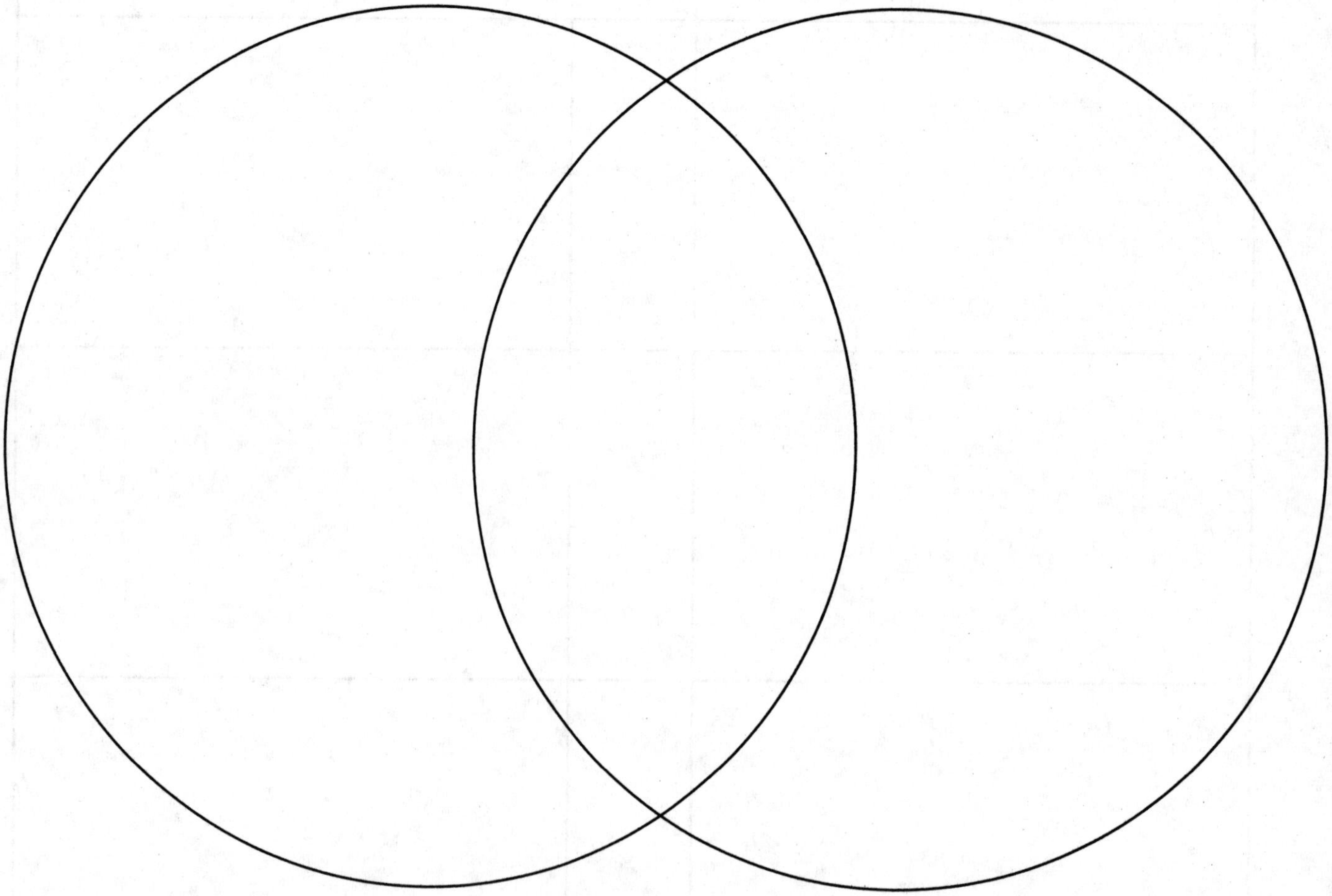

Evaluating Online Sources

The URL
What is its domain?

- .com = a for-profit organization
- .gov, .mil, .us (or other country code) = a government site
- .edu = an educational institution
- .org = a nonprofit organization

- Is this URL someone's personal page?
- Why might using information from a personal page be a problem?
- Do you recognize who is publishing this page?
- If not, you may need to investigate further to determine whether the publisher is an expert on the topic.

Sponsor:

- Does the web site easily give information about the organization or group that sponsors it?
- Does it have a link (often called "About Us") that leads you to that information?
- What do you learn?

Timeliness:

- When was the page last updated (usually this is posted at the top or bottom of the page)?
- How current a page is may indicate how accurate or useful the information in it will be.

Purpose:

- What is the purpose of the page?
- What is its target audience?
- Does it present information or opinion?
- Is it primarily objective or subjective?
- How do you know?

Author:

- What credentials does the author have?
- Is this person or group considered an authority on the topic?

Links

- Does the page provide links?
- Do they work?
- Are they helpful?
- Are they objective or subjective?

SOAPSTone:

SOAPSTone	Analysis	Textual Support
Speaker: What does the reader know about the writer?		
Occasion: What are the circumstances surrounding this text?		
Audience: Who is the target audience?		
Purpose: Why did the author write this text?		
Subject: What is the topic?		
Tone: What is the author's tone, or attitude?		

TP-CASTT Analysis

Poem Title:

Author:

Title: Make a Prediction. What do you think the title means before you read the poem?

Paraphrase: Translate the poem in your own words. What is the poem about? Rephrase difficult sections word for word.

Connotation: Look beyond the literal meaning of key words and images to their associations.

Attitude: What is the speaker's attitude? What is the author's attitude? How does the author feel about the speaker, about other characters, about the subject?

Shifts: Where do the shifts in tone, setting, voice, etc., occur? Look for time and place, keywords, punctuation, stanza divisions, changes in length or rhyme, and sentence structure. What is the purpose of each shift? How do they contribute to effect and meaning?

Title: Reexamine the title. What do you think it means now in the context of the poem?

Theme: Think of the literal and metaphorical layers of the poem. Then determine the overall theme. The theme must be written in a complete sentence.

TP-CASTT

Poem Title:

Author:

T		
P		
C		
A		
S		
T		
T		

NAME ______________________ DATE ____________

Active Listening Feedback

Presenter's name: ______________________

Content

What is the presenter's purpose? ______________________

What is the presenter's main point? ______________________

Do you agree with the presenter? Why or why not? ______________________

____

____

Form

Did the presenter use a clear, loud voice? ☐ yes ☐ no Did the presenter make eye contact? ☐ yes ☐ no

One thing I really liked about the presentation:

____

____

____

One question I still have:

____

____

____

Other comments or notes:

NAME ______________________________ DATE ______________

Active Listening Notes

Title: ______________________________

Who?

What?

Where?

When?

Why?

How?

NAME ______________________________ DATE ______________

Cause and Effect

Title: ______________________________

Cause	Effect
Cause: What happened?	**Effect:** An effect of this is
Cause: What happened?	**Effect:** An effect of this is
Cause: What happened?	**Effect:** An effect of this is
Cause: What happened?	**Effect:** An effect of this is

NAME ________________________________ DATE ____________

Character Map

Character name: ________________________________

What does the character look like?

How does the character act?

What do other characters say or think about the character?

NAME ______________________________ DATE ______________

Collaborative Dialogue

Topic: ____

"Wh-" Prompts

Who? What? Where?

When? Why?

Speaker 1

Speaker 2

NAME ______________________________ **DATE** __________

Conclusion Builder

Evidence

Evidence

Evidence

Based on this evidence, I can conclude

NAME ______________________________ DATE ______________

Conflict Map

Title: ______________________________

What is the main conflict in this story?

What causes this conflict?

How is the conflict resolved?

What are some other ways the conflict could have been resolved?

NAME ______________________________ DATE ______________

Conversation for Quickwrite

1. Turn to a partner and restate the Quickwrite in your own words.

2. Brainstorm key words to use in your Quickwrite response.

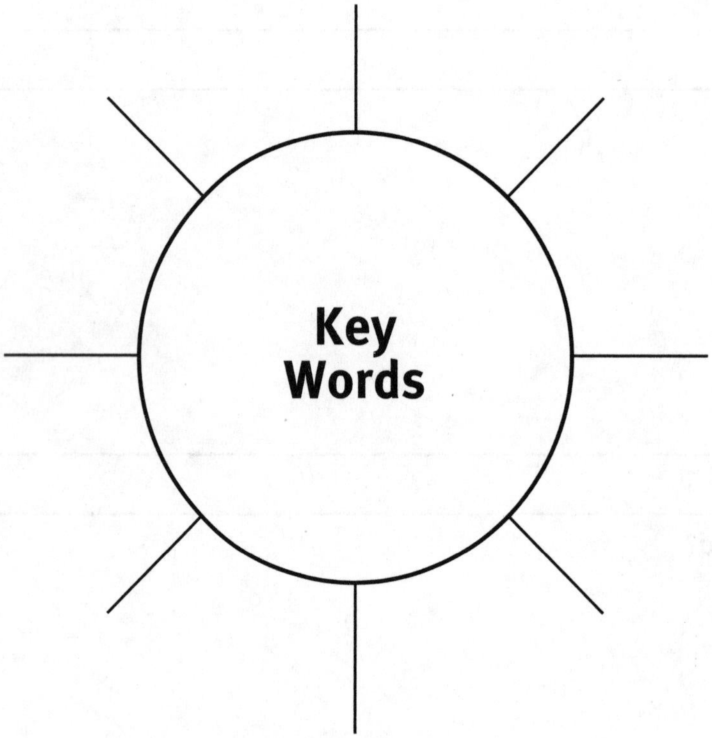

3. Take turns explaining your Quickwrite response to your partner. Try using some of the key words.

4. On your own, write a response to the Quickwrite.

NAME ______________________________ DATE ______________

Idea and Argument Evaluator

What is the author's idea or argument?

Supporting Idea from the Text

Does the author give a reason?

❑ yes

❑ no

Supporting Idea from the Text

Does the author give a reason?

❑ yes

❑ no

Supporting Idea from the Text

Does the author give a reason?

❑ yes

❑ no

NAME ______________________________ DATE ______________

Idea Connector

Directions: Write two simple sentences about the same topic. Next, write transition words around the Idea Connector. Then, choose an appropriate word to connect ideas in the two sentences. Write your combined sentence in the space below.

Sentence One

Sentence Two

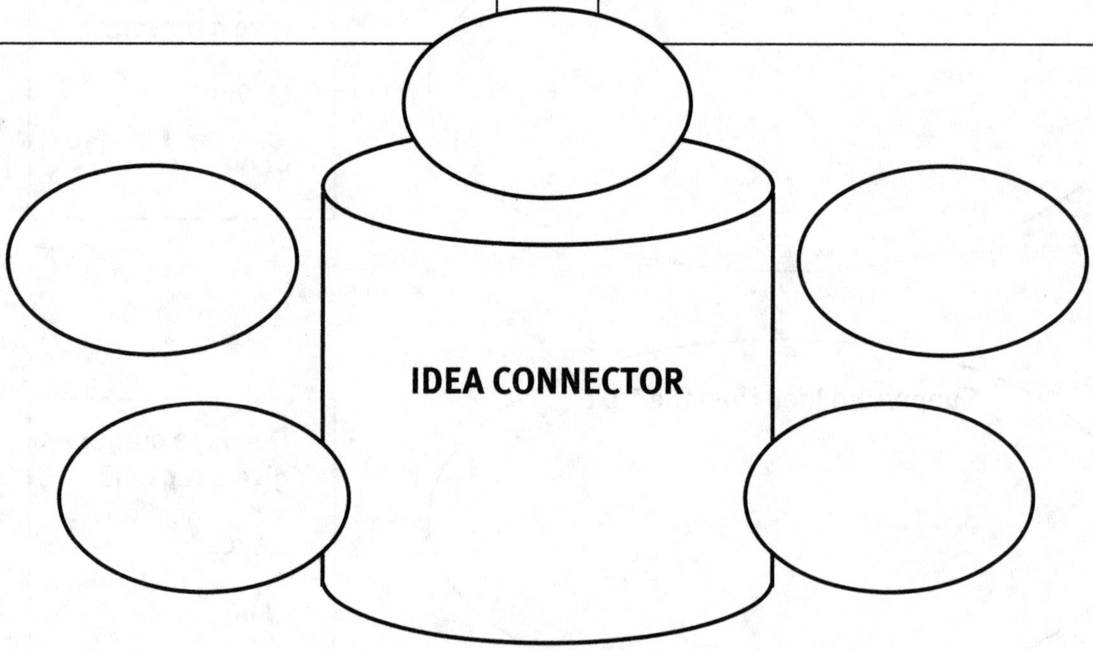

Combined Sentence

NAME ______________________________ DATE ______________

Key Idea and Details Chart

Title/Topic ______________________________

Key Idea ______________________________

____

____

Supporting Detail 1 ______________________________

____

____

Supporting Detail 2 ______________________________

____

____

Supporting Detail 3 ______________________________

____

____

Supporting Detail 4 ______________________________

____

____

Restate topic sentence. ______________________________

____

Concluding sentence. ______________________________

____

____

NAME ____________________ DATE ____________

Narrative Analysis and Writing

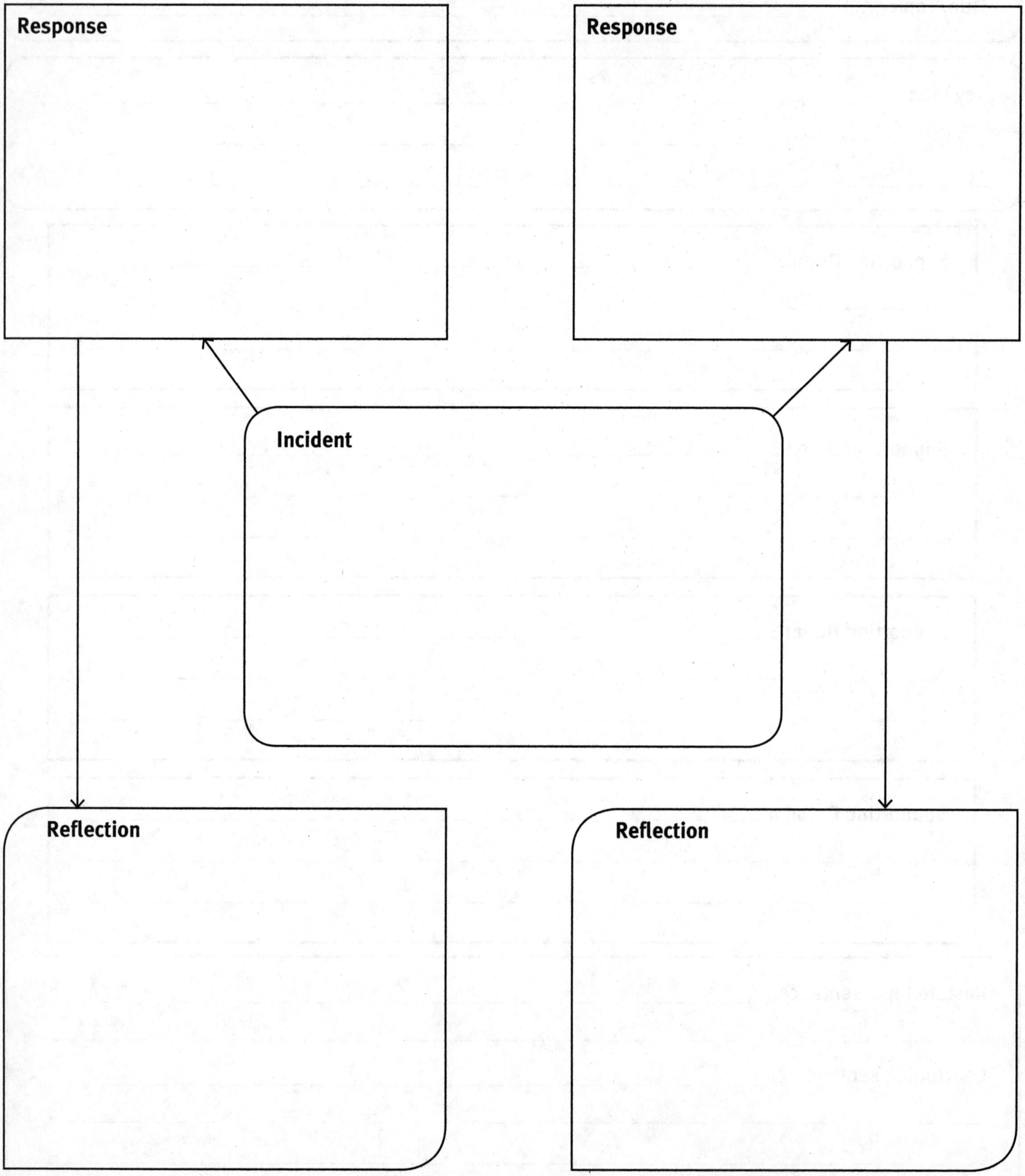

NAME ______________________ **DATE** ______________

Notes for Reading Independently

Title: ______________________________

The main characters are

The setting is

The main conflict is

The climax happens when

The conflict is resolved when

My brief summary of ______________________________

NAME ____________________ DATE __________

Opinion Builder

Reason

Reason

Based on these reasons, my opinion is

Reason

Reason

NAME ______________________________ DATE ______________

Paragraph Frame for Conclusions

Conclusion Words and Phrases

shows that

based on

suggests that

leads to

indicates that

influences

The ____________ *(story, poem, play, passage, etc.)* shows that *(helps us to conclude that)* ______________________________

____

____

There are several reasons why. First, ______________________________

____

____

____

____

A second reason is ______________________________

____

____

____

____

Finally, ______________________________

____

____

____

____

In conclusion, ______________________________

____

____

____

____

NAME ______________________ DATE ____________

Paragraph Frame for Sequencing

Sequence Words and Phrases

at the beginning

in the first place

as a result

later

eventually

in the end

lastly

In the ____________ *(story, poem, play, passage, etc.)* there are three important ______________________ *(events, steps, directions, etc.)*

First, ______________________

Second, ______________________

Third, ______________________

Finally, ______________________

NAME ______________________ DATE ____________

Paraphrasing Map

What does ______________ say?	How can I say it in my own words?	What questions or response do I have?

NAME ______________________________ DATE __________

Peer Editing

Writer's name: ______________________________

Did the writer answer the prompt? ☐ yes ☐ no

Did the writer provide evidence to support his or her reasons? ☐ yes ☐ no

Is the writing organized in a way that makes sense? ☐ yes ☐ no

Did the writer vary sentence structures to make the writing more interesting? ☐ yes ☐ no

Are there any spelling or punctuation mistakes? ☐ yes ☐ no

Are there any grammar errors? ☐ yes ☐ no

Two things I really liked about the writer's story:

1. ______________________________

2. ______________________________

One thing I think the writer could do to improve the writing:

1. ______________________________

Other comments or notes:

NAME ______________________________ DATE ______________

Persuasive/Argument Writing Map

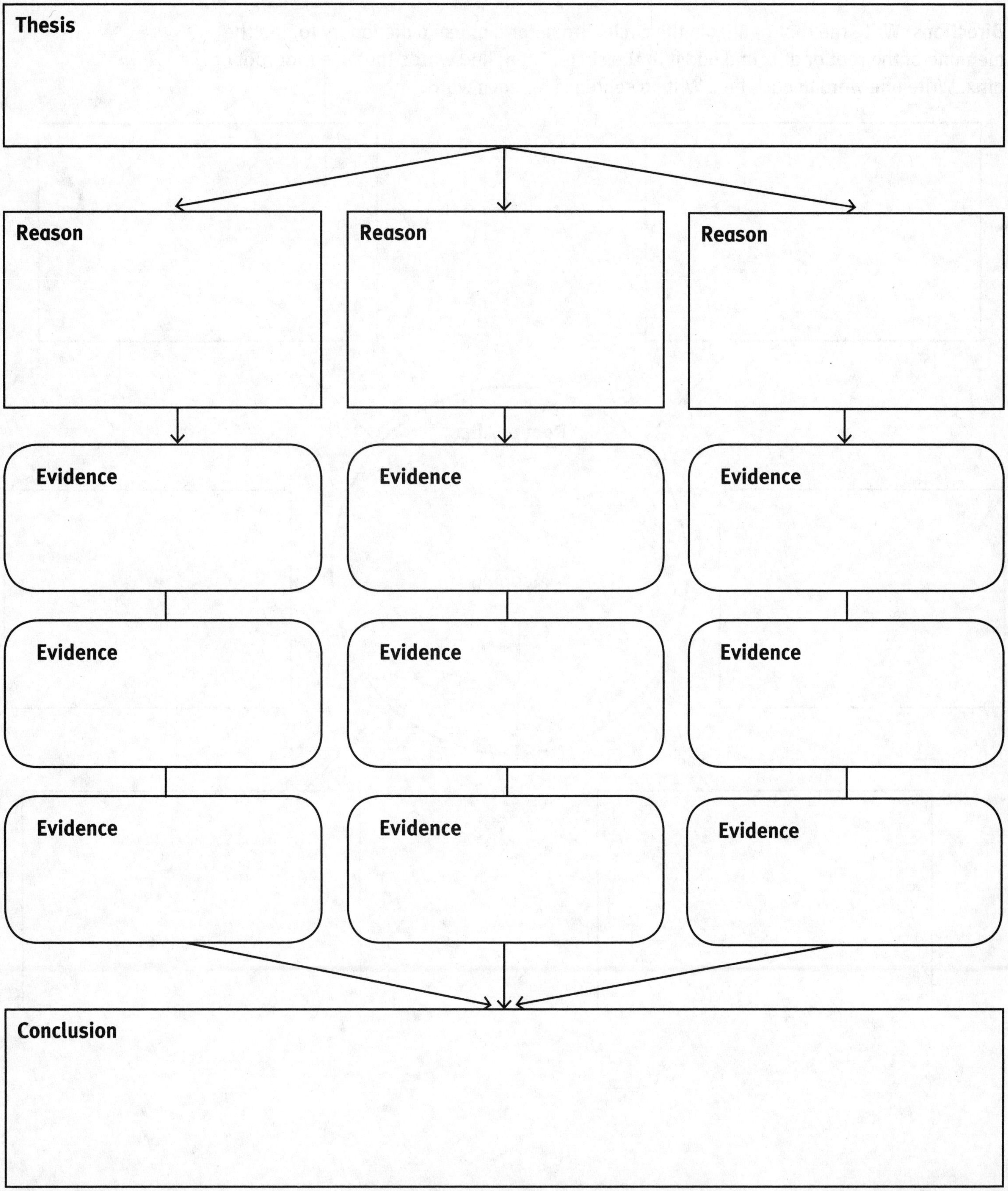

NAME ______________________ DATE ____________

Roots and Affixes Brainstorm

Directions: Write the root or affix in the circle. Brainstorm or use a dictionary to find the meaning of the root or affix and add it to the circle. Then, find words that use that root or affix. Write one word in each box. Write a sentence for each word.

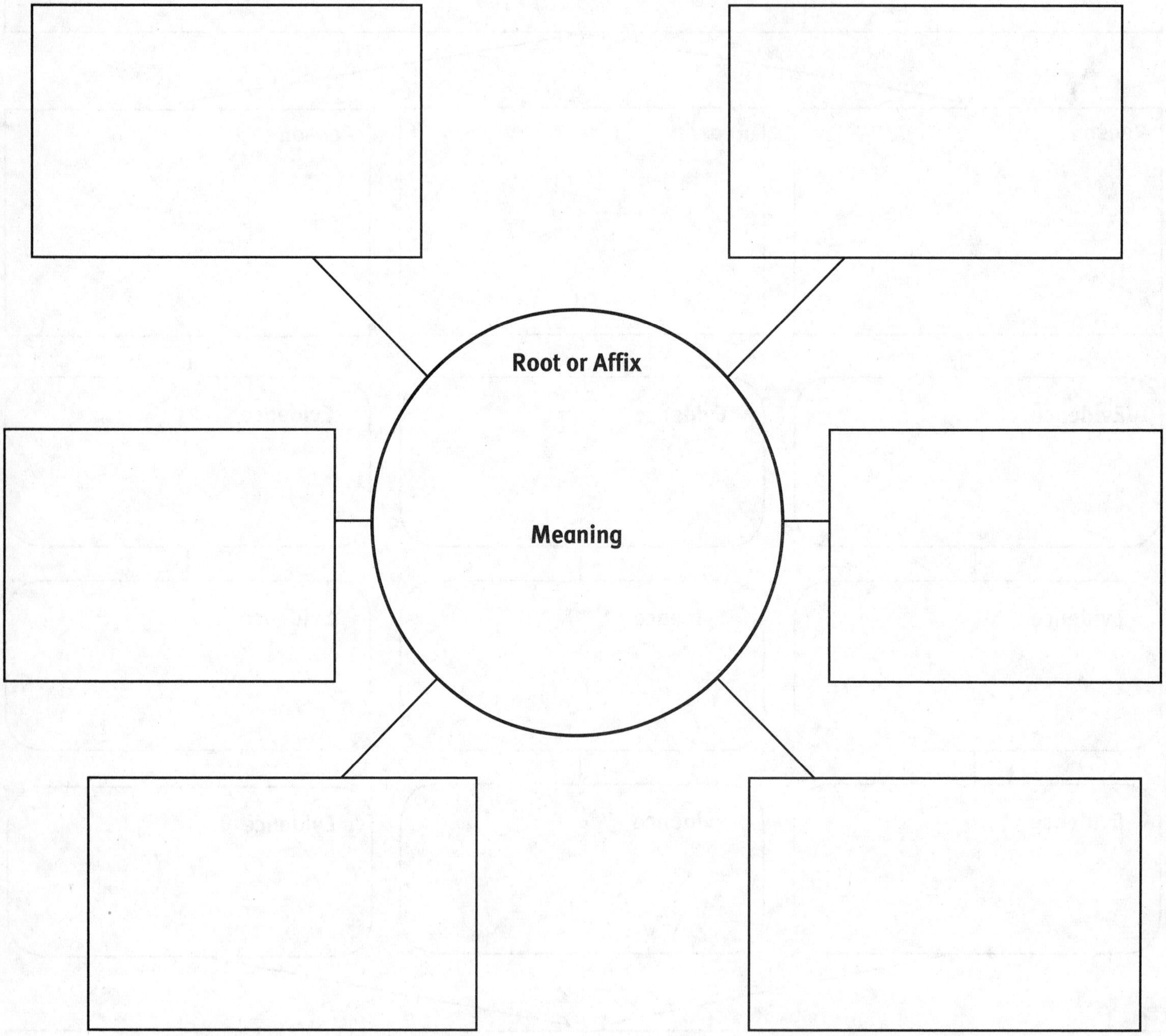

NAME ______________________________ DATE ______________

Round Table Discussion

Directions: Write the topic in the center box. One student begins by stating his or her ideas while the student to the left takes notes. Then the next student speaks while the student to his or her left takes notes, and so on.

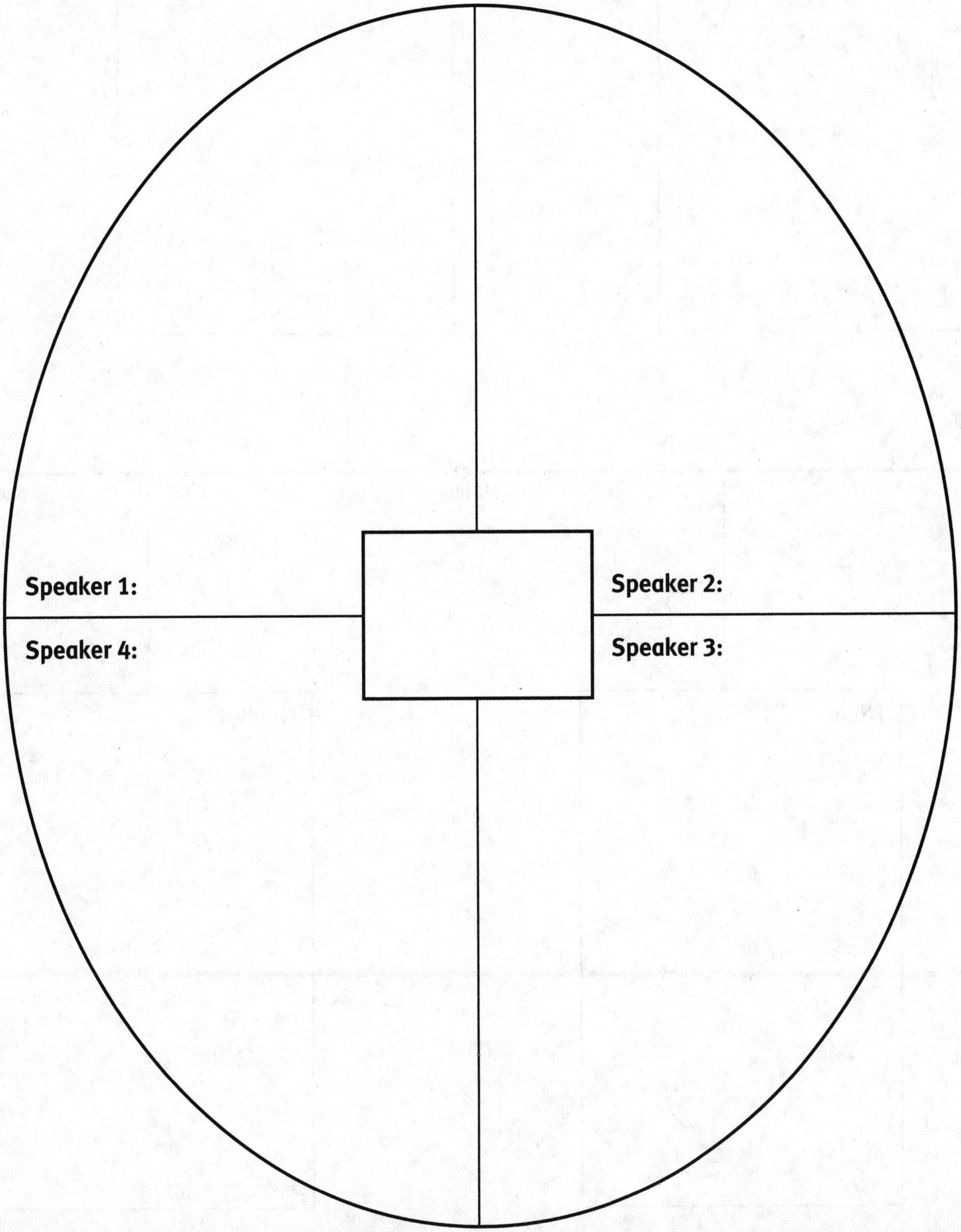

NAME ______________________________ DATE ____________

Sequence of Events Time Line

Title: ______________________________

What happened first?

Next?

Beginning — **Middle** — **End**

Then?

Finally?

NAME ______________________________ DATE ____________

Text Structure Stairs

What happened first?

Then?

Next?

Finally, what happened last?

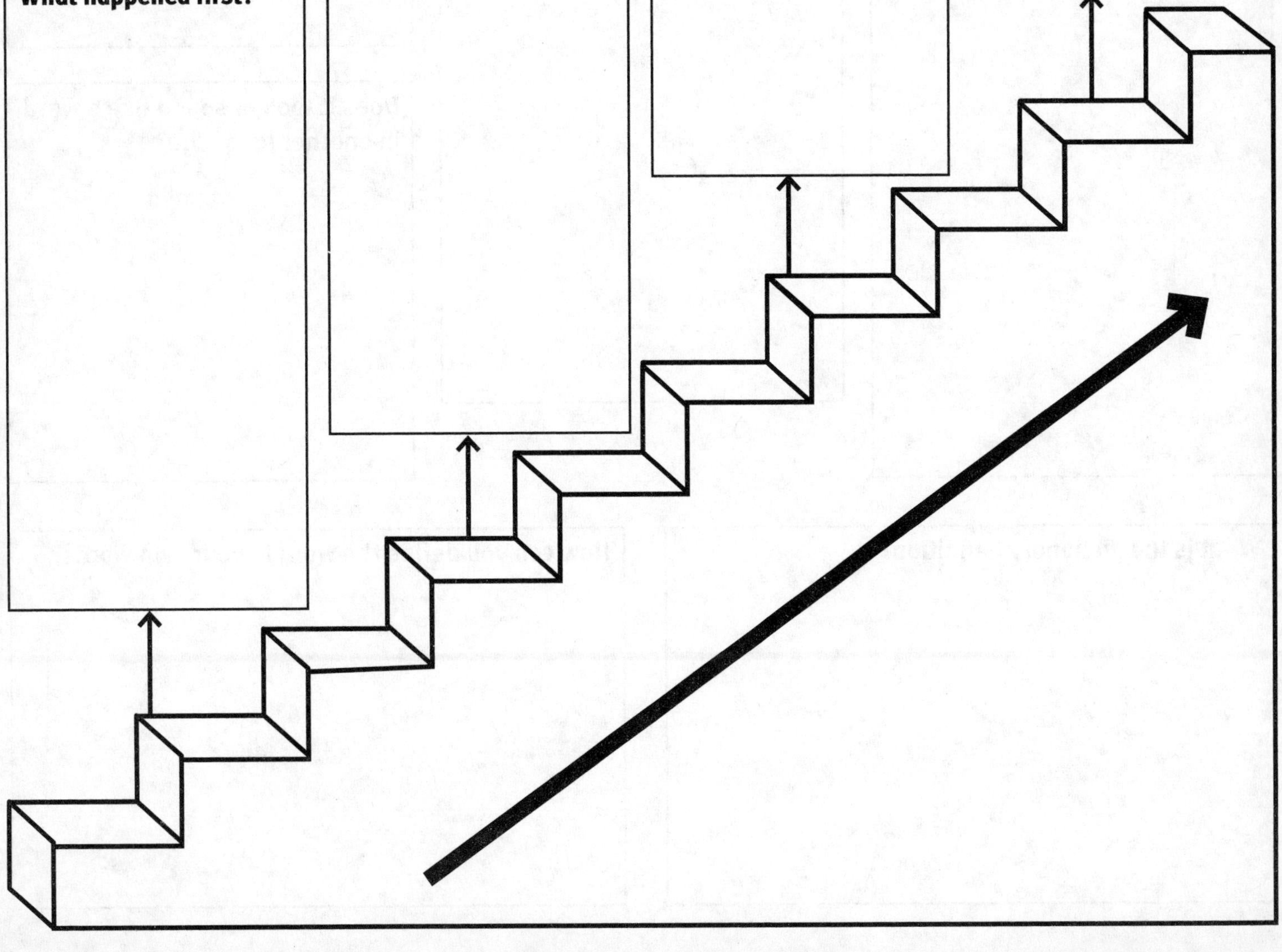

NAME ____________________ DATE ____________

Unknown Word Solver

Unknown Word

Can you find any context clues? List them.

Do you recognize any word parts?

Prefix:

Root Word:

Suffix:

Do you know another meaning of this word that does not make sense in this context?

Does it look or sound like a word in another language?

What is the dictionary definition?

How can you define the word in your own words?

NAME ______________________ DATE ______________

Venn Diagram for Writing a Comparison

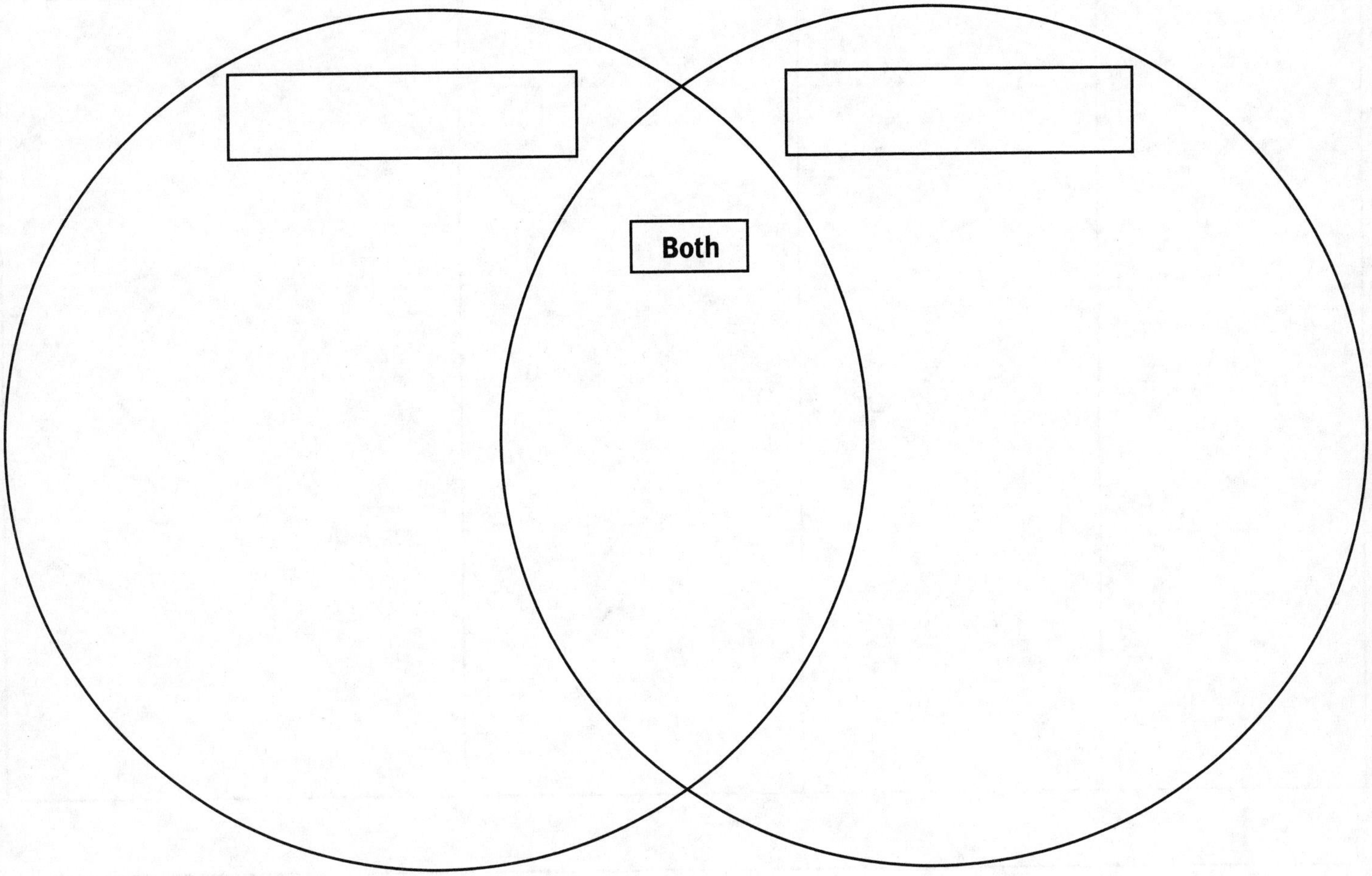

They are similar in that ______________________

They are different in that ______________________

NAME ______________________________ DATE ______________

Word Choice Analyzer

Word or phrase from the text	What does the word or phrase mean?	What is another way to say the same thing?	What effect did the author produce by choosing these words?

Explain Your Analysis

The author uses the word or phrase ______________________________, which means ______________________________

Another way to say this is ______________________________

I think the author chose these words to ______________________________

One way I can modify this sentence to add detail is to ______________________________

Glossary / Glosario

A

advertising: the use of print, graphics, or videos to persuade people to buy a product or use a service
publicidad: uso de impresos, gráfica o videos para persuadir a las personas a comprar un producto o usar un servicio

allegory: a story in which the characters, objects, or actions have a meaning beyond the surface of the story
alegoría: cuento en el que los personajes, objetos o acciones tienen un significado que va más allá de la superficie de la historia

alliteration: the repetition of consonant sounds at the beginnings of words that are close together
aliteración: repetición de sonidos consonánticos al comienzo de palabras que están cercanas

allusion: a reference to a well-known person, place, event, literary work, or work of art
alusión: referencia a una persona, lugar, obra literaria u obra de arte muy conocidos

analogy: a comparison of the similarity of two things; for example, comparing a *part to a whole* or the *whole to a part*
analogía: comparación de la semejanza de dos cosas; por ejemplo, comparar una *parte con un todo* o el *todo con una parte*

analysis (literary): to study details of a work to identify essential features or meaning
análisis (literario): estudio de los detalles de una obra para identificar características o significados esenciales

anecdote: a brief, entertaining account of an incident or event
anécdota: breve relato entretenido de un incidente o suceso

antagonist: the character who opposes or struggles against the main character
antagonista: personaje que se opone o enfrenta al personaje principal

antonyms: words with opposite meanings
antónimos: palabras con significados opuestos

archetype: a character, symbol, story pattern, or other element that is common to human experience across cultures and that occurs frequently in literature, myth, and folklore
arquetipo: personaje, símbolo, patrón de un cuento u otro elemento que es común a la experiencia humana a través de diversas culturas y que aparece con frecuencia en literatura, mitos y folclor

argument: facts or reasoning offered to support a position as being true
argumento: hechos o razonamiento entregados para apoyar una posición como verdadera

artifact: an object made by a human being, typically an item that has cultural or historical significance
artefacto: objeto hecho por un ser humano, habitualmente un objeto que tiene significación cultural o histórica

atmosphere: the feeling created by a literary work or passage
atmósfera: sentimiento creado por una obra o pasaje literario

audience: the intended readers of specific types of texts or the viewers of a program or performance
público: lectores objetivo de tipos específicos de textos o espectadores de un programa o actuación

B

balanced sentence: a sentence that presents ideas of equal weight in similar grammatical form to emphasize the similarity or difference between the ideas
oración balanceada: oración que presenta ideas de igual peso en forma gramatical similar para enfatizar la semejanza o diferencia entre las ideas

body paragraph: a paragraph that contains a topic sentence, supporting details and commentary, and a concluding sentence and that is usually part of a longer text
párrafo representativo: párrafo que contiene una oración principal, detalles de apoyo y comentarios, y una oración concluyente que normalmente forma parte de un texto más extenso

C

call to action: occurs at the end of an argumentative text to make clear what the writer or speaker wants the audience to think or do
llamado a la acción: ocurre en la conclusión de un texto argumentativo para establecer lo que el escritor o el orador quieren que el público piense o haga

caricature: a visual or verbal representation in which characteristics or traits are distorted for emphasis
caricatura: representación visual o verbal en la que las características o rasgos son distorsionados para dar énfasis

cause: an initial action; an event that makes something else happen
causa: acción inicial; suceso que hace que otra cosa ocurra

character: a person or animal that takes part in the action of a literary work
personaje: persona o animal que participa en la acción de una obra literaria

characterization: the methods a writer uses to develop characters; for example, through description, actions, and dialogue
caracterización: métodos que usa un escritor para desarrollar personajes; por ejemplo, a través de descripción, acciones y diálogo

citation: giving credit to the authors of source information
cita: dar crédito a los autores de información usada como fuente

cliché: an overused expression or idea
cliché: expresión o idea usada en exceso

climax: the turning point or the high point of a story
clímax: punto de inflexión o momento culminante de un cuento

coherence: the clear and orderly presentation of ideas in a paragraph or essay
coherencia: presentación clara y ordenada de las ideas en un párrafo o ensayo

comedy: an entertainment that is amusing or humorous
comedia: espectáculo que es divertido o cómico

commentary: explanation of the way the facts, details and/or examples in a paragraph or essay support the topic sentence
comentario: explicación de la manera en que los hechos, detalles y ejemplos de un párrafo o ensayo apoyan la oración principal

commercialism: an emphasis on gaining profits through advertising or sponsorship
mercantilismo: énfasis en obtener utilidades por medio de la publicidad o el auspicio

communication: the process of giving or exchanging information
comunicación: proceso de dar o intercambiar información

compare: to identify similarities in two or more items; *see also*, contrast
comparar: identificar semejanzas en dos o más elementos; *ver también*, contrastar

concise: brief and to the point
conciso: breve y al punto

concluding sentence: a final sentence that pulls together the ideas in a paragraph by restating the main idea or by summarizing or commenting on the ideas in the paragraph
oración concluyente: oración final que reúne las ideas de un párrafo, reformulando la idea principal o resumiendo o comentando las ideas del párrafo

conclusion: the ending of a paragraph or essay, which brings it to a close and leaves an impression with the reader
conclusión: fin de un párrafo o ensayo, que lo lleva a su término y deja una impresión en el lector

conflict: a struggle between opposing forces. In an **external conflict**, a character struggles with an outside force, such as another character or something in nature. In an **internal conflict**, the character struggles with his or her own needs, desires, or emotions.
conflicto: lucha entre fuerzas opuestas. En un **conflicto externo**, un personaje lucha contra una fuerza externa, como por ejemplo otro personaje o algo de la naturaleza. En un **conflicto interno**, el personaje lucha contra sus propias necesidades, deseos o emociones.

connotation: the suggested or implied meaning or emotion associated with a word—beyond its literal definition
connotación: significado o emoción sugerida o implícita que se asocia con una palabra—más allá de su definición literal

consumer: a buyer; a person who acquires goods and services
consumidor: comprador, persona que adquiere bienes y servicios

consumerism: the buying and consuming of goods and products; the belief that it is good to buy and consume goods and services
consumismo: compra y consumo de bienes y productos; creencia de que es bueno comprar y consumir bienes y servicios

context: the circumstances or facts that surround a particular event or situation
contexto: las circunstancias o los hechos que envuelven un suceso o situación particular

context clue: information in words and phrases surrounding an unfamiliar word that hint at the meaning of the unfamiliar word.
clave de contexto: información en las palabras y frases que rodean una palabra no conocida y que dan una pista acerca del significado de esa palabra.

contrast: to identify differences in two or more items; *see also*, compare
contrastar: identificar las diferencias entre dos o más elementos; *ver también*, comparar

controversy: a public debate or dispute concerning a matter of opinion
controversia: un debate público o disputa sobre una cuestión sujeta a opinión

copy: the actual text in an advertisement
texto publicitario: información actual en un anuncio publicitario

counter-argument: reasoning or facts given in opposition to an argument
contraargumento: razonamiento o hechos dados en oposición a un argumento

criteria: the facts, rules, or standards on which judgments are based.
criterios: hechos, reglas o estándares sobre las cuales están basadas las opiniones.

D

debate: *n.* a discussion involving opposing points of view; *v.* to present the sides of an argument by discussing opposing points
debate: *s.* discusión que involucra puntos de vista opuestos; *v.* presentar los lados de un argumento discutiendo puntos opuestos

definition: the process of making clear the meaning or nature of something
definición: proceso de aclarar el significado o naturaleza de algo

definition essay: a type of expository writing that explains, or defines, what a topic means
ensayo de definición: un tipo de escritura informativa que explica o define el significado de un tema

denotation: the exact, literal meaning of a word
denotación: significado exacto y literal de una palabra

denounce: declare something to be wrong in a public way
denunciar: declarar de manera pública que algo está mal

derision: strong disapproval of an attitude or topic
escarnio: fuerte desaprobación hacia una actitud o tema

detail: in writing, evidence (facts, statistics, examples) that supports the topic sentence
detalle: en la escritura, evidencia (hechos, estadística, ejemplos) que apoya la oracón principal

dialect: the distinctive language, including the sounds, spelling, grammar, and diction, of a specific group or class of people
dialecto: el lenguaje distintivo, incluyendo sonidos, ortografía, gramática y dicción, de un grupo específico o clase de personas

dialogue: conversation between characters
diálogo: conversación entre personajes

diction: a writer's or speaker's choice of words
dicción: selección de palabras por parte del escritor u orador

dissolve: the slow fading away of one image in a film as another fades in to take its place
desvanecimiento: desaparición lenta de una imagen en una película a medida que otra aparece progresivamente para tomar su lugar

drama: a genre of literature that is intended to be performed before an audience; a play
drama: género literario destinado a ser representado ante un público; obra teatral

dystopia: an imagined place or state in which the condition of life is imperfect or bad
distopía: lugar o estado imaginario en el que las condiciones de vida son imperfectas o malas

E

editorial: A short essay in which a publication, or someone speaking for a publication, expresses an opinion or takes a stand on an issue
editorial: ensayo corto en el que una publicación, o alguien que representa una publicación, expresa una opinión o toma partido acerca de un tema

effect: the result of an event or action
efecto: resultado de un suceso o acción

enunciation: how words are spoken so they can be clearly understood by an audience
enunciación: la manera en que se pronuncian las palabras para que sean entendidas claramente por un público

epic: a long narrative poem about the deeds of heroes or gods
épica: poema narrativo largo acerca de las proezas de héroes o dioses

epilogue: a section at the end of a book or play that extends or comments on the ending
epílogo: sección al final de un libro u obra teatral, que extiende o comenta el final

essay: a short literary composition on a single subject
ensayo: composición literaria corta acerca de un único tema

ethos: a rhetorical appeal that focuses on the character or qualifications of the speaker
ethos: recurso retórico centrado en el carácter o las capacidades del orador

euphemism: an inoffensive expression that is used in place of one that is considered harsh or blunt
eufemismo: expresión inofensiva usada en lugar de una considerada cruel o ruda

evaluate: make judgments based on criteria and standards to determine the value of something
evaluar: juzgar algo basándose en criterios y estándares para determinar el valor de algo

exposition: (*1*) a type of writing that explains, clarifies, defines, or gives information; (*2*) events that give a reader background information needed to understand a story
exposición: (*1*) tipo de escrito que explica, clarifica, define o entrega información; (*2*) sucesos que entregan al lector los antecedentes necesarios para comprender un cuento

expository essay: an essay that makes an assertion and explains it with details, reasons, textual evidence, and commentary
ensayo expositivo: ensayo que hace una afirmación y la explica con detalles, razones, evidencia textual y comentarios

expository paragraph: a paragraph that makes an assertion and supports it with details and commentary
párrafo expositivo: párrafo que hace una afirmación y la apoya con detalles y comentarios

F

fable: a brief story that teaches a lesson or moral, usually through animal characters that take on human qualities
fábula: cuento breve que enseña una lección o moraleja, normalmente por medio de personajes animales que asumen cualidades humanas

fact: a statement that can be proven
hecho: enunciado que puede demostrarse

fairy tale: a story that involves fantasy elements such as witches, goblins, and elves. These stories often involve princes and princesses and today are generally told to entertain children.

cuento de hadas: cuento que involucra elementos fantásticos como brujas, duendes y elfos. A menudo, estos cuentos involucran a príncipes y princesas y hoy se cuentan generalmente para entretener a los niños.

falling action: events after the climax of a story but before the resolution
acción descendente: sucesos posteriores al clímax de un cuento, pero antes de la resolución

fantasy: a story based on things that could not happen in real life
fantasía: cuento basado en cosas que no podrían ocurrir en la vida real

figurative language: imaginative language that is not meant to be interpreted literally
lenguaje figurativo: lenguaje imaginativo que no pretende ser interpretado literalmente

flashback: a sudden and vivid memory of an event in the past; also, an interruption in the sequence of events in the plot of a story to relate events that occurred in the past
narración retrospectiva: recuerdo repentino y vívido de un suceso del pasado; además, interrupción en la secuencia de los sucesos del argumento de un cuento para relatar sucesos ocurridos en el pasado

fluency: the ability to use language clearly and easily
fluidez: capacidad de usar el lenguaje fácilmente y de manera clara

folk literature: the traditional literature of a culture, consisting of a variety of myths and folk tales
literatura folclórica: literatura tradicional de una cultura, consistente en una variedad de mitos y cuentos folclóricos

folklore: the stories, traditions, sayings, and customs of a culture or a society
folclor: historias, tradiciones, dichos y costumbres de una cultura o sociedad

folk tale: an anonymous traditional story passed on orally from one generation to another
cuento folclórico: cuento tradicional anónimo pasada oralmente de generación en generación

foreshadowing: clues or hints signaling events that will occur later in the plot
presagio: claves o pistas que señalan sucesos que ocurrirán mas adelante en el argumento

formal style: academic writing that shows care and appropriate language
estilo formal: estilo académico de escritura que demuestra atención y lenguaje adecuado

found poem: verse that is created from a prose text by using the original words, phrases, images, and/or sentences, but manipulating them and reformatting them into poetic lines
poema derivado: poema creado o derivado de un texto en prosa usando palabras, frases, imágenes u oraciones originales, pero manipulándolas y reorganizándolas para formar versos poéticos

free verse: a kind of poetry that does not follow any regular pattern, rhythm, or rhyme
verso libre: tipo de poesía que no sigue ningún patrón, ritmo o rima regular

function: how something is used
función: forma en que usa algo

G

genre: a category or type of literature, such as short story, folk tale, poem, novel, play
género: categoría o tipo de literatura, como el cuento corto, cuento folclórico, poema, novela, obra teatral

global revision: the process of deeply revising a text to improve organization, development of ideas, focus, and voice
revisión global: proceso de revisar en profundidad un texto para mejorar su organización, desarrollo de ideas, enfoque y voz

graphic novel: a narrative told through visuals and captions
novela gráfica: narrativa que se cuenta por medio de efectos visuales y leyendas

H

headline: a short piece of text at the top of an article, usually in larger type, designed to be the first words the audience reads
titular: trozo corto de texto en la parte superior de un artículo, habitualmente en letra más grande, diseñado para ser las primeras palabras que el público lea

humor: the quality of being comical or amusing
humor: cualidad de ser cómico o divertido

hook: *n.* a compelling idea or statement designed to get readers' attention in an introduction
gancho: *n.* idea o afirmación atractiva diseñada para captar la atención del lector en una introducción

hyperbole: extreme exaggeration used for emphasis, often used for comic effect
hypérbole: exageración extrema usada para dar énfasis, habitualmente usada para dar efecto cómico

I

idiom: a figure of speech that cannot be defined literally
expresión idiomatica: figura del discurso que no puede definirse literalmente

image: a picture, drawing, photograph, illustration, chart, or other graphic that is designed to affect the audience in some purposeful way
imagen: pintura, dibujo, fotografía, ilustración, cuadro u otra gráfica diseñada para producir algún efecto intencional sobre el público

imagery: descriptive or figurative language used to create word pictures; imagery is created by details that appeal to one or more of the five senses

imaginería: lenguaje descriptivo o figurativo utilizado para crear imágenes verbales; la imaginería es creada por detalles que apelan a uno o más de los cinco sentidos

improvise: to respond or perform on the spur of the moment
improvisar: reaccionar o representar impulsivamente

incident: a distinct piece of action as in an episode in a story or a play. More than one incident may make up an event.
incidente: trozo de acción distintivo como un episodio de un cuento o de una obra teatral. Más de un incidente puede conformar un suceso.

inference: a logical guess or conclusion based on observation, prior experience, or textual evidence
inferencia: conjetura o conclusión lógica basada en la observación, experiencias anteriores o evidencia textual

inflection: the emphasis a speaker places on words through change in pitch or volume
inflexión: énfasis que pone un orador en las palabras por medio del cambio de tono o volumen

interpretation: a writer's or artist's representation of the meaning of a story or idea
interpretación: representación que hace un escritor o artista del significado de un cuento o idea

interview: a meeting between two people in which one, usually a reporter, asks the other questions to get that person's views on a subject
entrevista: reunión entre dos personas, en la que una, normalmente un reportero, hace preguntas a la otra para conocer sus opiniones acerca de un tema

introduction: the opening paragraph of an essay, which must get the reader's attention and indicate the topic
introducción: párrafo inicial de un ensayo, que debe captar la atención del lector e indicar el tema

irony: a literary device that exploits readers' expectations; irony occurs when what is expected turns out to be quite different from what actually happens. *Dramatic irony* is a form of irony in which the reader or audience knows more about the circumstances or future events in a story than the characters within it; *verbal irony* occurs when a speaker or narrator says one thing while meaning the opposite; *situational irony* occurs when an event contradicts the expectations of the characters or the reader.
ironía: un recurso literario que explota las expectativas de los lectores; la ironía ocurre cuando lo que se espera resulta ser muy diferente de lo que realmente ocurre. La *ironía dramática* es una forma de ironía en la que el lector o la audiencia conocen más acerca de las circunstancias o sucesos futuros de una historia que los personajes mismo; la *ironía verbal* ocurre cuando un orador o narrador dice una cosa para expresar lo contrario; la *ironía situacional* ocurre cuando un suceso contradice las expectativas de los personajes o del lector

L

legend: a traditional story believed to be based on actual people and events. Legends, which typically celebrate heroic individuals or significant achievements, tend to express the values of a culture.
leyenda: cuento tradicional que se considera basado en personas y sucesos reales. Las leyendas, que típicamente celebran a individuos heroicos o logros importantes, tienden a expresar los valores de una cultura.

limerick: a light, humorous, nonsensical verse of few lines, usually with a rhyme scheme of a-a-b-b-a
quintilla: verso liviano, humorístico, disparatado y de pocas líneas, normalmente con un esquema a-a-b-b-a

listening: the process of receiving a message and making meaning of it from verbal and nonverbal cues
escuchar: proceso de recibir el mensaje y comprender su significado a partir de claves verbales y no verbales

literary analysis: the process of examining closely and commenting on the elements of a literary work
análisis literario: proceso de examinar atentamente y comentar los elementos de una obra literaria

revisión local: revisar un texto a nivel de palabras o de oraciones
local revision: revising a text on a word or sentence level

logo: a unique design symbol used to identify a company visually
logotipo: símbolo único de diseño, utilizado para identificar visualmente una empresa

logos: a rhetorical appeal to reason or logic through statistics, facts, and reasonable examples
logos: apelación retórica a la razón o la lógica por medio de estadísticas, hechos y ejemplos razonables

J

juxtaposition: the arrangement of two or more things for the purpose of comparison
yuxtaposición: la disposición de dos o más cosas con el propósito de comparar

M

media: the various means of mass communication, such as radio, television, newspapers, and magazines
medios de comunicación: los diversos medios de comunicación masiva, como radio, televisión, periódicos y revistas

media channel: a type of media, such as television or newspaper
canal mediático: tipo de medios de comunicación, como televisión o periódicos

metaphor: a comparison between two unlike things in which one thing becomes another
metáfora: comparación entre dos cosas diferentes en la que una cosa se convierte en otra

monologue: a speech or written expression of thoughts by a character
monólogo: discurso o expresión escrita de pensamientos por parte de un personaje

mood: the overall emotional quality of a work, which is created by the author's language and tone and the subject matter
carácter: la calidad emocional general de una obra, que es creada por el lenguaje y tono del autor y por el tema

motif: a recurring element, image, or idea in a work of literature
motivo: elemento, imagen o idea recurrente en una obra literaria

multiple intelligences: the variety of learning styles that everyone has in varying degrees. In each individual, different intelligences predominate.
inteligencias múltiples: diversidad de estilos de aprendizaje que todos tienen en diversos grados. En cada individuo predominan diferentes inteligencias.

myth: a traditional story that explains the actions of gods or heroes or the origins of the elements of nature
mito: cuento tradicional que explica las acciones de dioses o héroes o los orígenes de los elementos de la naturaleza

N

narrative: a type of writing that tells a story or describes a sequence of events in an incident
narrativa: tipo de escritura que cuenta un cuento o describe una secuencia de sucesos de un incidente

narrative poem: a story told in verse
poema narrativo: historia contada en verso

negate: to deny or make ineffective
denegar: negar o anular

negation: showing what something is not in order to prove what it is
negar: demostrar lo que algo no es para comprobar lo que es

news article: an article in a news publication that objectively presents both sides of an issue
artículo noticioso: artículo de una publicación noticiosa que presenta objetivamente ambos lados de un asunto

nonprint text: a text, such as film or graphics, that communicates ideas without print
texto no impreso: texto, como una película o gráfica, que comunica ideas sin imprimir

nonverbal communication: gestures, facial expressions, and inflection that form unspoken communication
comunicación no verbal: gestos, expresiones faciales e inflexión que forman la comunicación no hablada

novel: a type of literary genre that tells a fictional story
novela: tipo de género literario que cuenta una historia ficticia

nuance: a subtle difference or distinction in meaning
matiz: una diferencia sutil o distinción en significado

O

objective: supported by facts and not influenced by personal opinion
objetivo: apoyado por hechos y no influenciado por la opinión personal

objective camera view: in film, when the camera takes a neutral point of view
visión objetiva de la cámara: en el cine, cuando la cámara toma un punto de vista neutro

omniscient: a third-person point of view in which the narrator is all-knowing
omnisciente: punto de vista de una tercera persona, en la que el narador lo sabe todo

onomatopoeia: the use of words that imitate the sounds of what they describe
onomatopeya: el uso de palabras que imitan los sonidos de lo que describen

one-liner: a short joke or witticism expressed in a single sentence.
agudeza: chiste u comentario ingenioso que se expresa en una sola oración.

opinion: a perspective that can be debated
opinión: perspectiva que es debatible

oral interpretation: reading aloud a literary text with expression
interpretación oral: leer en voz alta un texto literario con expresión

oxymoron: a figure of speech in which the words seem to contradict each other; for example, "jumbo shrimp"
oxímoron: figura del discurso en la que las palabras parecen contradecirse mutuamente; por ejemplo, "audaz cobardía"

P

pacing: the amount of time a writer gives to describing each event and developing each stage in the plot
compás: el tiempo que un escritor da para describir un suceso y desarrollar cada etapa de la trama

pantomime: a form of acting without words, in which motions, gestures, and expressions convey emotions or situations
pantomima: forma de actuación sin palabras, en la que los movimientos, gestos y expresiones transmiten emociones o situationes

paraphrase: to restate in one's own words
parafrasear: reformular en nuestras propias palabras

parody: a humorous imitation of a literary work
parodia: imitación humorística de una obra literaria

pathos: a rhetorical appeal to the reader's or listener's senses or emotions through connotative language and imagery
pathos: apelación retórica a los sentidos o emociones del lector u oyente por medio de un lenguaje connotativo y figurado

performance: presenting or staging a play
actuación: presentar o poner en escena una obra teatral

persona: the voice or character speaking or narrating a story
persona: voz o personaje que habla o narra una historia

personal letter: a written communication between friends, relatives, or acquaintances that shares news, thoughts, or feelings
carta personal: comunicación escrita entre amigos, parientes o conocidos, que comparte noticias, pensamientos o sentimientos

personal narrative: a piece of writing that describes an incident and includes a personal response to and reflection on the incident
narrativa personal: texto escrito que describe un incidente e incluye una reacción personal ante el incidente y una reflexión acerca de él

personification: a kind of metaphor that gives objects or abstract ideas human characteristics
personificación: tipo de metáfora que da características humanas a los objetos o ideas abstractas

perspective: the way a specific character views a situation or other characters
perspectiva: manera en que un personaje específico visualiza una situación o a otros personajes

persuasion: the act or skill of causing someone to do or believe something
persuasión: acto o destreza de hacer que alguien haga o crea algo

persuasive essay: an essay that attempts to convince the reader of to take an action or believe an idea
ensayo persuasivo: ensayo que intenta convencer al lector de que realice una acción o crea una idea

phrasing: dividing a speech into smaller parts, adding pauses for emphasis
frasear: dividir un discurso en partes más pequeñas, añadiendo pausas para dar énfasis

pitch: the highness or lowness of a sound, particularly the voice in speaking
tono: altura de un sonido, especialmente de la voz al hablar

plagiarism: taking and using as your own the words and ideas of another
plagio: tomar y usar como propias las palabras e ideas de otro

plot: the sequence of related events that make up a story or novel
trama: secuencia de sucesos relacionados, que conforman un cuento o novela

point of view: the perspective from which a story is told. In **first-person** point of view, the teller is a character in the story telling what he or she sees or knows. In **third-person** point of view, the narrator is someone outside of the story.
punto de vista: perspectiva desde la cual se cuenta una historia. En el punto de vista de la **primera persona**, el relator es un personaje del cuento que narra lo que ve o sabe. En el punto de vista de la **tercera persona**, el narrador es alguien que está fuera del cuento.

prediction: a logical guess or assumption about something that has not yet happened
predicción: conjetura lógica o suposición acerca de algo que aún no ha ocurrido

presentation: delivery of a formal reading, talk, or performance
presentación: entrega de una lectura, charla o representación formal

prose: the ordinary form of written language, using sentences and paragraphs; writing that is not poetry, drama, or song
prosa: forma común del lenguaje escrito, usando oraciones y párrafos; escritura que no es poesía, drama ni canción

protagonist: the central character in a work of literature, the one who is involved in the main conflict in the plot
protagonista: personaje principal de una obra literaria, el que participa en el conflicto principal de la trama

pun: the humorous use of a word or words to suggest another word with the same sound or a different meaning
retruécano: uso humorístico de una o varias palabras para sugerir otra palabra que tiene el mismo sonido o un significado diferente

purpose: the reason for writing; what the writer hopes to accomplish
propósito: razón para escribir; lo que el escritor espera lograr

Q

quatrain: a four-line stanza in poetry
cuarteta: en poesía, estrofa de cuatro versos

R

rate: the speed at which a speaker delivers words
rapidez: velocidad a la que el orador pronuncia las palabras

reflection: a kind of thinking and writing which seriously explores the significance of an experience, idea, or observation
reflexión: tipo de pensamiento y escritura que explora seriamente la importancia de una experiencia, idea u observación

reflective essay: an essay in which the writer explores the significance of an experience or observation
ensayo reflexivo: ensayo en que el autor explora la importancia de una experiencia u observación

refrain: a regularly repeated word, phrase, line, or group of lines in a poem or song
estribillo: palabra, frase, verso o grupo de versos de un poema o canción que se repite con regularidad

repetition: the use of the same words or structure over again
repetición: uso de las mismas palabras o estructura una y otra vez

research: (*v.*) the process of locating information from a variety of sources; (*n.*) the information found from investigating a variety of sources
investigar: (*v.*) proceso de buscar información en una variedad de fuentes; *también*, **investigación** (*n.*) información que se halla al investigar una variedad de fuentes

resolution: the outcome of the conflict of a story, when loose ends are wrapped up
resolución: resultado del conflicto de un cuento, cuando se atan los cabos sueltos

résumé: a document that outlines a person's skills, education, and work history
currículum vitae: un documento que resume las destrezas, educación y experiencia laboral de una persona

revision: a process of evaluating a written piece to improve coherence and use of language; *see also*, local revision, global revision
revisión: proceso de evaluar un texto escrito para mejorar la coherencia y el uso del lenguaje; *ver también*, revisión local, revisión global

rhetorical question: a question asked to emphasize a point or create an effect; no answer is expected
pregunta retórica: pregunta que se hace para enfatizar un punto o crear un efecto; no se espera una respuesta

rhyme: the repetition of sounds at the ends of words
rima: repetición de sonidos al final de las palabras

rhyme scheme: a consistent pattern of end rhyme throughout a poem
esquema de la rima: patrón consistente de una rima final a lo largo de un poema

rhythm: the pattern of stressed and unstressed syllables in spoken or written language, especially in poetry
ritmo: patrón de sílabas acentuadas y no acentuadas en lenguaje hablado o escrito, especialmente en poesía

rising action: major events that develop the plot of a story and lead to the climax
acción ascendente: sucesos importantes que desarrollan la trama de un cuento y conducen al clímax

S

satire: a manner of writing that mixes a critical attitude with wit and humor in an effort to improve mankind and human institutions
sátira: una forma de escritura que combina una actitud crítica con ingenio y humor en un esfuerzo por mejorar la humanidad y las instituciones humanas

science fiction: a genre in which the imaginary elements of the story could be scientifically possible
ciencia ficción: género en que los elementos imaginarios del cuento podrían ser científicamente posibles

search term: a single word or short phrase used in a database search
clave de búsqueda: una palabra o frase corta que se usa para investigar en una base de datos

seminar: a small group of students engaged in intensive study
seminario: grupo pequeño de estudiantes que participan en un estudio intenso

sensory details: words or information that appeal to the five senses
detalles sensoriales: palabras o información que apelan a los cinco sentidos

sequence of events: the order in which events happen
secuencia de los sucesos: orden en que ocurren los sucesos

setting: the time and the place in which a narrative occurs
ambiente: tiempo y lugar en que ocurre un relato

short story: a work of fiction that presents a sequence of events, or plot, that deals with a conflict
cuento corto: obra de ficción que presenta una secuencia de sucesos, o trama, que tratan de un conflicto

simile: a comparison between two unlike things, using the words *like* or *as*
símil: comparación entre dos cosas diferentes usando las palabras como o *tan*

slogan: a catchphrase that evokes a particular feeling about a company and its product
eslogan: frase o consigna publicitaria que evoca un sentimiento en particular acerca de una empresa y su producto

Socratic: adjective formed from the name of the philosopher Socrates, who was famous for his question-and-answer method in his search for truth and wisdom
Socrático: adjetivo derivado del nombre del filósofo Sócrates, que es famoso por su método de preguntas y respuestas en la búsqueda de la verdad y la sabiduría.

speaker: the voice that communicates with the reader of a poem
hablante: la voz que se comunica con el lector de un poema

speaking: the process of sharing information, ideas, and emotions using verbal and nonverbal means communication
hablar: proceso de compartir información, ideas y emociones usando medios de comunicación verbales y no verbales

stanza: a group of lines, usually similar in length and pattern, that form a unit within a poem
estrofa: grupo de versos, normalmente similares en longitud y patrón, que forman una unidad dentro de un poema

stereotype: a fixed, oversimplified image of a person, group, or idea; something conforming to that image
estereotipo: imagen fija y demasiado simplificada de una persona, grupo o idea; algo que cumple esa imagen

subjective: influenced by personal opinions or ideas
subjectivo: influenciado por opiniones o ideas personales

subjective camera view: in film, when the camera seems to show the events through a character's eyes
visión subjetiva de la cámara: en el cine, cuando la cámara parece mostrar los sucesos a través de los ojos de un personaje

subplot: a secondary plot that occurs along with a main plot
trama secundaria: argumento secundario que ocurre conjuntamente con un argumento principal

summarize: to briefly restate the main ideas of a piece of writing
resumir: reformular brevemente las ideas principales de un texto escrito

symbol: an object, a person, or a place that stands for something else
símbolo: objeto, persona o lugar que representa otra cosa

symbolism: the use of symbols
simbolismo: el uso de símbolos

synonyms: words with similar meanings
sinónimos: palabras con significados semejantes

T

talking points: important points or concepts to be included in a presentation
puntos centrales: puntos o conceptos importantes a incluirse en una presentación

tall tale: a highly exaggerated and often humorous story about folk heroes in local settings
cuento increíble: cuento muy exagerado y normalmente humorístico acerca de héroes folclóricos en ambientes locales

target audience: the specific group of people that advertisers aim to persuade to buy
público objetivo: grupo específico de personas a quienes los publicistas desean persuadir de comprar

technique: a way of carrying out a particular task; for example, visual techniques are ways images can be used to convey narration
técnica: una manera de llevar a cabo una tarea en particular; por ejemplo, las técnicas visuales son formas en que las imágenes comunican narración

tempo: the speed or rate of speaking
ritmo: velocidad o rapidez al hablar

textual evidence: quotations, summaries, or paraphrases from text passages to support a position
evidencia textual: citas, resúmenes o paráfrasis de pasajes de texto para apoyar una position

theme: the central idea, message, or purpose of a literary work
tema: idea, mensaje o propósito central de una obra literaria

thesis: a sentence, in the introduction of an essay, that states the writer's position or opinion on the topic of the essay
tesis: una oración, en la introducción de un ensayo, que plantea la afirmación u opinión del escritor acerca del tema del ensayo

tone: a writer's or speaker's attitude toward a subject
tono: actitud de un escritor u orador hacia un tema

topic sentence: a sentence that states the main idea of a paragraph; in an essay, it also makes a point that supports the thesis statement
oración principal: oración que plantea la idea principal de un párrafo; en un ensayo, también plantea un punto que apoya el enunciado de tesis

transitions: words or phrases that connect ideas, details, or events in writing
transiciones: palabras o frases que conectan ideas, detalles o sucesos de un escrito

TV news story: a report on a news program about a specific event
documental de televisión: reportaje en un programa noticioso acerca de un suceso específico

U

universal: characteristic of all or the whole
universal: característico de todo o el entero

utopia: an ideal or perfect place
utopía: lugar ideal o perfecto

V

verse: a unit of poetry, such as a line or a stanza
verso: unidad de la poesía, como un verso o una estrofa

voice: a writer's distinctive use of language
voz: uso distintivo del lenguaje por parte de un escritor

voice-over: the voice of an unseen character in film expressing his or her thoughts
voz en off: voz de un personaje de una película, que no se ve pero que expresa sus pensamientos

volume: the degree of loudness of a speaker's voice or other sound
volumen: grado de intensidad sonora de la voz de un orador o de otro sonido

W

juego de palabras: intercambio verbal ingenioso u ocurrente o un juego con palabras
wordplay: a witty or clever verbal exchange or a play on words

Y

yarn: a long, often involved, story, usually telling of incredible or fantastic events; an entertaining tale; a tall tale
narración: un historia larga, en ocasiones envolvente, que usualmente cuenta sucesos increíbles o fantásticas; un historia entretenida; un cuento fantástico

Index of Skills

Literary Skills

Reading Skills

Writing Skills

Media Skills

Speaking and Listening Skills

Language Skills

Vocabulary Skills

Index of Authors and Titles

Credits

Unit 1

From "The Happy Medium" from *A Wrinkle in Time* © 1962 by Madeleine L'Engle and Crosswicks, Ltd. Reprinted by permission of Farrar, Straus, and Giroux, LLC and Crosswicks, Ltd. All Rights Reserved.

"Saturday at the Canal" from *Home Course in Religion* by Gary Soto. Chronicle Books, San Francisco, 1991

"The Drummer Boy of Shiloh" from *Bradbury Stories: 100 of the Most Celebrated Tales* by Ray Bradbury. Copyright © 1960 by the Curtis Publishing Company, renewed 1980 by Ray Bradbury. Reprinted by permission of Don Congdon Associates, Inc.

From *The Odyssey* by Homer, translated by A. S. Kline. Reprinted by permission of A. S. Kline.

"A Man" by Nina Cassian, Roy MacGregor-Hastie, translator. Reprinted by permission of Peter Owen Ltd., London.

"Soldier Home After Losing His Leg in Afghanistan," by Gale Fiege, *HeraldNet*, July 9, 2012. Reprinted by permission of The Daily Herald, Everett, WA.

"Where I Find My Heroes" by Oliver Stone as appeared in *McCall's* Magazine, November 1992. Reprinted by permission of Steven R. Pines, CPA.

"Frederick Douglass." Copyright © 1966 by Robert Hayden, from *Collected Poems of Robert Hayden* by Robert Hayden, edited by Frederick Glaysher. Used by permission of Liveright Publishing Corporation.

Unit 2

"Grant and Lee: A Study in Contrasts" by Bruce Catton, *The American Story* by Earl Schenck Miers. Copyright U.S. Capital Historical Society, all rights reserved. Reprinted by permission.

"Harrison Bergeron" from *Welcome to the Monkey House* by Kurt Vonnegut, © 1968 by Kurt Vonnegut Jr. Used by permission of Dell Publishing, an imprint of Random House, a division of Random House LLC. All rights reserved. Any third party use of this material, outside of this publication, is prohibited. Interested parties must apply directly to Random House LLC for permission.

"Banned Books Week: Celebrating the Freedom to Read" from American Library Association. Copyright © 2012.

"Private Eyes" by Brooke Chorlton. Used by permission.

"Parents Share Son's Fatal Text Message to Warn Against Texting & Driving" by Jason Howerton, The Associated Press, April 11, 2013. Used with permission of The Associated Press. Copyright © 2014. All rights reserved.

"The Science Behind Distracted Driving," KUTV Channel 2, June 28, 2013, http://www.kutv.com/news. Reprinted by permission of KUTV Channel 2.

"How the Brain Reacts" by Marcel Just and Tim Keller as part of "Should Cellphone Use by Drivers be Illegal" by The Editors, *The New York Times*, July 18, 2009, http://roomfordebate.blogs.nytimes.com. Reprinted by permission of Marcel Just.

Brain images from "How the Brain Reacts" by Marcel Just and Tim Keller as part of "Should Cellphone Use by Drivers be Illegal" by The Editors, *The New York Times*, July 18, 2009, http://roomfordebate.blogs.nytimes.com. Reprinted by permission of Marcel Just.

"Cellphones and Driving: As Dangerous As We Think?" by Matthew Walburg, *Chicago Tribune*, www.chicagotribune.com, March 26, 2012. © 2012 Chicago Tribune. All rights reserved. Used by permission and protected by the Copyright Laws of the United States. The printing, copying, redistribution, or retransmission of this content without express written permission is prohibited.

Unit 3

Excerpt from *Night* by Elie Wiesel, translated by Marion Wiesel. Translation copyright © 2006 by Marion Wiesel. Reprinted by permission of Hill and Wang, a division of Farrar, Straus and Giroux, LLC.

From *The Diary of Anne Frank* by Frances Goodrich and Albert Hackett. Copyright © 1956, renewed by Albert Hackett, David Huntoon & Frances Neuwirth in 1986. Used by permission of Flora Roberts, Inc.

From "Chapter Twelve: Shmuel Thinks of an Answer to Bruno's Question" from *The Boy in the Striped Pajamas* by John Boyne, copyright © 2006 by John Boyne. Used by permission of David Fickling Books, an imprint of Random House Children's Books, a division of Random House LLC. All rights reserved. Any third party use of this material, outside of this publication, is prohibited. Interested parties must apply directly to Random House LLC for permission.

"January 13, 1943" from *The Diary of a Young Girl: The Definitive Edition* by Anne Frank, edited by Otto H. Frank and Mirjam Pressler, translated by Susan Massotty, translation copyright © 1995 by Doubleday, a division of Random House LLC. Used by permission of Doubleday, an imprint of Knopf Doubleday Publishing Group, a division of Random House LLC. All rights reserved. Any third party use of this material, outside of this publication, is prohibited. Interested parties must apply directly to Random House LLC for permission.

From The Nobel Acceptance Speech delivered by Elie Wiesel in Oslo on December 10, 1986, www.nobelprize.org. Copyright © The Nobel Foundation, 1986. Reprinted by permission of Nobel Media AB.

Excerpted from *Do Something!* by Vanessa Martir, Nancy Lublin, and Julia Steers. Copyright © 2010 by Do Something! Inc. Used by permission of Workman Publishing Co., Inc., New York. All Rights Reserved.

"Wangari Maathai," BBC News Profiles, BBC News, 2004, http://news.bbc.co.uk. Reprinted by permission.

Courtesy freerice.com © 2007–2014 World Food Programme. All Rights Reserved.

Courtesy Games for Change, http://www.gamesforchange.org.

KU Work Group for Community Health and Development. (2010). Chapter 3, Section 10: Conducting Concerns Surveys. Lawrence, KS: University of Kansas. Retrieved January 2, 2011, from the Community Tool Box: http://ctb.ku.edu/en/tablecontents/section_1045.htm. Reprinted by permission.

Public Service Notice: "Plant a Billion Trees" courtesy The Nature Conservancy.

Public Service Notice: "PLS DNT TXT + DRIVE" courtesy Alphabetica, Inc.

Address by Cesar Chavez, President United Farm Workers of America, AFL-CIO, at Pacific Lutheran University, March 1989, Tacoma, Washington.

Unit 4

From "Made You Laugh" by Marc Tyler Nobleman. Published in *READ*, April 1, 2005. Copyright © 2005 by Weekly Reader Corporation. Reprinted by permission of Scholastic Inc.

From "Brothers" by Jon Scieszka from *Guys Write for Guys Read*. Copyright © 2005. Reprinted by permission of the author.

"Take a Walk on the Wild Side" by Dave Barry, *The Miami Herald*, July 11, 2004. Copyright © 2004 by Dave Barry, Herald columnist. Reprinted by permission of Dave Barry.

"Underfunded Schools Forced To Cut Past Tense From Language Programs," November 30, 2007. Reprinted by permission of *The Onion*. Copyright © 2014, by Onion, Inc., www.theonion.com.

"They Have Yams" from *The People, Yes* by Carl Sandburg. Copyright 1936 by Houghton Mifflin Harcourt Publishing Company. Copyright © renewed 1981 by Carl Sandburg. Reproduced by permission of Houghton Mifflin Harcourt Publishing Company. All rights reserved.

"Mooses" from *Collected Poems for Children* © 2007 by Ted Hughes. Reprinted by permission of Farrar, Straus, and Giroux, LLC and Faber and Faber Ltd. All rights reserved.

"El Chicle" by Ana Castillo from *I Ask the Impossible*, published by Anchor Books, a division of Random House. Copyright © 2001.

"Is Traffic Jam Delectable?" from *It's Raining Pigs & Noodles* by Jack Prelutsky. Text copyright © 2000 by Jack Prelutsky. Used by permission of HarperCollins Publishers.

From "Fear Busters – 10 Tips to Overcome Stage Fright!" by Gary Guwe, August 9, 2007, http://garyguwe.wordpress.com. Reprinted by permission of the author.

Image Credits

Cover: Rapsodia/The Image Bank/Getty Images
1 (tr) i4lcocl2/Shutterstock; 58 (b) Tom Antos/Shutterstock; 69 (b) ra3rn/Shutterstock; 79 (tr) lynea/Shutterstock; 89 (t) thirayut/Shutterstock; 95 (b) Kovalchuk Oleksandr/Shutterstock; 96 (t) Stocksnapper/Shutterstock; 101 (br) pryzmat/Shutterstock; 115 (cr) Evlakhov Valeriy/Shutterstock; 140 (cl) Alan Poulson Photography/Shutterstock; 159 (tr) Christian Carollo/Shutterstock; 171 (cr) Brittany Courville/Shutterstock; 197 (t) Kristina Postnikova/Shutterstock; 217 (br) s_bukley/Shutterstock; 224 (cr) Sadik Gulec/Shutterstock; 229 (t) meunierd/Shutterstock; 233 (br) Sergey Furtaev/Shutterstock; 237 (b) Inc/Shutterstock; 248 (tr) Vladimir Korostyshevskiy/Shutterstock; 262 (cr) PavelShynkarou/Shutterstock; 276 (b) Jan Miko/Shutterstock